BERNADETTE SPEAKS

BERNADETTE SPEAKS

A LIFE OF
SAINT BERNADETTE SOUBIROUS
IN HER OWN WORDS

René Laurentin

Translated from the French
by John W. Lynch, SM
and Ronald DesRosiers, SM

Pauline
BOOKS & MEDIA
Boston

Library of Congress Cataloging-in-Publication Data

Laurentin, René.
    [Bernadette vous parle. English]
    Bernadette speaks : a life of Saint Bernadette Soubirous in her own words / René Laurentin ; translated from the French by John W. Lynch and Ronald DesRosiers.
    p. cm.
    Includes bibliographical references.
    ISBN 0-8198-1154-8 (pbk.)
    1. Bernadette, Saint, 1844–1879.   2. Christian saints—France—Biography. 3. Mary, Blessed Virgin, Saint—Apparitions and miracles—France—Lourdes. I. Title.

BX4700.S65 L3613   1999
282`.092—dc21
[B]   99–036942
                                                 Rev.

Originally published in French by P. Lethielleux and Médiaspaul, Paris, under the title *Bernadette vous parle.*

The photos and illustrations in this volume have been reproduced with permission from the following sources: Archives of the Abbey of Tournay (Dom Bernard), Archives of the Grotto, Archives of Nevers, private archives, Bibliothèque nationale, Lacaze and Viron, photographers at Lourdes, and Father René Laurentin.

Printed and published in the U.S.A. by Pauline Books & Media, 50 Saint Pauls Avenue, Boston, MA 02130-3491.

www.pauline.org

Pauline Books & Media is the publishing house of the Daughters of St. Paul, an international congregation of women religious serving the Church with the communications media.

1 2 3 4 5 6   05 04 03 02 01 00

CONTENTS

— ⚜ —

Part One
Her Childhood and the Apparitions
January 7, 1844 – July 16, 1858

Her Silence. Her Trials. "When God Wants It..." Small Talk and Legends. Childhood Prayers. At Aunt Bernarde's Tavern. The Heiress. Return to Lourdes.

Thursday, February 11. Friday, February 12. Saturday, February 13. The Apparition of February 14. Monday, February 15. Tuesday, February 16. The Third Apparition: February 18.

The Fourth Apparition: February 19. The Fifth Apparition: February 20. The Sixth Apparition: February 21. At Abbé Pène's. At the Commis-

Part Two

The Gathering of Evidence
July 16, 1858–July 4, 1866

Part Three

Nevers

or

The Fulfillment of the Message

July 7, 1866–April 16, 1879

Part Four

Bernadette's Significance and Relevance Today

ABOUT THE TRANSLATORS

— ⚜ —

The late Father John W. Lynch, S.M, was ordained a priest of the Society of Mary in 1943. He served for many years as a much-esteemed professor of English literature at the Marist Seminary in Bedford, MA. and in various ministries of his religious congregation. His final assignment was as a member of the pastoral team at the Lourdes Chapel in Boston, a center dedicated to fostering devotion to Our Lady of Lourdes, with a special outreach to shut-ins.

Father Ronald DesRosiers, S.M., ordained in 1963, holds a Master's degree in French and linguistics from Georgetown University. For over twenty-five years he served as a high school teacher in various Marist schools. His teaching apostolate has brought him as far afield as New Zealand and Senegal. Father DesRosiers is presently Assistant Professor of Philosophy and Ethics at Madonna University, Livonia, Michigan.

INTRODUCTION

— ⚜ —

This book contains all the makings of a story, you might even say of a novel. It is the fruit of an exhaustive, scientific study of the words of Bernadette—a study made from 1956 to 1971, with the collaboration of Mère Marie-Thérèse Bourgeade (†1971) and, beginning in 1965, Soeur Bernadette Chauvier.

The 857 words and conversations of Bernadette at Nevers were originally published in scholarly form in three volumes, entitled *Logia de Bernadette*. The dossier of her words at Lourdes had been previously unpublished.

Here in simple form, free of any scholarly apparatus, are the results of this painstaking work—a life of Bernadette, using her words, from her first baby-cry to her last breath. The "words" have not been limited to spoken words; we have included certain silences and meaningful gestures. Silence also has its expressive value, especially with Bernadette.

Since an informed reader reads with better understanding, let us make it clear that this book plunges us, without commentary, into life as it was lived a century ago. The style of piety at the time and the religious life practiced then were, as we say today, heavily "post Tridentine" and "pre-Conciliar." Bernadette lived within that context, in that environment. If she was ahead of her time, or if deep within herself she broke free from it, she nevertheless did not take issue with her world's limitations. She accepted them by voluntary, and at times difficult, obedience. It is in this chrysalis that the Holy Spirit caused a type of sanctity to flourish, a sanctity new enough to disconcert Bernadette's mistress of novices, who was an expert in her field and, for her time, one largely open to new ideas.

Trying to remain authentic, we did not want to discount the outmoded context nor the ordinariness, which, in a certain measure, characterized the life and words of Bernadette. To do so would have falsified the meaning of her spiritual adventure, where the exceptional took second place to the ordinary. The knowledgeable reader will be able to skim through these "gray areas," or may even choose not to read them at all! If one reads to the end, however, one will, as we did, grasp in its absolute clearness a new and hidden style, which makes some people consider Bernadette "the most secretive of all the saints." Hers was the secret of transparency.

Editor's note:

The cited documents have been enclosed within quotation marks so as to distinguish them from the connecting text of the author.

A brief glossary of French terms, the sources of the cited material, notes, and a map of Lourdes at the time of the apparitions will be found at the back of this volume.

The list of sources provides interested readers with numerous references for further study of the life of Bernadette.

PART ONE

— ⚜ —

HER CHILDHOOD AND THE APPARITIONS

January 7, 1844 – July 16, 1858

CHAPTER 1

— ⚜ —

BERNADETTE'S CHILDHOOD

Bernadette Soubirous was born in a flour mill to the sounds of grindstones crushing wheat. Was it a foreshadowing of the sufferings life had in store for her? Must we see this fact, at least, as a symbol?

Two days after her birth, she cried all during the baptismal ceremony of January 9, 1844. Her godfather was ashamed. On the way home he said, "All she does is cry. She'll be a bad one."[1]

But the wails of a newborn child are not yet speech. After that, many years were to pass before the least echo of her voice was heard. None of Bernadette's childhood words, admirable or comical as they may have been, have survived in anyone's memory.

Her Silence

The testimony of those who knew her during this period is banal or unsure: a little girl, "sweet and charming," reports her godmother, Bernarde Castérot. But this is a trite expression. Besides, its objectivity is suspect, coming from one who proudly boasted of having "served as mother to her from her earliest years."[2] "Aunt Bernarde" was Bernadette's mother's eldest sister. The marriage of the younger girl had frustrated the elder, for it flew in the face of custom.

3

The Boly Mill where Bernadette was born

The chain of mills on the bank of the Lapaca River. From left to right The Ravielle Mill; The Lacadé Mill, called the "Paternal Home"; The Dufo Mill; The Boly Mill

In 1843 their father, Justin Castérot, had been killed in a wagon accident on the road to Poueyferré. His death created a problem. How could the mill operate with only daughters there to run it? The solution was to marry off the eldest, Bernarde, aged eighteen, to François Soubirous, a bachelor miller of thirty-five. However, Soubirous irresistibly preferred her blond and blue-eyed younger sister, Louise, who was sixteen at the time. His stubbornness won out. But the eldest was to keep her thumb on the wife of François Soubirous, as was the matriarchal custom of the country. And so the first girl born at the mill became her godchild and was given the diminutive form of Bernarde's name: Bernadette. It was the god-mother who took charge from the first, until 1849, when the Soubirous household regained its independence. The favorable impression Bernarde had of "her" baby took on exaggerated pro-portions in retrospect—after the child became famous. In 1892, on his journey to Lourdes, the novelist Emile Zola, not without irony, noted this retrospective enthusiasm.[3]

Before anything else, the sparse testimony of this period vouches for Bernadette's silence. "Scolded, she would not answer," said her godmother. And that silence had its price, for Aunt Bernarde's scoldings were impressive. She herself proudly boasted of her effec-tiveness as a teacher: "I use the stick to make mine move...."[4]

From 1854, when ruin and hunger were the Soubirous' lot (they had been evicted from the Boly Mill and had gone from mill to slums), Bernadette knew how to be silent. So did her sister and brothers: Toinette, born in 1846, Jean-Marie in 1851 and Justin in 1855.

[Editor's note: the reference here is only to the children of Louise and François Soubirous who were living at the time of the 1858 apparitions. The couple actually had nine children altogether. A son named Jean, born in 1845, had died at the age of two months. A second boy named Jean-Marie, born in 1848, had died at the age of three. The Jean-Marie mentioned in the preceding paragraph was therefore the third son. Justin, who died at the age of ten in 1865, was followed by Bernard-Pierre, born in 1859. Another Jean, born in 1864, died within the year. A letter of Bernadette's tells us that an unnamed baby girl, born early in 1866, was the last of the children. The baby died almost immediately after birth.]

Louise

François

The cachot

A cousin, André Sajous, who took them into his own house—a former prison where they lived from 1857–1858 in the lowest and filthiest room, the dungeon—testified to the pride of the Soubirous children: "My wife often gave them millet bread. The little ones would never ask for any. They would have rather starved!"[5]

Marie Laguës, who became Bernadette's wet nurse when her own baby, Jean, died, and who later had her come to tend her sheep, confirms this: "She never complained of anything. Always docile, never a sassy answer."[6]

And yet, she had reasons to complain.

[Editor's note: As a result of an accident, in which she was burned by a falling candle in November of 1844, Louise Soubirous was no longer able to nurse Bernadette. The infant was consequently brought to Bartrès, about three miles from Lourdes. There, for ten months, she was nursed by Marie Laguës. When Marie returned Bernadette home to Lourdes, it was arranged that Monsieur and Madame Soubirous would bring her back to visit the Laguës family at least twice a year. In September of 1857, Marie, whose family at that point numbered eight children, sent her servant girl to ask Louise Soubirous if Bernadette could return to the Laguës farm to help with the children, the housework and the sheep. François and Louise Soubirous agreed, and Bernadette remained as a servant in Bartrès from September 1857 until January 1858.]

Her Trials

From her sixth year, Bernadette's health declined, says her mother.[7] She had "stomach trouble" and "a spleen disorder." Cholera, which ravaged Lourdes in the autumn of 1855, struck her cruelly. From that time on, she was asthmatic. Her queasy stomach rejected the "meal cakes," which were her ordinary fare. At home, they bought her wheat bread, when they could. At Bartrès, wheat bread was only for the masters.[8]

And yet, "even as a child she never complained about the food they served her," attests her schoolmate, Julie Garros.[9]

Bartrès was not the lush paradise of her childhood dreams that so enchanted Emile Zola. Bernadette suffered the harsh and laborious conditions of a child servant. To improve the situation, she sometimes invited Jeanne-Marie Caudeban, who shared the same fate, to accompany her to the Arribans meadow.[10]

*Marie Laguës, her wet-nurse, breast-fed Bernadette
in this room in the Burg House at Bartrès*

"Would you like to tend sheep with me?"[11] she would ask. When Jeanne couldn't come, it was endless solitude, in which Bernadette learned to pray her rosary, seeking other company with her hands and with her heart.

Another trial soon awaited her. In taking her on as a shepherdess in September 1857, Marie Laguës had promised her parents that she would send Bernadette to school and to catechism classes. But who would tend the sheep during those hours? Marie Laguës had reneged on her promise, and she became her teacher. She had absolutely no talent for teaching, however, but failed to realize this. As she saw it, Bernadette was "hard-headed...it was a process of forever repeating." She made her repeat "the same word three or four times," with no success. Then the nurse's temper began to rise. Finally she would end up throwing the book across the room shouting, "You'll never know anything!"[12]

And Bernadette would cry, but none of the words attributed to her on this matter bear credence. They are all literary fabrications, whose genesis may be followed in various authors.[13] "At least I can say my rosary and love God with all my heart," they have her saying. This reply and so many others only express her resignation. They leave her discreet and solid piety to be guessed at.

Marie "really loved" Bernadette, but with a divided affection. In 1844, the baby had been brought to her through misfortune. Bernadette drank the milk destined for Marie's dead child, the milk that caused her grief. Bernadette had been both a consolation and a thorn. From this fact came the rebuffs, which Bernadette never wanted to remember. When Marie's brother, Abbé Aravant stayed at the Burg house, he reproached his sister. "She'd change her behavior for a while...but then she'd revert to form,"[14] he later said.

Bernadette confided this problem to Jeanne Védère, her cousin and intimate friend. But in all other circumstances she had nothing but praise for her nurse.

"When God Wants It..."

On this same occasion she confided the secret of her resignation: "I thought God wanted this. When we think, 'God permits this, we don't complain.'"[15]

At the time of her stay in Bartrès, this was only a vivid concept, not yet spoken. It was the same with this other deep impression which she later confided to her childhood friend, Julie Garros: "When we wish for nothing, we always have what we need."[16]

Small Talk and Legends

For Bernadette, resignation was not a lack of feeling, for she was warm-hearted, even toward the sheep at Bartrès, and especially toward the little lambs to which she gave some of her bread. One day her father found her in a meadow looking very sad. "Look at my sheep, many of them have green marks on their backs," Bernadette pointed out.

"All the grass they ate has appeared on their backs…. They're going to die," her father joked.

At this, Bernadette began to cry. She had to be consoled…but it would only be a half-consolation. The green stain was the butcher's mark. Yes, her sheep were marked for slaughter.[17]

For the most part, her childhood words that have come down to us are either apocryphal or insignificant. Apocryphal words, inferred or transposed from later sayings, are meant to edify the reader. More spurious still are the golden legends that arose in Bartrès after the apparitions. There Bernadette became "the Miraculous Shepherdess." One day, it was said, she walked dry-shod, with all her sheep, across a torrent which barred the way; and although it was raining heavily she supposedly told the amazed farmers, "I'm not a bit wet. I haven't a drop of water on me. Only the wind gave me trouble."

The rest of these childhood tales are insignificant and hard to confirm. The oldest, the story of the ring that had to be sawed off her finger, cannot be dated. We will hear Bernadette herself retell this story at the twilight of her life, on December 13, 1878.

Here is one very shaky legend told to Emile Zola by the people of Bartrès on August 28, 1892.

Trembling and with watery eyes, an old woman looked at the novelist and said in *patois,* "That little girl often came to see me. The field where she tended sheep was near my shed. In the winter, since she was sickly, she came in to warm up. I had a statue of the Virgin on my mantle and Bernadette had fun dressing it up in a little woolen coat, which she had knitted herself.

"'Why are you doing that?' I asked.

"'It's so cold,' she answered, 'that I don't want the Virgin to be less clothed than I.'

"She always busied herself with my statue. In the summer, she wove crowns out of daisies. After the apparitions, she came to Bartrès and wanted to see my statue again.

"'Granny,' she said to me, 'the Virgin from heaven is very beautiful; but I like yours very much, because it's the first that I prayed before.'"[18]

Zola's journal itself[19] kept only this laconic note of the interview: "The little plaster statue which she dressed in winter so that she wouldn't be cold." And he added nothing more in his novel. Of Bernadette's childhood, he barely mentions anything except her silences: "A child not given to chatter, well behaved, not talking, always listening (he was told at Bartrès).[20] "It was difficult to teach her how to say the rosary, but once she knew how, she never left off saying it. Not very apt to learn, but nonetheless had common sense. A good little girl."[21]

Childhood Prayers

Can it be said that the best attested to words of Bernadette's childhood are her prayers? Yes, provided these are not exaggerated, as has sometimes been done. Lasserre [the most famous historian of Lourdes],[22] followed by other pious authors, declared that she recited the beads "anytime and anywhere." Zola fell victim to this theme, which went along with his own presuppositions. He expanded on it in his novel:[23] "It took infinite pains to teach her the rosary.... She said it from morning till night, so much so, that anyone meeting her with her sheep saw her with rosary in hand, thumbing the beads, saying Our Fathers and Hail Marys, etc."

In fact, the novelist's research had not proven his thesis of Bernadette always praying. "Bernadette was always fun-loving," a peasant woman of Bartrès told him. "Pious? About as much as any of us in the village."

"She didn't pray any more than the others," answered Zephyrin Laguës, her foster-brother.[24]

Other questions received similar answers. "Pious?" questioned Justine Laguës of Bartrès in 1913. "Eh, like anybody else. For me, I was just a child like her and I never noticed any of this."

"I don't remember seeing her with her rosary," Jeanne-Marie Caudeban, who tended sheep with Bernadette, maintained.

In 1878, a few months before Bernadette's death, some tried to resolve this doubt. On December 12, Père Sempé [superior of the chaplains at the grotto after the apparitions] asked her this question: "Did you recite the beads in the fields of Bartrès?"

The three investigators present noted her answer in analogous terms:

"I don't know."

"She does not know."

"She does not remember."

What seems certain, according to the unique testimony of her mother is this: Bernadette, from about the age of six, had a pronounced tendency to piety.[25] But it was a sober, ordinary piety, marked by nothing unusual.

In Lourdes, Bernadette said family night prayers in a loud voice, says her cousin Sajous, who heard her from the next room—"Shouting the prayers," was his way of putting it.

At church on Sundays, nothing in particular made her stand out. She was "like the children of her own age, sometimes turning around to see what was going on around her," says Louise Fourcade.[26]

During the month of May, she liked to put up little altars in the fields or near her bed, a local custom that did not make her exceptional.[27]

As for the rosary, two things are certain: since 1866, at least, she had a rosary, a "two-cent" rosary, bought at Bétharram.[28] She habitually took it with her, and so developed the familiar habit of grasping it, that we are soon going to see…. She knew how to say it in French, a language she could understand only roughly, similar to the way in which the laity understood Latin before the second Vatican Council.[29]

She had had trouble learning to say the rosary in French and knew nothing else except the invocation, "O Mary, conceived without sin…." She undoubtedly recited her beads, but without our being able to determine how often. Those close to her noticed nothing more about her piety. There was no show, nothing to distinguish her from any other little girl of her own age.[30]

At Aunt Bernarde's Tavern

Aunt Bernarde, Bernadette's godmother, ran a tavern at the corner of Rue du Bourg. When the Soubirous' troubles became acute—no work, no food—she would occasionally take Bernadette with her. Bernadette tended bar. She served wine with her natural generosity—at least when her aunt wasn't looking.

When Marie Camps or Jeanne-Marie Caudeban came for a liter, she gave good measure, and offered them what would not fit in the bottle urging, "Drink this, Marie!"[31]

Zola was familiar with this characteristic which we had gathered at Lourdes before the recent posthumous publication of his "Journal." He wrote as follows: "When her little friend came for a liter, and her aunt's back was turned, she said to her friend: 'Here! Quick! Take a good drink; my aunt isn't looking.' This showed a kind heart," he comments.[32]

It was one of those same friends who told Abbé Vergez the story of the wine secretly given. He reported it at the canonization process, but with this prudent addition: "I don't know whether Bernadette had permission."[33]

The Heiress

If Aunt Bernarde was able to give Bernadette room and board in this way, it was not because of her title of godmother, but because she was "heiress." This title was given the eldest daughter in any family of the matriarchal culture, still surviving in that part of France. The heiress held first place in the family and exerted an authority of the first order in family matters, even after the marriages of her brothers and sisters. Bernadette, the eldest daughter in the Soubirous family, was the heiress of her generation. Her personality was molded by this custom and influenced by the example of her aunt. From childhood, we see her exercising her role, in the authoritarian and moralistic style of her Aunt Bernarde.

Toinette, Bernadette's younger sister, gives this example: "I didn't stay at home. I went out a lot. Bernadette didn't like this. She wanted me home. Before the apparition, she used to scold me when I fell asleep during night prayers. She wanted me to recite a Hail

Abbé Ader

Interior of the parish church at Bartrès

The sheepcote where Bernadette tended sheep

Mary before I went to bed. 'If you should die, what would become of you?'"[she would ask].[34]

Bernadette was aware of sometimes accompanying her advice with arguments of a more forceful nature. This was part of her right and duty. Woe to her cousin, Jean Soubirous! At the time of the "Great Famine," they were playing together at "making soup"—a make-believe soup that fed only the imagination. Jean, twelve years old and much better fed than she, took the game a lot less seriously. For fun, he turned the pot upside down, but he soon found out that his cousin had a very quick hand.

Return to Lourdes

The last of her words in this hazy period occurred in mid-January. Bernadette was preoccupied. She wanted to make her First Communion. She had been promised she would be allowed to. At Bartrès, there was no progress. There was less hope now, because the "priest in charge," Abbé Ader, had left the parish on January 4, for a try at Benedictine life at La Pierre-qui-Vire, and he was not replaced. Bernadette could now take action without having to say anything against anyone. During these days, she confided to a visitor: "Tell my parents that I'm bored here. I want to go back to Lourdes to go to class and prepare for my First Communion."[35]

To Jeanne-Marie Garros, who was leaving Bartrès for Lourdes she said, "Tell my mother to come and get me."[36]

Jeanne-Marie was a good friend, a fellow-servant at the Burg house. When Bernadette washed her only handkerchief, Jeanne lent her one, for she was a little better off than Bernadette.

On Sunday, January 17, 1858, Bernadette left for Lourdes, "all alone." Monsieur and Madame Laguës were worried.

"Be sure to come back tomorrow, without fail," they insisted. She didn't return until Wednesday. When her employers asked for an explanation, Bernadette told them, "The parish priest wants me to make my First Communion, and if I go back home to Lourdes, I'll make it."[37]

Bernadette had made her decisions, calmly, step by step, like a peasant girl. She returned to Lourdes by the old road. On her right was the valley. On the other side of the Gave River, at the foot of the mountains, she could see the old rock ledges, Masse-Vieille, or as it was called, Massabielle, a steep cliff on the edge of the Gave, in the shadow of the north slope. Even if Bernadette had looked toward the shadowy site, where she had never gone before, she would not have noticed a certain, hardly visible grotto along the Gave. She could never have dreamt for a moment that this dark spot would soon brighten up for her, becoming an opening filled with living light.

CHAPTER 2

— ⚜ —

THE FIRST THREE APPARITIONS

Thursday, February 11

It was nine o'clock in the morning on Thursday, February 11, 1858. The rainy forenoon darkened "the dungeon" of the old prison, the last refuge of the Soubirous, who had been turned away from everywhere else. A bit of light came from the yard with its stinking manure pile. The two beds, where the family crowded in during the night, took up ten feet by fifteen feet of floor space. François Soubirous was lying on one of the beds, saving his strength on this day of enforced idleness. Louise, the mother—Maï as she was called in patois—was busy with the housework. Jean-Marie and Justin, the two boys (respectively six and three years old) were amusing themselves as best they could, while Bernadette and Toinette (fourteen and eleven years old) were unoccupied.

"My goodness! There's no more wood," exclaimed Bernadette.[1]

"What about the wood we gathered yesterday?" Toinette protested.

Indeed, the day before she had collected wood with her mother at four o'clock in the morning, but the bundle had been sold for six sous, to buy their daily bread.

PREMIERE APPARITION DE LA S⁺ᵉ VIERGE A BERNADETTE SOUBIROUS
dans la grotte de Lourdes le 11 Février 1858

A. DURUY.

The first apparition, a period print

At this point Jeanne Abadie, nicknamed "Baloume," because she was big and hefty, arrived. Coming in on the conversation about the wood, she offered to go with the Soubirous girls to get some.

"We need a basket to gather up the bones...." Bernadette suggested.[2]

This was a ploy to ask to go with Jeanne and Toinette. Maï didn't answer. Outside, it was misty and drizzling. She was worried about her daughter's asthma.

"I used to go out in Bartrès," Bernadette pleaded.

"Since you want to go, put on your hood," her mother relented.[3]

This hood, bought from a second hand dealer in front of the church, was white and patched. It had been washed and rewashed many times.

Three pairs of sabots clattered down the Rue des Petits-Fossés, then down the Rue du Baous and through the gate with its resounding arch. The girls gathered bones in Paradis prairie and then headed down toward the Gave River. In coming to the bridge, called "The Pont-Vieux," a kneeling silhouette by the water's edge attracted their attention. It was old Madame Pigoune, doing her strange laundry in the river. Coming closer, the girls saw she was washing some purplish-blue tripe.

"Auntie, what are you doing? Who are you cleaning the tripe for?"

"The tripe is from Monsieur Claren's pig," the peasant responded. "And you, what are you doing here in this bad weather?"

"We're looking for wood."

"Go to Monsieur La Fitte's meadow," Madame Pigoune directed. "He's had some trees cut down."

"No!" protested Bernadette, "We'll be taken for thieves."

"All right, then keep going toward Massabielle."[4]

All of this was said in patois, the local dialect.

The girls continued on. Walking over the ivy-covered bridge, then turning right, they crossed the canal on the wooden footbridge leading to the sawmill. Here they were in the "Ile du Chalet," a large triangle-shaped prairie bordered by a curtain of poplar trees. Neither Bernadette nor the other two had ever come this way before.

"Let's see where the canal joins the Gave," Bernadette suggested.

"And what if it joins the Gave at Bétharram!" retorted Toinette, who liked to contradict her older sister.[5]

In the end, there was no need to go so far. The prairie narrowed to an acute angle and ended on a sandy tongue where both branches of the waterways met: to the right, the swirling Gave; to the left, the canal. A rocky cliff rose about thirty feet on the other side, hollowed out at its foot by the grotto they had never seen before. Under the arch, they could see dry wood and bones. Baloume had thrown her sabots across the canal and crossed over. Toinette followed suit, but carried her sabots across.

For Bernadette, it was another story. Maï had warned her not to catch cold. She made her wear stockings, an unheard of luxury for the rest of the family. What was she to do?

"Help me to throw rocks in the water so that I can walk across,"[6] Bernadette pleaded.

But it was a useless appeal. On the other side, the two girls, squealing from the cold, were sitting on the rocks, briskly rubbing their frozen feet with their skirts.

"I could carry you on my back," Toinette suggested.[7]

"You're too small," Bernadette answered. "Baloume, you carry me,"[8] she begged.

Baloume, a healthy girl, strong like her father, the quarryman, wasn't a bit interested. "Hell's bells!" she yelled back. "Walk across like we did!"[9]

Baloume was angry with Bernadette, who hadn't gathered much of anything. She wasn't going to go out of her way for that good-for-nothing. She led Toinette along the Gave, where they continued to gather wood, skipping along to keep warm.

Bernadette took one last look around. There was no other way to cross over but to remove her sabots and stockings and wade through the shallow water. She began taking off her first stocking.

At that moment everything began. There was a blast "like a gust of wind," and yet the air was calm. Bernadette looked backwards, toward the Gave, opposite the grotto. The poplars were still. She bent over to remove the other stocking and again heard the same sound. This time she looked up. Above the grotto, on the right hand side, at the base of a niche-like cavity in the rock, some bushes were quietly shaking, their long brambles reaching to the ground. The dark cavity brightened and there in that light was a very young girl, dressed in white. She smiled in welcome.

Bernadette tried to brush the illusion aside. She vigorously rubbed her eyes. The apparition was still there. She reached in her apron pocket and took out her rosary. She tried to make the sign of the cross with the crucifix but could not. "My arm fell back," she was to say later. Fear took hold of her.

Then the young girl in the niche raised her arm toward her forehead. She too had a rosary. Following her example, Bernadette signed herself and with this gesture, all her fear disappeared. The girl in white passed the beads through her fingers, but without moving her lips. The rosary finished, she disappeared. And now the grotto was dark, the sky was gray, mist fell and the weather was foul again. But Bernadette was not the same. She removed the other stocking, which had fallen to her ankle. She crossed the brook and felt no cold at all.

The other two girls had finished their bundles. They were hopping about to keep warm, their sabots clattering against the frozen ground. Bernadette thought it unseemly to be playing about in that place. She interrupted them. "Did you see anything?"[10]

"And you, what did you see?" they rejoined.

Bernadette had the glimmer of an insight that what had happened was for her alone. She would have to keep the wonderful secret. She tried to change the subject.

"What a pair of jokers! You said the water was cold. I think it's warm."[11]

The other two girls became more and more puzzled. Bernadette, always susceptible to cold, acted as if she were warm. They came closer. It was true that she didn't seem uncomfortable.

"Well, now! You sure are lucky," said Toinette.

Jeanne got impatient. She resented this lazybones who hadn't yet gathered her bundle.

"Hell's bells!" she shouted once more to get things going.

It was only a mild oath, the equivalent of "By thunder!" But Bernadette didn't want to hear anything like that in such a place of mystery.

"Go swear somewhere else," she said calmly, rushing all the while to make up for lost time.[12]

While gathering wood, she kept peeking at the grotto, looking for some trace of what had happened. But it was useless. She

The grotto in 1858

saw only the ledge, the wet, reddish clay, and a few animal hairs clinging to the wall. (Herds of pigs were often pastured in the area of the
grotto.) The brambles, astir just a few moments earlier, now hung
motionless from the empty niche. The "pre-apparition" world had
returned without any break at all. Could she have been mistaken?
She couldn't help asking once again, "Didn't you see anything?"

"No. And you, what did you see?"

"Then, I saw nothing either."[13]

Jeanne grew more annoyed: "She saw nothing, but she didn't
want to gather any wood either. Maï will scold her."

At that point she picked up her bundle, took her basket of bones
and disappeared in the thicket up the slope. The two sisters were
left alone. Toinette tried to shoulder her heavy bundle of wood but
couldn't. Discouraged, she sat down. Bernadette, instead, had already hoisted hers onto her head. She arrived at the top of the hill
first, unloaded her firewood in the path and went back down to help
Toinette, who was dragging her bunch of wood behind her.

"But I'm the stronger one!" Toinette asserted.

"So what!" said Bernadette pointedly.[14]

Toinette was burning with curiosity. Going down the hill, she
came back to the attack.

"Tell me what you saw."

Bernadette kept silent.

"Just me! I promise I won't tell anyone, not even Maï!"

Bernadette believed in promises. She gave in. In a few words,
she told her sister everything. Toinette was afraid. She was also jeal-
ous, and frustrated by the privileges of her eldest sister, who was
entitled to wear stockings, eat wheat bread and exercise authority.
Her anger got the better of her.

"You're telling me this to scare me," Toinette yelled. "But I laugh
at it all now that we're on the road."

"No, you can believe me,"[15] Bernadette insisted.

"Hey, leave me alone!" Toinette snapped.

A short silence followed. Then Toinette stopped sulking and
questioned her sister again.

"I'm tired," replied Bernadette.[16]

They had reached the bottom of the hill in front of the sawmill.
The bundles were getting heavier. They sat down by the side of the
road.

"My, how I'd like to come back to the banks of Massabielle,"[17] Bernadette sighed.

Her unsharable happiness enraged Toinette, who beat her with "a stick from the bundle."

"All that stuff is nonsense!"

"You can believe me," repeated Bernadette as she warded off the blows.[18] "When I tried to make the sign of the cross, something stopped me from raising my hand, and when *Aqueró* (That) made the sign of the cross something made me raise my hand."[19]

Toinette was just itching to tell the secret. On their return to the dungeon, Louise Soubirous busied herself with her daughters' hair, which had become as dirty as the forest floor. This was part of her daily fight against lice and other vermin. While her mother combed her hair, Toinette acted mysteriously and kept clearing her throat to attract attention.

"Why are you doing that? Are you sick?" Maï asked.

"No, but I was thinking of what Bernadette told me...."

Then she poured out the whole story. "Bernadette saw a girl in white, perched on a rock at Massabielle...."

"Poor me! What are you saying?" Maï asked in alarm. To Louise, worn out by fatigue and troubles, bad news always took on the look of disaster. She tried to stay calm. "What did you see? Tell me! What did you see?"

"Something white...."[20] Bernadette finally answered.

A good beating followed for the two girls, with Bernadette receiving the lighter of the two.

"Your eyes deceived you! You saw only a white stone," her mother insisted.

"No, she had a beautiful face," protested Bernadette.[21]

Nothing more was said until that evening. Selling the bones, buying bread and finishing the daily chores filled the rest of the day. But that night, during the family prayers (was it while saying, "O Mary conceived without sin"?), Bernadette recalled the morning meeting. Her voice quivered. She began to cry. Maï was worried. She asked more questions. Bernadette was too overcome to answer. It was time to ask advice from Aunt Romaine, who lived upstairs with her five children. In the shadows of the night, the mother and the aunt grilled and lectured Bernadette.

"It's a dream. It's an illusion."

They finally tucked her in the bed she shared with Toinette—hoping that the dreams of the night would scatter her daydreams.

Friday, February 12

The next day, Friday, Bernadette rose, dreamy-eyed. She tried to keep to herself what was filling her mind, but it was too much to hold in. She ended up saying, "Something is pushing me to go to Massabielle."[22]

"Get to work!" her mother answered.

And for the day, that was that.

Saturday, February 13

At the parish church, the next day, Abbé Pomian was finishing with his Saturday confessions. Sliding back the grille for the next to last penitent, he heard, "I saw something white, having the form of a lady."[23]

The words were blurted out in patois. A confessor doesn't get shaken up by anything. Abbé Pomian thought, *Someone must have sent her to me.* He questioned her further.

Bernadette (he then learned her name) answered briefly but with strong conviction. The priest drew the story of the apparition out of her bit by bit. The child got louder and louder as she gained more confidence. Eléonore Pérard, the last penitent, heard her, in spite of her efforts not to listen. She ran away so as not to hear the confession.

What struck Abbé Pomian was this phrase of Bernadette's: "A sound like a gust of wind."[24]

Was this a biblical coincidence? Was this similar to the wind that revealed God to the prophet Elijah, hidden in his cave? Was it like the mighty wind of Pentecost? Or was it simply the tone in which Bernadette told him the story that deeply impressed him. He just couldn't pinpoint it. He tried to downplay what had happened, but, in the end, he asked, "May I talk about this with the pastor?"

Bernadette was not used to this much respect. Did the priest, who represented God, have to ask permission? She agreed without hesitation.

That same evening, Abbé Pomian met Curé Peyramale on the road to Argelès. He briefly presented the case. The Curé showed no interest. "We'll have to wait,"[25] he said.

The old church in Lourdes

The Apparition of February 14

On February 14, 1858, in the relaxed atmosphere of the last Sunday before Lent, curiosity was reaching its peak among Bernadette's classmates, all charity students at the hospice. Toinette had been spreading the news since the previous day. The little conspirators gathered together before and after High Mass. They just had to go to Massabielle.

Bernadette was torn between going and obeying. If only Maï would give permission. "We'll go ask,"[26] she said.

Louise Soubirous retreated behind her husband's authority. Just then he was working at Cazenave's stable. The children rushed to find him. The answer was no. His "boss," however, took the children's side: "A lady with a rosary—it's surely nothing evil...."

The father was forced to give in.

To be on the safe side, the children went to church to fill a bottle with holy water. Now they were on their way, ten poverty-stricken little girls. The scenery unfolded: The Baous Gate, the Pont-Vieux, the path through the woods.

On the steep path leading down to Massabielle, Bernadette started running. The others lost sight of her. They found her at the water's edge, holding her rosary and kneeling next to a rock that lay across the base of the grotto. Surprisingly, she was not out of breath. She was deaf to all their questions. At the end of the second decade, she merely said, "There is the light." And a moment later, "There she is! Her rosary is on her right arm. She's looking at you."[27]

Egged on by the others, Bernadette said a prayer of exorcism while sprinkling holy water on the lady. "If you come from God, stay; but if not...."[28]

At this mention of the powers of evil, a heavy object suddenly fell from somewhere above the girls, appearing to explode as it hit the ground and rolled into the Gave.

Jeanne Baloume, who had been left behind, was responsible for this dangerous practical joke. She had thrown a rock from the top of the cliff. Down below, the children didn't even know what it was. They panicked. Some ran off. Others tried to drag Bernadette away, but she seemed so heavy. It was impossible to budge her. She was pale as death, her eyes still glued to a spot above them.

To pull her away would take the strength of twenty-eight-year-old Antoine Nicolau, the strapping young miller whom the girls went to look for at the Savy Mill. He was more at ease carrying a bag of flour. Bernadette gently resisted his pull. For her, the everyday world had disappeared. She looked and saw nothing but this apparition from another world. The force of inertia in that smiling little body was amazing. With difficulty they pulled her up the steep footpath and then led her down the wooded lane.

On the threshold of the mill, she bowed her head. The color returned to her cheeks. It was all over. She was in contact again with the faces looking at her, happy and with no trace of fatigue.

The Nicolau family was worried. What had happened to Bernadette? She must rest. They laid her on a bed.

The miller made awkward jokes to hide his feelings. "What did you see there in that hole? Did you see something ugly?"

"Oh, no! I saw a beautiful young girl with a rosary on her arm."[29]

Bernadette, still filled with what she had seen, imitated *Aqueró's* gestures: hands joined, "flat together," as the miller expressed it.

News traveled fast. The townsfolk huddled together.

Maï came running, carrying a stick, the sign of her authority. People dissuaded her from using it, but not out of her lecturing her daughter: "You naughty girl! You're making everybody chase after you!"

"I didn't tell anyone to follow me," said Bernadette.[30]

From the mill to the dungeon, all she heard was Maï's tirade, which never let up: "What about the quarter of an hour it was supposed to last? And Vespers?... You would have missed it if I hadn't come to get you.... Is that what you're learning at the grotto? Will you be happy when they carry your father off to jail?"

At home, Cyprine Gesta, a single mother and a friend of Louise's, came to get firsthand news. Bernadette had to retell her experience. Maï listened and concluded, "It's an illusion. I don't want her to go back there anymore."[31]

At three o'clock Vespers, Bernadette tried to forget the grotto and to give it up forever. Circumstances were about to encourage her.

Monday, February 15

The next day, February 15, was the Monday before Ash Wednesday. At the sisters' school, annexed to the Hospice of Lourdes, Mère

The miller Nicolau and the Savy Mill, with the sawmill (bottom left)
and the rotunda (bottom right) built later

Ursule Fardes, the superior, came to inspect the "charity student class." She stopped in front of Bernadette, asking, "Are you all through with your 'shenanigans'?"

Later she would explain: "It's an illusion! Something like a dream; you mustn't dwell on it."[32]

On leaving school at the end of the morning session, an endless one for her, Bernadette received a slap in the face from Sophie Pailhasson, a crude and gaunt woman of about forty. "Look! Here she is, the clown!" Sophie cried. She had agreed to use this startling signal to point Bernadette out to Soeur Anastasie.

The sister took Bernadette's arm and shook her roughly saying, "Clown! Clown! If you go back to the grotto, they'll lock you up."[33]

Her classmates stood around snickering. Bernadette left stunned, but without any bitterness. What was happening?

The afternoon began well. It was sewing-class time. Here Bernadette knew her business. Her fingers were nimble. Success at sewing made her happy, whereas learning the alphabet was a hopeless struggle. The sister supervising the work was Soeur Damien Calmels, a good-natured nun, so recollected that she was unaware of anything going on around her. This was a great occasion for the students to embarrass the sister and at the same time, tease Bernadette. They began nudging each other, trying to draw Sister's attention: "Tell Sister what you saw," they prodded.

Bernadette didn't want to. "I don't know how to speak French,"[34] she answered.

That would never do. Her classmates told the story their own way, mixing everything up. Did they understand it that way or were they doing this for spite? Bernadette understood enough to protest vigorously: No, the young girl at the grotto didn't have a bouquet or shoes! And no she did not pursue her![35] Soeur Damien was puzzled. Like the rest, she said, "You must have been mistaken. Don't repeat this to a soul. They'll make fun of you."

But they had already begun: "the lady without shoes," "the swine of Massabielle," pasturing place for the common herds—so started a series of gibes which would be endlessly repeated for months ...variations on "the barefoot tramp" or "the pigs' cave." The mockers use the patois, *"Tute,"* a pejorative synonym for "grotto."

Bernadette was sorry she had ever let the secret out. She tried to be indifferent and thought she truly was.

Tuesday, February 16

The next day, when school let out, a servant girl came up to Bernadette and whispered, "Madame Milhet wants to talk to you."

Bernadette knew this wealthy middle-aged woman, who wore bizarre outfits she made herself with the help of Antoinette Peyret. What did Madame Milhet want with her? Probably more news of the grotto. Well, then, the answer was no. The servant girl returned all alone.

But Madame Milhet always got her way. That was how she came to marry her former employer, Monsieur Milhet, whose servant she had been. The present situation could be easily taken care of. She was one of the few women who gave work to Louise Soubirous. She had a hold on her. In the late afternoon, when school was over, the servant-girl was waiting for Bernadette with this new message: "Your mother wants you to stop at Madame Milhet's."

The Milhet house was on the Rue Saint-Pierre, next door to the commissioner's. In these wealthy surroundings, questions and objections fell thick and fast. Bernadette's answers came short, swift and to the point. Madame Milhet grew more and more intrigued.

"We'll go to the grotto together," she announced.

"I've been forbidden to go,"[36] Bernadette replied.

Bernadette had said good-bye to Massabielle. She accepted authority. But her questioner wouldn't give up, "Yes, yes, that will have to be straightened out. I'll take you home. I know your mother well. She won't be able to refuse me."

The Third Apparition: February 18

Thursday morning, February 18, found Bernadette on her way to the grotto. It was still dark outside. This trip had to outfox the curious. Madame Milhet had promised Maï, "No one will know." She was now accompanied only by her dressmaker-confidante, Antoinette Peyret, the bailiff's daughter.

At the top of the "neck-breaker"—the rough and slippery path that went down to the grotto—Bernadette was again gripped by desire. She broke into a run, in spite of the darkness.

"Wait, Bernadette!" Madame Milhet cried.

Bernadette waited impatiently, as Madame Milhet and Antoinette, slowly descended the slippery and dangerous slope, sliding down "on the bottom of their dresses."

Madame Milhet

At the edge of the canal beside the grotto, each took her place. Bernadette knelt down on a flat rock, in front of the niche, just a bit off to the side. The two others were on either side of her. To the left, Antoinette had just lit a candle and sheltered it under a jutting rock to keep the wind from blowing it out. To the right, Madame Milhet had also knelt down. The theory that came out of their secret talks held that the niche was the gateway to purgatory and was now in some mysterious way about to give vent to its suffering, its petitions. To record all this, Antoinette had brought along paper, pen and ink, the work tools of her father, the bailiff.

They began the rosary. "She's here!" murmured Bernadette.[37]

At the end of the rosary, Antoinette took out the writing materials.

Bernadette moved forward, paper and pen in hand. The others followed. She signaled them to move back. They huddled up against a rock on the right. The child went off in the opposite direction, took a few steps and stopped under a funnel-shaped hollow that cut into the stone arch, touching the niche of the apparition. Bernadette looked upward. She smiled.

Now she stood up on tiptoe and stretched her arms to offer pen and paper, repeating the words Madame Milhet taught her: "Would you be kind enough to write your name down?"[38]

Then she gave up the attempt and smilingly gazed at the hollow under the arch. Madame Milhet was growing impatient, standing there apart. What was Bernadette doing? What was she waiting for? She interrupted, "Bernadette! *Ask her* the way I told you to!"

The child came down to her, quite surprised. "But I did ask her, *very loudly!*"[39]

Surprise was equally strong on the part of the adults. Had Bernadette really spoken without being heard by the others?

"And her answer?" they asked.

"*Aqueró* began to laugh."[40]

Madame Milhet had felt hurt when Bernadette signaled her to

move back a moment before. Belittled in Lourdes by the common folk she had come from as well as by the wealthy, who closed their doors to her, the ex-servant had again felt in a flash that secret pain. Even here, she was being rejected!

"Ask your lady if my presence offends her," Madame Milhet directed. Despite her ever-present regal facade, her inner pain was evident.

"Ask her if we can come now," urged Antoinette.

Bernadette had an encouraging reply for both of them, "There's nothing to hold you back!"[41]

The women came forward, all smiles, as if they'd just passed an ordeal. Madame Milhet attached a high value on the approval of others. She knelt again and prayed. However, "the vision had already disappeared," rising to the upper cavity where the halo of light emerged for a moment longer. The vision had lasted less than a half hour.

Bernadette stood up. The other two did the same in a thoughtful frame of mind.

"*Aqueró* looked at you a long time," said Bernadette to Antoinette."[42]

Madame Milhet resented this special treatment. She said, "The candle was what she was looking at."

"No, it was you (Antoinette)," Bernadette insisted. "The lady looked at you and smiled."[43]

On leaving, Madame Milhet got even, "If you're lying, God will punish you," she told Bernadette.

On the way back home there were more and more questions. Why the comings and goings? The two women learned that after the rosary, *Aqueró* "glided" from the outer niche to the inner hollow, where Bernadette saw her again, closer at hand. And it was here that she spoke for the first time. But who was she?

"You didn't recognize Elisa?" Madame Milhet asked Bernadette.

Elisa Latapie—the two women's first guess—had been the president of the Children of Mary and had died a year before, in circumstances that had impressed the parishioners. A few hours before she died, she asked to be dressed for burial in simple garments: her sodalist's dress, without any lace or ribbons. The pastor gave her funeral "the greatest splendor and pomp possible." She still continued to edify her friends by her voluminous writings, even more astonishing than her life or death. It seems she was related to Madame Milhet.

Bernadette shook her head no. She knew Elisa well. "*Aqueró* doesn't look like her."

"In your opinion, who is she?" Madame Milhet pressed.

Bernadette didn't know, and she wouldn't guess.

"What if it's the Blessed Virgin?" asked Madame Milhet.

Bernadette remained silent. How would she know, since the lady had said nothing? And why would the Blessed Virgin put herself out for the likes of Bernadette Soubirous?[44]

Now the two escorts learned the purpose of the mysterious dialogue that had gone on in the inner cave. When asked to put her wishes "in writing," *Aqueró* had smilingly answered, "It is not necessary."[45]

That was the first time Bernadette had heard her voice, delicate and soft. *Aqueró* had continued, this time very seriously, "Would you have the kindness to come here for fifteen days?"[46]

Bernadette had promised,[47] and the apparition had also answered with a pledge: "I do not promise to make you happy in this world, but in the next."

Not in this world! Madame Milhet, who knew so well how to make her earthly fortune, was nonplused. How strange! The mystery of this child impressed her, but with her, impressions always took a practical and material turn. *In the meantime, I will fix it so that this little girl won't be so unhappy,* she told herself. She returned home elated at her success. (She had predicted rightly that no one would know of their grotto visit!) Madame Milhet then informed Louise Soubirous of her decision: "I'm taking charge of your daughter. I'm bringing her home with me."

CHAPTER 3

— ⚜ —

TWO WEEKS OF APPARITIONS

The Fourth Apparition: February 19

It was from Madame Milhet's house that Bernadette left for the fourth apparition. She was silent and calm. This time, she had to include some members of her family. Aunt Bernarde, her godmother, "the heiress," had not taken kindly to Madame Milhet's taking charge of her godchild. She was the one who was supposed to make the decisions.

"You have to take along something blessed," Bernarde told Bernadette.

"Would you ask Aunt Lucile for her sodalist's candle?" answered Bernadette.[1] She would take this candle along every day until March 3.

The Fifth Apparition: February 20

On February 20, the crowd had grown. Thirty people witnessed Bernadette's silent ecstasy.

On the Rue du Baous, with its timber-framed houses, Aunt Basile, Maï's sister, awaited Bernadette's return. Bernadette arrived looking serene and happy. But Aunt Basile showed her displeasure. "There's too much talk about you, my girl. You mustn't go there anymore!"

Bernadette's two aunts

Bernarde Castérot, her godmother

Basile Castérot

"Never mind. Let people talk," Bernadette answered.[2] A moment later she added, "If you want to come with me tomorrow morning...."[3]

Not wanting to admit it, Basile was dying to go. What troubled her was the crowd. "All right," she agreed. "But let's go earlier or later, when there are not so many people."

The Sixth Apparition: February 21

In spite of their much earlier departure on Sunday, February 21, there were many more people there. A hundred people filled the grotto space, right to the edge of the Gave. On their return, a group of women stopped Bernadette: "Abbé Pène wants to see you."

"I don't know him," Bernadette responded simply.

"He's asking for you."

At Abbé Pène's

Bernadette hesitated. This curate, Abbé Pène, lived in the house of the commissioner, the man who had jailed her father the previous year.

"He's a priest, you must obey him," the women insisted.

The real truth was, they were the ones who had offered to "bring her" to him. Now they had to carry out their plan.

The promise of happiness made by the lady to her on February 18 inspired Abbé Pène to set a "happy-trap." "So, Bernadette," he boomed, "now you can play all you want. You can put on airs. You can do what you want and not be afraid about your salvation."

Bernadette smiled. "Oh, that's not it at all. She'll make me happy only if I'm good."[4]

Asked about what she felt, she answered, "It seems that I am no longer of this world, and when the vision has disappeared, I am amazed to find myself right back here again...."[5]

This first visit greatly impressed the curate, but added to Bernadette's weariness.[6] Her troubles were not over.

At the Commissioner's

After Vespers, Constable Callet grabbed her by the hood, yelling, "Here she is!"

The man he called to was Commissioner Dominique Jacomet, thirty-six, tall, with a slim and athletic build—an impressive figure.

Bernadette's route from the church to the commissioner's house

He was dressed in civilian clothing, but was confident of his authority. He had been on the lookout for the young girl. He took Bernadette by the arm, courteously but firmly, saying, "Follow me."

"Yes, sir, wherever you wish,"[7] Bernadette responded.

Now she understood. She had seen this man with the alert and gentlemanly bearing last year in uniform. He was the man who had come to arrest her father, when he had been falsely accused of stealing flour. And yet, Bernadette felt surprisingly calm. Just before they turned the corner of the town hall, sympathetic bystanders came up to her. "Poor Bernadette! They're going to put you in jail."

She surprised herself by answering, "I'm not afraid. If they put me in, they'll have to let me out."[8]

She was now in the commissioner's office (his house overlooked the street to the church). He made her sit down.

"So you're the one who goes to Massabielle every day?" His manner was kind and warm.

"Yes, sir."

"And you see something beautiful there?"

"Yes, sir."

The child wasn't shy. She answered naturally. The commissioner ceaselessly took notes in pencil, without losing his air of complicity.

"What is your name?"

"Bernadette."

"Bernadette what?"

She paused a moment. "Soubirous."

"Who is your father?"

"François."

"And your mother?"

"Louise."

"Louise what?"

"Soubirous."

"No, I mean her maiden name."

She hesitated again, and then with the eagerness of a school girl who remembers answered, "Castérot."

"How old are you?"

"thirteen...or fourteen."

"Is it thirteen or fourteen?"

"I don't know."

"Do you know how to read and write?"

Commissioner Jacomet

"No, sir."

"Don't you go to school?"

"Not often."

"What do you do then?"

"I baby-sit my brothers."

"Do you go to catechism class?"

"Yes, sir."

"Have you made your First Communion?"

"No, sir."

"Well, now, Bernadette, you saw the Blessed Virgin?"

"I never said I saw the Blessed Virgin."

"Ah, well! You saw nothing!"

"Yes, I saw something."

"Well, what did you see?"

"Something white."

"Was it some 'thing' or some 'one'?"

"*Aqueró* has the form of a young girl."

"And *Aqueró* did not say, 'I am the Blessed Virgin'?"

"*Aqueró* did not say that to me."

"But that's what they're saying in town. It seems they even printed it in the newspaper."

Jacomet was embarrassed. The young girl's simple statements did not match public rumor. Everyone was talking of the Blessed Virgin, or at least a lady. It was more complicated than he had thought. He had better proceed in an orderly fashion.

"What day did you first see her?"

Bernadette hesitated, trying to find a point of reference. Yes, the wagons on the road....

"Tarbes' Market Day!"

"Good! Thursday, February 11. And how did it happen?"

"Jeanne Baloume came to get me to go gather bones...." The commissioner wrote it all down.

"And where were you when you saw this?"

"Along the canal at the mill...to go across."

"Then?"

"The other clowns went across."

"And you saw something?"

"I heard in the brambles a noise like a gust of wind."

"What did you see?"

"A bunch of brambles shaking."

"Then?"

"Then I saw *Aqueró*."

"Were there other girls with you at the time?"

"Yes, sir."

"Did they see?"

"No, sir."

"How do you know?"

"They told me."

On and on the questions went, short, to the point, often unexpected. Bernadette answered clearly and briefly, keeping up with the commissioner's pace. She never offered more information than the question required. She never got excited. She sometimes reflected for a moment, but always with conviction. Although she sometimes paused in responding to questions concerning dates and civil status, on the point of the apparition she never hesitated.

Occasionally, Jacomet stopped at an unclear expression, at something he thought might be a contradiction. The young girl was not upset. Her answers were unshakably consistent. Yes, what she saw was a real, living person, who smiled and talked like us. But Bernadette avoided and took exception to any identification or precise word to describe her. She kept falling back on *Aqueró* (That). If she seemed to accept, out of distraction, some term of comparison, as soon as Jacomet insisted, she rejected it with a compassionate attitude that got on his nerves. Jacomet was uncomfortable dealing with this kind of abstraction.

"All right then, this lady...er...this girl, she wears clothes?"

"A white dress, with a blue sash, a white veil on her head and a yellow rose on each foot...and rosary beads in her hands."

"She has feet?"

"Her dress and the roses hide them, except for her toes."

"Does she have hair?"

"Only a little bit of it can be seen, here." Bernadette brought her fingers to her temples, where she traced two oblique and symmetrical lines.

"Do you know who she is?"

"No, sir."

"Is she beautiful?"

"Oh, yes sir, very beautiful."

"As beautiful as who? Madame Pailhasson? Mademoiselle Dufo?"

The commissioner appreciated the local belles. He was a specialist in the matter. Bernadette could only feel sorry for him.

"They don't even come close."

"How old is she?"

"Young."

"And how did she appear to you?"

"I already told you."

"You didn't explain yourself very well."

He started over again. The mysterious apparition interested Jacomet less than did the physical human beings involved in the event. Madame Milhet particularly held his attention. He knew her to be a clever woman, a woman of leisure. Very interesting, that business with the pen and paper she had taken along to the grotto. What was more astonishing was that the paper didn't come back full of revelations in good and proper order. Yes, it was definitely more complicated than it seemed.

"Now then, this lady [Madame Milhet] took you to her house and told you what you must do?"

"No. Yesterday I returned home."

"Why?"

"My aunt did not want me to go back."

"Did Madame Milhet give you much money?"

"No money."

"Are you quite sure?"

"Yes, sir, quite sure."

Jacomet closely followed up on the list of initial confidantes in the affair: possible leads.

"To whom did you first speak about what you saw?"

Madame Pailhasson—"The beautiful chocolate-maker"—the Madame Bovary of Lourdes

"To the other clowns."

"Who then?"

"To my sister Marie [Toinette] on the way home and later that afternoon to Jeanne."

"And what did they say?"

"They made fun of me."

"Then whom did you tell?"

"My mother (Maï) that night."

"What did Maï say?"

"It's a dream. You mustn't go back there anymore."

"Who else?"

"To my Aunt Romaine, at the same time."

"Who is Aunt Romaine?"

"She lives above us."

"Oh, yes! Romaine Sajous" (*An honest woman but she drinks.* The commissioner, who knew everything, made a mental note.) "And what did Aunt Romaine say?"

"It's an illusion."

"Who else did you tell?"

"Cyprine, Sunday after Vespers."

"Cyprine who?"

"Gesta."

Jacomet shook his head. An unmarried mother with two children on her hands. Not too impressive, these relatives of the Soubirous!

"And the nuns, did you tell them?"

"The superior and the sister who teaches sewing."

"What did they say?"

"You can't dwell on this. You dreamed it."

"Yes, indeed, my girl, you dreamed it."

"No, I was wide awake."

"You thought you saw something."

"But sir, I saw *Aqueró* a number of times. I can't still be mistaken."

"Of course you can. Your imagination got the better of you. You told me that the others saw nothing. They have eyes, too."

"I can't explain it, but I'm sure I saw something."

"Listen, Bernadette, everybody's laughing at you. Everyone says you are mistaken, that you're crazy. For your own good, you must not go back to that grotto."

"I promised to go for fifteen days."

"There was no one to promise since you were mistaken. Come on! Be a good girl. Promise me—**me**—not to go back."

Bernadette remained silent, but her dark eyes clearly said, *Since I've already promised to go, I can't promise otherwise.*

Persuasion had failed. Besides, this calm, relaxed clear-headedness was not typical of a mad woman. Was it a put-up job? A lesson learned? The commissioner recalled something that had happened to his friend, Abbé Clouchet, back from South America. He had invited him to stay at his house last year, and some sanctimonious hypocrites had been scandalized, because the priest had gone pigeon hunting and had nibbled on a sausage, forgetting it was Friday. He had been driven out of Lourdes. Would these women, powerful enough to discredit a priest, carry enough weight to make people believe in an apparition? Now there was a trail to follow. But if that was the case, he mustn't beat around the bush.

Jacomet paused a moment. His face changed to that of the man "who knows all," a role he played well, one that had squeezed out many a confession for him since he began his career.

"All right, Bernadette, I've listened to you very patiently from start to finish. But I already knew your story and I know who prompted you."

He looked straight at her with those eyes whose power he knew. There was no harshness, only sympathy in his gaze, since he was looking for a confession.

"Sir, I don't know what you are talking about," Bernadette simply answered.

"All right, I'll make it clear. Who taught you the story of the lady in white at Massabielle? And who gave you hopes of a reward if you repeated it?"

"No one."

"And after that, who said it was the Blessed Virgin? Come on, you'd better tell me, since I already know. I'm only asking to see whether you will at last tell the truth."

"Sir, I've been telling the truth."

"No, you're lying.... And I'll be clear. If you confess I'll fix things up privately, and you'll never hear any more about it. If not, I'm going to take you to court."

She remained silent. Was it emotion? He took another sheet of paper, awaiting the crying spell he expected would follow. All he heard was this calm answer, "Sir, do what you want to."

"Too bad," he murmured, as if talking to himself, "it's her choice, she'll be punished."

He held up his sheet. "I'm going to write down everything you said, and we'll see if you're lying...."

He recopied everything, this time with pen and ink, on a large sheet of paper, the size of a notebook. The scratching of the pen and his grave movements accentuated the silence. He gestured threateningly in the air. He had almost reached the end of the third page, when he slowed down to let the ink dry. He came back to the first page.

"Let's summarize."

Bernadette tried to understand what "summarize" meant.

Jacomet read, "I am called Bernadette Soubirous, aged thirteen or fourteen. On February 11, market day in Tarbes, Jeanne Baloume came to get me...."

Bernadette listened attentively. So far, so good.

He continued, "The Blessed Virgin appeared to me."

"I didn't say the Blessed Virgin."

Jacomet brushed the correction aside with the back of his hand. *Then why do they say in town it was the Blessed Virgin?* Nevertheless, he conceded the point:

"Good...a twenty-year-old girl, dressed in white."

"No, I didn't say twenty years old."

"As beautiful as Madame Pailhasson."

The commissioner took pleasure in mentioning this lady, but without any more success.

"No, I said more beautiful than any of those ladies you mentioned."

"Her hair fell back like a veil."

"No, her hair could barely be seen."

The reading went on, interspersed every now and then with details he made up, some important, others insignificant. Every mistake was corrected.

"No, sir, you've changed everything," Bernadette pointed out.

Here and there the commissioner insisted, either pretending or because he really misunderstood.

"Yes, that's what you told me."

"No, sir."

"Yes."

"No!"

Their voices rose. The policeman in the next room thought he heard the words: drunkard...flirt...harlot....

The situation called for anger, but Jacomet's anger was too forceful to be entirely a sham. This little snip of a girl was irritating! Her simplicity left nothing to get a hold on. Jacomet hated to lose. He threatened with his eyes and with his hands: "You make everyone chase after you. You want to become a little wh..."

"I tell no one to go."

"Yes, you're quite happy to show off."

"No, I'm tired of all that."

"All right, if it tires you, say you saw nothing."

"But I did see something!"

He wrote a few lines with a shaky hand and by the fourth page his handwriting had doubled in size. Evidently, he had just gotten a brainstorm.

The interrogation had been going on for over an hour. In the street, in front of the commissioner's house, the people were starting to murmur. The crowd was getting more excited.

This had to stop. Who knew? Maybe Bernadette was getting worn out. Weren't those tears at the edge of her eyelids? Was she at last going to fold, as so often happened to those more hardened than she? For the last time, with gasping energy, Jacomet picked up the weapons which had fallen from his hands.

"Listen to me, Bernadette. I've listened to your stories, put up with your stubbornness. One last time, are you going to confess?"

"Sir, I told you the truth."

"Listen carefully, Bernadette! You're in a bad fix. I want to settle this privately, between just you and I, but on one condition: admit that you saw nothing."

"Sir, I saw something; I cannot say otherwise."

"At least, promise me that you won't go back to the grotto. This is your last chance."

"Sir, I promised to go back."

"Well, it's your choice. I'm sending for the police. You're going to jail."

Jacomet stood up. Bernadette didn't budge. Yet the threat

looked serious. Jean-Baptiste Estrade, an official in the Excise De-
partment, a fellow tenant in the Maison Cénac (where Jacomet had
both his office and his residence), had slipped into the room with
Jacomet's tacit permission. He intervened while Jacomet strode toward the door to the hallway.

"Come, Bernadette, don't be stubborn," Estrade urged. "The
commissioner is only looking out for your own good. Admit that
you could have been mistaken. Anyone can make a mistake. Or, at
least, promise not to go back there. What will you gain if they lock
you up?"

Estrade wanted to settle everything. Bernadette didn't answer.
She felt that it was none of his business. He gave up.

Why had Jacomet gone out? Because the murmuring out in the
street had increased. People were shouting and banging on his door
and window shutters.

"Let them come out!"

Tempers flared. On this late Sunday afternoon, the crowd in
front of the Maison Cénac had grown. It was getting more heated.
The arrival of François Soubirous, whom they had summoned,
touched off their anger.

"The commissioner is wrong!" someone yelled. "He hasn't the
right to question your daughter without you being present!"

"Go on in, if you're a man!"

Yes, François loved his daughter. It wouldn't be said that he
didn't know how to defend his own. He allowed himself to be
pushed up toward the front. He too got angrier and, like the rest of
the crowd, hammered away on the commissioner's door. He, the
weak one, the fearful one, crushed by his troubles, was ready to talk
boldly....

The door suddenly flew open and François found himself face-
to-face with the commissioner.

His own strength carried him inside, but he was alone. The door
closed behind him. In the hallway, shut off from the wave that had
been pushing him along, he felt his nerve dwindling. Under the eye
of the commissioner, all that was left was a big beret, twisting between embarrassed hands. The courage of François Soubirous died
even as it was being born. "I am the girl's father," he said.

Jacomet knew the legal basis for the father's intervention. He
adjusted to this and reacted accordingly: "Well, père Soubirous, I'm

glad to see you. I was about to send for you, because this comedy cannot go on. You draw people to your house."

"But...."

"I know everything now. The child herself is tired of all those people chasing her. She's fed up with being forced to go there to the grotto."

"Being forced? We were trying to stop her!"

"Listen, I've just questioned her, and I know what it's all about."

Jacomet took the sheet of paper and read the last lines he had written in large shaky letters. "Here's what she told me, through her tears: 'Papa and Mama are on the other side. You have to forbid them from making me go to the grotto. I'm tired of all this; I don't want to go back there anymore.'"

Uneducated François, with his one bad eye, stared in bewilderment at the mysterious writing. It looked like that which had gotten him thrown into jail eleven months before, even though he had been innocent. Bernadette protested. What more could they make her say? But the commissioner did not get entangled in this. He continued: "Listen, père Soubirous, I want to believe you, but you must not send your daughter back there. If you do otherwise, I'll know what to do. I don't believe you want to go back to jail and, for my part, I would hate to send you back."

"Good heavens, sir. All I want is to obey you. It's true we're sick of the remarks made about our daughter and having our house invaded. Your order settles everything. I'll close the door to people, and my daughter won't go to the grotto anymore."

Their session was over. On leaving, by the carriage-gate this time, Bernadette escaped as quickly as possible from all the questions hurled at her.

"What did he say to you?"

"What did he do to you?"

"Didn't he put you in jail?"

She was calm and relaxed. Now that she had left the commissioner, she found his shams and contradictions ridiculous. How could you say one thing one minute and the opposite the next?

She smiled as she remembered his tricks and his anger.

"What's so funny?" her father asked.

"He was shaking. His cap had a tassel that kept popping up and down!"[9]

February 22

The morning of February 22 brought back the problems in a more somber light. Bernadette's parents had promised the commissioner that she would not go back to the grotto; but she had promised to go "for fifteen days," and that promise remained.

"It saddens me. I must disobey either you or that lady,"[10] she told her parents. She forced herself to obey her father's orders to go to school "without straying right or left." She succeeded. Another scolding for her "shenanigans" by the sister superior reinforced her struggle against the lure of Massabielle.

At one o'clock in the afternoon, she returned to school, but in front of the white colonnade, just as she was about to cross the threshold, "an irresistible force" turned her right around. She went back down the hill she had just climbed and headed for the grotto, this time by the bridge over the canals and through the district where the mills stretch along the Lapaca River.

Her about-face was noticed at the police station, across from the Hospice. Two policemen followed her. The police sergeant joined her at the grotto. And while Bernadette prayed her rosary, he kept asking, "Do you see her?" Then he added smugly, "You see exactly what I see."

Bernadette's silence remained undisturbed. That day she saw nothing, and the shame was all she could focus on. It was even more intolerable because the alert had been given in town and a hundred people now crowded into the grotto.

Something had to be done. Aunt Bernarde blew out the candle Bernadette held and dragged her away. On the way home Bernadette was inconsolable. She murmured, "I don't know how I've failed the lady."

She was invited to rest at the Savy Mill. Emmanuélite Estrade, one of the last to leave the grotto, joined her and questioned her.

That night, under cover of darkness, Bernadette slipped into Abbé Pomian's confessional for a second time. He listened attentively and concluded, "They have no right to stop you."[11]

Against all expectations, in a few hours, the insoluble situation was resolved. Her father, touched by his child's dismay, took back his order.

Meanwhile, the mayor and the authorities deliberated, "How

can legal action be taken, since none of the proceedings fall under the law?"

The Seventh Apparition: February 23

The next day, February 23, the apparition kept its appointment. The crowd had grown at Massabielle. For the first time "gentlemen" from the town were present: Jean-Baptiste Estrade, Monsieur Dufo, a member of the Lawyers' Council and a Town Councilor, Monsieur Dozous, a doctor, and even Monsieur de La Fitte, a retired army officer and the head of one of the first families of the region. They made a deep impression.

Emmanuélite Estrade was surprised to see the candle flame come so close to Bernadette's fingers without making her wince.

In the afternoon, at the cachot, it was one visitor after another.

When school let out, Anna Dupin, the wife of Dupas, the hatter, was awaiting Bernadette. Her husband wanted to talk to this "clown." In the back of the shop, Bernadette bore the brunt of his rebukes: "You're quite a draw!"

"Why do people come?" Bernadette countered. "I don't go around collecting them!"

Anna's friends filled the room. With them, it was all admiration. Bernadette became their prey.

"I'll never have the joy of embracing the Blessed Virgin; let me embrace you!"

Seeing this undernourished child, Anna's thoughts ran in a more practical direction. She looked in the cupboard. Apples had been scarce that year. There was one "beauty" left. She offered it gladly. But Bernadette had learned to keep her distance, even when it came to nice juicy apples.

"Even though I begged and begged her to take it, she refused," the hat-dresser related.[12]

On leaving the hat shop, Bernadette was taken to the home of Eugénie Reval, the sister of Germaine who was a foster-child with Bernadette at Bartrès. She lived on the Place Marcadal. There were new faces, new questions. Bernadette answered straightforwardly, with no hidden motives. Why did she have to try twice to make the sign of the cross? Because she had tried to do it before *Aqueró* and so her arm fell back. What did the apparition tell her?

A prayer for her alone. After that they could get nothing more out of her. Was it weariness? It seemed so. They had mercy and let her go.[13]

At long last!

But no, it wasn't over yet. At the cachot, François was impatiently waiting for her. A little while before at the stable, his employer's sister, Dominiquette Cazenave, had ordered him in a tone reserved for the help, "After work tonight, bring your daughter to me!"

These apparitions bothered her. Secretly, she was obsessed, but she did not dare admit her attraction to them. She intended to unmask this young girl. That evening, when François brought Bernadette by the narrow, stairway-like alley, Dominiquette welcomed her by going on the offensive.

The Bernadette her father brought was but a shadow of herself. She was unresponsive, her mind a blank after so many questions, so much hugging and kissing. She "told in a few words what she saw," as if trying to get it over with. It was a great letdown as Dominiquette had secretly hoped it would be. To complete her victory, she made objections; but Bernadette was no longer listening. Her answers were vague. Besides, Dominiquette questioned her only to cut her short. She became ironical. "She made faces." Marie Pailhés stepped in, because she felt an attraction to the child, who had gently snuggled up against her: "Won't you give the little one a chance to talk?"

François also took a hand, becoming conciliatory. He would have liked to see his daughter a little more friendly toward his boss's sister. He assumed the responsibility of answering for Bernadette, as he had heard her tell the story, or at least, as he had understood it. But his way of telling it did not agree with Bernadette's. A peeved Dominiquette dismissed them. Why did everybody chase after that "clown"?

That night, she would have treated as a fool anyone who said that tomorrow she too would go to the grotto....

The Eighth Apparition: February 24

February 24 saw the end of the silent phase that characterized the four apparitions (February 19–23) that began the two week series. As on February 18, the day she had been asked to come, Bernadette went to the interior cavity, where the apparition came down to talk to her. This involved coming and going between the two cave-openings.

On the morning of February 24, her ecstasy included visible changes: color came to Bernadette's cheeks, then a pallor covered them "like a veil." The crowd got worried. Dominiquette touched the long branches that trailed down from the niche to the ground. Some women got angry: "Don't touch that rose-bush!"

They thought this was why "the Lady" did not come on February 22. Beneath the inner archway, Bernadette had found the apparition once again. She listened. She nodded "yes," "no."

"Her eyes still wet with tears...she burst out in sweet sounding ripples of laughter," observed Jacquette Pène.[14]

But there was something new. Bernadette walked on her knees and fell prostrate on her face. Beside her, Aunt Lucile, the youngest of the Castérot sisters, cried out and fainted away. Bernadette, who was about to bow to the ground again was brought back to reality. She interrupted her action and turned to Lucile: "Aunt, it's not good to get all worked up like that!"[15]

Her tone indicated a rebuke, yet at the same time it was reassuring. Bernadette looked again toward the grotto, as if to excuse herself, before continuing the interrupted movement. But her face, now back to normal, showed disappointment. Her pallor had disappeared. *Aqueró* was no longer there.

Bernadette rose, looking a little sad. She left with the quiet detachment that protected her from the curious.

On the way she said to Lucile, "Auntie, you mustn't come back with me anymore."

With that day's new developments many questions occurred to the spectators. For instance, on the way home, Fanny Nicolau, the schoolteacher, caught up with Bernadette and at the first favorable opportunity asked her, "Did the lady speak to you?"

Somewhat amazed,[16] Bernadette answered, "What! You were so close to me and you didn't hear?"

It suddenly dawned on Fanny—for Bernadette, the conversation was spoken out loud. Dumbfounded, the virtuous schoolteacher, herself a teacher of virtue, reacted professionally. *Do nothing that might add to this little girl's conceitedness!* So she made up a reason to justify her question. "Didn't hear? No, my dear...I was being shoved around so much, I was almost knocked down!"

Fanny continued, "How did she talk to you, in French or patois?"

"Oh, now you expect her to talk to me in French? Do I know French?"[17]

Deeply touched by the respect that the young lady had shown her, Bernadette added in a calmer tone, "She talks to me in patois and calls me 'vous.'"[18]

Fanny was struck by the respect shown by the Woman whom many believed was the Blessed Virgin.

That day Jacquette Pène made the same discovery. What intrigued her were the three progressive salutations, and especially the gestures, "yes" and "no" that Bernadette made toward the end of the apparition, before moving forward on her knees. Jacquette mentioned this to her brother, the curate. He was perplexed.

What did all this mean? Bernadette was called to the Maison Cénac (with the assurance that the commissioner was away!).

This was the explanation she gave: "Today *Aqueró* uttered a new word: 'Penance!' She also said, 'Pray to God for the conversion of sinners.'"

The lady had also asked Bernadette if she would kindly "get down on her knees and kiss the ground as a penance for sinners." The lady's face was sad. Bernadette answered "yes," her own face growing sad too. *Aqueró*, always respectful, asked her "if this would bother her."

"Oh, no!" she answered, "with all my heart."[19]

Bernadette felt ready to do anything to please her friend from another world, for the lady appeared to be so sad when she spoke about sinners.

The day's discussions gave Bernadette something astonishing to think about. First Fanny Nicolau, then the Dufos, Sajous, Tarbès and others had taken turns asking her questions about her morning conversation with the lady. It was very clear to Bernadette that there were secrets that had been confided to her in the intimacy of her heart; but it seemed to her the rest had all been said aloud. However, those words that Bernadette believed had been said aloud—both her own words and those of the lady—had been heard by no one.

During the day, Emmanuélite Estrade came to the cachot to get a closer look at Bernadette, whose ecstasy the previous day had upset her so much. She was struck by the poverty of the family's living quarters, a jail cell. Bernadette was upstairs at her Uncle Sajous. It was easier for her to breathe there. The visitor walked down the dark hallway, went through the small yard with its odorous manure pile, and climbed the open-air staircase, which was "pretty shaky." Bernadette was sitting near the "almost fireless" fireplace. Emmanuélite left a description of what she saw. "[Bernadette was] holding a child in her lap. The whole family was spread here and there about the room. Bernadette seemed the oldest. Seeing us approach their sister, the small family gathered around her."

In the group, Emmanuélite noticed a child of six, whom she had already met six months ago in church. She had been distracted in her prayers by what sounded like the scratching of mice. On his hands and knees on the stone floor, the little tike had been scratching up the wax candle drippings to stave off his hunger. Emmanuélite had hastened to give him a slice of bread and butter that day and on the days that followed, but the child had never gone inside her house nor whispered a word. Now she would learn everything....

"I put my hand on his head and gave it a gentle shake. 'Well, little one! You too have come to see Bernadette?' At this, I heard the child speak for the first time...."

"I am her brother."

"Bernadette also said: 'He's my brother....'"

One of the visitors asked, "You don't know the rumors that are flying? They say you're sick in the head, Bernadette!"

"No!" answered the child. "I'm not sick! They also said that I burned myself."[20]

Emmanuélite took advantage of this remark to examine the fingers licked by the flame, or so it seemed, during the previous day's ecstasy. Not a single burn mark could be found.[21]

On her part, Bernadette paid no attention to these unusual details. What counted for her was *Aqueró*, her unknown friend, and that morning's message. The thought of sinners, so far from her mind the day before, had been revealed to her, for the rest of her life, in the sadness of the lady's one look.

The Ninth Apparition: February 25

On Thursday, February 25, 1858, there was school. There were already three hundred people at the grotto when Bernadette arrived.

As soon as she went into ecstasy, she resumed walking on her knees, the action that had been interrupted the day before. She went back and forth a number of times between the exterior and the interior cave-openings. As she did this, Josèphe Barinque heard her murmuring in a full breath, then like an echo, one word repeated three times. Josèphe could barely make it out: "Penance... Penance...Penance."[22]

It was an echo of what Bernadette heard from above. At that point the comings and goings became complicated. Bernadette went down toward the Gave. But something stopped her. She came back, puzzled. She looked toward the niche and went back to the cave, but this time toward the left. She remained standing.

Finally, she climbed up the chute that rose to the back of the grotto. She stooped as the ceiling arched down to the ground at the back and to the left. Reluctantly she looked at the soil, a sort of reddish clay, a water-soaked muck. She cast an embarrassed glance toward the interior cave opening, as if to say, "What am I supposed to be looking for? There's nothing here."

Then, a sudden decision made her stoop down to the damp ground. She scratched with her right hand, scooped out a little "hollow," as they say in Lourdes, drew some muddy water from the very bottom, and brought it to her lips. She spit it out in disgust and seemed once again to be questioning with her eyes. She started scratching again a second time, then a third and each time was too disgusted to drink. The fourth time, it was not mud anymore. In the hollow of her hand was a bit of dirty water. She had a hard time swallowing it. Again she drew water, but this time to "wash" her face. Finally she gathered some leaves from a wild plant growing close by (golden saxifrage) and ate them. It was all over. She turned around to come back down from the grotto.

An uneasiness had gripped the crowd. They enjoyed the serenity of the ecstasies, but the day's incoherent and down-to-earth antics were disturbing. And now look—Bernadette had turned around, her face smeared with reddish mud!

Horrified, Aunt Bernarde quickly wiped Bernadette's face with a handkerchief while she continued down the incline. But her face was still dirty in spots, giving her a very weird look.

Estrade had become a believer only two days before when he had witnessed Bernadette's ecstasy. He too was there now, surrounded by friends, swept up in the wake of his enthusiasm. At the time, he did not have words adequate to describe the marvelous spectacle they were going to see "I have seen Mademoiselle Rachel at the theater in Bordeaux," he had said. "She is sublime, but infinitely inferior to Bernadette."

Now, here was Bernadette, the very picture of disgrace. Consternation seized everyone.

Bernadette then humbly withdrew to the foot of the niche, but that was not enough to erase the terrible impression she had left. The next issue of the *Lavedan* would talk of catalepsy....

On the way back home, Bernadette listened first to the tearful reproaches of her two aunts and then to the questions of Pauline Cazaux. "Why did you stop your sign of the cross at the end of the rosary?"

Aqueró hadn't finished.... I couldn't make it except when she did."

"In what language does she talk to you?"

"I don't know.... I understand her."[23]

But what puzzled everyone, especially those who believed "just the same," were the antics of Bernadette at the far end of the grotto. She would have to explain these many times that day—on the way home, at the cachot, and at the Maison Cénac in front of Abbé Pène and Monsieur Estrade. She explained without any embarrassment, with hardly any enthusiasm, in the simplicity of her awkward patois: "*Aqueró* told me to go drink at the spring and to wash in it. Not seeing any spring, I went to drink at the Gave; but she beckoned with her finger for me to go under the rock. I went and found a little muddy water, almost too little for me to hold in the hollow of my hand. Three times I threw it away, it was so dirty. On my fourth try, I succeeded."[24]

"Why did she ask you to do that?"

"She didn't tell me."[25]

"What did she tell you?"

Bernadette got her poor memory to concentrate and slowly remembered the words used by the lady that morning: "Go drink at the spring and wash in it."[26]

"And that grass you ate?"

"She asked me to do that too."

"What did she say?"

"You will eat the grass that is there."[27]

"But only animals eat grass!"

At a later date, Bernadette would have a reply to this objection she had thrown at her.

"And why all the movement today?"

"Yesterday *Aqueró* told me to kiss the ground as a penance for sinners."

"But do you realize that people think you're crazy for doing things like that?"

"For sinners...."[28]

There was a remarkable expressiveness in the way Bernadette looked and spoke: a reflection of the invisible "young lady" of the grotto. The sad thing here on earth is sin. To atone for it, to console *Aqueró*, Bernadette was ready to do anything. The rest was of little importance.

That afternoon, the dwindling number of visitors to the grotto noticed a new development. A thin trickle of water began seeping from the hole Bernadette had dug. The people, in turn, dug, drew water and drank. The rivulet grew wider. The water cleared up. The first bottles of water were taken to town that Thursday afternoon. Jeanne Montat gave some to her sick father. Those who drank the water felt happy and at peace.

The Interrogation at the Prosecutor's: February 25

The drama grew more serious and more complicated for Bernadette.

A policeman arrived at the cachot, where, on the previous March 27, another policeman had come to arrest François Soubirous.

"The Imperial Prosecutor asks Bernadette Soubirous to appear at his house at six o'clock this evening," the official announced.

The one who got this shocking news was Louise. François had not returned from market day at Tarbes. She went running to the quarry in search of her cousin Sajous, who owned the cachot. He left work and dressed in his Sunday best. At six o'clock, accompanied by Bernadette and her mother, he rang the bell at the prosecutor's house, the "Maison Claverie," on the Rue Marcaladouse (today, the Rue de Bagnères). Night was falling.

A maid answered the door. "Is the Prosecutor in?" Sajous asked. "Tell him Bernadette and her mother are here."

The maid was not about to let these common folk in. She left them on the doorstep. Prosecutor Vital Dutour came to the door.

He had the standoffish look of someone who's nervous, but he made it seem like an air of authority. His hair was curly, fluffed, parted on the right. He wore sideburns, which gave his weak, triangle-shaped chin a squarer look. Over all, there was something studied yet fragile about his appearance. Apprehensively, Monsieur Dutour eyed the unexpected man who stood between him and the two women. He went on the attack: "Are you her father?"

"No, I'm her uncle and the owner of the house where she lives."

"Bernadette, come in with your mother," Dutour directed. Then turning to Sajous, he added, "You, stay here a while. They'll be released."

Dutour's friendly and reassuring proposal was accompanied by a commanding gesture, which, without touching anyone, allowed the two women to enter and kept the uncle, who seemed ready for an argument, standing on the doorstep. Unprepared for this maneuver, Sajous found himself alone in front of the closed door—all dressed up with nothing to do but wait.

In his candlelit office, the prosecutor began his interrogation calmly, confidently, precisely, following a prearranged plan—to verify Bernadette's honesty and sincerity and, above all to convince her never again to set foot in the grotto. It seemed a simple matter. Her mother was already trembling. As for the little snip of a girl, obviously lacking polish, who couldn't even tell her own age, she would soon be trembling herself.

The prosecutor questioned Bernadette courteously, even kindly, in keeping with the rules of the game. All the attention was stimulating and made one want to talk. He got answers to questions that Bernadette usually avoided, because she found them trivial and senseless.

"Whom does this vision resemble?"

"Nothing."

"Come on, try! Whom does she resemble most?"

"For the face and dress, the statue of the Blessed Virgin in the parish church...but surrounded by light and she's alive."

"Her age?"

"Young."

"Tall?"

Bernadette's hand measured a height shorter than her own.[29]

Like Jacomet before him, Monsieur Dutour had a sheet of official stationery in front of him. From time to time he scribbled something, after carefully wiping the ink from his pen point against the lip of his inkwell.

He reread, but Bernadette found the account unrecognizable. From the very beginning, she protested, "Sir, I did not tell you that."

The prosecutor put on an extremely surprised look. They argued: "No!" "Yes!" He finally seemed to agree that he was mistaken. He scratched out words and reread...but always adding "new errors."

Suddenly he stopped and put his pen down. He triumphantly took a sheet of paper from his green case with the gold inlay work, a sheet already covered with writing, and called her attention to it with a wave of his hand. "I have here the commissioner's papers. You did not tell him the same thing."

A new cycle began.

"You told me one thing, but you told the commissioner something else."

"No, sir."

"Yes."

"No!"

"But the commissioner wrote it down!"

"If the commissioner made a mistake, that's his problem!"[30] Bernadette retorted.

The little snippet looked fragile, but she had a strong voice and an extraordinary self-assurance. The prosecutor raised his voice, but lost a bit of his authority in the process. Having taken her for someone simpler than she actually was, he had drawn some pretty striking answers from her. Attacking more subtly, he found this so-called idiot scoring more points.

In his self-assurance, Bernadette saw a patronizing attitude. She had noticed that he was altering the facts, and though she had answered politely, "No, sir," her dark eyes said clearly: *You're lying!*

The strict, scrupulous Monsieur Dutour, conscious of his reputation for honesty and of his legal ability, felt himself being judged and he experienced the sting. *Decidedly, this wild one is impossible,* he thought. *She understands nothing about the rules of interrogating!* He would like to explain to her: "I have to make changes to see if you tell a different story," but his explanations got all mixed up in his head, especially under that naive but steady stare. Monsieur Dutour was vulnerable. His powers of concentration were weak. His plan

The prosecutor, Vital Dutour

began to fade. He lost his thread of thought and began to use abstract and irrelevant phrases that the child did not understand. Under those dark eyes that judged him, the prosecutor lost ground. He got irritated. He wanted revenge. The sheet of paper on the desk gave him an idea for his attack.

"You ate grass like animals do."

The statement did not need an answer. Bernadette said nothing. She smiled innocently because his nervousness was becoming ridiculous. He had just missed the inkwell.

Seeing plan one—to establish lies or illusion—fail, he took up plan two: examine motives and influence.

"They give you money."

"No, no money."

"Nonetheless, you do what you do to get favors."

"I don't expect any favors in this life."

"Yet you profited from Madame Milhet's hospitality."

"She's the one who came to get me."

"The fact remains that you found life more comfortable there."

"I accepted to make her happy."

"But the pleasure was yours."

"I didn't think of myself. Anyhow, I haven't been there since Saturday."[31]

Dutour was getting nowhere. These irritating Soubirous! Their very wretchedness cried out, "Misdemeanor!" Yet, this year, just like the previous year in the theft incident, "the material elements of a felonious act" were missing.

Let's try intimidation. The prosecutor played this last card. "You are going to promise me not to return to the grotto."

"I promised to go for two weeks."

"That promise, made to a woman no one has seen, means nothing. You mustn't go."

"I feel too much happiness when I go."

"Happiness is a bad counselor! You'd do better to listen to the nuns, who told you it was an illusion."

"I'm drawn by an irresistible force."

"Well, suppose we put you in jail. What then?"

"Oh! If I can't go, I won't go."[32]

Monsieur Dutour had no legal right to make good on his threat, but even so, he would find a way to make this tough little girl give in. Her mother was visibly at the end of her stamina. It could not be said that she backed her daughter. As for the father, he was not so proud last year when it came to obtaining his release from jail. The prosecutor rang his desk bell. Madame Dutour answered immediately, curious to know what was going on behind that door.

"Send word to the commissioner to come fetch this little girl to have her sleep in jail."

A loud sob drowned out the last word. Maï, who a moment ago had been sniffling silently, suddenly burst out. The prosecutor stared at the speechless woman who now drew his attention. She was the very picture of misery. Bernadette approached her and whispered in her ear, "You are very kind to weep because we are going to jail. We haven't done anything wrong."

Louise seemed not to hear. Having stood for two hours, she began to stagger. She was about to fall. The prosecutor was not a torturer. "There are chairs; you may sit down," he said.

His condescension betrayed the scorn he would soon express in his reports.[33] Bernadette had not been schooled, but she caught the edge in his tone of voice. To hear her mother spoken to in that way revolted her. She heard herself answering without reflection, "No, we would dirty them."[34]

And while her mother sank into the chair, Bernadette, rather than taking the chair pushed forward by Madame Dutour, sat "on the floor, tailor-fashion."

It was impossible to question her anymore, so she squatted there with her tiny dignity intact, two feet lower than the table, ready to resist till morning. Moreover, a new development had arisen outside. A short time before, unfriendly murmurs had been heard outside the windows. Now there were shouts: "Let them out!"

The knocking against door and windows grew louder.

Sajous had gone over to the nearby café to salvage his dignity, all the while keeping an eye on the prosecutor's windows. He had explained the situation to the other quarrymen. At seven o'clock they had gone out to take a look. The group was getting excited. The noise had become deafening.

The prosecutor had to do something. He opened the window but lacked Jacomet's talent for improvising. All he could say was: "Easy there! Come on!"

He returned to Bernadette and tried to take up where he had

left off. "You're attracting everybody. I'll have to arrest you, if you keep this up."

"Stop the people from going [to the grotto]. I don't ask them to come."

"But you go!"

"Yes, but I made a promise."[35]

Monsieur Dutour was shaking more and more. He had definitely given up trying to find the mouth of his inkwell!

Outside, the banging got louder. This had to stop. Had Madame Dutour really gone to get the commissioner, or did she think her husband's order was simply another trick? The prosecutor was not quite sure. The important thing was not to lose face. He left for a moment and returned with this explanation: "The commissioner hasn't the time. This 'case' is postponed till tomorrow." And he added, "But it's understood, you are not to go back to that grotto."

"Sir, I do not promise you that."[36]

Monsieur Dutour put on an impassive face as he dismissed the two women. The door closed behind them, under the heavy silence of things left unsaid...the only weapon he had left. The imperial prosecutor picked up the pieces of his shattered plan and choked back his feelings, bitter to the soul of such a perfectionist. The interrogation had definitely not been a success. He would later destroy his rough minutes of the session.

That night, at least, he was delighted to learn something that bolstered his point of view, one that had been badly shaken. Barely out of his office, the woman and her daughter had gone into the café with the quarrymen. Extraordinary! These people have no money for food, yet they always have enough for drink! That fact would serve as a basis for his report of March 1. He would take his revenge by describing the Soubirous in the most unflattering way possible, even to the point of omitting that the arrest of François had ended in the dismissal of all charges: "Bernadette belongs to a poor family. Her father was arrested in 1857 for aggravated theft. The moral character of the mother is just as questionable. It is common knowledge that this woman is a drunkard. The combination of these miserable people—their language, especially their morals and their reputation—was certainly of a nature to destroy all attractiveness; they inspire not only doubt but disgust. They are indeed unworthy go-betweens for her who is considered the pre-eminently pure being."

Elsewhere we have rebutted these calumnies, which for the Soubirous, like so many others, were the consequences of losing everything. It is true that François Soubirous was arrested during the famine of 1857. As the police report clearly stated, it was "his poverty" that made him "a suspect in the theft" of flour from the Maisongrosse bakery.[37] No evidence was ever found to prove the charge, so it was dropped.

As for the mother's alleged "drunkenness," that too sprung from malice.[38] Wasn't Christ himself regarded as a "drunkard," because he occasionally drank wine? (Mt 11:19).

The truth is that the demonstrators had brought Bernadette and her mother to the café and offered them a glass of white wine (they preferred white to red), while they described the interrogation.

On leaving the café, the group ran into a policeman. "Hey, Callet!" someone shouted to him. "Where are you going at this late hour?"

"I've come to get Bernadette, to bring her to the police station."

At this stage the situation was tense. Callet, a decent man born of an unknown father, lacked the arrogance of the public officials. A voice from the crowd cried to him, "You can go to the prosecutor's if you wish, but all is changed; the case has been postponed until tomorrow!"

Back at the cachot, Dominiquette Cazenave, now a fervent believer in the apparitions, was eagerly awaiting news about the interrogation.

"Well now, did you confess?"

"Yes, I told the truth; *they* told lies," Bernadette responded. She remembered the deletions of the prosecutor. "Do you cross things out when you don't write correctly? The prosecutor was always crossing things out." She laughed.

"How childish you are," said her mother, tears barely dried.[39]

At the Espènettes, at Anna Dupas' house and elsewhere, rumors about Bernadette's interrogation were flying. The story was embellished and blown out of all proportion.

"The floor was shaking! The prosecutor was dancing!"

In the popular mind, the two small candles that were on the

table became "four large candles," appearing from nowhere.[40] To others, these four candles became a hundred. They lit themselves! And then, Monsieur Dutour, awakened in the middle of the night by a thunder clap, was attacked by a pillar of fire![41]

At the cachot, there was not a sign of such exciting fiction. The prosecutor's order and his threats loomed heavily on the horizon. The Soubirous were used to living from hand to mouth. This was what saved them from despair. Put problems off till tomorrow.

February 26

On the morning of February 26, a thorny question arose: Should Bernadette go to the grotto?

She felt attracted, but authority had spoken, even threatened. Maï believed it necessary to obey. She cried and moaned, but she didn't forbid Bernadette outright, as she had on Monday. The reason for this was another fear—fear of the mystery that gripped her. Aunt Bernarde, "the heiress," keenly aware of her duties as godmother and eldest daughter, was sitting at the table, puzzled. Suddenly, an inspiration seemed to hit her: "If I were in Bernadette's place, I'd go."

Without a word, Bernadette took her hood from the hook on the wall and went out. The waiting crowd followed her down the road.

But that day, as on that sad February 22, Bernadette recited her rosary in vain. She repeated the penitential actions that the apparition had requested two days before. Nothing. Still there was nothing. In her confusion, she gestured with her finger. The devotees immediately saw a meaning in this. "On your knees, everyone!" someone in the crowd exclaimed.

But the apparition had commanded nothing. There was no apparition.

Bernadette washed at the spring, as she had done the day before, and prayed again. Still there was nothing.

They finished by carrying her to the Savy Mill, her refuge on those unhappy days of February 14 and 22. Nothing seemed able to console her.

"What did I do to her?" she murmured, going back over the events of the last two days.

In the meantime, Louise moaned, "They're going to put us in jail!"[42]

The Tenth Apparition: February 27

Despite the disappointment of the two previous days, the crowd was even larger on the morning of February 27. Bernadette repeated her acts of penance, under the curious eye of Antoine Clarens, the director of the Secondary School in Lourdes. He was at the grotto for the first time.

No words of Bernadette have been preserved for this day.

The Eleventh Apparition: February 28

During the apparition of February 28, Bernadette repeated her penitential exercises before a larger crowd than the day before—1,150 people. A uniform stood out, heavy with gold braid. It belonged to Commandant Renault, a police official from Tarbes, who had heard that the crowd was increasing every day. What would it be like on Thursday, the last of the "fifteen days" when everyone was expecting great marvels? One must look things over and prepare for whatever would happen.

After High Mass, Bernadette was stopped by Inspector Latapie, who was in charge of all springs and fountains. She was not overly impressed by the man, who looked so embarrassed by this unaccustomed role. She teased him, "Hang on to me or I might slip away!"

Of the interrogation of February 28, a town official has left this picturesque and down-to-earth account:

"The judge said to her, 'You're here, you mischievous little girl?'

"'Yes, sir, I'm here.'

"'We're going to lock you up. What do you do at the grotto? Is someone pushing you to do this? We're going to put you in prison.'

"Here's how she answered, 'I'm ready—put me in, but it better be strong and locked up tight or I'll escape. I'm telling you!'

"Then the judge said, 'You have to give up going to the grotto.'

"'I won't give it up.'

"That little girl must be a saint or inspired to be as cool as she was. Then the Hospice sister, the stout one, the superior, came to get everyone out of this mess. Crying, she said, 'I beg you, gentlemen, give the little one to me; don't let her die!'

"The judge said to the commissioner, 'What will we do with her? Let's let her go, we have nothing to hold her for....'

"As she was leaving, she told me, 'I want to go; Thursday is the last day.'"[43]

In the afternoon, Antoine Clarens came to the cachot. Bernadette's actions at the grotto on the previous day—walking on her knees, kissing the ground and washing with dirty water—had made such a bad impression on him that he did not go back that morning. He did not come to form his opinion, which was already formed, but "out of charity," out of a sense of "duty," to "advise" the Soubirous. Wasn't he related to them on his wife's side? He intended to persuade Bernadette not to return to the grotto. First, he would convince her of her error. To do that, he would use his great powers of persuasion, which worked with his students, as well as with others.

He was quickly disarmed. Bernadette was very calm. She answered objectively, even "indifferently," "naturally," "clearly," "concisely," "confidently," in short, with such "charm" that Clarens' original opinion was shaken. Nothing smacked of hallucination.

He had her narrate the sequence of events. She did this seriously, strictly limiting her answers to the questions asked, and made the whole thing seem quite matter-of-fact. She even managed to give her strange behavior of the previous day a satisfactory explanation: "The vision ordered me to do these out of penance, first for myself, then for others."

Clarens was puzzled. Weren't these people right to expect a definite sign on March 4? He asked one last question: "Have you been given some message...some kind of mission?"

"No, not yet."[44]

One thing was sure: the child was untouched by the excitement going on around her. As he left, Clarens found his opinion changing. He later recorded his thoughts in a beautifully hand-written notebook which he would complete at his leisure on Thursday, March 4, and send to his beloved protector, the Baron Massy, Prefect of Tarbes.

The Twelfth Apparition: March 1

The March 1 apparition was no different from the previous ones, but a single gesture struck the crowd. At one point, Bernadette quickly lifted her rosary into the air, bringing it level with her eyes. Seeing this a woman cried out, "The Blessed Virgin must be blessing her rosary."

At this, all rosary beads were held out toward the niche of the apparitions, while Bernadette, unaware of the movement, resumed her prayer.

Jean-Baptiste Estrade and his sister reported this to Abbé Pène. Had Bernadette begun performing priestly functions? They didn't know.

"In any case," said Emmanuélite, "I don't know any way of interpreting this in a good sense."

Abbé Pène summoned Bernadette in order to put an end to such abuse. "So you're blessing rosaries now?"

Bernadette laughed. "I don't wear a stole."[45]

"What did you do then?"

She explained. That morning she had brought along to the grotto a rosary belonging to a woman named Pauline Sous. Devout, but too ill to go to Massabielle, Pauline was eager to be represented by her rosary. At the beginning of the apparition, Bernadette had two rosaries in her pocket. Forgetting all about Pauline, for at those moments she forgot everything, she unintentionally took out her own rosary. But the second time, after coming back from the spring, Pauline's rosary was the one she held in her hand. *Aqueró* seemed annoyed. She gestured. That is why Bernadette put Pauline's rosary back in her pocket and started all over again, this time using her own rosary. But first she held it out to show the apparition. Nothing even close to a blessing had taken place, still there was talk in town.[46]

The Thirteenth Apparition: March 2

On the morning of Tuesday, March 2, there were 1,650 people at the grotto. The first to arrive had been there since midnight. Fairly worked up by their long vigil, they were understandably anxious to hear from Bernadette's own lips her conversation in the interior cave opening.

"What did she say?"

To get them out of the way, Bernadette answered briefly as possible. "To go tell priests that people are to come here in procession."[47]

Then she hurried to get away, concentrating her weak memory on the message, which she had to then bring to the rectory.

But Bernadette hadn't told everything. *Aqueró* had also asked that "a chapel be built," and most probably, entrusted her with a secret.

The women to whom Bernadette revealed the apparition's message about the procession could wait no longer. They rushed to bring the news to their pastor, Abbé Peyramale, at about eight o'clock that morning. "Monsieur le Curé, the Blessed Virgin wants a procession this Thursday!"

For them, in keeping with common knowledge and the current interpretation, the lady in the grotto was the Blessed Virgin. And the procession Bernadette spoke of was obviously to be held that coming Thursday, "the big day," when there would take place "a marvelous or a terrible event," or so everyone thought. To their mind, everything depended on the procession....

At that stage, Abbé Peyramale was confused, unsure. On the one hand, a movement of grace was coming over his parish. Lenten services were attracting unaccustomed numbers of people. There was also, there was *especially* an increase in the numbers of confessions being heard. At certain times, yet always under the reserve his official capacity demanded, Peyramale believed in the apparitions. He said to himself, *I wouldn't even want my hat to know what I'm thinking!*

Nevertheless, the unusual events at the grotto, the exaggerations of some of his parishioners, the insignificance of this unpolished girl made him wary. Hadn't Abbé Pomian, just a few days earlier, while questioning Bernadette in catechism class, discovered that she had no idea about the mystery of the Trinity? Peyramale was torn between these rational objections and the stream that was pulling him along.

The prospect of a public procession put his feet back on the solid ground of his obligations and of his duty. This foolish order unleashed the authoritative side of his personality, which made him feared among the women of Lourdes. His tirade was immediate, overwhelming, unthinking. The faithful women now made a mad scramble for the door!

Meanwhile, Bernadette had gone to Abbé Pomian, her confessor, who was less intimidating than Monsieur le Curé. He listened attentively as usual, but his suspicions had only been growing stronger since the beginning. Bernadette's ignorance of religious matters, her odd antics in recent days, (the grass, the mud) and then the Curé's negative response—all made him leery. This last request for a procession was beyond him. He wasn't eager to be the go-between. He sent Bernadette back to the pastor.

Abbé Peyramale, the Curé of Lourdes

Bernadette got her two aunts, Bernarde and Basile, to go with her to the interview. They arrived at the rectory. Abbé Peyramale was walking back and forth in his garden, disturbed by knotty problems. He was furious with the women who had asked for the impossible and furious with himself for having refused them. What if this was a holy thing?

When his visitors arrived, he stopped his pacing. There was a little bit of a girl between the two women. It was the first time Abbé Peyramale had seen Bernadette. He brought them into the rectory.

"Are you the one who goes to the grotto?" he demanded.

"Yes, Monsieur le Curé."

To stand in front of the Curé was to lose all desire to be "the one-who-went-to-the-grotto!"

"And you say you see the Blessed Virgin?" the pastor continued.

"I didn't say it was the Blessed Virgin," Bernadette responded.

"Then what is this lady?"

"I don't know."

"Oh, you don't know, liar! And yet it's written in the newspaper and said by all those who chase after you: 'it's the Blessed Virgin.'"[48]

Peyramale, "the man of reason," had scored a point on Peyramale, "the man of faith." There was no possibility of having a procession for an anonymous apparition.

"Well, then what do you see?" he went on.

"Something...that looks like a lady"[49]

"Something!"

Repeated by the Curé, this word in patois exploded like a thunderclap. Some *thing!* Not even some *one!* This was the last straw! Under his tongue-lashing, Bernadette wavered, and what she meant to say was about to slip her mind. Before the message disappeared, she blurted out: "Monsieur le Curé, *Aqueró* asks that people come to the grotto in procession!"[50]

The Curé had hoped for a minute that the request had been something made up by devout, daydreaming women. But here it was again! His anger rekindled.

"Liar! How dare you tell me to order a procession? Only the bishop can order processions. If your vision were something good, she wouldn't tell you such foolishness. And when does she want this procession? Thursday, did you say?"

Here, Bernadette stumbled. Had the lady named a day? Was it

Thursday? She tried to remember where "Thursday" came from. Everything got hazy.

Just then, a priest, a stranger in Lourdes, arrived. Sympathizing with her, he broke the silence. "Be careful, little one. You must be certain."

The Curé strode up and down the room, saying, "Come on now! A lady! A procession!"

In the end Bernadette murmured, "I don't know when."

"And are you quite sure she asked for a procession?"

"I think so!"[51]

"Ah! You think so! You're not sure. All right, when one isn't sure, one stays home! Go home and don't go out anymore. It's a sorry thing to have a little one like you who makes people chase after her. All right, we'll give you a torch. Go start your procession; they'll follow you. You don't need a priest!"

Aunt Basile shook at the outburst. It was "frightening to watch the Curé" striding like that "up and down his room," shouting "like during his sermons," and "even louder as he grew hoarse."

"It's a scandal!" the priest boomed. "And they say you ate grass like an animal!"

Bernadette tried to disappear under her hood, and Basile felt as helpless as "a grain of millet." The pastor noticed the two trembling aunts. He knew them both. They had both been expelled from the Children of Mary for having conceived or given birth before they were legally married. Even though this hastiness had been mended by respectable marriages later on, they were a shabby recommendation for Bernadette.

"Are you related to this child?" he questioned.

"Yes, Monsieur le Curé, we're her aunts."

"It's pathetic to have a family like this sowing disorder in town. Keep her at home and don't let her budge!"

Abbé Pomian's entrance refueled the pastor's energy. Peyramale called upon him to bear witness. "See that little girl! She's the one who goes to the grotto every day. She comes here to tell lies."

More gently, Abbé Pomian asked, "Did you just tell lies, Bernadette?"

"No, Monsieur l'Abbé, I came to tell what *Aqueró* said."[52]

The Curé interrupted, "Get out of here! Send her to school and don't let her go to the grotto anymore. Let this be over and done with."

After bowing deeply, Bernadette and Basile walked quietly out of the room. Alone in the street again, they hurried homeward. Aunt Bernarde had already slipped away. In tears, Basile finally said, "No one will ever catch me going back to Monsieur le Curé's."

She was angry at having been dragged into a situation where she had expected a little more consideration. She turned on Bernadette. "You see how you got yourself scolded!"

Bernadette seemed calm, not sorry at all. "Oh, if he doesn't want to believe, he doesn't have to. I ran my errand."[53]

After a few more steps, Bernadette suddenly stopped. "Oh, Aunt Basile, we must go back to Monsieur le Curé."

"Go back! Oh, no!"

"I forgot to mention the chapel."

"Don't count on me any longer! You're making us all sick."[54]

While the discussion continued at the rectory, Bernadette searched in vain for someone to accompany her. She was about to give up when Dominiquette Cazenave came along looking for news. "What did she [the lady] tell you this morning?"

"To tell the priests to have a chapel built here."

"And you didn't tell Monsieur le Curé?"

"My parents won't come with me, neither my mother nor my aunt. Would you be willing, Dominiquette?"

"All right!"[55]

Tactful by nature, Dominiquette would lay the groundwork at the pastor's house. She knew how to handle him. The appointment was made for seven o'clock.

At nightfall, Bernadette and Dominiquette headed for the big, isolated house, the last one on the left, at the edge of town. The windows, golden in the candlelight, pierced the moonless night. Never in her life had Bernadette's heart beat so fast. This time she couldn't hide it. "I hope Abbé Serres is present,"[56] she said.

Abbé Serres was another curate in the parish, the most quiet and unobtrusive of the priests.

The atmosphere in the rectory was relaxed, but impressive. The whole household was there, in the candlelit parlor. Bernadette counted four cassocks: Abbé Peyramale and his two curates, Pène and Serres, as well as Abbé Pomian, the chaplain at the Hospice. They were full of questions and armed with all their theology. Abbé Peyramale invited the young girl to be seated. She was as impressed by the armchair as by the "tribunal" about to interrogate her. She hastened to "complete her errand."

"Monsieur le Curé, *Aqueró* told me: 'Go tell the priests to have a chapel built here.'"[57]

Abbé Peyramale raised his eyebrows. A procession wasn't enough! Another problem! Bernadette could see the storm coming, and in her panic, she improvised and added to the words of the message, for the only time in her life: "A chapel...only that...even if it's only a little chapel."

She was pitiful to see and the pastor intended to stay calm. He was cold as ice.

"A chapel? Like the procession? Are you quite positive?"

"Yes, Monsieur le Curé, I'm positive!" These words rushed out in a great surge of conviction.[58]

"You still don't know her name?"

"No, Monsieur le Curé."[59]

"Well, you'll have to ask her."

The pastor was through. The other priests then asked their own questions according to their personal suppositions, for or against. The interrogation took place half in French and half in patois. Bernadette knew only a few words in French. She got lost.

"Have you ever heard of fairies?" asked Abbé Pomian.

"No, Monsieur l'Abbé."

"Have you ever heard of witches?" asked another.

"No, Monsieur l'Abbé," said Bernadette.[60]

All this was in dialect.

"That is not very likely," remarked the Abbé (in French). "Everyone in Lourdes has more or less heard something about witches...."

Dominiquette stepped in. "Monsieur l'Abbé, Bernadette didn't understand you. Use the word 'Brouches,' not 'Soucièros.' Your word doesn't mean a thing in the dialect of this area." (The dialects differed from valley to valley.)

Abbé Pène, taking his turn, knew he was not well versed in the various dialects. What interested him was the message of the apparition. "What are the words the lady said?" he asked.

"This doesn't involve a pot," Bernadette answered.[61]

"What do you mean no *words!* What about the chapel? The procession?"

Dominiquette jumped in once more, "Monsieur l'Abbé, Bernadette didn't understand you. In Lourdes, we say *'parolos,'* not *'paraoulos,'* as they say in your valley. Bernadette understood you to say *'paraou,'* which means 'pot'! Monsieur le Curé," she added, "let her go!"

"Yes, that's enough."

Dominiquette kept a charming recollection of their return home. The little girl skipped along beside her, happy to have accomplished her mission.

"She [Bernadette] took my arm and said, 'I'm very happy. I ran my errand.'

"I said to her, 'You'll have to ask the lady her name.'

"'Yes, if I can remember.'"[62]

Bernadette was worried. She knew from experience that when she saw the apparition, she forgot everything and everyone else, including what people had asked her to do. Would she remember? Dominiquette insisted, "They won't have the chapel built if they don't know her name."[63]

The Fourteenth Apparition: March 3

"The little one saw no apparition this morning!"

"Yes, she did!"

"She didn't see her, because someone broke her candle."

"She felt a movement."

"It's because Laborde, the innkeeper, did nasty things at the grotto...."

This was what people were saying in Lourdes on the morning of March 3. What exactly had happened? Bernadette had taken her usual place at the usual time—but not without difficulty. She had to pass through a crowd of three thousand people packed beyond description between the Gave—into which more than one person fell—and the cliff, where they were hanging on like bunches of grapes! As she struggled to reach her place, her candle got broken. She prayed her rosary but "said nothing" that morning.

At the Savy Mill, her Uncle Sajous gave her some advice: "There are too many people. Come, have something to eat, and then, if you want to go back, we'll go by the road at the foot of the castle so they won't follow us."

When they went back, there were no more than one hundred people at the grotto, and Bernadette saw the apparition.

That night she visited the Curé Peyramale, just back from Tarbes. "Monsieur le Curé, the lady still wants her chapel."

"Did you ask her name?"

"Yes, but all she does is smile."[64]

"She's really making fun of you!"

The pastor was puzzled. It occurred to him to ask for a sign. "All right, if she wants a chapel, let her give her name, and let her make the rosebush at the grotto bloom!" He paused, then added, "If she gives her name, and if she makes the rosebush bloom, we'll have a chapel built, and it won't be a little one, believe me! It'll be a big one!"

Once outside, Dominiquette took Bernadette home with her because the late arrival of the Curé had caused Bernadette to miss her supper. While she ate her codfish on that Wednesday of Lent, Jean-Marie Cazenave, the owner of the stagecoach arrived. He was returning from Bagnères with a full coach. There was a great rush on the eve of "the big day at the grotto." He had heard contradictory rumors. He asked Bernadette, "Did you see her?"

Bernadette put down her fork. "Yes, I saw her."

Jean-Marie stood tall in the strength of his thirty years. He had the confidence of a man used to giving orders to horses, to passengers and to the clumsy coachmen who blocked up the road. His appearance had earned him the great-sounding nicknames of "Ganço" or "Rotchil," by which he was better known. Bernadette looked up at this strong man whom even her father obeyed. She began thinking, *Now here is someone better than my aunts to open up a way through the crowd on the final day.*

"Ganço," she asked, "will you come with me to the grotto to-morrow?"[65]

He accepted.

At that point, François Soubirous came to get his daughter. Her aunt and cousin Jeanne Védère had just arrived for two reasons: to go to the grotto as well as to attend the funeral of Aunt Jeanne Soubirous, who had died at five o'clock that morning. Bernadette was very fond of her cousin Jeanne, a schoolteacher in Momères. And besides, she was the sister of Bernadette's godfather, Jean-Marie Védère, then stationed in Lyons with the fifth infantry, complete with sergeant's stripes. Bernadette's first words were of him: "How is my godfather?"[66]

But the cachot had been invaded by the curious and those who had advice to give. It was getting late. The family got rid of them and closed the door. Jeanne could now talk in peace with her cousin. She knew the apparition had failed to take place that morning. She was worried. "Maybe you won't see her tomorrow either?"

"I didn't see her this morning, but I did see her during the day."[67]

Jeanne also worried about the crowd. In that crush she would never reach the site of the apparition. Bernadette reassured her, with conviction in her voice, "Don't worry, you'll be there."[68]

With that reassurance, they snuffed out the resin torch. Silence and sleep overtook the cachot.

The Fifteenth Apparition: March 4

On Thursday, March 4, the morning of the big day, Bernadette went to Mass, celebrated for the repose of the soul of her Aunt Soubirous. Just before the end of Mass, she slipped off. Jeanne noticed this and caught up with her in the church square. "So, you're abandoning me!" she exclaimed.

"It's because I'm very busy."[69]

They left in silence. The group included Bernadette's father, his sister Thècle, who was Jeanne's mother, her godmother, and especially "Ganço" (Jean-Marie Cazenave), whom Bernadette had recruited the day before. On the way Bernadette's silence would be broken three times.

Having arrived behind the castle, Jeanne pressed close to her cousin, whom she was afraid of losing, and murmured, "I'll never be able to see you at the grotto. The crowd will separate us."

Bernadette renewed her promise of the night before, "Don't worry, you'll be near me."[70] She used the respectful *"vous"* to her cousin the schoolteacher, who, that morning, seemed to be the little follower.

A man from Luz approached. "Pray for my child who is blind," he begged.

The little child was there in a red hooded cape, the color of her valley. She was frail and had a bandage covering her eyes. Bernadette looked at her and said, "Go make her wash in the spring."[71]

A little further on was a lady, accompanied by her servant who was carrying a lame and mute child of about three or four in her arms. "Take this candle," the woman said. "Offer it to the Virgin for my child."

"Madame, I'll pray for your child. As for the candle, put it in the grotto or in the church yourself."[72] Bernadette answered gently but firmly. She revealed an authority her cousin never knew she had. The lady tried to force the candle on her, but she refused to take it.

At the grotto, the press of the crowd was unbelievable, but Bernadette's arrival had been anticipated. Tarbès had created a sort of aisle with girders. The commissioner was there with his entire force. That was how Bernadette managed to get to her usual place without any trouble. But Jeanne's way had been blocked. She had sadly resigned herself when she heard a loud voice announce, "The little one is asking for one of her cousins."[73]

Jeanne answered, "I'm here, but I can't move ahead."

The commissioner and a policeman came over to her and pointed her out to Bernadette. "Is she the one?" they asked.

"Yes," answered Bernadette.

They brought Jeanne right up to Bernadette, under the crevasse that pierced the ceiling of the grotto.

The apparition took place as usual: rosary, bows, smiles. The commissioner kept a tally in his notebook, with little lines.

The apparition was over. Nothing miraculous had happened. Packed together on both sides of the Gave since the night before, the crowd was disappointed. But something insignificant was all that it would take to fire up the enthusiasm of the volatile gathering.

Bernadette and her group climbed the hill and had reached halfway. Gança was holding her right hand, while with the other he gestured the crowd to make way. But Bernadette slowed down.

"What are you doing? Get going!" Gança urged.

The small opening in the crowd was about to close up again. Bernadette's eyes were staring toward the right.

"What are you looking at?" he asked.

"That Maïnade over there," Bernadette replied.[74]

It was the little girl in the red hood, whose father had pleaded for her on the way to the grotto. The girl who seemed so unhappy appeared to be Bernadette's own age. Gança also recognized her. He was the one who had brought her to Lourdes in his coach.

More than pity, an outpouring of affection showed in Bernadette's eyes and voice.

"You like that poor girl?" Ganço asked.

"Oh, yes!"

"Well, then, give her a kiss!"[75]

Ganço called over a neighbor. "Young man, bring that *toye* here.
(*Toye* is the name given to the people of Barèges.)

The red silhouette approached, walking haltingly, her eyes bandaged. She wore the bandage both to conceal the ugliness of her
diseased eyelids and to shield her eyes from the light, which hurt
them. She felt a strong emotion at being called that way, she, the
little girl nobody wanted, the one made fun of at school because
even in the simplest games her eyesight hampered her.

Bernadette came before her, filled with the riches she had received that morning. She took her hands and gave her a big kiss.
The little girl, no longer embraced by her friends, now felt reborn.
Both girls burst out laughing, holding each other's hands. Bernadette
kissed her a second time and left without even asking her name.

With joy, Eugénie tore off her bandage to look at her wonderful
friend, who was moving off. She could stand the daylight now, without pain. The crowd gathered around. A miracle!

While Bernadette disappeared on the path into the woods, the
word spread. The girl from Barèges was filled with a warm sense of
blessing. She didn't suffer anymore. She believed that she'd been
cured. Her parents soon shared her belief. In the afternoon, an
enthusiastic group would bring her to the prosecutor, who would
methodically interrogate her and remain more puzzled after his
examination. Some weeks would have to pass before the illusion,
born of a moment of joy, vanished. Eugénie died the following year
on June 15, 1859.

On the way home, Jeanne questioned her cousin about her behavior during the apparition: "Why did you try three times to make
that beautiful sign of the cross?"

"*Aqueró* had not made hers yet. I couldn't bring my hand to my
forehead...."

"Why were you happy one minute and sad the next?"

"I am sad when *Aqueró* is sad; and I smile when she smiles."

"And why did you go look in that hole?"

Jeanne still felt the emotion she had experienced when Bernadette had gone to talk at the interior cave opening. She had thought she felt a presence and, by instinct, she had drawn back.

"*Aqueró* had gone down there," answered Bernadette. "If you had reached out your hand only a little bit, you would have touched her."

"And why were you talking so softly that I couldn't hear a thing?"

Bernadette looked surprised. "We were talking the way I'm talking to you now."[76]

They arrived at the cachot. Visitors poured in. The family closed the door. The crowd increased in the tiny street and asked more and more loudly to see Bernadette. She appeared at the window once, twice, then a third time...and finally, they had to open the door. The crowd pushed its way up the shaky staircase, toward cousin Sajous' room where Bernadette was hidden. Among the first to get there was Jeanne Adrian, a schoolteacher from Gavarnie, who had spent the whole night at the grotto. She gave Bernadette a hearty hug and, happy then, headed back to her village.

Bernadette was a captive of the crowd: more women than men, and a number of children. All kinds of lips kissed her cheeks and her hands. Hidden scissors snipped threads from the lining of her dress. The group was carried away by the presence of their idle. She protested. "Why touch me? I have no power whatever."[77]

But it was a wasted effort!

Some wanted more than this. It was not enough that they touched their rosaries and medals to her. She must touch them herself. She protested laughingly, "And after I touch them, then what?"[78]

New groups kept arriving and Bernadette was afraid that it would go on until nighttime. She grew weary. If only by going along with all this she could bring it to a sudden halt! She made an attempt to stop it. "What do you want me to do? Bring them all at once, and I'll touch them for you."[79]

It was useless. The only thing the crowd understood was that she had agreed, and more rosaries than before were brought for her to touch. This ritual offended something inside her, but necessity spurred her on. She made an impromptu compromise, whose explanation would become clear to her cousin.

Yes, Jeanne was still there. She had also joined the line in the staircase, caught in the spirit of things. Because she had to return home that same day, she wanted to take something back with her.

She held out her rosaries to Bernadette to be touched, three of them, a whole arsenal: the rosary of the Seven Sorrows, the Camaldolese rosary, and the rosary of Saint Dominic.

"You too!" murmured Bernadette. "What do you want me to do to them? I'm not a priest!"[80]

She resigned herself, but would put things in proper focus. "I will touch them to the beads I had at the grotto."[81] With great seriousness Bernadette mixed Jeanne's rosaries with her own. She wanted to give credit to "the lady of the ledge" for what was unfortunately being attributed to herself. But Jeanne interpreted this otherwise: wasn't it because the Virgin herself had touched that rosary?

That "two-cent" rosary was coveted by many. Two women wanted to trade theirs, which were beautifully wrought in gold. Even the rich were waiting in line; hoopskirts, jewels and shiny hats stood in stark contrast to the poverty of the cachot. One of the wealthiest families of Pau arrived. Together with their chambermaids they waited their turn to embrace "this poor child." No longer did they find it shameful to enter this house, this jail, this "shanty," this "filthy hovel," to use the words of the prosecutor in the report of the preceding Monday. It had become a sacred place. People were tearing off bits and pieces as relics.

From then on, the Soubirous' poverty, which had been so taken for granted, seemed unbearable. The visitors offered "large donations." Bernadette refused them all. Insisting or trying to slip them by her was useless.

Lacking money, one man offered oranges. He had to take them back.

A serving-maid presented a child of six or seven to Bernadette. The child, whose arms and hands were partially paralyzed, was the daughter of Monsieur Sempolis of Tarbes. She had been brought to the grotto the previous night, given that a "miracle" was to occur. Standing in line in the street and on the staircase, the serving-maid seemed exhausted. Louise Soubirous, who knew what weariness was, offered her a chair in front of Bernadette. The paralyzed child looked back at Bernadette, then down at her apron pocket. Something red was sticking out of it. It was the apple Bernadette hadn't had time to eat. The little arms jerkily beat the air in the direction of the fruit. Bernadette understood and skillfully placed the apple in the hollow of the little hand with the bent fingers. At the first jerk of motion, the apple fell. Someone picked it up. Bernadette gave it to her again. Another series of jerks sent it rolling off. The sick little girl began to cry. A third try was just as unsuccessful. The serving-maid picked up the apple and left, shaking it in front of the eyes of the now smiling child. That smile would make people talk about a new miracle.

Impromptu security guards sped things up. The dinner hour reduced the numbers of people. At last, the family managed to stem the flow and close the door.

"Ten thousand people must have come by," estimated Sajous, with no exaggeration.

There was only one woman left. She took advantage of being the last one. She had gotten into a conversation with Bernadette and wanted to buy her rosary. Bernadette categorically refused. The woman offered the money anyway. She still had no luck. Well, then, since Bernadette was so disinterested, why not just give her the rosary?

"I'll neither sell it nor give it away!"[82] Bernadette responded.

They couldn't get rid of this woman, even though it was well past mealtime. The visitor had a sudden thought. She offered them oranges, insisting that they take them. Bernadette, who had so stoutly resisted thus far, was not merciless. "All right, provided that you eat with us," she agreed.

The woman was seated at the table with the Soubirous and Tarbès, who organized the security guards. She had never eaten such a sparse meal in such humble company. At the same time, she had never been so happy.

For Bernadette the meal did not last too long. She had to take advantage of the respite to report to the rectory what *Aqueró* had confided to her. Disguising her as best they could, they took her there.

Abbé Peyramale was anxiously waiting for her. He had hopes.... "What did the lady say?"

"I asked her name.... She smiled. I asked her to make the rose-bush bloom and she smiled again. But she still wants her chapel."

"Do you have money to build this chapel?"

"No, Monsieur le Curé."

"Me neither. Tell the lady to give you some...." Then he added, "She didn't tell you to come back?"

"No, Monsieur le Curé."

"She didn't say she would not be back?"

"She did not say."[83]

Disappointed, the Curé had turned his back. Bernadette's heart was heavy at not having received the hoped for answer on that final day. But at least she had delivered the message. All she had to do now was to go to "cousin" Clarens' house, which he shared with Isidore Baudéan, the candle-maker, at 15 Rue du Bourg. Clarens had proposed this as a place of refuge from the crowd. Here, no longer worried over the latest developments, she immediately began to play games with the director's young children. Her host, quite pleased at receiving the personality of the day, couldn't get over it. Who would believe she went into ecstasies? Perplexing, this young girl who laughed heartily with these little children with whom she had made friends so quickly.[84]

But Bernadette's peace could not last. The "miracle" of the blind girl from Barèges created a movement that ended at the cachot. The red hooded cape of Eugénie Troy, who was overjoyed and thankful, aroused the people's enthusiasm. The street was jammed. The Soubirous were swamped. Between three and four o'clock, François went to the home of the Director of the Lourdes Secondary School where another crowd had begun to assemble. Just in the nick of time, Clarens escaped a situation that was beginning to get out of hand.

The waiting line formed again at the cachot. It got longer. Night fell. Bernadette was exhausted, her cheeks sticky from being kissed. She was having difficulty breathing. Her asthma, dormant for the past three weeks, threatened to return with a vengeance. She pleaded for mercy. "Lock the door."[85]

As Bernadette's friend, Dominiquette, the sister of François' employer, slipped inside. She noticed how drawn Bernadette looked. "You're very tired?" she asked.

"Oh, yes! What with all that kissing!"[86]

That night, the breath of the miraculous blew over Lourdes. One group, returning to Angles, saw a bright light pierce the darkness, "Like a fire in the air." Another group of six or seven people including Lacoste, the bailiff, on their way to Saint-Pé, observed something glowing opposite the grotto. It was a freakish occurrence caused by the weather, no doubt. Capitayne, the poacher, was stunned. He stopped at the first shelter and didn't leave until day-break.

Meanwhile, Bernadette had fallen asleep out of weariness, not clearly understanding why the young lady at the grotto asked her there for two weeks. She was very happy to have seen her and now promised herself to obey the human authorities. She would not go back to the grotto.

CHAPTER 4

— ⚜ —

THE LAST THREE APPARITIONS

Bernadette Disappoints

The day after March 4, Bernadette again found some degree of calmness. The crowd was disappointed. The "big day," so long awaited, had brought nothing spectacular. The "miracles" labeled as such by popular enthusiasm proved to have no foundation. Anxious for a while, the opposition was now reassured. The press orchestrated the triumph.

"What fakery! How many naive believers have been humiliated. How many! People have finally understood too late, alas! the foolishness of their behavior and now deplore their extreme gullibility..." wrote the *Lavedan* of March 4.[1]

Even though the flow of visitors to the grotto and the spring continued, Bernadette herself did not go. She was no longer drawn to Massabielle. She was preparing for her First Holy Communion and was trying to learn the catechism, whose answers her poor memory failed to retain. To overcome this handicap the nuns called on the help of nine-year-old Julie Garros, a little girl of extraordinary energy who knew everything by heart. Despite her warmhearted nature, Bernadette was more discouraged than cheered up by this effort, much like someone paralyzed watching an acrobat do

87

his stunts. The sisters remarked, "You would have been better off asking your lady to teach you your catechism."

That didn't help either.

There were fewer and fewer visitors. Bernadette discouraged them by the briefness of her answers. She claimed no mission for herself and acknowledged nothing out of the ordinary. She didn't know who had appeared to her. At a time when everyone was talking of "the Virgin," she always spoke of *Aqueró*. She refused to give the lady any other identification.

Her childish behavior threw people off. Uncomfortable with schoolwork, she seemed to like nothing better than to laugh and play, appearing to be completely unconcerned about what the enthusiasts of the grotto were discussing.

Miracle at Piqué?

A chance occurrence would get her back in the harness. After classes on March 9, her schoolmate Joséphine Doucet came up to her very politely and said, "My little brother would like to see you. He's been sick a few days. He thinks only of seeing you."

Bernadette was willing to go home with Joséphine after school the next day, Wednesday, March 10.

Scarcely five minutes up the steep hill leading to Bartrès, among the trees on the right, sat a square house, flanked by two sheds, smelling of sheep and hay. It was the Piqué Farm.

In the parlor, to the right of the fireplace, Bernadette saw a strange sight: a huge mouth, open wide like an oven. It seemed to be devouring the face of a sickly child, seated near the fire in some sort of cradle. His name was Jean-Marie, and he was nine and a half years old. Since Christmas, he had been the despair of his family. He could no longer walk. His body jerked without warning. As for that mouth, he barely closed it once a day to take a bit of food. Doctors Lacrampe, Peyrus and Bordères couldn't make heads or tails of the boy's condition. They had never seen anything like it. They used fearsome words like "neuralgic" and "incurable."

Seeing Bernadette, the sick child uttered a happy yelp, "like the barking of a little dog." He had a sharp eye and a fresh, rosy complexion. But certainly the only thing one could see was that mouth! The tongue was dry and raspy. The saliva drooled down to his knees.

Le jour ont me mettait dans un petit matelas au coin du feu

PAR là miséricorde de Dieu jean-Marie Doucet Infirme, le 4 Avril 1861.

Jean-Marie Doucet in his chimney corner
(A reproduction from his handwritten diary)

His body jerked. He was shaken by hiccups. All in all, it was a heart-rending sight to see.

Bernadette put on a brave face. She looked right at him with a friendly smile and said, "How are you?"[2]

With another kind of yelp, which his mother translated, he answered, "Not too good."

"Are you the one who made this?" she asked, instinctively choosing the right topic for conversation.

Next to him was a little chapel made of fir branches, decorated with several colorful pictures—a real collection, which, with the gifts of visitors, grew from day to day. He was indeed the creator, for his mind worked too much rather than not enough. He untiringly drew strange faces on sheets of paper that he should have used sparingly. This pastime gave him comfort and lifted his spirits.

Bernadette's visit was short, because it was lunchtime and classes resumed at one o'clock.

"Well, I have to go. Take care of yourself."[3]

Jean-Marie kept looking at her and began to yelp again, frustrated at not having been understood. His mother interpreted, "He says that you must come back."

She promised she would.

At this answer, the rigid mouth of the sick child happily came to life, and as Bernadette left, his lips trembled. After "three big yawns" his mouth closed. "Now I'd like something to eat and drink," he said in a normal voice.

His mother, who for months had been crying at the thought of losing this child, was overjoyed with hope. It had been so long since he has asked for anything to eat. It was a "miracle" performed by this "saintling!"

But the "miracle" was not to last. Jean-Marie later described it in his *Journal,* complete with French misspellings: "the meal was barely over when all the torments began again with the same violence as before. From that night on, I could not close my mouth, nor eat, nor drink."[4]

It was the same during all the next day. His mouth closed just long enough for a snack, around noontime.

Two days later, on Friday, March 12, Bernadette returned. But this time she had companions. Joséphine had spread the news of the "miracle" of that first visit, and her friends from the "charity class," Thérèse Courouau, Marie Chouatou and company were in

Visite que me rendait les bourjeoises, à Pique.

par la miséricorde de Dieu, Jean Marie Doucet Infirme

Par les paroles que me disait Bernadette, je pu plusieur fois marquer

Visites que me rendit la généreuse Bernadette Soubirous, le mois de mars, a Pique en 1858.

par la miséricorde de Dieu Jean-Marie Doucet Infirme, le 11 Février 1882.

La Solitude devint mes délices...................

par la miséricorde de Dieu Jean-Marie Doucet Infirme

Au doux souvenir de mon enfance p. m. m.

par la grâce de Dieu jean-Marie Doucet Infirme à la Touloube

Jean-Marie Doucet and his chapel of pictures
(Reproductions from his diary)

the habit of going out together in a group. Bernadette cheerfully greeted the little invalid. "How are you?"

"Not good," he answered. (This would become the refrain of all the visits.)

"Are you hungry?"

"Yes."

"Well, force yourself to close your mouth and eat!"[5]

Whereupon, as had happened two days before, after "three or four yawns," his mouth closed. Jean-Marie was at once able to question Bernadette about the apparitions. Time flew, but before she left, his mouth was again agape.

At eleven-thirty, on Saturday, March 13, the group paid the Piqué Farm another visit. Bernadette instinctively felt that improvement in the invalid was up to her. She became very sharp with him. The Soubirous and Castérot families were characterized by a "no-nonsense" attitude, where whims were given short shrift. Bernadette turned to these familial methods, without reflection, but she did it in her own pleasant manner. "So, you never want to get up. It's always up to me to come to see you!"

"Oh, if I could get up, I really would, really!"

"Oh, you are a lazybones; otherwise, you would get up. And you would dance around the room. Look, you're a rascal. You act sick to get good food to eat. Well, as for me, I don't like you anymore, because you're a lazybones."[6]

"Come on, Bernadette, make him close his mouth!" his mother urged her. "He hasn't eaten anything today."

"You haven't eaten anything?"

"No."

"Well, now, eat, lazybones!"[7]

These scoldings did wonders. Jean-Marie happily ate his meal. His mother suddenly noticed something she had forgotten. "This cheese has to be brought to Minjote Théas for President Pougat! Will you take it there, Joséphine?"

There was little time left before the start of school. Joséphine, Thérèse, and Marie ran off on their errand, in spite of the ominous-looking clouds, while Bernadette continued to feed the invalid. They would pick her up on the way back. There was time enough.

But they were too optimistic! Time passed and the girls didn't return.

"It's time to go," said Bernadette, "I'm leaving."

"Wait a bit! They won't be long. Look at the weather outside; it wouldn't be reasonable to leave now," Madame Doucet advised.

A soft snow was already falling. It soon turned to a downpour, and when the errand-runners finally returned at one o'clock, they were soaking wet and chilled to the bone. The problem was that it was time for classes to begin.

"You'll have to stay here and dry off," Madame Doucet decided.

Many of these poor little girls had no change of clothing and the woman of the house was not unhappy to hang on to Bernadette, her "good luck charm."

Happiest of all was Jean-Marie. What he had not foreseen was that, after having done all she could for him, Bernadette would go to the barn to join the other girls, now dry and having a good time.[8]

"Then," Jean-Marie relates in his journal, "my intellectual and redoubtable furies returned to harass me with their reproaches, as if I had paid them some insult."[9]

At three o'clock, Madame Doucet went out to get Bernadette, telling her that Jean-Marie was asking for her.

"And what does he want?" Bernadette questioned.

"The joy of seeing you."[10]

No! Bernadette wouldn't simply make an appearance. She believed in the virtue of strong action.

"Hey! You won't eat anything, lazybones!" She began again.[11]

This had an immediate effect on the little boy. He yawned three times and then spent fifteen minutes eating. Afterwards, however, he wrote that all his pains returned.[12]

At four o'clock, the girls left, not at all unhappy to have skipped classes...under the protection of the Doucet family.

At the Doucet's, hope had revived. Jean-Marie's mouth closed twice a day. Yes, Bernadette had to return.

On Sunday morning, Bernadette agreed to pay them two visits: on her way to and from Bartrès. She discovered a telling argument to make Jean-Marie eat: "All right, since you won't eat, I'm leaving. Adieu! I don't like you anymore."[13]

The door was hardly closed when his mouth closed too. They ran to call her back. In this high-handed fashion, she fed him two meals in one hour.

This time the improvement held, whether Bernadette came

or not. Jean-Marie began eating, not two or three, but four meals a day.

This success had an effect in town that Bernadette did not suspect. A new "miracle" was proclaimed. The rectory was alerted.

On Monday, March 15, Monsieur le Curé, with the Abbés Pomian and Pène beside him, came to make an inquiry at the Piqué Farm. With Eugénie Troy, "the blind girl cured on March 4," the deception was complete.[14] Abbé Peyramale hoped for better things in the Doucet case. He was puzzled at what he saw, but there was still hope. That very day he wrote to the bishop: "An interesting case...quite an improvement. If he is thoroughly healed we can say with Saint Augustine: *Causa finita est* (Case closed).

But the verdict hung on an "if."

Nevertheless, the authorities were worried. The popular "movement," whose decline they had watched with pleasure on the day after March 4, threatened to begin again. Romain Capdevielle, engaged to the charming Marie Dufo, an enthusiastic admirer of Bernadette, had published two successive articles in the *Mémorial de Pau,* on March 9 and 16. This young and talented lawyer sang the praises of the visionary of the grotto: "Just as simple and unspoiled today as before." Popular feeling reawakened. The number of candles at the grotto increased. This had to be attacked at the root: at the Soubirous' house!

The Soubirous' public image was not good. Despite François' acquittal, being charged with larceny remained a mark of shame, as had been shown by the prosecutor's report. Indeed, the family was discreet, quiet and polite to a T. Was this a ruse, the ability to camouflage "the material elements" of the crime, to use the prosecutor's words? What were they hiding?

Now, here they were, supported by a movement that reached up to the highest levels of society.

Monsieur Dufo, president at the bar and town councilor, showed an interest in Bernadette, pushed to fever point. "He kissed her hand and called her the saint," noted the Imperial Prosecutor Dutour, in his report of March 17.[15]

This was far from being an isolated case. There was worse! Monsieur Pougat, President of the Tribunal, a gentleman fond of good living, who had reached the bench through his political ties, secretly counseled the Soubirous. Threats made little impression now, given the reassurances of this highly placed person. Prosecutor Dutour had assumed his most knowing and enigmatic air to tell Bernadette, "Be careful! Bernadette! There is a certain gentleman around the Porch who gives you advice. He may not be able to keep you from going to jail."

The reference to the president's home, the "Place du Porch," was quite clear. But Bernadette answered, "You have to stand up to talk to that gentleman."

It was an awkward situation. In his March 17 report, Monsieur Dutour tried in veiled terms to denounce the scandal to the attorney general in Pau. After mentioning the Dufo case, he wrote on his rough copy, "I could mention other men whose position is even higher...."

But he stopped there. The sentence was left hanging, half crossed out, half-erased.

Direct and official action had to be taken.

The Interrogation of March 18

Bernadette was summoned on Thursday, March 18. Present that day were a whole court of officials: the prosecutor, the commissioner and the mayor, assisted by Joanas, secretary for the mayor's office, who recorded the official minutes.[16]

Bernadette acted naturally. She confirmed what Capdevielle said in his articles: *Aqueró* asked her "to have a chapel built," and told her some secrets. She refused to say anything more.

"*Aqueró* has forbidden me to reveal them to anyone. However, I can say they contain nothing to be frightened of and they concern only me."

Quite briefly Bernadette described her visits to Jean-Marie Doucet, affirming (what the inquiry would prove to be true), "I have not gone to see any other sick people."

"But did they bring them to you?"

"Only one, Monsieur Sempolis' daughter."

She talked about the apple given to the half-paralyzed child on March 4, and concluded, "The child left the way she came."

Asked about the girl with the red-hooded cape from Barèges—the alleged "blind" girl miraculously cured—she said even more clearly, "I don't think I've cured anyone whatsoever, and besides I haven't done anything for that reason."

They had her describe the apparitions one more time, which she did in shortened form. (For this part of the "court statement," Jacomet relieved Joanas, official secretary for the mayor's office.)[17]

"Those first days, I merely knelt to pray to God, and *Aqueró* would appear to me at the exterior cave opening, which is above the main grotto. She would smile, she would bow to me; I'd smile back and bow to her. She held a rosary in her right hand."

Here, the interrogators asked for precise details.

"Did *Aqueró* wear shoes, as the newspapers said?"

"No, a yellow rose on each foot."

"An apron?"

"No, no apron."

She continued (according to the official minutes), "Later *Aqueró* told me to walk on my knees, kissing the ground as a penance for sinners. Finally, *Aqueró* told me to go drink at the spring."

"Why?"

"I don't know."

At this point, obsessed by the secrets, Jacomet interpreted, "I cannot reveal the reasons for this command."

Bernadette continued, "Tuesday, March 2, I went to the grotto as usual. *Aqueró* told me to ask...."

Here Bernadette hesitated. Abbé Peyramale's anger had clouded this recollection. Jacomet took down her remarks as follows: "I don't know whether it's a procession or a chapel, I'm not sure. I went to tell the Curé, who said that nothing could be done until there was some unusual thing or other; that the Virgin, for example, would make the rosebush in front of the grotto bloom."

She cautiously concluded, "I don't know whether I'll go back to the grotto again."

Her tone of voice was so conciliatory that Prosecutor Dutour thought himself authorized to interpret this statement as a straight out promise to the attorney general: "She promised not to go back, nor to invite the abuse which credulity and bad faith make of her actions and of her person."[18]

Just when detailed and repeated inquiries established that the Soubirous received no profit whatever from popular enthusiasm, the interrogation of March 18, tended to confirm that, as far as Bernadette was concerned, the affair was over. Optimism was reborn among town officials.

The Sixteenth Apparition: March 25

During the night of March 24, the vigil of the Annunciation, the problems started up again. Bernadette awakened. It was not due to the difficulty in breathing brought on by her asthma attacks; it was because of the joy of an attraction she quickly recognized. She felt an urgency to go to the grotto. The clock struck many times. It was nowhere near morning. She went back to sleep without saying a word.

Awake again before four o'clock, she gropingly dressed in the dark, awaited the first sign of the family's awakening and told them of her attraction, "I must go to the grotto. Hurry, if you want to come with me."

"Come now, that would be bad for you," her mother cautioned. Bernadette's asthma had been acting up the previous few days.

"I'm all better now," the teenager maintained.

"Wait till sunup."

"No, I must go and go quickly."[19]

Her parents gave their permission and began getting ready themselves. A little before five, Bernadette and her mother and father were on their way to the grotto. It was still dark. This time, nobody knew of the trip ahead of time; they wouldn't be bothered, thought Monsieur and Madame Soubirous.

But they were in for a surprise! There was a crowd at the grotto. The feast of the Annunciation had sparked enthusiasm and high hopes. For a few days before, rumors had been flying. "Bernadette is going to leave for Rome," they were saying in Lourdes beginning on Saturday, March 13.

"She's leaving with a priest next Friday (March 26)," others specified.

"The priest is her confessor, and on the day before they leave, the Annunciation, Bernadette will go to the grotto."[20]

Even though these rumors had no basis in fact, about one hundred people had gathered at Massabielle. The commissioner was there too; nothing escaped him.

The young lady in white was faithful to the rendezvous that she had set—for Bernadette alone.

The joy of being reunited with the young lady did not distract Bernadette from the answer she had to get at all costs. During the three weeks of the lady's absence, she had mentally prepared a beautiful, formal and reverential way of asking her question: "Mademoiselle, would you have the kindness to tell me who you are, if you please?"[21]

But this lovely turn of phrase was too complicated! Bernadette got mixed up and said "willingness" *(boulentat)* instead of "kindness" *(bountat);* She had a hard time distinguishing between those two words. The longer word seemed much more polite.

The young lady in light smiled. Could she be mocking her, as Monsieur le Curé had said? No. There was so much gentleness and kindness in her gaze. Bernadette must start over: "Would you have the kindness..."

Aqueró said nothing. Nevertheless, she was there, quite close. She had come down into the interior hollow where she came when she wanted to speak. So why this silence? Bernadette persisted, "Would you have the kindness..."

Aqueró smiled all the more. But Bernadette was determined. Nothing would stop her. She would try ten times if she had to, since the young lady took no offense.

There was no need to go that far. At the fourth attempt, *Aqueró* no longer smiled. She had just slipped her rosary over her right arm. She unfolded her hands and extended them toward the ground. She then folded them at her breast, raised her eyes to heaven and said, "I am the Immaculate Conception."[22]

The apparition had lasted close to an hour. The color returned to Bernadette's face. In the brightness of daybreak, she stood up elated, overflowing with thanksgiving, not thinking at all.

Before leaving the grotto, she got the urge to leave something there as a sign of her thanksgiving. Unfortunately, she had nothing to leave—it was impossible to leave her heart! She looked at the burning candle in her hand. She would have liked to put it with the countless others already burning beneath the vault, a whole forest of them, sputtering and flickering in the breeze created by the mysterious hollows of the grotto. But the candle she held was not hers. It was her Aunt Lucile's sodality candle. She was given permission to leave it there. She wedged it between the rocks under the cavity where the answer she sought had finally burst forth.

"What did she tell you?"

From every side, questions arose, bringing her back to face the problems she had temporarily forgotten. Just a short while before, the young lady's answer had been so marvelous and clear. Bernadette then realized that those words, never heard before, were obscure. She didn't even understand them. Their harmony had vanished with the light. They would slip her mind, like the words in class...especially the second. What was it now? *Cou-che...siou.... Counchet-siou?*

She felt the words eluding her. She ran off, repeating softly, painstakingly: *"Immaculada Coun...chet...siou, Immaculada Coun...chet...siou."*[23]

Intrigued, a few people followed her. What was she saying? Was it still a secret? Right next to her, twelve-year-old Jeanne-Marie Tourré made out the strange words on her lips and repeated them under her breath.

The sky had brightened. Behind the little group, the last stars disappeared. In front of them, the castle, perched against the open sky, cut out from the brightness of the dawning light a strange silhouette broken here and there by a curious light. The sun was starting to shine on the hillside.

Ursule Nicolau, heading the group, caught up to Bernadette, took her by the arm without missing a stride and kissed her, saying softly, "Do you know something?"

Bernadette laughed. Ursule could see she was happy.

"Do you know something?"

"Don't tell anyone, but she said, 'I am the Immaculate Conception.'"[24]

Ursule ran to tell Eugénie Raval, urging her not to tell anyone else. Eugénie told her sister Germaine, who repeated it to Dominiquette Cazenave, each, of course, telling the other not to repeat it to anyone else.

Meanwhile, Bernadette had gone up the Rue de Baous and crossed the "Place du Porche," repeating the words she didn't understand. What in the world was *"Counchetsiou"*?

She pushed the rectory door open and flung her words in the Curé's face, almost at the top of her lungs: *"Que soy era Immaculada Counchetsiou!"*[25]

Peyramale, the rock, wavered under the shock whose significance he miscalculated. His authoritarian anger, which rose up within him in trying circumstances, clicked in like an automatic reflex. He was about to say, "You are the Immaculate Conception!" or "You little show-off!" But the words stuck in his throat. Having just realized the bluntness of her message, Bernadette repeated more precisely, "*Aqueró* said, 'Que soy era Immaculada Counchetsiou!'"[26]

Monsieur le Curé had pulled himself together. The words came out, heavy and gruff, "A lady cannot bear that name!"

He tried to recall his theology. Let's see now, the Virgin was conceived without sin...her conception was immaculate...*but how can she say she is her conception?* He returned to the attack. "You're mistaken! Do you know what that means?"

Bernadette pathetically shook her head.

"Then how can you say that, if you didn't understand?"

"I repeated it all the way here."[27]

Peyramale was at a loss. The weapon of his authority, those short-lived outbursts of anger, which he wielded to produce good results, abandoned him. From the bottom of his heart and breast, a tide had risen, submerging him, as in his childhood days. Was he sick? He choked back his sobs.

During the lull, Bernadette murmured, "She still wants her chapel."[28]

The pastor gathered his strength to utter a final face-saving statement, "Go on home. I'll see you another day."

Bernadette left confused. If Monsieur le Curé didn't know what the lady meant, who would? She went home, where the curious awaited her. Dominiquette, the brave one who had accompanied her to the rectory on March 2, took her aside in the shadows, "next to the door with the big bolt."

"Do you know the Lady's name?" Dominiquette questioned.

"Who told you that? I only told Ursule."

"Tell me."

"I'd like to tell Monsieur l'Abbé first."

"Tell me!"[29]

To get rid of her, Bernadette gave in and told her, then went to see Abbé Pomian. The curate listened with his usual calm, but this time, he was puzzled. He would talk about this with Monsieur le Curé.

Leaving his house, Bernadette still did not know the meaning of those words which caused disappointment one minute, joy or anger the next. No one had yet thought of explaining them to her.

That afternoon at Monsieur Estrade's, understanding came. She recounted the morning apparition: *Aqueró's* smile, the four repeated petitions and, finally, the answer. Here she acted out the words. She extended her hands out toward the ground, then joined them at her breast, while she gently lifted her eyes toward heaven. Seeing this acted out, a thrill passed through her audience. Estrade and his sister were on the verge of tears. But the oracle who had just steeped them in wonder did not give them time to dwell on it. The under-privileged child hadn't even understood the words she had just re-peated. She hesitatingly asked the question that finally brought her enlightenment, "But what do these words mean: *'Immaculada Counchetsiou'*?"

Annunciation Day ended in joy for Bernadette. It had really been the Blessed Virgin.

The Medical Inquiry of March 27

During the next few days Bernadette again underwent questioning by friends and acquaintances—Marie Dufo, in particular, who wrote down the account of the crucial apparition.[30]

On Saturday, March 27, she underwent an interrogation and an examination by three physicians: Doctors Balencie, Lacrampe, and Peyrus. The prefect's confidence in them was the basis for their hav-ing been chosen to authorize her confinement. These three set great store by administrative authority. It had its reasons, they knew. It also governed the Hospice where Doctor Balencie worked. He and his colleagues would not want to betray the trust that civil au-thorities had put in them. After consulting those opposed to the grotto and compiling the file for the prosecution, they proceeded to examine Bernadette. The session lasted more than two hours and dealt first with the physical then with the psychical. At first, the doc-tors said nothing but platitudes: "The young Bernadette is of a deli-cate constitution, of a lymphatic and nervous temperament; aged thirteen, looks no more than eleven; her face is pleasant; her eyes have a vivid expression; her head is of a regular shape, but narrow, small rather than large."[31]

They then looked for symptoms of a nervous disorder:

"Do you occasionally have headaches?"

"No."

"Have you had nervous attacks?"

"Never."

"Yet your health seems mediocre."

They noted the "breathing, slightly constricted and wheezing" and diagnosed "asthma." She felt trapped. She replied, "I eat, drink and sleep perfectly."

They made her recount the events of the grotto, beginning with the first "rush of wind." They were surprised that she was unaware of things everyone else was talking about. Was she pretending not to know, or had she forgotten? The problem was solved when she answered the following question, "Aren't you frightened when you see so many people surrounding you, throwing themselves at you?"

"At those moments, I don't see a thing around me," answered Bernadette.[32]

The doctors remained confused. They spent four days trying to agree on the wording of their report. An important factor from the start was the question asked by the prefect. They put it as follows, "Is this child suffering from a mental disorder? Is treatment necessary for her?"[33]

After this, things got muddled. They resolved one editing difficulty only to fall into another. After much time, they settled on the following diplomatic wording:

"There is nothing to indicate that Bernadette wanted to deceive the public. This child is of an impressionable nature and *could* have been the victim of a hallucination; a reflection of light, *no doubt,* drew her attention to the side of the grotto; her imagination, *under the influence of a moral predisposition,* gave it a form that impresses children. Must not the young child's state of mind have been more and more affected and her over excitement reached its peak? What at first was but a simple hallucination exercises more control. And here we find a genuine state of ecstasy, that lesion in the mind, which places the one affected under the domination of the idea that obsesses him. Examples of this type are, moreover, reported by the authors."[34]

But the prefect wanted a practical conclusion, and so the doctors went on in this vein:

"Does this ailment require treatment? *We have little to say on this subject. The* sickness that we believe can be assigned to Bernadette *offers no risk to the health* of this child within the limits observed. It is likely, on the contrary, that when Bernadette is no longer harassed by the crowd, when they no longer ask for prayers, she will stop thinking about the grotto and the wondrous events she describes."[35]

"The sickness...offers no risk to her health." The three doctors, entangled in their editing difficulties, did not stop short at the strangeness of their wording. The problem was administrative, not medical. In this regard, their language constituted a minor master-piece of tactfulness. In a hypothetical mode, they paid their respects to the thesis of the prefect, but discreetly advised postponing any confinement.

Years later, when Doctor Balencie was no longer under the thumb of Prefect Massy and was visiting the Bureau of Medical Sta-tistics in Lourdes, he loved to recount what he could best remem-ber of this particular interrogation: Bernadette's openness and the quality of her "good judgment."

Two sentences were engraved on his memory: "Of course, I see her as I see you. She moves, she talks to me, she holds out her arms."[36]

He also retained this fragment of dialogue: "Aren't you afraid when you see so many people around you?"

"I don't see anything around me."[37]

In those later days, Doctor Balencie repudiated the report of 1858.[38]

At the Tardhivails'

The next day, Sunday, March 28, the three Tardhivail sisters, Antoinette, Marie and Théotiste, had an interview with Bernadette.

She "laughed a lot" in telling of the doctors' interrogation and their embarrassment: "They wanted me to think I was sick, but I'm not sick at all."

"Weren't you afraid of those gentlemen?"

"No."

"The commissioner? The prosecutor?"

"No one."

"But what if they put you in jail?"

"I couldn't care less."[39]

The indifference Bernadette admitted here was confirmed by other testimonies, whose dates are unknown. Louise Fourcade, for instance, reported this extract from some interrogation or other:

"We will put you in jail."

"Yes, but the bolts won't hold too long..."

"Your father went to jail."

Doctor Peyrus

*The Tardhivail sisters: Antoinette, Bernadette's tutor (standing), and Marie (seated).
The empty chair recalls the memory of the third sister, Théotiste.*

"Yes, you put him there, but you had to let him go."[40]

On March 28, the three Tardhivail sisters asked Bernadette once again the question that had been put to her by the doctors, "When you see the Blessed Virgin, do you also see the people?"

"No, only the Blessed Virgin."

"But she speaks to you very softly?"

"As loudly as you are doing right now."[41]

In a letter dated March 29, 1858, Antoinette Tardhivail added another detail from that evening. Two gentlemen, moved by the poverty of the Soubirous cachot, tried to slip quietly into Bernadette's hand "a forty-franc piece and another worth twenty francs," but the little one pushed them away and would accept nothing. The unselfishness of the Soubirous caused Antoinette to make this comment, "And nevertheless, they are poor, as poor as our Lord when he was on this earth, and on this little girl Mary has cast her eyes, preferring her to so many rich young people, who, at this very moment, envy the lot of her whom they would have looked at with contempt. They now consider themselves lucky to be able to kiss her and touch her hand."[42]

At Blazy's

There were few visitors after March 25. The Soubirous had closed their door. They made themselves as inconspicuous as possible.

However, on Good Friday, April 2, rumors began to fly, "The little one is going to the grotto."

In the blink of an eye three hundred persons gathered, but Bernadette was not there. On April 6, the same rumor was repeated. The next morning, as early as four o'clock, there were people on the road to Massabielle.

This last alert was not without foundation. On the morning of April 6, Bernadette had left Lourdes with her family to go to Adé, four kilometers from Lourdes, at the invitation of Blaise Vergez, nicknamed "Blazy," a wine merchant and the former mayor of Adé. Afflicted by painful and persistent rheumatism, he had found relief in the icy water of Massabielle. Now he wanted to see Bernadette and show her off to his parish priest. That is where she had lunch on April 6.

But she didn't let herself get carried away at the beginning of that afternoon. She hastened the departure. By four o'clock, she was back in Lourdes. Once again the grotto drew her. She went to church to pray and entered the confessional.[43]

From the sacristy, where she was preparing the vestments for Vespers, Antoinette Tardhivail noticed the stratagem. She sounded the alarm in town. The Soubirous were swamped with questions. Fear seized them. What would Jacomet do?

Blazy's son offered a solution: he would bring Bernadette back to the village of Adé. Then they could say, without lying, that she was not in Lourdes. Police as well as busybodies would both find that tough to crack! But Blazy swore he would have Bernadette before the grotto at daybreak the following day, even earlier, if she so desired.

The Seventeenth Apparition: April 7

On Tuesday, April 7, at five o'clock in the morning, Blazy's son kept his promise. Bernadette was kneeling at Massabielle. About a hundred people were already there. In front was Antoinette Tardhivail, wearing her "double spectacles." She had not gone to bed the previous night for fear of sleeping through. She spent the night "on a trunk," counting the hours.

Blazy had provided Bernadette with a large candle,[44] which would be the focal point. It was so heavy that Bernadette had put it on the ground. She held it by the top between her palms, cupping her hands like a shell to protect the flame. During her ecstasy, the flame seemed to lick her fingers. Doctor Dozous was completely overwhelmed. At the end of the apparition, which lasted half an hour that day, he took Bernadette's two hands, turned them around, wiped one of them on the back of his sleeve and murmured in patois, "There's nothing there![45] I don't know what you see, but now, I believe that you do see something."[46]

"The Miracle of the Candle," as they called it from that day on, the heavily publicized conversion of Doctor Dozous, who spread the news everywhere, even in the face of the commissioner,[47] brought the curious back to the cachot. To escape the renewed fervor, Bernadette fled. The Tardhivail sisters gave her refuge and questioned her about the apparition.[48]

"Who taught you to bow so nicely?" asked Marie.

"I don't know how I bow."

"But at the grotto?"

Doctor Dozous

*In his notebook, Commissioner Jacomet, on April 9, jotted down
the doctor's enthusiastic deposition on the "Miracle of the Candle."*

"I do what the Lady does."

"And why did you go under the arch?"

Indeed that morning, a new conversation had taken place between Bernadette and the apparition, under the interior vault. Bernadette answered, "The Lady came inside to talk to me."

"To talk to you?"

Antoinette was dying to know more.

"That's where she talks to me."

"And how do you know when to go?"

"She points with her finger."

"But what did she tell you?"

"She still wants her chapel."

"And you seemed to be talking. What were you saying?"[49]

Having undergone a running fire of questions since morning, Bernadette showed signs of weariness. Antoinette thought she understood that Bernadette had asked for a miracle to convince the unbelievers. Was it the blossoming of the roses for Monsieur le Curé? Antoinette went on, "Did the Lady tell you anything else?"

Worn out, Bernadette grew more and more concise, evasive. Antoinette concluded that she was hiding some secret or confidence.

"But why did you put your hand like that on the flame? Weren't you afraid of burning yourself?"

Bernadette looked astonished. She had not yet clearly understood why Doctor Dozous examined her fingers with such a stunned look on his face after she came out of her ecstasy. Antoinette now took Bernadette's hands. She examined them. She was surprised to find they weren't even rough. Only Bernadette's index finger showed needle marks from sewing. No, this certainly was not the skin of a lizard!

The assistant-sacristan Tardhivail got a devilish idea: "Put your hands together like this morning...like this!"

Taking advantage of the concentration that made Bernadette look down, the woman slipped a lighted candle under the girl's fingers. Immediately Bernadette pulled her hands back crying, "I'm burning myself!" Little seven-year-old Marie Duserm, who was there for a catechism lesson, was no doubt petrified.

Bernadette took her leave as quickly as possible.

What was wrong with people? As she came out of the Tardhivails', someone else grabbed her. It was Madame Garoby, who was inconsolable at having missed the morning's apparition (her husband was sick). She too wanted to test Bernadette. She brought out a candle. This time Bernadette pulled her hand back in time. These people must all be crazy! She slipped away in a hurry.

Objections from a Member of Parliament

On April 10, Monsieur de Rességuier came to Lourdes. He was a former legitimist (supporter of the Bourbon claim to the French throne over that of the Orléans line) and representative in the legislative assembly of 1849. He had also been one of the signers of the declaration that deposed Emperor Louis-Napoleon—a public figure who would come to the fore again in 1871. He came with a gift: a chasuble for the church in Lahitte. In the presence of Abbé Peyramale, he had a long interview with Bernadette. Peyramale summed up the interview: "Everything about this girl struck him vividly; he subjected her to a most detailed, thorough and tricky interrogation, and this child answered all his questions with explanations beyond her years and, it seems to me, beyond her understanding."[50]

From this whole interview, unfortunately, only one *exact* statement has come down to us. The deputy was asking about the "tongue" spoken by the apparition. Bernadette did not seem to understand. He insisted, "You do know, don't you, what a tongue is?"

She answered yes by innocently sticking hers out at him! He rephrased the question. "She spoke patois," Bernadette answered.

Monsieur de Rességuier objected authoritatively, "The Virgin could not have spoken patois. God and the Blessed Virgin do not speak that language."

"How would we know it, if they didn't?" Bernadette answered.[51]

Monsieur de Rességuier tried particularly to trap her concerning the apparition's words of March 25, "I am the Immaculate Conception." That expression had not yet been introduced in Lourdes. People corrected what they thought was a lapse on Bernadette's part, and it was these softened versions that found acceptance:

"I am Mary Immaculate."

"I am the Virgin of the Immaculate Conception."

"I am Mary, the Immaculate Conception," etc.[52]

Abbé Peyramale had been the first to be shocked by the straightforward statement. He had expressed his objections in his March

25 report to his bishop. That report is no longer extant; it was probably burned when the Curé got rid of all papers containing his
obsolete objections. His letter of April 10 underscored the difficulties shared by both the politician and the priest. Unfortunately,
Bernadette's answer was left out.

In the same letter, Peyramale reported another item to his bishop. At that time, Bernadette was asked, in the presence of a large
number of radiant young beauties, if the vision was very beautiful.

"Oh, yes!" she answered, turning around toward the ladies,
"much more beautiful than all these."[53]

It is clear that the last two words were softened. Bernadette probably said, "all that stuff!"

A somewhat feverish fervor gave rise to an epidemic of visionaries.

An Epidemic of Visionaries

After April 10, 1858, Bernadette withdrew into the background.
This was what she had hoped for. An outside event made her disappearance easier.

A few days after Monsieur de Rességuier's interrogation, five
women visited the grotto in the midst of mounting excitement. They
went inside the "upper cavity." This was not the wide-open passage
right in the center of the vault by which the Immaculate Lady would
come down to talk with Bernadette. It was, rather, a narrow, shadowy opening, about ten feet above ground, at the bottom of the
right side of the grotto. The women had borrowed a ladder. Shiver-
ing with fear and emotion, they crept into the rocky depths. After
crawling a few yards under the lower arch, they stood up. And what
did they see? A dazzling white shape, standing upright, with a
head...without a head....

What caught their attention was nothing but a white stalactite,
still visible today to anyone who would risk going on the same spe-
lunking expedition.[54] It had the form of a decapitated statue, standing on a pedestal. The devout women were emotionally excited.
Flickering candlelight, the play of shadows and their imagination
did the rest. They believed that they, too, had seen the Blessed Virgin. Thus began the epidemic of visionaries.

This new fad replaced Bernadette, for it satisfied the hunger for
the extraordinary that Bernadette now disappointed. These women
stirred up a great deal of enthusiasm. "Those who won't believe are

Lourdes, April–July, 1858
A somewhat feverish fervor gave rise to an epidemic of visionaries

*The visionaries' stalactite at the rear of the interior cavity of the grotto.
Bernadette never went in as far as this rocky passage.*

worthless scum!" shouted Estrade on April 22, upon witnessing the ecstasy of Joséphine Albario.[55]

Visits to the Soubirous home had grown fewer. Jacomet noted only this in his notebook, dated April 22, 1858: "M...went to see Bernadette around noon. He found her in bed. A priest...translated...her answers."[56]

In the days that followed, Brother Léobard, the Director of the Catholic school in Lourdes, questioned her in similar fashion. Brother Cérase acted as his interpreter. The purpose of the interview was to draw up a continuous narrative of the events. We will not go into the substance of this interview or of others like it. The study was valuable in establishing the history of the apparitions. It would be tedious in this "collection of words," because Bernadette always told the same story in the same way, with the same expressions, marked with variations caused by two factors analyzed in the *"Histoire authentique"* (Official History): the questions of each questioner and his freedom to improvise.[57]

Bernadette at Cauterets

Was concern for her asthma the reason why Bernadette, sick in bed since April 22, was sent to Cauterets from May 8–22? Or was it to get her away from police visits and investigations? The second reason seemed to have played a part following the decision made by Prefect Massy during his visit to Lourdes on May 4: "Any person claiming to be a visionary will be arrested immediately and brought to the Hospice of Lourdes."

Strictly speaking, Bernadette could have been arrested at once. She had seen the lady and she would say this plainly if asked. There would be nothing more to do except to confine her as a "visionary." Bernadette had just been sick to the point of receiving the sacraments, according to Adélaïde Monlaur.[58] The waters of Cauterets would do her good. Four days after the prefect's splendid speech, she was in Cauterets. The decision to go probably reflected the well-founded worries of those around her as well as the suggestions of President Pougat. As for Bernadette, she remained unconcerned about the danger. Shortly before leaving she declared, "I fear nothing because I have always told the truth."[59]

Although Adélaïde, in the remoteness of her village of Angles, had known of Bernadette's departure since May 11, the prefect

learned of it only on May 15. When he got the news, he sent the
Commissioner of Police in Cauterets a message with these orders,
"Put Bernadette and those around her under a discreet surveillance
and watch all their movements. Send me a report."[60]

On May 22, the commissioner sent the following report:

"Bernadette Soubirous...has been the subject of a very active surveillance. This girl went regularly to bathe at the Bruzeaud Baths.
Several people questioned her about her so-called visions. She keeps
to her original story. Several sick people spoke to her, but she limited her answers to saying that, if they believed in God, they would
obtain their cure; she has always refused any remuneration."[61]

Bernadette's absence weighed heavily on Lourdes. On her return, the visits resumed. This renewed outbreak worried the commissioner. In his report of Tuesday, May 23, he wrote:

"Young Bernadette returned from Cauterets Saturday morning;
they call her to various houses; they show her off to strangers; in a
word, they never miss an opportunity to bring her out. For example,
yesterday at nine o'clock Mass was being said for a women's group;
it was a policeman's wife's turn to distribute the blessed bread.
Do you know, Monsieur le Préfet, whom she chose to bring it to the
altar in church? Bernadette, of course, who naturally attracted the
attention of all the people in church. That's all it took to make
Bernadette the topic of conversation for the rest of the day for those
very people who had almost forgotten all about her."

Nevertheless, Jacomet concluded by acknowledging: "No trouble.
No disorder to report."

Visitors in May 1858

During this same month of May—the month of Mary—Bernadette
had set up "a big altar in front of her house," a kind of roadside
shrine decorated with flowers, like she used to make in the fields of
Bartrès, according to popular custom. Marie Fourcade brought her
a crown of flowers from the nuns of Bagnères. She found Bernadette
at the front door. "Thank you very much," Bernadette said, "I'll
place it on my Blessed Virgin right away."[62]

The beautiful weather brought more visitors, often bothersome,
either for their flattery or for their opposition. Abbé Vincent Péré's
visit was one of the latter kind. He himself gives us this testimony:

"On May 29, 1858...still fresh from my priestly anointing...I went to Lourdes, to my godmother's. There I let it be known that I wanted to see Bernadette to question her. 'Don't do it', my godmother told me, 'the bishop has just forbidden all priests to talk to her,' I satisfied my conscience reasoning that, as a priest from Landes, I was not under the jurisdiction of the bishop of Tarbes and, consequently, his ban did not affect me.... I went to Bernadette's home. She had attended my Mass that morning. So I went in and in a loud, harsh voice I said, 'Are you the little clown who claims to see the Virgin on rocks of Massabielle?'

"'Yes, I am.'

"'You're lying, you insolent girl! It's not true, that...'

"'Yes, it's true.'

"'I say again, you're lying and if you keep this up, we're going to have you sent to jail.'

"At the word 'jail,' her mother burst into tears. Neither the child's expression, nor her color changed.

"'Aren't you ashamed,' I then said, 'to make your mother cry like this?'

"'Yes, it hurts me, but the Blessed Virgin ordered me to say what I say.'

"Little by little, the house filled up. People had come in after me. I looked around and saw that I was surrounded by laborers coming home from work, whose faces were none too reassuring. It was easy to see they sided with the child. I understood the danger. Toning down my voice and still talking to Bernadette, I said:

"'I can't believe that it is the Blessed Virgin who spoke to you. You just thought she did, that's all. I went to the rocks of Massabielle myself yesterday, and I thought I heard something move. It must have been the same with you. You probably heard some bird who was hiding there and you imagined it was the Blessed Virgin who spoke to you.'

"But she replied, 'If it was a bird, it wouldn't have spoken.'

"Her answer floored me! A workman came up to me and with his fist under my nose said, 'Are you done torturing this child?'

"I turned to leave and came face to face with Doctor Dozous.

"'Monsieur l' Abbé,' he said, 'your words and actions are hardly those of a man of the cloth. What has just passed between you and this child is for me irrefutable proof that she is not lying. I am immediately going to draw up a statement of this scene, and I ask you to come and sign it with me.'

"'Me? Sign a written statement?... Give you my name? Never!'

"That said, I turned on my heels. That's why I think I am the first priest to talk to Bernadette, to subject her to a long interrogation."[63]

First Communion

On June 3, the day of her First Communion (at long last!) Bernadette would have willingly passed up the many embraces, mentioned in a letter published June 12, 1858 in the *Rosier de Marie* (Rosebush of Mary). The document, it seems, came from the Dufo family whose unreserved devotion to Bernadette the imperial prosecutor had described. The letter read: "Today, little Bernadette made her First Communion in the chapel of the Hospice of Lourdes. You should have seen her, Monsieur l'Abbé! She's an angel from heaven. I see her every day and still can't have enough, for I would like to hold her in my arms constantly. She too is a little mystical rose who intoxicates us with the aroma of her innocence and simplicity."[64]

During the retreat preparatory to her First Communion, Bernadette had been questioned in the presence of Abbé Peyramale by a woman who had been dying to see her. The Curé used this occasion to remind Bernadette that "he forbade her to go" to the grotto. The woman asked her this question, "Monsieur le Curé forbids you to go to the grotto. Suppose the Blessed Virgin ordered you to go, what would you do?"

"I would come and ask Monsieur le Curé's permission."[65]

The day after her First Communion, Emmanuélite Estrade asked Bernadette this question, leaving her no escape, "Which made you happier, your First Communion or the apparitions?"

She answered, "These are two things that go together, but which cannot be compared. Both made me very happy."[66]

Saint John's Day at Bartrès

On the feast of Saint John (June 24, 1858) Bernadette went to Bartrès. People asked her to tell them about the apparitions. She concluded as follows, "Godmother, don't go if you haven't much faith. You must have much faith to go."[67]

Jeanne Aravant, to whom this was said, explained, "She called me 'godmother,' as the others here call me and repeated the answer in its clearest form, 'You must have faith or else you must not go.' "[68]

Fences and Criminal Charges

On Thursday, July 1, Bernadette went to Tarbes to stay at the home of her aunt, Madame Deluc, who took her to Canon Ribbes, the director of the seminary. The priest declared that he was "very satisfied with the simplicity and the correctness of her answers," which unfortunately he did not take down in writing. What he carefully pointed out was Bernadette's amazement at the swarm of cassocks.[69]

"It was market day. The seminarians were going to the parlor in groups. When Bernadette saw them coming, she interrupted her account, 'Oh!' she exclaimed.

"And without further thought about her questioner, she leaned forward and went to the window to get a better look at the seminarians. As soon as one group had passed, Bernadette went back to her place and resumed answering my questions; but she would stop again, make the same cries of surprise and go back to the window to look at a new group of seminarians, more taken up with this spectacle than with the part Divine Providence had given her to play. As I left her, I said to myself, 'Bernadette is no deceiver.' "

During this period, things were growing more intense at the grotto. On May 4, the prefect had ordered the removal of those objects which established the site as an "illegal place of worship." On June 7, at his request, the mayor of Lourdes, Monsieur Anselme Lacadé, drew up a decree ordering that the grotto be closed. On June 15, fences were set up. But they were torn down during the night (by the same men the commissioner had conscripted to erect them!). Set up again on the twenty-eighth, they were torn down once more on the night of July 4, then rebuilt on the tenth.... More and more criminal charges were drawn up against the trespassers.[70] The people were getting worked up. They petitioned the authorities; they defied the ban.

Bernadette didn't lead this crusade. At a time when people considered it an honor to be charged with a crime—almost as if they were being granted the honorary degree of "Confessor of the Faith" —she advised against going to the grotto.

One Thursday in the summer of 1858, at the end of a prolonged illness, her cousin, Jeanne Védère, visited her.

Jeanne recalled, "As soon as Bernadette saw me, she said, 'Have you come to go to the grotto?'

"'No, I've come to visit you.'

"'Oh, don't go to the grotto. You'd be arrested. It's forbidden to go in there.'

"But just to see what she would say, because I had no desire to go, I said, 'I can go there to pray; I won't cross over the fences.'

"'Don't go.'

"And turning toward a statue of the Blessed Virgin which was in the room, she said, 'Pray to her and be patient. Soon you'll be able to go to the grotto without danger, the fences will soon be taken down.'

"'The fences will fall down?'

"'No,' she said, 'those who had them put up will have them taken down.'

"I said to her, 'I don't approve of the commissioner's conduct.'

"She answered, 'We shouldn't pay too much attention to men. God permits this. We should be patient.'"[71]

Jeanne's memoir has highlighted the prophetic aspect of Bernadette's words. The heart of what she remembered was the invitation not to defy authority. Bernadette was no less sympathetic toward those who had gotten caught. Cyprine Gesta, a single mother, was found guilty at the Lourdes Tribunal of having visited the forbidden grotto.[72] She appealed to the tribunal in Pau, following legal advice, inspired, it seems by President Pougat. Cyprine, deathly afraid of the thought of standing before such a high court, went to seek the support of Bernadette, who assured her, "Don't be afraid! It won't amount to anything."[73]

In fact, on Thursday, July 15, a little before midnight, the defendants returned in triumph. They had been acquitted! "The prefect lost his case!" They would never have believed that possible. The very next day, Cyprine went back to thank Bernadette. "I told you so," she answered.[74]

The Last Apparition: July 16

On the evening of July 16, while the acquittal, spoken of on every doorstep, inspired jokes and "irrepressible laughter," Bernadette had something else on her mind.

Once again she began to experience the inner feeling she had learned not to expect anymore. The Virgin (she now called her by this name) was drawing her to the forbidden grotto. Torn between the interior invitation and the official prohibition, she reflected. How could she ask advice without embarrassing her parents, without beginning a family discussion, as on February 26, which would attract crowds? Only one thing was clear: that night's meeting had to avoid the commotion going on in Lourdes.

It was 8:00 P.M. Just a few minutes earlier, the sun had gone down behind the chestnut grove on the right bank, casting on the grotto, which emerged from the shadows only when the summer solstice drew near, a last reflection of its fiery red rays. It left in its wake a trail of mauve that little by little darkened in the sky. Two shadows hurried down the lower street. The taller was Lucile Castérot, Bernadette's young aunt. And the other? It wasn't the well-known hooded cape of the visionary. Nevertheless, under that oversized cloak, under the bonnet that concealed three-quarters of her face, was indeed Bernadette Soubirous! Safe in this disguise and the semi-darkness, she was finally able to follow her heart.

She hurried, not on the road to the grotto, but along the other bank. On their knees in Ribére's meadow, where groups were praying here and there, facing the rocks of Massabielle on the other side of the Gave, Bernadette, her aunt, and two other sodalists were just one group among many. In the dusk brightened by candlelight, the smile of ecstasy lit up Bernadette's face. For prayer had enabled her to see clearly. She found the Immaculate Lady once more in her usual place. All distance was erased. After the rosary, she stood up. The others questioned her: "What did she say to you?"

"Nothing."[75]

Bernadette was not disappointed. Just having seen the Virgin had been enough. And never had she looked so beautiful![76]

"But how could you see across that distance and over that fence?" asked Antoinette Tardhivail, who never missed a trick.

"I saw neither the boards nor the Gave; it seemed to me I was at the grotto, no farther away than at the other times. I saw nothing but the Blessed Virgin."[77]

This bit of news was kept secret within a small group. The commissioner, who usually missed nothing, never knew a word about this. The Episcopal Commission had no knowledge. Thus did this last apparition almost pass history by, unnoticed.[78]

Where Did Bernadette Live during This Period?

When did the Soubirous family leave the cachot? The study of Bernadette's words permits us to specify exactly what had been said about this.[79]

The two basic facts are the following:

1. The dire warning of the doctors on March 4, 1848: "If you want to keep your children alive, you can't stay here."[80]

2. The deposition of Uncle Sajous, owner of the cachot: "They were removed from here two months after the apparitions, because of the stench of the manure-pile. They went to live at Deluc's."

This note poses a problem: do the "two months" begin after the "fifteen days," that is on March 4, 1858, or after April 7, the date of the last public apparition? At first, we thought they were calculated from the April 7 date.[81] But that hypothesis was eliminated by the testimony of Jeanne Védère[82] who pointed out that the Soubirous "were still in the Rue des Petits Fossés" during the period of the "fences" and "arrests," which began during the second half of June. (This seems to be confirmed by a statement made in July, 1858, about "the wretched conditions in which the Soubirous live.")[83] Therefore, it was around mid-September, two months after the last apparition, the one on July 16, that the Soubirous found a room to rent at the home of Jean Deluc, the baker and café owner. Monsieur Deluc was married to a daughter of Bibie Castérot, the sister of Bernadette's maternal grandmother.[84]

PART TWO

— ⚜ —

THE GATHERING OF EVIDENCE

July 16, 1858 – July 4, 1866

CHAPTER 5

— ⚜ —

GIVING PUBLIC TESTIMONY

The night of July 16, 1858 brought the apparitions to a close. Bernadette, returning little by little to ordinary life, was now forced to bear testimony. She was left "hanging in the wind" with no protection whatsoever. She lived with her parents, who still didn't grasp what was going on, in a house open to all. She roamed through the streets. She was invited into people's homes, even to neighboring villages. People liked to see her and show her off. She found herself subjected to all kinds of questions, offers, and influences. She faced all this with no attempts to dazzle or to appear as a wonder-worker, but simply with her common sense and openness.

How many interrogations did Bernadette undergo? What percentage of these left any mark? One in a hundred? One in a thousand? Bernadette must have answered "the questions of thirty thousand people," said the Curé of Lourdes on May 12, 1859.[1] This obviously referred to the number of *visitors,* often in groups, and not the number of *visits.* Nonetheless, what remained of the one-per-hundred or one-per-thousand gives us an insight into this heroic and busy period. We will ordinarily spare the reader those visits whose sole contribution was just one more index card, e.g., the minor seminary professors who visited the home of André Labayle, their student from Lourdes, to talk with Bernadette. We will bring up only

the ones in which significant words or actions were reported. We
will not repeat Bernadette's account; it remained consistent and followed an unchanging format, more or less accurately reproduced
by the witnesses.

Visitors: July 1858

One of the best interviews we have from this period is that of "the
lawyer from Dijon." This mysterious person still remained anonymous at the time we were publishing his account in Volume 3 of the
Documents authentiques (Authentic Documents). As a matter of fact,
Père de Lajudie, who transmitted his account, did not take down
his name nor the date of his visit (between July 16 and July 28),
because he could not remember them. After a search of many years,
the enigma was solved. The visitor of July 1858, was thirty-two-year-
old Charles Madon. He was indeed a lawyer, but in Beaune, not
Dijon (a fact that had clouded the trail). He had been a seminarian
with Père de Lajudie, whom we shall meet again later on, and was
preparing to be appointed to the bench.[2] What impressed him most
on entering the cachot was the "abject poverty" of the Soubirous.
(This is a new indication that they did not move out of the cachot
before the end of summer.)

"However," Attorney Madon underscored, "no one has yet been
able to make the little one accept the smallest sum of money, even
for her parents."

The visitor soon forgot the misery around him to concentrate
only on Bernadette.

"Intelligent face...appearance both charming and modest, which
does one good to see. She answered with a great deal of good will,
and when she was afraid of not being able to make herself understood in French, she said, 'I would rather speak patois.'"[3]

Her asthma gave her much trouble. "She often coughed." He
asked her, "Have you prayed for a cure?"

"No."

Attorney Madon, who was preparing to be a judge, conducted
the conversation methodically. His report followed, without transposition, the chronological order of the apparitions. The key words
were the very ones Bernadette would use three years later in her
written accounts.

The young man dwelt especially on the three secrets. Might this not be a vague recollection of Maximin and Mélanie? He asked, "Do you know what happened to the little shepherds of La Salette?"

Bernadette did not know.[4] As to "the secrets," her answer was clear: "They concern only me."

"If the Pope asked you, would you tell him?"

"No."

"What if your confessor would not allow you to make your Easter Duty because you refused?"

"No."

Bernadette could anticipate no exception. The friendly, relaxed atmosphere of the interview lent itself to a number of questions on this topic.

"I know one of your secrets. You're going to be a nun," Madon suggested.

Bernadette laughed and replied, "That's not it; they're more serious than that."

"Does it bother you that people ask you about your secrets?"

"No, but the apparition told me not to tell."

The attorney extracted some rare and sometimes unique details: The secrets were spoken "in patois...on several different days." "The apparition spoke more carefully than I." She, "did not cry."[5]

"Did you ask to see her again?" asked the young man.

"Yes!"[6]

A Roll of Gold Coins

Jean-Baptiste Estrade told another story that took place at his house about this time. "A lady, an outsider with well-bred manners, came knocking at our door asking to see Bernadette. We invited her in. She could not thank us enough. She made Bernadette talk and hung on every word that fell from her lips for over an hour. When this stranger was getting ready to leave, with the tactfulness of those who know how to give, she kissed the child and secretly slipped a roll in the folds of her apron. As if struck by a hot coal, Bernadette jumped up and dropped the lady's gift on the floor. Embarrassed by her own behavior, she picked up the roll of gold and kindly gave it back to the charitable stranger. No amount of pleading could make her accept this treasure."[7]

Bishops at Lourdes

At one o'clock in the afternoon of July 17, 1858 a carriage from
Cauterets arrived in Lourdes. It stopped quietly near the rectory. A
young priest stepped down and entered the large house. Almost
immediately he came out again with the Curé of Lourdes, who appeared excited and very attentive. A second, older priest then
stepped down from the carriage. The three priests lost no time helping a fourth, wearing a sash. (The changing of its color to purple,
which would then turn to red, had not yet begun.) The three visitors who exited the carriage were, in hierarchical order, Abbé Euzet,
private secretary, Canon Baudassé, Vicar General and Monseigneur
Thibault, Bishop of Montpellier. On his way back from Cauterets,
the bishop wanted to inquire about the apparitions.

At home with the patois of the Pyrénées, the bishop questioned
Bernadette himself. Abbé Peyramale translated for the benefit of
the others. The bishop asked more and more questions full of pit-
falls to "test" the young girl. Bernadette's answers were short and to
the point, respectfully punctuated with the words, "Monsieur le
Curé." This was the first time she had spoken to a bishop. "May
Monseigneur forgive her—to her, all priests are 'Monsieur le Curé,'"
Abbé Peyramale explained.[8]

The more difficult, disconcerting or tricky the question, the
more relevant was her answer. The prelate was won over. In the presence of this radiant and sickly child, undernourished yet steady, his
emotion got the better of him.

The rectory maid brought "a snack for Monseigneur." He invited
Bernadette to eat with him. She flatly refused; she would not be persuaded.

"That child is poor, isn't she, Monsieur le Curé?" the bishop
asked, continuing to eat.

"Yes, Monseigneur, very poor," Abbé Peyramale responded.

Bishop Thibault was more and more moved. He "took Bernadette's
hands in his" and surreptitiously fixed it so that they would "touch
his rosary." He murmured: "Oh, no, Bernadette, you are not poor;
you are blessed, yes, blessed!"

He would have liked to offer her something. Money would have
been improper. He tried to think of the right gift, one that she
couldn't refuse. He was still holding his rosary with its golden chain.

He urged her to accept it. Canon Baudassé here noted, "None of us could look on this precious object without being affected."

Bernadette stepped back. Anything "gold" seemed like fire to her. "Thank you, I have one,"[9] she said.

The bishop tried tempting her with the spiritual favors attached to the rosary, pointing out, "This rosary has been given indulgences by Pius IX."

She remained unshakable.

"Since you don't want my rosary for nothing, let's exchange; give me yours and take mine." The bishop was thinking about the gift that he wanted to make, as well as the relic he would own through this exchange.

Bernadette remained unmoved. "No, Monsieur le Curé, I prefer mine."

She understood, nevertheless, that her refusal might hurt his feelings, so she tried to soften it by adding gravely, "Yours is good for you."[10] She concluded, "I thank you very much."

The bishop understood that she was right.

Abbé Peyramale didn't like the tone of admiration that was creeping into the conversation. He did what he could to end it. Regretfully the bishop dismissed the young girl in the worn-out skirt. He himself left, two hours after his arrival, saying, "I had not intended to stop at Tarbes; my conscience today makes it a duty. I shall go see Bishop Laurence."[11]

He would find his colleague quite "impassive," but already preparing an inquiry into the happenings at Lourdes, which he meant to conduct with all the deliberation such a delicate matter required.

In the next few days, another visitor to the Soubirous family, Henri Fontan, a seminarian, stated, "The poverty of the family...the meal...more than frugal: there was only...water on the table."

Bernadette's mother told him, "We would be comfortable if my daughter had accepted the rolls of gold that were offered her, and with insistence."

She told him about the recent episode of the rosary; in refusing it, Bernadette had supposedly said to the bishop, "The Blessed Virgin doesn't like vanity."[12]

On July 20, Monseigneur Cardon de Garsignies, the Bishop of Soissons, came in the footsteps of the Bishop of Montpellier to the rectory of Lourdes. Was it all in innocence or to spring a trap? He asked Bernadette this odd question, "Tell me, dear child, what goes on up there in heaven? You can tell me, for I know all about it."

Bernadette answered, "I don't know anything, Monseigneur, I'm ignorant."[13]

Immediately after this interview, the bishop took the road to Tarbes, where he met with Bishop Laurence. The next day, the two went to consult the Archbishop of Salinis. The following day, July 22, the three of them returned to Tarbes to hold a council meeting there. A fourth party accompanied them. This was Louis Veuillot, editor-in-chief of the *"Univers,"* who was taking advantage of the mineral springs, said to have curative effects, at Bagnères with the archbishop.

A few days later, on July 28, at eleven o'clock, Bishop Laurence signed and dated his "Ordinance creating a commission of inquiry into the apparitions."[14]

A Lady from the Imperial Court

On July 28, Bernadette was summoned by Abbé Pomian, at the request of a lady whose titles made no more of an impression on Bernadette than did the coats-of-arms of the bishops. The woman was the wife of Admiral Bruat and governess to the Imperial Prince. She was accompanied by her three daughters and a nun, Soeur Saint-Antonin. In the absence of the Curé, who was also visiting the mineral springs at Bagnères, with the archbishop and Louis Veuillot,[15] Abbé Pomian received them. Monsieur Lannes, the tobacco warehouse keeper and a co-tenant of the rectory, had slipped in to act as interpreter. He helped the curate translate Bernadette's answers. The visitors took him for a schoolteacher. It didn't matter to him, as long as it gained him access to the "inner circle." The nun asked, "Are you happy to have seen the Blessed Virgin?"

Bernadette, who had taken a particular liking to her, disclosed the recent apparition, "Oh, yes! Very happy, and I saw her two weeks ago."

This event had passed so unnoticed at Lourdes, and Bernadette had said this so unassumingly, that the nun mistakenly took this to mean in the future, "I *will see* her again in two weeks."[16]

"A priest from Rome," Abbé Labayle, also present at this interview, asked her some tricky questions, such as, "The Blessed Virgin, married to Saint Joseph, must have been wearing a ring?"

"No, Monsieur l'Abbé, she wasn't."[17]

At the end of the interview, after the inevitable embraces, the ladies asked Bernadette to go with them to the grotto. She absolutely refused, "No! No! I'm forbidden."[18]

She took them only half way and turned back at the Pont-Vieux.

Press Conference

A few minutes later, she was summoned to the pharmacist Pailhasson's for an interview that would have far-reaching effects. It was actually a "press conference," before the French language borrowed this expression from the English. Louis Veuillot was the one who wanted to see her. Abbé Peyramale and the three bishops, in addition to his contacts in Lourdes (which had begun multiplying the previous week) had kept him informed. The meeting was crowded, for an entourage of admirers followed the journalist, then at the height of his glory. Bernadette wasn't impressed.

On first meeting her, Veuillot noted, "an intelligent face, without guile—beautiful eyes." She told her story in patois, segmented, piece by piece, to give Abbé Pomian time to translate. Then Veuillot asked questions, always through an interpreter. The secrets preoccupied him. "Many people think badly of this mystery," he told her.

Bernadette "did not defend herself,"—the secrets concerned only her.[19]

"Have you heard about the children of La Salette?" Veuillot asked.

"Yes, since the visions."

"If you were lying, do you know to what extent you would be guilty?"

"They've already told me."

"And what do you intend to do? Don't you think that some day a few charitable people will care about what happens to you?"

Looking at her poor clothing, she smiled.[20]

The curate finally dismissed her. Then Veuillot abandoned the impartial tone of his interview. "She is ignorant, but she's worth more than I am. I'm worthless."[21]

Opposition

Other confrontations were more severe. Toward July 30, Père Hyacinth Loyson, the famous preacher who would soon leave the Church, summoned her to his hotel room.

"He questioned her...in French, distorting everything she said," reported Antoinette Tardhivail.[22]

He may well have been mocking the incorrect speech of the young girl, who was trying for his sake to express herself in French.

"The Lady would have done better to teach you to speak," Loyson told Bernadette.

"What she did not teach me was to make fun of people who didn't know any better," she responded.[23]

"There was indignation, public resentment," noted Antoinette Tardhivail.[24]

A similar scandal, caused by Père Nègre, a Jesuit renowned for his knowledge and piety, would go even further.[25]

His visit took place about the same time: between July 20 and August 20, 1858, according to his own letter, dated March 9, 1879.[26]

Bernadette arrived at Antoinette Tardhivail's, who had volunteered to teach her how to write, but this time she came for a different reason. "A priest wants to see me at Monsieur Pailhasson's. I don't want to go alone," Bernadette explained.

She knew what to expect unless a third party was present to restrain the whims of strangers. Here they were then at the house of the pharmacist, a man famous for making chocolate and even more so for his beautiful but sad wife. "He lost his fortune through his wife's misbehavior," said Antoinette, who described the interview as follows:[27]

"Bernadette got next to me. She didn't want to go near Père Nègre. He questioned her.

"'My poor child! You saw a lady? You saw the devil!'

"She turned toward me and said, 'The devil isn't as beautiful as that.'

"'Tell me, little one, you didn't see her feet, did you? You can't see the devil's feet!'

"'Yes, I did; she had very pretty bare feet.'

"He claimed this was false. Bernadette remained peaceful and calm.

"'But you didn't see her hands! Wasn't there a shadow hiding them?'

"'No! I could see them and they were pretty.'"

Père Nègre was no doubt confused in situating this visit at the

Hospice, in the presence of a nun, in his letter of September 18, 1890, in which he tried to dismiss what had happened.

Antoinette reported that, "The priest's tone of voice showed his conviction that the vision was false. He made a long speech about the deformities of the devil. He refused to believe that Bernadette saw the feet or the hands.

"Bernadette said to me, 'He doesn't want to believe. Let's go.'

"I left indignant; she left hurt."

Antoinette was "very indignant," according to her own testimony. Did she exaggerate? Certainly not, for Père Nègre's three letters (June 11, 1878, March 9, 1879 and September 18, 1890, preserved in the Archives of Père Cros)[28] confirm his prejudices at the time. His inquiry led him from one disappointment to another.

He later explained that three facts had "prejudiced him against Bernadette." First, he had met the so-called "blind-girl from Barèges," whom public opinion considered "miraculously cured." Like Abbé Peyramale, he had learned that the girl had never been really blind, and that she was not cured. Secondly, at the grotto, Père Nègre had found not "the clear spring people had boasted about to him," but "a slow trickle of muddy water." The pipe that collected the water, as well as Castérot's basin had been destroyed by the police. He noted in his letter of September 18, 1890 that the illicit pilgrims drew water from the bare ground, heavily covered with rocky debris. Lastly, they brought before him the most famous visionary of Lourdes, a nineteen-year-old-girl. "I recognized the devil's hand by the uneasiness that the vision had left behind in the soul of this young girl," the priest wrote in his letter of March 9, 1879.

Was he speaking about the same interview as the one described by Antoinette? We can very well wonder, since he places the interview at the Hospice in the presence of a nun and not at the Pailhassons' in the presence of Bernadette's volunteer teacher. But except for this mix-up (whether his or Antoinette's) Père Nègre's other references to the interview with Bernadette agreed with the description left by Antoinette Tardhivail. It was a "short visit…lasting no more than a quarter of an hour."

Most of all, Père Nègre's correspondence confirmed the theme of his interview with Bernadette—as bizarre as it might seem today.

"I was inclined to believe it was a counterfeit of the apparition of La Salette, brought about by God's monkey, Master Satan," he wrote in his letter of June 11, 1878.

His third letter clearly showed the importance he attached to the question about the "feet of the apparition." "I know that the devil, in his appearances, ordinarily takes the feet of the beast. Ever since the Incarnation of the Word, God won't permit the devil to take a completely human form. He must betray himself by something belonging to the beast" (letter of September 18, 1890, p.6).[29]

This nightmarish obsession did not blind Père Nègre to the undeniable qualities of the girl he was questioning. "The impression she gives of simplicity and innocence keeps me from thinking that she is lying," he wrote in his letter of March 9, 1879. "I judged her entirely incapable of deception," he confirmed in another letter of September 18, 1890. But, he added, "I was inclined to believe she was deceived by the devil. What shocked me...was the command she got to eat grass like the animals."[30]

Thus had he charged at the "beast"...for the greater glory of God.

This affair had repercussions in the Paris press. Alerted, apparently by an item in the *Siècle,* dated September 18, 1859,[31] the *Charivari,* the *National Enquirer* of that era, treated the incident like a farce. The author of the article presented himself as a fan of "miracles," fascinated by the "telegrams" coming from Lourdes:[32] He wrote: "My dear friend, it's all over—our miracle is caving in; the Reverend Jesuit Father has just declared that it was 'a false miracle, brought about by the machinations of the evil one.' He said that, to the people impatiently awaiting his opinion, it seems that the evil spirit, envious of the miracle of La Salette, wanted to stir up some competition and he chose as his instrument the demoiselle Bernadette Soubirous. Thus, instead of proclaiming this young person to be a first-class miracle worker, it would be better to exorcise her. It seems that the town of Lourdes is in a state of great turmoil: half the people are on the Jesuit Father's side while the other half claim to accept the miracle anyway and see in the Reverend Father an emissary of Beelzebul, some even calling him 'his private secretary!'"

Père Nègre's was not an isolated case, judging from the August 10, 1858 declaration of Abbé Peyramale, who observed similar incidents. "Bishops and priests threatened her with hell fire. They told her that if she said she saw the Blessed Virgin on earth, she would not see her in heaven. She smiled, her face showing no sign of emotion."[33]

On August 28, 1858, another opponent, Abbé Fonteneau, the future Bishop of Agen, was converted. He summarized his interview with Bernadette as follows:

"She answered our complicated questions and our various objections with admirable clarity. She ended with these words, which struck me deeply: 'I can't force you to believe me; I can only answer by telling you what I've seen and heard.'"[34]

The future bishop was captivated, revealed his companion, Abbé Moreau. A detailed account of the interrogation was published in a "little Bordeaux newspaper," which has eluded every inquiry, Père Cros' as well as our own. Apparently it had been an offensive article.[35]

In August 1858, Monseigneur Plantier, Bishop of Nimes, was likewise won over. Brought to the hospice of the Sisters of Nevers by the Curé of Lourdes, he had approached Bernadette as a judge, but left converted.[36]

In the case of the Count of Bruissard, "a hardened sinner," as he called himself in the article published by Guy de Pierrefeux, meeting with Bernadette seemed to have brought about a true conversion. One, no doubt, must take into account the literary flights of fancy of this writer, author of commissioned articles, who was quick to embellish an event by means of contrasts and clever generalizations. Nevertheless, we are dealing with an article published during the Count's lifetime, the very same year he confided it to the journalist "with all the good will in the world."

"I was at Cauterets," the Count wrote. "I no more believed in those apparitions than I did in God. I was morally corrupt and what was worse, an atheist.

"Having read in a local newspaper that on July 16 Bernadette had had an apparition and that the Virgin had smiled at her, I resolved to go to Lourdes out of curiosity and catch the little one in a barefaced lie. So I went to the Soubirous home and found Bernadette on the doorstep, mending a black stocking. She seemed common to me; her sickly features, however, had a certain sweetness. At my request, Bernadette told me about the apparitions with a simplicity and self-confidence that struck me.

"'Well, now,' I said, 'how did that beautiful lady smile?'

"The little shepherd girl looked at me in surprise and after a moment of silence answered, 'Oh! Monsieur, one would have to be from heaven to make that smile again.'

"'Couldn't you make it for me? I'm an unbeliever and don't believe in the apparitions.'

"Her face was clouded over and took on a severe expression.

"'So Monsieur, you think that I'm a liar?'

"I felt defenseless. No, Bernadette was not a liar, and I was on the verge of...asking her forgiveness.

"'Since you are a sinner,' she answered, 'I will make the Blessed Virgin's smile for you.'"[37]

Meanwhile, on August 4, Bernadette made her second Communion at the parish church, two months after her first:[38] her viaticum "to walk another forty days and forty nights."[39]

Summer's End

The visits continued in September, in a charged atmosphere, because the grotto was still banned.

On the fifth, Bernadette was solemnly introduced to Raphael Ginnasi, a very distinguished Italian whose mere presence in the Pyrénées made the news. Ginnasi was said to be "a relative of the Pope"—no doubt, he was a "regular visitor" at the papal court. He was most interested in Bernadette and an ardent admirer. She had to give him an autograph for the Holy Father. She wasn't too impressed. Despite the visitor's skillfulness and social rank, she accepted no gift nor did she surrender her rosary or her medal to him.[40]

How then can we explain Estrade's notation in his first *Memoir* (1858–1859)?

"She will receive one of your medals (and)...will give you one of hers with charming simplicity."[41]

It all depends on the terms of the exchange. Bernadette consented quite willingly whenever an offer involved religious objects of little value, and when the offer was made sincerely with no misunderstanding.

On September 8, Feast of the Nativity of the Blessed Virgin, three devout pilgrims visited the forbidden grotto and were arrested. They were Abbé Néréci, Abbé Delherm and Doctor Magnié. They received permission to see Bernadette, who was admitted that same day into the Sodality of the Children of Mary. The Curé introduced her to them in these words, "Here is the little girl you are looking for! The Virgin has given her graces she doesn't deserve. Many of her companions would have been more worthy."

As a matter of fact, in April, the Curé had more readily believed the other "visionaries" of Lourdes.[42] Now, it was a different story. He meant to protect Bernadette's humility. To do this, he fell back on the artificial methods then in use, describing the meeting as follows: "During this lecture, Abbé Néréci studied the little peasant girl, wearing a calico kerchief on her head...frail constitution... gentle face, transparent eyes.

"She blushed, lowered her head modestly and, bowing wordlessly, sat down on the chair they offered her, without saying a word, with that charming awkwardness workmen have when they find themselves among well-bred people. We left it to the eldest among us to question her. He had her tell about the apparitions. As she progressed, he would ask her leading questions to trip her up but in vain. With a surprising relevance, Bernadette would answer everything and finish by leaving her adversary nonplused!"

This "long and tiring,"[43] interview ended in two new trials: the affectionate outpourings of Madame Campardon, who had been present at the meeting, and her very persistent offers of money. Bernadette suffered the former and victoriously resisted the latter. At last she left, happy at having completed a chore, childishly happy, like a schoolgirl who has just finished with a written punishment.

Abbé Sempé, at Lourdes to preach the Children of Mary's retreat, happened to be close by when she left. He saw Bernadette, unaware she was being watched, laugh for a long time, rubbing her hands together and looking at the child who was with her.

"Already believing in the apparitions, I was somewhat shocked at what I thought was mischievousness, and my faith was a bit shaken by this,"[44] he stated.

Given this prejudice, Abbé Sempé questioned Bernadette the next day. He too was won over by her simplicity, but made a point of hiding his enthusiasm. He ended the interview with a stern lecture on humility and the dangers of illusions "with personal references, strong enough to hurt her feelings," as he himself stated to Abbé Burosse.[45]

"Whether the Blessed Virgin appeared to you or not, you must always fear the temptation of pride and of being lost by giving in to it," he specifically stated.[46]

Her head lowered, Bernadette listened very attentively; and when he had finished, she said: "You are quite right, Monsieur l'Abbé. I thank you, and I'll do my best to put what you told me into practice."[47]

Marie Courrech, the mayor's housekeeper and the best known among the visionaries,[48] had her last ecstasy on September 8. Her piety gave her much credibility among the clergy. A few days later, someone asked Bernadette, untouched by the slightest tinge of envy, the following question, "The Blessed Virgin told Marie Courrech that she would not see her again in this world. Since then, Marie does nothing but cry. How come you're not sad?"

"She never told me that I would never see her again," answered Bernadette.[49]

Step by step we are eliminating words of doubtful authenticity. For example, we can give no credence to the anonymous correspondent of the *Rosier de Marie* (Rosebush of Mary) who claimed that Bernadette, in seeing people cut branches from the rosebush at the grotto for relics, cried out, "Now where do you expect the Virgin to stand, if you cut away her rosebush?"[50]

The author placed this "two weeks ago," therefore shortly before September 15. We cannot see how Bernadette could have been a witness to the ravaging of the rosebush, since she had no longer been going to the grotto for months. The witness seems to be attributing to her the words of some other visionary.

On September 23, there occurred in Lourdes one of the seven cures that the bishop's Commission would later acknowledge as authentic. Four-and-a-half-year-old Jean-Marie Tambourré, suffered from first degree coxalgia (a hip disease). His parents brought him to the grotto, placed him under the jet of the spring water and the child, who had not been able to walk since June 13, went on his own toward the grotto. "His mother didn't want to leave Lourdes without seeing Bernadette. As soon as Bernadette saw the child, she asked him if he was cured, and the young Tambourré said yes. She embraced him and made him promise to recite some prayers, said his parents."[51]

But Jean-Marie placed the event at a much later date, in 1865. In his undated letter to Abbé Liesta, he wrote, "I declare that Bernadette made me promise to say three Hail Marys and three Our Fathers in Mary's honor, the year before she left for Nevers" (which would bring us to 1865).

Were there two meetings or rather some confusion? It is pointless to involve the reader in this unimportant difficulty.

On September 24, Bernadette artlessly dealt with a difficult party. A reporter from the *Courrier Français* came to catch her in a mistake, but he would truthfully write an altogether different article than he had anticipated.[52]

The article began with this description:[53] "Bernadette will soon be fourteen years old, but she looks more like ten. She is very small. She must have often suffered hunger and thirst. Her face, very pale, exudes goodness and kindness. Her eyes are bright and alert. She is dressed very humbly and carelessly in a calico dress whose original color has faded, heavy shoes which have never known a brush, and something like a cotton shawl over her shoulders; on her head is an old turban with neither taste nor grace. She speaks bad French and expresses herself more readily in the patois of the region. Her ease and calmness in the presence of strangers is surprising in a young girl her age. She gives the impression of being neither bashful nor boastful, and the curiosity she arouses does not seem to embarrass her in the least."

"It seems," the reporter said to her, "that you are made much of in this region. I heard about you in Bagnères, did you know that?"

"So I have heard."

"Does that make you happy?"

"I couldn't care less."

"Many newspapers have published your name; did they tell you that, too?"

"Yes."

"Have you seen the papers?"

"No, I can barely read."

"And does that make you happy?"

"Oh! Not too much! No."

The reporter tried to dazzle her with the prospect of becoming wealthy. "Listen, Bernadette. You must come to Paris with me and in three weeks you'll be rich. I'll take care of your fortune."

"Oh! No, no. I want to stay poor."

"My child, what you're saying is unreasonable. I'm not asking you to come with me by yourself; your parents will come too; you won't be separated from them."

"It's no use, I don't want to."

"Yet, if before leaving you were given sixty thousand—one hundred thousand francs? Think of it, one hundred thousand francs! That's a fortune. You would be almost as rich as the mayor and richer than Monsieur le Curé."

"Don't talk about that anymore or I'm leaving," Bernadette answered.[54]

Around the same time, the Courrèges d'Agnos family, traveling through the Pyrénées, asked the Curé if they could please see Bernadette. He gave them this telling answer, as reported by Henri de Courrèges: "You are eager to see Bernadette? You are not the only one, Madame. This summer, at the height of the season, I had to reply to thousands and thousands of these requests. People kept coming and going, and I assure you that these numerous visits were not without weariness for the child, who is not strong. Yet I didn't think I had the right to decline these interviews which are permissible if they help you to believe. You think that I can't treat you any differently than I do complete strangers. I shall send for the child; the only thing I ask is that you not make the interview too long."

Monsieur de Courrèges continued the account: "A quarter of an hour later, the rectory maid brought in a little girl dressed like a peasant. Her head, a bit big for her size, was wrapped in a brown and yellow checked kerchief, tied tightly over her forehead. A shawl was neatly crossed over her breast, its ends falling onto a dark-colored dress. A pale complexion; large, gentle eyes; she was neither forward nor shy.

"The Curé spoke to her: 'Look, Bernadette. Here are some people who wanted to see you. You will answer whatever questions the lady chooses to ask.'

"My mother then asked if she would rather speak in French or in patois. The little visionary was more fluent in her native tongue, so the conversation took place in patois. All I remember is that the child said the Lady was the most beautiful woman she had ever seen. One phrase has stayed with me quite vividly, the description of what the Virgin was wearing: a white dress, tied with a blue sash and a yellow rose on each foot. Her answers were always clear and precise; she never hesitated. I was just a little child myself; but even at that age children judge one another, especially when it comes to sincerity."[55]

In this same summer of 1858, a "diocesan missionary" from Tarbes questioned Bernadette on the promise of "being happy, not in this world but in the next": "So Bernadette, since the Blessed Virgin promised you heaven, you don't have to worry anymore about taking care of your soul?"

"Oh, Monsieur l'Abbé, I'll go to heaven if I do what I ought."

"What do you mean by 'do what you ought'?"

"Oh, that doesn't have to be explained to you, Monsieur l'Abbé."

"Fine! Let's say then that I understand. But what if someone ignorant asked you what one must do to go to heaven, what would you answer?"

"Oh, Monsieur l'Abbé, I don't know even how to read; there's no one more ignorant than I...."[56]

From that summer on, the flood of visitors became so large and uncontrollable that it caused problems. It was all too easy to see Bernadette without stopping at the rectory. Both pilgrims and the merely curious could meet her in the street or at her house, at her friends' or even at the hotel. The Curé was growing anxious. One day he met Bernadette at the convent of the Sisters of Charity at the Hospice and suggested a solution to her. "You must stay here; see, the good sisters will take care of you and teach you to read; you will be well fed and clothed; and at your house, you know...."

"Oh! I quite understand, Monsieur le Curé, but I love my father and mother so much! Besides, I need so little!"[57]

The end of the summer brought a certain calm and allowed a little respite. Furthermore, the grotto, finally reopened on October 5 at the command of the emperor, was now the center of attraction. And that is where an event that would have a considerable effect on future pilgrimages would unfold.

The Interrogation of November 17

At eleven o'clock on the morning of November 17, 1858, a group of clergymen left the rectory in Lourdes and headed toward the grotto "in a roundabout way." They were the members of the Commission of Inquiry appointed by the bishop to help him prepare his decision about the apparitions. They hoped to escape the attention of the crowd, but it was quite difficult for four very important canons to pass unnoticed. "In the twinkling of an eye, four hundred people" gathered at the grotto; they witnessed the examination of the site. The onlookers were also helpful in answering questions about the previous condition of the spring. Bernadette kept the members of the Commission waiting.[58]

They had asked her to arrive a quarter of an hour after them, for reasons of privacy. Unaware of the time, she arrived only at noon—overdoing her obedience to orders! The investigators questioned her about the layout of the site: the niche on the cliff where the Virgin would appear and the interior cavity opening where "she sometimes came down" to talk to her.[59] The little girl made a favorable impression: "Respectful modesty...and yet self-confidence. In the midst of this large gathering, in the presence of distinguished priests she had never seen before (she behaved) with the same calm, the same freedom, as if she were alone or with her parents."

But in spite of its quiet attentiveness, the growing crowd interfered with the interrogation. Then again, it was lunchtime. The canons adjourned the meeting. Before leaving the scene of the apparitions, they knelt down on the pebbles and prayed. Bernadette sat down on a rock saying, "I'm really tired!"

This lack of self-consciousness took Mademoiselle Lacrampe by surprise.[60] Today we find it reassuring. An actress would have staged a moving show of piety. The tiniest bit of concern about appearances would have produced such an act. Bernadette couldn't have cared less. Her task done, she rested.

And well she did, for the meeting resumed around four o'clock in the sacristy of the parish church. Bernadette gave an orderly account of the apparitions, along the lines she usually did. She grouped the Virgin's words together—except for "I am the Immaculate Conception"—as if they had all been spoken on one day, February 18. The stages she had still been able to distinguish so clearly on March 18 were now lumped together in a tightly structured abridged version. She paid no heed to months and dates, and she said this straight out to the Commission. What counted for her was not chronology, but the apparition, the message.[61] On that score, her story was clear, exact and precise. It drew out the essential.

The members of the Commission reread the deposition.[62] They especially reviewed two points: "How is it that the vision ordered you to tell the priests that the very next day a solemn procession be made to the grotto, yet you did not affirm that later?"

Here Bernadette hesitated, as she had on March 18 before Jacomet. The confusion of March 2, 1858, and Abbé Peyramale's anger had obscured her memory on this point. She limited herself to saying, "I'm not sure that this order was given to me, but as for building the chapel, *that* I've always been sure of and I still am."[63]

As had the police commissioner, so did the bishop's commissioners question her about "the blind girl of Luz," the child with the bandaged eyes to whom Bernadette had sent a stroke of "inspiration,"—as people coming home from the apparition on March 4 had put it. It was thought that the girl had been miraculously cured. This incident that had made such a bad impression on Père Nègre also troubled the Commission, because it was clear from then on that no miracle had been involved.[64] Bernadette answered, "I didn't send for the girl from Luz. I didn't have the slightest inkling that she was in the crowd. But finding her on my way, I felt drawn to her, I don't know why, and I embraced her."[65]

The interrogation was over, to the full satisfaction of the investigators.

Difficulties in School

What a contrast there was between the maturity of Bernadette's testimony and the constant difficulties she had in the classroom! In those last months of 1858, Bernadette sometimes despaired of ever remembering elusive letters and numbers.

"I'll never learn anything. You'll have to shove the book into my head!"[66]

Anxious to learn, Bernadette desperately sought the causes of her inability. Might it be her eyesight? She ran to the water at the grotto. "I've got to wash myself since I can't see."

"What do you mean you can't see?" asked Elfrida Lacrampe, her volunteer tutor.

"No, since I can't learn how to read...."[67]

A New Trial: Autographs

Her troubles in class coupled with those brought on by visitors seemed to culminate in a strange episode on January 1, 1859. We can only draw our conclusions from six of her own documents, whose handwriting is hesitant and relatively uniform, six "Happy New Year" letters. Some were addressed to Doctor Dozous, some to her sister and one with compliments to the official chaplain of the Imperial Court!

We can reconstruct the scenario as follows: the doctor who treated Bernadette's asthma free of charge asked for an autograph. Bernadette barely knew how to write. It didn't matter! He traced out samples for her to copy. That was all she knew how to do, according to the testimony of Azun de Bernétas [who interviewed her later that year].[68] So one sample was given to her, then others; both the text and quality of paper improved. She got help; they started over. They had to fill one more page on which a dried flower had been glued. Then another, decorated with painted roses, for the "Imperial Chaplain," thanking him for the "lovely letter" he had written to Bernadette. What did she do herself and what was done for her? The answer, it seems, is anyone's guess![69] That day, Bernadette set a new task for herself: writing autographs. This would soon become her daily bread.

Change of Address

By mid-September, the Soubirous family had left the cachot. Now that people no longer slammed the door in their face, they found a room to rent at Deluc's, the baker and café owner, who was married to a "daughter of Bibie Castérot's husband." (Bibie was the sister of Bernadette's maternal grandmother.) That is where in December of 1858, they were visited by Marie Moreau from Tartas, one of the seven miraculously cured women, acknowledged by the bishop's Commission.

This young woman came to give thanks for having regained her sight. As far as we know, she was the only visitor to the Soubirous who managed to leave Bernadette a gift. "Vowed to wear blue for a year in honor of the Blessed Virgin,"[70] she left her old apron "on the bed." Since no one knew to whom it should be returned, Bernadette made use of it.[71] André Sajous assures us that once she became a ward at the Hospice, Bernadette sometimes had to accept similar gifts, through obedience.[72]

At a time difficult to date, during the first three months of 1859, there was another change of address. Freed from the social obstacles that had condemned his family to poverty, François Soubirous was able to rent the Gras Mill, situated on the Lapaca River. Now that people listened to him instead of turning their backs on him, he could take his chances like anyone else. The misfortune brought on by poverty seemed to have been banished...for a while. As a matter of fact, shortly afterwards he was again a "brassier," i.e., a handyman, reduced to "renting out his arms" at 1.50 francs a day; a much lower fee than that paid for a horse, whose "horsepower" was obviously superior!

In one of these last two homes that year, it seems that fifteen-year-old Bernadette wanted to fast at the beginning of Lent (March 9, 1859). She wanted "to do penance," as the Virgin had asked her. She also dreamed, perhaps, of preparing herself to enter Carmel. Louise Soubirous forbade the fast. Bernadette had to be satisfied with the penance of obedience.[73]

The 1859 "Season"

With the beginning of spring, 1859, the tourists and visitors returned. The first to arrive on April 19, was R.S. Standen, a young English Protestant who made a hobby of "Psychical Research." This is what drew his attention to Bernadette. On the Gras Mill road, he met François Soubirous, in the calm satisfaction of his restored honor—"serious-looking and respectable." The miller very gravely bowed to Standen as if to say, "I know where you're going."

Standen was a skeptic. The believers in the grotto had astonished him with accounts of the miraculous. During the apparitions, he was told, Bernadette's clothes never got soiled, even when they were dragged through the mud. She repaired her broken candle one day, merely by passing her finger over the cracked part; her hand was not burned by the flame....

In contrast to this enthusiasm, Standen was very impressed by Bernadette's calm simplicity. "A very pretty looking girl," he wrote. He told her of the "miracles" with which public rumor glorified her. She answered abruptly, "There is *nothing* truthful in *any* of that."[74]

"Not a single thing," is saying a great deal, since myths always rest on some foundation. Bernadette could have offered shades of meaning or given some background. She rejected everything that wandered from the truth. It was her way. One has to know this in order to understand her remarks accurately.[75]

Standen continued:

"She welcomed us as though she had a long habit of receiving strangers. She invited us to follow her to a room on the second floor of the humble dwelling, next to her father's mill. Two youngsters, alert and happy, her brothers, were playing here and didn't seem a bit upset by our arrival. Neither father nor mother was at home. The child offered us chairs, while she stayed near the window and briefly answered the questions I put to her. She volunteered very few remarks of her own.[76]

"She refused the small gift we offered her and would not allow us to give anything to her little brothers. And we were sure that neither the parents nor the children ever accepted anything from strangers.

"She led us downstairs, and as we were crossing the room where the millstones were, she saw us looking at this apparatus with some curiosity. She then sent the little boy whom we had brought along as guide to open the dam. Then she herself explained the mechanism very intelligently.

"We left her, with the strong conviction that we had just finished talking to a most amiable little girl, and one superior to her age and station, both in manner and education. Whatever the true nature of the apparitions, we were totally convinced of the sincerity of her faith."[77]

On May 10, 1859, the Cornulier-Lucinière family, on vacation in the Pyrénées, received Abbé Peyramale's permission for an interview with Bernadette, in the rectory parlor, a room "of imposing dimensions but furnished with the greatest simplicity."[78]

Eighteen-year-old Marie, wrote an account of their visit on May 12, while it was still fresh in her mind. Her enthusiasm glorified the visionary a bit. She saw her as having "beautiful blond hair," thanks to I don't know what stroke of sunlight or imagination. The rest is objective: "Bernadette speaks little, briefly and simply but sometimes gets excited."

Marie de Cornulier-Lucinière also noted "her subtle smile," which must have broken out, particularly when Marie's parents asked her if the privilege of seeing the Blessed Virgin did not make her proud.

"Oh, no!" she answered, "for I am only her servant."

"But then how much does she pay you?"

"We never agreed on anything."

"What are your secrets?"

"I will never tell; besides there are some that are only for me."

"But if you don't at least reveal what concerns others, what good will the apparition be?"

"The chapel won't be only for me."

"If the Blessed Virgin told you to return to the grotto, even though Monsieur le Curé has said no, would you go?"

"I would first ask Monsieur le Curé's permission, and if he refused to give it, I'd go anyway."[79]

Bernadette was here thinking of the "irresistible force," which drew her to the grotto on February 22, 1858, in spite of her own resistance.

Marie de Cornulier-Lucinière also noted the following answers. The first concerns the "secrets":

"Would you tell them to the Pope?"

"He doesn't need to know them."[80]

The other concerns the apparition: "She was surrounded with light like the sun, but easy to look at; on appearing, she stretched her hands out and while speaking would fold them. She held a rosary and passed the beads through her fingers, but without moving her lips."[81]

On August 8, 1859, Bernadette was forced to stay in bed because of an asthma attack. The benefits of a stay in Cauterets (probably in May, 1859) did not last.[82] Was she worn out from the many visitors? Even so, they kept on coming.

On Friday, August 12, when Père Dominique Mariote, a forty-three-year-old Oratorian priest, and Paul de Lajudie, a twenty-year-old seminarian appeared at the Soubirous home, Bernadette's mother brought them upstairs without any questions or objections. This was fortunate for us, because these two visitors made careful notes of their conversation. Père Mariote, the more precise of the two, even used initials to identify the speaker:

D=Dominique Mariote, Oratorian, native of Lamarque-Pontacq, then professor at the college of Saint-Pé.

P=Paul de Lajudie.

B=Bernadette Soubirous.

We can do nothing better than to reproduce here a side-by-side synopsis of these two accounts, whose very differences vouch for their value and fidelity. The two visitors were next to the bed, where asthma left Bernadette "free enough that day to carry on a conversation perfectly."

[Editor's note: The left column indicates the dialogue between Bernadette and the visitors as recorded by Père Mariote. The right column provides the notes taken by Paul de Lajudie.]

D. "So, my child, you're sick? You have to stay in bed?"

We asked about her health. She told us she had to stay in bed.

B. "Yes, Monsieur l'Abbé" (the usual formula found in most of her answers.)

D. "How long have you been sick in bed?"

B. "Since last Monday."

"Since Monday." (Our visit took place Friday the 12 or 13 of August.)

D. "And what ails you?"

B. "My chest." (Her cough indeed indicated a considerable weakness in the chest.)

A frequent cough seemed to indicate a bit of asthma.

D. "We aren't tiring you?"

B. "Oh, no, Monsieur l'Abbé; today I can talk."

D. "And are you asking the Blessed Virgin for a cure? Hasn't the water from the grotto cured many people? Why wouldn't she cure you? She has cured others; didn't the Blessed Virgin promise to cure those who drank the water?"

I asked her if she was drinking water from the spring; she answered, "Yes, Monsieur l'Abbé." I then asked her why this water cured others, but not her.

B. "Perhaps she wants me to suffer."

"The Blessed Virgin perhaps wants me to suffer," she said.

D. "Why does she want you to suffer?"

"And why?"

B. "Maybe I need to suffer."

"Oh, because I need to."

D. "Why do you need to?"

"And why would you have to [suffer] more than others?"

B. "Ah! God knows."

She answered so as to avoid this subtlety, but very politely.

D. "Do you sometimes go to the grotto since you last saw the Blessed Virgin there?"

I asked her if she still went to the grotto.

B. "Yes, but I cannot go without Monsieur le Curé's permission."

D. "Why were you forbidden?"

B. "Because everybody was following me."

D. "So you don't go without permission? But how come, even without permission you used to go anyway? You were forbidden, weren't you?"

B. "Yes, Monsieur l'Abbé."

D. "Well, then! How come you don't go now as you did then?"

B. "Oh! Then I was *very pushed*" (very emphatic).

D. "Were you very pushed?"

B. "Oh, yes! I was very pushed."

D. "But what was pushing you?"

B. "I don't know, but I was pushed, and I couldn't stop myself."

D. "Whereas now you aren't pushed anymore?"

B. "No, Monsieur l'Abbé."

D. "And have you seen the Blessed Virgin since then?"

B. "No, Monsieur l'Abbé, I have not seen her anymore."

D. "Not even on your First Communion Day? You have made your First Communion, haven't you?"

B. "Yes, Monsieur l'Abbé."

"When Monsieur le Curé allows me."

"He doesn't always allow you?"

"No, because too many people come with me."

"And yet, in the beginning you went, even when they had forbidden you?"

"It's because I was driven (or pushed)."

"Maybe if I were pushed again (or driven) in the same way, I would go again; I was very driven (or pushed)."

"Have you seen the Blessed Virgin again this year?"

"No, Monsieur l'Abbé."

"When you receive Communion, do you see her?"

"No, Monsieur l'Abbé."

D. "A long time ago?"

B. "Almost a year and a half ago."

D. "And you don't see the Blessed Virgin in your Communions?"

B. "No, Monsieur l'Abbé."

D. "Not even on your First Communion day?"

B. "No, Monsieur l'Abbé."

D. "When you go to the grotto, don't you see her anymore?"

B. "No, Monsieur l'Abbé."

D. "Were you the only one to see the Blessed Virgin?"

B. "There was the mayor's girl [undoubtedly, the servant] who also saw her the last day I saw her."

P. "The Blessed Virgin must have been very lovely!"

B. "Yes, Monsieur l'Abbé."

D. "What was she like?"

B. "She wore a white dress, with a rosary on her arm, a blue sash, and two yellow roses, one on each foot."

P. "Did you see her face?"

B. "Yes, Monsieur l'Abbé."

P. "Was she sad?"

B. "No, Monsieur l'Abbé."

P. "She didn't cry?"

"When did you make your First Communion?"

"Last year."

"And the day of your First Communion, you didn't see the Blessed Virgin?"

"No, Monsieur l'Abbé."

"Do you receive often?"

"Every two weeks."

"When you go to the grotto, do you feel a strong emotion?"

"Did others besides you see the Blessed Virgin?"

"The mayor's servant girl."

"Do you remember what happened? Can you picture the Blessed Virgin quite clearly?" She answered these questions by describing the Blessed Virgin's clothing. (She became absorbed and recollected.)

"She wore a white dress, a white veil, a blue sash, yellow roses on her feet."

B. "No, Monsieur l'Abbé."

P. "What was she doing?"

B. "She was smiling."

D. "And didn't she have light around her head?"

B. "Yes, Monsieur l'Abbé."

D. "And that light didn't keep you from seeing her?"

B. "No, Monsieur l'Abbé."

D. "What kind of light was it?"

B. "It was like the sun when it reaches the earth."

P. "How did she hold her hands?"

"How were her hands? Were they crossed over her breast? Or were they by her side?"

B. "She had them open, and she extended them."

P. "Like the picture of the Immaculate Conception?"

B. "Yes, Monsieur l'Abbé."

D. "Did she look the same as when she appeared to a Daughter of Charity?"

B. "I don't know, Monsieur l'Abbé."

P. "Did rays come from her hands?"

B. "No, Monsieur l'Abbé."

D. "So she was not exactly like the Miraculous Medal?"

B. "Oh, no, Monsieur l'Abbé."

D. "She carried a rosary. How was she holding it?"

B. "She had it on her arm; and then sometimes she slipped the beads through her fingers, like us, or faster."

"No, she held a rosary, telling the beads rapidly, one by one, as if she were saying the rosary."

D. "What did this rosary look like?"

"What did the rosary look like?"

B. "The beads were white and the chain yellow."

D. "Was it big?"

B. "Yes, Monsieur l'Abbé."

D. "Bigger than ours?"

B. "Oh! yes, Monsieur l'Abbé, bigger than a full rosary."

D. "Was it like ours with five decades or with fifteen?"

B. "I don't know, I didn't notice."

D. "You didn't see it?"

B. "No, Monsieur l'Abbé."

D. "Did the Blessed Virgin speak to you out loud?"

B. "Yes, Monsieur l'Abbé."

D. "What did she say?"

B. "She told me to tell the priest (or priests) that they must build a chapel."

D. "Didn't she say something else? People say that she told you that you would suffer very much."

B. "Yes, but she promised me I would be happy in the next life."

D. "So you're sure of going to heaven?"

B. "Oh, no!" (excitedly).

D. "What! The Blessed Virgin promised you!"

B. "Oh, but that makes no difference. If I do good."

"The beads white, the chain yellow."

"Was it like ours? With five decades?"

"Much bigger, like a full rosary."

"With fifteen decades?"

"I didn't count them."

"What did the Blessed Virgin tell you?"

"The Blessed Virgin wants a chapel. She told me to tell Monsieur le Curé that she wanted a chapel."

"Did she promise special graces to those who would pray in that place?"

"She didn't say, but without a doubt yes, since she wants a chapel."

"That I would not be happy in this world perhaps, but I would be in the next."

"So you're sure of going to heaven?"

"Ah, if I do good."

"But the Blessed Virgin promised you."

"Only if I do good."

D. "So it's conditional. Didn't the Blessed Virgin tell you what you had to do to go to heaven?"

B. "No, Monsieur l'Abbé; we already knew that!"

D. "Didn't she tell you any secrets?"

B. "She told me three."

P. "The newspapers say she told you four."

B. "No, she only told me three."

P. "People say these secrets concern you alone. Will you reveal them some day?"

B. "If the Blessed Virgin wants me to."

D. "How will you know if the Blessed Virgin wants you to?"

B. "She will know how to let me know; she will tell me."

D. "So you're not sure that you will tell them?"

B. "No, Monsieur l'Abbé."

D. "Do these secrets concern you alone?"

"Did she tell you how to get to heaven?"

"We already knew that; we didn't need any more."

"Did she speak to you often?"

"Yes, Monsieur l'Abbé."

"Every time?"

"No, not always."

"Was she very lovely?" (She answered softly and seemed tired.)

"Did the Blessed Virgin tell you secrets?"

"Yes, Monsieur l'Abbé."

"How many?"

"Three secrets."

"Three or four?"

"Three."

"Will you reveal them?"

"If the Blessed Virgin tells me to reveal them."

"Do these secrets concern you alone or others?"

"They're for me."

"But they concern others too?"

D. "And didn't she tell you you would go to heaven?"

B. "Ah! But, if I tell you, it would no longer be a secret!"

D. "Besides, we don't want to know them."

P. "Where were the Blessed Virgin's feet? In the air? On the ground?"

B. "On the moss, Monsieur l'Abbé."

P. "And where did you see her?"

B. "On the spot where there is a rosebush and some brambles."

D. "Is your medicine good?" (She began to laugh.)

"No, only me."

"Only you?"

"And did she tell you the surest way for you to get to heaven?"

"Ah! Those are secrets; if I told you they wouldn't be secrets anymore."

"But it's not to make you violate your secrecy."

"Indeed!"

"Don't worry; we don't want you to reveal them."

At the end of the month, one of the two interviewers of August 12, Paul de Lajudie, questioned Bernadette once more. The acts of penance (kissing the ground, eating grass) seemed eccentric and unreasonable, he objected. "She answered...without getting excited ...as if it were a natural thing: 'For the conversion of sinners.'"[83]

Paul also got a few answers concerning the "irresistible urge" that drew Bernadette to the grotto on February 22, even though "her parents had told her not to go."[84]

During a third visit, that most probably took place on September 28, he came back to the secrets: "Might they involve something sad? Did they concern the world, the Church, France?"

"No, Monsieur."

"Did they concern you personally?"

"Oh! Yes, Monsieur." (She answered as if to get rid of an unwelcome question.)

"So she spoke to you of your vocation?"

"Ah!" (She smiled).

"How did the Blessed Virgin bring this up? Did she talk to you about heaven?"

"Yes" (vaguely, hesitatingly).

"Did she speak every time during the two weeks?"

"Yes!"

"What did she say?"

"Ah!"

"Well, what did she say?"[85]

Bernadette had become distant. To try to get her to talk again, Paul de Lajudie reminded her of one of the Virgin's statements: "I do not promise that you will be happy on this earth, but you will be in heaven."

"How did the Blessed Virgin introduce these secrets? Did she say, 'I am going to tell you a secret?'"

"Yes..."(vague and noncommittal).

"In what language?"

"In the local patois."

"Would you tell the Pope your secret?"

"The Blessed Virgin forbade me to tell a single person and the Pope is a person."

"But the Pope has the authority of Jesus Christ."

"Yes, that's true; the Pope is very powerful on earth, but the Blessed Virgin is in heaven."

"How do we know if it's really the Blessed Virgin who appeared to you, that it's not an illusion, a trick of the devil?"

"Oh, no! I threw some holy water at her and the apparition made the sign of the cross. She told me, 'I am the Immaculate Conception,' and said the rosary with me."

"Just the same, the devil could have done all that."

"Ah! Well, that's not my business anymore; I believe it was the Blessed Virgin."[86]

On entering the house, one of the visitors who was with Lajudie wanted to give the Soubirous family medals. He took out his purse. The children, seeing something white and thinking it was money, refused the offer that was about to be made.

"No, Monsieur, I don't want anything," Bernadette protested.

"Human justice has plagued you, persecuted you," the visitor sympathetically commented.

She answered with simplicity, "I don't remember."

"Did they change the meaning of your words?"

She gave the same answer.

Bernadette, who forgot being annoyed, paid the marvelous no more attention.

"To your knowledge, did anything miraculous happen, were cures performed miraculously?" the visitor questioned.

"I've been told there were miracles, but to my knowledge, no!"

Lajudie was so surprised that he rephrased the question. She gave him the same answer, "Not to my personal knowledge; I didn't see them."

"People say you had something to do with some of these miracles. Is that true?"

She answered with a smile, "Oh! No, Messieurs! No Monsieur! Not a single one!"[87]

In October 1859, there was a brief conversation between thirteen-year-old S. Carrère, accompanied by his grandmother, and Bernadette:

"So you have had the pleasure of seeing the Blessed Virgin?"

"Yes, and without deserving it."

Visitors asked her to make the sign of the cross as the apparition did; they asked for her prayers and then let her go. She was happy to be released so quickly, and would run back to her companions to rejoin their games.

At the Mineral Springs of Cauterets

On October 20, 1859, Bernadette was sent to Cauterets for the third time, it seems, again because of her asthma. Père Paul de Dieu, who was there from October 20 to All Saints' Day, saw Bernadette receive Communion, the final day at "six o'clock in the morning, at the first Mass." She went to Mass early, so as to avoid the curious. This witness explains more precisely: "She was constantly being asked to spend the day, sometimes at Monsieur le Curé's; at other times with pious families who called for her every morning to have her tell and retell what happened at the apparitions. They asked her for medals and for the booklet, entitled, *Vision of Lourdes,* (Paris, Palet, 1858), which told of the event.

"Twice they had her come to Cauterets to satisfy the curiosity of the residents and of visiting bathers.

"Whenever anyone went directly to Bernadette to ask her for

medals or booklets, she would answer, 'I'm not in business.' It pained her to see all these marks of respect and esteem. As much as she could, she ran away from these forced visits, but visitors would ask those close to her to have her come. She obeyed, but anyone could see on her face the pain she was suffering."[88]

That is why some visitors found her looking a bit sad, at least when she first arrived.

"If people did not force her to go here or there, she would stay at her aunt's house and never went out. She would never talk about the apparition, except when questioned. Her simple pleasure for recreation was to have fun with a two or three-year-old child belonging to the family.

"At Cauterets, continues Paul de Dieu, "she went to Mass every morning and would stay in church after Mass, until her aunt came and said to her, 'Come on, let's go.'"[89]

This distant aunt, the wife of the police constable of Lourdes, tells of an extraordinary happening (for many other people were still caught up with the extraordinary). "A woman told me in confidence...that twice she saw Bernadette's bedroom in Cauterets all lit up with a brilliant light. She told this to no one else."

Monsieur le Curé of Cauterets questioned her about the chapel the apparition requested (about which nothing yet had been decided): "Wouldn't you be happy to see it built?"

"Yes, very much."[90]

Meeting with Azun de Bernétas

On November 12, 1859, Bernadette suffered the assaults of a strange visitor named Azun de Bernétas. De Bernétas was an educated man from a good family, who had haunted religious orders and major religious centers without ever settling down, except for a short spell in the vicinity of the Curé of Ars. He was eager to offer Bernadette one of his books: *La Retraite* (The Retreat).

He had been warned, "The Soubirous accept nothing." His answer was, "Yes, they will accept this, because they are religious people and my *Retraite* produces spiritual benefits."[91]

He offered the book to Bernadette. Here, as de Bernétas described it, is what happened: "With a quick gesture of her hand, she refused it and with a look as firm as it was dignified, she said, 'Thank you.' A critical and painful moment." Turning toward her mother, he then said, "Madame! You couldn't possibly refuse such a simple object! Think of the spiritual benefits this book will bestow on you. It confers on you, as well as on your whole family, fifty-two Masses a year, forever, by an approved foundation attached to it. Do you think yourself rich enough in graces to boldly turn down those being offered to you? That would be far from edifying...."

He was just as persistent then about the future of his "mission." Bernadette, he said, must offer special prayers, even sponsor this enterprise.

"Without doubt, you want devotion to the Blessed Virgin to spread everywhere, and, according to the desire she expressed, see the conversion of sinners?" continued de Bernétas.

"Yes, Monsieur."

"Well then! I intend to write a book with that in mind. Promise that you'll pray for the people who buy the book, and especially, in a particular way for those who distribute it. As a guarantee of your promise, give me your signature."

Bernadette did not yet know how to write without tracing. "Make a sample and I'll sign," she answered.

This visitor was, no doubt, irritating because of his stubbornness and the fanatical quality of his fervor. But these are the very qualities needed by an investigator. De Bernétas had an obsession with documents and also with objectivity—in short, a kind of naïveté which made him Bernadette's faithful echo.

On November 12, he methodically took down the account of the apparitions, which she gave "partly in French, partly in patois." He rewrote it "under her dictation." He made a polished copy of her deposition, submitted the text to her the next day, made the corrections she suggested, and submitted the amended text the following day. This time, "she acknowledged it to be an accurate statement of the exact truth." In fact, this is one of the best-written statements of Bernadette's story, the fifth in order of accuracy, among those that stretch from February 21, 1858, to the very last day of her life. This document[92] is precious for three reasons: 1. It confirms the stability of Bernadette's testimony; 2. It reveals one stage in her memories and oversights; and 3. It preserves a few rare or original details, for example, the following about the third apparition on February 18, 1858. Bernadette told him that after the recitation of the rosary, "the vision called me, and I immediately wanted to alert my two companions, but I could barely begin saying the first word: Ah! My tongue could say no more. With her finger, she beckoned me to come closer. I instantly obeyed and I went to the back of the grotto. The apparition let herself drift through the opening, which cuts the ledge, approached me and said, 'Would you have the kindness to come to the grotto for fifteen days?' I promised her I would."

Asked to describe what went on around her and within her at the grotto during those fifteen days or stations, Bernadette answered, "I can tell you almost nothing about that, because the presence of that object (in patois, *Aqueró*) would usually captivate me completely."

This was an excellent detail, which confirmed what the doctors had noted on March 27, 1858: during the apparition, Bernadette not only lost sight of her su rroundings but even forgot herself; she was not focusing on her "condition" but on the one who was appearing to her.

Azun asked her again, "You no doubt have heard about the children of La Salette?"

"Yes, Monsieur."

"Well, then, it is *my* opinion that they were flattered too much on the apparition of the Virgin at La Salette. Maybe they will not be so good. The favors God grants a soul in the quiet of prayer are for that soul's benefit alone. Don't you go around and persuade yourself that you are better, and if people shower high marks of esteem on you, let them kiss the rosary so that the just veneration due to the Blessed Virgin will redound to her who is entitled to it. Furthermore, you are not the only one here to whom the Blessed Virgin has appeared. People say that Monsieur le Maire's servant (Marie Courrech) has also seen her. These external manifestations, in my view, do not constitute true and solid virtue."

"Monsieur, I thank you for your good advice; I'm going to put it into practice," Bernadette responded.

This answer was not given out of ordinary politeness. Bernadette profited by the lesson.

"She has since shown us her thankfulness" (insisted the writer).[93]

Toward the end of 1859, it seems, Bernadette had a conversation with "a Protestant judge, a wise jurist," whose name has not come down to us. Abbé Boyer, who reported this, especially guaranteed its accuracy. He assured us that the speaker was moved "to tears."

"Monsieur l'Abbé," the judge said on coming out of his meeting with Bernadette, "people can object, they can try to explain the cures attributed to the water of the grotto. The force of conviction for me is here. That child amazes me; she moves me. There is truly something there."[94]

That same year, when François Soubirous regained his position as miller, Jeanne Védère was stunned by the generous welcome given to customers at the mill. "From morning till night, none of the women who came to have their wheat ground left without getting some refreshment. [Louise Soubirous] spent more [this way] than she received as payment for the miller. I saw something wrong about this. Bernadette disapproved as much as I did. She told me one day to talk to her mother about it. Of course I couldn't do that. The first time I came back to Lourdes, I knew Bernadette had told them that I didn't approve of this practice, because my aunt said to me, 'You must be amazed to come here and always find women eating; but we cannot act otherwise. It's the custom in Lourdes.'"[95]

1860—Abbé Junqua's Visit

At the beginning of 1860, Bernadette was visited by Abbé Junqua, an educated priest, but a bothersome one due to his impulsiveness and his lack of tact and moderation.

As soon as he arrived in Lourdes at the end of January, Abbé Junqua took steps to set up a meeting with the "privileged child," as he called her. He sent "a pious person, known to her" to present his request.

The answer came back: Bernadette is ill with asthma; but she will come if her confessor permits. Junqua obtained permission from Abbé Pomian and immediately sent two messengers in the pouring rain, who clop-clopping in heavy sabots, brought back a white hooded cape under a "heavy cotton umbrella"—Bernadette.

Her two companions left her at the threshold.

Junqua was surprised at her youthfulness, "a face barely twelve years old." The interview took place in his hotel room and lasted two hours. Junqua relates what happened:[96]

"My child, concentrate. I can be useful to you if you tell me the truth; but tell me only what your conscience and especially your eyes have seen. Is it true that you have seen a strange person in the little mountains?"

"Yes, Monsieur, I did."

"How was she dressed?"

"She had a white dress, a white veil, a rose on each foot."

"What did you feel when you saw her?"

"A great deal of pleasure, so much that I can't put it into words."

"And since?"

"A great desire to see her again."

"Did you see her again after the first time?"

"Yes, for fifteen consecutive days."

Here Junqua somewhat confused what Bernadette told him about the fifteen days. He did better on what concerned the spring.

"The vision [this is the name which in her language, half-patois, she gave to the apparition] told me to drink there, pointing to the deep end of the grotto. I ran to the Gave to drink, but the vision called me back: 'I did not say that you had to drink at the Gave, but over there.' She indicated the deep part of the grotto where there was no water, only dust and rocks."

"And what did you do?"

"I obeyed. I went back to where the vision wanted and I scratched at the ground."[97]

The word *scratched* is significant (though poorly rendered). Bernadette used the verb *scratch* (scrape, claw), commonly used throughout southern France. The author, Marcel Pagnol, used it in the last act of *Marius:* "I will scratch him," says Honorine to César, speaking about the boy whose belt she found in her daughter's room.[98]

Junqua went beyond the truth when he specified with emphasis, "I scratched at the *very dry* ground." Bernadette always spoke of damp and muddy ground. But the interviewer could not resist the myth, and it is from him that Lasserre took this legend, which is refuted by both the written accounts and the Commission of Inquiry. After having thus conformed to the "miraculous" Junqua resumed his more accurate account of Bernadette's remarks:

"I scooped out a handful of damp soil; I didn't dare drink that. I scratched again, with the same result; I didn't dare drink that either. Finally I scratched again, and this time there was more wetness in my hand. At that moment, I obeyed and drank it all."

"Tell me, my child, did this person speak to you?"

"Yes, she did, just as you and I are speaking now."

"Did you answer her?"

"Yes, as I'm answering you."

"What did she tell you?"

"To *pray for sinners,* to come to the same place for fifteen days and a few other things."

"Tell me those other things the vision told you."

"I can't, it's *secret,* it's...."

"How many secrets?"

"Three."

"Tell them to me. I'll bring them to a great archbishop, a friend of the Pope and a cardinal of the Church. I'll be seeing him tomorrow, and he will do some good for the mountain and for the miracle."

"Since it's a secret, I can't tell you."

"Yes, you can, provided you tell nobody but me."

"Then it wouldn't be a secret anymore."

"Yes, it would; I'll keep silent like a confessor."

"My confessor can't know either."

"Your confessor neither?"

"No, unless the vision orders me to tell him."

"But you can at least tell me whether the secrets concern the Church, France, or the Pope."

"No, they concern only me and are not about the Church or France or the Pope."[99]

After a few digressions, followed by a misunderstanding about the "age of the apparition," which he tried to set at the respectable age of "twenty years," Junqua continued:[100]

"Was she beautiful?"

"Oh! Oh! Yes indeed! And even more than that!"

He here described her mimicry. "She smiled and turned her head to show what she meant, quite sure of herself."

"My child, did the vision keep on talking to you?"

"No, sometimes she prayed and sometimes she spoke to me."

"What prayer was she saying?"

"She prayed her rosary."

"How?"

"She went from one bead to the next without ever moving her lips."

"My child, stand up and show how this fascinating person acted, especially when she was praying the rosary. Pose like the vision did at other times, too."

Junqua recorded this description: "Here Bernadette got up, standing with her hands folded, her fingers intertwined, one thumb over the other. She acted out praying the rosary, going from one bead to the next with the thumb and index of her right hand, while her lips were silent like the vision's."

"My daughter, when the vision was not praying the rosary, how did she look?" Junqua asked.

Again he described what happened next: "Here, Bernadette took a new pose. She straightened her arms, let them hang by her side and turned her hands around with palms open, perfectly imitating the pose of the Virgin on the Miraculous Medal. At this moment, I said, 'Would you say that the vision posed like the Virgin on this medal?' (I showed her a Miraculous Medal.)"

"Yes, exactly, but she didn't have those things on her hands."

"She pointed to the rays coming from the hands on the medal, and which the Virgin did not have and never had in any of her apparitions to Bernadette."

"My daughter, why did the vision choose this place to appear to you?"

"Ah! Because she wants a chapel built there in her honor."

"Who told you that?"

"She did."

"How did she tell you?"

"She told me, 'You will tell the priests that I want a chapel built here.'"

"What did the priests say?"

"My priest said, 'We cannot build this chapel without knowing who the person is who talks to you; ask her who she is.' Then I went to the mountain and asked the vision who she was. She told me."

"What did she say?"

"*'I am the Immaculate Concetcion.'*(I spell it the way she pronounced it.)"

"You are deceiving the public, my child, because you are still ignorant; you were even more ignorant twenty months ago, and it's impossible for you to have remembered these words: *Immaculate Conception,* since you couldn't even understand them. Isn't it true that you did not understand them?"

"Yes, that's true, but on my way home I kept repeating them, right up to the rectory. Every step I took I kept saying, '*Immaculate Concetcion,*' because I wanted to bring the vision's answer to Monsieur le Curé, so that the chapel would be built."

"My daughter, I understand, and you are right. Now stand up and imitate how the Virgin stood and spoke on that occasion."

Abbé Junqua described the scene that followed. "Bernadette rose again and placed her hands as explained above (when the Virgin was not praying the rosary) and said: 'I asked the vision, "Who are you?" The vision smiled, but did not answer.'"[101]

Here as elsewhere, we have eliminated the commentary with which Junqua filled Bernadette's testimony. Bernadette's statement, "The vision smiled" became "with a gracious smile which would have been haughty had it not been provocative." Fortunately, the differences of style between those remarks faithfully written down and those of the writer himself are sharp enough that we can sort things out quite well.

The account continued: [Bernadette explained,] "I asked again: 'Who are you?' The vision smiled again in the same way. But the third time I asked, she raised her arms and her hands (something like the priest at Mass when he says, 'The Lord be with you'), joined her hands close together, raised her eyes to heaven and keeping them focused there, forcefully said these words: 'I am the *Immaculate Concetcion,*' and disappeared."

"My child, I have tired you greatly. Take these three coins as payment."

"No, Monsieur, I don't want anything."

Abbé Junqua noted that, "Here Bernadette expressed herself with an energy that showed I had insulted her integrity and unselfishness. I insisted, but with an eloquent silence mixed with pain and indignation she let me know that I had better quit. I put the money back in my purse, then continued."

"My child, show me the medals you wear in honor of Mary."

"I have them at home. They were just torn from me to be placed on some sick people, and the strings that held them were all cut apart."

"Show me your rosary. (The girl showed her beads, a simple rosary with a medal attached.)"

"Will you give me this rosary? I'll pay you later."

"No, Monsieur, I don't want to give or sell you my beads."

"But I'd really like to have a souvenir from you. I traveled so far to see you! Truly, you owe me your rosary."

"And Bernadette gave it to me. I seized this heavenly quarry upon which the tears of the child fell more than once, for she actually used these beads in the presence of the vision. What a treasure! Oh, if anyone were to take this precious relic from me, he would be the cruelest of enemies!"[102]

Was it indeed "the rosary of the apparitions," as Junqua claimed? Specifically questioned about this on January 12, 1879, Bernadette answered, "One day, I put it in my pocket. That night I couldn't find it. This caused me great sorrow. If someone is sure he has it, it's because he stole it from me. I never wanted to give it to anyone."

The rosary of the apparitions, no doubt, had already been stolen. Abbé Junqua received another rosary from Bernadette.

"May I pay you for this rosary, my daughter? Here's a coin."

"No, Monsieur, I'll buy another one with my own money."

"At least here, take these three silver medals."

"No, Monsieur."

"But they are of the Virgin of Loretto, whose shrine I am restoring. Take them and give them to your companions, waiting for you at the door of the hotel."

Junqua added in his notes, "Bernadette took the medals. I blessed them in her hands."

"My child, here is my scapular. Is yours made like this?"

"No, Monsieur, it's double."

"Show me."

The priest recorded, "Bernadette reached modestly for one end of the scapular, which in fact was double, in the sense that it was like an ordinary scapular, except that it had a double lining."

"My daughter, blessed by God! I know a very pious soul who would be happy to have half of your scapular, which can indeed, be separated. Oh! please forgive me, but give me half. There'll be enough left for you, since you'll still have a complete scapular."

"Monsieur, would you split the rosary I gave you in two?"

"No."

On February 5, 1860, Bishop Laurence,
Bishop of Tarbes, saw Bernadette for the first time.

"Neither will I split my scapular."

"I realized [he concluded] that I had to give up and not persist."[103]

At last! Abbé Junqua ended the interview with a long exhortation encouraging Bernadette to be pious, and especially to pray for him and not to forget him. "I shall return. Remember me! Promise you'll remember me!"

He wrote her answer in indirect style, obviously toned down. She may well have said something like, "I can't promise you that! I see so many people, all kinds of people."

This visitor was a sorry specimen. Involved in an opposition movement, he was soon to leave the Church. For this reason the pious literature of the day, out of a sense of decency, attributed his memoirs to a believer in Lourdes, a Père Hermann. But Père Hermann, who also questioned Bernadette, did not leave any notes. Neither did Père Sibillat, who interrogated her at the grotto itself in June, 1859, in front of three hundred people, the reports of which would reach as far as the Imperial Ministry.[104]

Let us render to Junqua what belongs to Junqua!

Bernadette's Confirmation

A few days after Junqua's visit, on Sunday, February 5, 1860, Bernadette received Confirmation. From that day on, she was allowed to receive Communion once a week—an exceptional favor in those days.[105] On the day of the ceremony, Bishop Laurence asked to see her personally. It was the first time. He jotted it down in his diary—the notation exhibited his usual terseness.

The Secrets Again

One of the last visits in this crowded period was that of an unidentified ardent ecclesiastic, indiscreet and full of his own importance. He had Elfrida Lacrampe bring him to the Soubirous house. (She operated the Pyrénées Hotel, where he was staying.) The "secrets" distracted and disturbed him.

"The Blessed Virgin has no right to impose on you," he declared. Bernadette remained silent.

"Well, let's take it as a given then. As a priest, I have the right to ask you, I who have the right to know and 'to forgive sins.'"

Bernadette looked at him with a smile but remained silent.

"Look, I understand your scruples about telling me. All right, let's try another way. I will question you. If I discover the secrets, say nothing. And if it isn't what I say, you just have to answer 'No!'"

She remained silent.

"Let's get on with it! The secret, is it that she told you the hour of your death?"

This time Bernadette answered "mischievously." "Do you know 'the hour of your death?'"

"I? No. But you must know yours! Come, come. The Blessed Virgin must have forbidden you to accept any gifts?"

Bernadette had returned to her smiling muteness. She was a solid wall of silence. Not learning any "secrets," the visitor asked for a souvenir. Here Bernadette was more agreeable.

"You give it to him," she said to Elfrida Lacrampe, untying the worn metal chain on which her medals hung.

But they had to give up trying to make her accept a silver chain in return.[106]

Headed in Four Directions

In the spring of 1860, the flow of pilgrims intensified, following the rhythm of the seasons. Bernadette found herself bound to four sets of almost incompatible duties, which she fulfilled without seeming to be inconvenienced.

1. She worked for a living. She spent her days as a "baby-sitter" for Armantine Grenier.[107]

2. She tried to complete her missing schoolwork under the direction of Antoinette Tardhivail, her unpaid teacher.

3. She helped out at home.[108] She played the part of eldest daughter. This was not an empty expression, according to regional custom. Under this title, she corrected her flighty younger sister Toinette with authority, "Don't do that!"

This quality of character has been attested to by Isabelle Aiguillon, a classmate Bernadette used to meet on her way to the grotto.[109]

After the apparitions, Bernadette was the one who would recite family prayers, morning and night, reported her brother Jean-Marie. She insisted that everyone be reverent. "One day when I went to bed too early, intending to say my prayers lazily in bed, she forced me to get up."[110]

4. Lastly, she met visitors of all kinds, opponents or believers,

who were determined not to leave Lourdes without "seeing the eyes which saw the Blessed Virgin," as Agnes Veuillot put it.[111]

No one knew how to relieve her from this crushing burden, for keeping her in her room would only create idle speculation. But above all, her testimony was decisive, even indispensable for the pilgrimages that were beginning.

Available to everyone, she edified some and amazed and confounded others, noted Abbé Peyramale in his letter of May 17, 1860.[112]

And Abbé Pomian said, "The best proof of the apparition is Bernadette herself."[113]

But at what a cost! How much weariness, confrontation, unwholesome or disturbing contact, flattery and vexation were involved. She also had to travel frequently, since people were not satisfied with going to see her, but showed her off "at Cauterets, Pau, at Bagnères."[114]

All this bustle did nothing to take care of the Soubirous' business. The coming and going cramped their work and used up their money. Their lack of concern and their patience helped them not to lose heart in this confusion. But it could not go on. Not for Bernadette's sake either. Her refusal to leave her family, which up to that point she had maintained, could no longer be defended. Dominiquette Cazenave's tact would overcome any final opposition.

Decision

From the hills of "The Espénettes," during the week of July 9–15, Dominiquette came down to the Soubirous' mill. Louise took advantage of her visit to ask her to teach Bernadette to sew.

"Not here!" Dominiquette protested. She had witnessed the constant hubbub that interfered with any organized activity in the house. "Let her come to the quiet of my house."

That needed authorization. Monsieur le Curé had limited Bernadette's visits in town (a salve to his conscience!). His permission had to be obtained. That did not bother Dominiquette. She knew how to handle her Curé. She took advantage of the occasion to describe to the pastor the difficult position of the Soubirous and their daughter. "You cannot think of leaving her in the world," she concluded.[115]

Dominiquette had not been the first to mention this to Abbé Peyramale. The Curé now went back to his plan of autumn 1858. Bernadette would be placed with the Sisters of Nevers. They operated a school and a home in the same building. Bernadette would receive her schooling as well as room and board at the hospice.

All that remained was to settle her legal and financial status. Mayor Lacadé, who subsidized the institution, was, here as elsewhere, as kind as he was clever. To satisfy the administration, Bernadette could be there free of charge, as a sick person, for example, unable to pay.[116] Behind this arrangement, a suitable schedule would be set up for her to finish her academic and domestic education.

Despite her persistent doubts about the apparitions, Mère Ursule Fardes, the superior, willingly agreed to accept Bernadette and entrusted her to the care of Soeur Victorine Poux. Monsieur le Curé set up rigorous rules for this mission of trust. Bernadette had to be protected. She was to visit no one without explicit permission from the rectory. Mère Ursule immediately made a request. The following day, Monday, July 16 (the anniversary of the last apparition) she was going to Bagnères, where "our Sisters" would really love to see Bernadette.[117] Permission was granted by way of exception.

Bernadette's parents were opposed to this separation. A permanent exception was made in their favor: their daughter could visit them anytime, but always accompanied by a nun.[118]

Now all the problems had been taken care of.

On Sunday, July 15, 1860, Bernadette moved into the hospice, which she would never leave—except for a few nearby visits—until her departure from Lourdes.

Shadows

Over this "carefully arranged" matter, one shadow remained: Doctor Dozous. The hospice, from which he had been fired in 1856,[119] stirred up the darkest experience of his life. He was furious and exploded, "What! Entrust Bernadette to that superior, an unbeliever! who begins by taking her to Bagnères, when she was confided to her care to keep her out of circulation! Bernadette is in bad hands. She must be removed from there at all costs!"[120]

Peyramale took all this philosophically.

To Dozous, the superior was once, "that incomparable woman." Now, she was his "pet peeve."

There were bitter regrets too at the Tardhivail sisters, Bernadette's former teachers. They had difficulty seeing her given over to someone else's care.

In October, 1860, Azun de Bernétas returned to the Soubirous as a bearer of a new pious intention: a way of being present at the grotto without going there. In Bernadette's absence, he asked her mother to make a novena at the grotto for the success of his projects and insisted on paying her something. To overcome Louise's refusal, he improvised an argument that Bernadette would surely have rejected.

"You can't refuse this. It isn't a gift or a salary. I knew you would refuse that. It is compensation. Look, I take an hour of your time every day: twenty minutes to go to the grotto, twenty minutes there and twenty minutes to return. In conscience, I feel that I must make good for this."

Louise hesitated. Never had one sou entered the house because of the grotto; but every one of her objections stimulated Azun's eloquence. "Even to help out a neighbor, you have no right to neglect the duties of your state, the interests of your large family. This compensation is justice, and you have no more right than I to pass it up."[121]

For the visionary too, the move involved a few drawbacks. In leaving her family, Bernadette was further removed from her role as "eldest," which had given her a useful and responsible place both in the family group as well as in her social milieu. From now on she found herself protected, but cut off from the kind of human relationships in which her fundamental qualities had blossomed. Bernadette, an open-air plant had been transplanted to a hothouse.

CHAPTER 6

— ⚜ —

BERNADETTE THE BOARDER

We now find Bernadette a boarder at the sisters' home. The school year was about to begin. There was great excitement among "the demoiselles of the boarding school": the visionary was to leave the class of charity cases, from which they were separated. They were at last going to have her to themselves. Marie Mouret was especially happy about this.

"Second Class"

Bernadette was much less happy. She was sorry to see herself in the category of the privileged—desirable though this might be. By instinct and by grace, her place was among the poor.[1] She would have opted for the charity-case class, but this did not fit in with the class schedule. Reasons of correctness and morality kept the charity-case students outside the regular organization of a house already made complex by the fact that it served as both school and hospital. Only two options presented themselves for the new boarder: the first class, which comprised "the demoiselles of the bourgeoisie," and the "second class," made up of girls from families of more modest means, but of established good character. Unable to get her first

The Hospice of Lourdes, where the Sisters of Charity of Nevers taught school: Bernadette's last residence in Lourdes (1860–1866).

choice the charity-case class, Bernadette, more docile than her reputation for stubbornness would suggest, accepted the latter choice.[2]

The School Girl

The uprooting had at least one advantage. For the first time, she
could (at last!) complete one school year, with almost regular attendance.[3] Of course, at sixteen, the experience was hard and progress
was slow. On December 31, 1860, she still found it hard to write a
short New Year's note[4] to her parents, who, luckily, could not read.
It was a time when sympathetic companions felt sorry that she had
trouble finishing her homework. "Let it go, I'll finish it for you,"
suggested one of these understanding friends.

Bernadette's solid common sense reacted, as did her conscience.
"No, the good sister will know and she'll scold me," she answered.[5]

At the beginning of 1861, her diligence bore fruit: her academic
development was under way. She no longer faltered in reading or
fought to recall an alphabet running about helter-skelter like a flock
of crazed sheep. The letters were now clear. They had at last become for her a means of self-expression. And the discovery brought
her joy. On May 28, 1861, Bernadette drew up, on her own, her first
account of the apparitions, still peppered with delightful phrases in
patois.[6] (The account included rough copies, now unfortunately
lost.)

As for sewing, she already had more than just experience. She
possessed rather a kind of gift: nimble and tireless fingers and a
knowledge of stitches and materials. She was marvelous at embroidering.[7]

At recreation, she was the life of the party.[8]

"Not exuberant, but always happy," recalled her young companion, Philomène Camès.[9]

She joked and laughed whole-heartedly. At ease with people of
all ages, she enjoyed playing with the youngest. Her small size and
simplicity saved her from the embarrassment of being a backward
"grown-up" among the children.

"No one would have given her age as more than eleven. In the
schoolyard, she often played games with those of us who made up
the youngest class. She was easily winded," said Philomène.[10]

Jumping rope was too much for her, but she liked to swing the rope for her companions and was able to keep up with the others playing games like "knucklebones, hide and seek and blindman's bluff."[11]

Bernadette's "Faults"

This playfulness raised more than one eyebrow, for Bernadette was under constant supervision. Suspicion? No, on the contrary. She was considered to be a "saint," and the smallest prank appeared unseemly or sacrilegious, as if a church statue had come to life and did a pirouette!

Bernadette knew what she wanted. She had her stubborn moments.

Without reason, the sisters wanted her to change her Sunday dress. Well, she wouldn't! They would not allow her to visit her family and yet they had promised that she could go there freely! She objected and would not give in. We must at least admit that she only reacted privately, and "not in the presence of the children."[12]

She was "sensitive" to "small injustices."[13] This was seen as weakness, as a lack of serenity. As for her mischievousness, they counted it squarely among her faults, because there was a bit of a wild streak in Bernadette.

At the beginning of the summer, we find her at the second floor window of the hospice with lively, ten-year-old, Julie Garros. Both were gazing at a patch of tempting red strawberries, the first of the season. It was forbidden to go into the garden, but there was no formal ban on strawberries (even though this went without saying). Bernadette got an idea: "I'll throw my sabot out the window. You'll have to go fetch it, of course, and bring back some strawberries."[14]

The sabot dropped and Julie went downstairs. Unfortunately, we don't know the rest of the story, except for what happened much later. Half a century later, a respected moralist focused on this story after being told of it innocently by an old and wrinkled nun, whose name was Soeur Vincent Garros (the "Julie" of 1861). He was what is commonly called the "Devil's Advocate" in Bernadette's canonization process. This was the most serious accusation that he could bring against Bernadette. After laborious dissertations on insignificant events, he now took the triumphant tone of the seeker who has finally found what he was looking for: "De malitia, in casu, dubitari nequit, apertaque est disciplinae violatio." ("Here the desire to do wrong is beyond doubt and a clear breaking of the rule.")[15]

Luckily for the canonization, it was only a sin of youth!

Soeur Victorine Poux surprised Bernadette in "flights of fashion." One day, for example, she was struggling to "puff out her skirt" to make it look like crinoline; another time, she was putting "a bustle in her corset: a block of wood."[16] Bernadette was seventeen. She was no stranger to natural inclinations. Would not the contrary have been more disturbing?

Where she was intransigent was in respect for God and for prayer. At church, quite a few girls, apparently absorbed in their prayerbooks, were secretly reading cheap romantic novels, about which they later sentimentally spoke among themselves. Bernadette was scandalized to the point of turning her natural repugnance to such reading into a matter of principle. "Don't learn how to read," she told her sister, Marie one day. Soeur Victorine caught her giving this bad advice by the hospice's hall window.

"Bernard! (that is how she sometimes called Bernadette) Why are you saying that to Marie?"

"Ah! We come from a family where it's better."

"But why?" insisted the nun.

Even in her anger, Bernadette wouldn't betray her companions for all the world.

"That's the way it is. It's better that way."

Definite stubbornness. Soeur Victorine would never learn the reason for the strange advice.[17]

Although she was an admirer of the visionary in her care, Soeur Victorine was surprised to find her quite ordinary, even in piety.[18] Bernadette was irreproachable on this point: she always made her sign of the cross "like at the apparitions," large, perfectly gestured, simple—even when she "thought herself unobserved."[19] She diligently said the rosary on her own, "several times a day," and took it with her at night to say while going to sleep. Yet this was not unusual among Children of Mary.[20] Her confessor allowed her to receive Communion every Sunday and sometimes, even during the week.[21]

There was nothing more. When Soeur Victorine suggested that

she add the practice of meditation, Bernadette answered, "Ah well! I don't know how to meditate!"

"But in the end, she tried," admitted Soeur Victorine.[22]

The sisters sometimes found her repugnance to money excessive. But one needed money. Refusing it, without exception, a practice Bernadette had imposed on her family, could not be continued at the sisters' home. When money was intended for the Church, didn't it become holy? At the beginning, when a visitor tried to slip her an offering, Bernadette "dropped" the wicked money about which the Gospel speaks, and "they had to scold her to make her pick it up."[23] Later, she would say a bit unpleasantly, "There's a poor-box...."

The poor box was for the sisters at the home. Or she would hasten to put the money into the hands of the superior.[24]

She was attached to nothing and willingly gave away what she had.[25] Personal things didn't pile up in her little boarder's locker, where there was nothing worth noticing, except a vial of wine, which surprised Soeur Victorine. Her parents brought her some from time to time.[26] Wine was rather uncommon in Lourdes. To have it gave one prestige. It was supposed to give strength. Bernadette took a bit for medicinal purposes, with no hint of abuse. The sisters overlooked it because it was a "family and regional" custom.[27] But where was the asceticism of the Desert Fathers!?

Then again, Bernadette took snuff. True, it was for her asthma and prescribed by Doctor Balencie. However, in catechism class one day, Soeur Marie Géraud heard fits of sneezing, followed by suppressed laughter.

"What's going on back there?"

The commotion was coming from Bernadette's end of the classroom. She was the last person anyone would suspect in such a situation. However, she was the one who stood, holding her snuffbox.

"I'm the one, Sister! I offered a pinch of snuff to my neighbors."[28]

Bernadette was a gentle child, simple, patient and friendly toward all. It always appeared that her pleasure was to please others, rather than to find her own enjoyment in their games. She seemed to avoid the most serious things, even during the recreations of the Children of Mary, whose meetings she attended every two weeks. She never spoke about the apparitions "on her own."[29] She was not vain about this. She acted "as if somebody else had received these favors." When anyone wanted to bring up the subject, she changed the topic. "Please, leave me alone," she begged. "I have to tell it to so many strangers."[30]

She insisted "that they draw no attention to her, for fear of the curious,"[31] especially on excursion days to Bétharram.[32]

The sisters recognized her devotion for Communion. "She prepared herself well," said Soeur Victorine. "Even when she was suffering, spending sleepless nights, she still got up to go to Communion. [Sometimes at night] I offered her lozenges. She would say, 'No, Sister. I might fall asleep before I swallowed it, and then I couldn't go to Communion.'"[33]

In those days, it was not scrupulosity but respect for the rules she had learned.

First Photos of Bernadette

Photography has enabled us to see what Bernadette looked like at this time, that is, at the age of seventeen or eighteen. There are no snapshots from "the year of the apparitions," regardless of the claims printed on later, touched up pictures.

During the first months of her stay at the hospice, sometime between October 1861, and the first months of 1862, Abbé Bernadou took six photographs of her. He was the chemistry teacher at the minor seminary and had taken up this new art form,[34] not for commercial reasons—only for art and history—but he had extremely high ambitions. He wanted nothing less than to capture on film an image of Bernadette in ecstasy, even at the risk of distorting the young girl's spirit by leaving to posterity the portrait of an actress! Bernadou kept pushing with the enthusiasm of an impresario, obsessed with his own ideas, possible or impossible:

"No, that's not right! That's not the expression you had when the Virgin was there."

"Well, it's because she isn't here!" retorted Bernadette.

A further difficulty was that the pose had to be maintained for several minutes. In every picture Bernadette appears simple and natural; she is a bit stiff only because of the effort she made not to move—even her eyes or her lips—under the magic eye of the camera. This was a performance very few girls her age could have carried off.[35]

A Bernadou photo

Her Health

What was most worrisome was Bernadette's health.

Soeur Victorine, assigned to watch over her from All Saints' Day, 1861, kept her eyes open for symptoms, which she described as follows: "Regularly short of breath, she experienced all kinds of troubles: toothaches, frequent rheumatism in her leg; one Good Friday, a painful shoulder, almost causing her to faint...a chronic cough, vomiting or coughing up blood (frequently), occasional palpitations. Several times a year, violent asthma attacks. She would stay in bed a day or two, suffering very much; she had to be brought to the window to help her breathe. [She would say] 'Open my chest!'"[36]

"In sickness, she was never impatient," noted Soeur Victorine.[37] "She was in constant pain but you would have scarcely suspected it unless you knew her well."[38]

Soeur Victorine pointed out a connection between Bernadette's physical discomfort and other annoying problems: "Lengthy interrogations gave her trouble; all that stress affected her chest; then she had asthma attacks; they had to carry her to bed; but she did not blame the visitors."[39]

The sister was not quite so understanding when it came to Bernadette's faults: "When she was disobedient or stubborn (or exhibited any kind of fault), she would be sick that night or the following day. We used to say, 'She'll soon come down with some illness or attack.' God would immediately make her do penance for her sins."

When her attacks were acute, it was feared she might choke. Someone would keep an eye on her during the night, but she found enough breath to tell her nurse to go to sleep.

"Sometimes," recounts her brother Jean-Marie, "her asthma attacks were so violent...that they thought she was dead and several times they came from the hospice during the night to get my parents. We would all get up and go to the hospice. We would kneel beside my sister's bed, as if we were witnessing her final moments."[40]

Visits at the Hospice

Were those asthma attacks Bernadette's greatest trial? No. She herself supposedly said one day when she was sick, "I much prefer this to receiving visits."[41]

Another Bernadou photo from 1861 or 1862

And these visits were frequent. "At school, she was disturbed by visitors almost every day," said Soeur Victorine.[42]

These surprise visits no longer took place in the freedom of an unscheduled life, but within the routine context of a life laid out by timetable. Constant calls to the visitors' room were becoming unexceptional exceptions! As much as possible, the sisters kept class time from being interrupted, but her recreation period was completely swallowed up. It was a thorn in her side for Bernadette to stop playing (and play was something she needed), to face the unpredictable mix of politeness, enthusiasm, devotion, nosiness and absurdity which at that point was her fate. It reached the point of making her sick. She would leave recreation obviously against her will. The other girls would say to her, "Why are you going?" She would answer, "Because they order me to."[43]

"The apparitions did not take place for your amusement but for the people," the sisters would tell her by way of encouragement.[44]

That argument didn't lessen her repugnance.

"I saw her weep at the door, when there were twenty, thirty, forty people waiting for her in the sitting room," said Soeur Victorine. "Big tears filled her eyes. I would say, 'Courage!' She would wipe her eyes, go in, bow graciously and answer [their questions].[45] Once back from these meetings, she simply resumed playing or working, as if nothing unusual had taken place."[46]

Supervising those visits enabled the sisters to size up more closely the risks run by Bernadette, who was being exalted like some character in a stained glass window.

One day, according to Soeur Victorine, a Carmelite friar from Bagnères knelt down before her...

"Bless me," he asked her.

Bernadette was washing her hands in the kitchen....

"I don't know how to bless...."

"[Well, then] say, 'Blessed Virgin, who appeared to me, bless this priest and this family!'"

There was a lady with two children present.

Bernadette repeated [his words].[47]

People would make her touch their rosaries. She touched them, turning them in her hands, or taking them in one hand, she would touch them with the other. Abbé Pomian forbade her to do this.

From then on, she no longer did, and when people insisted, she answered, "I am forbidden."[48]

After that, visitors changed tactics. They gave her medals to distribute. Her own disappeared as if by magic, so did her rosary beads, when she forgot them in bed in the morning. To make it easier for her to refuse, she was forbidden to give "snippets from her hair" or other "relics..."[49]

We must acknowledge the name of miracle-worker that people were starting to give her. Indeed, countless stories were going around. For example, this tale told by Philomène Camès:

"For several days, my mother had a very painful finger. One Sunday, after Vespers, she said to Bernadette, 'Listen, squeeze my finger.'

"'What do you want me to do for you?'

"'I'm asking you to squeeze my finger.'

"Smiling, Bernadette did, and that very night my mother was healed."[50]

When she went out, it was another story. "Women" came up to her "from behind," tells Soeur Victorine. [Their intention was,] "If only I could cut a swatch from her dress."

One day, Bernadette overheard [a similar saying]. She turned around and said, "How silly you are!"[51]

Some people "knelt before her at the grotto." Others said aloud, "She'll be raised to the altars!"[52]

One day, some visitors showed her the latest thing from the local store: "Her picture in a rose," like "a mystical rose," for her to sign. She signed, but said, "What foolishness!"[53]

People asked her, "Bless these rosaries for us."

"I don't have permission," Bernadette answered.

That day "There were some soldiers present," riflemen "dressed in hooded white military cloaks."

Some women said, "Here come some Carmelite friars!"

"Yes," replied Bernadette, "go get their blessing!"

Some old women were talking with her about things of a delicate nature and asking her advice. She showed no reaction. She told them that she would pray.[54]

Bernadette seemed to take no foolish pride in these compliments: neither "feelings of self-satisfaction," nor "credit to herself."[55] Nevertheless, the sisters feared she would grow spoiled, so they made it their duty to humiliate her in public. Even Soeur Victorine Poux, who was so fond of her, did this. "I would say in her presence, 'She's worth nothing. She's done nothing, etc.' She never held this against me."[56]

Some were harsher: "She's just a charity case; she still has many faults; and if the Blessed Virgin has appeared to her, it's certainly not because she deserved it."[57]

Bernadette accepted this well enough[58] and showed "neither dissatisfaction nor satisfaction"[59] "Has she no feelings?" wondered Soeur Victorine for a long time. She did, for one day Bernadette admitted to her, "It humiliates me."[60]

This moral "compensation" did not soften Bernadette's ordeal; it made it all the harder. Blowing hot and cold like that, they added bite to the burn. Bernadette, wounded both in her humility and in her legitimate pride, kept the hurt to herself by radiating joy. Only a few subtle signs betrayed how traumatized she was.

Another problem created by the visits concerned all those pilgrims who asked for "very special and daily prayers." How could one fulfill so many requests? Bernadette found a solution, which she explained, without any mystery, to Madame Fontan, in the summer of 1860: "Every day I say a rosary for all those who ask me to pray for them."[61]

In certain special cases, however, "she quickly ran to the chapel and knelt in front of the statue of the Blessed Virgin which was on the altar and which she loved very much."[62]

In 1863, the authorities made it a rule that she would pray "twice a day, morning and evening," for the benefactors of the chapel.[63]

In return, Bernadette asked people to pray for her. A very young visitor was surprised at this. "Does she need prayers?" he asked his mother.

Bernadette didn't cater to the pilgrims' inclinations toward magic. She brought them back from the incidental to the essential, from signs to basic realities. Looking back, Monsieur Moisset, a pilgrim from Pechprunel, found in the words she had spoken to him the solution to a difficulty that had been raised by an eminent personage. "People take water from the grotto like medicine," the bishop of Montauban had objected.

Had this abuse come from Bernadette? Moisset wondered. No it

Louis Veuillot

couldn't have, for she had emphatically repeated to him, "You must have faith and pray with perseverance.... This water would have no power without faith."[64]

Visitors of 1860

So much for the prevailing climate and atmosphere. With this as background, let us pick up the chronological thread of visits to Bernadette, beginning with her admittance to the hospice.

Shortly after July 15, 1860, three Jesuits, Pères Sacareau, Durand and Kerskaver, had Bernadette describe the apparitions once again. She spoke without emotion or affectation, as if the experience had "happened to a third party." What interested them most was the message. They wanted to know everything about what the Virgin said.

"Pardon me," [Bernadette said,] "she told me something else, but it's a secret."

"So, it's a useless revelation."

"It's useful to me."

"Will you at least have to tell your confessor?"

"No, not at all...the Blessed Virgin told me not to tell anyone."[65]

In the summer of 1860, Madame Dufourc-Bazin came with her eight-year-old daughter Claudie. The child fixed her eyes on Bernadette. When Bernadette imitated "the gesture of the *Immaculate Conception*," the little girl threw her arms around her neck. This memory would ease Claudie's insomnia in her dying days in 1933. [66]

On September 1, Louis Veuillot visited together with his sister Elise and her two daughters, Agnes and Luce. The collapse of his newspaper had given the journalist a martyr's halo. *L'Univers* had died "fighting the good fight." The great man was welcomed like a prince and his remarks were considered the voice of God at the minor seminary of Saint-Pé. At Tarbes, the bishop invited eighteen guests to a dinner in Veuillot's honor. On his own, Abbé Peyramale proposed, by way of exception, to summon Bernadette to the rectory. He introduced the visitor to her, saying, "He is a great defender of the Church, you must pray for him."

But before Bernadette arrived, Peyramale had told the journalist, "Talk to her about anything you like, except the apparitions."

This instruction allowed her nothing but small talk, none of which has been recorded, except to note the atmosphere of fervor. [Veuillot's niece] thirteen-year-old Agnes, stared at Bernadette as if the visionary were an icon. This was too much, Peyramale, anxious about Bernadette's "humility," thought. He abruptly told her in his rich bass voice, "You can go!"

The brusqueness of this dismissal astonished the young admirer. "To get rid of" this living saint like that! Seventy-eight years later, Agnes still remembered.[67]

On October 26, there was another visit from Azun de Bernétas. This time he did not come as an investigator and limited himself to congratulations.[68]

At the end of the month, it was a Jesuit, whose initials, "M.M.," are the only identification given. He entered, accompanied by Abbé Peyramale and M. Laffaille, director of the major seminary. The Jesuit was an experienced debater. He kept bringing up objections, including this final one, "You say the Blessed Virgin spoke to you in patois. That is impossible. The Blessed Virgin does not know patois. She was from Judea and spoke Hebrew."

Bernadette instantly answered, "God...is...the Author of all languages. Couldn't he have taught the Blessed Virgin patois, just as he did me?"[69]

This answer "put an end to the interrogation," and Bernadette took advantage of the silence to beg with her eyes to be dismissed. Returning to recreation, she asked Soeur Victorine, "What did this Curé come here for, since he doesn't believe what I tell him?" And she added, "He might just as well have stayed home!"[70]

At the Bishop's

On December 7, 1860, Bernadette was summoned to Tarbes. This summons involved a solemn court appearance, a last official deposition before the episcopal judgment on the apparitions.

Here we have Bernadette before Bishop Laurence: a clean-shaven, emotionless "mask," surrounded by twelve members of his Commission, their faces like sharply chiseled sculptures. At the secretary's desk, Canon Fourcade took down her words as she spoke and compared them with the written statement of November 17, 1858. They agreed perfectly. The commissioners pressed her for details and set snares for her.

"Did the Blessed Virgin have a halo?" asked one.

"Halo?" Bernadette looked around for an explanation of this strange word. Then, once she understood, [she announced,] "She was surrounded by a soft light."

"Could you see her clearly?"

"Yes, clearly."

"And did this light appear at the same time as the apparition?"

"It came before and stayed a bit after."

Another commissioner observed, "It does not seem like an idea worthy of the Blessed Virgin to make you eat grass."

"We eat salad, don't we?"[71]

Bishop Laurence was deeply impressed by the way she imitated the gesture of the Immaculate Conception.[72]

Visitors of 1861

In mid-August 1861, under a sun hot enough "to fry eggs on ice" (in the words of one witness), a gentleman from Brittany visited her. First, he spoke to the Soubirous. Struck by their poverty, he tried discreetly and persuasively to get them to accept his offer of money, with no success. He received permission for an audience in the sitting room of the hospice. Full of enthusiasm for the young girl who had seen the Blessed Virgin, he had not come to question her but to confide in her, to be heard. He was a widower with a fourteen-year-old daughter, who was now his whole life, the only thing he loved in the whole world. Bernadette listened so calmly that he spoke longer than he had intended. He finally realized he had taken up so much of her time, though she had not complained, and exclaimed, "How good you are! How kind you must be to those around you! In fact, I'm sure you've never even gotten angry."

"Well, you could be wrong, Monsieur!" Bernadette replied.

The visitor took this statement for false humility; but Monsieur le Curé, on being asked, related an example of Bernadette's anger caused by her concern about avoiding all trace of self-interest within her family. One day one of Bernadette's brothers had accompanied some strangers to the grotto. For his troubles, he accepted a small coin. His big sister angrily told him to go back immediately and give back to those people what he never should have accepted in the first place. He hesitated and got a slap on the cheek. When he re-

An old view of Lourdes, Place du Marcadal

turned, Bernadette gave him a kiss and said, "Don't ever let that happen to you again."[73]

On October 13, 1861, there was an excited, impressive priest, who vehemently insisted that Bernadette recognize him right away. Had he not made her promise to remember him? He hastened to remind her, "I'm the one who...."

Bernadette's recognition seemed proof enough to him that she was "quite happy" to see him.[74] It was Abbé Junqua. He showed her the rosary that he had almost forced from her at his last visit. "You recognize it, don't you?" he asked. "Well, I had it blessed by the Holy Father," he went on, "and in thanksgiving for this gift, I recommended you to his prayers. I presented him with the account of my first visit to Lourdes, when I took notes of your answers. He placed it carefully among his secret papers and promised me to examine it closely."[75]

Unfortunately, this is the only document[76] we have concerning what went on between Lourdes and Rome before 1862. Its contents can be trusted, because Junqua, a doctor of theology, was at the time assigned to the Shrine of Loretto and had official duties in Rome. He had Bernadette repeat the account of the apparitions, but this time he took no notes. He was amazed that her story never changed.[77]

Among other visitors who left only minor impressions,[78] let us mention only two priests, renowned for their sanctity.

The date [of the first visit] is uncertain, but it seems [to have taken place] a little before the episcopal judgment. Bernadette was sent by carriage to Bétharram to be examined by Père Michel Garicoïts. Nothing would emerge publicly from this confidential interview except the priest's enthusiasm for Lourdes.[79]

As she was leaving, two religious teased her, "Well, my child, you've been very lucky; the Blessed Virgin has promised you heaven!"

"Yes," she answered, *"if I earn it."*[80]

In April 1862, she was visited in Lourdes by a Capuchin Friar, Père Marie-Antoine, the "saint of Toulouse," one of the future pillars of what was becoming a place of pilgrimage. This holy man had a minor fault, quite typical of his time: eloquence.[81] His account shows an inexhaustible enthusiasm for what Bernadette told him, without ever indicating the reason why!

The oldest photo of the spring.

The basin with the three taps (left) had been made on his own by Castérot, the tinsmith, on April 14, 1858, with the help of Lourdes quarrymen.

"Mary Has Truly Appeared"

January 18, 1862 marked a new stage in the affair whose only witness had been Bernadette. The bishop signed the episcopal document wherein he declared, "We judge that Mary Immaculate, Mother of God, has truly appeared to Bernadette."[82]

Four days later, on January 22, Abbé Peyramale himself came to question Bernadette.[83] The bishop had personally asked him to verify a few details for the publication of the document and for the written account of Canon Fourcade, secretary of the episcopal commission.

"Did the Virgin speak of a 'spring'?" Peyramale asked.

Bernadette repeated [in patois] the words, *"Anat beoue an-a hount..."* (*hount* means spring, fountain).

"And what did you do then?"

For the bishop, it was a matter of being certain of the verb he used in the following sentence: "The young girl, seeing no water in the grotto was making her way *[s' acheminait]* toward the Gave, when the apparition called her back...."

Bernadette specified, "Not seeing a spring, I headed *[je me dirigeai]* toward the Gave, but she gestured to me with her finger, showing me the spring...."

"S'acheminait" was then the proper word.[84]

Abbé Richard, who was also an engineer, a hydrogeologist, [specializing in the study of the occurrence and distribution of underground water] was present at this interview.[85] Listening to Bernadette, he made such a funny face that Bernadette stopped, taken aback, her eyes seeking an explanation. That was exactly what he was waiting for. "Well, if the Blessed Virgin gets together with you to uncover hidden springs, you'll undoubtedly be more than a match for me!"[86]

Sickness—Spring of 1862

The spring of 1862 was an emotional one for those around Bernadette.[87]

On March 25, Antoinette Tardhivail had received Mother Superior's permission to take Bernadette to the grotto. This was a praiseworthy concession on the part of the sisters, because Bernadette's ex-tutor had shown some resentment toward them ever since they had taken her place with the visionary. However, the day after this visit, an "inflammation of the lungs" occurred, one of the most serious, according to the doctor.

Bernadette's friends were very worried, none more so than Antoinette, whom public rumor strongly accused of causing Bernadette to come down with a fatal illness by exposing her to the draughts at the grotto of Massabielle. Antoinette broke out in tears and prayers,...which were answered.

By about April 20, Bernadette was back on her feet, despite a persistent pain in one leg. To console the Tardhivail sisters, a decidedly forgiving Mother Superior allowed them to take Bernadette back to the grotto, this time in thanksgiving.

What kind of bad luck kept hounding Antoinette? The very next day, Bernadette had a relapse! This time "both lungs" were affected.[88]

Lina's Visit

Despite the scare of the previous week, Bernadette received another visit on the morning of April 28, 1862. Elfrida Lacrampe, the daughter of the owner of the Pyrénées Hotel, forced her way in.[89]

Her fervor was long in coming. Taken to the grotto by Jean-Baptiste Estrade, on February 25, the day of the discovery of the then muddy spring, she had described her unfortunate impression in the rather crude language of the hotel coach drivers, even going so far as to call Bernadette a little "liar."[90] Elfrida had gone from a militant unbeliever to a self-proclaimed convert.

A young woman trailed after her, almost reluctantly. Her name was Lina. She was a servant to an English family living in Pau, while her husband, Joseph, was employed with another family near Lourdes.[91] Lina was a charming woman, far above her class, who could have been taken for her employer. She was Protestant, and, at Joseph's request, Elfrida had taken up the task of converting her.[92] Their friendship had come about easily, but Elfrida's religious militancy annoyed Lina and put her off. The previous day, April 27,[93] she had been made to go to the grotto but had refused to pray or drink of the water there.[94]

On their way back "a terrifying storm" forced Elfrida and Lina to find shelter. "Grace is going to fall on you like this rain," Elfrida laughingly told Lina. This violent image of grace hardened Lina's defenses. She refused to visit the visionary. She had to leave for Pau. Besides, at that hour, Bernadette "might perhaps be dead." Elfrida's persistence made her change her mind. Lina postponed leaving until the afternoon, and that was how she arrived, unwillingly, at the visionary's bedside on the morning of the twenty-eighth, accompanied by her husband, Joseph.[95] Elfrida, who had the run of the hospice, marched right in.

At Bernadette's bedside she came upon a pitiful scene. The patient was choking. Her face was flushed. Elfrida drew closer. "Don't talk, just touch these objects," she said. Joseph, Lina's husband, was the one who wanted this favor.[96]

Elfrida kissed the sick girl and was about to leave. But just then Lina fell to her knees in the spot where Elfrida had been standing and sobbed. Bernadette, though panting, was able to speak. "Madame, get up, I beg of you, it makes me feel sad."

Elfrida brought Lina a chair.

"Madame Joseph, stay here if you wish, but please sit down," pleaded Bernadette.

Lina sat down, still in tears, her head in her hands.

"Madame, I beg you, it makes me so sad to see you like this," Bernadette repeated. And after a moment, she added, "I would like to give this woman something. What can I give her?"

All she found at hand were the cross and medals around her neck.

"No, no, nothing. I'm unworthy," answered Lina, still deeply moved but calmer now.

Elfrida came up and cut the string holding the objects. "Choose yourself what you want to give her," she told Bernadette.

Medals were hardly appropriate for a Protestant, but Bernadette knew nothing about such matters. And ecumenism had not appeared yet on the horizon. How did she handle the situation?

"Here, Madame, the cross is for you; and the medal is to remind you of me."

Elfrida didn't think she had to push the matter any further. Hadn't she seen the tears of conversion? On a return trip to Lourdes "fifteen days" later, Lina would disappoint her.

"It was the emotion of the moment," she explained.[97]

The epilogue of this visit? Joseph returned to Lourdes with the cross and medal Bernadette had given Lina. He was now a widower.

Lina converted to Catholicism a few months after her stay in Lourdes, and died two years after.

The Anointing of the Sick

Bernadette's condition worsened after that visit. During the afternoon of the same day, April 28, 1862, Louise Soubirous was sent for. Death seemed imminent. Doctor Balencie, the hospice physician, had to call in a consulting doctor.[98] The examination lengthened. Abbé Pomian awaited the doctor's departure. He was afraid of arriving too late to administer the sacraments. The two doctors left, shaking their heads pessimistically. The chaplain took their place at the patient's bedside. Bernadette made a very difficult confession because she could not talk. The priest asked her to respond with gestures. Should he offer her Communion? She seemed unable to swallow. He decided to give her a particle of the Host with a little water from the grotto.

That was when the dying girl's expression changed.[99] The obstruction had suddenly disappeared. She began breathing freely. Bernadette felt like laughing and crying but held back in order to make a prayerful thanksgiving. Finally, she said, "I'm cured. It's as if a mountain has been lifted from my chest."

Nothing impeded her speech. She added, "Monsieur l'Abbé, you brought me a good doctor."

She laughed, she talked, she asked for something to eat, she wanted to get up. The superior objected, "No, it's already nighttime. That can wait until tomorrow."[100]

The patient slept all night long without the slightest cough. The next day, April 29, it was she who greeted the doctor in the visitors' room. Taken aback for a moment, Doctor Balencie quickly recovered his professional calm. "Say, those medicines we prescribed did their job!" he commented.

"But I didn't take any," Bernadette said.[101]

"Well, my little one, no matter, you're cured. You weren't as sick as we thought, no doubt."[102]

In town, people were talking miracle. Was this word justified? Without a doubt, the coincidence was striking. But asthma is a strange sickness, subject to sudden remissions, which would produce other surprises in Bernadette's life. Today, the Medical Bureau would not entertain a moment's thought of opening a file on such a case.

As for Bernadette, she didn't believe in the miraculous any more readily than she did in the expertise of Doctor Balencie, whose confusion she had already sized up. She concluded in her own words, "If I'm sick again, I'll ask the doctor to pay more attention. He mistook one sickness for another, and I could have died."[103]

That was her last word on the matter.

We would be more understanding today. A specialist, Doctor B. Lancieux, has written that with asthma we are dealing with "a sickness...which is in many respects a mystery.... It is absolutely impossible [he has concluded] to codify the treatment of such a baffling sickness, where so many elements are interspersed: allergy, environment, biological factors, multiple triggers, psychological factors, etc."

After her cure in April, 1862, Bernadette resumed her various occupations: daily class, sewing, housework, cooking, care of the sick. Sometimes they even put her in charge of the children in the youngest class.[104]

Visits During the "Season" of 1862

With the return of the beautiful weather, the flood of visitors began anew. In August 1862, at the end of a stay in Barèges, Père Lataste, a Dominican, questioned Bernadette at length:

"What was the Virgin's expression when she spoke of sinners?"

"Serious, but...not severe or irritated...at all other times she was smiling."[105]

Bernadette specified that she had not had "an ecstasy or a vision in a long time." The priest admired her agreeable "simplicity," but found her "sickly."

In October 1862, Abbé Corbin visited her. He was a specialist in iconography. He was preparing a book on "The Apparitions of the Blessed Virgin at the Grotto of Lourdes from the Viewpoint of Christian Art." With him came Monsieur Rouy, a town counselor and a retired officer, who abruptly asked her to, "Make the sign of the cross as you saw the Virgin make it at the first apparition."

"That is impossible," Bernadette replied.

"I'm not asking you to make the sign of the cross *as well* as the Virgin, but nearly so."

Bernadette repeated her refusal: "Even nearly so."[106]

The Abbé then followed this with his questionnaire on the vi-

Asthma, a Baffling Illness

Dr. B. Lancieux noted the following in *La Croix,* May 24, 1969:

The word...comes from a Greek term meaning "difficult breathing." We find descriptions of this sickness in the ancient writings of Galen and Paul of Aegina. They were already speaking of "air canals" obstructed by "thick humors."

Precise descriptions...came...with Laënnec and especially Trousseau, himself an asthmatic.

An asthma attack generally breaks out in the middle of the night, surprising the sick person during sleep. Yet it gives warning the night before by minor preliminary difficulties, such as nasal stuffiness, faintness of voice, watering of the eyes, migraine or itchiness.

Awakened during the night by a choking feeling, the patient sits up or gets up. He literally suffocates; he perspires. It is as if his thorax is blocked by forced inhalations made with great difficulty. It is the exhaling which is long, difficult, and is accompanied by wheezing which is audible when the lungs are osculated.

In general there quickly appears a cough—at first dry, then more and more "phlegmy" with emissions of thick, whitish and viscous sputum.... The attack usually lasts from one to two hours. It leaves the patient exhausted, dejected but without any respiratory discomfort.

These attacks occur in a particular context, hereditary in nature. Asthma...a lifelong sickness...most frequently starts in infancy, between two and ten years of age. The onset is rather deceptive.

In certain cases of ancient asthma, secondarily infected, there may appear, independently of paroxysms of suffocation, an authentic chronic respiratory discomfort.

There is also what is called the condition of asthmatic disease, that is to say, a severe asthma attack, which contrary to what usually happens, does not disappear in a few days but lasts for several days. In such a case...the patient runs a real danger of asphyxiation or heart failure.

The diffuse but transitory obstruction of the intrapulmonary bronchi is linked to several additional phenomena. There is first the bronchial spasm, caused by the contraction of the surrounding muscles, which considerably narrows the diameter of the bronchi. The passage of air through the bronchi is made all the more difficult by the congestion and swelling of the mucus membrane that lines them. Finally, this membrane begins to secrete a much thicker and stickier mucus than usual, congesting the bronchi.

Contrary to a very widespread belief, asthma is not necessarily an allergic illness.

Asthma, somewhat similar in this respect to a stomach ulcer, is an illness in which the organic elements, location, heredity, bronchial irritability and psychological elements closely overlap. An outburst of anger or frustration can trigger an asthma attack. The great Trousseau, himself an asthmatic, was sensitive to the scent of roses. He tells of one day having an attack upon catching sight of some roses in the sitting room, before realizing that they were artificial!

sual details of the apparition: "Did she have a cloak on her shoulders or a scarf around her neck?"

"No, Monsieur, but her dress went up to her neck, had no collar, and was tied around her waist with a blue sash, the ends of which hung down the front."

"What color were the roses on her feet?"

"Like the chain of her rosary, yellow and shining like gold."

"Do you know what the roses meant?"

"No, Monsieur."

"Did you notice the shade of the Blessed Virgin's hair?"

"I didn't pay any attention; besides, her veil covered it almost completely."[107]

On top of all his questions, the priest had her repeat the gesture that they now asked her for almost daily—the one the Immaculate Virgin made when she gave her name.

Abbé Corbin ended it all with this tricky question, "What if the bishop of Tarbes...had judged that you were mistaken, what would you have answered?"

"Never could I say that I didn't see or hear her..."[108] answered Bernadette.

He stopped there so as not to tire her out, because "she had just gotten over a sickness." This comment places the visit around May-June, which fits in well with the publication of his book in October 1862. Very much impressed by his meeting, Corbin, in expert fashion, noted, "It is easy to see that with her, imagination plays no role whatever."

Her Godfather

The year 1862 was highlighted by a great joy for Bernadette.

A wondrous, almost legendary figure became a reality in her life. At the end of August, her godfather, Jean-Marie Védère, arrived on furlough at Momères, wearing the medal of the Legion of Honor that had been awarded him in 1859 at Solferino. Bernadette saw him for the first and last time.[109]

The winter of 1862–1863 was a good one for her. She worked in a relative calm on all fronts, schoolwise and otherwise. She was maturing....

Abbé Alix, "converted" by Bernadette

The "Season" of 1863

With the spring, the visits resumed, more numerous than ever.

In June 1863, Abbé Alix, an influential and self-confident man and a noted preacher and professor at the Sorbonne, was completely overwhelmed when he met Bernadette.

"She was not afraid to answer me twice, 'It's the Blessed Virgin, Monsieur; it's the Blessed Virgin who did this.'"[110]

After this visit, he canceled his trip to Spain, made a general confession and profoundly underwent a thorough conversion.[111] He became one of Bernadette's advisors at the decisive phase that would begin that year.

Many sick people came to see the "visionary" of Lourdes. Bernadette protested that she had no power. She could only pray for them, like anyone else. That was all. She sent them to the grotto. Cures took place, about which it is impossible to make a judgment today. Here is one, for example, which Abbé Peyramale described to Bishop Laurence in a letter dated July 26, 1863:

"Yesterday, a girl from Marciac (Gers) arrived in Lourdes at four in the afternoon. She immediately went to the hospital. Her arm was in a sling. A fall she had while tending her mother had deprived her of the use of this arm. The arm was immobile but very painful. The slightest touch would make this poor girl scream. The fingers were contracted and thin; one would have said lifeless. After seeing Bernadette, this young girl went to the grotto. There, after praying awhile, she washed her arm, and at that very moment it began to move and come to life. The fingers became supple again; the sensitivity disappeared; the arm had returned to normal. The coachman who had brought the girl was present. According to his own patois expression, which rendered well exactly what he felt, he was frozen on seeing the girl all of a sudden raise and stretch out her arm, then open and close her hand, which had been completely useless only a few moments before."[112]

Likewise, on August 5, twenty-three-year-old Catherine Duros arrived in such a bad state that Bernadette was asked to come to the Hotel Maumus to see her in bed. Bernadette sent her to the spring, where she was cured on the spot.[113]

On Friday, August 7, Bernadette received the Count de La Ville-marqué, a member of the French Institute, and his wife. Bernadette came alone to the meeting. The Count recognized her from her photographs.

"Are you Bernadette?" asked Madame de La Villemarqué.

"Yes," Bernadette answered graciously, asking them to be seated. "Mother Superior is busy; she will be here in a little while and has asked me to welcome you."[114]

The Count noticed her "shortness of breath" and inquired about her health.

"It's better."

"Would you like to be a nun?"

"Yes, but I haven't the health."

He asked about the apparitions. "You are very happy..."

"Oh, yes!"

Madame de La Villemarqué then noticed her "beautiful, velvety black eyes." She said, "Everyone would have liked to be in your place."

"Ah! (said her husband) we will be, in the next world, I hope."

"Yes," said Bernadette, smiling.

"Wouldn't you like to go to heaven to see her again?"

"Oh, yes!" she answered.

"[Make] the sign of the cross the way the Blessed Virgin made it," asked Madame de La Villemarqué.

"I cannot make it like her."

Monsieur de La Villemarqué insisted, "and got the same answer."

Then he himself made "a large sign of the cross," like Père Ravignan.

"Was it like that?"

"Yes," she answered.

He went back to the apparitions: "[Was she] very beautiful?"

"Oh, yes!"

"More beautiful than anyone you have ever seen?"

"Oh, yes!"

"Did you see her close enough to tell the color of her eyes?"

"Yes...blue."

"And her hair?"

"I couldn't see her hair very well, because of her veil."

"Do you see her sometimes in your dreams?"

"I have never seen her since."

"Was she on the stone that's in the niche?"

"In front of it."

"Was she tall?"

"She didn't look very tall."

At this point the superior came in. She would describe the apparition of March 25, as she herself had heard it described so often by the visionary. The visitors got Bernadette to speak again by asking her to repeat the main words of the Virgin. She did so mechanically, as if "rattling off a homework assignment."

"Don't you get tired of always repeating the same thing?"

"Sometimes," she said smiling.

Madame de La Villemarqué then came to the object of their visit: an *Ave Maria* for her husband's cure.

"Yes," said Bernadette eagerly.

"We knelt down in front of the picture of the Virgin. Bernadette began in French. She said two 'Hail Marys,' to which we responded, and three times the invocation:

"'O Mary, conceived without sin....' We stood up again and I asked the superior if I might embrace Bernadette. With (Sister's) permission, I kissed her heartily on both cheeks; she allowed this very graciously, almost emotionally, seeing that I was so moved. I would have kissed her feet. My husband bowed and we left. She slipped into an adjoining room, where we heard her cough.

"'It's always that way', the superior told me, 'as soon as she has talked a bit. I don't believe she will live long.... When her mission is accomplished, God will take her.'"[115]

Another visitor this same month of August 1863, Père Hamard, a Vincentian, was surprised to find her so "puny" (his own word). "I have never seen such an expression," he would say in 1878, "except at the hospice of Enghien." (That was where he had seen Catherine Labouré in 1876.)[117]

On September 7, Père de Langlade, S.J., asked her, "So you saw the Blessed Virgin?"

"I'm not saying I saw the Blessed Virgin, I saw the apparition...."[116]

At the end of September, Bernadette met Achille Jubinal, a deputy from the Pyrénées. He wrote to the bishop to let him know the deep impression this left on him.[118]

In October, the bishop of Nantes, Bishop Jacquemet,[119] went to see her at Bagnères. Bernadette was staying at the boarding school.

Here she met Julie Duboé,[120] whom she would meet later at Nevers, under the name of Soeur Emilienne. Bernadette joined the boarders in their games. She was still a bit of a child.

One day at the hospice she was singing at the top of her lungs in a classroom. She thought she was alone. She heard an impressive voice say, "Who is that little bird singing?"

She found herself facing three bishops, who had undoubtedly come to see her.

"I could have stuffed myself down a rat hole!" she later exclaimed. "A beautiful bird? A crow! My singing is enough to chase all the nightingales from the forests!"[121]

That same summer, Louis de Combes visited. He was in the waiting room with some other visitors. Among them, he noted:

"was...a peasant woman...nursing in her lap an almost ghost-like child wrapped in a filthy blanket.

"A few moments later, the portress brought in a priest, strongly built, with brusque gestures...a soldier dressed up as a priest...his cassock all threadbare. He strode up and down the room, as if he could not stand still. It was Abbé Peyramale.

"At last, through the half-open door, we heard footsteps, then the sound of labored breathing, heavy, struggling, wheezing. The superior appeared, followed by a small child, who looked thirteen or fourteen years old: she was really nineteen. The young girl was dressed like a peasant. The kerchief, typical of Gascony kept back her dark hair, barely visible above her bare forehead. A colorful shawl covered her breast and was tucked under the dark apron she wore around her waist. Her face, oval, full and regular, was unremarkable. The effort it took to walk while struggling to breath turned her cheeks the crimson color often found in those suffering from pulmonary tuberculosis and asthma.

"In his rough voice, the Curé said, 'Well, Bernadette, things aren't going too well? Would you like to be pushing up daisies?'

"Without giving her time to answer, because any fatigue, even the slightest, could bring on an attack, he told of the apparitions in a few words.

"'Do you remember,' he continued, 'how I welcomed you? You told me you came on behalf of a Lady! What Lady? I don't know! You don't know? Then you're lying. And when I had you ask the Lady, if she was really the Blessed Virgin, to make the rosebush blos-

BERNADETTE À 14 ANS
d'après son 1er véritable portrait en prière

p.p. *Bernadette S.*

NOTRE DAME DE LOURDES. PRIEZ POUR NOUS
Vierge immaculée inaugurée dans la niche de la grotte le 4 Avril 1864

p.p. *Bernadette S.*

GROTTE DE LOURDES
(HAUTES-PYRÉNÉES)

GROTTE DE LOURDES
(HAUTES-PYRÉNÉES)

Apparitions nombreuses de la Très-Sainte Vierge à la jeune BERNADETTE SOUBIROUS, du 11 février au 5 avril 1858.

Une source jusqu'alors inaperçue s'est manifestée limpide et abondante.

Des grâces singulières, des guérisons réputées surnaturelles ont propagé et propagent encore la dévotion à Notre-Dame de Lourdes.

Une Commission nommée par l'autorité ecclésiastique a constaté les faits et fait son rapport.

Monseigneur l'Évêque de Tarbes a porté son jugement sur l'apparition.

Une souscription a été ouverte pour construire à

la Grotte, la Chapelle demandée par la T.-S. Vierge.

Un don personnel ou collectif de 500 fr. confère le titre de FONDATEUR.

Un don de 20 fr. celui de BIENFAITEUR principal, leurs noms seront conservés et déposés dans un cœur de vermeil placé au maître-autel du sanctuaire.

Il est dit, chaque semaine, et à perpétuité, deux messes pour les Fondateurs et les Bienfaiteurs principaux et une messe pour tous ceux qui auront fait une offrande si minime qu'elle soit.

Mandement de Mgr l'Évêque de Tarbes
du 18 janvier 1862.

PAUL DUFOUR, LIBRAIRE-ÉDITEUR, A TARBES

A. Chardon Jne Photo, Paris

A few of the hundreds of pictures, autographed on the reverse by Bernadette for pilgrims:
"P(riez) p(our) [Pray for] Bernadette."

som in the middle of February! The Mother of God smiled. The rosebush did not blossom, but the spring bubbled up...that was the answer.'

"Bernadette, still standing, remained silent, her face showed no emotion.

"The poor waiting mother was growing impatient. What did she care about all this chatter? Suddenly she got up, held out that little creature and cried out with tears in her voice, 'Mademoiselle, my little girl is very sick. In the name of the Good Lady, touch her with your hand.'

"The young girl stepped back a bit. The superior said to her, 'Give this poor woman the favor she asks.'

"The nun had her give us a photograph, on the back of which the visionary wrote, in our presence, 'Pray for Bernadette.'"[122]

On September 23, 1863, Père Mariote, an Oratorian had another experience. In front of Abbé Pomian and Abbé Miégeville,[123] he transcribed, under Bernadette's dictation, the Virgin's words in patois: all of them, except the secrets. It is the earliest transcription that has come down to us.

At the beginning of October 1863, Monsieur Billard-Perrin took a number of photos of Bernadette with the bishop's permission.

The date is certified by the angry complaint registered with Bishop Laurence by a competitor, Monsieur Dufour of Tarbes:

> *M. Laporte (is) surprised that the face of that child has been entrusted to...M. Perrin...for his own advantage. His first business was that of a juggler, traveling from town to town and singing in cafés! He has never been a professional photographer—he married the daughter of a traveling photographer and his wife is the one who gave him a few lessons in this art. He has no permanent residence, etc., etc.*

In fact, Billard-Perrin's photographs show that he knew his business well enough for that time.

Here are a few of his pictures of Bernadette at nineteen:

CHAPTER 7

— ⚜ —

THE SHEPHERDESS
AND THE SCULPTOR

A Project

On September 17, 1863, Bernadette was snatched away from recreation in the schoolyard for a meeting that would create quite a stir.

This came about as a consequence of a pilgrimage to Lourdes in July 1863 by the de Lacour sisters, ladies of the consular nobility in Lyons. Seeing the small plaster statue of the Virgin that people had placed on their own in the niche of the grotto, they got the idea of "a statue which would depict as accurately as possible the dress and posture of the apparition." They sent their priest companion, Abbé Blanc, to the rectory. They were ready to lavishly underwrite the project, providing seven thousand gold francs, plus all the sculptor's expenses. They recommended a well-known candidate, Joseph Fabisch, professor at the School of Fine Arts and member of the Academy of Sciences, Arts and Humanities of Lyons. He had already sculpted the statue of La Salette and the Virgin gracing the steeple of Fourvière: in a word, he was an expert. His reputation as a "religious sculptor" had been confirmed among the clergy by the statement of one Minister of Fine Arts, with a sentence that might have come from a play by Flers and Caillavet: "Even his muses are 'clerical.'"

*The grotto before the Fabisch statue. A little statue of the Virgin,
held in place by wire, had been put in the niche of the apparitions.*

Bernadette—autumn of 1863
(Photo by Billard-Perrin)

This remark delighted Abbé Peyramale, who remarked, "Clerical muses! They are the best of their kind and an artist's highest praise!"[1]

That September 17, 1863, Fabisch was nervous about meeting Bernadette. He was reminded of the difficulties he had had to overcome at La Salette. The "bizarre" clothing described by the visionaries there violated all the rules of classical art, and the artist was as sure of these as he was about the Last Judgment. So he had used all his diplomatic skill with Bishop de Ginouilhac of Grenoble for permission to *interpret* the children's description in a way that "would approach, as much as possible, the *traditional* dress" of the Blessed Virgin. "Interpret," "traditional": these two words, chosen from hundreds, had allowed him a free hand.

In Lourdes, it would be more difficult to work. The contract, which set his handsome fees, specified that the apparition would have to be depicted "as accurately as possible." The sculptor would have to "adjust the expression and attitude" according to Bernadette's description.[2] They insisted on this in Lourdes, and Peyramale had already interviewed the visionary. He wrote to his bishop on August 19, "This statue will be remarkable from an artistic point of view and will reproduce the Immaculate Virgin exactly as Bernadette saw her."[3]

Was her description compatible with the rules of art? The sculptor had another fear, a common one, but one that he never grew used to: the artist's vision. He was always on the lookout for that unpredictable stroke of inspiration without which beauty could not be born.

Bernadette's Description

To nurture this inspiration, he scribbled twenty questions on the left side, front and back, of a sheet of stationery. The right side was left blank for the answers.

He met Bernadette and watched her. His professional observation: "Though lacking that regularity of features the sculptor looks for, her face has something very friendly…an attractiveness that commands respect and inspires trust."[4]

He was amazed at how young she looked and was moved by her frail health—"consumptive down to her fingertips" was his interpretation.[5] It was during this initial meeting that the following episode

Bernadette—autumn of 1863
(Photo by Billard-Perrin)

most probably occurred, according to Père Clavé, who got it from Abbé Peyramale.

"Someone took a box full of engravings, in which the Blessed Virgin was represented every which way...and gave them to Bernadette to look at. She was barely looking at them, when, all of a sudden, seeing a print or lithograph of the Virgin of Saint Luke, she quickly put her hand on it, saying, 'There's something there.' Then she added, 'But that's not it! No, that's not it.'"[6]

Once the preliminaries were over, the sculptor began his methodical questioning:

"Was her body standing straight or leaning forward?"

"Straight, but not stiff."

"Did her head lean toward the side or the front?"

"Straight, too."

"Her hands, how did she fold them when she said, 'I am the Immaculate Conception'?"[7]

Here the sculptor noted: "Bernadette stood up with great simplicity, folded her hands and lifted her eyes toward heaven!... I have never seen anything so beautiful...Fiesole, Perugino, and Raphael never created anything so sweet and at the same time so profound as the expression of that young girl who had not the slightest doubt in the world about the unique favor she had received."[8]

At that moment Fabisch, according to his own words, "felt that electric jolt that stirs up enthusiasm and creates in the loftiest regions of the mind, the perfect model for a work of art."[9]

He could already see that moment of perfection set in marble. Relief number one. He continued methodically, "How old would you say she was?"

"Young."

He wrote this word down automatically, though it ran contrary to his own ideas. Like his contemporaries, he thought the Virgin had to be a "grown-up." He wrote the letters, with no thought for the meaning of the word.

In 1878, when he "recreated" the interview for Père Cros, he changed the offensive remark. The question and answer became: "Did she look young?" "No, Monsieur."

As a matter of fact, the statue he sculpted was not "young." For the time being, he went on, "Did she look slender or stout?"

"Rather slender."[10]

He now reached a touchy subject: the clothing. Here is where the "details furnished by Bernadette herself"[11] risked contradicting the "rules," which for him were the Law and the Prophets.

"Was the veil long?"

"Not quite to the bottom of the dress."

"What material?"

"I never saw anything like it."

"And the dress?"

"Same material as the veil."

"Were the sleeves full or tight?"

"Gathered at the wrist."[12]

Here the sculptor turned the page for the last ten questions, written on the back:

"Was the waist smooth or pleated?"

"Pleated."

"Many pleats? Did the dress look plain?"

At this point Bernadette showed by gestures the fullness and simplicity of the dress.

"What material did the dress seem to be made of?"

"The same material as the veil."

"Was the sash wide?"

Fabisch gave Bernadette's gestures and comments the following interpretation: "Six inches wide, gathered at the middle and falling down the front."

"Was it pleated or smooth?"

Bernadette specified that the sash was pleated where it was fastened; the tips were tied once and fell down the front "growing wider toward the bottom."

"How low did it go?"

"Like the veil." ("That is," noted Fabisch, "halfway down the legs.")

"What material," the sculptor asked once more, following the previous words used at question eighteen.

"It is impossible to say."

"The roses on her slippers?..."

Here the sculptor was referring to the famous "yellow slippers" that newspapers in 1858 gave to the apparition. But Bernadette stopped him.

"Her feet were bare."

Joseph Fabisch

"Did the roses look embroidered or natural and projecting out?"

"They were resting on her feet."[13]

At last the interview was over. The twentieth and final question concerned the "size of the roses." The sculptor, very relaxed, made a rough pencil sketch of the bottom of the dress with the two flowers hiding the feet.

He was visibly relieved. The Curé noticed this: "As you can see, there's nothing really strange."

"That's right! Except for the sash, it's the description of a Virgin by Fra Angelico."[14]

Art Is Eloquence

Briefly put, there were no awkward details. As to the character of the description: youth, smile, simplicity, fullness of the dress, there was nothing materially restrictive. The artist felt free. The transposition had already taken place in his mind. Was not art "eloquence"? Was not its purpose to "perfect" and to "civilize" a person as he had said in his acceptance speech at the Academy of Arts and Humanities of Lyons? Fabisch already had an inkling of how he would add dignity to the far too simple little girl Bernadette so candidly described. He would make her youthfulness solemn and grave and her smile serious. He would make her taller, incline the head toward the right, and curve the folded hands which Bernadette had shown quite flat, palm against palm. He would portray upward movement of the silhouette with elaborate contours, subtle designs, and soft gracefulness. He felt himself to be the master of the techniques that would tilt a foot, bend a knee, and create so many folds down the dress that the eye would get lost. Wasn't this, for him, the very heart of aesthetics?

That evening, in a letter to Madame Fabisch, he was sorry not to have made, right away a "rough sketch" of the image that had come to him at the time. Would it have come closer to what Bernadette had seen? The question was almost meaningless, because Fabisch was too narrowly wedded to the traditional rules for naturalness to break through. Under the most favorable conditions, simplicity for him would have been the result of haste, something he would have carefully avoided.

The very next day, Friday, September 18, he made a preliminary sculpture.[15]

On the nineteenth, after seeing the Minister of State, Monsieur Fould, and the bishop, who kept him for dinner ("lunch" for people in the north), Fabisch went home early and worked on his sketch.

Criticism of the Sketch

On Sunday, the twentieth, he had two meetings with Bernadette. The first was at the grotto. Fabisch had cut a silhouette out of cardboard. He tried it in the niche. Bernadette gave some "yeses" and also some "noes," but no one took note of the questions.[16]

At the hotel, the sculptor submitted a clay model to Bernadette. The silhouette was simple—it gave the general contours but not one detail. Nevertheless, Bernadette asked for "corrections." The sculptor, optimistic and tactful, went into raptures over what agreed with his thinking—a nice way to let the rest slip into the background. Tact was second nature to him. That very night he wrote, "She pointed out some corrections to me, which even from an artistic point of view bettered my work. I challenge the most gifted member of the Institute to have better ideas on the suitability of these corrections than this poor shepherdess..."[17]

Bernadette, however, supposedly had this reservation, "Oh, Monsieur, how cold it is!"[18]

Jean-Baptiste Estrade, who told this story, artificially reconstructed the "thousand details that Bernadette allegedly criticized." What is clear is that the atmosphere of enthusiasm was somewhat ambiguous. Misunderstanding lay hidden beneath the surface, but the emotional excitement of the sculptor from Lyons overcame disagreements and misunderstandings. Music would add to his euphoria.

"When I arrived at the grotto a choir of young girls from the region were singing the 'Magnificat' in three part harmony. I couldn't begin to tell you how much this music moved me. During the hotel interview, the choir of young girls came to sing beneath our window. Bernadette showed me how the Blessed Virgin *looked* when she said, 'I am the Immaculate Conception.' It was enough to make one weep with emotion."[19]

Once again there was a misunderstanding. Seeing the clay model, what Bernadette meant was that the Virgin kept her head straight when she raised her eyes to heaven. Fabisch, however was not about to sacrifice the movement of the head in the direction of heaven. Later he was sorry for this, especially since the neck of the statue, seen from below, becomes quite over exaggerated. But this problem had not yet crossed his mind.

Leaving Bernadette he said, "I see your Virgin; I'll show her to you and when the statue comes, I want you to say, 'That's her!'"[20]

Criticism of the Clay Model

In November 1863, a letter containing a photograph arrived at the Lourdes rectory. Fabisch had completed the plaster model, two-thirds the final size. He submitted it for approval to the donors and to Bernadette.

At the chateau of Montluzin, the de Lacour sisters and their secretary, Abbé Blanc, had found a few discrepancies. "According to Bernadette, she was short rather than tall." But this objection was coupled with so many nuances and swamped under such a flood of praise and compromise that it amounted to giving the sculptor a blank check.

Abbé Peyramale, who received the full blast of Bernadette's criticisms, transmitted them more precisely: "The face doesn't seem young enough or smiling enough. On the right side, the veil adheres to the head and neck, creating a curve from the head to the shoulder. On the left side, it doesn't cover the shoulder; and also, on both sides, it gets caught up in folds under the arms. According to Bernadette, the veil came down *perpendicularly, smoothly* and covered both shoulders and elbows.

"The dress doesn't come high enough, or, if you prefer, it isn't clerical enough: it leaves too much of the neck exposed. The hands [of the Virgin] were folded more closely, the fingers pressed together; the left foot is too far off to the side. Lastly, to give you an overall criticism, it would be better if the whole outfit were fuller. You forgot the rosary."[21]

These words reveal Bernadette's harsh and concise criticism. The Curé kept back a few artistic details that were expressed too vaguely to have any effect. Was asking for a "fuller" look enough to show that Bernadette took exception to the slender figure and wanted a flared dress? On the other hand, as a priest, Peyramale backed up anything that concerned modesty, certain of being understood by the man who had once spoken of "clerical muses."[22] He toned down the heart of what Bernadette was insisting on, as she clearly demonstrated by her whole attitude, her gestures, her per-

*The model (above)
and Fabisch's statue
(right).
Bernadette's comments were
virtually ignored. The
sculptor merely simplified
the fall of the veil.*

son and the simplification, even her verbal comments, that is to say, the composition of the apparition was simple, smooth and upright. This was something a simple soul, a village sculptor could have understood, someone like Senatori, who had portrayed so well on canvas the Emperor's visit to Biarritz in 1858, with the ingenious eye of Henri (le Douanier) Rousseau.[23] That, however, was not Fabisch's gift.

Finally, Peyramale cloaked these substantial criticisms in such praise and especially with so many compromises that the sculptor felt completely free. Did not the Curé go so far as to say, "I don't know whether the rules of art will permit you to pay attention to all these observations. I am convinced that, inspired by your talent and by the Immaculate Virgin, you will bring us a remarkable work of art, etc."[24]

More severity would have greatly embarrassed the sculptor, because before receiving his answer, he had already begun the final version in marble.[25]

The Misunderstanding

We are approaching the fourth act of this well-disguised misunderstanding. Peyramale was already preparing the minds of the sculptor and the shepherdess, as the conclusion of this letter shows: "I, who have never had the joy of seeing the Queen of Heaven, consider your model perfect. As for Bernadette, it's something else! I strongly doubt that when she sees your statue, *no matter how astounded she may be,* she will cry out: 'That's her!' Don't be angry. It will in no way be a criticism of your work. Eye has not seen...."[26]

These last words go beyond the superficial misunderstanding to a much deeper problem, a double problem.

To begin with, as Peyramale rightly said, the ineffable cannot be reproduced.... That is evident!

Then, too, the function of art is not to reproduce reality but to point to it.

Has official art ever been an authentic expression of the Christian mystery? That could be debated. Of course, it has been able to express certain aspects, but an excessive concern about imitating nature by idealizing it has made it ill-equipped to express mystery and the existential relationship between God and humanity. As for the personal apparition of the Blessed Virgin to the little girl,

Bernadette, official art could only be an interpretation in the wrong direction. An authentic expression would have required either abstract art, as Hartung did at the "Lourdes '64" Exposition, or a particularly naive and transparent representational art, something similar to what Dubos sculpted for the same Exposition.

It was highly unlikely that Fabisch, schooled in the traditional rules of art, could follow such a path. With the kind acceptance of his partners, little by little he departed not only from the spirit but also from the specific physical details supplied by Bernadette.

In this respect, the inaccuracies grew worse from the plaster model to the final statue. The model, preserved at the Sisters of Nevers in Montluzin, was younger looking, had more of a smile and was also shorter (five feet).

The First Shock

After working feverishly "night and day," Fabisch took the express train from Lyons to Lourdes on March 30, 1864. He finished the trip by stagecoach. The statue arrived with him as accompanying freight. Early in the afternoon of the next day, March 31, the crate was delivered to the hospice. Père M.J.H. Ollivier, a Dominican, who had preached the Lenten sermons at Bagnères, and Canon Fourcade, the bishop's secretary-general,[27] had been invited by Abbé Peyramale for the opening of the crate. The preacher had asked to meet the visionary. Peyramale had at first categorically refused, "Bernadette is unwell...and besides, it's not good for her to be shown off," etc.

His justification was "eloquent," inexhaustible, but his first reason fell immediately. Bernadette, whose asthma had been so bad they *feared losing her*,[28] had the usual sudden remission. There she was "beneath the window," happily playing games with the other girls, said the preacher.[29]

"A moment later," she came in, annoyed at having to leave her friends and her games once more.

"She was greeted with a scolding on the danger of getting herself all perspired like that, then was invited to tell us briefly about the apparitions. The meeting was interrupted by the news that the statue had been placed on a piece of furniture in the next room. Monseigneur Peyramale brought us in.... After an examination of some length, he called for Bernadette.

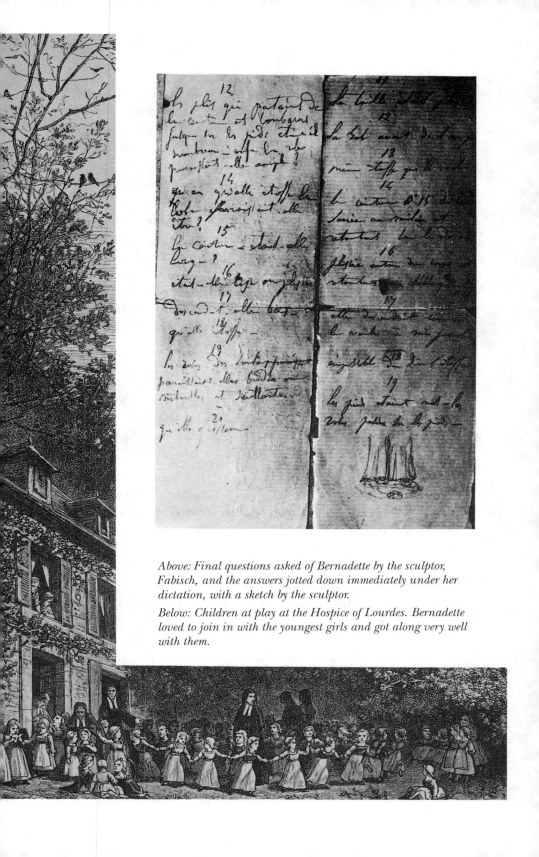

Above: Final questions asked of Bernadette by the sculptor, Fabisch, and the answers jotted down immediately under her dictation, with a sketch by the sculptor.

Below: Children at play at the Hospice of Lourdes. Bernadette loved to join in with the youngest girls and got along very well with them.

"'Is that it?' Monseigneur Peyramale asked a bit anxiously."

Caught up in the overall excitement, the child "folded her hands" and forced herself not to lose patience—something that did not escape Père Ollivier. She "muttered" the expected answer, "That's it, all right...."

Then after a moment of silence and with a touch of sorrow, almost resentment, [she added] "No, that's not it."[30]

Her reaction was suppressed in official circles, as usually happens in such cases. On April 4, 1864, the unveiling was a triumph.

However, the sculptor himself was disappointed. Later he admitted, without realizing the full significance of his failure, "That day I felt one of the greatest sorrows of my artistic career."[31]

As for Bernadette, she remained quiet, but not to the extent of keeping silent at Elfrida Lacrampe's direct question, "Are you happy with the statue?"

"No!" (scornfully).[32]

Likewise, two years later, when Père Cros asked her, "Does the statue over there (at the grotto) look like the Blessed Virgin?"

"'Not a bit,' [she] said with a look I can't describe."[33]

Later, as we shall see, she was to be much more explicit.

The Dedication of April 4, 1864

Bernadette could not be present at the April 4 dedication. The Curé found her insufficiently recovered and wanted to preserve her humility. She obeyed without reservation, but obedience cost her, as this was a great religious celebration.

The Curé himself had to absent himself. In March, he had had an attack of rheumatoid arthritis, accompanied by fever. On March 6, his condition had worsened to such a point that they telegrammed his brother: "Curé of Lourdes very sick. Some hope."[34]

Doctor Dozous had treated him, had bled him, to no avail.[35] Even Bernadette's novena for him seemed to have had no effect. But she didn't give up; she had tied a golden heart around the neck of the Virgin in the chapel. Someone mentioned to her, "The Blessed Virgin doesn't seem to hear your prayer."

"If he dies, I will pull that heart off," she supposedly answered, if we are to believe Dubosc de Pesquidoux.[36] A short time after, they tolled the death knell.[37]

A holy card of the period

However, the robust constitution of the Curé got the upper hand, although convalescence had its ups and downs. And that is why on April 4, 1864 he had to stay in his room.

Among the visits Bernadette received that day, the most pleasant was surely that of Jeanne Védère. Arriving before the procession started (she recounts), "I went directly to the hospice, and I told my cousin how sorry I felt that she couldn't attend this beautiful ceremony. She said to me, 'I'm as happy to stay in bed as I would be to go to the grotto. I would like to go...God does not want me to. His will be done.... Don't feel sorry for me; when we do what God wants, no one should feel sorry.'"[38]

After the procession was over, Bernadette asked her cousin, "You went to the grotto; give me a bit of that cloth that the statue of the Blessed Virgin was wrapped in."

Jeanne answered her, "I saw them remove this big blue cloth that covered the statue...but I don't know what became of it. No one gave me any."

"All right! I didn't go to the grotto," Bernadette responded, "but I'll give you some."

At this Bernadette spoke to a sister, probably Soeur Marie Géraud, who had come from Bagnères for the dedication.

Jeanne continued her account:

"'Get what I asked you to put in the closet.'

"The sister brought back a pretty little box with a big piece of material used to wrap up the statue. She gave me some. I cut it up into pieces to share with more than twenty people."[39]

All day long, pilgrims rang the bell at the hospice to see Bernadette. Among others, was a "lady from Bagnères.... At first, Soeur Olympe refused. Then, giving in to the lady's insistent demands, she agreed, provided Bernadette would not talk. The visitor said she would be happy if she were permitted only to kiss the hem of her dress...(which she did) without saying one word."[40]

That holiday was marked by a decision that would require a life-long commitment from Bernadette.

CHAPTER 8

— ⚜ —

BERNADETTE'S VOCATION

Bernadette chose the April 4, 1864 festivities to make a major announcement to Soeur Alexandrine Roques, the superior at the hospice. After Mass, she went up to her and said, "I know now, dear Mother, where I am to be a nun."

"Where, my child?"

"With you, dear Mother."

"That's fine, my child, we'll go talk about it to the bishop."

Soeur Marie Géraud (in Lourdes for the unveiling) was convinced that Bernadette had found the light that would convince her of her religious vocation in the Communion she had just received.[1]

In fact, the decision had come before that, long before that. We must go back to a series of conversations that show how it developed.

The definitive studies on her vocation are Dom Bernard Billet's, found in volume seven of *Documents authentiques,* (Authentic Documents) pp. 78–127 and *La Vocation de Bernadette,* (The Vocation of Bernadette) Paris, Lethielleux, 1966; 2nd edition, 1972, *Bernadette, une vocation comme tout le monde* (Bernadette, a Vocation Just Like Everybody). In keeping with the aim of this present volume, we shall concentrate on her "sayings."

Bernadette with Soeur Alexandrine Roques, the superior of the Hospice of Lourdes

Since the 1861 Bernadou photo above, an "un-tamed" Bernadette had matured (Billard-Perrin photo of 1864, or perhaps 1866, if there were two Billard-Perrin photo sessions).

At the Time of the Apparitions

Before the apparitions were over, Adélaïde Monlaur wrote in a letter dated April 8, 1858:

"The mayor of Lourdes and several other gentlemen asked her what line of work she wanted to pursue. If she wanted to train as a seamstress, they would pay for this; or if she wanted to be a clothes ironer, they would also be willing to pay for that.

"After a moment's thought, she answered that she wanted to be a nun. The mayor replied, 'But what if you change your mind? Meanwhile, you must learn a trade.'

"She said, 'I won't change my mind; however, I'll do whatever my father and mother want.'"[2]

This had to have happened in March, or at the very latest during the first few days of April 1858, before the eighth, the date of Adélaïde's letter. The timing cannot be refuted.

Looking toward Carmel

"Bernadette was first drawn to the contemplative life," affirmed her godmother, Bernarde Castérot. "Soon after the apparition, she got the idea of being a nun; she wanted to be a Carmelite."[3]

Her other aunt, Basile Castérot, confirmed this, "I understood that Bernadette wanted to become a nun. I even heard her say that she had been longing to enter the convent, without being able to say just when the idea came to her. But I think she was considering entering a more cloistered convent and a stricter order, and that it was the Curé Peyramale who advised her, because of her health, to go with the Sisters of Nevers."

Bernadette "said" the same thing to Marthe du Rais: "that after her First Communion (June 3, 1858), she thought of entering religious life and that she was approached and encouraged to enter Carmel."[4]

Carmel.... Very early, as early as springtime of 1858, she had heard talk of Carmel from Antoinette Tardhivail, her volunteer tutor. On September 21, 1858, she had met a renowned Carmelite, Père Hermann. This musician, a convert from Judaism, whom many called a saint, had stirred up great excitement in Lourdes, with his "loud and hearty" rendition of the *Magnificat,* and one of the psalms, and then by preaching at the forbidden grotto.[5] He had made an impression on Bernadette. In February 1865, when she received his picture, she announced, "I've really wanted to have this...."[6]

The Carmel of Bagnères was not far away. Bernadette must have been brought there shortly after the apparitions. We don't know when. The silence, the convent grille, passing things through a turnstile, nuns hidden behind black veils, were for her signs of a mysterious life sheltered from the sights of the world. Carmel satisfied her desire for the hidden life, in contrast to her present daily ordeal. But this idea was quickly discarded.

"She was made to understand that her health would not permit her to be a Carmelite," her godmother Bernarde revealed.[7]

Later attempts at recruitment served only to annoy her. One day, on the pretext of a pleasure trip, one lady unexpectedly brought her to the Carmelites at Bagnères. The Curé was displeased. "That's not what she said to me! The next time I won't let her take you again."[8]

Another time, a visiting Carmelite mentioned the subject head on, "My child, you should be a Carmelite."

"Father, if I become a nun, I'll join a congregation where I can follow the rule without exemptions."[9]

"But we can grant dispensations."

"I don't want any dispensations. I want to be able to follow the rule without exemptions."[10]

The Carmel of Rennes sent her "a certificate of spiritual affiliation" which entitled her to share in "six Masses and one corporate Communion each year for twenty years."[11]

"Saint Bernard"

The intimate conversations between Bernadette and her cousin Jeanne Védère in 1860–1861 inform us of the next stage. Bernadette was still drawn to the contemplative life, but in another direction. Jeanne's own religious vocation was being opposed at this time. Her mother, and especially her father, were applying all kinds of pressure, including bribery. Following the apparitions, they thought a word from the visionary of Lourdes would carry much weight, so they entrusted Bernadette with presenting their case. She faithfully conveyed what they had told her, but without taking sides.

"You know, of course...pray with all the fervor you can..." Jeanne told her.[12]

Jeanne also confided to her "that she had had this desire [to become a nun] ever since her First Communion, that is, since [1837 when] she was ten years old."

At their next meeting,[13] Jeanne asked, "Have you thought of me?"

"After a moment's reflection, (Bernadette) told me, 'Yes, you have to be patient; you will succeed, but not yet.'[14]

"Then she told me, 'I feel sorry for you; you must be suffering?'

"I answered, 'No.' I thought God was permitting this.

"At that time I didn't know about the Trappistines [also known as the Cistercian nuns]," continued Jeanne, a member of this order when she composed her memoirs. "I had always had the idea of entering Carmel...but my father assured me that he would do his utmost so that I wouldn't stay.

"'As soon as I speak to them,' he told me, 'they will quickly send you home; and, before God, you will be responsible for what I tell them. I'll really insult them.'

"That scared me. I thought, 'If he's going to insult those good sisters, God might well get angry.'

"I had made another resolution. It was to go to the Sisters of Saint Vincent de Paul with the intention of entering Carmel later on. That would have been easier than staying home with my parents.

"When Bernadette said, 'have patience, you will succeed,' I told her all this. She immediately replied, 'Don't! Don't do that!'

"She told me things...the way one of the most experienced [spiritual] directors would have done."[15]

A little further on, Jeanne reconstructs Bernadette's words as follows: "Oh! Don't do that! Stay home instead. It's as if you intended to deceive others and God. God cannot be deceived. He is the one who's giving you the attraction you think you have for the cloister; but he's not giving you the idea of joining the Sisters of Saint Vincent de Paul, with the intention of leaving later on to go somewhere else. Believe me, God sees the difficulties and permits them. He'll know how to smooth everything out when the time comes."[16]

Jeanne continued: "My cousin had not spoken to me yet about her own vocation. This is when she spoke about it with me for the first time. There was one religious order she could not praise highly

enough, one I had never heard of before. She told me that this order practiced vigils...fasts...self-flagellation...self-mortification.

"'I'd like that very much,' she told me, 'if I were a little healthier.'[17]

"She spoke to me about Saint Bernard, but since I had never
heard of that order, I paid little attention to what she was telling
me. She noticed this and said, 'You don't appreciate what I'm telling you. If I were you, that's where I'd go. I'd be left alone, no one
to bother me. But they told me they wouldn't accept me because of
my poor health. I wouldn't be able to do anything prescribed in
their rule...they'd send me home.... I wouldn't want to go back into
the world; once I leave it, I never want to return to it.'"

However, Bernadette seemed to have had some hope. Only in
the following conversation did she clearly affirm, "I'll never be able
to go; they only accept people who enjoy good health, people who
can observe the rule. I've got to give up this idea."[18]

"In the religious order I've talked to you so much about, they
follow the rule of Saint Benedict," Bernadette made clear a little
later on, in October 1864.[19]

This is how Jeanne became convinced that Bernadette had
heard about the order that Jeanne wound up entering: the Cistercians.[20] She thought she remembered that Bernadette had used the
word, but had "not spoken about the Trappistines."[21]

Bernadette could possibly have learned of the Cistercians before Jeanne, at the time Marie Fourcade left to enter the Sisters of
Nevers, on November 18, 1860. But this was not the order about
which Bernadette was speaking.

The religious family of "Saint Bernard" which attracted her was
a foundation established at Anglet, near Bayonne, by Père Cestac,
for those among the Servants of Mary—the congregation he had
founded—who desired to lead a more austere and secluded life.
According to Marie Auros, a young girl from Lourdes who entered
at Anglet in 1861, Bernadette is said to have come there, it seems,
before July 15, 1860. She apparently asked to be admitted to the
novitiate. The founder supposedly refused Bernadette for reasons
of health. But he had another reason, perhaps an even more convincing one which touched on the internal life of the community:
"I don't want people to come chasing after her at Notre Dame."[22]

Bernadette's presence would have threatened the solitude that
inspired the foundation—that hidden life which attracted her.

The following incident highlights that environment. When the emperor came to visit Anglet in 1858, he asked one sister to lift her veil. Père Cestac could not very well refuse. The sister complied, but without raising her eyelids.

Père Michel Garicoïts is said to have been the one who, at one point, directed Bernadette toward Anglet. But this and many other details like it have been gathered from an oral tradition whose authenticity is hard to measure.

Attraction to the Active life

A positive attraction came to take the place of the obstacles which had turned Bernadette's thoughts away from the contemplative life: the desire to serve the sick and the poor. Working at the hospice, beginning in the summer of 1860, she became aware of this; and only then, according to Soeur Victorine, did she state, "No, I don't want to become a Carmelite to stay 'inside.'"[23]

From then on, she replied to those who spoke to her in that vein "that she was not made for that, and that her health was an obstacle, that she liked the active life."[24]

And so in 1860 or 1861, "neither sooner nor later,"[25] Bernadette told Jeanne Védère quite simply that "she didn't feel any attraction for Carmel."[26]

From 1861, she seemed to be firmly decided in favor of the active life. However, around this time, according to her confessor, Abbé Pomian, "She had little inclination toward the Sisters of Nevers."[27]

"She wasn't keen on the Sisters of Nevers," her Aunt Bernarde also said.[28]

But these remarks were made in 1878, at a time when Lourdes was saddened over Bernadette's absence. This explains and makes even more suspect a remark attributed to her, "If I became a sister, I would not become a Sister of Nevers."[29]

Invitations

Perhaps the thought of entering religious life seemed quite simply too far out of reach—given the idea she had of her own inability. "She would have liked the Sisters of the Cross," said her confessor Abbé Pomian.

Had he noticed some attraction for that community? Or had he rather tried to draw her toward that local congregation? We don't know. The only reference we have along those lines is Bernadette's reaction one day when the sisters wanted her to try on their huge cornette: "I don't want anything to do with this tunnel!"[30]

Did Bernadette feel some attraction to the Sisters of Saint Vincent de Paul, as Jeanne Védère said? There is no other evidence. In any event, certain proposals she received concerning this left her cold. In the summer of 1861, Germaine Reval, one of her friends present at the apparitions, had made her postulancy with the Sisters of Saint Vincent de Paul. She returned to Lourdes for the last time, according to their custom, to see her family before leaving for the *séminaire* (novitiate) on the Rue du Bac in Paris. She had no trouble getting Abbé Peyramale's permission to invite Bernadette, who gave her self-confidence about her vocation. In fact, (according to one tradition reported by the Superior General of the Daughters of Charity to Bishop Théas), Germaine, wavering for a moment, had asked for prayers and advice from the visionary. The answer she received was "to follow her attraction...to the community of Saint Vincent." Bernadette, it is claimed, even said, "That is surely her vocation."[31] Thus it was that at the age of twenty-one (in 1859), that Germaine "told her father...of her unshakable intention to leave. He was sick at the time and asked for a cure as a sign. He was cured, resigned himself, and gave his permission"(from a letter to Bishop Théas, cited above).

Given the situation, the sisters from the hospice of Tarbes, and the superior herself came as a group with Germaine for her final visit to Lourdes. The sisters were overjoyed at seeing this visionary, who was so well disposed toward their Congregation. Who knew? Wasn't this a sign of an attraction that might be encouraged? The outcome of the meeting was contrary to their hopes.

"I got very bored today," Bernadette said. "The day seemed very long. Those sisters had me try on their habit, but I don't feel the least bit attracted."

"Ah! This will give you the vocation, Bernadette!" they answered her.

"Oh, no! Quite the contrary! I don't feel one bit attracted to that Congregation."[32]

Yet Bernadette had given the Daughters of Charity such a warm welcome that entreaties on that score would spring up again, as we shall see.

A Decisive Experience

In short, by 1863, Bernadette had had the opportunity to come to know different orders. She had left the contemplative vocation behind for two reasons: one negative, her health; the other positive, a desire to serve the poor and the sick. Abbé Pomian added some details on this essential point, "She practiced taking care of a few old and 'very repulsive' people. She lovingly worked hard at it. She came to like it."[33]

We don't know the name of the elderly woman involved. It may perhaps be the one Jean Barbet, the schoolmaster at Bartrès, describes this way, "An old woman in rags who liked her wine, had fallen head-first onto some glowing coals and had suffered severe burns. Bernadette asked to see her and to take care of her. She received permission. Bernadette carried out her work like an experienced nurse. When the woman was about to leave the hospice, Bernadette laughed and said to her, 'From now on, you mustn't *snort down* so much!'"[34]

This is only one case among many; there was also, for example, an old woman with cancer, whose condition was particularly sickening.

Bernadette took care of many anonymous sufferers, and there her life found meaning. She said so to her cousin Jeanne: "I love the poor very much; I like nursing the sick. I'll stay with the Sisters of Nevers. They gave me a patient to tend. When I'm well, no one takes care of her but me. I'll stay with them."[35]

Bernadette still held back because of certain material factors. She was poor and had no dowry. She would have had to beg for admission. As we shall see, she was worried about this. She was afraid to be a burden on account of her poor health, and also because of her "disability."[36] This idea had been driven into her head through repeated zealous scoldings made to keep her humble. In those days, those in authority failed to realize the dangers of such treatment.

On August 24, 1862, Père Lataste, a Dominican, questioned her on her vocation. He jotted down her answer, "She feels called to the religious life, but does not know where yet."[37]

According to Barbet, Abbé Pomian introduced her to various "religious orders":

"Do you like this one?"

"I don't know."

"That one?"

"I have no preference; and besides, I haven't yet made a decision."

"In that case, let's stop. You let me know when you reach your decision. Pray hard to the Blessed Virgin to enlighten you."[38]

"I haven't made a decision,"—this was Bernadette's position in the middle of 1863. The decisive phase came on September 25 of that same year.

Conversation with Bishop Forcade

That day Bishop Forcade came to Lourdes. Bernadette was assigned to ring the bell announcing the prelate's arrival. She did her job well, maybe too well, since the bishop, walking next to her, exclaimed: *"Prou, prou!"* (Enough, enough!)

That word, said in the local dialect, greatly amused Bernadette. Coming back to the community, she laughed heartily and said, "The bishop can speak patois!"[39]

The ice was broken; conversation became easy...on Bernadette's part, for the bishop was unaware of who the bell-ringer was.

"After that," he relates, "My first word to the superior was, 'You will show me Bernadette.'

"Using good judgment, the superior replied, 'As soon as you wish. But so as not to expose the little girl to any temptation of vanity, it might be better to wait...'"

So she cleverly arranged a chance meeting in the kitchen, where Bernadette was working.

The bishop continued, "My eyes fell on a young girl wearing a kerchief, poorly dressed and frail looking, sitting on a block of wood in the corner of the fireplace peeling a carrot.

"The superior whispered in my ear, 'That's the one.'

"Bernadette continued her work, while I seemed to be inspecting the area and exchanged a few words with the sister in charge, who fell at my feet and asked for my blessing. I invited Bernadette to do the same. She got up without saying a word, likewise knelt down, kissed my ring and went back to her carrot.

"This first conversation seemed short to me. So I did my best to make the superior understand that I had not come so far for so little....

"Bernadette was assigned to help my servant wait at the table during lunch. But that was not the right place to have a more ordered, serious conversation with her. After the meal the most urgent thing for me to do was to ask the superior explicitly to bring her to the parlor and to leave me alone with her.

"I began by questioning her at length about the apparitions."[40]

The bishop was in for a surprise! Bernadette, who had not said a word until then, "spoke a correct, clear and precise French, without for a moment groping for words." Trick questions left her "unshaken and nothing confused her." After her account, the bishop asked her, "And now, my dear child, what do you plan to do?"

After a moment's hesitation she answered, "Why nothing!"

"What do you mean? We all have to do something here on earth."

"Well, I live with the sisters."

"Of course, but you can only stay there for a while."

"I will stay forever."

"That's easy to say, but not always so easy to do. The fact that they took you in for a while out of charity, shouldn't lead you to think that they'll keep you forever."

"Why not?"

"Because you're not a sister, and it is essential to be a sister to be admitted permanently into the community of sisters. You're not even a servant here. Right now, you're exactly what a moment ago you said you are. You're *nothing,* and on this footing you won't last long anywhere."

The bishop's account of the meeting continues:

"Bernadette seemed thoughtful and couldn't answer anymore. After a moment of silence, I picked up the conversation again, 'You're not a child anymore; perhaps you'd be pleased to find a small but suitable business in the world?'

"Sharply [she answered]: 'What? Certainly not!'

"'Well, then, why don't you become a sister? Haven't you ever thought about it?'

"'It's impossible. You know very well that I'm poor. I'll never have the necessary dowry.'"[41]

The bishop swept the objection away by his authority as superior of the Congregation: "Whenever we recognize a true vocation in poor girls, we don't hesitate to accept them without a dowry."

Bernadette then brought up her health, her weaknesses still ringing in her ears to keep her humble.

"I don't know anything...I'm good for nothing."

"You fail to recognize your talents. This morning, I saw with my own eyes that you're good for something."

"What then?"

"For peeling carrots..."

Bernadette burst out laughing. "Bah! That's not so hard!"

"No matter. They'll find some way to make good use of you, not to mention the fact that in the novitiate they won't fail to give you much of the training you now lack."

"Since that's the way it is, I'll think about it. But my mind doesn't feel made up yet."

"Yes, of course, think about it. Consult your confessor, and pray especially to the Blessed Virgin who was pleased to appear to you.... Then if you feel like it, you will ask Mother Superior to notify either Mother General or myself and I'll take care of the rest."

"That was the end of our conversation," said Bishop Forcade.[42]

Conversation with Jeanne Védère

Bernadette thought about joining the Sisters of Nevers during the asthma attack that struck her toward the end of the same year, 1863. She was thinking about it at the time her cousin Jeanne Védère was visiting. When Jeanne arrived at the hospice, Soeur Marie Géraud took her aside and asked, "Do you intend to become a nun?" Jeanne recalls what happened next:

"Yes, Sister."

"Come with us."

"I smiled and said, 'I don't feel drawn to be a Sister of Nevers.'

"The sister began to cry and answered, 'Don't take Bernadette with you.'

"I said to her, 'My dear Sister, you don't need to cry; my cousin won't go anywhere because of me, nor I because of her. Bernadette will not leave the Sisters of Nevers.'

"'You don't think so?' she asked.

"'No, you can rest easy.'"

Then Soeur Marie, passionately devoted to the visionary, opened her heart to Jeanne. She confided that during Bernadette's asthma attack, she had wanted to watch over her; but Bernadette had told her, "Sister, go to bed. I don't need you; please, go. You make me feel bad, seeing you here. Do me this one favor—go away!"

The sister left, but came right back. And Bernadette went into her routine all over again to get her to leave.

"But Sister," Jeanne told her at this point, "you tired her out instead of comforting her."

"What do you expect?" she said. "If I can only touch her pillow, I am content. I feel no need to rest."

"I don't think God will leave you with her long."

"Do you believe that?" the sister asked.

"Yes, you are too attached to her," Jeanne replied.[43]

As a matter of fact, that was the year Soeur Marie was transferred to the hospital in Bagnères. Jeanne made it clear that "Bernadette was very fond of her too."

The two cousins talked vocations once more. According to Jeanne, Bernadette said, "Since I don't have the health to enter where I would have liked, I'd prefer the Sisters of Saint Vincent de Paul to the Sisters of Nevers. But how can I tell them? I don't have the heart to hurt them." And she added, "It's not because of my own little self that they're anxious for me to stay; I understand that very clearly, because I would be good for nothing. What would you expect them to do with me? Yet, I know they wouldn't be happy if I went somewhere else. And besides, I think they both have about the same responsibilities: to care for the poor and the sick. I love the poor very much; I like taking care of the sick. I'll stay."[44]

The touch of criticism in this passage, referring to the Sisters of Nevers, has to be at the very least qualified, keeping in mind the following observation by Soeur Hildegarde in her memoir to Père Cros: "Jeanne Védère, who is a good soul and not given to imagining things, thinks she noticed at Lourdes that the Sisters of Nevers did not take kindly to her rather frequent visits to Bernadette. Sometimes they even refused to let her go to the parlor. But noticing this, Monseigneur Peyramale got angry, it seems, and advised these sisters never to keep Bernadette from Jeanne Védère (etc.) and to leave the two cousins alone so that they could talk about their pious aspirations to the religious life."[45]

The criticisms mentioned above and below regarding [the Daughters of Charity of] Saint Vincent de Paul likewise make us take Jeanne's testimony with a bit of caution. The competition between Congregations, very intense at that time, creates a few shady areas that are hard to clear up.

Reflection

In the months following her conversation with the bishop, Bernadette considered everything carefully. If the determining factor in her decision was the vocation to care for the sick, two other factors also played an important role. Her health improved during the winter of 1863–1864. Then too, Bernadette thought highly of the sisters who had taken her in. She appreciated their simplicity in dealing with her, as compared to the way she had been treated by other sisters.

"I'm going to Nevers, because they didn't entice me," she later said.[46]

Final Choice

Her reflections came to full maturity the day of the inauguration of the statue, April 4, 1864, the date we have now reached. From that time on, Bernadette's decision was firm. When she was approached by other Congregations, her invariable answer was, "Soeur, you followed your vocation, I have to follow mine."[47]

"The Sisters of Saint Vincent de Paul made her many offers and invited her to lunch," says Soeur Marie-Joséphine Viguerie. "She always refused. The superior of the hospice scolded her and obliged her to accept one of these invitations. On that occasion, one of the sisters of Saint Vincent de Paul took the liberty to say: 'So, Mademoiselle, you want to go with the Sisters of Nevers?' The immediate answer was, 'Yes, indeed, Madame.' The sister of Saint Vincent de Paul said no more."[48]

Shortly before her decision, when they announced to her the visit of a sister of that same Congregation, she said, "I'm going to turn toward the wall." And she pretended she was asleep.[49]

It was the same with the Sisters of the Immaculate Conception, with whom Père Sempé, the first superior of the chaplains, would have very much wanted her to go. She answered, "I am called to the Sisters of Nevers."[50]

Still, one of Père Sempé's reasons impressed her, "[You should] have chosen a Congregation dedicated to devotion to the Virgin." This obviously meant the Sisters of the Immaculate Conception, founded by Père Peydessus.

"Bernadette did not answer but reported this comment to Abbé Pomian, who told her, 'Every congregation is dedicated to devotion to the Virgin. One can honor the Blessed Virgin in every Congregation.'"[51]

"A Secret" from the Apparition?

The rumor was going around that Bernadette's vocation had been suggested to her during the apparitions, that it was one of the secrets from the Virgin.

"I know at least one [secret]," Brother Léobard told her, "it's that you must become a nun." Bernadette bowed her head and said nothing.[52]

This reaction suggests that the statement hit its mark. But such an interpretation would overlook Bernadette's peasant cleverness in this matter. She generally avoided saying "yes" and "no" when it would have inevitably revealed what she had to keep to herself. Her silence, unassuming and non confrontational, often tinged with humor, simply meant, "I don't have to answer you, and that was not a nice question to ask me." To Père de Lajudie, who had provoked her this way at the end of August 1859, she merely replied, "Ah!" and she "smiled."[53]

Was that an admission? Not in the least! The interviewer took note of this throughout his account on the secrets: "She answered that way as if getting rid of an unimportant question."[54]

As for her smile, she clarified its meaning in July 1858, when Charles Madon, the lawyer from Beaune, said to her, "One of your secrets is that you will be a nun."

That made her laugh, and she said, "That's not it; they're more serious."[55]

Victoire Cassou would turn toward a somewhat different mystical explanation, "Before joining the Sisters of Nevers (in May 1862),

I went to Lourdes to say good-bye to Bernadette, with three other companions who wanted to become nuns in the same Congregation. I asked her if she would be joining us soon at Nevers. She answered, 'I am to be a nun, but I don't know the order. The Blessed Virgin hasn't told me. I'm waiting.'

"Later in 1871, when I saw her at Nevers, I said to her, 'So, the Blessed Virgin has spoken?' she answered me emphatically: 'Of course!'"[56]

This testimony tends to suggest that Bernadette might have been privileged with a word from the Virgin between 1862 and her entrance at Nevers. What was that message? We must exclude a new apparition. Bernadette clearly said over and over that she had none after July 16, 1858. Was it an interior message? The tendency on the witness' part to interpret this her way and Bernadette's style of life invites one to think that it was simply the "direction" she saw the course her life was taking, exteriorly and interiorly.

Bernadette's vocation was not the result of a decision that fell from heaven, but of a submissive and careful consideration at the level of the human realities in which she was actually rooted, especially in her experience as a nurse serving the poorest of the poor.

CHAPTER 9

— ⚜ —

THE YEAR 1864

Telling the whole story of the statue unveiled on April 4, 1864, and Bernadette's vocation, which we had to trace from its inception in April 1858 to the same date April 4, 1864, has interrupted the chronological thread of Bernadette's sayings. Let us take up where we left off: at the beginning of 1864.

Births and Deaths

On February 4, a little brother was born to Bernadette at the Baudéan Mill. He was named Jean. Bernadette was eager to go see him, but permission was refused.

"She showed a bit of bad temper, but that did not last very long," says Soeur Léontine Villaret.[1]

The same month, she learned of the death of her godfather, Jean-Marie Védère on February 20, 1864. She had seen him only once, in August 1862.[2] She loved him very much. She was reported to have said at the time, "I knew he wouldn't live long; they told me not to get so attached to him."[3]

Beginning in March 1864, she was assigned a new task: writing letters to pilgrims who requested prayers. Up to now, others had answered for her. Now they handed over to her those that seemed most urgent. So between March 4 and August 22, 1864, she wrote seven of these letters.[4]

Visitors

On March 29, 1864, she welcomed a scholarly Jesuit Father, who would soon use his prodigious talent as a researcher and historian to tell the story of Lourdes—Père Cros. If only he had known at that time how advantageous it could have been for him to speak freely with Bernadette! This was permission that he would fail to obtain at the very peak of his work. Now he came as an ordinary visitor, with no particular plan in mind; but he could see, listen, feel and observe. He wrote up his impressions of the trip for a friend.[5]

Walking from Pau to Lourdes, his breviary under his arm, he arrived at night. From afar, on the other side of the Gave, he could see the grotto all aglow with candles. He felt overwhelmed. He did not even ask to see Bernadette. Someone suggested it. At the sisters' request, Bernadette "agreed" to "tell him about all the apparitions," but he "wouldn't hear of it."

"I believe. Just tell me what the Virgin expects of us."

"That a chapel be built there and that we pray for sinners."

The priest looked at Bernadette. Later he wrote, "She is very sick. She will probably die soon. Everything about this young girl of twenty expresses innocence. I've seen a photograph of her, but it's a very poor picture. If you should happen to come across one, don't think you have seen Bernadette!"[6]

Giving her his blessing, he left. "Pray for me," he told her.

Père Cros took notes of the unrestrained enthusiasm that certain visitors lavished on her:

"Some priests knelt down before her and had her bless them (one at least did this very flamboyantly…and other similar things). Women snipped off locks of her hair or pieces of her clothing. Country folk cried out, 'What a saint! What a sweet little virgin! Anyone can see she is a saint!'"[7]

In such a situation, he admired her "simplicity." This word recurs several times in his account: "She does not seem to have the slightest idea of how extraordinary her situation is. After these visits, her usual words are 'Oh! What a nuisance those women are.'

She used the word *'embêter,'* which is the only word these people commonly use to express annoyance" [he explained at the end].[8]

On April 12, 1864, the Duke de La Rochefoucald was puzzled by his meeting with Bernadette. "I did not deny (the apparition)...but I admit I had my doubts. I had seen nothing up to now to convince me. I was struck by the simplicity of the little peasant girl, timid without being embarrassed, answering my questions without ever making a mistake or contradicting herself."[9]

On April 27, there took place a visit of another kind: Romaine Mengelatte, about to be married that very day to Lucien Poueyto, the farmer from Espelugues, (a farm barely one hundred yards from the grotto) came to the sisters to borrow an umbrella to protect her wedding gown. She dropped in to see Bernadette, who was ailing, "resting on two pillows, which raised her up to let her breathe."

"What do you want, Romaine?" Bernadette asked.

"I've come to see you. I'm getting married in a little while. I'm going to live at Espelugues, near the grotto...."

"Oh, you'll go to the grotto often, won't you? You'll go pray to the Blessed Virgin for me...I hope you'll be happy. Adieu!" All this was in patois.[10]

We will set aside the elaborations that this visit to the future nun stirred up in the young bride who became the mother of sixteen children.[11]

On July 14, 1864, another account of the apparitions was given to Madame A. de Minvielle, who dwelt on the "famous secrets." Like Père Cros, she found the photograph she was sending "badly taken": Bernadette was "better-looking."[12] This visit took her from "doubt" to "full and absolute belief."[13]

On Saturday, August 20, there was the visit of eight priests, among whom was Abbé Cabane, who drew up an account.[14]

The priests asked the sisters of the hospice for an interview. To see Bernadette? That was easy. To question her? That was another matter, given the large number of visitors during vacation season.

"A lot of them came today! (said the superior) but yesterday even more...well over nine hundred people."

She nevertheless allowed them to "question Bernadette on a few details of the vision." The most important of the priests—the one Abbé Cabane called "our president"—opened the conversation. He asked, "Do you have a perfect recollection of what happened?"

"Yes, Monsieur le Curé."

"Did the Virgin speak loudly? Did she raise her voice?"[15]

At this point one of the observers indicated that the question did not make much sense. It grew more confused. A discussion arose on how a glorified body can make itself heard. They called Bernadette to witness. She replied simply, "I could hear her very clearly."

"Was it an inner or audible voice?"

"Audible," she answered, bowing her head.

The first questioner added, "Then the Blessed Virgin appeared to you in flesh and blood as a living person?"

"Yes, Monsieur le Curé. She had on a white mantle, a white veil, a blue sash, a yellow rose on each foot."

These words were pronounced fairly rapidly, like an oft-repeated formula, with Bernadette keeping her eyes lowered.

"Did her feet touch the ledge?" asked someone.

"I don't know; at her feet there was some moss that kept me from seeing."

When Bernadette coughed painfully two or three times, one of the priests said, "Did you ask the Blessed Virgin for good health?"

The one who presided took this up, "Oh! No doubt Bernadette prefers asking for spiritual favors."

She remained silent.

"Can you sleep?" asked the president.

Bernadette responded with a smile, "Yes, Monsieur."

After a moment's reflection she added, "Except when I cough" (smiling again).

Her voice was very weak and a little strained.

Questions and comments multiplied, some trivial or improper.

Bernadette saw so many people, someone said that she must end up feeling embarrassed by it all. She seemed not to understand.

"Bernadette, all those who come must be asking you for prayers," said the acting president of the group. "It is true we can pray for everybody with only one prayer."

A smile was her only reply.

While this was going on, a sickly old man, dressed like a beggar, opened the door a bit without saying a word. The superior, who was near the door, opened it wider and asked the old man to come in. Silently he approached Bernadette and gazed at her, his eyes filled with tenderness and veneration. Bernadette hastened to bring him a chair. Several of those in the room thought it was her father.[16]

The man Bernadette welcomed so warmly because he was sick and poor had come merely to have her sign a "worn, ragged-edged picture." She did this for him in the adjoining room. The eight visitors got the same idea.

"She'll sign whatever you want," the sister said.

Most of the visitors left to buy what they needed at the door of the hospice. Nothing was sold in the house. The superior then came and took her place next to the priest at the center of the semicircle. He was the one who seemed to be presiding. "Bernadette must really love the Blessed Virgin," he said, "after the privilege she has received."

"Oh! Yes indeed!" quickly answered the sister (careful to avoid any touch of praise); "it would be a crime if she didn't."[17]

At that point, the sister was called out. "Two or three" stayed with Bernadette. "In order not to drop the conversation," Abbé Cabane had her give an overall account of the apparitions and paid attention to a few details.

"Is it true that the Blessed Virgin entrusted you with a secret that concerns you alone?"

"Yes, Monsieur l'Abbé"

"But," said someone, "you didn't think you had to keep it secret from your confessor?"

"It's not a sin," Bernadette retorted with a smile.[18]

The others returned. Bernadette, still in the room adjoining the parlor, signed her name slowly and came back "with a playful eagerness" to give each one her picture "smiling innocently." They recommended themselves to her prayers. One of the visitors asked her for "A special *Ave Maria.*"

She seemed to think about what she should answer; then raising her eyes and smiling she responded, "You pray for me, too."

The priest visitors left reluctantly.[19]

As it was, "other visitors had entered the parlor to take their turn." Looking at his autographed picture, Abbé Cabane was puzzled by the two letters that preceded Bernadette's signature. He thought he read "P. P." He returned to the parlor, now open to one and all, and asked Bernadette to "explain the initials in front of her name."

"*Priez pour*' (Pray for) Bernadette Soubirous," she said. Then with a smile she apologized for poorly writing the first letter of her name and sat down again.

At the end of August 1864 (between the twentieth and the twenty-sixth,)[20] there was a visit from the future historian of the apparitions, Henri Lasserre. He came to Lourdes for the first time in thanksgiving for his cure of October 20, 1862. Was he very anxious to question Bernadette? Neither the Lasserre archives nor the account of Léonce Dubosc de Pesquidoux contain explicit evidence that would support this possibility. Lasserre did see Bernadette. He was aware of "the visionary's expression that no actress, no artist's model could have produced so surely, with such total perfection!"

Once again, she demonstrated for him how the Immaculate moved. But the future history of Lourdes was still only a distant project. Henri Lasserre's worries and combats were somewhere else. His history would be based on the collection of official documents loaned to him by Lourdes and on the spur-of-the-moment conversations with a few witnesses, not on a methodical investigation.[21]

On September 11, 1864, sorrow visited Bernadette. Her little brother, Jean, born on February 4, 1864, died before having reached his first birthday.

A Stay at Momères

On October 3, 1864, Bernadette received an unexpected visit from Jeanne Védère, who was still awaiting her parents' consent to enter the convent. She had come from Momères with them. Was it because Bernadette's departure for Nevers was already in the works? She ventured to ask permission to take Bernadette to Momères. The superior objected saying, "Bernadette has been sick for a week, and I'm afraid that if she goes out she'll get sick again."

"Madame, I wouldn't want that to happen," Jeanne responded.

A priest accompanying them gave Jeanne an encouraging sign and said to the superior, "Madame, the little one doesn't seem to be suffering today."

"If her cousin wants her to go out, I don't want to refuse her; the only thing I ask is that you bring her back before you leave (town)," the superior replied.

"Yes, Madame, you know that's what I do every time she comes out with me."

With this first success, Jeanne suddenly had an idea that she immediately shared with her father. "I really would've liked to bring Bernadette home (to Momères)..."

"You're telling me now? If you had told me this morning, I would've gone to Monsieur le Curé to ask his permission."

"Be kind and go now, and let Uncle (Bernadette's father) go with you."

But first, they had to make sure of the willingness of the interested party. "If Monsieur le Curé agrees, Bernadette, do you want to come?" Jeanne asked.

"Good heavens!" Bernadette answered. "What an idea you've got! You didn't mention anything to me this morning. I'd be delighted to go. I'd be very happy."[22]

The plan worked. Bernadette received permission to spend three full days in Momères, until Friday, October 7. She was happy; the superior was less so: "What if she gets sick?"

"We have Doctor Peyramale; he will take care of her. Don't worry."

There was also the trip by night...but the superior willingly concluded, "Since Monsieur le Curé has spoken, it is useless to say anything. We'll give her nothing, because, if she has a change of clothing, you would perhaps keep her for a week."

"It isn't necessary to give her anything. Monsieur le Curé has limited the time she can stay and I won't disobey his orders," Jeanne assured her.

"They weren't expecting Bernadette at home, and it was a pleasant surprise," continues Jeanne. "The next morning we went to the six o'clock Mass. Imagine our surprise at seeing the Curé of Lourdes, who was finishing his Mass. He was at the last Gospel. (Monsieur le Curé of Lourdes came from Momères; his parents lived there.)

"Once we had left the church, Bernadette said, 'Did you see Monsieur le Curé? Who knows? He may have come to tell you to send me back to Lourdes. Let's go see him.'

"The house of Doctor Peyramale, the Curé's brother, was quite near the church. At the doorway, we met the doctor as he was leaving. He said to me, 'Ah! You have Bernadette?'

"'Yes, Monsieur.'

"'Come in.'

"My cousin said, 'I would like to see Monsieur le Curé.'

"He answered, 'Monsieur le Curé left right after Mass. He came here on a small errand.' Then, addressing me, he added, 'How long can you keep your cousin?'[23]

"'Monsieur, I have permission until Monday....'"

"Monday" was October 11 and no longer the seventh. It had now become an extended permission.

The doctor interrupted, "Monsieur le Curé told me to tell you that you can keep her for two weeks if you want. Even longer if she isn't sick."

Jeanne replied, "If she's sick, we'll take care of her."

"You can keep her more than a month, if you want," the doctor said.[24]

Bernadette's stay lasted seven weeks, in the warm family atmosphere made all the more lively and congenial by her presence. For her, it was an oasis of happiness.

She spent the time praying, working and reading, though she preferred meditating to reading.[25] She was, "very punctual in following her little schedule. She went to Mass every morning and received Communion three times a week: Sundays, Wednesdays and Fridays. She made a daily visit to the Blessed Sacrament and recited her rosary every day. When she prayed, you would have thought she was almost in ecstasy, she was that pious and recollected....

"She did everything people wanted her to, both in and outside the village; she was well liked by all who knew her. She was lively and playful. She greatly enjoyed joking with one of her cousins."[26]

Her sole trial was the curious and the intrusive. The first few days, Bernadette went to school with her teacher-cousin.

"She loved the children very much and was beloved by them," continues Jeanne Védère. "We were often disturbed by visitors, and the children suffered from it. So I made her stay at home."[27]

Of course, Bernadette could not escape visitors, even in that isolated corner. On one of the very first days, on the way to class "at the town hall," the two cousins were stopped. Jeanne described what happened:

"The 'Grand Vicar' (Laurence, nephew and confidant of the bishop[28]), the Curé of Momères and a lady were waiting for us near the rectory, which was on our way. As soon as Bernadette saw them, she said to me, 'Oh! There's the lady, I think, who wants me to go to the Carmelite Fathers.'

"They invited us in. After we answered a few questions put to us by the 'Grand Vicar,' the lady said to me: 'Mademoiselle, please let your cousin come with me. I'll bring her back to you tomorrow.'

"'Madame, I can't let her go anywhere unless I go with her. I promised the Curé of Lourdes that she would not go out without me.'

"'All right! I'll take you both and I'll come along with you.'

"'Madame, today is not a holiday; I can't leave.'

"'Monsieur le Curé will give you time off.'

"'I'd need time off from the mayor and he's not here.'

"She pleaded earnestly to get to take Bernadette. On my part, I did the same to keep her from going. The lady was not happy. The 'Grand Vicar' told her she shouldn't get angry: 'She promised Monsieur le Curé Peyramale not to let her go out alone.... She does well not to let her go.'"[29]

Alone at last, Bernadette then explained that this was the lady who had already kidnapped her one time to take her to the Carmelites at Bagnères, without Peyramale's knowledge and to his great displeasure.

Again Jeanne recorded: "The second Sunday Bernadette was with us (October 16), a gentleman stepped out of his carriage in front of the house. He came in and placed a package on the table. He left without saying a word. The house was crowded. When the people left, we examined the small package, which contained medals, pictures and stationery with a beautiful letterhead on each sheet, representing Our Lady of Lourdes. There was a short note, which read: 'Bernadette, I've found out that you are in Momères. I bring you these little objects for you to distribute among the children of the parish and any who want them. When you run out, I will give you some more.'" Signed Dufour.[30]

Monsieur Dufour was a photographer and at the same time a publisher in Tarbes. He specialized in promoting the pilgrimage to Lourdes. Since October 1862, he had already sold several thousand pictures or photos of Bernadette. He circulated the first prints made by Abbé Bernadou (1860–1861). Since 1863, he had opened a second store in Lourdes. Part of the profits went to him, and part went toward the construction of the chapel, in keeping with an agreement reached with the diocese.

At the beginning of October 1863, a second photographer,

Billard-Perrin, had made the same arrangement with Bishop
Laurence. Monsieur Dufour saw his monopoly disappearing. He
wrote to Bishop Laurence to discredit his competition: "a one-time
juggler, traveling from town to town and singing in cafés...a bank-
rupt (with no) permanent residence. In 1862 and even in 1863,
when I had publicized my extensive plan for the grotto, Monsieur
Perrin and his friends ridiculed me by saying these miracles were a
hoax.... Today, he changes his tune and is stealing the fruits of my
initiative away from me."[31]

Having lost the monopoly, Dufour then asked to take some new
pictures. He had, in fact, taken some in October 1863: Bernadette
in ecstasy, Bernadette kneeling before the grotto together with the
sisters. These different subjects "reduced into photographs on visit-
ing-cards sell for one franc," as the advertisement read.

"Do you think they're selling you at a high enough price, Bernadette?" asked Elfrida Lacrampe.

"More than I'm worth."[32]

This time, Dufour wanted to renew his stock of pictures by having Bernadette come to his studio in Tarbes, where he would use all
the resources of his art. This would be the fourth time Bernadette
would sit for the camera.

These gentlemen always got their way, regardless of any obstacle.

On Monday, October 17, Monsieur Dufour returned to get
Bernadette.

"I'm very angry, Monsieur," Jeanne Védère objected, "but I cannot go with Bernadette. For that, I need permission from the Curé
of Lourdes and from the bishop."

"I have everything you want," he answered.[33]

And indeed he had the authorization from both the Curé and
the bishop.

"I can't go until Thursday," Jeanne replied. "The children are
back in school. I'd need permission from the superintendent."

"I'll see him tonight, and I'll be here at eleven o'clock tomorrow. Be ready!" Dufour responded.[34]

In fact, the next day Jeanne "received a letter from the Inspector." Not only did he authorize this absence, but he added: "I give
you permission to take all the time off you want for as long as
Bernadette stays with you, provided that someday you bring her to
my house."[35]

Dufour photo, October 18, 1864

So Monsieur Dufour returned Tuesday "At eleven o'clock." "Bring another outfit for her to put on before sitting for the camera," he told Jeanne.

"No, that wouldn't be right. You must let her keep what she's wearing or it wouldn't be her."

He understood and said, "You're right."

Jeanne explained, "I wanted to test Bernadette...to see if she wouldn't like to fancy up...I went to her room [and said], 'Monsieur Dufour told me to make you look pretty. You'll have to change your clothes.'"[36]

Ordinarily, Jeanne noted, Bernadette would "always go along with what others wanted," but at this point she reacted: "If Monsieur Dufour doesn't think I'm pretty enough, tell him to leave me here. I'll be much happier.... Let him be satisfied with the way I'm dressed. I won't even add one more pin."

Bernadette, who in another era would have been named "patron of cover girls," on this October 18, sat through the longest and most meticulous photo session in her life. The technical conditions were good for the times, but the ideas were not. Dufour directed the poses. He tried to re-create the ecstasy with the help of projectors. He arranged theater sets and staged the first apparition with two companions and a bundle of firewood in front of a mass-produced backdrop painted with a romantic landscape.

Finally, since the lighting could not quite catch Bernadette's unpatterned clothing, he got her to wear a series of checkered skirts, whose folds he carefully arranged.

When the fifteen pictures were taken, Dufour wanted a sixteenth with Jeanne Védère.

"Both of you must be taken together."

Jeanne recounts: "That pleased Bernadette, who whispered to me, 'We'll do one to keep at your house and one for my parents when we're in the convent. Our parents will always see us together, and that will make them happy.'

"To humble her a bit (I was afraid that some conceited thought might arise in her heart because of the veneration everyone had for her) I said to her, 'Oh no! I wouldn't like being seen behind glass with you.... When our parents want to see us together, all they'll have to do is put our pictures side by side.'

"'You're right,' she said."[37]

Bernadette as posed by Dufour in a "re-creation" of the original apparition scene

During Bernadette's stay in Momères, one of the most frequent visitors was Doctor Peyramale. He brought up the subject of his brother's sickness at the beginning of that year. He had spent several nights keeping watch over him, "I then found out," he confided, "that all the money the Curé of Lourdes had in the world amounted to forty centimes...and thirty-five rents to pay for the poor, which he paid regularly."

In addition Abbé Peyramale had taken it upon himself to back an honest but incompetent hotel owner. All of this could have been charged to the doctor, who also had to buy his brother's medications....

Jeanne Védère relates:

"Laughing heartily, Bernadette said to him, 'You didn't have to buy him any.'

"Monsieur Peyramale then said, 'But Bernadette, didn't you say that Monsieur le Curé would not die?'

"Instead of paying attention to this question, she replied, 'Oh, good heavens! One day when you came [to Lourdes] from Momères, the servant girl didn't follow the doctor's orders....'

"And the doctor said, 'Yes, I had already raised my hand to give her a good whack with my cane. The Blessed Virgin is the one who stopped me.... But didn't you say Bernadette, that my brother would not die?'

"'Oh,' she replied again, 'Monsieur Dozous was angry....'

"We understood that she did not want to answer that question."[38]

What Jeanne is suggesting here is that her cousin, through humility, wanted to hide a gift of prophecy.

On this same subject, Jeanne thought she witnessed something extraordinary during Bernadette's stay at Momères, which she confided "under the seal of secrecy" to the insatiable Père Cros. We quote here Jeanne's own written account, for which she alone bears responsibility and which she herself undertakes "with no guarantees."

When I was at Momères, we had a custom, on weekdays, of covering the statue of the Blessed Virgin, which is in church in the chapel of Our Lady, with a veil. We would remove it on Sundays and feastdays and put it back again that same evening.

The Monday after Bernadette arrived at Momères...in the morning, we discovered that the veil they had covered the statue with the night before was at her [the statue's] feet, laid out like a muffler

Dufour took dozens of rest breaks…

Bernadette was tired, really tired of it all

people wear in winter. I had seen this without paying much attention to it; but after one lady mentioned it to me, I too made it a point to look. The next day, Tuesday, Monsieur le Curé said to me, "Haven't you noticed that the Blessed Virgin doesn't want her veil anymore now that Bernadette is here?"

He went on to tell me that he would go once again that evening to cover the statue and we would see if the same thing happened again. And so our Good Mother was covered with the veil Tuesday evening; and the next morning, to our great surprise, the veil was again removed and at her feet. From that moment, Monsieur le Curé said that the veil was not to be replaced and they didn't replace it until my cousin left. Once she was gone, they again covered the statue as usual, and the veil no longer fell off.

After discussing the causes of this phenomenon, which for her had no explanation, Jeanne recounts her conversation with Bernadette about this: "Haven't you noticed that the Blessed Virgin no longer wants her veil since you've been here?"

Bernadette answered: "Oh! Then again, why put a veil over the Blessed Virgin? Why hide her?"[39]

Here, as she often did, Bernadette practiced evasion: a method that most swiftly eliminated trivial questions. She dismissed more sharply the exaggerated stories of Bartrès, which had been making the rounds since 1858, the episodes of which Jeanne referred to her. Here are some examples:

"Watching her sheep one day while she was at Bartrès, Bernadette crossed over the stream without touching the water...the shepherds in the area, it was said, had seen her and spoke about it."

"On another occasion, her wet-nurse had trouble making dinner. She wanted Bernadette to go get flour at the mill. The child, they said, told her not to worry about the flour, but to give her the small amount she had and she would make dinner. The flour increased; there was more left after dinner than her wet-nurse had given her....

"Bernadette answered that this was false, maintaining that there was no truth in any of it."[40]

"No truth in any of it," ("Rien de vrai en tout cela."). This expression must have been recorded word for word, since the Englishman Staden wrote it down literally on the occasion of a similar denial.

During Bernadette's stay at Momères, the two cousins had fur-

NOTRE-DAME DE LOURDES
« Je suis la Vierge Immaculée »
La T. Ste Vierge à Bernadette

The apparition to Bernadette
(A period print)

ther occasion to talk vocations. When Abbé Portalet visited, he offered them medals of Saint Benedict. That was when Bernadette said to Jeanne, "In the religious order I told you so much about, they follow the rule of Saint Benedict."[41]

But while they were talking, people from the region came and interrupted them. As a result, Jeanne did not understand what order Bernadette had in mind.

Jeanne's parents still objected to her vocation. Bernadette supposedly told her, "The biggest difficulty will soon disappear."

"This big difficulty was my poor godmother," Jeanne recorded, "who more than anyone opposed my entrance into the convent. She was sick at the time. Four days after my cousin left, my godmother died; it was November 23...."[42]

During Bernadette's stay, there was one visitor from Lourdes who was especially regular—it was François Soubirous, her father. Any opportunity was a good one...like the time when Bernadette was being nursed at Bartrès. He missed his daughter, and he felt more comfortable at Momères than at the hospice. He could have her all to himself. Twelve and a half miles one way did not faze him in the least.

Bernadette's Preference

It must have been on this occasion that Bernadette told her cousin this secret, "It seems to me that I have a preference for my father. I love my mother very much, but I feel more drawn to my father. I don't know why, unless it's because my father came to see me [at Bartrès] every day, and my mother seldom did."

Bernadette made this confession with a hint of regret. She would have liked to "re-order her affections," as people used to recommend in those days.

François came to see Bernadette three times at Momères. On his fourth visit, Jeanne adds, "we had to give her back to him."[43]

Return to Lourdes

On November 19, 1864, Jeanne, who had held herself responsible for her cousin, brought Bernadette back to Lourdes in good health, accompanying her right to the rectory. There Abbé Peyramale recalled those heroic days when Bernadette had asked him "to build a

François Soubirous and his youngest children, in front of the paternal home

chapel." He repeated what he had said at that time: "Do you yourself have any money to build a church?" and "If this Lady wants a
church, let her give you the money."

The Curé was going through his first worries as a builder. This
was but the beginning. Things would get harder.

Mysteries and Secrets

Jeanne Védère reported two other secrets, of uncertain date, which
might best be situated during their long conversations at Momères.

One was about Bernadette's trials in Bartrès. She never told anyone else about them. Whenever anyone referred to them, she
changed the subject or began praising her wet-nurse who was so
attached to her (which was quite true). One day, however, she entrusted herself more openly to Jeanne's discretion. "I was with
Bernadette," Jeanne recounts. "A priest stopped us, and began talking familiarly with her. When he was gone, I asked her who this
priest was. She said, 'He's so good! I like him a lot! He's my wet-
nurse's brother. He always took my side when I was in Bartrès. My
wet-nurse wasn't always pleasant. This priest, when he came during
vacations, was more friendly to me than to the other children. So,
after Monsieur l'Abbé had reprimanded her several times, my wet-
nurse changed her ways as long as he stayed home. Afterwards, she
would resume her usual behavior. In order to get me to go back a
second time, she promised my parents to have me prepared to make
my First Communion. She did nothing.'"

"But seeing that you were uncomfortable, why didn't you tell
your father?"

"Oh, no! I thought it was the good Lord's will. When we think,
'the good Lord allows it,' we don't complain."[44]

Jeanne's other recollection concerns a "fastday," perhaps the
vigil of June 29, 1866, when they said their good-byes. But this is
only a guess. In any case, Jeanne came to Lourdes; the two cousins
went down "to the grotto together" and stayed there "until about
three o'clock in the afternoon. At that hour Jeanne still had not
eaten anything. When someone mentioned this to Bernadette, she
got a bit upset: 'Oh! Look!' she said; 'she's going to God through
fear and not through love. You think God is very wicked; he's so
good! Come on! He would've been more pleased with you if you

had eaten something. The next time, if you come on an empty stomach, I won't go to the grotto with you.'"[45]

Where the Final Obstacles Fell

On her return to Lourdes, Bernadette received some good news. Her request to be admitted to the Sisters of Charity of Nevers, made that April 4, had been granted. The superior of the hospice had forwarded it to Bishop Forcade.[46] The bishop had been delayed by the Superior General, Mère Joséphine Imbert, who "hesitated a long time." He "was annoyed," reports Mère Joséphine Forestier.[47]

From the end of September to October 3, he went to Toulouse to preach the retreat for the superiors from the south of France. Mother General was present. "He was emphatic with her" on getting a definite answer, according to Mère Forestier's well-founded surmise.[48] The superior of Lourdes (or her delegate), present at this retreat, did not return to the hospice until Bernadette left for Momères. She must have given her the news on her return or shortly afterwards.[49]

Bernadette informed her parents. She "let it be known that she was happy," noted Jean-Marie Soubirous.[50]

Relapse

Bernadette's religious formation could now begin; but at the start of December, less than two weeks after her return, she had a relapse. She had to stay in bed until the end of January. The prospect of the novitiate grew dim. It was only at the beginning of February that she was able to get up, she tells us in her letter of February 7.[51]

There was also sad news at the beginning of this same month—Justin, the little brother she had so often held on her lap, died at the age of ten. The doctors summoned on March 4, 1859, had warned the Soubirous of the consequences of their unsanitary living conditions—conditions about which they could do nothing—saying, "You will not be able to keep your children."

Chapter 10

— ⚜ —

The Year 1865

With the coming of beautiful weather, the visits to Bernadette resumed.

On May 27, 1865, there came two Jesuit novices: Clauzel and Clavé. Following a custom started by Saint Ignatius, they had been sent out on the road to live as beggars for a month. The custom fell into disuse between the two World Wars, because this clerical begging met with too generous a response in rectories.

Such was the case in Lourdes. Before anything else, the generous Abbé Peyramale offered the two visitors "a Capuchin shirt," as he called it, referring to a large glass of wine for refreshment. He spoke to them about Bernadette, brought up the "scandalous" objections Père Nègre (also a Jesuit) had made when he visited in 1858,[1] and the American bishop who supposedly fell to his knees before her![2]

He then sent them off to see Bernadette at the hospice, where the superior warned them more explicitly: "I'm as concerned about Bernadette's humility as I am about my own eyes—no praise, I beg you. Don't look too impressed. Just imagine, last week I had to step in to control the devotion of a priest who was placing his breviary and his rosary in the child's hands! I think, God forgive me, that he was asking her to bless them...."

The two novices knew this priest quite well. With enthusiasm, he had shown them the objects he had had Bernadette touch.

All at once, the visionary found the two novices, intimidated and speechless. Contrary to her usual custom, she was the first to speak. They wrote down "the answers, pretty close to the actual words," as follows:

"We prayed at the grotto this morning, but the Blessed Virgin wasn't there."

"Ah, yes! Only her statue [was]," Bernadette answered.

"The statue is really beautiful. They told us you had described the details."

"Oh! I don't know what they did; but they couldn't have made it the way it actually was."

"Do you remember the features of the Blessed Virgin?"

"Yes, to the last detail."

"And you'll recognize her when you get to heaven?"

"Of course, if she hasn't changed!"

"Did the Blessed Virgin speak audibly?"

"Yes, I could hear her with my ears, like any voice."

"So she had a voice like Father's?" said Clavé, pointing to Clauzel. "Ho!"

According to Père Delhostal, who got it from Père Clauzel, she exclaimed, *"Bou Diou!"* ("Good Lord!")

Correcting herself, she added, "Oh, no! Her voice was delicate, delicate!"

When Bernadette brought up the apparition on March 25 and the pose struck by the Immaculate Lady, the Fathers began to grow more excited. Bernadette's superior then took command of the conversation. "Listen, Fathers," she said, "let me complete your instruction by telling you what the Blessed Virgin hasn't done for Bernadette yet: obtained her final conversion. With all these unearned privileges, she's laying up time in purgatory for herself, poor Bernadette, and you'd be doing a charitable deed by praying for her to become better. Would you believe that just a moment ago, mademoiselle and I had quite a little argument? She wanted to throw her peels into the basket on the right instead of the one on the left. And I realized that I'd have to give in!"

"Dear Mother," Bernadette said with tears in her eyes, "I ask your forgiveness again."

"Yes, yes," answered the superior, smiling in spite of herself as she looked at the Jesuits over Bernadette's head, "don't start up all over again! And now I order you to autograph two pictures of the apparition for these Fathers. Write down that they are to remember Bernadette in their prayers."[3]

On July 26, Abbé Boyer visited. He was writing the first book for the pilgrim to Lourdes, *Une visite à la grotte* (A Visit to the Grotto). Visitors were waiting, and he himself had come with others. So in the middle of a large "circle," Bernadette described the apparitions, then answered questions.

"Didn't you notice anything in [Our Lady's] expression?"

"She smiled at me, except when she told me to pray for sinners."

"From the time of the privilege you were granted, haven't you ever had temptations to pride, self-importance, or self-satisfaction?"

Bernadette smiled as if this were all new to her.

"Oh, no! Monsieur!"

"But when you encountered people, even priests, who refused to believe what you were telling them, didn't you feel any anger, or some resentment?"

"No, Monsieur. I told what I had seen and heard, and then if they didn't want to believe me, they were free not to; it was none of my business."[4]

At noontime the visitors left, after the usual autograph session [in which Bernadette signed whatever she was requested with] "P.P. Bernadette," or, for a change, "union of prayers."

On leaving, the visitors expressed a desire to meet Bernadette at the grotto itself.

"She rarely goes," the superior answered.

It was the permission that was rare, given the reverence she was shown and the crowds all this attracted. On exceptional occasions, however, permission was granted.

The visitors examined the grotto, now enclosed by a grille, and the esplanade along the Gave, then they began to pray....

"[There was a] stirring within the crowd, [then] everyone stood up." Bernadette was arriving.

Above: the grotto at the time of the government "fence"

Below: the "grille" set up by Church authorities in 1864
(Period prints)

"Without saying a word," Abbé Boyer recounts, she covered her head with her hood (protection from the curious) and came to kneel right up against the grille, facing the Madonna. I was near her; it seemed to me that I was praying more fervently than before; but it didn't take long for someone to interrupt her....

"'Come on, Bernadette, show us exactly where you were when the Blessed Virgin appeared to you.'

"'Everything is so changed that I hardly recognize it. However, I was over there....'"[5]

Questions about the spring led to others, particularly about the secrets:

"Wouldn't you tell the Pope if he asked you?"

"I don't know what I'd do."

"'Immaculate Conception:' did you know what that meant?"

"I didn't know; I had never heard those words before."

"How did you manage to remember them?"

"I kept repeating them all along the way."

"Have there been many miracles since that time? Cures, conversions?..."

"Yes, Monsieur, there have been."

"Was it people you prayed for who received such favors?"

"I know nothing about that."

"But didn't you ever pray for people who obtained some great favor?"

"I don't know; maybe, but it wasn't my prayers that got them these favors."

"Here Bernadette seemed uncomfortable..." Abbé Boyer recorded. "The moment had come for us to leave."[6]

Bernadette's conversation provided a new insight into a few Gospel verses in the mind of one visitor who wrote: "She puts into practice...'Confine yourself to a simple yes or no.' Listening (to her)...you would think you were reading...the answers that the sick whom Jesus healed gave to the Jews who were questioning them" (cf. Jn 9).

Abbé Boyer's book was submitted to Bernadette in February 1866. She corrected three details: the days without apparitions were not "a *Monday* and a *Wednesday*," but "a *Monday* and a *Friday*"; the apparition "always kept her hands folded"; and lastly, it was not accurate to say that the visionary was living "at the hospice, where the township pays for her support." This last correction was written in a style different from Bernadette's:

"I owe the happiness of living in this dear haven solely to the charity of the Sisters of Nevers."

After careful consideration, Boyer had not invented this last item. He had gotten it from Abbé Peyramale; other witnesses confirm it.[7] What is true is that the situation he was informed about in July 1865 had changed by the time he submitted his book. Bernadette was now a postulant. She was completely under the authority of the sisters, who were anxious to make the correction.[8]

On September 7, 1865, the Vigil of the Nativity of Mary, Abbé Montauzé came to see Bernadette, accompanied by Abbé Vergès, dean and pastor of Saint Vincent in Tyrosse and Abbé Salomon, professor at the Seminary of Bazas. They joined the line of visitors that had gathered at the rectory, where a Spanish lady was already waiting. The wait grew longer. The Abbé took advantage of the time to read a manuscript, left for the guests: Henri Lasserre's account of his own cure. The overworked Curé Peyramale arrived home at last. He accompanied the visitors to the hospice.[9]

"Bernadette was in pain, very sick," says Abbé Montauzé. "She was able to get up, however, when Monsieur le Curé sent word that someone wanted to see her. He advised us to conserve her strength. The poor child was brought to the parlor, where we were waiting. [Her face bore] a suffering, but with expression...no pose or affectation. There we all were, looking at her, not daring to question her for fear of taxing her weary lungs with efforts and words that would wear her out. Nevertheless, the Spanish lady began...

"First came questions about the Lady's sash. Then, the hair. 'How was it arranged?'

"Bernadette said nothing.

"Monsieur le Curé of Lourdes then answered for her. 'Her hair was covered by her veil, Madame. You women spend a lot of time on your hair.'

"This remark silenced the lady, and I took advantage to ask my question: 'Tell me, please, how did the Blessed Virgin make the sign of the cross in front of you?'

"Bernadette said nothing and remained motionless.

"Thinking that she had not understood my question, or that she wanted to know why, I repeated it and added, 'Being a priest,

I'm sometimes required to teach people how to make a good sign of the cross. And if I could say how the Blessed Virgin makes it, it seems to me that I could persuade my audience to make it more devoutly.'

"Bernadette still made no movement and said nothing. I was quite astonished.

"Monsieur le Curé of Lourdes then said to her, 'Bernadette, make the sign of the cross because Monsieur l'Abbé asks you to.'[10]

"At this order, Bernadette obeyed immediately and made the sign of the cross...simply...calmly. I'd never seen the sign of the cross done better. I'll remember it. But I noticed that Bernadette had said nothing while she was making the sign of the cross.

"'Didn't the Blessed Virgin say anything when she made the sign of the cross?'

"'I couldn't hear anything,' she answered.

"'Were you afraid when you saw the apparition?' then asked Abbé Vergès.

"'At first, yes, but after I made the sign of the cross, I wasn't afraid anymore.'

"While I was questioning Bernadette, I saw Mother Superior talking to Abbé Vergès, but I couldn't hear.

"'What was Sister telling you a moment ago?' I asked him.

"'She told me that Bernadette always experienced difficulty when she was asked to make the sign of the cross the way the Blessed Virgin did.'

"'Why?'

"'I don't know, Sister didn't say.'

"And we began to imagine all kinds of reasons."[11]

At this point Abbé Montauzé went to the grotto. He prayed for a long time. He also observed, as one who understood intimately, the behavior of the pilgrims—the young man, for instance, who stood there stiffly, kneeling first on one knee, then on both, and bursting into silent tears. The Abbé returned to the hospice to clear up the question that was haunting him. Bernadette's reluctance to make the sign of the cross came quite simply from "the perfection with which the Blessed Virgin made the sign of the cross. She doesn't dare attempt to act out what she saw," the superior told him.

"And is Bernadette the one who gave you this explanation for her difficulty?" the Abbé asked.

"Yes, Monsieur," she answered.[12]

At this, the visitors requested an additional interview with the visionary, on behalf of Abbé Salomon, "professor in the diocese of Bordeaux," who had missed that morning's.... "He *only* wanted to tell her that tomorrow he would celebrate Mass for her."

"And will there be a *memento* for us?" asked the superior.

"Yes, Soeur, and another Mass Sunday for all of you."

"Fine, then. Permission granted!"[13]

Coming back from this visit, Abbé Salomon revealed his impression: "That child is going to die."[14]

At the beginning of September 1865, Bernadette's health was evidently not robust. On March 29, 1864, Père Cros had issued the same judgment.

On October 23, 1865, however, he saw a startling change: "Last year, I saw her at the point of death; today she's well again."

In these more convenient circumstances, Cros was captivated by Bernadette. He experienced for himself the truth of what the superior of the major seminary had told him: "The most striking proof of the apparition is Bernadette."

On his own authority, Père Cros added: "She herself is an apparition. There is something of the supernatural in her features. I think that it's impossible to keep in the imagination a clear picture of a supernatural apparition. Well, I've been unable to keep Bernadette's face in my imagination, and after much reflection, I'm incapable, right now, of picturing her; and even when I was with her I could not recall that face. Yet I have many other pictures hanging in the galleries of my mind...."[15]

The meeting took place in the parlor at five o'clock in the afternoon. This time Père Cros was heading toward history. He had prepared a list of questions, but he was only looking for edifying material for his preaching. Before beginning, he recited a Hail Mary with Bernadette "so that the Blessed Virgin would be with us," and then began. "I am going to make you weary, Bernadette, but the purpose is to make many children love the Blessed Virgin; they're the reason why I'm questioning you. As for myself, all I need is what you told me last year."

"With pleasure, Father," Bernadette responded.

It was evidently a conversation about the most widely known de-

Père Léonard-Marie Cros, S.J. (1831–1913)

tails, but Cros took exceptional care to write down Bernadette's answers: her words, her gestures, her style.

"Before the apparitions, did you sometimes see extraordinary
things?"

"I'd never seen anything extraordinary."

"Were you very well behaved?"

Père Cros noted that, "Bernadette answered with a little shrug
of her shoulders and a half-smile; her eyes remained lowered. All of
this suggested: 'Well, I don't really know how to answer.'"

"The Lady was very beautiful?"

"Oh, yes!"

"Have you ever seen a face that looked like hers?"

"Not one."

"Have you ever heard a voice like hers?"

"Oh, no!"

"Did she use 'tu' with you?" ["Tu" in French is the familiar form
for "you." It is used, for instance, when speaking to little children.]

"No, never."

"How did the Most Blessed Virgin hold her hands?"

"Not always the same way. When I said the rosary, she held one
in her hands."

"Would the Most Blessed Virgin recite the rosary?"

"She would slip the beads through her fingers."

"Did she go fast?"

"She went at my pace."

"Did she move her lips?"

"No, she didn't."[16]

While asking Bernadette to repeat the Virgin's words, the idea
came to him to determine the original patois text. Then and there,
in the little parlor, Père Cros put the plan into effect.

"She was on one side of a small round table and I on the other.
She dictated. I wrote, then read back to her what I had written. Then
I asked her to transcribe these words on the back of a picture."[17]

"Is that Saint Aloysius Gonzaga?" she asked.

"No, it's Blessed John Berchmans."[18]

And with a scholar's enthusiasm, Cros explained the connection
between these two persons. He was deeply involved in a historical
study on Berchmans: "How happy he is!" Bernadette concluded.

Père Cros left her the sheet he had written under her dictation so that she could recopy it in her own hand. She said: "I don't know whether I can finish tonight, but I will finish before eight o'clock tomorrow."[19]

The following day, October 24, Cros celebrated Mass in the hospice chapel. He wrote: "I gave Communion to a child who seemed to me to be between twelve and fourteen years old. I got the impression that it was Bernadette, but I couldn't be sure, the brief instant when I caught a glimpse of the communicant's face. I found the face so childlike that I could not believe that it was she. After Mass, I wanted to see her again; the superior said, 'She's in the chapel making her thanksgiving.' I knew then that it was she. What simplicity!"

Overwhelmed by the strong impression so weakly expressed by this commonplace word, "simple," Cros here mimics the not quite developed style of Charles Péguy [1873–1914], the French author whose style was to create an overall impact by the accumulation of synonyms and repetitions:

"I wish you could see this simple, this altogether simple, this totally honest, quite worthy, especially simple thing, that earthly nature could never manage to simulate. She came to Communion shrouded in the long veil of sturdy white wool, worn by the women and girls of the region."[20]

These sharp impressions gave rise to a new project: to establish "an authentic record of the fact" of the apparitions from Bernadette herself. Before leaving Bernadette, Père Cros asked her, "Would you be willing to answer in writing a series of questions that I will send you? If you were willing, I'd ask the bishop."

She accepted with pleasure.[21]

At the end of the retreat he preached at the major seminary in Tarbes, Père Cros submitted the idea to the bishop, who gave his approval. "I want to give you my blessing for that...."

The project haunted Cros, even as he was preaching a retreat to the children of Montauban. He came up with the novel idea of having "each child draw up a questionnaire for Bernadette." He was hoping for "a great deal of insight coming from the innocence of children."[22]

But his Father Provincial, who considered Père Cros too enterprising, brought the project to a halt: "Leave that to others; you work on your Berchmans."[23]

Taking into consideration Bernadette's lapses of memory con-

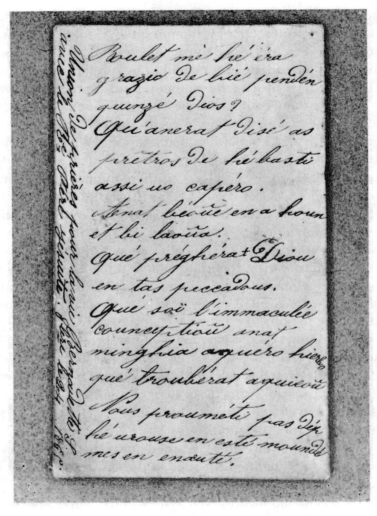

The Virgin's words in patois, written by Bernadette for Père Cros on October 24, 1865

cerning external details and chronology, how sorry we are today about that decision. Had he been allowed to, Père Cros would have begun looking for witnesses twelve years earlier than anyone else. We can only imagine the testimony that might have been given by Bernadette's father and mother, whom no one ever thought of interrogating before their death; by Mayor Lacadé (†1866); by Germain, the veterinarian; by Dufo (†1872), and so many others, at a time when memories were fresher, younger, and when countless letters were still being preserved within families.

The Apparent Age of Bernadette

A number of visitors underlined the contrast between Bernadette's apparent age and her real age:

"13 years old"—appeared to be "10 or 11": Peyramale, March 9, 1858.[24]

"13 years old"—appeared to be "10 or 11": Capdevielle.[25]

"13 years old"—Appeared to be "11": doctors on March 31, 1858.[26]

"14 years old"—appeared to be "10": Balech, September 24, 1858.[27]

"16 years old"—appeared to be "12": Junqua, February 20, 1860.[28]

"17 years old"—appeared to be "13–14": Junqua, October 20, 1861.[29]

"17 years old"—appeared to be "13": Lataste in 1862.[30]

"18 years old"—appeared to be "16": Villemarqué, August 7, 1863.[31]

"19 years old"—appeared to be "13": L. de Combes, summer of 1863.[32]

"19 years old"—appeared to be "13": Cabane.[33]

"21 years old"—appeared to be "13": Cros, October 24, 1865.[34]

But there is always a bit of literary license taken by writers who seek to concoct a contrast. Abbé Poisson, a visitor in 1863, spontaneously put Bernadette's age at "18–19 years old," her true age.[35]

A related observation: in 1858, several visitors saw her as "a child of 12."[36]

But these comments carry no weight because Bernadette, who had turned 14 on January 7, 1858, usually gave her age as "13." Furthermore, she was so used to doing this that she continued to give this as her age at the time of the apparitions.[37]

It seems clear that Bernadette had not reached puberty at the time of the apparitions. The doctors who examined her in March 1858, hint at this. The journalist, Balech de Lagarde, said as much on September 24, 1858: "She has all the appearances of a child...she is sickly and rickety-looking. She is very small. It is obvious that very often she must have suffered from hunger and thirst."

In centuries past, puberty occurred much later than today. "In cities and in wealthy families," writes Buffon, "children accustomed to abundant and nourishing food arrive at this stage much sooner; in the country and among the poor, the children develop more slowly because they are poorly and inadequately nourished. They require two or three more years."[38]

Jean-Jacques Rousseau, who cites this observation in Emile, attributes this delay, not to undernourishment, but on the contrary, to favorable natural circumstances:

"In countries where the villager eats well and abundantly, as in the Valais and even in certain hilly cantons of Italy, like Friuli, the age of puberty for both sexes is also later than in cities, where, to satisfy vanity, they are often excessively frugal when it comes to food. It is astonishing in these mountains to find full grown boys strong as men, still with a high voice and beardless chin; and full grown girls, in other respects quite mature, but without the periodic symptom of their sex."[39]

We know how Rousseau idolized childhood.

For Bernadette, the delayed onset of puberty must have followed closely on the apparitions, even though, lacking documentation, we cannot say for certain. Nevertheless, in the photos of 1862– 1864, she clearly looks like a girl. And it is significant that in 1863 Madame de la Villemarqué—a woman—put Bernadette at 16.

Significant also was Cros' comment on Bernadette's youthfulness in 1865.

"I do not think it is possible to come across a child who looks younger at 13 than Bernadette does at 21; and her youthfulness has a supernatural charm that is impossible to ignore," etc.

What he meant to describe was a youthfulness "in the face" and thereby a state of Gospel-like childhood.

Other visitors, impressed by her maturity, strike another note. On April 19, 1859, the Englishman, Staden, put Bernadette at "14" (she was barely 15) and noted in her "a calm and composed demeanor that adds a few years to her appearance."[40]

CHAPTER 11

— ⚜ —

THE FINAL MONTHS IN LOURDES

1866 was the last year Bernadette began in Lourdes. Before she left, there were so many requests to see her here and there!

The Journey to Pau

It seems that in the spring of 1866, (though it could have been the preceding autumn[1]), the superior of the hospital, accompanied by Soeur Victorine Poux, took her to Pau as quietly as she could, "to show her to our sisters. Unfortunately, one person recognized her by her hood. In no time, our house was besieged. We had to call the police. A line of mothers with their children gathered in our sisters' courtyard. The police kept order. She went around touching the children. This cost her much hardship and fatigue."

"From Pau, I brought her to Oloron," continued Soeur Victorine.

The same thing happened. A crowd flocked to see her, to touch her. Abbé Souviron, who witnessed the spectacle, asserted that curiosity "sometimes reached fever pitch."

Bernadette was tired, listless; yet she could still react. Someone tried to slip some coins into her hand. She quickly threw them away "with horror."

A procession to the grotto, before the construction of the crypt

The sisters had her climb up into the pulpit in the large recreation hall (today turned into rooms for domestic science classes). She began with the sign of the cross and told the assembled children (at least, this is how they summarized her remarks):

"Always make it that way. This is how the Blessed Virgin made it at the time of her first apparition."[2]

Then she said a few words about the Virgin and recited the rosary. On the way out, she saw the chaplain. He had already spoken to her three years before. He had warned her against the danger of being "the object of so much talk and so many visits."[3]

She still remembered. He was amazed.

But she was visibly exhausted. An asthma attack had started up. The sisters would have liked to keep her, to take care of her. They called for the community doctor, Doctor Casamayor; but Bernadette would not give in. "She was anxious to get back to the hospice." Soeur Victorine brought her back "terribly sick"; she herself would take care of her.

Acceptance

It was time to get Bernadette away from this self-destructive existence. In Nevers there were still some reservations. In a circular letter, the Mother General had warned about admitting postulants "who should be sent home to their families," or subjects who would be "burdensome to the institute."[4] Furthermore, vocations were plentiful, so it was better to be selective.

In April of 1864, Bernadette had written her request for admission to the Sisters of Charity of Nevers.[5] The influence of Bishop Forcade, ecclesiastical superior of the Congregation, had swept away all hesitation. Mère Marie-Thérèse Vauzou, mistress of novices, openly expressed her delight: "It will be one of the greatest joys of my life to see the eyes that have seen the Blessed Virgin."[6]

The house at Nevers was ready to receive Bernadette, who wrote April 28 to announce that she would be leaving Lourdes "before long."[7]

But Bishop Laurence insisted that she be present at the dedication of the crypt, which formed the substructure of the "chapel" requested by Our Lady. Mère Alexandrine, the superior in Lourdes, wrote on May 1, 1866, "Bernadette longs only for the moment of

The "Postulancy" at Lourdes

At Lourdes, Bernadette began "her apprenticeship in the religious life," according to the expression of her Aunt Basile.[8] *This was, in other words, what Bishop Dufêtre, Bishop of Nevers, commenting on the sisters' constitutions of 1852, already called "the postulancy."*[9]

When did it begin?

1. Bernadette could have begun her postulancy no earlier than the end of the year 1865, writes Père Copéré in the articles of the Process of Beatification.[10] *Such is the version in the obituary notice, published April 19, 1879 in the* Conservateur de Nevers (Conservator of Nevers).

2. Her "postulancy" may have started as early as the beginning of 1865, according to Julie Garros, who says, "Bernadette told me that she began her postulancy at the hospice with another girl, Léontine Mouret."[11]

Léontine was indeed at the hospice on February 7, 1865. Bernadette too confirms this in a letter bearing that date. She herself was able to take up her normal life again on January 31, 1865, after having been bedridden during December–January.[12]

3. In his article "Vocation de Bernadette" (The Vocation of Bernadette) (published in Litérature et Religion,)[13] *Dom Bernard introduces some new elements. It was toward the end of Bernadette's stay in Momères (October 3–November 19, 1864) that the superior in Lourdes received an affirmative answer from the Superior General. Bernadette's postulancy would therefore have begun on her return, i.e., the end of November 1864.*

4. Mère Bordenave claims an even earlier date. Bernadette supposedly "shared the life of the community for almost two years, as if she had been a religious," from the day when "she manifested her desire to be received into the Congregation."

Mère Bordenave, followed by Mère Forestier,[14] *was in error, it is true, in dating the event from August 1864, when it was really*

April 1864; but this is obviously a simple misreading. [Note:
Août (August) Avril (April) are words more similar in French
than English.]

    What is to be concluded from all of this?

    Dom Bernard's research has firmly established that the time of
her postulancy was long. It was extended because Bishop
Laurence was eager to have Bernadette attend the dedication of
the grotto crypt, first set for August 15, 1865, then postponed un-
til September 8, then December 8, 1865 and finally to May 19,
1866.[15] The last postponement certainly delayed her departure
from Lourdes.

    Ultimately, it seems artificial to want to date the start of
Bernadette's postulancy mathematically. This initiation was un-
derstood flexibly and progressively in day-to-day living, rather
than in prefabricated rules. The juridical tentacles of the Congre-
gation of Religious had not yet spread out, thanks to inadequate
communications, and it would be an anachronism to impose on
Bernadette the canonical requirements for postulancy.

    The initiation was gradual, with no preliminary ceremony nor
specified duration. It is significant that at that time people never
used the word "postulancy."

    "The years she spent with the sisters at the hospital in Lourdes
were considered sufficient probation," says Abbé Perreau.[16]

    "She shared the life of the community as if she had been a reli-
gious," says Mère Bordenave.[17]

    Thus, Bernadette left the group of boarders to follow the life of
the religious community sometime around her return from
Momères (November 20, 1864) or at the end of that winter, when
she was well again (January 31), and when Marie Mouret [the
sister of Léontine] arrived. In any case, her sickness during De-
cember–January kept her out of community life.

her departure, which I fear will be delayed, if the bishop requires her to remain for some time longer for the good of the grotto.

"Pray hard to the good Lord, dearest Mothers, that this doesn't happen, if it is God's will, so that this child may be protected from vanity and from the greedy eyes of all the religious orders, who, even in our presence, often come with attractive proposals, not realizing that that very thing puts her off and gives her a greater desire to be one of us, even though we have never done anything to recruit her, although we do understand the advantage this can, in some small way, bring to the Congregation."[18]

The Dedication of the Crypt

"There will probably be such a crowd that it will be impossible for us to attend," wrote Mère Alexandrine Roques of the dedication of the crypt in her letter of May 1, 1866.[19] Under such conditions, and in this place where she would be the central focus, how could Bernadette be protected?

On May 17, two nights before the dedication, Bernadette was permitted to go pray at the grotto incognito, with Mère Ursule Court, the superior in Bagnères. A pilgrim asked Mother where the visionary was. Just as the superior was about to answer, Bernadette tugged at "her apron." She understood and gestured evasively.[20]

For the ceremony on the nineteenth, the first day of the triduum, the sisters found it best to put her in the middle of the closed ranks of the Children of Mary. She was shielded by the uniform that made all the girls look alike.

"From the road to the entrance of the hospital and even in the courtyard," said Jeanne Védère, who arrived just as her cousin was coming, dressed like the rest, "you couldn't move because of the *press* (meaning the pressure from the crowd). Several people from Momères told me, 'Make her come out a bit just so we can see her.' Madame la Supérieure made me go into the parlor; she sent for my cousin. When I saw her, I asked Madame la Supérieure to please let her go out a little...because all the people in the courtyard and in front of the cloister wanted to see her. She very readily agreed, provided I wouldn't let anyone come near to touch her. As soon as they saw her, some said:

"'Oh! What a pretty saint!'

"Others, 'The pretty virgin!'

"Still others: 'How happy she is!'

"Poor Bernadette paid no attention at all to what they were saying."

What was on her mind was making sure that her cousin had a good spot...as at the apparition on March 4, 1858.

"'Come with us,' she said to me. 'Otherwise you won't be able to see a thing or hear the sermon; put yourself next to me.'

"'Do you expect me to go with the girls dressed up in white so I'll stand out?'

"'I will tell our dear Mother...to lend you a white uniform.'

"'No, thank you.'

"The sisters agreed with her. I thanked them as well as I could. They wanted me to wear their habit. They told me no one would pay any attention: 'They'll take you for one of our sisters.'

"All I did to make them happy was to remain in Lourdes until the next day. 'If you stay, they told me, we can go out by pretending to accompany you; otherwise, we won't be able to see anything.'

"So to make them happy, I stayed."[21]

The sermon on May 21, 1866, spoke in praise of the bishop, of Curé Peyramale, but made no mention of Bernadette. Despite this discretion, the sisters had to surround her to protect her. Some people even went so far as to snip her veil. She hid herself as best she could among her companions and said, "How stupid they are!"[22]

That evening at the hospice, the crowd gathered in front of the colonnade, slipped through and could not be prevented from shouting for her.

"We had closed all the gates so that the courtyard would not be invaded," relates Mère Ursule Court, "but that did not stop a few people from climbing over the wall to reach Bernadette. The superior [of Lourdes] made me responsible for parading her under the cloister to satisfy public curiosity. Those who had succeeded in getting inside came over to touch her and gave her pictures to touch (too), so they could take them back as souvenirs."

"Meanwhile, Bernadette said to me, 'How really foolish they are! Let them go get those objects touched at the grotto and leave me alone.'"[23]

To protect her from assaults, she had to be put "in the midst of the sisters," and soon they themselves had to be surrounded "by a cordon of soldiers" who were there. They were mobilized. They had "a great deal of trouble maintaining order." Bernadette did not like this at all. She said: "You're showing me off like a rare coin."[24] And again, "You're putting me on display like a prize-winning ox."[25]

At last she was allowed to go back inside.

"The moment we were going through the doorway," Mère Ursule relates,[26] "a soldier approached, clasped Bernadette's hand, then left immediately saying: 'They could've put one hundred francs in my hand and it wouldn't have made me as happy as touching that little girl's hand.'"

The dedication generated much publicity. Pilgrimages multiplied.[27] The problem this created led to the decision to postpone Bernadette's departure no longer.

Another Obstacle

Only one obstacle remained. Along with Bernadette, the sisters were to take Léontine Mouret, her fellow postulant, to Nevers. But Léontine's father objected to her leaving. She was barely seventeen. So, on May 26, 1866, Bernadette wrote to Monsieur Mouret.

"My father was deeply moved on reading this letter," relates Marie Mouret, Léontine's sister. He even shed tears and no longer dared to oppose my sister's vocation."[28]

In the final days, Bernadette was invited to visit the Mouret family with Léontine.[29]

"We left the day before, very happy at the thought of spending a whole day in the country," writes Marie Mouret. "Bernadette was as happy as a lark. We arrived at our parents' [house]. They had prepared a little snack for us. We were barely seated at table, when a servant girl from the hospice came running up. 'Quick, quick, Bernadette,' she urged, 'my dear Mother wants me to tell you to come home as soon as possible. The Bishop of M... has just arrived and wants to see you.'

"A slight reaction of disappointment, quickly suppressed, appeared on Bernadette's gentle face. Then she answered, smiling, 'All right, I'm coming.' And she set out again with the servant."

At the end of spring 1866, everything was settled. On June 15, Bernadette wrote to Mère Ursule Fardes, the former superior (the one who didn't believe in the Lourdes apparitions and who had left the hospice in October 1862). Bernadette informed her that she would be setting out at "the beginning of next month, with Léontine."[30]

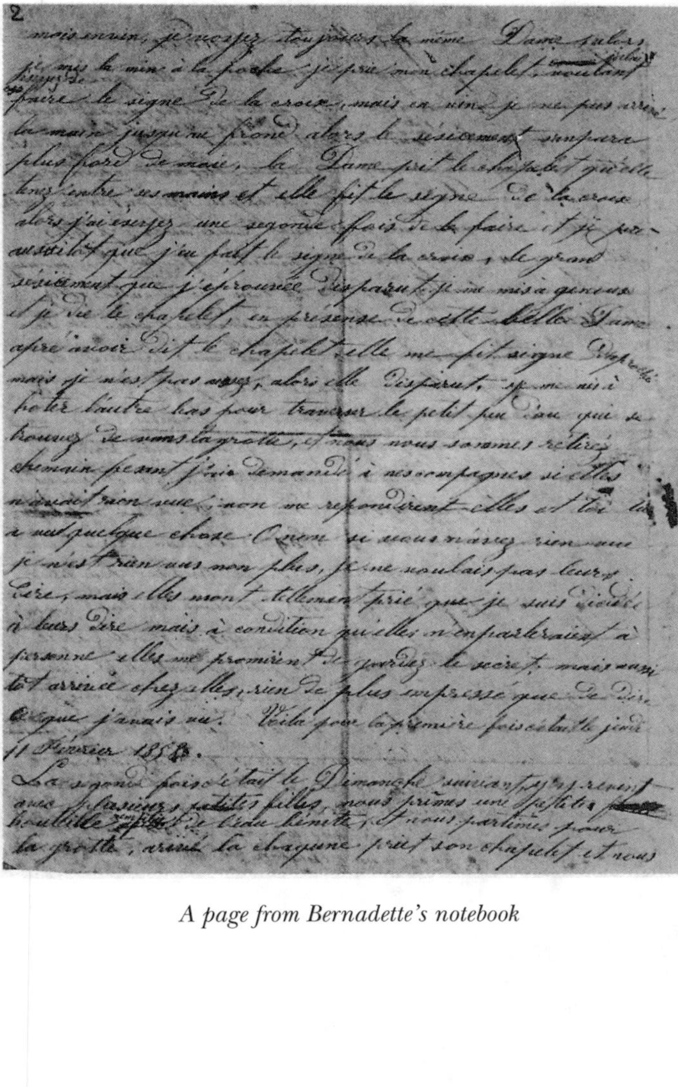

2
mais en vain, je voyez toujours la même Dame alors
je mis la main à la poche je pris mon chapelet, voulant
faire le signe de la croix, mais en vain je ne pus arrivé
la main jusqu'au front alors le saisicement s'empara
plus fort de moi, la Dame prit le chapelet qu'elle
tenez entre ses mains et elle fit le signe de la croix
alors j'ai essayez une seconde fois de le faire et je pus
aussitôt que j'eu fait le signe de la croix, le grand
saisicement que j'éprouvée disparut je me mis à genoux
et je dis le chapelet, en présence de cette belle Dame
après avoir dit le chapelet elle me fit signe d'approcher
mais je n'ai pas osez, alors elle disparut, je me mis à
hoter l'autre bas pour traverser le petit peu d'eau qui se
trouvez devant la grotte, et nous nous sommes retirés
chemin faisant j'ai demandé à mes compagnes si elles
n'avaient rien vue; non me repondirent-elles et toi tu
a vut quelque chose. O non si vous n'avez rien vue
je n'ai rien vus non plus, je ne voulais pas leurs
dire, mais elles m'ont tellement prié que je suis décidé
à leurs dire mais à condition qu'elles n'en parleraient à
personne elles me promirent de gardez le secret, mais aussi
tôt arrivé chez elles, rien de plus empressé que de dire
ce que j'avais vu. Voila pour la première fois c'était le jeudi
11 Février 1858.
La 2e seconde fois c'était le Dimanche suivant, j'y revint
avec plusieurs petites filles, nous primes une petite
bouteille remplie d'eau bénite, et nous partimes pour
la grotte, arrivé la chacune prit son chapelet et nous

A page from Bernadette's notebook

This affectionate letter recalls the memory of an otherwise unknown conversation that seems to indicate her vocation and whose
date must not be much before October 1862: "I like to recall the
day when we were at the woodshed, when you spoke to me about
my vocation. How often I've recalled that little chat. It seems I can
still see you sitting on one step and I on another. I look at it every
time I go there...."[31]

The last days were very busy. Departure time was no time to re-
lax.... Bernadette tried to write in a notebook her final draft of a
journal dedicated to the Queen of Heaven, a detailed account of
the apparitions, already written in a rough draft. She did not have
time to finish the transcription. The notebook, begun on May 12,
1866, stops at the discovery of the spring.[32] Bernadette only had
time to make one copy for Soeur Elisabeth Rigal, who was helping
her with this project. This document has since been lost.[33]

CHAPTER 12

— ⚜ —

GOOD-BYES AND DEPARTURE

The time for farewells had arrived. The news had spread. Lourdes was sorry to be losing Bernadette.

Philomène Nicolau came to shake hands.[1] A mother brought her deformed child, hoping for a miracle. On Corpus Christi, the little Lasbareille boy, his face disfigured by a large wen destroying his eye, was brought to her with the same hope. She kissed him and sent him to the grotto, where he would be cured.[2]

A Marriage Proposal

Bernadette even received a proposal of marriage. The suitor was Raoul de Choisne de Tricqueville. He lived in Nantes and he was a medical intern. He applied to Bishop Laurence, whom he considered morally and to the highest degree the young girl's father: "It seems to me that the best thing I can do is to get married, and I would like to wed Bernadette. If I were not to wed her, I think I would leave the world; I would ask God for the grace to go die in seclusion."[3]

This was not his first letter. It was his last appeal, desperate, polite and already resigned. In fact, the suitor added, "I am grateful to you for the way in which you told me the unvarnished truth. In ac-

Bernadette at her departure from Lourdes on July 2, 1866

tual fact, I am submitting my judgment to yours. I did not think my wishes could jeopardize a work desired by the Blessed Virgin...."

We do not know whether the proposal was forwarded to Bernadette. The fact remains that it was preserved in the archives. Is this the same suitor who made a second attempt at Nevers? We do not know. Might Bernadette have been notified simply as a formality, as Maria Claudia has it in *La Croix* (The Cross) of August 15–16, 1936? This particular detail is more than doubtful.[4]

Final Days

At the end of June 1866, the last visits began. On the twenty-fifth, Mère Alexandrine took Bernadette to Tarbes to see Bishop Laurence, but he was away on a confirmation tour. Two letters, one from Bernadette (June 26),[5] the other from the superior,[6] had to suffice.

Another day was reserved for Bagnères. Mère Alexandrine had promised to visit the local superior, Mère Ursule Court, advising her "Not to extend many invitations," relates Mère Ursule. "However," she continues, "I had invited a few close friends, and in particular Madame Labayle, our doctor's wife. As she left, this lady (now deceased) shook Bernadette's hand and left her a twenty franc coin. Immediately the child handed this coin to me, saying 'Take it, it's burning me!'"[7]

From then on, the sisters got Bernadette to control her reaction, which was to throw the firebrand across the room!

As they were leaving, the two superiors agreed to meet in Tarbes on July 4. From there, they would set off together for Nevers, with their respective postulants.

During these last days, Bernadette paid a visit to Jean-Marie Doucet, the little invalid of March 1858. Fifteen years old now, he was working for Monsieur Dufour, applying color to prints of the apparition and pictures of the visionary.

Jeanne Védère, it seems, then paid a final visit. Bernadette gave her "some rosaries, medals and other small religious objects she had received."[8] She gave her books to the sisters at the hospice: to Soeur Aurélie, *Le combat spirituelle* (The Spiritual Combat); to Soeur Damien, *Amour et confiance* (Love and Trust), with the inscription, "Union of prayer and suffering." The two volumes are kept today in the museum at the convent of Saint-Gildard in Nevers.

A Viron photo, July 2, 1866

Sophie Pailhasson came to ask forgiveness for slapping her on February 15, 1858, but Bernadette had already forgotten that offense, like all the others. She never quite managed to remember them.[9]

With Julie Garros, her fellow-student and tutor, she talked vocation: "Me? A nun? A Sister of Nevers? Absolutely not!" answered the impetuous Julie.[10]

To Jeanne-Marie Garros, formerly a servant with Bernadette at Bartrès, now living in Azereix, "two and a half hours from Lourdes," she gave a present of "a rosary" and of a "medal given to her by a cardinal."[11]

The Departure Photos

On July 2, 1866, two days before she left Lourdes,[12] there was a fifth photo session...the last, thought Bernadette. Philippe Viron, city official and amateur photographer, on his way to setting up shop professionally, got permission to take pictures of the visionary. Viron found out that the bishop had been a barber in the days of his youth. He made references to their common background in order to strike an emotional chord with the bishop. "Imagine, Your Excellency, a poor barber, obliged to work on the holy day of Sunday, eking out his daily bread—obliged, I say, as a result to deprive myself of something for which I shall one day have to account to Almighty God: not keeping holy his holy days. Repenting my best failures up to this very day, and wishing in the future to find another way of living, I come very humbly to implore your assistance by begging you to grant me the same privilege you have granted others and under the same conditions, if there is cause."[13]

So with tripod, black cloth and "magic accordion box," the photographer arrived at the hospice. Viron spread a carpet and hung tapestries, while Bernadette, in anticipation, donned the habit of the Congregation. For the first pictures, seven sisters from the hospice were gathered around her. They had overlooked, on the left within lens range, a broom, on top of a bag or some canvas.

Bernadette changed back to her peasant clothing. More pictures were taken. Except for Soeur Olympe, who got between Soeur Aurélie and Soeur Elisabeth to make room for Bernadette, the sisters remained in place, standing this time.

Farewell photos
Bernadette wore a religious habit (above), then civilian clothes (below).

Standing left to right above are: Soeurs Aurélie Gouteyron, Elisabeth Rigal,
Olympe Bessac and Damien Calmel. Seated are Soeur Victorine Poux,
Bernadette in the habit, Soeur Alexandrine Roques, superior, and Soeur Gilbert Janton.

Below: Soeur Olympe has moved between Soeur Aurélie and
Soeur Elisabeth to make room for Bernadette, standing in the back row.

There was a pause between pictures and several sisters changed places. Soeur Olympe went to Bernadette's left. Soeur Ambroise, who came in late, joined the group.

For the next picture, the photographer added a small round table with a crucifix. This was the last picture taken with the sisters.

Now it was time for the Children of Mary who had wheedled special permission out of Abbé Peyramale. They took the sisters' places around Bernadette, their hands linked in a friendship chain. The tapestries were replaced. To give the scene that wealthy and noble look suitable for respectable young middle-class girls, the photographer set up a balustrade of which only half a pillar can be seen on the edge of the picture. The rest was hidden by flared skirts. These young ladies tried to out do one another in rigidity, in order to hold the pose, especially the completely inflexible Sidonie Méau, who had fluffed up her ample dress as if she were wearing a petticoat. There was something intoxicating about this tempting forbidden fashion—the clergy even looked upon it as "diabolical"!

Finally, the photographer took three pictures of Bernadette by herself.

Was it actually Viron who took all these pictures? Didn't Billard-Perrin also come (right under Dufour's nose!) to take a few photographs? The problem arises because the photos taken of the sisters at the hospice are stamped "Billard-Perrin" and everything, including the presence of Elisabeth Rigal at the hospice, indicates they were taken in 1866.[14]

Internal criticism allows us to credit Viron (who later re-did some negatives of his colleagues) for three photos of Bernadette by herself as well as for the family group. To include everyone, he had taken two separate pictures: her mother's family, then her father's. This latter photo, however, either did not come out or was irretrievably lost; and the first has come down to us in a very defective condition. The rest come from some other source.

That same evening, according to Marie Mouret's testimony, Viron brought the twelve prints Bernadette had asked for. He wanted to give them to her as a present.

"No, no, I want to pay for them, because if you gave them to me, they wouldn't really be mine," Bernadette responded.[15]

She gave them out to her relatives and friends:

"One to Soeur Victorine, one to my sister, Léontine.... I was there," continues Marie Mouret, "and as I watched, silent, looking worried and nervous, she said, 'Ah! what a pretty face you'd make if there weren't one for you! But calm down, I haven't forgotten you. Here, this is the one I've set aside for you....' And she gave me a photograph (on the back, she had written with her own hand, 'Pray for Bernadette Soubirous')."

On the eve of her departure, July 3, 1866, she received a visit from thirteen-year-old Justine Laguës, her wet-nurse's daughter, whom she had held in her lap.

"Doesn't it bother you to leave?" Justine asked.

"With the little time we're here on earth, it must be well spent," Bernadette replied.[16]

Good-bye to Massabielle

That same afternoon, it was good-bye to the grotto. Authors have unjustifiably dramatized the scene. They attributed to Bernadette many memorable words she supposedly uttered on tearing herself away from those "sacred precincts."

"Grotto, I shall see you no more."[17]

"Oh, my Mother! How can I ever leave you?"

"Oh, for mercy's sake! It's for the last time."[18]

"Let me be for one more moment."[19]

"It's the last time."[20]

"It's all over. Never again in my whole life will I come back to Lourdes."[21]

And best of all, Bernadette was supposed to have given this answer to a bystander, who was astonished at her "excessive grief": "Do not be so surprised. In Lourdes, the grotto was my heaven."[22]

Indeed, there are too many such remarks and on too hackneyed a theme for any of them to be trusted. Barbet, the teacher, spoke of Bernadette's "sobs," "flood of tears," of her prostrating herself with "her face flat on the ground, against the earth," "heart-rending scream," etc.

*Above, standing: Soeurs Aurélie Gouteyron, Damien Calmel, Victorine Poux,
Bernadette and Soeurs Savinien and Olympe. Seated are Soeurs Gilbert Janton,
Ambroise and Alexandrine.*
*Below: the Children of Mary. Standing are Sidonie Méau, Bernadette, Sophie Francez,
Adéle Moura. Seated are Ida Ribettes and Philomène Méau.*

Bernadette's farewell to the grotto
(Period print based on Dufour photos)

Indeed Bernadette was deeply attached to the grotto, and leaving it behind was a wrenching experience. But no eyewitness reported such displays of emotion and Mère Bordenave flatly denied them.[23] Even the style of these dramatized accounts shows how contrived they were. As for the words themselves, insofar as they have any foundation at all, we must search for them later, at Nevers, where we will find them in their proper context. Let us trust the closest witness, Basile Castérot, Bernadette's aunt, who spent the evening with her and saw her again the next day: "I was not at the grotto when she went for the last time. I know she felt hurt to be leaving it; but she proved herself to be courageous."[24]

The Last Family Meal

On the evening of July 3, the whole family was gathered for a "farewell dinner" that went on and on. "At eleven o'clock at night, a large crowd was waiting for Bernadette in front of our door, and when she came out, everyone was closing in around her, considering themselves fortunate to be able to touch her."[25]

*The Lacadé Mill, where Bernadette's parents
were living at the time of her departure from Lourdes*

Her close relatives went up to the hospice the following morning for their last good-byes: her father, her mother, "already sick,"[26] her godmother Bernarde, her Aunt Basile and a few others.

The Traveler

Bernadette wore a blue dress she had been given.[27] She must have accepted it, "at the command of the superior of the hospice" contrary to her usual practice, for she refused everything. Now she was a postulant; she must obey.

From Lourdes, which she was leaving forever, she took very little. She had given away all she could. The rest, the essentials, were in a rough canvas bag with vertical rainbow-colored stripes—a functional peasant model that would make a comeback a century later. But the sisters had anticipated a trousseau filling a trunk almost to the breaking point.[28] Entering religious life was like entering married life: the middle-class family, in a time of stability, provided the woman with enough linen to last the rest of her life.

"We were all crying," said Bernadette's six-year-old brother, Bernard-Pierre. "I acted like the rest, without knowing the reason for these tears."[29]

Those tears were not completely shared. "She was very happy to be leaving for Nevers," reported her Aunt Basile. "We were crying, but not her. 'How good of you to cry,' she told us, 'but I can't stay here forever.'"[30]

This eyewitness testimony once again dispels those tasteless fictitious dramas, fabricated by Estrade and Barbet: "Sobs from Bernadette, fainting in her mother's arms or on her lap," etc.

Family photo of July 2, 1866

As with certain difficulties found in the synoptic Gospels, the historian is dealing with the fragmentary nature of the evidence and the inevitable influence of more or less mythic "composition" without which there is no human speech. Here, the catalyst is the "reality-and-myth" of leaving for good and the final separation. The witnesses' statements are like sunlight shimmering on the waves.

Was it the carriage driving away that "tore Bernadette from the arms of her parents," as the historians put it? Yes, it was, according to Marie Mouret.[31] No, it was not, according to Ida Ribettes, who said the *"adieux"* took place at the railroad station, where Bernadette gave her a medal.[32] To reconcile all this, should we say it was the railroad station at *Tarbes?* Ida Ribettes or someone else might have brought Bernadette there by carriage. What brings up this possibility is the fact that Aunt Bernarde, Toinette and Soeur Victorine went there,[33] no doubt because the carriage that left Lourdes with Bernadette would be returning immediately. They took advantage of the unoccupied seats.

The fact remains that a large group was present as she set off from Lourdes. Bernadette had a word for each familiar face: "Adiou, Maria!" she said to Marie Camps.[34]

Lourdes and its mountains faded away in the blue of the horizon.

At Tarbes, they were joined by the superior of Bagnères and her postulant, Marie Larrotis. Aunt Bernarde, Toinette and Soeur Victorine[35] stayed on the platform, with a group of friends and bystanders. A puff of smoke and a flutter of handkerchiefs—this was the second good-bye.

It was not the last, for the Mourets had taken the train with Léontine as far as Andrest (near Vic), where they owned a piece of property. At this stop, Marie Mouret recounts: "A crowd of friends had come to say good-bye to my sister, and they expressed a strong desire to see Bernadette. To satisfy them, she went and stood at the door of the car. But the whistle was already blowing, and they had to leave. They wept as they kissed good-bye, and the train disappeared, carrying the two future sisters toward Nevers."[36]

The castle as seen from the north and the west (above).
Below, X marks the bridge over the rivulet.

Above, the Pont-Vieux (the Old Bridge).

Below, the castle as seen from the east and the south.

PART THREE

— ⚜ —

NEVERS

OR

THE FULFILLMENT
OF THE MESSAGE

July 7, 1866 – April 16, 1879

Chapter 13

— ⚜ —

Arrival at Nevers
and Postulancy

First Stop: Bordeaux

"Let me tell you how we made the trip. We arrived at Bordeaux, at six o'clock in the evening, July 4, 1866, and stayed there till one o'clock Friday. Believe me, we made the most of our time to go sightseeing and in a carriage, if you please! They brought us to see all our houses. I have the honor of telling you that none is like the one in Lourdes...especially the Imperial Institute: you could call it a palace rather than a religious house!

"We went to see the Carmelite church; from there, we set off for the Garonne to see the ships. We went back again to the Botanical Gardens. I must tell you that we saw something new. Guess what? Fish: red, black, white and gray! That's the most beautiful thing I came across: seeing those little creatures swimming in front of a crowd of little children, who were watching them..."[1]

That is how Bernadette described her journey in her letter to the sisters at the hospice of Lourdes (July 20). From this objective account, two impressions emerge:

First, the impressive architecture of the religious houses in Bordeaux, especially the "Imperial Institute" for the education of the deaf. Did Bernadette approve? Did it bother her, given her under-

Bernadette, Dufour photo

standing of evangelical poverty? Here, as elsewhere, she does not judge; but her perceptive and prudent observation gives the reader cause to catch the note of ambivalence, a little like some of John XXIII's talks: conservative out of deference and progressive out of conviction.

What she found "most beautiful," that is, the most moving in the popular meaning of the expression, were the goldfish. Why? Here again we have to guess. Was it the amazement of the village girl who had never seen much of anything? The strong impression "these little creatures" made on her came from a kind of bond she felt with them. Have we not heard her complain about being put on display herself "like some strange creature"? With a very Franciscan sense of kinship, she identified with these "little creatures," fearlessly swimming in front of "a crowd" of onlookers....

Next Stop: Périgueux

On Friday, July 6, the little group of travelers made its second stop at Périgueux. Bernadette's short stay had not been publicized. Nevertheless, they showed her off at Sainte-Ursule's where teachers and students gathered in the parlor; also, at the Miséricorde, the Mercy Home for orphan girls. There Bernadette caressed "the littlest orphan."

At the hospital, where she spent the night, Abbé Plantier, vicar at the cathedral, came to question her about the Virgin's beauty. She supposedly gave this answer, which comes to us in two forms:

"Ah! If men only knew!"

"Ah! If sinners only knew!"[2]

Initial Contacts

The journey from Lourdes to Nevers was quite a trek.

On Saturday, July 7, the third and final stage of the journey, Bernadette took the seven o'clock morning train; she arrived at 10:30 that night. At the Nevers railroad station a carriage was waiting for the two superiors and their three postulants: Marie, Léontine and Bernadette. Just before reaching the top of the hill, the coachman turned left and drove through the convent gate: the one leading to the kitchen steps. The house was silent; the sisters had been asleep since eight o'clock. The welcome was quick and quiet.

Only on the next day did Bernadette and her two companions

Bernadette, Dufour photo, 1863

It was through the old gate leading to the facade (below) and not through the new gate (above) that Bernadette crossed the threshold of Saint-Gildard's Convent.

discover what that large, solidly built house, overlooking the roofs of the lower city looked like. The newcomers were introduced to the Mother General and then led, in keeping with custom, to the statue of the Virgin at the novitiate.

The arrival of Bernadette was an event. Mère Marie-Thérèse Vauzou, mistress of novices, had read the visionary's letter to her novices. In emotional terms, she spoke strongly of the "grace...of receiving Mary's privileged child...."

She allegedly went as far as to say: "For me, it will be the greatest joy of my life, to see the eyes that have seen the Blessed Virgin...."[3]

The novices' eyes were also on the lookout for those eyes. Which of the three new arrivals was Bernadette?

Even as she prayed before going off to do her "morning assignment," Hélène Chautard kept asking herself that very question, scrutinizing the trio furtively. "It's the smallest one," she rightly guessed.[4]

The famed visionary took part in recreation. Soeur Lucie Cloris[5] was astonished that "she was no different from the other postulants," except, perhaps, that she was much "shyer."

The Account of July 8

The difficulty for the superiors was to keep Bernadette from becoming once again the "strange creature," the "goldfish" that everybody could observe in the aquarium of the motherhouse. That would be unhealthy for her as well as for her companions. They had to anticipate the feverish and emotional epidemics that threaten to run through any house of solitude and prayer. Interest and curiosity are nevertheless legitimate. To govern is to organize, to channel. Therefore, Bernadette would tell her "story," once and for all, in front of the entire assembled community. Afterwards, no one was to speak to her anymore about the apparitions.

On Sunday, July 8, at one o'clock in the afternoon, the novices and postulants were assembled in the novitiate conference hall. The whole community was invited, including the sisters of the two other communities in Nevers—about three hundred persons in all. Mother General presided, surrounded by her Council and the two superiors from the Pyrénées.

Usually, postulants were dressed as such as soon as they entered. On this day, however, an exception was made for a touch of local color. This way, the sisters could see Bernadette's famous hooded cape, popularized by the photos of Bernadou, Dufour, Billard-Perrin, and Viron. This would also be a way to make a clean break between the "before" and the "after": the past in Lourdes, which Bernadette would describe for the last time, and the silence that she would observe on taking the religious habit.

Bernadette stood in front of the mistress of novices, facing the large audience of nuns. A less than cordial Mère Joséphine Imbert gave her the floor. She was anxious and determined not to give Bernadette any occasion for pride. The visionary sensed her coolness. She hesitated, then spoke first in patois, listlessly giving a few boring points from the usual narrative: gathering wood, the gust of wind, the lady in the white dress and blue sash. Mère Marie-Thérèse Vauzou and, perhaps Mother General asked a few questions to goad her into expanding on her story.

When Bernadette spoke of the muddy water she had thrown up three times on February 25, in spite of the order to drink it, Mère Alexandrine Roques, superior in Lourdes went through the ritual humiliation: "You can determine from that her lack of mortification."

Mère Marie-Thérèse Vauzou drove home the point: "You were not very mortified!"

In a playful tone, Bernadette answered innocently, "It was because the water was so dirty!"[6]

Asked about what happened on March 25, Bernadette spontaneously reenacted the Virgin's gesture. This emotional moment was recalled by five witnesses.

The "secrets" preoccupied Mère Vauzou. She liked openness in her novices; Bernadette sidestepped the question, as usual.

Then Bernadette was asked how she came to Nevers. She explained that two Congregations in particular had made overtures. "There was even one which bore the name of the Immaculate," she specifically stated. The sisters in question had been founded in 1863 by Père Peydessus.[7]

"Don't you know, my child," replied Mère Marie-Thérèse, "that our Congregation was one of the first to be dedicated to the Immaculate Conception?"[8]

On December 8, 1854, the day this dogma was promulgated, the Congregation had indeed consecrated itself to the Immaculate Conception and every year, on December 8, renewed this act.

The novitiate conference hall and the celebrated hooded cape of the apparitions

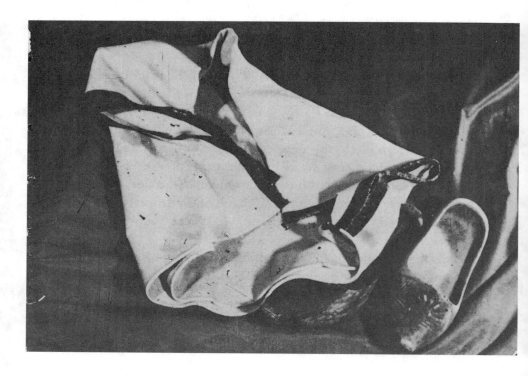

The meeting was over. Mother General firmly took the floor again: from then on, the sisters were no longer to mention the apparitions, either to Bernadette or among themselves.

Already news had gotten around town. The bell at the convent gate never stopped ringing. The townsfolk were asking to see the visionary. It was definitely not easy to have a Bernadette in the house! The superior general gave no permissions.[9] However, the students at the boarding school of Notre-Dame des Anges (Our Lady of the Angels) were allowed to attend Vespers in the community chapel. The girls were hoping to see Bernadette. But the new postulant had now put on a postulant's uniform. It was impossible to pick her out in the compact group wearing shoulder capes and fluted caps. The boarders did not give up that easily. On the way out, according to Soeur Emilienne Duboé, they went and stood "in a row along the community's passageway," and secretly stuck their skirts out and in that way brushed against each of the postulants who passed in front of them, so they could say that their clothing had been touched by the visionary.[10]

Orientation

According to custom at the motherhouse, two novices were entrusted with initiating the new arrivals during the first week.

Bernadette's two "guardian angels" were two Pyrénéennes, originally from Bagnères: Soeur Emilienne Duboé, who had met her in 1862, and Soeur Philomène Tourré.

"I helped her unpack the trunk she brought from Lourdes," relates Soeur Emilienne. "The good sisters had included some chocolate and other goodies.... Bernadette said to me: 'They'll take me for a glutton when I bring these edibles to our mistress.'

"The trunk also contained flannel shirts that the sisters in Lourdes had packed because of her asthma. She thought they had been overly considerate about her because she said, 'the other sisters couldn't use flannel.' She also thought they had packed too many linens, saying 'she'd never live long enough to wear them all out.'

"Lastly, we found a box of snuff and some colored handkerchiefs. She made a big fuss because she'd be the only one to take snuff and to have colored handkerchiefs. Although the doctor had prescribed the use of snuff for her, she was afraid of making herself conspicuous. Her superiors wanted her to follow the doctor's order...

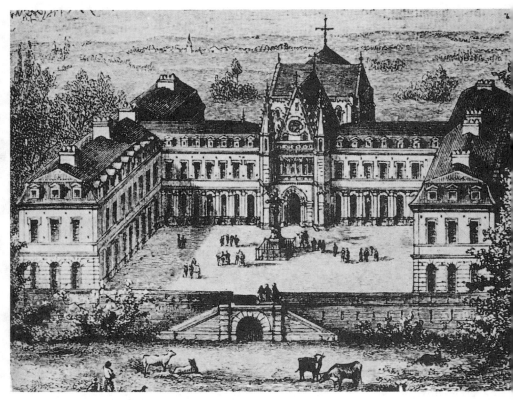

The Convent of Saint-Gildard in Nevers

"During these first few days...Soeur Marie-Bernard was feeling very bad and...would often weep. I asked her why, thinking she was upset at being separated from her parents. She answered that she had already sacrificed her family but that she missed her visits to the grotto. She didn't think she could ever get used to this loss."[11]

"She added," Soeur Emilienne said somewhere else, 'If you only knew what a beautiful thing I saw there!' I was tempted to ask her about it, but she answered that she could say nothing, that our mistress had forbidden it. 'If you only knew how good the Blessed Virgin is!'"[12]

Bernadette herself confirmed the difficulties she had in getting accustomed to her new life. Eleven years later, in July 1877, she still remembered and told Procule Borot, a postulant suffering from a similar depression: "Oh! I was very upset at the beginning. Whenever I got a letter from home, I waited till I was alone to open it, because I felt I couldn't read it without bursting into tears."[13]

In her letter of July 20, 1866, she shared this tearful memory with the sisters in Lourdes: "I must tell you that Léontine and I gave a

The "fluted bonnet" worn by postulants fell out of use in 1942

good watering to the whole of Sunday with our tears! The good sisters encouraged us by telling us that was the sign of a good vocation"[14]

In those days, this was a typical occurrence among those stay-at-home girls who never left their family or their country and who thought they would never see them again.... At the time Bernadette wrote this, however, the crisis was over. She concluded, "I assure you that now it would be a far more bitter sacrifice if we had to leave our dear novitiate. We feel this is the good Lord's house. We have to love it in spite of ourselves! Everything there sustains us, and especially the directions of our dear mistress. Every word that comes from her mouth goes straight to the heart."[15]

Thus did Bernadette, for Soeur Philomène's use, confirm with conviction, as early as the first few days, the definition of the novitiate that she had drawn up in her letter of April 28, 1866: "A genuine heaven on earth."[16]

Soeur Emilienne said that, most of all it was the grotto Bernadette missed. Her July 20 letter to the sisters of the hospice in Lourdes gives evidence of this:

"I beg you, my very dear sisters, to be good enough to offer a few prayers...for me...*especially when you go to the grotto.* That is where you will find me in spirit, *clinging to the foot of that ledge I love so much...*"

At this time then, the grotto was at the origin of her tears and of her consolations. She took comfort in another grotto. Indeed, she continued:

"For my part, I never forget you before Our Lady of the Waters, which is at the foot of the garden, *in a kind of grotto.* That was where I went to unburden my heart those first few days and since then, our dear mistress has been kind enough to let us go there every day."[17]

The grotto inspired her to invent a game during those early days: "She picked up three little stones in the novitiate courtyard. 'These are my companions whom I love,' she said as she showed them.

"On one she had written 'Lourdes'; on the second, 'the grotto'; and on the third, 'Nevers, motherhouse.'

"To those who asked her why she indulged herself in this whimsical ritual, she replied, 'It's fun, it relaxes me and brings back many memories.'"[18]

It was a way of changing her sadness into smiles, and of brightening the monotonous recreations, as she used to do in Lourdes.

Our Lady of the Waters, at the foot of the garden at Saint-Gildard's

"Do they play jump rope in the novitiate?" she asked in the early days.

"No, but our recreations are always very enjoyable."

"It's because I really like swinging the rope for others to jump."[19]

In sorrow as in joy, Bernadette was all ears for Soeur Emilienne's instructions.

She insisted on knowing what she had to do, asserting that she didn't want to fall short in any of her duties.[20]

She couldn't understand why people were not on time for community exercises.[21]

Innately compassionate, she was attentive to others. At the novitiate, she met a novice from Gannat, Soeur Emilienne Chataignon. Bernadette initiated the conversation:

"The sisters in Gannat had written to me in Lourdes asking me to pray for a sick novice...."

"I'm the one!" answered Soeur Emilienne.

"I went to the grotto three times to pray for you...."

"And, little by little, I got better, after receiving the water and the medal you sent me."

"If the good Lord gave you back your health, it was so you could work for the Congregation, but above all for your own perfection," Bernadette finished.[22]

In the early days, Bernadette suffered from the food that was "too rich for her delicate stomach."

"But she forbade anyone to tell any superior.... She would rather suffer than appear finicky,"[23] reported her other guardian angel, Soeur Philomène.

It was hot. Bernadette was thirsty. Soeur Emilienne Duboé noticed.

"Seeing her suffer, I didn't want her to drink anything except water, but not being bold enough to go to the kitchen for the key to the refectory, I went through an open window on the side of the cloister.[24] Bernadette was not pleased. 'That's acting just like thieves,' she said. She got very angry.[25] From then on, even though she would again suffer from thirst, she wanted no more help from me."[26]

Her guardian angel also remembered Bernadette's lectures on her slipshod signs of the cross: "'You must pay attention,' she told me, 'because it's quite an achievement to make the sign of the cross well.'"[27]

"She also said, 'If we had faith, we would see God in everything.'"[28]

Trials of the Novitiate

Concerned about the humility of her far-too-famous novice, Mère Marie-Thérèse often reproved her...and missed no opportunity to reprimand her. "One day, I asked Soeur Marie-Bernard if the way they treated her made her feel sad," a fellow novice relates.

"'Oh, no!' she answered. 'The mistress of novices is quite right, because I have a lot of pride; but now that I'm here, I'll work on mending my ways. It's not like in Lourdes, where I was surrounded by too many people.'"[29]

At the novitiate, Bernadette experienced another trial for the second time—academic difficulties. In the early days, she was given a grammar assignment that went over her head:

She stood up and with simplicity replied, "Dear Sister, I don't know how to do a verb."[30]

As to the ordeal of visits, they were lessened but not abolished.

On July 12, her first Thursday at Nevers, Mother General took Bernadette to the sisters' house in Varennes, a little over four miles from the motherhouse. En route, they came upon a squad of minor seminarians from Pignelin, led by Abbé Benoit:

"Look, children," he exclaimed, "the young girl you see over there is Bernadette, the visionary of Lourdes."

The carriage was immediately surrounded.[31]

On Thursday, July 19, Bernadette was called to the parlor. There were three bishops there: Bishop Forcade (was this the first time she had seen him since the decisive conversation of 1863?); Bishop de Marguerye, Bishop of Autun; and Bishop de Mérode, titular archbishop and "Chaplain to the Holy Father." She gave an account of the apparitions one more time.[32]

Bernadette was still wearing the fluted cap of a postulant, which she would put aside before the end of that month, in favor of the cornette of the Sisters of Nevers.

Retreat before the Clothing Ceremony

The next day, July 20, the Council met in chapter. Bernadette was to receive the religious habit and become a novice.

The retreat was opened by a Marist, Père Douce, chaplain at

The novitiate garden

Saint-Gildard's and a devout and austere man.[33] He would be Bernadette's confessor and director until September 28, 1876.

The rest of the retreat was preached by Père Raccourt, also a Marist priest.

Bernadette led the procession on the day of her reception of the habit.... This was not to make her conspicuous, but the novices went according to height, and she was the shortest: four feet, six inches.[34] During the clothing ceremony her partner was Soeur Emilie Marcillac. They both noticed one novice "who always kept her eyes closed out of devotion." This made Bernadette laugh. She said, "Look...if she didn't have her partner to guide her, she would've had an accident by now. Why close your eyes, when you ought to keep them open?"[35]

Soeur Emilie emphasized that Bernadette, on the other hand, "was very natural, without any affectation. She behaved like everyone else, but better than everyone else."

What Bernadette received at the grotto, she felt she had received through her eyes. At Nevers, as in Lourdes, she remained the woman with open eyes: the eyes of the body and the eyes of faith.

CHAPTER 14

— ⚜ —

THE NOVITIATE

On July 29, 1866, the feast of Saint Martha, forty-four postulants took the habit, while nineteen novices made their profession.[1]

During the ceremony "the people looked first to see Bernadette, but...they could not distinguish her from her companions, except by her extreme shortness of stature," noted Count Lafond.[2]

Bishop Forcade presided over the ceremony. After the general questions, answered by one postulant in the name of all, the forty-four "little bonnets" left chapel briefly to put on the religious habit, while the congregation sang Psalms 126, 132, and 140. They returned wearing the white veil, a loosely fastened bridal veil, to be replaced by the black veil. The bishop addressed the group in French: "You are about to receive a new name, which will remind you that you are separated from the world and that you belong to Jesus Christ, whom you desire to choose as your spouse."[3]

After this, he gave each sister her veil, pronouncing in Latin the ritual formula, taken from Saint Paul (Eph 4:24) and from the rite of tonsure: "Soeur Marie-Bernard, may the Lord clothe you with the new self, created according to the likeness of God in true righteousness and holiness. Amen."

This was the first time Bernadette had been called by her religious name. Mère Marie-Thérèse Vauzou had explained this choice to the novices as follows: "It was only right that I give her the name of the Blessed Virgin, whose child she is; I wanted her to keep the name of her patron saint, of which Bernadette is a diminutive."[4]

Bernadette left the chapel, coifed in the cornette with the two white bands hanging loosely in a diagonal line beneath the chin; the cornette disappeared a century later, following the Second Vatican Council.

Before taking the habit, each retreatant had solicited prayers.

Soeur Charles Ramillon[5] related: "Soeur Marie-Bernard asked me for an *Ave Maria*.... She was to say one for me. On the morning we were to take the habit, she whispered to me: *'Ave Maria.'*

"I answered, *'Ave Maria.'* And on the spot, we recited this prayer, each by herself. The intention we had made was that we would persevere."[6]

Soeur Charles worded her prayer [to the Blessed Mother] as follows, "My good Mother, I am going to recite this *Ave*, only to keep my part of the bargain, because you have already assured her of her salvation; but hear the prayer that Soeur Marie-Bernard is offering you for me."[7]

Bishop de Mérode, the Archbishop of Mélitène, who was at Pougues, availing himself of the mineral springs, came to Nevers for the clothing ceremony. He celebrated Vespers and asked to see Bernadette. He was accompanied by Count Lafond and his wife, who were entertaining him at the Chateau de Nozet near Pouilly. The Count and Countess wanted to give Soeur Marie-Bernard an offering of one hundred francs for Lourdes. But she was no longer bound by obedience to accept it as she was at the hospice. She answered decisively: "I wish neither to accept nor to forward this money."[8] They would send the offering directly to Bishop Laurence.

No sooner had the habit been taken than the novices were dispersed among the various houses of the Congregation. They were receiving their training by doing hands-on work: an energizing approach that involved the local communities in the formation of the young sisters...until the Roman Congregation suspended this practice.

Bernadette now became a problem. Her presence risked creating a difficulty for the community that received her as well as for herself. The motherhouse was best suited to shelter her. It was de-

Bernadette and the Convent of Saint-Gildard

cided to keep her there. But being an exception weighed heavily upon her. To Soeur Emilienne Duboé, who was displeased at being assigned to Clermont-Ferrand, she replied, "After a retreat like the one we just made, you're not very generous! How happy I'd be to be able to go out and work! But I'm forced to stay here and do nothing."[9] [Here Bernadette used *vous,* the formal French word for *you.*]

After saying this, she comforted Soeur Emilienne and went back to using *tu,* the familiar form of *you.* "Promise me you'll say your rosary every day."[10]

Bernadette was thankful for the new habit that shielded her by making her look like the others, especially the veil, which kept her hidden from pryers. She liked to bring the veil forward, as she had done with the hood on her cape at the time of the apparitions;[11] she wrapped up in it during her thanksgiving. But the novitiate was no place for complacency. To the mistress of novices who asked her why she did this, and to the novices, who teased her, she replied, "It's my little house."[12]

Had she not, in those days, expressed the motive that had brought her to the motherhouse? "I came to hide myself."[13]

August 15–October 30, 1866

We know about the August 15–October 30, 1866 interval from the novices who returned to Nevers to prepare for their profession on October 30. The new arrivals had not heard Bernadette's account, nor had they received the order not to mention the apparitions. The association of ideas brought them back to Lourdes and to the grotto:

One day Soeur Anne-Marie Thomas asked Soeur Marie-Bernard, "Why won't you say what the Blessed Virgin told you?"

"Then it wouldn't be a secret anymore."[14]

Though the tear-filled days had come to an end, Bernadette still felt a smidgen of nostalgia. To one of her companions, Soeur Dominique Hostalot, she said one day, "Ah, Soeur Dominique! How I'd like to see the grotto again!"[15]

In the Infirmary

Around August 15, Bernadette entered the infirmary. At the time, the reason was only fatigue. She helped out as a nurse's aide. At the beginning of September, however, her asthma grew worse, and she had to remain in bed.

The first few days, her neighbor in the next bed was another postulant, Annette Basset, whose health seemed insufficient for the religious life. Doctor Robert Saint-Cyr advised that she be sent home. Tearfully, she confided her sorrow to Bernadette. She affirms that she then got this answer, "Don't cry, Mademoiselle. The good Lord wants you to be a nun. And you will be, but in another Congregation."[16]

Annette left the following September 3 and entered the Sisters of Saint Joseph of Cluny, where she ended her days, sixty years later, under the name of Soeur Bertilie (†April 25, 1926).

One day during recreation, Soeur Julienne Cayssalié noticed Bernadette halfway down the Saint Gertrude staircase. She called her: "Come with us!"

"I don't have permission to come down,"[17] Bernadette responded.

Soeur Emilie Marcillac, nurse's aide, testified that Bernadette's sickness became serious: "Several times, I was on the verge of getting Mother Mistress of Novices. I thought she was going to choke at any moment. She didn't complain."[18]

"You're suffering a great deal, my poor Sister!" said Soeur Emilie.

"It's necessary; it's nothing," Bernadette answered.[19]

Soeur Eléonore Lacroux was assigned to keep watch over her during the night. But Bernadette was concerned over Sister's sleep, as she had been at Lourdes about Soeur Marie-Géraud.

"Rest in that armchair," she told her. "I'll call you when I have to."[20]

Her concern for others won out over her own suffering. "She apologized for the fact that her coughing might keep me from sleeping," relates her fellow-patient, Soeur Emilie.[21]

What struck Soeur Victoire Talbotier, another fellow-patient of Bernadette's, was her patience during the long nights of choking, more painful episodes than those that occurred during the day, confirmed another witness.[22] She could not help but voice her admiration. Bernadette answered, "The good Lord sends it; I must accept it."[23]

Bernadette took no pride in her courage. Soeur Hélène Sutra, whom she advised to be patient, answered her one day: "It's quite easy for you...after all the graces and privileges you've received...."

"It's true, I've been very spoiled...privileged.... If I didn't act accordingly I'd be really sinful."[24]

Soeur Hélène was surprised at the poignancy of this reply, because Bernadette always thought people "did too much for her." Soeur Hélène also reported that Bernadette said to her: "Don't disturb yourself. You might need it more than I do."

If Bernadette complained of anything, it was that she was too well taken care of: "The poor aren't treated like this."[25] She often repeated these words during her bouts of illness.

What weighed on her the most was inactivity, uselessness. When Soeur Emilie asked her for a prayer, she agreed, adding, "But you pray for me, too; I'm good for nothing."[26]

She was still appreciative of friendship and didn't hide this fact.

Soeur Emilie relates, "Whenever I needed a helper in the infirmary, I would choose a novice from Lourdes, knowing this would be pleasant for both of them."

She was, no doubt, referring to Léontine Mouret, Bernadette's traveling companion, now Soeur Alexandrine.

Soeur Emilie continues: "But one day, the mistress of novices asked me the reason for my choice and forbade me from then on to take Bernadette's friend. The next day, seeing another novice, Bernadette asked me if her companion from Lourdes was sick. I told her, 'No, but the mistress of novices forbade me to take her.'

"'Ah! I understand,' she replied.

"From the slight cloud that came over her face, I understood that the sacrifice was painful, but she did not complain."[27]

Food still gave her trouble, but very few were those who noticed.

"When I brought her breakfast," Soeur Marcillac relates, "she would say, 'You're bringing me my penance.' And she took it without saying another word.[28] She never refused anything I brought her."[29]

In her greatest suffering, when "fits of coughing tore at her chest," she kept herself from groaning and complaining, and only said, "My Jesus!"

"At the same time, she looked at her crucifix...and there was in this look an expression that spoke volumes," Soeur Marcillac testified.

As soon as Bernadette was better, she mobilized her strength and her infectious happiness for the service of others.

"One day," Soeur Emilie recalled, "I had taken a postulant to help me carry supper to the patients in the infirmary. The postulant, moving a bit roughly, dropped the board she was carrying, and everything spilt into the corridor...I cried out: 'We're lost!'

"Soeur Marie-Bernard came running at the noise. 'My poor Soeur Emilie, why feel sad like that? You are not lost; calm down! I'll take care of things with my dear Soeur Marthe' (who was the first infirmarian).

"The next day when I came to the infirmary, she said to me, laughing, 'You're not lost yet!'"[30]

She loved "to tease" and to joke during recreations.

"She sang songs in the patois of the Pyrénées; she was happy and laughed heartily seeing that I couldn't understand a word," remembered Soeur Emilie Marcillac.[31]

This attentiveness toward others was inseparable from her attentiveness toward God. "Everything brought her back there; it was her center," Mère Bordenave noted.[32] "She used to say, 'God is so offended![33] All this is good for heaven.'"[34]

And when she was unable to carry out the exercises prescribed by the Rule, she explained simply, "The good Lord doesn't want it, *fiat!* (so be it)."[35]

Profession in Danger of Death

On October 25, Bernadette was at her worst. Mère Marie-Thérèse Vauzou had visited her every day.[36] She marshaled prayers at the novitiate. Countless candles burned in front of the Virgin's statue. Soeur Emilienne Vallat informs us that they made as many as "nine novenas in one day." It seemed all was in vain. Doctor Robert Saint-Cyr, the community doctor, announced that she would not last the night. Soeur Marcelline Lannessans, her infirmary roommate, was transferred to another room. Mère Marie-Thérèse prepared Bernadette for death and had her receive the Anointing of the Sick, called at that time Extreme Unction.

The Council, in emergency session, made the decision to admit her to religious profession. The bishop's dispensation was needed for this, but he was on a Confirmation tour. As soon as he returned, around seven o'clock in the evening, he was apprised of the situation. He himself describes what followed:

"My valet came to tell me that two Sisters of Nevers had come running to the bishop's house, asking to talk to me right away on an urgent matter. I hastened to see them....

Bishop Forcade, Bishop of Nevers

"'Soeur Marie-Bernard won't last the night,' [one sister explained], 'and Mother General sends us to ask your permission to admit her to profession.'

"'I am unwilling to yield the honor of receiving her profession to anyone.... Go back to Saint-Gildard's and announce me. I'll be right behind you.'

"As a matter of fact, I got there almost as soon as they did, and I hastened to go up to the infirmary. I found the patient panting, if not at her last gasp. She had just vomited a basin of blood, which was still there by her bed. I went over to her [and said],

"'You're going to die, my dear child, and I'm told that you wish to make your profession. Here I am to receive it.' Then in a faint voice she answered,

"'I won't be able to say the formula...no strength.'

"'That's no trouble; I will say it for you. All you'll have to do is say: "Amen...So be it!"'

"And so it was. I spoke a few words of encouragement to her. I blessed her. I begged her not to forget me in heaven, and I left, deeply moved, convinced that I would never see her alive again.

"The superior general stayed at the foot of the bed, with the devout intention of closing her eyes. Scarcely had I left, when the dying nun recovered her speech, and said smilingly to the superior, 'You had me make my profession because you thought that I was going to die tonight; well, I won't die tonight.'

"'What's that?' the superior snapped back sharply. 'You knew you weren't going to die tonight, and you didn't tell me? And so you caused the bishop to be sent for at such a late hour, and everything has been thrown into chaos because of you. You're nothing but a little fool. I tell you that if you're not dead by tomorrow morning, I'll take away the profession veil you've just received, and I shall send you back to the novitiate with the veil of a simple novice.'

"Remaining calm and continuing to smile, the sister said, 'As you please, my dear Mother.'

"The next morning, Soeur Marie-Bernard was not dead, and soon after, she humbly returned to the novitiate as a novice and with her novice's veil."[37]

Bishop Forcade's enthusiastic account has shattered the actual time frame and spiced up the superior's dressing-down. We shall not linger to discuss the minor adjustments found in the *Logia*.[38]

As for the canonical problem, vows taken "at the point of death" became invalid if the person recovered, but the decision committed the Council from then on in regard to Bernadette. At the regularly scheduled date of her profession, her case would not be reexamined. The Council would simply refer to the deliberations of October 25, as the registers prove.

As for the rest, one fact remains: Bernadette kept the insignia of her profession during the first few days, as Soeur Charles Ramillon attested:

"I recall seeing on her bed her crucifix, her profession veil and some books [probably the Manual and the Rule, two books given on profession day]. I said to her with a smile, 'You thief!'"

"She answered, 'Fine, a thief! But in the meantime, they are mine; I'm keeping them. I belong to the Congregation and they can't send me away.'"[39]

This was no act...Bernadette was jubilant, because being professed eliminated the fear that had kept her in suspense. Would the sisters keep her? Would she have to be sent away like others, more robust than she, had been? There was no longer a possibility of dismissing her for "reasons of health." It was a heavy load off her mind, as Soeur Marcelline confirmed: "I shall never forget how happy she looked when she showed me her crucifix and said, 'I've got it. I'm hanging on to it. It's mine. I belong to the Congregation! They can no longer send me away!'"[40]

She loved to look at the crucifix, to hold it in her hands in times of suffering. "My real support," she would say from that time on.[41]

Soeur Emilie continues, "For a few days, she kept her worsted veil. (reserved for the professed sisters) on her bed. She'd show it to me and keep saying, 'I'm in!'"

"Then I said, 'It's really nice, Soeur Marie-Bernard, to play tricks like that!'"

"She was happy, and she'd laugh...."[42]

She seems to have said something similar to the then chaplain, Père Douce: "I've got my veil. I won't let go of it."[43]

To Soeur Emilie, Bernadette merely said, "The good Lord did not want me. I went up to the door, and he told me, 'Go away; it's too soon.'"[44]

To Soeur Louise Lanchèze: "I'm still much too wicked; the good Lord wanted no part of me."[45]

Her Mother's Death

The year ended on a sad note: Louise Soubirous' death. Soeur Victorine Poux, on her way to Vespers, had gone to see the sick woman. She had been edified by Louise's resignation.

"I talked to her about Bernadette," she relates. "I said I'd write to her. She made a sign of approval. When I returned from Vespers, she was dead."[46]

These Vespers of the Immaculate Conception were the first to be celebrated in the crypt. Louise was 41 years old. She completed a life prematurely worn down by toil and poverty. On February 12, 1867, Bernadette wrote to Abbé Pomian, "I cannot tell you the sorrow I felt upon suddenly learning of my mother's death. I learned of her death sooner than her illness."[47]

She had received word of her mother's death on December 10 or 11. She asked when it had occurred and, on hearing it had taken place on the feast of the Immaculate Conception, she said, "Well done, for now she's in heaven."[48]

Friendship with Jeanne Lannessans

The above statement of Bernadette has come down to us through the most intimate witness of this period, Jeanne Lannessans, who came from the Basses-Pyrénées. She had arrived at the motherhouse in August, 1865. In Lourdes she had consulted Bernadette about her vocation that was encountering some difficulties. She had received this answer: "Pray, persevere. I'll pray for you. You'll be successful."

The sisters' Chapter of September 27–28, 1866, admitted Jeanne to profession, but as she was nearing her goal, her difficulties began again. She fell ill and left the novitiate for the infirmary, where she became Bernadette's roommate. During recuperation, they used to sing together in patois to encourage one another. On October 24, Jeanne had been transferred to another room to spare her the emotion of Bernadette's profession and probable death.

When things got better, their separation weighed heavily on them. One day, at mealtime, the infirmary was deserted relates Jeanne. "She called me...asking me to come see her; I told her I couldn't because they had taken away my clothes. Finally, I looked around the room; I saw a mantle hanging from a nail.... I got up.... She told me to hurry so no one would catch us. We were not dis-

Louise Castérot, Bernadette's mother

obeying, for no one had told us not to. We embraced each other and parted company—both very happy."[49]

Soon after, Bernadette and Jeanne were again put in the same room; where they convalesced together over several months.

"On confession day, we teased each other," Jeanne recounted. "I wanted her to go to confession first. I asked her to talk a little loudly, not to hear her sins, but to learn how to go to confession myself. Quite calmly she replied, 'My dear friend, "give honor where honor is due": you are the elder, you should go first.'"[50]

"I asked her to pray for my recovery. She set about it and made a novena. At the end of the novena she said, 'You will not recover from this sickness, but you won't die either. The only thing is, you will suffer. You'll have to work hard to win heaven.'

"Since that time, I have never stopped suffering from this same sickness. I have always devoted myself to my work, except during extra violent attacks, and I do hope to win heaven."[51]

Jeanne's health improved, at least enough for her to make her profession on February 4, 1867. That morning the bishop came for her and her alone. She took the name Soeur Marcelline.

The Shadow of Lourdes

In the intimacy of common life in the infirmary, where the ban on speaking about Lourdes was not observed, Jeanne Lannessans had tried to satisfy her curiosity about the apparitions.

"Wasn't one of the Blessed Virgin's secrets that you were to join the Sisters of Nevers?" she asked.

Bernadette answered, "You're too nosy; you won't find out a thing."[52]

Bernadette told her that she "hated the visits," and that "the superior general had truly to tell the dear visiting sisters not to ask her...useless questions," seeing "that anyone could get the account of the apparitions at little cost." The account referred to here cost "one franc," or by mail, "one franc ten." It was the work of Canon Fourcade, secretary of the commission of inquiry on the apparitions. Bernadette considered it an accurate, well-balanced, and faithful copy of her own description of what her memory had gleaned from the experience.

When visiting sisters came to the infirmary to question her about the apparitions, Bernadette answered in Soeur Marcelline's presence, "I'm not allowed."

Going back over a singular past would have only distracted her from the rigorous path of faith that from then on would be hers. This was something she was well aware of.

It was quite enough that she would be summoned to judge images of the Virgin, in particular the statue at the novitiate: "Isn't she beautiful?"

"You think so? I don't."[53]

To Mère Marie-Thérèse Vauzou, who couldn't keep from asking a question on the same subject, she gave a similar answer: "Mère, I can find no beautiful image of the Virgin."[54]

Bernadette made an effort to speak in generalities, which would provoke no discussion. "The Blessed Virgin cannot be depicted here on earth," she told Soeur Joseph Caldairou.[55]

Jeanne Lannessans described Bernadette's piety during this period in the following words: "Nothing out of the ordinary...[except] her preparations for Holy Communion and her thanksgiving, which she made beside my bed.... Gazing on her face, it was easy for me to do it, too. She had lively faith in the Eucharist. She preferred to read books...on the Eucharist, on the Passion...the New Testament, and the Imitation of Christ."[56]

Jeanne still remembered those trivial or comic touches: "One day, Bernadette [was praying to the Blessed Virgin for me, but she] knelt down before [the statue of] Saint Joseph. I pointed this out to her. She answered, 'In heaven there's no jealousy.'"[57]

To Mère Alexandrine Roques, superior of the hospice, Bernadette was to write in the same vein (on April 13, 1872) in connection with a novena to the Blessed Virgin: "I wouldn't like to hurt Saint Joseph's feelings; I love him very much, but in heaven they don't get angry."[58]

Lastly, on being informed about the battles being waged at that time against the Papal States, even Bernadette grew inflamed, saying of the "principal" aggressor (was she thinking of Cavour or Garibaldi?):

"The good Lord should send him a good bellyache!"[59] According to popular folklore in Lourdes, intestinal disorders were heaven's way of sending a harmless and humorous reminder to the presumptuous.[60]

Soeur Marcelline remembered a few edifying—but a bit ideal-ized—traits from that period. Bernadette would delight, it seemed, in wearing worn out, mended clothing. This is a mistake, as we shall see later. In any case, while carefully doing her mending, Bernadette said: "Patching is our business."[61]

One day, Soeur Marie-Bernard was munching on a pear. Soeur Marcelline was prohibited from eating any fruit. She begged Bernadette to give her a small bite. Bernadette "pretended to give her some, then ate the piece she had been holding out." Her reply to the exclamation that followed was, "What! You would've liked me to disobey the doctor and our superiors who forbade it!"

Soeur Marcelline thought she could also remember that, as early as 1866, Bernadette had given her a prophetic description of the stained-glass windows which were to be installed at the Basilica in Lourdes in 1877, including the fact that they would depict Bishop Forcade, Bishop of Nevers. No doubt she was confusing a conversa-tion that had taken place in 1868 with one that took place later. In fact, she did see Bernadette again in 1878, after the windows had been installed.

In Mère Vauzou's Hands

Bernadette left the infirmary on February 2, 1867, and returned to the novitiate to follow the life of a novice, but not without a few problems. On August 16, 1867, she wrote to Mère Ceyrac of Figeac, "I'm still a pillar of the infirmary."[62]

On Bernadette's return, Mère Vauzou was determined to make up for lost time:

"Well, Soeur Marie-Bernard, we are going to enter into the time of testing," she told her.

With a shy smile, Bernadette answered, "Oh, Mère, I beg you not to go too fast."[63]

According to Soeur Léontine Villaret, Mère Marie-Thérèse was even supposed to have said severely but no doubt jokingly, "Now we're going to beat you."

And Bernadette instantly replied, "I hope you'll do it gently."

"Mère Marie-Thérèse told me that she was not edified by this remark," comments Soeur Villaret. "Mère Marie-Thérèse did not like privileged souls and always endeavored to humble them. In her case it was a matter of temperament."[64]

Jeanne Lannessans was not the only one to enlighten us on what followed. Many of her fellow-novices testified forty and fifty years later, at the beatification process, idealizing a bit. Statements like these abound:

"Seeing her pray, you would have said that she was no longer of this world."[65]

"When Soeur Marie-Bernard crossed the cloister...you would have said that her eyes were glued to the ground, but it is probable that her spirit was soaring higher."[66]

"She had something in her expression that was exceptional."[67]

Setting aside those conjectures, what struck them was Bernadette's recollection, her strict obedience, her reserve and her personality, but also her disposition, her "vivacity,"[68] and more than anything else, her "cheerfulness," her "enthusiasm."[69]

"We were in the same class and same profession group. I never noticed anything...that made her stand out from the others, except her fidelity to the Rule, her strictness, her silence and especially her extreme charity," attests Soeur Joseph Caldairou.[70]

Something else is clear: Bernadette was the center of attention. "We always had our eyes on her," said Soeur Stanislas Tourriol.[71]

This was a vulnerable position, where faults were quickly spotted. But Bernadette's unpretentious nature, her preference for "the lowliest duties," for "works of humility,"[72] and her patience in accepting correction "without saying a word,"[73] discouraged any fault-finding among her companions. She was visible when she was called on to perform some duty, but inconspicuous when she was required merely to be present.

Her fellow novices' criticism took a somewhat different turn, though silent and reverent. It focused on the way Mère Vauzou treated Bernadette.

"The mistress of novices was harsh with Soeur Marie-Bernard," says Soeur Bernard Dalias. "She corrected her curtly, without feeling. The Servant of God felt this keenly. You could see her turn pale, but she never made a gesture nor said a word expressing discontent (despite her) natural quick temper."[74]

Very few of these admonitions have been recorded. The ones that have been preserved allude to Bernadette's lowly background.

"One day, during a prescribed reading at the novitiate," Soeur

Stanislas Paschal relates, "Soeur Marie-Bernard was sitting on a step, close to the mistress of novices and was mending Mother's apron. One passage in the reading had to do with the apparition of the Blessed Virgin to a shepherdess. At that, Mère Marie-Thérèse Vauzou turned toward Soeur Marie-Bernard and said, 'That's the way the Blessed Virgin always acts with shepherdesses, isn't it, Soeur Marie-Bernard?'

"She answered politely, 'Yes, my dear Mother.'"[75]

Reporting a recollection of Mère Isabelle Descazeaux, the same sister recalls that on another day, "They had drawn lots for a statuette of Saint Germaine Cousin; Soeur Marie-Bernard won it. Mère Marie-Thérèse Vauzou then observed sarcastically, 'A shepherdess could only fall into the hands of another shepherdess.'"[76]

Soeur Stanislas adds this related incident: "Soeur Marguerite Challiès saw Soeur Marie-Bernard at the door of the mistress of novices' office. She was holding a statuette in her hands...filled with fear. It was her day for [spiritual] direction."[77]

"At instructions, she was seized with a fit of coughing...Mère Vauzou sent her out. It must have embarrassed her, but it didn't show," testified Soeur V. Mirambeau.[78]

It would be a caricature to paint Mère Marie-Thérèse Vauzou as being a harsh, quarrelsome and obnoxious woman, and the novitiate as a place of torture. Bernadette's letters freely express just the opposite, "happiness at being there, and an affectionate reverence toward Mère Marie-Thérèse." Her companions confirmed this. Soeur Justine Pélat, for example recalls, "When her health permitted her to resume the different exercises of the novitiate, (Bernadette) would arrive...content, happy...especially when the main hall of the novitiate was set to receive our revered Mère Marie-Thérèse. Oh! Then you would see her light up; her joy was complete. Our venerable mistress's motherly look seemed eager to draw all our hearts to herself and to wrap them in her own."

Bernadette reacted instinctively against being "wrapped up" like that, but she did feel an overall attraction, according to the testimony of Soeur Stanislas Paschal: "One day, when the mistress came home from a journey...we were waiting for her in the cloister to bid her welcome. When she appeared, Soeur Marie-Bernard ran into her arms like a child long separated from her mother...and Soeur

Mélanie Monèry [mistress of studies at the novitiate] said to her, 'Well, Soeur Marie-Bernard! What enthusiasm on seeing your mistress again!'

"'Oh, yes, my dear Sister!' she answered; 'it was much too human...I'm very sorry.'"[79]

If Mère Vauzou's harshness hurt so much, it was partly because of the strong affection the novices had for her. We must keep in mind this was a time when the emotional bonds between a young girl and her mother were stronger and lasted longer than nowadays. It happened then that a transfer of affections, sometimes quite pronounced, was made to the mistress of novices.

Bernadette should not be pictured as having been humiliated in everything. She was the one in charge of "blessing the hour,"[80] that is, of reciting the obligatory prayer when the hour struck. It was a serious responsibility. Clearly, Mère Vauzou had chosen Bernadette not only for her strong and distinct voice, but for her radiance.

Other Trials

What were Bernadette's other trials at this time? Her homesickness for Lourdes remained carefully concealed, gently surfacing only on occasion. Going through the poplar-lined meadow which then existed "on the kitchen side of the convent," she found herself saying, "Oh, those poplar trees! They remind me of the Gave...."[81] Upon which, according to Soeur Bernard Dalias, she immediately became silent, remembering, no doubt, that she was entering forbidden territory.

From her own experience, Bernadette was able to sense when others felt uprooted. She would then do something to divert them.

Marie Paschal, a seventeen-year-old novice, assigned to Bernadette for orientation week, was asked by her, "Did you cry for your mama?" Then Bernadette added with a big smile, "Shed tears for your mama, give the mice a drink!"[82]

To Soeur Emile, who was looking sick before her profession, Bernadette said, "My poor Soeur Emile, you need a breath of your native air to make you better!"[83]

But in this case the banter had a different meaning. Soeur Emilie was fearful of not being admitted to profession because of

The poplars at the grotto (above, 1872),
which Bernadette loved, would disappear in 1877 (below).

her health. She answered back (as if to reassure herself), "I'm not afraid."

And with her mischievous look, Bernadette laughingly repeated, "Native air! Native air!"

As soon as she was admitted to profession, Soeur Emilie ran to the infirmary crying out, "Well, Soeur Marie-Bernard, my native air! It's still pretty far away!"

Bernadette burst out laughing and answered, "I was only teasing you."[84]

According to her companions, Bernadette's academic difficulties continued in spite of her constant and continuous progress.

"Soeur Marie-Bernard was placed in the lowest class. She understood nothing about arithmetic," relates Soeur Joseph Caldairou.[85]

"She was uncertain of her grammar and spelling. She sometimes came to have me correct (her) letters," recalls Soeur Marie Bastide.[86]

To overcome this difficulty, the superiors tried assigning Bernadette to the bursar's office, from February to October 1867, during the hours the novices spent learning the different jobs to be done in the house. Mother General even specified that she must "be trained to write letters."

"But she had no liking for this and showed rather some annoyance," reports Soeur Valentine Gleyrose, who supervised this office. "Reverend Mother then told me to find something else for her to do, so I had her file and go over our print shop accounts and other papers."[87]

Nevertheless, the drudgery of writing would continue in other ways, made more burdensome by requests from important people and benefactors, who wrote to the superiors, asking for "a letter from Bernadette."

"If it weren't for obedience, I wouldn't answer," Bernadette told Soeur Brigitte Hostin.[88]

Visits

More oppressive were those unbearable visits; Bernadette thought she had escaped when she passed through the gates of the motherhouse....

But it was very difficult for the sisters to turn away a mother in tears, who had brought her sick child (a baby boy three months old), convinced that contact with the shepherdess of Lourdes would cure him. Bernadette felt strongly that what was being asked of her in visits like this was totally beyond her. After kissing the child, she tried to channel hope in the right direction: "Let's go to the chapel and pray to our good Mother...." And likewise in taking leave of them she advised, "Pray hard, Madame, and get others to pray...."[89]

After the child got well, how could the sisters turn down the requests of other inconsolable mothers? How could they refuse an interview by Henri Lasserre, who was preparing the *Histoire de Lourdes* at the request of the diocese of Tarbes? A very busy man besides, he only stopped over briefly at the motherhouse on August 15 or 16. At the time he attached more importance to official documents than to Bernadette's own testimony. If he took any notes at all, which remains to be proved, we find no trace of them in his archives, nor any distinguishable echo of them in his work.[90]

Bernadette felt herself under no obligation to give in to unscheduled visits when she was being tricked into them.

One day a preacher expressed a desire to see Soeur Marie-Bernard; the superior tried to find a pretext to show her to him.... She said, "Look, here's a novice; look at the difference between her veil, which is made of silk, and the professed sisters, which is made of wool."

Soeur Marie-Bernard was not taken in. She concealed her face as well as she could. Shortly afterwards, she said, "I understood clearly what they tried to do, but he didn't get to see very much."[91]

Likewise, Soeur Augustin Faur, who was in the cloister with her brother, wanted to find a way that might allow him to see her; but they could never get Soeur Marie-Bernard to walk in front of him a second time. She had caught on to their trickery.[92] "That's why Bernadette tried to conceal herself when she was praying," related the witness.[93]

When it was a matter of obedience, she tried to "make a good impression" by clinging to this motive: "I have to go speak about my heavenly Mother!"[94] But on that very point, she couldn't hide her sorrow. "I have to go to the parlor again," she said one day to Soeur Joseph Caldairou. "If you only knew what an effort this is! Especially if they're bishops!"[95]

Among these, the most persistent was the local ordinary, Bishop Forcade. He accompanied his colleagues and came personally to hear the confessions of the sisters in the infirmary...when Bernadette was there. She said, "It's funny that a bishop would take the trouble to hear the confessions of the sick sisters."[96]

Confident in his position, Bishop Forcade did not hesitate to ask Bernadette questions, as he himself admits: "On two or three separate occasions, I asked her if she had seen the Blessed Virgin since the famous apparitions, or received some other extraordinary favor. 'Never!' she answered very plainly. 'Right now I am just like everybody else.'"[97]

On another day, the bishop went further. Going through Saint Gertrude's, the novices' workroom, he shot this question point-blank: "One of your secrets is your vocation to the Sisters of Nevers —isn't it?"

She only answered, "Ah! Monsiegneur!"[98] As if to say, "What kind of a question is that, for you, a bishop, and one who hears my confessions?"

All for God

Apart from the visits, Bernadette cheerfully put up with everything else.

To Soeur Isabelle Laverchère, who admonished her for her lack of progress in reading, Soeur Bernard Dalias remembers hearing her reply quite joyfully, "Thank you, dear Sister."

"Given the work...of cleaning toilets," she answered Louise Brusson, who felt sorry for her. "But it's my job!"[99]

The secret of this simple and joyful forbearance was that Bernadette referred everything to God. Sometimes she said so explicitly. "We must know how to do everything for God," she used to say.[100]

"Let us seek only the glory of God and his will."[101]

"Could this offend the good Lord?"[102]

The superior general, Mère Joséphine Imbert, about to leave for Paris, thoughtfully asked the sisters what she could buy for them:

"And you, Soeur Marie-Bernard, what do you want me to bring back for you?"

"Mother, bring me back the love of God!"[103] came the answer.

The cloister at Saint-Gildard

Novitiate "Blunders"

Let's set our minds at rest. There was nothing inflexible about Bernadette's flight toward God. It affected neither her good humor nor her natural whimsy.

"Her vivid imagination provided her the wherewithal to entertain those around her and make them laugh, almost beyond measure," said Soeur Justine Pélat.[104]

What she herself called her "novice's blunders" amused her companions before and after the novitiate, for she recalled them later on to brighten up the monotony of their recreations.

There was the story of the faucet that Soeur Claire Bordes narrates: "Soeur Marie-Bernard had gone to the kitchen for some hot water. Seeing no one there, she took some from the faucet. Soeur Cécile, the sister in charge of the kitchen, and a stickler for rules, happened to be working in the small refectory adjoining the kitchen with Mother Assistant, Mère Louise Ferrand. Soeur Cécile suddenly appeared and asked Bernadette, 'What are you doing here?'

"'I came to get some hot water for a sister,' Bernadette replied.

"'So that's it! You should've asked for permission. Put that water back where you got it.'

"'My dear Sister, it's from the faucet,' Bernadette explained.

"At that moment, Mother Assistant came into the kitchen and asked what was going on. The kitchen sister said, 'See that little sister, she came to get water without permission.' Mother Assistant tapped Bernadette on the shoulder and said, 'Take that water to your patient.'

"On her way out, Soeur Marie-Bernard could not help laughing at the strange thought of putting the water back up the faucet. Soeur Cécile noticed her laughing and said to the Mother Assistant, 'Look at that wisp of a sister. She's laughing. An older sister would be sniveling.'"[105]

Soeur Claire Bordes also relates the story of the matches:

"Once, Soeur Marie-Bernard, responsible for the same patient's room, went to the kitchen to get matches, which she had forgotten to get. The bell had just rung, summoning her to the novitiate. The kitchen sister said to her, 'What time is it, Sister?'

"'4:05.'

"'At what time are novices supposed to come for matches?'

"'3:30.'

"'Next time, try to be here on time....'

"Bernadette left with the box. Noticing this, the kitchen sister said, 'What about the others? What will they have if you take the whole box? Take what you need and put the box back where it belongs.'"

"See what a bungler I was," said Bernadette, telling the story to Soeur Claire, ten years later, on December 26, 1877.[106]

The story of the mirror we owe to Louise Brusson, eye-witness and accomplice:

"One day, a very ugly postulant was in the linen room and kept looking at herself in a mirror, which was in a small decorative box she kept next to her linen. I came into the room. Immediately, Soeur Marie-Bernard gestured to me and, looking at the postulant, said, 'For her own sake, put something over that mirror.' I took some paper and a pencil and wrote, 'Look at your soul.' Then I put the paper over the mirror and closed the lid.

"That evening or the following day, the postulant opened the box to look at herself again, but seeing the paper stuck there, uttered a cry of surprise, 'Oh! Who put that there?'

"No one answered. Soeur Marie-Bernard and I weren't there. The sisters who were there got a good laugh. I had forgotten all about it, when, at the next recreation, Soeur Marie-Bernard softly said to me, 'Mother wants to know who the guilty party is.' I answered, 'I am, of course, and I'll go tell her. How about you, Soeur Marie-Bernard?' She smiled at me and gestured that she had already confessed. That same day, we made our *culp** together."[107]

Louise Brusson also tells of one of those spells of uncontrollable laughter in the novitiate:

"One day when we were on refectory duty, we sat down at table after the rest had gone. That day there was a platter of carrots, sliced into thin circles. They were hard. Soeur Marie-Bernard picked at the plate with the fork, and sent the carrots rolling down the table. It was impossible not to laugh. Soeur Marie-Bernard was laughing so hard that we all did too. We couldn't eat anymore. At the end of the meal, Soeur Marie-Bernard turned to me and said, 'Let's go.'

---

*A practice in some religious communities of confessing before the assembled community, faults committed in public. It was done once a week at a community ceremony. One could go to the superior on one's own in case of a major blunder—like this one here!

"I understood. We left to make our *culp* to the mistress of novices."[108]

According to Soeur Madeleine Bounaix, Bernadette told this story about the cornette:

"The sister in charge of the workroom had given me a cornette to repair; it was torn from end to end. I brought the cornette up to the infirmary and showed it to the sister in charge of the sick, saying, 'I will never manage to mend this cornette.'

"She answered, 'Don't worry, I have some that I use for dressings; they're not as bad as that. I'll give you one.'

"I took it and mended it as best I could; then I took it to the sister in charge. She said to me, 'But that's not the one I gave you.'

"I answered, 'No, Soeur Marthe exchanged it for another less torn.' This was reported to the mistress of novices, and I was severely scolded."[109]

To Madeleine Bounaix, who wanted to find excuses for Bernadette when she finished telling the story, Bernadette said, "No, I was wrong...I didn't bring back the cornette I had been given...."[110]

Was it because they had discovered a weak spot on that score? The fact remains that afterwards, Bernadette seemed to have been doomed to torn cornettes. One day, teasing Soeur Elisabeth Manhès, she said, "They give you the most beautiful cornettes. Mine are for the birds. Look!"

There must have been more resentment in her voice than she intended, for Soeur Elisabeth felt the sting. "I blushed," she relates, "and I was a little offended, for Bernadette seemed to be saying that I was conceited. Seeing that I wasn't taking the joke very well, she said, 'Oh! So your virtue isn't any stronger than all that!'"[111]

These small incidents open a perspective on what could be called Bernadette's technical skills. She excelled in sewing. This, with her gift of repartee, was one of her strong points, a prominent element in her personality. She had an appreciation of work well done and a horror of mending. In those days when they pushed to extremes the mortification of the will, her spontaneous reactions were easily attributed to "self-will," or to "movements of nature," that were incompatible with sanctity. Today, we would instead consider them signs of health.

*The southern facade of Saint-Gildard's Convent. It is
probable that the episode with the egg took place at the foot of this drive.*

It is equally a good sign that her "blunders" and "whimsies" carried on beyond the novitiate, when Soeur Marie-Bernard gave free rein to her natural high spirits to add life to the sisters' recreations, periods that could so quickly become routine within an enclosed group. "One day," relates Soeur Eudoxie Chatelain, "I saw the kitchen sister take a fresh egg out of her apron pocket and offer it to Soeur Marie-Bernard. She broke it, and as quick as a wink, she drank it down, to the great amusement of her companions. But immediately I heard her say, 'Ah, that's it! You made me drink an egg, and now I've got to go find Mother Assistant *to ask her permission.*'

"I saw her leave and go off toward the community room."[112]

What is reassuring in all this is Bernadette's backing away from her public persona. In this way she avoided an ever-present pitfall. She had her sight intently set on holiness, but the fervor of others (already prepared to set up a statue of her) would have inclined her to present a conventional and artificial image. Humor as much as humility kept her far from such temptations.

Bernadette had a good laugh when she learned that her photo was being sold in Lourdes "for ten centimes." "That's really all I'm worth!"[113] she joked.

With a smile she accepted her own shortness of stature. Of all the novices, she was the shortest. Even her partner in line, Soeur Joseph Caldairou, was a bit taller. Similarity of stature coupled with a subtle but comical caricature of the dignity that was a part of their training enabled them to even out their height—"Bernadette, by standing a little taller and I by stooping just a bit," relates Soeur Joseph Caldairou.

To make the others laugh, Bernadette decided to have fun one day by standing between the two tallest novices, who were particularly tall that year. "See what I am," she said. "I really think I'm something!"[114]

We can picture that same smile when she made this remark one day to her group. They urged her to take the place of the absent sister who usually gave them motivational talks, so they could hear her give an edifying talk on the Blessed Virgin. Bernadette replied, "I couldn't say anything. I can't give a talk. I'm a stone; what could you get out of a stone?"[115]

We find the same sense of humor in her first meeting with Soeur Bernard Dalias, on May 16, 1867. During recreation the day she arrived, the new postulant expressed her desire to meet Bernadette. Soeur Bernard describes what happened.

"'Bernadette?' said Mère Berganot immediately. 'Why, here she is!'

"'What!' I exclaimed.

"Bernadette graciously held her hand out to me and said, 'Why, Mademoiselle, that's all there is!'

"And from that moment on she treated me with genuine friendship."[116]

Bernadette as sold for ten centimes

CHAPTER 15

— ⚜ —

PROFESSION OF VOWS

Bernadette made her profession of vows on October 30, 1867, during the Mass celebrated by Bishop Forcade at Saint-Gildard's. Before receiving the Body of Christ she pronounced the words which committed her to practice the "vows of poverty, chastity and obedience...and charity." This fourth vow,[1] which dated from the very beginning of her congregation (1683) was suppressed a little later, when Rome revised the sisters' Constitutions, for charity has always defied legal formulation.

Soeur Véronique Mirambeau reported that Bernadette's voice trembled a bit; but Soeur Bernard Dalias noted that "her intonation was steady and...without any affectation."[2]

After the profession ceremony, each religious received her "obedience," which assigned her to a position in one of the houses of the congregation. And immediately after, they were scattered all over France, each to her new assignment.

What happened then greatly impressed the witnesses, and as always in such cases, the many reports that have come down to us—that of the bishop and those of the sisters—present several variants, which are analyzed in the *Logia*.[3] Here, as elsewhere, we present a distillation.

The novitiate chapel and the statue of the Virgin in Bernadette's time.
"You think she's beautiful? I don't," Bernadette remarked to Soeur Stanislas Tourriol.

The ceremony took place in the afternoon, in the conference hall of the novitiate. Following custom, Bishop Forcade presided. Bernadette's forty-three fellow novices were called one by one. Each one received her "crucifix, book of Constitutions, and letter of obedience."[4] Bernadette waited for her turn, but it did not come. All the rest had been called.

Here the bishop paused. Bernadette leaned over to her neighbor, Soeur Anastasie Carrière and said, "Everyone got something.... Still, I would've liked to have been treated like everyone else."[5]

At that moment, Bishop Forcade turned toward Mère Joséphine Imbert, the superior general, who was next to him. He asked her (the actual words differ among the witnesses), "What about Soeur Marie-Bernard?"

Mère Joséphine answered, "Monseigneur, she is good for nothing."

This was said "with a smile," says Soeur Joseph Caldairou,[6] and softly.

"I heard nothing of this conversation," says Soeur Emilie Marcillac, "but I did hear the bishop say aloud, when the Servant of God approached, 'Soeur Marie-Bernard! Nowhere!'"[7]

Whereupon, Mère Joséphine sat down again.[8]

Bernadette had come forward.

"Is it true, Soeur Marie-Bernard, that you are good for nothing?" the bishop asked.

"It's true."

"Well then, my poor child, what are we going to do with you?"

"I told you in Lourdes when you wanted me to join the community; and you answered that it would make no difference...."[9]

The bishop was not expecting this answer, and many of those present did not hear it, for the conversation was carried on softly. Bernadette was kneeling in front of the bishop to receive her book and her crucifix. At this point, the superior general intervened, according to plan: "If you wish, Monseigneur, we could keep her here at the motherhouse, out of charity, and somehow use her in the infirmary, if only for cleaning up or preparing herbal teas. Since she's nearly always sick, it would suit her just fine."

According to Soeur Marie Bastide, the superior even added: "She's only good for blowing embers into flame."[10]

The bishop agreed and spoke to Bernadette, who replied, "I'll try."

She then received her profession crucifix and Rule, affirms Soeur Joseph Caldairou,[11] a rosary, too, but no letter of obedience.[12]

The bishop then blessed her and loftily announced, "I assign you to the post of praying."[13]

During the recreation that followed, Bernadette kept her good humor.[14] With some regret but with no bitterness, she acknowledged the lack of talent that others remarked about her. She was friendly to those who were going away. Several of them experienced her words of encouragement and her affection.[15]

Distributing pictures on the occasion of the profession, she said to one of her classmates, Soeur Louise Molénac, who was "touched" by it: "Soeur Louise, I'm going to give you the cross."[16]

This staging of the "obedience," offensive by today's standards, has to be placed in its own time, but also in the concrete situation. The problem for everyone, including the bishop, was this: on the one hand, the daily difficulties at Saint-Gildard's made it obvious "that a small house, open to all comers," could not "protect Bernadette from the prying public." On the other hand, "posts at the motherhouse were considered the plums of the Congregation." Never was a newly professed sister assigned to the motherhouse, except on rare and extraordinary occasions. The drama played out on October 30, 1867, solved the dilemma by making the honorary assignment take on the appearance of a humiliation. Bishop Forcade explicitly told this to Count Lafond, who wrote it in his book, published in 1879.

There were, therefore, reasons for this solution; it also had its advantages. This can be judged, by comparison, with the absence of any protection for the visionaries of La Salette—especially Mélanie. But such shocks to the personality of a young girl from a poor background involved other risks. Bernadette experienced a hurt that some later statements will allow us to guess at.

What she used to tell herself is no doubt reflected in this piece of advice Bernadette gave to one of her first patients, Louise Brusson, who was in bed with bronchitis at the infirmary. Louise couldn't bear "mustard plasters" and "blistering."

"Come on, you big clown," Bernadette told her, "it's for the good Lord. We have to suffer for him; he suffered enough for us."

CHAPTER 16

— ⚜ —

BERNADETTE EMPLOYED

Once professed, Bernadette entered into a new phase: the active life. Before following her in her daily chores, we must examine a few unusual incidents that disturbed her, for she was still a celebrity. It sometimes became impossible to protect her privacy against the invasions of people working for Lourdes who, at all costs, wanted to exploit this golden treasure.

The Photographer's Victory

On February 4, 1868, J. Provost, a photographer, arrived. The bishop of Lourdes had recommended him to the superior general as "a respectable gentleman and father of a family." The bishop hoped that the sisters would let him take a few pictures of Bernadette in order to help subsidize "the construction of the chapel of the apparitions," and "to put an end to bootleg photos."[1] Regretfully, Mère Joséphine gave her consent.

For the sixth time, then, Bernadette had to pose for the camera, in the very cloister where she had come to hide.

She had second thoughts about coming downstairs. Soeur Marie Mespouilhé found her in a bad mood, putting her cornette back on.

Bernadette, Provost photo, February 4, 1868

Bernadette "secularized" by Provost, February 4, 1868

"Is everything all right?" Soeur Marie asked her. She then recalls what happened:

"Replying in the affirmative, she [Bernadette] shook her head impatiently and rumpled her cornette."

"'That's not nice,' I told her.

"'You're right; forgive me.'"[2]

"That said, she came downstairs, overcoming a strong impulse 'to make faces' to hinder the process."[3]

The bishop was confident that Monsieur Provost would not misuse the recommendation he had been given.

"He will be satisfied with the clothing that you select," the bishop had written to the superior of Nevers.

Provost started out with the religious habit; that was his purpose, since there were as yet no photos of this kind, at least nothing authentic.

He shot several poses: Bernadette standing, kneeling, with the crucifix, without the crucifix, etc.—in all, eight good exposures.

He also managed to get a picture of Bernadette in peasant costume. Outrageous? Not at all. It was quite simple. She could keep her religious habit, which included a skirt like any other, and sleeves not much fuller than others. All she had to do was throw on a shawl and replace her cornette with a kerchief, all dark colored; in that way she would not even have to "set aside her religious habit."

It was a victory! They more or less twisted a lighter colored fabric over her head. The final photo was taken. It took but a moment, but Bernadette's expression, caught forever by the camera, speaks volumes about her feelings as well as her weariness. She literally "made a face" like nothing we ever see in any of the sixty-three other pictures of her.[4]

Bishop Chigi and Bishop Machebeuf

The visits continued one after another. They were carefully sorted out, and only the inescapable were accepted.

In particular there were the guests of Count Lafond: Bishop Chigi, on November 16, 1868;[5] and a priest, Abbé de M., who asked a great many questions about the Virgin of Massabielle. Bernadette confirmed[6] once more that she "never saw her again."[7]

On October 6, the visitor was Bishop Machebeuf, the Vicar Apostolic of Colorado, "come to Lourdes seeking a cure." He made

Bernadette as a religious, Provost photo, February 4, 1868

the trip to Nevers "specifically to see Bernadette." "During his visit," according to an article published in the United States,[8] "a mother rushed into the convent, carrying a crippled child, unable to walk. She begged that Bernadette be permitted to tend the child. The mother superior placed the child in the arms of the saint and told her to take him into the garden. Bernadette came back in tears a few moments later. 'The child escaped from my arms and is running around the garden,' she announced."

This story caused us much concern. It is but one of the numerous versions of the miracle of "the child who could not walk." And these versions differ significantly. Emile Zola had an opportunity to present one version to Henri Lasserre on August 31, 1892, and heard himself saying, "It's not true."

According to the accounts, sometimes it involves a girl, at other times a boy or a newborn. Other versions say a child of three or older escaped from Bernadette's arms to walk or even run for the first time. These are but different distortions of one and the same event, whose origin we finally tracked down: the documentation kept in the family by the child himself, Ferdinand Paquet. He was two and a half years old when his mother, one day in March 1867, brought him to the parlor of Saint-Gildard's and successfully got Bernadette to carry him over to the Virgin's altar.

After a moment of silence, Bernadette gave the child back to his mother, saying, "Pray and get others to pray."[9]

Five days later, the child's condition improved. He survived, far beyond all hope, until July 23, 1946, when he died in his eightieth year.

Henri Lasserre's *"Protest"*

On October 13, another matter arose, about which much ink would be spilt: Bernadette's *"Protest"* against *La petite histoire des apparitions*, edited by the chaplains in Lourdes.

Bernadette's comments on this subject must be put into context.

Henri Lasserre, the most famous historian of Lourdes, had been cured of an eye disease in 1862, after washing with water from the grotto. In 1864 he had been assigned to write the history of the apparitions. But at the time, he was swamped with a thousand and one things to do—public debates, newspaper articles—and the project was continually being postponed. In Lourdes, people were growing

I

ENDANT toute ma vie j'ai joui d'une vue excellente. Je distinguais les objets à une immense distance ; et, d'autre part, je lisais couramment un livre, quelque rapproché qu'il fût de mes yeux. Des nuits passées à l'étude ne

Cured of an eye disease by washing with water from the grotto in 1862, Henri Lasserre, Lourdes historian, was convinced he had a mission, illustrated by this engraving from his book.

impatient. This is how the writer came to publish the first chapters of his history in the *Revue du monde catholique,* dated December 10, 1867, but the rest was delayed a few more months.

Meanwhile, the chaplains at the grotto, Pères Sempé and Duboé, had themselves drawn up an account of the apparitions from sources almost totally different from Henri Lasserre's. He had official documents from the diocese; they only had a few duplicates. For their part, the two chaplains had recourse to eye witnesses, whom they rubbed shoulders with every day in Lourdes: Toinette Soubirous and Jeanne Abadie, Bernadette's two companions at the first apparition, Nicolau, the miller, a witness at the second, etc., humble folk whose memory needed no promoting and whom Lasserre had not bothered to interview.

In August 1868, therefore, the two missionary chaplains began publishing their own *Petite histoire* in the *Annales de Notre-Dame de Lourdes,* while Lasserre continued his writing in the *Revue du monde catholique,* not without interruption, because his marriage (on September 8, 1868) and other subsequent issues, took up his time. He completed his writing in June, 1869, and *Notre-Dame de Lourdes* came out as a book at the beginning of summer, 1869.

Lasserre had strongly requested—in a way, even demanded—that his history would henceforth be the only one. The bishop had rejected this monopoly and even withheld official approval, for the account severely criticized the magistrates and public officials of 1858, most of whom were still living.

But Henri Lasserre of Monzie had connections. He went higher. Through the intervention of Cardinal Pitra, he received a "brief of praise" from Pius IX, on September 4, 1869. The bishop had been short-circuited!

Now it was a matter of getting the missionaries' account censured by Bernadette herself. This was the scheme that brought Lasserre to Nevers on October 13, 1869. The climate was in his favor. His book, published without an imprimatur in July 1869, met with phenomenal success and had also occasioned the first papal document in favor of the apparitions at Massabielle. The gratitude of his friends in Lourdes was heartfelt, and his prestige as an historian at its peak. He was convinced that he had produced a "work of justice and of truth," for the chaplains' picturesque details were foreign to both his documentation and his sense of the sacred. He considered them apocryphal and absurd. Finally, this aristocrat looked good and spoke even better. He expressed his honest piety warmly and ably. He was gifted with the kind of vigor and proverbial tenacity that his friend Édouard Drumont, the anti-Semitic journalist, could not find words enough to praise.[10] With his "quietly stubborn doggedness that no obstacle could discourage," he obtained permission to interview Bernadette. Lasserre was received without any distrust or suspicion.

The visionary had never read a book on the events of which she was the central figure, with the exception of Fourcade's booklet: an extremely well balanced copy of her own testimony, as we have seen. She was kept away from everything written about Lourdes—luckily for the authors, for she had little patience for conjectures and literary embellishments. Bernadette had lived the event from the inside, and to describe her ecstasy from the outside clashed with her intimate experience as well as with her sense of propriety. She reacted passionately in this area...as she did to statues of the apparition.

The account of Pères Sempé and Duboé, woven from picturesque elements borrowed from the unrestrained popular imagination of the early witnesses, was in this regard, particularly exasperating for her, especially in the first few pages, where the chaplains had given free rein to the vivid impressions and expressions of Toinette Soubirous and of Nicolau the miller. For the rest, Henri Lasserre's threats had stopped them. They had given up on detailing the chronology and had fallen back on cautious generalities. And so it was primarily the beginning chapters of the chaplains' work that Henri Lasserre submitted to Bernadette on that October 13, 1869.

He brought her the first six installments of their account (covering August 1868–January 1869). He began his reading with the description of Bernadette,[11] followed by the arguments among her brothers and sisters, just as Toinette had described them to the missionaries with innocent enthusiasm. Facing Bernadette, seated between Mère Elénore Cassagnes and her secretary, Henri Lasserre began to read:

"Her sister, three years her junior, says with tenderness and respect that Bernadette would often scold her for her scant inclination to prayer, for her brusqueness and for her determined ways. The younger sister was more forceful; when these complaints made her angry, she stirred up her little brother, and both of them would fall on their poor elder sister, who defended herself poorly, cried a bit, soon forgot everything, and never complained to her parents."

"We sometimes argued, of course, but without hitting one another," Bernadette corrected.[12]

Lasserre chalked up his first point. He went on, "Often beaten, her inexhaustible goodness nevertheless made her love tenderly...."

"She didn't beat me," said Bernadette. "I gave my brother a few taps, but he never gave me any."[13]

In fact, according to local custom, the eldest daughter, the heiress, had the right to hit the younger ones, but not the other way around. There were a few exceptions, however, clearly confirmed by Toinette herself,[14] and which had been buried in Bernadette's memory, quick to forget abuse.

Lasserre read on: "In the evening, since her return from Bartrès, Bernadette had been saying night prayers out loud for the whole family."

"That's not right," Bernadette interrupted. "By no means did I get the family together. I only knew my rosary. My mother was the one who said the prayers when we said them together."

"She would not start," Lasserre continued, "until everybody was kneeling...."[15]

Bernadette interrupted again. "That's not true; I never thought about all that."

An encouraging start! What came next was less fruitful. Bernadette even forgot to correct the wrong date the *Annales* quoted for the first apparition (February 12, instead of February 11). She reacted once more at the following passage: "Marie and the other child hurried to take off their stockings."[16]

"They weren't wearing stockings!" exclaimed Bernadette.

A little further on, Lasserre scored again reading this incident that Toinette, swept along the path of hagiography, had told more than once: "Bernadette, with her instinct for modesty, delicate to the point of severity, was shocked that her companions did not observe strict rigorous modesty as she wanted, and she sharply told her sister, 'Marie! Come on! Better to let the hem of your dress get wet.'"[17]

"Oh, now that's not true!" exclaimed Bernadette.

It didn't take her long to dispute yet another incident, confirmed several times by Toinette: "Her sister volunteered to return to carry her on her back."[18]

lait souvent, pendant le jour, à la Sainte Vierge Marie qu'elle connaissait à peine. La Vierge Mère de Nazareth aimait Bernadette, la laissait grandir, humble et pieuse, et l'attendait.

Le prêtre qui gouvernait la paroisse de Bartrés, à l'époque où Bernadette allait quitter le village pour se préparer dans sa famille à la première communion, la rencontra un jour, conduisant son troupeau. L'air d'innocence et la candeur de l'enfant allèrent à son âme. Il la salua avec respect et se retourna pour la regarder encore; il dit :

— Les enfants à qui la Sainte Vierge s'est montrée sur la montagne de La Salette devaient être comme cette petite.

Le prêtre ne se doutait pas que dans cette parole il y avait une lueur de prophétie.

Première Apparition

Le 12 février 1858, vers le milieu d'une froide journée, Bernadette, avec sa sœur plus jeune, Marie, et une troisième compagne, descendait le bord du Gave par la prairie voisine de Massabieille, en cherchant des débris de bois pour le foyer de famille.

Le canal qui meut le moulin et la scierie tournait alors le rocher; et comme le Gave était faible à cette époque, un petit banc de sable et de cailloux restait à sec entre les deux courants; il allait, en se rétrécissant toujours, se perdre à la jonction des eaux par delà la Grotte.

A l'extrémité de la prairie, Bernadette dit à ses compagnes :

— Allons, par ces pierres, voir où le canal finit.

Elles descendirent jusqu'en face de la Grotte. L'excavation était alors pleine de sable, et le sable parsemé de petites branches que le courant avait entraînées. Bonne fortune pour les glaneuses.

Marie et l'autre enfant s'empressent d'ôter leurs bas. Bernadette hésite.

Je n'ose pas me mettre à l'eau, dit-elle, enrhumée comme je suis.

71

— Reste là, dit Marie d'un air décidé; je vais, moi seule, finir notre charge.

Les deux filles troussent dans leur tablier bas et sabots, prennent leur léger fagot sous le bras et entrent dans le canal. L'eau, mal tarie pour la réparation du moulin, était assez haute en cet endroit, et embarrassait un peu les enfants. Bernadette, avec son instinct de pudeur délicat jusqu'à la sévérité, fut choquée de ce que ses compagnes ne gardaient pas la modestie rigoureuse qu'elle voulait, et elle dit vivement à sa sœur :

— Marie, allons ! laisse plutôt mouiller le fond de ta robe.

La cadette n'osa désobéir; son vêtement toucha la surface de l'eau et se glaça ensuite.

Les deux enfants crièrent en traversant que l'eau était très froide, et en toute hâte elles allèrent s'accroupir pour réchauffer leurs pieds.

⁂

Bernadette voulait passer. Il y avait à sa portée beaucoup de cailloux ; elle jeta dans le courant le plus gros qu'elle put soulever, afin de se faire un chemin praticable en sabots. Elle ne réussit pas.

Sa sœur s'offrit à repasser pour la porter sur son dos.

— Oh ! tu me jetterais à l'eau, dit Bernadette, non non, tu es trop petite.

L'autre compagne était plus robuste et plus grande. Bernadette se hasarda à lui demander de la venir chercher sur ses épaules.

— Non !... dit-elle en accentuant énergiquement un de ces jurons auxquels les enfants du peuple se familiarisent trop aisément.

— Ah çà ! lui dit vivement Bernadette, si tu veux jurer, va-t-en ailleurs qu'ici.

— Et pourquoi pas ici comme ailleurs ?

— Allons ! c'est très mal, et tu ferais bien mieux de prier le bon Dieu.

La jeune fille riposte en la traitant dérisoirement de

tutions et Ordonnances Apostoliques, et, autant que besoin sera, nonobstant les statuts, les coutumes de la susdite Confrérie, même corroborés par le serment, la confirmation Apostolique, ou tout moyen quelconque de confirmation, nonobstant enfin les autres choses contraires quelles qu'elles soient.

Donné à Rome, près Saint-Pierre, sous l'anneau du Pêcheur, le XIV Juillet MDCCCLXVIII, la vingt-troisième année de notre pontificat.

Pour Monseigneur le Cardinal PARACCIANI CLAVELLI,
J.-B. BRANCALEONI CASTELLANI, prêtre.

PETITE HISTOIRE
DE NOTRE-DAME DE LOURDES
(suite)

Deuxième Apparition (*)

Bernadette pensait avec effusion à la douce Dame; elle la revoyait dans son souvenir, belle, bonne, souriante. Elle sentait cet appel du doigt et du regard auquel, défiante encore, bien que charmée, elle n'avait pas osé obéir. Voir la Dame du rosier! c'était un besoin. La Vierge, en allumant ce désir ardent par la puissance de sa virginale beauté, commençait à prendre possession de l'enfant qu'elle avait choisie pour se manifester. Mais la défense de sa mère, ses paroles affligées, son air de tristesse détournaient Bernadette de solliciter la permission d'une promenade à la rive de Massabieille.

Le dimanche, 14 février, au sortir de la grand'messe, vers onze heures, plusieurs petites filles viennent trouver Bernadette.

(*) Par une erreur d'impression, la livraison d'Août met au 12 février la première Apparition de la Vierge. C'est le 11 qu'elle a eu lieu.

Quelques lecteurs pourraient être surpris de la forme dialoguée de notre récit. Nous racontons et n'imaginons pas. Les paroles transcrites dans nos pages nous ont été rapportées, comme nous les donnons, par les acteurs mêmes de cette histoire, ou par des témoins chez qui nous trouvons ces souvenirs vivants encore.

Une jeune fille se détacha pour aller chercher du secours au moulin.

Il n'y avait rien dans le visage de Bernadette qui dût effrayer. Elle n'était pas livide, et ne s'affaissait point. Mais son immobilité, son œil fixe, une sorte de transparence du visage qui aurait ravi des regards plus attentifs, frappaient de terreur ces imaginations d'enfants. Dans cette suspension de la vie vulgaire, elles voyaient la mort.

La petite Marie entendant dire : «Elle pourrait mourir,» eut une grande frayeur et se prit à pleurer.

— Sortons-la d'ici par force, s'écria-t-elle au milieu de ses larmes, aidez-moi ! — Les jeunes filles saisissant Bernadette par le bras, essaient de la faire lever. Mais elle :

— Oh ! vous n'en faites rien, je ne m'en irai pas... je la vois toujours... je veux rester...!

Tirée vigoureusement par ses compagnes, elle se cramponne avec ses doigts au rocher détaché qu'environnaient les enfants. Quand on l'en arrache, elle tourne la tête du côté du rosier.

Les enfants l'emmènent se débattant toujours.

— Vous n'en faites rien, répéta-t-elle, tenez, je la vois, je la vois encore; elle me suit...

Une femme arrivait du moulin pour la prendre. On lui fait gravir la pente, on l'entraîne sur le chemin de la ville, on la fait entrer dans le moulin.

♉

Bernadette était toujours hors d'elle-même; elle s'élançait quand on la laissait libre, elle tendait les bras, avec de petits cris inarticulés et tendres, elle se signait quelquefois. Un jeune homme lui couvrit les yeux; elle voyait encore.

La famille du meûnier remarquait avec étonnement la beauté de l'enfant. Elle se souvient toujours de la blancheur de ses joues, de la lumière de son regard, de ce doux visage qui semblait être de fine cire. Bernadette souriait, et des larmes détachées et brillantes roulaient parmi ses sourires.

A few pages from the "Petite histoire," published by
Pères Sempé and Duboé in the Annales de Notre-Dame de Lourdes

QUELQUES FEUILLETS DE LA « PETITE HISTOIRE »,
publiée par les pères Sempé et Duboé,
dans les « Annales de Notre-Dame de Lourdes ».

"That's not true!"

Lasserre went on reading: "The other companion was sturdier and bigger. Bernadette ventured to ask her to come carry her on her shoulders."[19]

The historian looked for the visionary's reaction. "No, I don't remember at all," Bernadette answered more softly.

In reality, if one of the preceding stories was incorrect, and the other doubtful, Bernadette's request to Jeanne Abadie is abundantly borne out by Toinette, by Jeanne and by Bernadette herself, who soon forgot this incident.[20]

Lasserre quickly resumed the conversation reconstructed by the missionaries as follows:

"'No,' said Jeanne forcefully spitting out one of those mild vulgarities with which the children of the lower class grow comfortable too readily.

"'Oh, no!' Bernadette sharply said to her; 'if you want to swear, go somewhere else.'

"'Why? Here's as good a place as any.'

"'Come on! That's very wrong, and you'd do better to pray to the good Lord.'"[21]

Bernadette interrupted the reading. "Pray to the good Lord! That's not true."

What is true here is Jeanne's swearword, a very mild familiar curse, that she had learned from her father, the quarrier: "Pet de périclé," meaning, "By thunder!" It was also well enough established that Bernadette did scold her, not at that very moment, but a little later, when Jeanne repeated it.[22]

"We did not have an argument," Bernadette stated briefly. "After looking for a way across [the river], farther down, I merely asked them to kindly bring me some stones."

What followed drew no comments from Bernadette until the beginning of the apparition, which the missionaries described in this way: "A shining, young, wondrously beautiful lady bowed to her, her arms by her side, gracefully bending toward her."[23]

"She didn't hold her arms by her side, but was praying," Bernadette said. "She extended them only to say, *'I am the Immaculate Conception.'*"

Bernadette's reaction here was to an ambiguity in Père Sempé's edition. Reading it, we would think that the Virgin was set in the

Miraculous Medal pose. In fact, the gesture of welcome with open arms lasted but an instant, then the hands were folded immediately for prayer, as substantiated by Bernadette's first statements, the ones closest to the event. Lasserre's hasty writing of *"The Protest"* brought in another ambiguity by seeming to exclude the gesture of welcome.

The account of the apparition itself brought *no criticism* from Bernadette. But on the following page, she was surprised that the time the apparition lasted was estimated to be "one hour or more."[24]

"The time it takes to say one rosary," she corrected.

This brings up another problem. According to the estimate of Toinette, who is our source here, the rosary would have lasted "one hour or more." No doubt, this is an exaggeration. Then again, how long might a rosary, said in ecstasy, last? Bernadette did not commit herself in this area.[25]

Lasserre then read the dialogue about the water in the river, which her two companions found ice-cold, and to which Bernadette had replied, "'Oh, what liars you are! You claimed that the water was very cold, but I find it quite warm.'

"'Yes, awfully warm!' the children answered. 'The waters of the Gave warm in winter!'

"'Well, I'm telling you, I find it as mild as dishwater.'

"'Come on now,' said little Marie, 'my feet are swollen and they're bleeding.' And she bent down to touch Bernadette's feet. They were warm. Her surprised companion also came to touch them, etc....."[26]

At this, Bernadette commented, "I only said that I didn't find it cold, because the others were complaining about the icy coldness. All the rest never happened."

Indeed the account was gratuitously embellished. What remains true, and Bernadette's own reaction proves it, is that she did not find the water cold. Like the other two, she often described this incident, which, strictly speaking, contained no miracle. Numerous declarations acquaint us with the precise word Bernadette used: she found the water *"mild."* "This word *[douce]* is pronounced the same way in patois as in French," Jeanne Védère specified.[27] Bernadette later conceded that she might have said, "mild as dishwater," *"duço comma er'aygua d'era bachera,"* according to the transcription of Estrade, whose spelling I accept here. This local expression does not mean warm water. A farmer's wife in Espelugues, talking to Père Cros about the Brioulante spring, where she did her washing winter and summer, told him: "It is *mild* in winter, *like dishwater*, and during the summer, *heavy* and *cold*.[28]

We're talking here about a cold spring with a constant temperature, which feels different on cold days and extremely hot days.

In short, after being in ecstasy, Bernadette was not bothered by the water of the Gave; from this comes the incident that Toinette and the missionaries embellished a bit.

Bernadette also seems to have reacted to the story of the bundle of twigs, too heavy for Toinette, which she herself supposedly "carried on her head."[29]

"We dragged the bundle. I didn't carry it by myself," Lasserre here noted.

But this incident did not seem very convincing to him. He didn't have Bernadette "circle" it, and did not keep it in the definitive text of *"The Protest."*

Like the account of the apparition, the return home provoked no criticism. But Bernadette reacted to the evening episode:

"She was saying out loud the prayer she had learned in patois in the village. As was her custom, she was about to say several times: 'O Mary, conceived without sin, pray for us....' but at the first invocation, a sob choked the words."[30]

"Not at all. I wasn't leading the prayers and I did not burst into sobs," said Bernadette.

It was the expression "burst into sobs" that embarrassed her, because she did acknowledge, a moment later, that she did cry that evening. Henri Lasserre went on with his reading: "She continued. Sobs again cut off the syllables in her throat."[31]

"I don't remember that at all," said Bernadette. "*I think I cried,* but no longer remember about what."

In reality, the tears that Bernadette vaguely remembered were often attested to by herself and by others. It was night, bedtime. Was it during prayers? Was it during the invocation, "O Mary, conceived without sin," (said in French, as was the whole of night prayers)? This is more difficult to determine.[32]

Lasserre had come to the account of the second apparition, which would bring him livelier satisfaction.

Bernadette first reacted when they had her saying, before leaving for the grotto, "That lady, maybe she's something evil...."[33] In fact, she was not the one who said this.[34]

The number of girls from the charity-student class seemed exaggerated to her:

"Nearly twenty," Sempé said,[35] following Toinette.

"We weren't that many: five or six," said Bernadette.[36]

Indeed, the number was exaggerated but we must include a minimum of eight girls and more probably ten or twelve. They came in two groups: five or six with Bernadette; the others arrived late,[37] during the ecstasy, which had removed the visionary from the outside world.

Bernadette responded more intensely to the beginning of the apparition, which Lasserre read from the missionaries' *Annales* as follows:

"The child said to the others: 'When I sprinkle holy water on her, she raises her eyes to heaven and bows to me.'

"Reassured and won over, she stopped sprinkling the rosebush, stayed a moment with her arms half-lowered, and continued to watch.

"'What are you doing, you fool?' the children shouted.

"'You don't see her?' repeated Bernadette listlessly filled with wonder and deeply moved. 'But she's there, she's looking at us... she's smiling.... Now she's turning her head.... Look at her feet...her toes...her sash is swaying...see, her rosary is wrapped over her arm.... Oh, she is beautiful!... She has a small face, which looks waxen... she's blessing herself....'"[38]

Bernadette objected. "Never did I say that. I couldn't even see the others at that moment."

Indeed, this was a work of pure fiction, due in part to Toinette and in a larger measure, to the editorial efforts of the missionaries. Nevertheless, at the first moment of ecstasy, Bernadette seems to have announced the presence of *Aqueró*.[39]

Bernadette was even more stunned by the episode at the mill, described at some length by the chaplains,[40] according to the testimony of a number of Bernadette's companions and especially the miller Nicolau, who brought the visionary in ecstasy from the grotto to the Savy Mill.

"I don't remember a thing about all that," said Bernadette.

As we see it, the words swiftly jotted down by Lasserre are not an explicit rejection. Bernadette did not deny; all she said was that she had no recollection. It occurred to her that she had already been struck by these accounts and had felt a certain discomfort. And so she added these words, which Lasserre also took down: "They asked me that at the time. There were lots of rumors going around."

Now we enter upon a murky situation which scientific criticism of the witnesses' statements has cleared up with certainty from documentary evidence, as we have proved in the *Histoire authentique*.[41]

What happened at the second apparition? Bernadette gradually fell into ecstasy before her companions, troubled by her loss of speech and her pallor in the shady isolation of Massabielle. An unexpected object seemed to fall from the sky, exploded in their midst and rolled into the Gave. This was the last physical event that Bernadette remained aware of, before going more deeply into ecstasy. Several of her companions fled, not realizing that it was simply a large rock, thrown from the top of the cliff by Jeanne Abadie.

In their panic, they thought the object was chasing after them. That's what Brother Cérase Escoubas heard them shouting from across the river. Others wanted to drag the ecstatic Bernadette away. The world around her had vanished. They thought she was sick or dead. "You've killed her!" one of them said to Jeanne Abadie.[42] They tried but failed to move her. Neither could the girls who came with Jeanne, nor two women whom they met on the road move her. It was miller Nicolau who managed to carry Bernadette to the mill. The ecstasy lasted right up to the threshold of the mill. That is why *the witnesses' recollections are so unlike Bernadette's, who was cut off from what was happening around her.*

That much would have been easy to ascertain, but the object of this interview was to compile evidence against the *Petite histoire* written by the missionaries. Keeping this one aim in focus, Lasserre made the most of his success by going over each detail in the narrative of Bernadette's removal to the mill. This account was all the more open to attack because the recollections of those moments of panic were, to some extent, very confused. A few girls even went so far as to put their own reactions into Bernadette's own mouth; the missionaries had her saying things like, "I see her, I can still see her; she's following me."[43]

The truth is that it was the girls running away who shouted, "It's following us!" Bernadette did not have that experience at all. She never heard her companions scream and was *never even aware of being moved from the grotto to the mill,* where she finally regained consciousness.

Henri Lasserre

Was Lasserre now getting tired of all this? Was he pressed for time? The fact remains that at this point, he began taking fewer and fewer notes.

Concerning the third apparition, Bernadette's only reaction was to this passage:

"The sodalist (who accompanied her) said to Bernadette, 'Go ask her if it's a problem for us to come with you.'

"Bernadette started to go, but she stopped and suddenly said, looking sadly surprised, 'Oh, she's not there anymore!'

"'No matter,' said the young girl; 'go back to the foot of the rosebush; maybe she'll come back.'

"Bernadette obeyed. Taking a step, she said, 'She's back.'"[44]

Bernadette corrected that. "Never did she appear and disappear. When she disappeared, it was over."

It seems, in fact, that the apparition did not come back after the dialogue between Bernadette and her companions. The girls were confused on the subject, as explained in the *Histoire authentique*.[45] According to Bernadette, *Aqueró* "glided" from the outer niche to the inner hollow, but did not disappear then reappear.

Bernadette again reacted to passages where the beginning of each apparition was described in these words: "First, a soft light cast a golden glow over the niche and the ledge. Then everything was bathed in the ever-brightening light and on the wild rosebush (the bramble, Bernadette called it) the lady appeared."[46]

Was Bernadette tired? Still upset over the previous inaccuracies? Did Lasserre misread or miswrite? We do not know. Nevertheless, this is what he wrote: "Vision first, light afterwards."

In the final draft of *"The Protest,"* he was more specific: "It is inaccurate that I saw the light first and the vision afterwards; what happened was just the opposite."

The additional contradiction has her regressing. Actually, Bernadette did not react when just a few minutes earlier he had read about the February 11 apparition, where the missionaries had also written: "All of a sudden, the niche and the rosebush lit up, and in the middle of the brightness, under the arch of the ledge, a lady, radiant, young, wondrously beautiful...."[47]

Was it at that very moment or later? In any event, Lasserre noted in his own hand at this spot on the copy he had submitted to Bernadette: "The apparition first and the light after."[48]

Here the writer, carried away by success, contradicts Bernadette's *constant* testimony, numerous echoes of which can be found in the *Histoire authentique*.[49]

A more serious consequence for himself: he thus contradicted his own history, where he had faithfully reported Bernadette's constant affirmation. On this point, therefore, by challenging the work of the missionaries he was simultaneously challenging his own. The most curious thing is that they had borrowed this detail from him. In this instance, Henri Lasserre's weapon became a boomerang.

The interview went along more rapidly because the rest of the account did not greatly lay itself open to criticism.

Bernadette reacted again at the point in the account at which the missionaries said that the Virgin asked her "to leave her candle... at the grotto."[50]

"That's not true," she protested. "*She* never asked me for a candle."

What's true is that Bernadette did indeed *leave* a candle at the grotto, March 25, with all those that were already burning there. It was her Aunt Lucile's sodality candle. Bernadette had asked her aunt for permission, but she was acting on her own initiative and not at the request of the apparition, as popular devotion had it.[51]

Bernadette's final reaction took place two installments later in response to the passages describing, December 1868.

"Bernadette, as was her habit, heard holy Mass before leaving," said the *Petite histoire* concerning the morning of March 4 (day of the last apparition of the fifteen days).

"I would go to Mass sometimes, but not every day," Bernadette here observed.

She spoke the truth, but it is also certain she did go that day. Her aunt, Jeanne Soubirous, had died the day before and the Mass was being celebrated for her.[52]

Lasserre jotted down one last notation, imperfect and incomplete, concerning page 148 of the January 1869 *Annales*. We will omit this, for the passage is without interest and Lasserre himself deleted it from the rough draft of *"The Protest,"* as he did in the final version.

Now he moved quickly to rework Bernadette's remarks into a format that would deal a crushing blow to the missionaries. Recasting in his own style the notes he had jotted down so hurriedly, he toughened, transposed, and turned observations that had been limited and most often qualified, into generalizations. Anxious to have a juridical instrument, in due and proper form, against the missionaries, he invited the visionary to circle the passages to which she had objected. He reread the definitive text, which begins like this:

"I, the undersigned, Bernadette Soubirous, in religion Soeur Marie-Bernard, having received notice from Monsieur Henri Lasserre of the *'Petite histoire de Notre-Dame de Lourdes,'* contained in the *Annales* (published by the missionaries of Lourdes), I owe it to the truth to protest against this account, of which a large number of details are fabricated and imaginary, as much in what concerns me as in what concerns the very fact of the apparitions. I declare to be contrary to the truth specifically the passages contained on pages: 69, 70, 71, 72, 73, 74, 75, 76, 86, 88, 89, 90, 93, 103, 114, 132, 148."

This language was certainly foreign to Bernadette. She was obviously unfamiliar with the word "fabricated." The phrase "as much in what concerns me as in what concerns..." also exceeded her vocabulary and syntax. Lastly, this wording eliminated the subtle distinction between what Bernadette had declared contrary to the truth and what she had said she had forgotten.

In conclusion, Lasserre had her saying: "Of various *other* details, I have no recollection, but all these things are enough for me to protest against the overall quality and particular character of this account."

Assuredly this was going too far. Bernadette had reacted against a few minute details which were fairly external to the very fact of the apparitions, against conjectures, editorial clumsiness and excess, which affected the particular *character* rather than the *overall quality* and substance of the account.

But at the time when Lasserre completed his writing, that was not the difficulty. What the sisters called into question was the very principle of getting Bernadette's signature. They did not want her to get involved in this dispute. They took shelter behind the bishop, who obviously would refuse to let her sign the statement. "Bernadette cannot sign without Monseigneur's permission," the sisters told Lasserre.

No matter, Henri Lasserre was invited to dinner that evening at 6:30 at the bishop's house. The meal had been arranged in his honor, to celebrate the success of his book in Rome and through-out the Christian world. It was time. Lasserre was in a hurry. He was one of the last to arrive at the bishop's house. It was impossible to start out by talking about what was on his mind. He knew how to exercise self-control. He observed the rising warmth of the conversations at this banquet, the center of which was himself. But as he left the table, he asked the bishop for a few words "in private." Lasserre showed the bishop the protest drawn up in his own *hand-writing,* and asked him to authorize Bernadette's signature.

"What need have you of a signature?" replied the bishop. "You told me this morning that your only goal was to assure the accuracy of your account. This goal has been achieved. What more do you want?"

The writer was persuasive. He had an answer for everything.

"You must be anxious to return to my guests, who were invited here in your honor," the bishop continued. "We'll continue this conversation after they've gone."

"But it will be too late. Bernadette will be in bed, and I won't be able to get her signature."

"Well then, if she doesn't sign tonight, she can sign tomorrow morning.... There's no great danger in waiting, is there?"

"But that's impossible, I have to take the midnight train home."[53]

Then Lasserre added an irrefutable argument: "My wife is about to deliver and...I don't know whether I'll get home in time even if I leave tonight...." (Note: The date was October 13, 1869, and Marthe M. Lasserre was born on October 31, 1869).

The private conversation between the host and the guest of honor could not go on any longer. For the sake of peace, the bishop came up with a solution. "Very well, I agree to give Bernadette permission to sign, but on condition that you promise to transmit this document to the bishop of Tarbes and never publish it."

The bishop wrote down this condition on the document...which, he admitted, he never even took "time to read."[54]

It was late, almost the sisters' bedtime. Lasserre hurried over to the motherhouse with his magic paper. The bishop's "permission" became an agreement, if not an order. Bernadette put her signature at the bottom of the page. Lasserre also had her initial his rough draft, as on a notarized document. He was an expert in matters of law and court proceedings.

Père Sempé's *"Counter-Protest"*

Emotions ran high in Tarbes and Lourdes when the bishop received the text of the explosive *"Protest."*

Père Sempé, superior of the missionaries and co-author of the *Petite histoire,* stopped at Nevers a month later, on November 16, 1869. It was his turn to interview Bernadette "in the presence of the superior general and two assistants."[55]

The atmosphere was tense. The sisters had endured being reprimanded by the bishop of Tarbes. They were quite apprehensive. Bernadette, now aware of the broader impact of this affair, had lost her composure. She arrived "in tears," acting under obedience and visibly upset at being there.[56]

While it was impossible to see things clearly in such an atmosphere, Sempé tried to restore calm, to set their minds at rest. He had no intention of exploring the arena of legal depositions and litigations. He was simply conducting an informal inquiry to uncover the truth, hidden among so many contradictions. Once calm had been restored, he questioned "Bernadette at length." He showed her the details of the *Petite histoire* that were in dispute. Here is how he summed up the results of the interview in his letter the following day:

"It is impossible that she intended to protest against the character and overall quality of the account in the *Annales,* which she had never read nor heard read—no more than against the other facts which had never been submitted to her."[57]

Here, the testimony of the superior general, Mère Joséphine Imbert, witness to both examinations, agrees with Père Sempé's. On December 10, 1869, she wrote to Henri Lasserre: "Soeur Marie-Bernard had no intention of protesting against the overall quality and particular character of the general account, *Histoire de Notre-Dame de Lourdes,* but only against those facts you pointed out to her. She has never read the *Annales de Lourdes,* no more than she had your book; you know that, Monsieur! She cannot object to something she does not know."

This correction seems to indicate that Lasserre's reading had been incomplete, that he sometimes pointed out or referred to facts mentioned by the missionaries, more than actually *"reading"* them.

Père Rémi Sempé, superior of the Chaplains of the Grotto

Be that as it may, Lasserre finally abandoned his blanket. In editing *"The Protest,"* in 1870, he deleted the contested phrase in his memoir to the Holy Office, and reduced it to a note with cumbersome explanations aiming at justifying it.

Concerning the various details about which he had talked to Bernadette, Sempé concluded in these words: "She remembered yesterday, in our presence, that, before the apparitions, she did not know the ordinary morning and night prayers; that her mother sometimes said night prayers with the family; but she did not deny, even though she had no memory of this, that the night of the first apparition she might have said aloud, amidst sobs and tears: 'O Mary, conceived without sin....'

"She remembered that on that day, February 11, she compared to dishwater, the water in the river, which her two companions had found ice-cold."[58]

If all these details are inconsistent with the text of *"The Protest,"* composed by Lasserre, they were, on the contrary, quite consistent with what he had *jotted down hurriedly in the interview notes* we have already referred to. Likewise for the following:

"She remembered that the following Sunday, the day of the second apparition, there had been question between the children and her, about bringing holy water to the grotto; but she could not remember at all who first came up with the idea, she or the children."

Basically, what she denied to Henri Lasserre was the sentence he attributed to her: "This lady, perhaps she is something evil!" Naturally, she never had such an idea. Nevertheless, she was indeed the one who wrote in her own account in 1864: "Then I began to sprinkle holy water at her, telling her that if she came from God, to stay; but if not, to go away...."[59]

As for being taken from the grotto to the mill on February 14, Bernadette was more negative; and Sempé, who did not understand the key to the problem (loss of contact with the outside world connected with the state of ecstasy) recorded her negative reaction, unaware both of its cause and its meaning:

"She...*does not remember*...what happened that day on the road from the grotto to the mill, nor even at the mill...."

In actuality, the problem was not that Bernadette *did not remember,* but that *she had perceived nothing* of what the others had seen and done on the way.

Sempé clearly felt that there was something defective in his wording. He crossed out what he had just written and started over.

"She denied having been carried to the mill, and having seen the Blessed Virgin there."

That was no better, because the word "deny" was too strong to describe Bernadette's confused state.

The next version was better: "She does not remember the many witnesses who saw and heard her, but she would not be so bold as to deny what these witnesses say; and she does remember that her mother came to the mill to get her."[60]

This states the essential, though not with perfect accuracy. The short trip to the mill had gone undetected by Bernadette who was in ecstasy.

Bernadette remembered being at the grotto and even seeing the rock (her last recollection of the outside world). She also remembered finding herself at the mill. Between the two, she was aware only of the apparition, neither of reality around her nor of the short walk.

In a word, even on that apparently most serious detail, *"The Protest"* was a tempest in a teapot. Bernadette's statements, made to the two men who questioned her one after the other agree, if we accept them for what they are, and if we place them in the overall context, rigorously established by analyzing the evidence.

As for the rest, Sempé summed up the results of his cross-examination:

"Regarding the other details called into question...such as her companions' stockings, their dresses raised up too high, Jeanne's swearword, her own comments and objections—she has no recollection of these at all, and, still innocent as a child, says that she does not believe them, but she does not venture to say they are not true."

Seeing Bernadette's emotion and wanting to avoid another river of tears (the first had dried up during the interview), Sempé abandoned the idea of drawing up a notarized document, as Lasserre had done. This was his explanation: "It would be a genuine and useless act of cruelty to force her, as has been done, to write a signature which would then trouble her timid conscience and be the cause of many tears. The word of a priest who affirms before God that this is the outcome of the November 16 interview—his affirmation, I believe, suffices. Moreover, these lines read and reread today in the presence of witnesses to this interview, who bear witness to their accuracy, prove that I have not been mistaken. Also proved is something we already knew, something Monsieur Lasserre himself said: 'Bernadette has largely forgotten the little details.'"[61]

On the well-known question of the light, where Lasserre's suggestions had confused her, Bernadette *appeared the most discomfited.* On this subject, Sempé first wrote: "The question of the light disturbed her a great deal; she stated only that she saw..."

He crossed out that sentence and started over: "As for the light, Bernadette, very disturbed by this question, merely affirmed that she still saw it for a moment after the Virgin's disappearance."[62]

This disturbance on something she had affirmed so often and so consistently during the early years[63] proves to what extent her treatment at the hands of others finished up clouding her memory, and details disappeared.

The Balance Sheet on *"The Protest"*

Has history been the loser because a more methodical debate, conducted by third parties, was never carried out? Without a doubt; but we have lost very little. In the first place, *"The Protest"* affects only minor details. Secondly, the considerable weight of the evidence has allowed us to satisfactorily untangle the skein as has been done in *Histoire authentique des apparition.*[64]

At the end of this critical analysis we pointed out some conjectures and editorial conclusions in the writing of the missionaries. But we found that the same things, as well as some misleading generalizations, were also noted in the composition of *"The Protest."*

This was already evident when we compared this final version with the interview notes, taken by Henri Lasserre himself, and to a greater extent when we contrasted the notes with the many earlier statements of Bernadette and the other witnesses.

Lasserre also seems to have considered the inaccuracy and the approximation of the document he had managed to have Bernadette sign. On the one hand, he had stopped trying to hang on to the conclusion rejected by the Sisters of Nevers. On the other hand and most glaringly, he never corrected his own history on the points where Bernadette had objected, saying, according to *"The Protest,"* "It's the opposite that is true."

The historian knew how to correct his works when they met

with a denial. For this reason, he corrected his fanciful account of Bishop Dupanloup's visit to Nevers, following criticism from Bishop Forcade (volume 1 of the *Logia*[65]). On the other hand, Lasserre retained the passage where he had Bernadette stating that light preceded the apparition. These lines were reproduced, without correction or retraction, in more than a million copies of his *Notre-Dame de Lourdes,* which were printed in several dozen languages, for this book was the "best seller" of the nineteenth century, at least in the field of religion. On this point, then, *"The Protest"* appeared to Lasserre to be without purpose.

We will not spend any more time on the aftermath of this affair. Lasserre published *"The Protest"* in a confidential memoir, addressed to the Holy Office in Rome, where he denounced the account of the Chaplains of Lourdes and their "commercialism at the grotto." The whole affair backfired on him, because the decision of the Holy Office went against him, and the denunciations made in town against him caused his translation of the gospels (reviewed by the English exegete, Alfred Plummer, as "uncritical but interesting") to be wrongly placed on the *Index of Forbidden Books.* Édouard Drumont recounted this episode at length in his *"Testament d'un antisémite"* (Testament of an Anti-Semite).[66] But let us remain within the limits of this volume.

Bernadette's Tears

What concerns us here are the words spoken by Bernadette and the trial she experienced, even to the point of weeping. Tears also speak a particular language, and they are solidly substantiated in this case...though with differences that, at first sight, are perplexing. Let us judge from the two excerpts that follow.

On December 10, 1869, Mère Joséphine Imbert, the superior general and witness at the interview, wrote to Henri Lasserre: "Soeur Marie-Bernard was not distressed after your visit. But she was very troubled in the presence of Père Sempé. She wept and contradicted herself through lapses of memory on certain points of little importance."

By contrast, one of the two sister assistants told Père Sempé, just before his meeting with Bernadette: "Soeur Marie-Bernard...wept a great deal after Monsieur Lasserre's visit...and it made her sick."[67]

These two statements are apparently contradictory. According to the first, Lasserre's visit did not cause any distress; according to the second, it provoked tears. They are reconciled by what Sempé honestly declared in his account of the day itself, as in the memoir of 1873: "I found the good Sister (Bernadette) in a state of extraordinary sorrow. *She arrived in tears.* She did not want to say anything and kept repeating that she had forgotten—that they had written down her answers at the time; that it was necessary to stick to what had been written then...."

The three texts and the context lead to the following outline of events: after the interview with Lasserre (October 13) and before the interview with Sempé (November 17), Bernadette learned of the turmoil caused by the way her statements were being used. She pondered and felt lost; she considered how much she had forgotten. According to the sister assistant's testimony, she wept over this. She received word of Père Sempé's arrival. She was about to meet the superior of the missionaries in Lourdes; he had been hurt by her remarks. She thought about it, and the sobbing recurred. She arrived "in tears," according to the words used both by Mère Joséphine and Sempé himself. This was her condition when he first met her. So he endeavored not to add to her distress but to calm her down. He seems to have succeeded.

Beyond the personal confrontations and the tears, the ordeal had been very demanding on Bernadette. As a result, she discovered that the simple event at Massabielle had become a source of conflict. She also discovered how fragile and fleeting were her memories. Up to that point, she had been self-assured in her testimony; but now the event was slipping away from her; she was filled with uncertainty; the best in her was coming undone and growing more distant. In this way, she found herself cast into the thick darkness of a night that is difficult to get used to: the night of pure faith.

CHAPTER 17

— ⚜ —

BERNADETTE THE INFIRMARIAN

episcl

12 62
change

The ordeal of photographers and of historians were only intermittent episodes in a life of hard work.

Assistant Infirmarian

On October 30, 1867, Bernadette began working in the infirmary. She was no longer limited to minor physical duties, as during the time of her novitiate, while she was convalescing. After her profession, she was assigned the position of assistant infirmarian.

All the little chores rested on her shoulders. She was the one who filled the flower vases for the statue of the Virgin in the infirmary. She replenished them at the fountain near the Saint Gertrude stairway and politely begged pardon of Soeur Marthe Clamens, assigned to keep that area clean.[1] She also had less charming chores, along the lines of her previous duty of cleaning toilets....

But she quickly took on added responsibilities. She had influence over the sick. She could brighten up recreations and just as easily remind them of times of silence with a no-nonsense "Shh!"[2]

"No self-control!"[3] she said to Soeur Pélagie Laborie, who had trouble holding her tongue.

"She always had the kind word that relaxed, reassured, and got them to take their medicine,"[4] stated one of her first patients, Soeur Bernard Dalias, who was under her care from August to October 1869. Bernadette had formed a friendly partnership with her, that she connected with the closeness of their names: Bernadette and Bernard. She said to her young patient, "You're asking me for something.... I wouldn't do it for anyone else; but it's for a Bernard...."[5]

On days when everything went wrong, Bernadette addressed her friend with the familiar *tu* (you): "My poor Bernard, you can't take any more? But you're only halfway done!"[6]

She gave her a collection of hymns popular at Notre-Dame de Lourdes, which she had received as a gift: "Here, take it; it's more your cup of tea than mine. I have permission to give it away...."[7] Bernadette kept nothing.

Her advice was short and simple. To Soeur Cécile Pagès, who was very impatient to have her prayers answered after one novena, Bernadette said, "Oh! The Blessed Virgin...wants us to pray to her a long time."[8]

Soeur Dominique Brunet was worried about some dental surgery—done, in those days, without anesthesia. "So, Mademoiselle, you don't want to suffer?"[9] Bernadette asked her.

Her patients remembered her maxims, which were, besides, the classic ones:

"See God in your superiors."[10]

"When you obey, you can't go wrong."[11]

Head Infirmarian

Bernadette's proficiency was as great as her moral authority. She was known for her dexterity, firmness and precision. Her patients bore abundant witness to this.[12]

By accepting the whole job, quite simply, Bernadette settled a difficult situation. The official infirmarian, Soeur Marthe, was sick. She could no longer be relied on. On April 12, 1870, she went home to rest until June 9. On her return, she was unable to continue with her work. After December 23, her condition worsened. The bishop came to bless her on March 22, 1871. She died on November 8, 1872. Without fanfare, Soeur Marie-Bernard took on all the duties and responsibilities. She had become head infirmarian at the motherhouse, a position she would hold until October 30, 1873.

The infirmary at Saint-Gildard's.
These jars and instruments are the very ones used by Bernadette.

Bernadette had patiently learned her craft, including complex pharmaceutical measurements, which at that time were midway between the traditional French units and the metric system—a changeover much more difficult than converting from "old" to "new" francs (something that many lawyers in France never managed to get used to, even after ten years).

Bernadette diligently absorbed the new measurements. She wrote in her infirmary notebooks:

One *grain* equals 5 centigrams

Three *scruples* or one *dram, 4 grams*

One *ounce, 32 grams*

She also noted, "Since a change in the position of a decimal point can involve significant differences, it is desirable that, in formulas, quantities in grams, decigrams, centigrams and milligrams be written out in full."[13]

As an added precaution, she always wrote down the amounts in both measures. She did this in the record book she had drawn up for the various illnesses: coughing up blood, dysentery, cold humors, scrofula, king's evil.

S'il y a en même temps des centigrammes et des milligrammes, chacun d'eux conserve sa place.

0,1018 grammes. = 18 milligrammes ou 1 centigramme et 8 milligrammes
0,1046

S'il y a en même temps des décigrammes, des centigrammes et des milli..., on les écrit à la manière suivante:

0,138 grammes. = 138 milligr. ou 1 décigr. 3 centigr. 8 milligr.
0,836

S'il y a des grammes 1 gramme 1 décigr. 3 centigr 6 milligr.

S'il y a des grammes et des fractions de grammes, on suit la même règle. 1,236 grammes = 1 gra 2 décigr. 3 centigr. 6 milligr.
6,348

Comme un changement dans la position de la virgule peut entraîner des différences très graves, il est à désirer que dans les formules les quantités en grammes, décigrammes, centigr., et milligr. soient inscrites en toutes lettres.

Miquel a indiqué un moyen mnémonique qui lui sera fort utile aux praticiens; il donne une approximation tout à fait suffisante. Pour la transformation des gros en grammes, pas de difficultés; il suffit de multiplier le nombre des gros par 4 pour avoir le nombre des grammes qui y correspondent.

Bernadette painstakingly adapted herself to the metric system, as shown here by her notes.

For the pains of rheumatoid arthritis (misspelling this last word *articulères* instead of *articulaires*), she wrote down, following Dr. Robert Saint-Cyr:

Three cups of elderberry tea
Add to each, 5 drops of distillate of monkshood
Monkshood liniment: 18 grains...1 gram
Olive oil: 35 grains, 2 grams
Lard: one ounce, 32 grams.[14]

Even outside the infirmary, Bernadette kept an eye open. In March–April 1870, she ran into Soeur Angèle Lompech, who was attending to her duties, her hands chapped and bleeding. "You put me to shame with hands like that. You must come to the infirmary and I'll take care of you," Bernadette told her.

"For a few days, I did indeed go up to the infirmary. She put honey on my hands, and a few days later, I was cured,"[15] Soeur Angèle recalls.

This "honey," no doubt, was beeswax.

A little later, she had to treat Soeur Angèle's eyes. "She used an eyedropper and put one drop of collyrium in each eye, which made me cry. Then she said, 'What! I give you one drop and in return you give me several!'"[16]

Bernadette's advice covered both the physical and the spiritual. "Accept willingly what the good Lord sends,"[17] she told Soeur Angèle. And another time: "Don't let the water run needlessly."[18]

"Don't push yourself forward,"[19] she recommended to Soeur Madeleine Bounaix. "Ask our Lord for a good memory so you won't forget what I tell you," she told this same sister who was inclined to be flighty.[20]

Bernadette knew how to listen, how to understand. One Thursday, while scrubbing down a statue that needed cleaning, Soeur Julienne Capmartin, who gave her a hand with the heavy jobs, unburdened herself of a dream that had been haunting her for a few months:

"Being in the house, I dreamed, I told her, that I was back in the novitiate....

"The Blessed Virgin had placed the infant Jesus in my arms.... Walking along with him, I met Mère Thérèse Montagné.... He looked at her with pleasure. Further on was a sister I liked very much; and as I was trying to draw the Holy Child's attention to her, he turned his head away so abruptly that his movement woke me up. Quite struck by this refusal, I realized it was just a dream, and I was relieved.

"Barely back to sleep, I found the Infant Jesus in my arms again, but as lifelike as if he had been real. A sister about whom I was rather indifferent happened to come along.... I was astounded to see the little Jesus stretch his small arms out to this sister, happy to let her fondle him. Then the Blessed Virgin gestured me to return the Divine Child to her and I immediately did.

"I was very surprised that Soeur Marie-Bernard did not tell me to be quiet, for it often happened that she would call me a chatterbox! But not at all. She looked at me from time to time, then smiled and said to me, 'You like that sister too much. Baby Jesus has given you a lesson by showing you that what we like too much, he doesn't like. He didn't say anything to you?'

"'No. I was really quite happy to carry him and see him smile.'

"'To whom have you told this dream?'

"'So far...only you.'

"She gave me a smile that I can still see...."[21]

Why did Bernadette listen that day? No doubt, because this conversation was, in reality, a liberation of the spirit. She sensed the sister needed to talk. Hence, her friendly attention, her dream interpretation and her smile.

But she could also give a clean and perfect rebuke. Thus it was for Soeur Claire Basset, who recalls: "I had practically wrung a permission from her [Bernadette] to attend a lecture by our mistress (Mère Vauzou) at Saint-Gertrude's...with the order to return at a specified time. But the lesson was followed by an informal, motherly talk which I did not have the heart to leave. Back at the infirmary, I gave the extenuating reasons for my tardiness, which carried no weight at all. I can still see the harsh look on the dear infirmarian, scolding me the way I deserved and ordering me to go confess my fault to the appropriate person."[22]

Bernadette firmly intervened one day when the order to stay in bed had not been carried out: "Not understood?... Not received?..." Soeur Claire relates that "A full investigation began and then the two guilty parties were thoroughly admonished. I seem to remember that because of this the sick novice spent two days in bed."[23]

A similar scene occurred for Soeur Eudoxie Chatelain, on August 10, 1872:[24] "I had had two severe bouts of fever, and they dreaded a third. Our Mother Mistress, who understood me, had come that night to comfort me, and I spent an excellent night. In the morning, finding myself well, I got up and went to hear holy Mass from the choir loft. I returned about 8:30, when I had finished my prayers. On my return, Soeur Laurent Debiard said to me, 'You know, Soeur Marie-Bernard is very displeased because you left the infirmary without permission.'

"'But,' I answered, 'I'm not sick anymore.'

"'All the same, she said, you should've stayed.'

"When I did get to see (Soeur Marie-Bernard), I gave her my reasons, which I thought were good; but she spoke to me about religious obedience as binding in the infirmary as at the novitiate....

"Despite my independent spirit, which was very strong at the time, I said 'What should I do?'

"'Go back to bed.[25] Sacrifice is worth more than prayer,' added Bernadette.[26]

"The next day, I asked her for permission to get up.... She gave it to me and that evening I went back to the novitiate," said Soeur Eudoxie, ending her story.[27]

Soeur Julienne Capmartin relates a similar incident: "She caught me reading my Children of Mary manual, after she had told me to keep well covered in bed, in order to perspire.... She snatched the book away from me. 'Now, here's a bit of zeal sewn up with disobedience,...' Bernadette said.

"Try as I might to ask for my book back, I never saw it again."[28]

Once she was on her own ground, Bernadette suffered no lack of authority, even before the venerable mother general. At the beginning of winter, 1871, during a cold spell, Soeur Alexis Féral, then a novice, relates: "Soeur Marie-Bernard lit a big fire.... During recreation, finding it was getting too hot, she opened the window.... Along came Mother General, who...was surprised at this and scolded Soeur Marie-Bernard, [saying] 'Doesn't that make you feel guilty?'

"'Oh no, my dear Mother!' Bernadette responded.

Only afterwards did obedience take the upper hand.

"She closed the windows and a quarter of an hour later...went to the community room to make her *culp*."[29]

The infirmarian's day began regularly at "7:45 A.M.," Soeur Eudoxie Chatelain tells us. Upon arriving, "she would inquire about our condition and would serve us breakfast, which a novice brought from the kitchen. She went from one infirmary to the other, with no time to sit down or to do sit-down work. From time to time, she would say something spiritual, like, 'Really love the good Lord, my children. That says everything.'"[30]

Bernadette's nights were spent watching. When she had to, she spent them near the seriously sick, but she had help for this duty. At the beginning of October 1871, Soeur Clémence Chassan was sent to sit up with an aged sister who was dying.

"If you see her getting worse, come get me," Bernadette directed.

"At eleven o'clock, I called her," Soeur Clémence recalls. "She came right away. I was amazed at the kindness and gentleness she showed her patient.

"After seeing to it that the Last Rites had been administered, she asked our Mother Assistant's permission to spend the rest of the night. The time seemed quite short to me.... I was impressed by her fervor, especially when she said prayers to the Blessed Virgin."[31]

Another night that same month, it was Soeur Joseph Ducout who was sent to sit up with this same gravely ill religious. She has left us with the sister's name: Mère Dosithée Vielcazal.

"I was...very nervous about caring for the patient, who was strongly agitated, troubled at the thought of death.

"Not knowing what to do, I went to get (Bernadette).... She got up and came immediately. She said to me, 'We'll give her some Lourdes water and pray for her....' Instantly, the patient grew calm, physically and emotionally. She died most peacefully two hours later."[32]

Bernadette liked these duties and responsibilities. She wanted to carry them out in their full human dimension, among the poor. She still had hopes of doing this in the autumn of 1871, when she introduced Soeur Clémence Chassan to "certain medications," with a view to her future duties.

"I'd love to go take care of the sick in hospices," she said. "I'm afraid...that my health may not permit me to be sent; but I submit myself to the good Lord's will, to do with me as he pleases."[33]

On September 3, 1872, Doctor Robert Saint-Cyr, the mother-house doctor, physician and president of the *Société des médecins de la Nièvre* (Medical Society of Nièvre), drew up this evaluation of Bernadette: "An infirmarian who does her work to perfection. Short, frail looking, she is twenty-seven years old. Possessing a calm and gentle nature, she cares for her patients with great intelligence, overlooking nothing she has been ordered to do. Accordingly, she enjoys great authority and, for my part, my complete confidence."[34]

Infirmarian and Patient

Everything was going along fine. There was only one dark shadow: the health of the infirmarian.

In a letter of April 6, 1869—Bernadette's only letter that year, recently discovered—she wrote, "The good Lord judged it best to make me spend the Easter holidays in bed. The attack was severe... but it didn't last long."[35]

In October 1869, she was again sick in bed. To help her, the superiors kept Soeur Cécile Pagès in the community for three weeks, though she had been called to exercise her nursing duties in Paris.

"Bernadette was then in bed," Soeur Cécile relates, "spitting up blood by the half-basinful. I was applying blistering agents.

"'You can pull hard,' Bernadette directed. 'I'm used to pain... like a cat with nine lives.'[36]

"Our venerable Mère Imbert used to come see her. They'd chat.... Bernadette would tell us, 'If you offer up your life in sacrifice, don't you go to heaven?...'

"I jokingly said, 'We'd have at least one saint, instead of having none in our Congregation.'

"And our venerable Mother said, 'You think there aren't any? I think there are.'

"'But not canonized,' I told her.

"As she was leaving, our venerable Mother asked me what I thought of Bernadette's condition. I told her that I thought she was doing very poorly, and she added, 'Yes, the doctor thinks that she could easily die coughing up blood.'"

On November 6, 1869, the *Journal de la Communauté* (the Community Journal) has this entry: "Soeur Marie-Bernard is sick. She is chronically ill."

On April 12, 1870, the two infirmarians were sick in bed at the same time.[37] For Bernadette, it was serious.

"We thought her nearing the end," Soeur Honorine Laffargue relates. "One morning, I was in the cloister, a little before 5:30 A.M., awaiting the signal to go to chapel.

"Our mistress, coming downstairs from her room, said to me, 'Soeur Honorine, go see how Soeur Marie-Bernard's night went.'

"I went into the infirmary and found this dear sister, so to speak, at death's door. It seemed to me she had but a few hours to live.

"'My dear sister,' I said to her, 'our mistress has sent me to ask you how your night went.'

"'Tell her not to worry, I won't die today.'[38] Bernadette replied."

A prophecy? No, it was rather the usual remission that followed her asthma attacks, as on the day she was professed "at the point of death."

From May 15, 1870 to the beginning of 1872, except for the usual setbacks of the two winters in the period from January–February,[39] Bernadette had a good spell, during which she showed what she was capable of. This was even the only time she wrote without further comment, "My health is pretty good,"[40] and perhaps even (though this letter is no doubt apocryphal), "My health is marvelous" (1872?).[41] Yet there were setbacks; from March–April 1871, for more than a month, she "suffered terribly." Her asthma attacks were such that she had to be kept under constant supervision; but "not one complaint," only short invocations, noted one of her night attendants.

In January 1872, Bernadette herself drew this picture to reassure people: "My health is no worse than it was last year. Only the bitter cold this winter has been a bit of an ordeal. I breathe less easily...."

The attack the following winter, 1872–1873, was more serious. On January 17, "she was admitted to Saint Julienne's infirmary." [42] On February 3, she was still "very sick."[43]

She could attend Mass only on Easter Sunday, April 13. A relapse followed; she "had to stay in bed" for two weeks.[44] On May 12, 1873, she was well on the mend at last.

Mère Joséphine Imbert, also convalescing, was able to take her by carriage to the orphanage in Varennes.

The nine laundresses, who were beating the laundry in the wash house abandoned brushes and paddles to see Bernadette.[45] She was seated in a wheelchair, and in this position she delivered an exhortation on the month of Mary to the orphans: "My children, love the Blessed Virgin.... Pray hard to her; she will protect you."[46]

June 3 brought a more serious relapse: Bernadette received the Anointing of the Sick for the third time, at least.[47]

Jeanne Jardet, then a young employee at Saint-Gildard's, recalled Bernadette's long absence, for she liked to see her when she came to the kitchen to order meals for the infirmary....

When Bernadette returned, Soeur Cécile Fauron, treasurer in charge of the domestic staff, congratulated her on her recovery. She answered, "They didn't want me up there."[48]

And so Bernadette was relieved of her duties on October 30, 1873.

With the Novices

During this active period of her religious life (1868–1873), Mère Vauzou made good use of Bernadette's radiant personality—whether she was sick or in good health—for the novices' benefit. This was proof both of her appreciation and her good judgment.

"I can certify that, during her eighteen months at the mother-house, in 1869 and 1872, Bernadette never stopped coming up to the novitiate, and circulating among us, although she had been professed since October 1867. I saw her at almost all our noonday recreations and often enough in the evening."[49] Thus spoke Soeur Julienne Capmartin. She specified that this was the only detail "where the superiors relaxed our customs in favor of the saint...."

Actually, professed sisters and novices lived separately, in keeping with the Canon Law of the times.

Bernadette's visits to the novitiate allowed the superiors to "solicit" her prayers, without letting it show. They made their requests to whatever group Bernadette was in. In serious cases, they insisted, "My dear Soeur Marie-Bernard, you heard that, didn't you?"

"Yes, yes, I heard."

"One day, they asked us to pray for a little girl from Nevers, who had disappeared and who was found a few days later in a Gypsy caravan near Vierzon."[50] Soeur Julienne noted.

They also resorted to calling her in to dispel homesickness and other gloomy moods. This was the trouble with Amélie Poujade, who had just arrived from her native Aveyron on May 15, 1873.

"Would seeing Bernadette make you happy?" Mère Marie Thérèse Vauzou asked her.

Such a welcome and embrace were more effective than any sermon, the young girl in question later affirmed.

Bernadette had a sharp eye and could offer pointed words of advice. Soeur Justine Vergeade, a postulant assigned to help with the "general cleaning of the infirmary," had long focused her perfectionism on polishing the copper balls atop the iron bedposts. She innocently called attention to her success. Bernadette replied, "Yes, they're certainly shiny. You worked hard on that job because it shows."

The postulant recalls, "She made this observation so kindly that I didn't feel hurt; but all the same, I felt that little cut of the lancet piercing my swollen pride, and I left with this lesson: the work that is not seen...is seen by God alone...did you do it equally well?"[51]

Bernadette was so simple, so cheerful, so removed from anything hinting of esoteric, dark, or distorted mysticism, that on June 1, 1869, they ended up (by what happy combination of circumstances?) having her repeat the story of the apparitions to four new arrivals.

"Mesdemoiselles," said Mère Vauzou, "I imagine that you would enjoy hearing Soeur Marie-Bernard describe the apparitions in Lourdes.... I'm going to send for her. But afterwards, I want there to be no more talk about these things, at least with her. You will speak to her no more about this."

Soeur Julienne Capmartin was one of the four. "Not once did Bernadette raise her voice," she relates, "and even when talking about the Virgin, she did not get excited. No sign of rapture...or of personal pleasure...answers always precise and short.

"At the end of five or ten minutes, our mistress said to her, 'That's fine, daughter, you may go now.'"[52]

"Go now." That Bernadette was very willing to do, for she didn't like to see certain kinds of fervor get stirred up.

Her presence was even more "desired by the novices" because it was rare. "Sickness too often kept her in the infirmary," relates Soeur Clémence Chassan, a novice from August to November 1871. That's why after a long absence, "we waited for her and greeted her with a deep bow. She got angry and said, 'Since you pay me honors I don't deserve, I won't stay with you during this recreation.'

"And it was with great difficulty that we kept her there. We had to promise to be more simple with her; then she edified us by her simplicity and good humor."[53]

This was the atmosphere Soeur Victoire Girard found in February, 1871. "The first day I arrived at our motherhouse, during the evening recreation (at the novitiate) I asked the sister next to me to point out Soeur Marie-Bernard. She replied, 'Yes.' That's as far as I got until the next day. I made the same request of another sister who answered 'Why, you were right next to her last evening....'"[54]

What Soeur Eléonore Bonnet, a postulant from August to November 1871, remembers was Bernadette's hearty laughter during a singing exam. "To show off her beautiful voice," like the crow in the fable, Eléonore had chosen the hymn:

Etoile,	*O Star*
sans voile,	*unveiled,*
Fais à mes yeux	*show to my sight*
éclore l'aurore	*the breaking dawn*
d'un jour radieux.	*of day so bright.*

To Bernadette, this "cuteness" was irresistibly funny.

L'APPARITION

A LA

GROTTE DE LOURDES

EN 1858

NOTICE RÉDIGÉE

Par M. l'abbé FOURCADE

Chanoine, Secrétaire de la Commission

Approuvée par Monseigneur l'Evêque de Tarbes

ET CONTENANT

L'ORDONNANCE ET LE MANDEMENT DU PRÉLAT SUR LA QUESTION

TARBES

J.-A. FOUGA, IMPRIMEUR DE L'ÉVÊCHÉ

— 1862 —

Avec réserve de tous droits.

Fourcade's brief account. The only book on the apparitions ever read by Bernadette.

"You embarrassed me," Soeur Eléonore later told her.

"It's true, I really laughed. But you must admit, there certainly was good reason...."[55] Bernadette replied.

During the classic crying spell of the first few days, Bernadette told her, "Don't worry, you'll soon get used to it. Everybody's nice here."[56]

If Bernadette automatically ran away from honors, it was painful for her to leave when certain books were being read. Although, theoretically, "she was unaware of what had been written about the apparitions,"[57] it was easy for her to see that the topic was Lourdes. On that score, the superiors were on the alert. They pleaded with Henri Lasserre not to paint "a flattering picture of Bernadette." He paid no attention. But to beg their forgiveness, on January 16, he sent them a *manuscript* of the first installment of the *Revue du monde catholique*, No. 10, December 1867—just out that very month— together with a moving letter, in which he supported their views, but from another angle. He begged them to promise that *Bernadette would never read this book*. To what extent was Bernadette's humility his primary motive? To what extent was it a tactful means of gaining the sisters' goodwill or of keeping Bernadette's blunt critical spirit from shattering his stained-glass window into a thousand pieces? The fact remains that the principle was ratified. Bernadette never read anything except Fourcade's *Notice* (Review), appearing in 1862[58] and the passages from the *Petite histoire*, selected by Henri Lasserre at the time of *"The Protest."*

Mère Vauzou

When Lasserre's first installment was read at the convent in mid-January 1868, Bernadette had been excluded.

The scene repeated itself in June 1868, when Père Sempé sent the first installment of the *Annales*. "You're tired, go lie down," Mère Vauzou would say, whenever this reading came up.

Bernadette was not fooled by these periodic dismissals. In August 1871, when Julie Garros saw Bernadette "go back up to the infirmary before the end of recreation," something that had happened "several times," she asked her, "Why so early?"

"Since they want to read something on Lourdes, they're sending me out,"[59] Bernadette replied.

How did they go about it? One day Soeur Julienne Capmartin

saw what happened. Between May 29 and July 15, 1869, Bernadette came, as usual, to take part in the recreation at the novitiate; but her arrival interrupted a reading.

"Soeur Marie-Bernard," said the mistress of novices, "this is no time for you to be here. Your place is in the infirmary." She added, "Kiss the floor and leave."

To kiss the floor was a widely accepted practice at the time. "I'm still looking for a brick I haven't kissed," said Soeur Julienne, who has left the following account:

"Soeur Marie-Bernard fell to her knees and kissed the pavement, stood back up, and without a word, headed toward the door. Mother Mistress stopped her and asked her what she wanted.

"'My dear sister,' Bernadette answered, 'I've come on behalf of Mademoiselle Irène. She's feeling better today and asks your permission to get up before noon.'

"'I permit her to get up,' replied Mère Marie-Thérèse, 'but only this evening, after she has eaten something.'

"Then, with a gesture of tenderness and protection, she laid her hand on Soeur Marie-Bernard's head, saying, 'Go now, my daughter.'"[60]

Was she sent away because the reading concerned Lourdes? The fact remains that, between July and November 1869, whenever Bernadette came "to hear a lecture," that Mère Vauzou was about to begin, she was told, "Go away, Soeur Marie-Bernard."

"Oh, Mother!" she pleaded.

"Go away!" the answer came.

And Bernadette left immediately.[61]

Relations between Bernadette and the mistress of novices were complex. On Mère Vauzou's side, we perceive a mixture of inflexibility and attraction, of disparagement and thoughtfulness, expressed on the one hand, by a certain hostility and, on the other, by the way she entrusted Bernadette with her novices.

The tension stemmed partly from Bernadette's secrecy. The other sisters would open themselves up to the novice mistress; Bernadette was evasive. It was not only a question of our Lady's three secrets. What kept thwarting the mistress of novices was Bernadette's secrecy: a certain transparency of life and love that did not express itself in conversations, or even in meditations, let alone in self-analysis. Bernadette seemed as resistant to self-reflection as she was to self-revelation. In short, she didn't conform to the traditional religious model and only half-fit the patterns of that period, despite an obedience beyond reproach and an all-out effort to assimilate the established values. There was about all this something irritating to Mère Vauzou, a woman who excelled in molding a generation in the image of what she herself had achieved; all the more irritating because Bernadette enjoyed immense prestige. But the misunderstanding arose from a deeper cause. The young professed sister was unknowingly following a different path. The Holy Spirit was forming in her a new kind of sanctity, based solely on the Gospels, without works or words, "hidden from the wise and the learned" (Mt 11:25). The scholar who has written this book has himself also run up against this wall for a long time. Bernadette's writings and sayings do not express the essential. Their meaning is a simple radiance that is grasped intuitively and is obscured by commentary.

Bernadette strongly shared the community's affection and devotion toward Mère Vauzou. She had nothing to say against her. Somehow she instinctively sensed a variance before which her enormous goodwill was helpless, there were also, of course, the deliberate trials or the involuntary sternness which were her fate at the hands of the novice mistress.

A minor episode—which occurred between August and November 1871—shows the ambiguity of this relationship, where reserve and affection combined to create a certain apprehension.

One day, in the infirmary, relates Soeur Joseph Durand, "Bernadette told me 'that she knew our Mother Mistress' footstep perfectly.'

"'Besides,' she added, 'whenever she walks by the infirmary...she usually coughs. Last night, I didn't answer her, because it was the time of silence.'"[62]

Without insistence on either side, we can here surmise an attraction, a need to communicate. Powerless to knock the wall down, Mère Vauzou and Bernadette turned to the substitute language—often elemental—of those who never manage to carry on a real conversation. This episode seemed surprising to those who knew Mère Vauzou. It could not have been fabricated. It denotes a secret space hidden from others and from herself. We will come back to it at the end of this study.

The War of 1870

The major event of this period was the Franco-Prussian war. On September 1, 1870, Napoleon III surrendered at Sedan, bringing on the disaster. Mother General, who had been in Rome since March 26 to have the Constitutions approved, returned on July 7, 1870. As early as the month of August, she put the sisters at the disposition of the Ministry of War. A field hospital was installed at Saint-Gildard's. The bright colors of the military uniforms mingled with the black and white silhouettes of the sisters in the courtyards and corridors of the motherhouse.

On September 6, twenty-five novices were sent to communities in the south; the postulants were sent home to their families. The Prussians were coming. Nevers was on the alert, ready to defend itself. About a hundred militiamen came to replace the sick and wounded in the convent. The military authorities installed cannons on the inner terrace of the motherhouse and in the novitiate gardens, which overlooked the northern part of the city. Rumors were flying in France: Bernadette had been favored with new visions; she had a mission to fulfill with the government. The bishop published a denial in the *Semaine religieuse* (Religious Weekly) of October 10.[63]

"The night of October 24, 1870," relates Mère Eléonore Cassagnes, secretary general of the Congregation, "a strange phenomenon appeared in the sky. The horizon was all ablaze. You might have thought it was a sea of blood."

What lay behind this description, reduced to a metaphor of blood suggested by the circumstances? A particularly brilliant sunset? More than that: "an aurora borealis," which lasted "from seven to nine o'clock at night."[64] The display was very impressive, and Soeur Marie-Bernard was struck by it like everyone else. According to witnesses, they heard her murmur, "And still, they will not be converted."[65]

This is the only hint of earnest emotion we find in her words during this period. Bernadette here expressed a general feeling. She did it by connecting the distinctive nature of this event to a basic theme of Lourdes and of the Gospels: conversion. With this one exception, we do not see her give in to excesses of emotion. Her hardy and simple faith understood providential events according to a system of interpretation common in those days, just as it was in biblical times. But she did this not self-assertively but looking upwards, with dignity, clinging as much as she could to God's point of view.

Around December 9, 1870, when the Prussians were at the departmental borders, the Chevalier Gougenot des Mousseaux interrogated her:

"At the grotto of Lourdes or after...did you get any revelations concerning the future and the destiny of France? Might not the Blessed Virgin have entrusted you with some warning, some threat to France?"

"No."

"The Prussians are at our gates; don't they inspire you with terror?"

"No."

"So there should be nothing to fear then?"

"I only fear bad Catholics."

"Do you fear nothing else?"

"No, nothing."[66]

Soeur Madeleine Bounaix describes another event that occurred toward the end of 1870. "One night a fire broke out in the motherhouse pharmacy. The novice in charge, deeply affected, suffered violent pains, which made her cry for twenty-four hours.... Soeur Marie-Bernard, filled with pity and finding no medicine to tranquilize her said to me, 'We'll give her some Lourdes water and pray to the Blessed Virgin to soothe her....'

"We prayed together. Indeed, a few minutes later, the poor sister's pains subsided, and she stopped screaming."

"There was in Bernadette's voice," later added the witness, Soeur Madeleine,[67] "a note of energy and a supernatural confidence which struck me."[68]

But what struck her most was Bernadette's calm in that apocalyptic atmosphere. She continues: "In May, 1871, during the Commune, learning that *Les Tuileries* (the royal palace) had been burned down, I hurried to go tell (her) about it. She answered me very calmly, 'Don't worry; it needed to be whitewashed. The good Lord is wielding the paintbrush!'"[69]

What information could Bernadette have gotten about the morality of the Tuileries? We do not know.

In any case, the metaphor is certainly hers. She used it in her 1875 letter on the floods: "The good Lord chastises us, but always like a Father. The streets of Paris were soaked with the blood of a great many victims, and it wasn't enough to touch hearts hardened in evil. The streets of the south also had to be washed and have their victims, too."[70]

The following is a related text from a letter Bernadette had written to her father on November 1870, of which Père Cros has saved us this fragment: "People say the enemy is getting closer to Nevers. I could easily do without seeing the Prussians, but I do not fear them. God is everywhere, even in the midst of the Prussians. I remember, when I was very little, after one of Monsieur le Curé's sermons, I heard people saying, 'Bah! He's just doing his job.' I think the Prussians are also just doing their job."[71]

Her Father's Death

The above letter reveals Bernadette's ability to bounce back from events. It was the last letter her father received from her: her father, whom she loved so much, whom she was afraid of loving too much, who had visited her so often when she was being nursed in Bartrès, in 1844, and again during her stay in Momères in 1864. He had planned to come visit her at the end of 1870. Bernadette had discouraged him, because she thought she would be going to Lourdes in the near future.[72]

"About March 6, 1871," relates Soeur Madeleine Bounaix, "I went up to Saint Catherine's infirmary, where I found our dear sister, leaning against the fireplace, crying. I knelt down next to her and asked, 'What's wrong, dear sister? Have I hurt you without even knowing?'

"She answered, 'Oh, no! But two weeks ago you were sad (I had lost a brother of mine) and I consoled you. Today, it's my turn. I've just learned of my poor father's death. He died Saturday.'"[73]

He had died quite suddenly in Lourdes on Saturday, March 4, 1871, at nine o'clock in the evening, after having vomited blood.

"'My Sister," Bernadette added, 'always have great devotion to the agonizing Heart of Jesus, for it's a consolation when we lose loved ones and are absent, to think that we prayed for them. That's what I did Saturday night, without even knowing; by praying for the dying, I was praying for my father, who was beginning his eternity at that moment....'

François Soubirous and the Lacadé Mill, his last home

"She fell ill during those days and for more than a month suffered horribly...."

She did not hide her sorrow.

"I come to weep with you," she wrote to her sister Toinette on March 9, 1871. "Let us, nevertheless, always remain submissive...although heavily afflicted, to our Father's hand which has been striking us so hard for some time. Let us carry and kiss the cross."[74]

In 1871, bereavement followed bereavement in the Soubirous family. Bernadette, Toinette's daughter, died on February 12. On March 16, Lucile Castérot, Bernadette's youngest aunt, the one closest to her, passed away. Bernadette had seen this sorrow coming. She had written on March 6, "It seems Aunt Lucile is quite sick, perhaps even dead at this moment? I'm ready for anything. Write me, I pray, and don't hide anything from me. If my aunt is still alive, tell her I am praying for her, as are all our dear sisters.... I would willingly sacrifice my life to our Lord for her, if it is his will."[75]

On August 23, Toinette lost another son, little Bernard. Although she named her children after Soeur Marie-Bernard, she still could not keep any. She would lose five during Bernadette's life as a religious, and the ordeal touched her deeply.[76]

The visits of friends brought some light to these years of war and sorrows. On April 23, two postulants arrived from Lourdes, where there were then countless vocations: Jeanne Barbazan and Marie Tuhat. They showed her "two photographs of the grotto."

Bernadette leaned over to look at them. "Oh! How the poplars have grown since I left!" she exclaimed and she slipped away.[77]

She loved those poplars on the banks of the Gave: the ones she had seen on February 11, 1858, on the occasion of the "famous gust of wind," announcing the apparition.

The Initiation of Julie Garros

On August 4, 1871, an arrival even more delightful for Bernadette took place. Julie Garros, the young tutor who had taught her catechism in the springtime of the apparitions came to Nevers to enter the Congregation.

How many memories they shared, from the event at the grotto to the sabot thrown into the garden so they could go gather strawberries.... They had been classmates and they made a good pair: Julie's sense of responsibility for Bernadette's schoolwork channeled

Toinette Soubirous, also called "Marie,"
Bernadette's younger sister, lively, bossy, and good-hearted

her excess energy, and Bernadette's serenity was a good influence on Julie, whose peevish moods the sisters thought "terrible."[78]

"There you are, you naughty thing! You finally gave in!" said Bernadette, welcoming Julie to the novitiate dormitory.[79]

This was in reference to one of their last conversations in Lourdes. They had been talking vocations, then Julie said: "Me, a religious? A Sister of Nevers? Absolutely not!"

Bernadette was the one assigned to guide Julie's first steps as her "guardian angel," according to custom. She arrived too late to help her unpack her bags, which the sisters in Lourdes and her family had generously stuffed with provisions: "a pound of chocolates ...pictures, statues, etc."

"I had turned everything in to the mistress of novices," relates Julie.

"Bernadette made this observation, 'Ah, my poor one! I'll never see any of it!'

"I replied, 'You mean, everything disappears here?'"[80]

Their first concern was news of their village. "What are they saying in Lourdes?" Bernadette asked.

"They say you're coming back."

"Oh, no! Never! Lourdes isn't heaven."[81]

Bernadette is said to have added—but Julie seems to be inserting here, in hindsight, the attempt made by Père Sempé in 1879, to have Bernadette's body brought back to Lourdes—"They'll make many attempts to get my poor body, but to no avail."[82]

"I remember that as if she had just finished telling me," states Julie. But in her testimony of 1907, her words were not the same. She had Bernadette saying, "After my death, Monseigneur and Père Sempé will attempt to get my miserable body, but without success."[83]

The least we can say is that Julie added this detail after the fact. In 1871, Bernadette could not have called her parish priest "Monseigneur," for he was not yet a monsignor. In her deposition of 1909, Julie went back to being indefinite, coming closer to the truth: "After my death, *they may* try to get my miserable body, but to no avail."[84]

Bernadette supposedly also asked her: "Is Père Sempé converted yet? Is he behaving better toward Monseigneur Peyramale?"[85]

These words referred to a tense situation. In 1866, Bishop Laurence had entrusted the Lourdes pilgrimages to the Missionaries of the Immaculate Conception. The Curé of Lourdes had found himself forced out of the work he had founded, limited to his parish, now cut off from Massabielle, its very heart. His work was falling into other hands and in a direction that, fatally, did not coincide with his. Local interests and Henri Lasserre's influence stirred up the latent opposition of Abbé Peyramale to Père Sempé, superior of the grotto Fathers. For lack of crosschecking, it is difficult to reconstruct exactly what Bernadette said, for examination of the opposing evidence in this matter often reveals surprising differences.

In that month of August, 1871, Bernadette was especially preoccupied over the situation of her sister Marie, better known as Toinette, the one who had lost so many children. She was now selling religious articles in Lourdes. The sisters would have liked to discourage her from doing this. They had written to Soeur Marie-Bernard to lend her support in her role as elder sister.

"I've written to her but she does nothing about it," observed Bernadette.[86]

Between the two friends, Bernadette and Julie, memories continued to flow. "La Croisine," as she was called, the mother of little Justin Bouhort, one of the seven whose miraculous healing was recognized by the episcopal commission of Bishop Laurence, was brought up in the conversation. On July 6, 1858, she had plunged her baby naked into the ice-cold water of the spring.[87] That was how he was cured.

"Her faith was as strong as her face was ugly. This was one of the good Lord's families," Bernadette moralized.[88]

Julie brought news about everybody, beginning with Mère Alexandrine, superior at the hospice. "She's like a mother to me," said Bernadette.[89]

Then Abbé Pomian.

"There's a priest!" Bernadette exclaimed.[90]

Bernadette asked specifically about Mademoiselle Claire, a Child of Mary, overwhelmed by sickness and woes. "Not only does she suffer patiently," answered Julie, but she says something that greatly amazes me: 'If this is not enough, may the good Lord add more.'"

Soeur Marie-Bernard made this observation, "She is very generous; I wouldn't do that much. I'm satisfied with the ones I'm sent."[91]

Bernadette mentioned a sister at the hospice in Lourdes, who used to smile and happily welcome correction, even when unjustified.

"Do you remember Sister So-and-so? You wouldn't have done the same; you wouldn't have allowed yourself to be falsely accused."

"Maybe not...."[92] Julie replied.

The two friends had the same reaction here: a healthy reaction, counter-cultural to the abundant excesses of the times. To desire pain for its own sake and to enjoy being treated unjustly do not square with the meaning of creation, nor even of redemption. Christ himself accepted suffering as something to be endured: "Father, if it is possible, let this cup pass from me" (Mt 26:39,42).

Those who would have liked to see in Bernadette approved models of sanctity found her "dull and ordinary," even as the Holy Spirit was at work within her, giving shape to another style. She did not belittle the cross, but respectfully gave it its proper place.

"Suffering passes, but having suffered lasts," she also said to Julie.[93]

Memories of Bartrès also came to life. "The favorite lamb...white ...spotless." "And yet, he gave me lots of trouble," said Bernadette. He had often tipped over her Month of Mary altars and "when she led the flock...he would set out in front, butt her behind the knees, and knock her over."

"To punish him, I'd give him bread and salt, which he was very fond of," recalled Bernadette.[94]

The "bread" was the cornbread that her stomach could not tolerate but which was her fare in Bartrès.

Bernadette forgot her foster mother's severity just as she did so many others'. All she remembered was her affection. However, she had not forgotten the reason why her parents had packed her off to Bartrès in 1857: "It was one less mouth to feed at home."[95]

Without bitterness, she recalled those words that reflected the poverty of her family, among whom she was one too many; for bread, unlike affection, grows smaller for each one when it is shared, so that each "mouth to feed" takes what is needed away from the others.

Traveling down memory lane with Julie led to the topic of the apparitions. "It's because God loves shepherd girls," declared Julie (later known as Soeur Vincent).

"And the proof?" Bernadette replied, shrugging her shoulders to show that she attached no importance to this.[96]

They were not there to devote themselves to nostalgia. Among

Sheepcote and sheep at Bartrès

those memories, which were not forbidden to their friendship and the closeness that the role of "guardian angel" allowed for, they recalled above all their "blunders" and inexperience. How had Bernadette been so bold as to throw holy water like that at the second apparition, asking the *"Demoiselle"* (young lady) of light if she came from God? What about holding out that sheet of paper to *Aqueró* so she could write down her name?[97] And the crucial words that followed: "I do not promise to make you happy in this world."[98] Then the fruitless search for the spring; the disgust at drinking the muddy water despite the apparition's insistence.

"But I couldn't see any spring," said Bernadette, laughing.[99]

Julie recalled the handkerchief with which Bernadette had wiped her face, when she returned from the "spring"....

"It was clean,..." said Bernadette.

"But it wasn't embroidered," Julie retorted.[100]

"Do you like salad yet?" Julie asked further.

"Why?" Bernadette responded.

"Because at the grotto, I saw that you had no appetite for the grass that the Blessed Virgin told you to eat. You took a little bit and spit it out right away.... You were a *"gourmande."* She used the word *"gourmande"* in its local sense, which meant "fussy or delicate."

"But it was hard and foul," Bernadette answered, still laughing.[101]

Bernadette also recalled the sharp confrontations with Peyramale, especially that of March 25, when she flung in his face the "message," repeated all along the way: "I am the Immaculate Conception."

"He answered me," she recalled, 'What are you saying, you arrogant creature?'

"Then I thought better of it and told him, 'The Lady is the one who said these words.'[102]

"I still didn't know that it was the Blessed Virgin's name," Bernadette clarified.[103]

Good-natured and terrifying Peyramale! He had forbidden her to attend the procession at the grotto in 1863. "Yes, but the Blessed Virgin really got him!" Bernadette exclaimed. "She sent him a good bellyache, that kept him from going himself."[104]

A few more intimate impressions also cropped up in these "free" conversations between Bernadette and Julie,[105] permissible during the orientation period.

"I felt attracted to the Lady," said Bernadette. "I don't know how or why; I can't explain what was stirring within me at those moments."[106]

And again: "When the commissioner was asking me questions, I was no longer myself. I wasn't afraid and yet, they turned me every which way. I was sure of what I was saying.... There was something within me that enabled me to overcome everything."[107]

On this favorable approach, Julie Garros recalls how she ventured right up to the "secret garden."

"What were your secrets?"

"She [Bernadette] laughed in my face and said, 'That's my business.'[108]

"'And since then, you've had other apparitions?'

"'Never.'"[109]

Bernadette didn't expand on this subject and "said nothing special," Julie noted.[110] If the association of ideas brought up the subject of the apparitions in the presence of other sisters, "she observed the greatest caution." She discouraged the conversation with a curt "Yes...no."[111]

Julie was sick during her postulancy, in 1871, when Bernadette was in charge of the infirmary. That was an opportunity for sharing more confidences.

"In my missal," Julie relates, "I had a photograph of the grotto and another of Bernadette.... She looked at them and said, 'Ah! Now that's the grotto; I recognize it.'

"I said, 'And that?' [It was] her picture...very poorly done.

"She made a pouting grimace and said nothing. Meanwhile, the mistress of novices came to the infirmary and noticed the two photos in my missal.

"'Above all,' she said, 'do not show them to Bernadette.'

"I replied, 'But dear Sister, I already have.' At that point, Bernadette came back. I told her what Mère Marie-Thérèse Vauzou had just said.

"'The prohibition came too late,' Bernadette said, and she began laughing."[112]

The fun they were having together did not come easy. Being uprooted was hard on Soeur Vincent (Julie); the inactivity of the novitiate, still harder; and even more so, life behind walls for this

Bernadette, Provost photo, 1868

creature of the open air! Did this have something to do with her being sick?

"Two weeks after, I arrived," Soeur Vincent recalls, "I grew very unhappy. I couldn't adjust. They kept me in the infirmary out of charity. I said to Soeur Marie-Bernard, 'I'm going to leave. I'm too unhappy.'

"'Too bad you're unhappy,' Bernadette said. 'Go find the mistress and tell her you want to leave.'

"So I did and the mistress sent me to the sister in charge of the linen. In the linen room sister told me to wait until tomorrow, that it was too late. Then I went back to Soeur Marie-Bernard, who told me, 'Go pray before the Blessed Virgin in the novitiate and sleep in peace.'

"I followed her advice and the next day, I changed my mind."[113]

This nondirective method was helpful for Soeur Vincent, who also relates,

"I considered her [Bernadette] my mother and told her all my troubles. She would answer, 'Now what's that? Foolishness! Don't forget that the novitiate is heaven on earth.'"[114]

Julie also remembered these minute cautions: "Don't waste a crumb of bread."[115]

"The first impulse does not belong to us, but the second one does."[116]

And this remark about her hasty signs of the cross: "Is your arm sore? Are you anxious to get it over and done with?"[117]

It was the memory of the apparitions that was Bernadette's inspiration here. On the other hand, she got the following aphorism from a trend traceable to Bernardine of Siena and popularized in France by the Curé of Ars: "Between a priest and an angel...one should greet the priest first, because the priest is the representative of our Lord, who is himself obedient to him."[118]

She also said: "Never abstain from Communion."[119]

"Purify your intention."[120]

"Never seek to stand out from others."[121]

"Work for heaven."[122]

She explained, "If you work for the creature, you'll have no reward and you'll get very tired."[123]

Bernadette meant not that we should be unconcerned about

others, but that we should not expect anything in return, nor focus on our own satisfaction.

"Don't wait for compliments," Bernadette advised.[124] She also told Julie, "When we've done some work that turned out well, we should not grow vain over it."

"God uses us like instruments. We mustn't expect a compliment when we submit our work to Mother Mistress, otherwise we lose our merit."[125]

Bernadette practiced what she preached. "In May 1873," relates Soeur Eléonore Bonnet, "I saw her working in the community room. She was embroidering a magnificent alb, intended for Bishop Forcade...named to the archdiocese of Aix.... He had not yet left Nevers. I approached the embroiderer and admired her work...."

Where is this alb today? We don't know, for Bernadette left three embroidered with fine threads, but all justified Eléonore's admiration of the embroidery and needlework. However, Bernadette showed no self-satisfaction. "She smiled at me," Soeur Eléonore continues, and said, 'Any other sister could do the same.'"[126]

Like Bernadette, Soeur Vincent experienced difficulties in meditation. With her, too, it was service, patience, fidelity, and the total gift of self, which plowed the furrow in secret. Unable to resist, she followed not the paths to self-fulfillment, but those which led to self-emptying.[127]

Bernadette somehow or other shared with Julie the fruits of what she herself found most helpful in meditation. Soeur Vincent chose from these methods, and even developed them—undoubtedly in a more imaginative way than that of Bernadette.

Julie recalls: "'Go to the Garden of Olives or to the foot of the cross and stay there. Our Lord will speak to you. You will listen to him.'

"Sometimes I told her [Bernadette], 'I went there, but our Lord told me nothing.'"[128]

Julie also asked her, "How do you manage to stay so long in thanksgiving?"

"I picture the Blessed Virgin giving me the child Jesus. I receive him. I talk to him, and he talks to me."[129]

There was always the question of giving flesh to invisible and fleeting presences. The following are some of the recommendations that Julie remembered and perhaps "improved on."

"Consider yourself the errand girl of the Holy Family.... See first the child Jesus, then the Blessed Virgin and don't forget Saint Joseph."[130]

Bernadette also said, "When we can't pray, we call on Saint Joseph."[131]

"When you are before the Blessed Sacrament, you have near you the Blessed Virgin on one side to inspire you what to say to our Lord, and your Guardian Angel on the other to keep track of your distractions."[132]

"When you walk by the chapel with no time to stop, tell your Guardian Angel to bring your messages to our Lord in the tabernacle. He'll bring them and then will have time to catch up with you."[133]

"We must receive the good Lord well; we have every reason to give him a good welcome...for then he'll have to pay us our rent."[134]

It is not impossible that in quoting Bernadette, Julie is here expressing her own spirituality, for these flights of imagination are isolated cases among both Bernadette's sayings and writings.

What follows corresponds more precisely to her lived experience. It happened one night in the infirmary. Julie says: "I was tossing about in my bed. She noticed and said, 'When we're in bed, we must stay still and see ourselves like our Lord on the cross.'[135]

"'We must break our wills,' she also said."[136]

To shake her companion out of her melancholy, Bernadette would tease her mercilessly. She would make Julie give vent to her natural aggressiveness, which could be self-destructive when kept bottled up inside.

Julie recounts: "One time in the infirmary, she told me, 'I'm going to give you a fine snack.' There were candied fruits. She offered me one and said, 'Today is Saturday. We won't eat any. We'll do this little mortification for the Blessed Virgin.'"[137]

Soeur Vincent paid her back in kind. "One day," she relates, "I had brought her some burnt chocolate. I tasted it as I sometimes did and said to her, 'Oh, how good it is! It's delicious!'

"After taking some, she replied, 'You're quite right, it's better than usual.'

"Even as a child, she never complained about the food she was offered," Julie underscored here.[138]

"I was not used to getting up at five o'clock," Julie also confided.

"One morning in chapel, I fell asleep during prayer and fell over. The infirmarians carried me out and Bernadette was one of them. They gave me a cordial, which I gladly accepted without saying that I had fallen only because I was sleeping. I later explained it to Soeur Marie-Bernard, who said, 'You took advantage of your infirmarians' kindness? You lacked humility.'"[139]

"I happened to make some mistakes, and I had to pay for them. She said, 'All that, why it's sugar!'"[140]

"When she was reprimanded or received some humiliation, she would say to me, 'I've just been given a piece of candy.'

"'What kind?'

"'Ah! That's my business!'"[141]

"When she had her asthma attacks...it was pitiful to see. Never did she complain; and once the attacks were over, she would say, 'Thank you, my God.'"[142]

Was Bernadette patient? Not by nature. Julie was all the more aware of this because they had the same Bigorre strength of character. "She was quick of temperament, a little irascible," Julie reported; "but it wasn't that noticeable, so well had she learned self-control. Sometimes we could see a small sign of impatience appear on her face; it was gone as quick as lightning, without ever expressing itself by deed. I'd say, 'You're very lucky to be so patient.'

"She answered, 'Ah, yes!'"[143]

Soeur Vincent caught a glimpse of the power underlying this patience: it was a self-forgetfulness that directed all suffering toward serving the redemption of others. Bernadette used to say, "Let us pray for such-and-such a family, that the Blessed Virgin convert it."[144]

"For the souls in purgatory."[145]

All this in and for God: a deep root that we will come across again.

One day, close by the confessional, Soeur Vincent watched Soeur Marie-Bernard, "all wrapped up in her veil." A little later, she said to her, "You hide yourself well. One might have said you were wearing your hood...."

She answered, "I love being alone when I visit the good Lord...."[146]

Hers was the secret of a flame. In the infirmary, Soeur Vincent often heard her say these words, "My God, take my heart. Make it burn!"[147]

The New Constitutions

August 20, 1871 was a red-letter day for the congregation. After long negotiations, Rome approved the sisters' new constitutions. These were to last almost a century, up until the days following the Council. The old books were burned;[148] the new ones formally distributed. Henceforth, these constitutions would govern Bernadette's religious life.

On September 8, 222 superiors came to the motherhouse to pronounce their perpetual vows, according to the new Rule.

Mère Sophie Cresseil thus met Bernadette for the only time in her life. She was surprised to find her doing the ordinary tasks of an assistant infirmarian. (Soeur Marthe, the head infirmarian, was still living in September 1871.)

Bernadette answered simply, "That's all I'm good at; I'm no good at anything else."[149]

This was an echo of the humiliating words she had heard on the day of her profession. They had stayed with her.

"Haven't you ever experienced some temptation to self-satisfaction for having been so favored by the Blessed Virgin?" asked Mère Sophie, who had not received the order to be silent about the apparitions.

"What do you think?" answered Bernadette "If the Blessed Virgin chose me, it's because I was the most ignorant. If she had found a girl more ignorant than I, that's the one she would have chosen."[150]

In December 1871, a sister from Lourdes, Soeur Victoire Cassou, a distant relative of Bernadette's, arrived. Having entered the Congregation before Bernadette, she was passing through Saint-Gildard's on the way to her new assignment. She remembered this secret of Bernadette's at the time of her departure, on October 15, 1863: "I must be a nun, I don't know in what congregation; the Blessed Virgin hasn't told me yet. I'm waiting."

So the conversation began with this dialogue:

"Well! So the Blessed Virgin has spoken?"

"Of course."[151]

The visiting sister was feeling sad. On Christmas Eve, Bernadette said to her, "At midnight Mass, sit next to me. There's room."

Soeur Victoire recalls: "I was very happy. That's when I was able to see for myself how recollected she was. Hidden within her veil, nothing could distract her. After Holy Communion, she fell into such deep recollection that everyone else left, and she never seemed to notice. I stayed next to her, because I had no desire to go to the refectory with my companions. I gazed on her a long time, without her realizing. Her face was radiant...like during the ecstasy at the apparitions. When the sister in charge of locking the doors of the church came to do her job, she jangled the bolts vigorously. That's when Bernadette emerged from that state. She left the chapel and I followed.... In the cloister, she leaned over toward me and said softly, 'You didn't take anything?' (in the refectory).

"I answered, 'Neither did you.' She withdrew in silence...."[152]

Bishops Come Visiting

This period also brought its share of episcopal visitors. The visit of Bishop Dupanloup left hardly a trace except the following literary piece and the episcopal denial it provoked:

"One winter's night," wrote Lasserre, "a tall, austere and distinguished looking priest appeared at the convent of Saint-Gildard ...and sent for the superior general.

"'I've come rather far,' he told her, 'and I purposely made this trip to see and meet Soeur Marie-Bernard.'

"'Alas, Monsieur le Curé! I cannot in this circumstance lift the cloister, except with the explicit authorization of the Bishop of Nevers; and I mustn't hide from you the fact that he doesn't give it very readily.'

"The priest seemed annoyed.

"'I specifically wanted to see her incognito. But since I must, I will tell you who I am.'

"He opened his black overcoat, and the sister caught sight of the episcopal cross. 'I am the Bishop of Orléans,' he said.

"The superior bowed, begged the renowned prelate's blessing, and went to get Bernadette. Bishop Dupanloup had a long conversation with the visionary. Despite the superabundance of evidence, which had established the truth of the Christian faith...he was afflicted with doubts....

"When he left her, the bishop's eyes were filled with tears and doubt had left his heart forever.

"'I have just seen the innocence of a soul,' he said, 'and the irresistible power of truth.'"[153]

Bishop Forcade, bishop of Nevers, in his *Notice sur la vie de soeur Marie-Bernard,* (Account of the Life of Sister Marie-Bernard) published in 1879,[154] offered the following corrections:

"An outrageously imaginative account. [This visit] is said to have occurred *during the episcopacy of Bishop de Ladoue;* it took place during mine; *in winter* and it was spring; *at night,* and it was in broad daylight. Bishop Dupanloup is described as a *tall, austere and distinguished looking man.* We will see shortly whether he appeared in that imposing guise. To disclose his identity, this prelate, with a dramatic gesture, *opened his black overcoat* and *revealed his episcopal cross.* He was wearing a lined greatcoat and had neither cross nor ring. *The superior bowed, begged the renowned prelate's blessing and went to find Bernadette.* The superior was sick in bed, which could not have made these various activities very easy for her. The renowned prelate did not even see her.

"Here is the true story:

"On April 16, 1872, between four and five in the afternoon, there appeared at the door of the convent, by himself and very humbly, an older cleric of average height, on his head an old hat, over his shoulders an old greatcoat, and under his arm an old umbrella. He asked to see Bernadette. The sister portress answered, as usual, that 'my permission was necessary and there was no way of getting it, since I was making my Confirmation visits and, in any case, I granted it only to bishops.'

"'Lucky for me, then,' the old man replied. 'I am the bishop of Orléans....'

"The sister brought him into the parlor and rushed to get one of the assistants, to whom she said something like this, 'There's an old priest at the door, who's asking to see Soeur Marie-Bernard and says he is the Bishop of Orléans. But he doesn't look like a bishop at all; he's so pathetic....'

"Sister portress' doubt was shared by the sister assistant.... She went to the superior general's room.... Now the superior was worried...and after a few moments of hesitation, made up her mind to allow the stranger to see Bernadette, but strongly advised the assistant to deal very cautiously with him and not to leave him for an instant. This prudent command was strictly obeyed.... They were not entirely certain until the next day about the identity of this person.

"Such a cold reception did not bother Bishop Dupanloup. With his usual enthusiasm and his well-known determination, he put

Bishop Dupanloup of Orléans (top right)

and Bishop Forcade of Nevers (bottom left)

Bernadette through a long and rough series of questions and did not let her go until he had learned everything he wanted to know."[155]

Bishop Forcade found equally doubtful the "tears" and the "overstrained" sentence attributed to Bishop Dupanloup....

Bishop Forcade wrote: "The great bishop of Orléans did not shed tears so easily, and even less, express himself so pretentiously. He spoke very simply in conversation, as do all truly superior men. Be that as it may, we at least have the certitude that he went away satisfied with his interview with Bernadette, and that his convictions on the miracle of Lourdes, if they had not been positively established yet, were settled from that moment on."[156]

So many bishops came that it required great effort to show them Bernadette without her noticing. That was the case with Bishop Dreux-Brézé, bishop of Moulins, who "had already met Bernadette," but "wanted to see her again."

"So they drew up a strategic plan.... I was put in charge of carrying it out," says Soeur Julienne Capmartin. "One of our mistresses, Soeur Mélanie...told me, 'Go to the infirmary and tell Soeur Marie-Bernard to be good enough to go to the linen room and get the dinner napkins we need and have her bring them to me....'

"She added, 'You will take her by the flower beds, and when the two of you are facing the bishop's parlor, you will make her stop, by pointing out a flower, a stone, an insect, whatever; but you will position yourselves so that she's facing the parlor. The bishop of Moulins will be on the threshold and will be able to see her without being seen....'

"I went to the infirmary and did my errand. Soeur Marie-Bernard left her work and followed me.... Once we arrived in front of the parlor window, I stole a glance through the window and recognized Mère Marie-Thérèse and Soeur Eléonore, and beside them, framed in the doorway, a vague shape, like the silhouette of an observer trying to conceal himself. I immediately took my companion by the arm and, showing her a daisy, said softly, 'Oh, my dear sister! Tell me if this wild flower isn't delightful! It is more beautiful than the flowers in the garden. Don't you find that the good Lord knows his business better than men do?'

"She broke away and headed for the linen room saying: 'Blabbermouth!'"[157]

Bishop de Léséleuc de Kérouara experienced Bernadette's intensity in another way. It was February 22, 1873. She was sick and he had to be brought to the infirmary.

"The Bishop of Autun was standing...his violet skullcap dropped onto the bed.

"The Mother Assistant had the impression it was done deliberately.... Obviously, the prelate wanted to put Soeur Marie-Bernard ...in the position of having to pick up the skullcap and return it to its owner.... Therefore, the skullcap dropped onto the bed, and there it stayed.

"The bishop made no move, neither did Bernadette.

"The conversation dropped...like the skullcap. The resulting silence made the situation more critical.... The bishop felt obliged to take the offensive. 'Sister,' he said to her, 'would you give me my skullcap?'

"She answered, 'Monseigneur, I didn't ask you for it...you can pick it up yourself.'

"To save the situation, Mère Ferrand intervened, 'Come now, my dear sister,' she said laughing, 'give the bishop back his skullcap.'"[158]

To See Lourdes Again?

In June 1873, a sister coming in from Lourdes "placed on Bernadette's bed a photograph of a pilgrimage or of the basilica of Lourdes....

"'You'd be happy, wouldn't you, to go to the grotto of Massabielle?'

"All smiles...despite an asthma attack...she answered, 'No, that doesn't tempt me. I made the sacrifice of not seeing Lourdes again .... In heaven it will be more beautiful.'"[159]

The same question would be asked of her time and time again during the course of the year 1873, especially by the sisters who were going to Lourdes to attend the consecration of Bishop de Ladoue, appointed to Nevers to replace Bishop Forcade, who had been elevated to Archbishop of Aix. Shortly before their departure, on September 16, Mère Marie-Thérèse Vauzou asked, "Well, now, Soeur Marie-Bernard, would you like to come along with us?"[160]

The possibility had been so favorably considered in 1870, as we have seen, that Bernadette had discouraged her father from coming to Nevers himself. "Our venerable Mother promised that she would allow me to see the whole family when the chapel at the grotto was blessed," she had written at the time. "I would have been very happy to see my father, but my happiness will be greater when I see all of you at home...."[161]

At the time that Mère Marie-Thérèse asked the question, the possibility was gone. Bernadette summed up her thoughts: "Ah! If only I were a little bird."[162]

Emile Zola expanded on this remark, which he had received in Lourdes on August 26, 1892 from the lips of Henri Lasserre: "Ah! If only I were a little bird how I would fly away to have another look over there...."[163]

This interpretation falls in line with the novelist's hypothesis: Bernadette, kept far away by outside influences, would have liked to fly to Lourdes. Lasserre gave a better interpretation when he said: "What she wanted...was not the swift wings of the swallow, but rather the power to see without being seen."[164]

She would bring up the same idea with other visitors: Soeur Aurélie Gouteyron, on October 30, 1873, then Soeur Victorine Poux in 1874 and Soeur Sophie Pasquine in 1876.

During the same visit on September 16, 1873, Mère Vauzou commanded Bernadette again, "You will give me your messages for the Blessed Virgin."

Was she hoping for a closely guarded secret? Here as always, Bernadette fled straight up: "Oh, I'll see her in heaven!"[165]

The same day, she told Soeur Nathalie Portat, who was also in the group going to the consecration, "Oh, my dear Sister! If I had to go back to Lourdes, I wouldn't choose a pilgrimage day."[166]

The ceremony on September 21, 1873 and the photos that circulated during those days were an opportunity to ask Bernadette many questions bordering on the "secret garden": "Where did the Virgin appear? Where did the spring gush from? etc."[167]

The New Bishop

A few days later, on October 16, 1873, Bishop de Ladoue, the new ordinary of Nevers, came to visit the motherhouse for the first time. Soeur Vincent Garros questioned Bernadette, who saw him at closer range: "Well now! What do you think of our new bishop?"

She reported the answer this way: "He's short; he's cold; but he won't stay long."[168]

As a matter of fact, he did not have the jovial spontaneity of Bishop Forcade. He died suddenly while celebrating Mass, less than four years later on July 23, 1877. However, it was only in 1918, looking backward, that Soeur Vincent reported this prophecy. In the meantime, Bernadette was to see this short-lived bishop more than once.[169]

News from Lourdes

At the end of October 1873, Bernadette received other visitors from Lourdes.

First came Soeur Aurélie Gouteron and Soeur Damien Calmels, her former teachers at the hospice. Among other things, they conveyed the complaints of her friends in Lourdes: "They're not happy that the letters they write to you go unanswered."

"Tell those young ladies, dear Sister, to leave me alone in my solitude," Bernadette replied, "I pray for them. That's all I can do."[170]

This was an old sore spot. Bernadette did not feel called to a letter-writing mission. She had to guard against spreading herself too thin; and communicating by letter seemed quite trivial to her. "What do you want me to say, if not to constantly rehash the same things, not knowing anything new," she wrote to her sister on December 25, 1870.[171]

Furthermore, she didn't like to see her letters passed around, as was being done. Bernadette inquired about her relatives, especially her younger brother, Bernard-Pierre...her godchild.

"I don't ask that they be rich," she said, "but that they love the good Lord, and that they be well-behaved."[172]

Her letter of May 29, 1872, bears out this concern: "I've been told that Joseph had some idea of having my younger brother Bernard-Pierre run some kind of shop, if he withdraws him from Garaison. Tell him from me, that I'm expressly opposed to this, because it's not suitable and the good Lord won't be happy with you."[173]

Leaving Soeur Aurélie, Bernadette asked her for prayers, now and for the future. "When I'm dead, they'll say, 'She saw the Blessed Virgin, she is a saint'; and all that time I'll be broiling away in purgatory."[174]

This was a sentence she would have many, many opportunities to repeat.

Soeurs Aurélie and Damien, who visited Bernadette at the end of October 1873, had been photographed with her at the time of her departure from Lourdes on July 2, 1866.

Above: standing from left to right are Soeurs Aurélie Gouteyron, Elisabeth Rigal, Olympe Bessac, Damien Calmel. Seated are Soeurs Victorine Poux (who nursed Bernadette with somewhat nervous devotion) Bernadette, dressed for the occasion in the religious habit, Alexandrine Roques, the superior, and Gilbert Janton

Below: standing from left to right are Soeurs Damien Calmel, Savinien Besseyre, Bernadette, Elisabeth Rigal Gilbert Janton and Aurélie Gouteyron. Seated are Soeurs Victorine Poux, Alexandrine Roques and Olympe Bessac.

Julie Garros Again

Between July and October of 1873, Julie Garros came back to the motherhouse "for reasons of health." She "remained as a patient in the infirmary."

Getting used to religious life was definitely very hard for this exuberant girl from Lourdes. "I was then affected by my sickly condition and persuaded that I could not be allowed to make profession," she relates.

"Don't worry," was all Bernadette said.[175] And again, "Don't get discouraged, I'll pray for you."[176]

More than these recommendations, what put Julie back on her feet was to find the shoe on the other foot: she had to encourage Bernadette, brought down by an asthma attack. At that time she received this exceptional disclosure from Bernadette, brought about by an excess of suffering and the sweetness of friendship: "It's really painful not to be able to breathe, but it's much more agonizing to be tortured by spiritual distress. It's terrifying."[177]

As early as 1871, it seems, Julie had gotten a glimpse of this abyss from the way Bernadette had spoken to her about this petition in the "Our Father": "Forgive us our trespasses, as we forgive...."[178] She gave no further details.

Julie had guessed Bernadette's hidden "distress," but understood that she must not go further. "I didn't dare," she confided. Again in 1873, she knew how to respect Bernadette's privacy.

CHAPTER 18

— ⚜ —

BERNADETTE'S FINAL ACTIVITIES

Assistant Infirmarian and Sacristan

On November 5, 1873, Charlotte de Vigouroux, in religion Soeur Gabrielle, a young twenty-eight-year-old professed sister, was named infirmarian. Bernadette became assistant infirmarian again. She inwardly showed great courage in adapting to this new situation. Responsibilities had suited her generous nature. Now, she missed them. Furthermore, it is always difficult to take second place when one has been in charge. Now, when she had her own notion on how things should be done and defended it, she found herself being called arrogant.[1]

There was "some uneasiness between them," noted Soeur Philippine Molinéry.[2] Hence, this resolution written in Bernadette's retreat notes: "Work on becoming indifferent to everything my superiors or companions say or think about me...."[3]

At the beginning of January 1874, the superiors gave Bernadette an additional duty: that of serving as assistant sacristan. Julie Garros added this detail, "She vested the altar boys."[4]

Good-byes to Julie

In the month of June, her friend from Lourdes came back to the motherhouse for the third and last time. This time Julie had overcome her difficulties. She was there to prepare for her profession, which would take place on July 13. On June 4, she attended the Corpus Christi procession, which took place at the hospital of Nevers: "As I did not know the garden, I wanted to use this opportunity to see it.... Besides, someone had told me jokingly that it had a pond and you had to be careful not to fall in.... My veil was lowered like my companions'...so...with a large pin, I made a hole big enough to look through. The Venerable found out and said to me, 'You showed a lack of respect...and also a lack of poverty.'

"I answered, 'How did I lack poverty?'

"'Why, by making a hole in your veil.... From now on, show more respect for the Blessed Sacrament.'"[5]

Here is another reprimand related by Julie: "I was in charge of tidying up the office of our dear Sister Mistress (Mère Vauzou). I had forgotten to put holy water in the font. To avoid humiliation, I secretly took a little saliva from my mouth with my fingertip, then dipped it into the dry font and offered it to our mistress. A sister in the novitiate told Soeur Marie-Bernard, who told me that I had shown a lack of respect toward my superior and toward a holy object.

"I answered, 'I didn't intend to show a lack of respect; I just wanted to avoid a humiliation.'

"'You would've kissed the floor—so what! Well, now you'll go to confession and you'll tell Mother Mistress.'

"'Yes, I'll go to confession, but tell Mother Mistress! Oh, not that!'

"I went to confession, and I made up my mind to tell Mother Mistress after all."[6]

Bernadette put her friend in some demanding situations. Julie was like the kind of metal that has to be heated white-hot to achieve an all-resistant temper.

Julie recalls, "Mère Anne-Marie Lescure was stricken with breast cancer. (Bernadette) nursed her.... One day, she gave me the responsibility of taking this patient, who was also blind, for a walk. She said to me, 'You will take as good care of her as though she were the good Lord.'

"I answered, 'Oh, there's quite a difference!'

"I asked her why this patient didn't wear her entire religious habit. She answered, 'Oh, come and see tonight.'

"I went. I saw the patient's sore, covered with worms, which Bernadette was putting into a dish. I couldn't stand the sight. Bernadette said, 'What a Sister of Charity you'll make! What little faith you have!'

"The next day I came back and helped her with the patient's dressing, but without touching the sore.... (Bernadette) applied the dressing very tenderly."[7]

When this sister died on June 29, 1874, Julie happened to be passing by the infirmary as Bernadette was beginning to prepare the body. Bernadette called to her, "Come and help me."

Julie recounts, "I didn't want to because I was disgusted. Bernadette said, 'You're a coward. You'll never be a Sister of Charity!'

"When the deceased was clothed, the sisters came to kiss her. It was an effort for me to do like the others. Nevertheless I did it, but felt sick. Then Bernadette said to me, 'A Sister of Charity who cannot touch the dead, what kind of a nun is that?'"[8]

Julie Garros was one of the rare witnesses who saw Bernadette doing her work in the sacristy. She attested only to Bernadette's attention to order and her care to observe the established rule: "I wanted to touch a purificator, she stopped me and said, 'You're not at that point yet.'

"And I saw her take the purificator with great reverence and put it back in the burse."[9]

On June 3, 1874, the admission of Soeur Julie Garros was settled: "They called...'the novice from Souillac'.... I stepped forward, afraid of being sent home, because I had been sick a long time in this house; but nothing was said. I related this to Soeur Marie-Bernard, who said, 'Don't worry, I didn't clothe you just so you could abandon the holy habit.'"[10]

Indeed, on November 10, 1870, no one had refused Julie a privilege, eagerly sought at each clothing ceremony: that of being clothed for the first time by Bernadette, before going to receive the veil and rosary from the bishop.

On November 8, 1870, Soeur Marie-Bernard had thus pinned up Soeur Marcelline Revel's cornette and had assured her, "You will never leave."[11]

On November 20, she could already say with a smile to Soeur Eléonore Bonnet, "All the cornettes I put on are solid."[12]

Bernadette took a liking to this job and to the joy she gave in doing it. Sometime during July 1874, she met in the cloister a very young novice who had been careless in arranging her veil. "'Oh, dear Sister!' [she called out.] 'Your veil's all crooked! Come over here.'

"In the nearest room...she removed it, set the long cornette... fixed the pin under her chin, arranged the veil on the white cornette, and, lastly...smoothed the folds of the veil down over her shoulders.

"'Now, you are a genuine Sister of Nevers,' she said to Soeur Thérèse Portal, the novice in question."[13]

On July 13, Julie was professed. Departure day was set for the fourteenth. On that day she had her last conversation with Bernadette and received these last words of advice: "If you're assigned to a hospital, be moderate in speech in the beginning. Don't put up with an unbecoming gesture."[14]

Having undoubtedly been taught at a very early age while working at her Aunt Bernarde's tavern, she offered this advice, "When you're in a room with men, make sure the door is always open."[15]

But it was the patients she underscored: "When you nurse a patient...you must withdraw before receiving thanks.... We are sufficiently rewarded by the honor of being attentive to him."[16]

"Don't forget to see our Lord in the person of the poor...the more disgusting the poor man, the more you must love him."[17]

Julie recalls, "I asked her for a souvenir, but she answered, 'You don't have to exchange souvenirs when you love each other.... We must love one another without measure and be devoted to one another without keeping count.'"[18]

The last moments arrived. "Let's embrace for the last time,..." said Bernadette.

Julie continues, "Then she added the following recommendations: 'Accept sickness like a caress. Spend yourself in the service of the poor, but prudently. Don't ever give way to discouragement. Love the Blessed Virgin very much. Pray for my sister who worries me and count on the help of my prayers. We'll be thinking of each other every morning at the Holy Sacrifice.'[19]

"Embracing her, I said, 'See you again.'

"She replied, 'Not on this earth.'

"It was, in fact, the last time I saw her."[20]

Bernadette and Her Stained Glass Window

On August 15, 1874, the sisters from the motherhouse participated in a solemn procession at the cathedral. In sending Bernadette, had the superiors forgotten what she was about to see?

On the preceding January 21, a stained glass window in honor of Lourdes had been installed. One of the panels depicted Bernadette's clothing ceremony. Mother General had sent her assistants to the bishop to ask to have the window corrected or changed, but the delegation had failed. The stained glass window would remain in place until the bombardment of 1944....

On their way through the cathedral, the sisters from the motherhouse examined the new work of art, all the while watching their companion, who came face to face with her own likeness.

Bernadette also looked at the window, but said nothing. Not daring to question her, the sisters turned to Soeur Antoinette Noireau, the assistant mistress of novices. Bernadette told her that she found "the stained glass window not very close to reality...that she herself had not been flattered, that there was nothing there to be conceited about."

Supposedly, she even said more explicitly, "They made me look pretty ugly."[21]

The Decline

In September 1874, the visit of Soeur Victorine Poux, so devoted to caring for Bernadette during her days in the hospice of Lourdes, occurred. She gave up a one-on-one conversation by bringing along one of her former students, Soeur Véronique Crillon, who was so very eager to meet the visionary.

"When we entered the room," relates Soeur Véronique, "she was hidden at first behind a bed curtain. When Soeur Victorine asked her why she was hiding herself, she answered it was because there were many people in the community that day and she wanted to avoid being questioned by them all.... She welcomed me graciously. Pointing to Soeur Victorine, I told her that we were both students of the same teacher."[22]

Soeur Victorine recalled Bernadette's strong reactions to "little wrongs" and "false accusations." "Now, I'm pretty indifferent," Bernadette replied honestly.[23]

This indifference was not at all passive; she would experience the resurgence of her natural temperament, as we shall see.

This month of September 1874 marked the end of Bernadette's active life. She could no longer serve except from time to time. She felt herself failing in her position as sacristan. It would even happen that she fell "motionless on the steps of the sanctuary," according to Estrade.[24] But one must take into consideration the inordinate attraction this writer had for swoons. The fact remains that Bernadette could no longer carry out her duties as assistant sacristan, her last active function. On October 6, we find her back in bed in the infirmary.

Despite the tense relationship with her replacement, Soeur Gabrielle de Vigouroux—or perhaps to overcome this tension—she indulged in a rare revelation: "While I was nursing her," relates the infirmarian, "she told me the story of the apparitions. I remember that she kept staring at a picture of the Lourdes grotto, placed at the foot of her bed.... (That night or the next day) I put down in writing what she told me in my little personal notebook."[25]

This account, fragmentary but accurate, was entered into evidence at the canonization process. Bernadette ended her story as she had ended the letter of August 22, 1864, to Abbé Bouin: "Her eyes were blue...."[26]

CHAPTER 19

— ⚜ —

THE LAST ASSIGNMENT

1. Encounters

With the winter of 1874–1875, Bernadette entered a final phase, a distressing but necessary one. She no longer had regular duties. Her story would now blend with the account of her illnesses. From now on, these would become "her assignment," as she said to give her the courage to accept them.

If we consult the memories of her contemporaries, however, this period seems particularly rich and fruitful in contacts.

Bernadette and the Novices

Bernadette's healthy and refreshing influence on the novices and postulants was affirmed. She solved their problems. Mère Vauzou had become aware of this and sent more and more of them to her. It was a regular parade. It would be tedious to cite them all. If, indeed, each visitor whose testimony is preserved was deeply affected by this contact, the words exchanged were usually unexceptional. Bernadette's presence and pointedness were more effective than the contents of her conversation. The words were like the shadow show of a live production, or like the imperceptible drop of water that remains in the hand when we try to capture a snowflake.

Let us present, however, the more striking testimonies before following the thread of suffering with which Bernadette's lively conversations were woven—the price she paid for the influence that was hers during the years 1875–1878.

From April to June 1875—a difficult period healthwise—a newcomer, Soeur Rosalie Pérasse, had the duty of cleaning her room in the infirmary.

"She stayed in bed all this time," she relates, "but never did I hear her complain; and each morning, I would find her smiling, despite her suffering and sleepless nights. Every day she sent me for news of another patient, Soeur Joséphine, who was in a nearby room. She would instruct me to bring Sister some reading material, after carefully marking the interesting pages herself so that Sister would not have to look for them.

"When she received Holy Communion, she observed our custom by wearing her veil, which she then put down on the bed. So I had to fold it myself. The first time...I did it awkwardly. She noticed and said, 'Come here so I can teach you how. You must know how to fold a veil, since you'll soon receive one of your own.'"[1]

If Bernadette encouraged many sisters to persevere in the religious life, it was not done systematically. Her advice came from looking and assessing, not from a recipe.

At the beginning of September 1875, they brought her about fifteen postulants. Bernadette "took a long look at one of them," relates Soeur Juliette. It seems to have been nineteen-year-old Marie Champagnan, who had arrived on August 31, 1875. When Soeur Ursule Millien asked her for her impressions, Bernadette answered, "She still needs her mother."[2] In fact, this postulant returned home the following September 14.[3]

Bernadette discouraged misplaced admiration.

"Soeur Madeleine Mespouilhé...in charge of the infirmary where Soeur Marie-Bernard was staying...while making the bed one morning, discovered a string rosary that Bernadette usually used.... She really wanted to keep this rosary, at least for a while, and she put it in her pocket.... During the day, Soeur Marie-Bernard asked her, 'Little Sister, I've mislaid my rosary. Perhaps you've found it? It's funny, rosary beads can't seem to stay in my pocket.'

"Soeur Madeleine gave it back to her, admitting her desire to keep it.

"'I can't let you keep it,' she said simply. 'My dear Sister Assistant gave it to me. When you leave, I'll give you a little souvenir.'

"And she did; a short time later she gave her a holy picture."[4]

Bernadette was especially lavish with words of encouragement.

"After spending seven months in the infirmary, because of an eye ailment," relates Soeur Marcelline Durand, "I went down to the novitiate. But the next day, there was pressure in one eye and I had to go back to the infirmary. I was grief-stricken, saying to myself that, this time, they wouldn't keep me in the congregation. I had already been notified, and several times at that, that I would have to go home or join the Visitation Sisters, who were willing to accept me.

"I immediately let Bernadette know of my deep anguish and she told me, 'Rest easy, you'll be cured and you'll be received into the Congregation. The Blessed Virgin doesn't want me to observe my month of Mary in the infirmary by myself. And here you are. We'll do it together. Let's pray hard to her and she will cure you....'

"We observed the month of Mary.... On June 1, I left the infirmary and never went back. I was admitted to profession."[5]

In her complementary deposition, Soeur Marcelline detailed the program they had drawn up and followed, in keeping with the practices in those days. "Bernadette had a small statue of the Blessed Virgin between the bed curtains. On either side was a little candlestick and, in front, a little paper basket she had made herself. I did the exercises of the month of May with her in front of this statue. We recited a few Ave Marias and she designated a practice for the day. If we were faithful, she placed two little paper discs in the little basket; if we slipped up, we had nothing to put in the basket and we did a penance that she chose herself. On the next day, if we managed to redeem ourselves by making sacrifices—doubling what had been required by the practice—we'd put two paper discs in the basket, so that we would each have thirty little paper discs at the end of the month. Actually, on May 31, the basket held sixty little paper discs, with which we made a 'bonfire' in honor of the Blessed Virgin."[6]

Bernadette's words of encouragement were those of her day; sometimes they were conventional.

"Because of my eye-disease," relates Soeur Madeleine Durand a bit before June, 1876, "the doctors had ordered me to take snuff. I was loath to do it for fear of developing the habit. Soeur Marie-Bernard, who used snuff on doctor's orders, offered me her snuffbox, and I refused. Then she insisted, saying, 'Take some; that's an order.'"[7]

For Soeur Claire Salvy, it was more serious.

"One day, feeling very sad with tears in my eyes, I went to the infirmary to bring the patients something to drink," she relates. "She asked me why I was sad. I told her...'I made a careless mistake at work and one of the older sisters told me I'd never be able to become a religious.'

"She smiled and seemed to close her eyes, as if she didn't want to answer me; then looking at me, she said, 'Since you really want to do the good Lord's will, you will be a Sister of Nevers. Don't be sad! But you must learn to bear little crosses.'"[8]

For Soeur Joseph Cassagnes, suffering from homesickness the first few months, she used the language of the Curé of Ars: "Don't you see that it's that 'ugly little grapnel?'" She paused and then playfully went on, "When he comes near, spit in his eye!"[9]

That postulant became Assistant General and often recalled this memory, until her death in 1949.

To Soeur Marcelline Boyer, who had torn herself away from her family "against her parents' wishes," she said, "Mademoiselle, dry your tears; your parents will come around in a little while. Your head will be shaved and you'll be a fine religious."

This prediction came true, for four months later, her mother came very happily to attend her clothing ceremony.[10]

Soeur Casimir Callery's father died suddenly. "Don't grieve," Bernadette told her. "The good Lord does not permit the parents of religious to be damned. He gives them a special grace in view of the sacrifices we've made."[11] She added, "My mother died December 8, 1866. The Blessed Virgin wanted to make me understand that I must love her alone and rely on her alone...that she would replace my mother."[12]

On another day, Soeur Casimir also fell sick. The superior general, Mère Joséphine, met both of them. She made a point of humiliating Bernadette, to keep her from becoming proud.

"She treated us as useless people," Soeur Casimir recalls. I began to cry, but Soeur Marie-Bernard said to me: "For that little thing? You have more kindness than you need. You'll be seeing lots more of these."[13]

This comment marks a step forward, more than it seems, for

regarding this same superior, Bernadette acknowledged: "Mère Joséphine! Oh, how I fear her!"[14]

Likewise, Soeur Eugénie Calmès regained her courage beside Bernadette's bed: "I was so lonesome that I was thinking of leaving.... But Bernadette said there was nothing to fear about my persevering.... She repeated this a number of times, with such certainty in her voice that I was deeply affected. Moreover, she promised to pray for me and invited me to come and see her if I felt myself weakening. But I think the power of her prayers was so great that the lonesomeness stopped all of a sudden. I didn't even think about it again. And truly, I'm almost sorry today, that's how I lost the opportunity of seeing her again."[15]

To Soeur Valentine Borot, who came to her in a similar state, Bernadette confided: "Oh!... In the beginning I was very lonesome. Whenever I'd get a letter from home, I waited until I was alone before opening it, because I felt incapable of reading it without crying my eyes out."[16]

To Henriette Viquerie and Justine Barat, whom she met in the cloister as they were arriving, she said, "You will be very happy in religious life. The good Lord has given you a very great grace."[17]

And to Soeur Gonzague Cointe, "I like your sister a lot. Come, be as fervent as she is."[18]

Bernadette comforted Soeur Charles Estanave, who had to be sent home in 1877. She would come back in 1880, after Bernadette's death, and make her profession in 1885.[19]

To Soeur Claire Bordes, sick and fearful of not being admitted for reasons of health, Bernadette gave herself as an example: "I was sick and they accepted me just the same. If the good Lord wills it, you'll be a religious. He will know how to knock down all obstacles."

"From that moment on," relates Soeur Claire, "I found myself totally resigned to accept what the good Lord wanted. I was no longer worried, and I even found myself feeling better."[20] Bernadette sustained her by inviting her "to make spiritual communions with her."[21]

Sometimes she spotted novices in difficulty and took the initiative to approach them. That was the case with nineteen-year-old Adèle Martin from Château-Chinon, who arrived in Nevers on May 2, 1878. The whistle of the trains near the motherhouse were a heart-rending reminder for this novice of her family home.

"I became unable to swallow a single mouthful," she relates. I was asked, 'Mademoiselle, perhaps you don't like this dish?'

"'Yes, I do, but there's something choking me.'

"What was choking me was sorrow.

"One day they assigned me to clean the novitiate staircase. I was going downstairs backwards, crying and sobbing, sweeping each step, my face turned up toward the landing, but my heart was in Château-Chinon with my little brothers. I thought I was alone, but I must have given myself away by sobbing out loud, for all of a sudden, I felt that there was someone on the landing, looking down at me. And I heard a gentle voice saying to me, 'Who's that little postulant crying like that?'

"'It's me.'

"'Who's me?'

"'Adèle Martin.'

"'Where do you come from?'

"'Château-Chinon.'

"'Why are you crying?'

"'Because I'm lonesome.'

"'But Mademoiselle, you're close to home. Château-Chinon isn't all that far.'

"'I'm lonesome for my little brothers. If you only knew how much I love them! I'm afraid they'll be neglected.'

"'Your little brothers are not abandoned, Mademoiselle. Be reassured.'

"She added, 'I promise to pray for them and also for you.' She said this in a low voice and withdrew.

"A sister who happened to come by at that moment whispered to me, 'Do you know who spoke to you? It's Soeur Marie-Bernard.'

"And since that name meant nothing to me, she made it clear, 'The one who saw the Blessed Virgin eighteen times at Lourdes.'"[22]

For those who grew used to the novitiate, it was often a second uprooting to leave the motherhouse for the houses to which they were assigned. This was why Bernadette consoled Soeur Anastasie Carrière on October 25, 1877.[23] This is also why she addressed this word of encouragement to a group of professed sisters, who, on June 8, 1878, were being scattered to Bagnols, Marcillac and Béziers: "I promise to pray for the exiles."[24]

"For her, as for everybody," comments one of the three, Soeur Rosalie Pérasse, "home and homeland were the motherhouse."

This comment was particularly strong for Soeur Marie-Joséphine Viguerie, still not fully detached from her own self-will. She was afraid of going to another house and strongly hoped to stay at the novitiate. It became an obsession. She confided this to Soeur Marie-Bernard, who "put her hand on sister's head" and answered "mischievously": "You! You need to go to another house to get your head together!"[25]

If Bernadette was often helpful, it was doubtless because they sent her all those in distress, but also because she had good judgment.

"Despite her desire to go unnoticed, she used the times of 'mingling' to seek out the new arrivals and speak a sisterly word," noted Soeur Marguerite Chardon, the postulant from Beaucaire, who arrived on November 7, 1878.[26]

In this way, Bernadette used one of her very last "expeditions" outside the infirmary to comfort the new postulant.[27]

Then again, Bernadette was attentive to each sister's wishes. She knew how to put herself in their place, how to listen to them.

"We never failed to go up to the infirmary to see dear Soeur Marie-Bernard, always gracious and always cheerful, even though most often we found her bedridden, or sometimes working, seated on her bed," relates Soeur Philomène Roques. "I roused her interest by telling her stories of little incidents concerning the children....

"[I told her] about the frequent showers on Sundays when we went to the forge at Imphy, or the parish church for High Mass.

"She said to me, 'I'll pray for good weather.'"[28]

Special Visitors

During the period of 1875–1878 the flood of outside visitors tended to diminish. The reason was that sickness confined Bernadette more and more to the infirmary, where visitors were not allowed. It also came from her reluctance and her growing insistence that the sisters honor their promise of keeping her hidden. She was growing less and less tolerant of being admired. She was becoming more and more skillful at slipping away. "On June 7, 1877," relates Soeur Bernard Dalias, "on the occasion of the Sacred Heart procession, when the public was admitted to Saint-Gildard's, as people were going back into chapel...Madame de Falaiseau found herself between Bernadette and me. Looking at Bernadette, she said to me, 'How happy I am!'

"Bernadette heard her and whispered to me, 'I'll fix her.'

"Then she went between the wall and the pew and disappeared in the back of the chapel. The elderly lady noticed and sadly said to me, 'Oh! Oh!'

"I answered her, 'You talked too much.'"[29]

The need for recollection became urgent for Bernadette. In 1876, she was in Saint Joseph's Infirmary. It was 7:30 A.M. She had received Communion at 6:15. She was alone with Soeur Marcelle Vialle. The bell rang for the second sitting of breakfast. "My dear Sister," said Bernadette, "I am very annoyed. I would like...to extend my thanksgiving while you're gone, but they won't allow me. The sisters from the first sitting will come and knock at the door on their way up to their rooms, and I'll have to receive them."

"Is that what's bothering you?"

"Yes, what would you do in my place?"

"Oh, I wouldn't be embarrassed, and if you permit me, I'll apply the remedy right away by locking you up."

"Very well," she said. "Lock me up."

Soeur Marcelle locked the hallway door, left by a second side door leading into an adjacent room, locked that door, put the key in her pocket and went downstairs. When she came back, a quarter of an hour later, Bernadette thanked her. But she was not comfortable with this ruse.

"That night," added Soeur Marcelle, "when I showed up to offer my services, she beckoned me over and said to me very gently, 'You won't lock me up again?'

"She didn't give me her reasons, and I didn't ask for any."[30]

Visitors at that time were strictly limited: close relatives and exceptionally important people.

Here are the main ones in chronological order:

Abbé Pomian saw Bernadette twice during this time, on the occasion of his two visits to Saint-Gildard's. The first was on July 29, 1875 for the temporary profession of his niece, Soeur Mathilde Pomian. That visit left not an echo.[31]

The second visit occurred on September 15, 1876.[32] Abbé Pomian returned to negotiate the construction of the orphanage in Lourdes.

Abbé Pomian, Bernadette's confessor, was the first priest to receive news of the apparitions.

To the right, a drawing by Yan Dargent.

Below, a later photograph. The holy man reluctantly consented to be photographed. He was panic-stricken at the thought of being in front of a camera. Because of this he allowed his hair to be combed differently than usual.

The only evidence of this tedious visit is the letter of apology Bernadette sent to him three months later: "I'll try to be more sociable
next time. I still get embarrassed every time I think of how disagreeable I was when I received you. I beg a thousand pardons. I hope
that you will not hold it against me."[33]

Might Bernadette have given her former confessor the cold
shoulder? Not at all.... The key to the riddle is found in her correspondence at that time. Her stomach rejected all food.[34] Consequently, she offered the visitor a sorry sight, which she wished to
spare him.

Coronation Celebrations

The celebrations held in Lourdes from July 1–3, 1876, for the consecration of the basilica and the coronation of the statue, brought
about another series of visits. Bernadette received the pilgrims from
Nevers. She entrusted them with her letters to Lourdes, one of
which was for the Virgin herself, one for the Curé, one for the
bishop, who was looking after her family; others for her family.[35]

Abbé Perreau visited her. He was the "assistant chaplain" at the
motherhouse—unassuming, spiritual and understanding. She regarded him highly as indicated in the letter she entrusted to him
for Mère Alexandrine Roques, superior of the hospice: "You are
going to get the very latest news...through...our assistant chaplain,
who is coming to Lourdes for his health. I recommend him to you,
as well as to Abbé Pomian. He is very bashful, and since he is sickly,
we are afraid that he will have to stop en route, as he did the last
time. I feel so bad for him. Knowing how much he's been wanting
to make this trip, I hope the Blessed Virgin grants him this grace."[36]

Bernadette encouraged him before he boarded the pilgrimage
train on June 30. He himself relates, "She asked me to pray for her
family and more especially for one of her brothers, her godchild
Bernard-Pierre. She asked not so much for their health and prosperity as for their virtue and their faithfulness to their Christian duties. She was partial to her younger brother. She had recommended
him to me and asked me to watch over his religious education."[37]

Indeed, Bernadette worried greatly about her family. It was generally believed at that time that justice was meted out here and now.
She saw a connection between her family's doing business on Sun-

day and the bereavements afflicting them. "She considered certain trials that had come upon them as chastisements because, she said, God could not bless that."[38]

The ceremonies of July 1–3, 1876, were elaborate and enthusiastic. A crowd without precedent was in attendance: thirty-five bishops, three thousand priests and nearly one hundred thousand pilgrims, from all over the world, assembled at the grotto. This was twice as many as had come to the "Banner Pilgrimage" (forty thousand people in 1872) and ten times the largest crowd drawn by the apparitions in 1858.

Abbé Perreau had a good trip and got blanket permission from Mother General to give Bernadette all the news of Lourdes.

Bernadette had many questions about her family. Their budding fortune bothered her. For her it was like a muddy stream, flowing from the pure spring that she had brought gushing forth in Lourdes. "She put a great deal of emphasis on asking me if they were not to become rich," attests Abbé Perreau.[39]

He enthusiastically described for her the "beatification" of the site, the coronation, the crowds. She listened gleefully.

"You would've enjoyed being there?"

"Yes," she answered at first. Then, she "immediately" took it back: "No, my place is here," she said, pointing to her sickbed. "I was much better off in my infirmary."[40]

Before the ceremonies, Soeur Ambroise Fenasse, superior of the Hôtel-Dieu in Saint Etienne, had already asked her, "Wouldn't you be happy to attend?"

"Oh, no! I prefer my little corner of the infirmary a thousand times over...."

She added, "If I could transport myself down to the grotto 'in a balloon' and pray for a few moments when there was no one there, I'd gladly go; but if I have to travel like everyone else and find myself in the middle of the crowd, I'd rather stay here."[41]

She was dreaming of a quick visit like the one Pius XII almost made a month before he died, on August 15, 1958.

Bernadette had said in a similar vein to Bishop de Ladoue before his departure, "If only I could see without being seen."[42]

But her heart's desire was beyond these dreams. Before leaving, the bishop had asked her, "Would you like to come to Lourdes?"

She answered simply, "Oh, no, Monseigneur! I'd rather be in my bed."[43]

She gave the same answer to Soeur Marthe du Rais, who asked, "Had you no wish to take part?"

"Oh! Not at all! I'm staying in my corner."

We hesitate to record another remark ascribed to her by Henri Lasserre on this same occasion: "Don't feel sorry for me. I've seen lovelier."[44]

On her own, Bernadette never spoke of the apparitions, as every witness testified. She focused on the future: "I gave up Lourdes. I'll see the Blessed Virgin in heaven; it will be much more beautiful."[45]

Leaving the past behind is one of the constants of this period. Bernadette held fast to her destiny. She accepted it; she accepted herself without a backward glance. If she still spoke of her "dear grotto," she was remembering, not anticipating.

To Soeur Pérasse, she said, "I love my brothers and my sister very much; and yet, it would be a very great sacrifice for me to go back to Lourdes."[46]

"That answer really astonished me," said the witness.

Beyond these intimate reasons, Mère Ursule Lassalle reveals one of the minor elements in this conviction. "She showed her a photograph of the grotto. [Bernadette] looked at it a moment and made this remark, 'Oh, my poor grotto! I wouldn't recognize it again.'"[47]

Mère Ursule continued, "Would you be happy to see it again?"

"My mission in Lourdes is done. What would I do there?"[48]

That was her heart's desire: to stick to the message that Curé Peyramale had given her on November 9, 1868: "Your mission at the grotto is finished; work on your sanctification."[49]

This is what occupied her conversations with the pilgrims from Lourdes. One superior began to recall "the wonderful things going on there." But, she relates, Bernadette folded her hands and simply said: "Sacrifice!"

"I had the impression that we would have made her sad by staying on that subject.... We took our leave."[50]

We will understand later [51] that the sacrifice Bernadette endured went further than that simple word seems to indicate.

To the piercing question that Soeur Joseph Caldairou again

asked her in 1878, she answered in the same way: "I have left Lourdes forever."[52]

And when sister continued, "Would you be happy to see the grotto again?"

"No...I'd be overwhelmed by the crowd, and I don't want that."[53] She also added, "I don't want to go; I'm comfortable here, and I'm happy to stay."[54]

Bernadette sounded the same note to Soeur Marcelline Lannessans, also assigned to Lourdes on September 22, 1878: "No, they'd look at me like some strange animal. Besides, they'd leave the Blessed Virgin to follow me. Pray for me at the grotto."[55]

Years later this was to be the problem Pope Paul VI would have in Bogotá: the crowds of August 1968 ran out to see him; but when he left, they abandoned the ceremonies of the Eucharistic Congress being held there.

Soeur Joseph took advantage of her return from Lourdes to ask Bernadette some questions on the apparitions: "'Was it through the hole in the rock that the Blessed Virgin arrived and disappeared?'

"With a smile, she answered, 'Why, no, she vanished like a cloud.'[56]

"'Did she speak to you in French?'

"'She couldn't speak to me in French. I couldn't understand it. She talked to me in patois.'"[57]

"Monsieur le Curé"

When Abbé Perreau had left for Lourdes in 1876, for the consecration of the basilica, Bernadette had given him particularly warm messages for her former Curé: "Go see Monseigneur Peyramale. Tell him I think of him every day, that I pray for him and I ask for his blessing...."

The Curé of Lourdes was already in deep distress when Bernadette's message reached him, Abbé Perreau here notes.[58]

What distress? We have seen that Abbé Peyramale found himself evicted from the grotto. Afterwards, he tried to make his parish one of the pilgrimage "stations"; he had thrown himself into the construction of a new church and was head over heels in debt. Construction had been halted by higher authority. And the whole situation had been recklessly aggravated by some indiscreet friends. Peyramale, shrouded in the prelate's purple with which he had been honored in 1874, a generous man, but one who was sensitive and suspicious in adversity, was overwhelmed with suffering. He sent his

This construction site, looking like ruins overgrown with grass behind the locked gate and the standing crucifix, symbolizes Abbé Peyramale's trials. The grotto had been entrusted to the "Missionaries" in 1866. Peyramale found himself evicted, cut off from the source of revenue. At the request of higher authorities, the Curé of Lourdes had to halt the construction of his new parish church and be content with the old one, often too small, where he celebrated Mass until his death.

answer to Bernadette in this simple message: "Tell her that she is still my child and I bless her."[59]

The following year, on Saturday, September 8, 1877, feast of the Nativity of the Virgin, a telegram arrived in Nevers: Abbé Peyramale was dying. Bernadette wrote Abbé Pomian these simple words, the starting point for all the fanciful elaborations in later literature: "On the day of the Nativity, at nine o'clock, Soeur Nathalie Portat came looking for me in the choir loft and told me they had just received a dispatch notifying us that the Curé of Lourdes was in critical condition."[60]

At this message, Bernadette said only, "Oh! Monsieur le Curé!"[61]

"The next day," the letter continued, "a second" dispatch "announced his death."

The telegram was opened during the community meeting, when Soeur Marie-Bernard was present.

"I was next to her," relates Soeur Victoire Cassou, a relative of Bernadette's and a witness of the apparitions. "Immediately on hearing the news, in order not to burst into sobs in front of the sisters, she gave me a sharp tug and we left. She sobbed to me, 'He did the work I couldn't do.'"[62]

Reporting this praise of Peyramale, Soeur Victoire included Père Sempé, who had continued the work in his place and in a different manner. She has Bernadette saying: "These are the *two* people I've loved the most on earth; they did the work I couldn't do."[63]

A statement like this makes one hesitate. Bernadette had known Père Sempé over a long period of time, and she had turned to him trustingly in certain family difficulties.[64] But she did not share with him the same bond that united her to her childhood Curé. Could Soeur Victoire have had the pious intention of reconciling in death and through Bernadette these two priests, whom so many ups and downs had set at odds?

Soeur Elisabeth Rigal, the former teacher who had encouraged Bernadette to put down in writing her own accounts of the apparitions, came to Nevers a short time later on October 17. She remained at the motherhouse until October 25, making during that period the retreat in preparation for her perpetual vows. Bernadette talked with her about her old Curé, "her eyes filled with tears," saying "Do you think I could ever forget him?"[65] She also said, "Oh! Soon it will be my turn; but before, I have to undergo another death."[66]

"What if I've Made a Mistake?"

This other death was already in progress. It was tied up with the mysterious ordeal to which we shall return at the end of this book. The visit of Bishop Bourret, bishop of Rodez and former professor at the Sorbonne, allows us to catch a glimpse of this trial.

"Bernadette thought she could avoid this visit," relates Soeur Victoire, an eyewitness.[67] "One day, the Bishop of Rodez, having come to Saint-Gildard's, wanted to see Soeur Marie-Bernard. To show her to him without her knowledge, they fell back on a ruse. They assembled the whole community in the novitiate hall, and after the bishop had delivered a few edifying words, the superior called out for the sisters from Aveyron. They stood up. Then those from the Pyrénées, who likewise stood up. Then the bishop went down the line to have them kiss his ring. At the same time, the superior or the mistress of novices gave a few details on each sister, saying, 'This one is from Aveyron, that one from the Pyrénées.'

"Soeur Marie-Bernard then understood what was going on. I was next to her and she whispered to me, 'Don't say a word, I know what I'm going to do!'

"And right away, she slipped through a small door not far from her. I said to her, 'What about the forty days indulgence?' [Editor's note: This was the indulgence granted at that time for kissing a bishop's ring.]

"She answered, 'My Jesus, mercy! There's three hundred!'"[68]

Bishop Bourret would not accept disappointment. He got even more than he had originally expected: a private conversation and even a disclosure. Let us allow him to describe in his own words this meeting on Saturday, September 1, 1877.

Bernadette admitted her reluctance to talk "about the vision of her youth." "It's already far away...very far...all those things I don't remember anymore. I don't really like to talk about it because, good Lord! What if I've made a mistake?..."[69]

And yet, she talked about it convincingly as shown by the continuation of this same letter: "Making an effort to describe for me how the vision looked, she told me, almost word for word and with no uncertainty, what occurred during the transformation.... What struck me most from all the accounts that I've read was:

"'I saw a dazzling light.... But a light like nothing here on earth, even the sun. In the midst of that light, I saw a wonderful form, but not like any earthly form. It was physical and it wasn't. I heard a melodious voice and I looked, without noticing anything else around me. There I was, and when it was over, my vision was blurred, like someone coming into a room after looking at the sun for a long time. The woman's form I saw there looked nothing at all like what has been reproduced!'

"Then she exclaimed, 'Oh, if only I were a painter!'"[70]

The negative part of this disclosure, "What if I've made a mistake?" brings out what for Bernadette at that time was the fading away of her memories of 1858. This darkness can surprise only people unfamiliar with any experience of the spiritual. To understand, think of what one feels during a long spell of rainy days when it looks as though the sun will not return again. So too, did the cave dwellers in the Far North wonder every year whether they were not plunged into endless night, and whether they would ever see the return of the endless days of summer.

2. Sickness and Remissions

It remains for us to examine the course of her suffering—and acceptance—which constitutes the intimate story of this period: Bernadette's "assignment" at the foot of the cross. This suffering was not at all passive nor self-absorbed; it was attentive to others. Bernadette constantly guarded against letting herself sink into suffering. She was ready to use the least bit of physical or psychical strength as a gift and a humble service.

1875

In 1875, she kept to her bed from April to mid June.[71] Summer brought about an improvement, but she relapsed in October.[72] Given her ups and downs, she did what she could. One day in November 1875, Soeur Dominique arranged for her to come down, on the pretext of "taking care of a group of children." The truth was that they had come to see her.[73] On November 19, her coughing up blood aroused fear for her life,[74] and after that, she was confined to her bed until the month of May 1876.[75]

1876

On February 29, 1876, the bishop came to see her.[76] In a letter, written that day, she acknowledged her "usual state of suffering."[77]

The warm days of 1876 restored her life once again. In June, she was able to attend Sunday Mass; she had been deprived of it for six months.[78] What she did not tell her family was that she could not go to Mass by herself. She admitted this to Soeur Victorine Poux: "I have completely lost the use of my legs. I must undergo the humiliation of being carried, but our sisters do this with such good grace that the sacrifice is really not as great. I'm always afraid that they will hurt themselves, and when I tell them so, they begin to laugh and, I'd even say, to make fun of me! They tell me they could carry four people my size."[79]

The fact is that Bernadette had grown very, very light. Her stomach could not tolerate much.

I am "always worn-out," she wrote on June 25, 1876, to Mère Alexandrine Roques. She softened the picture a little by adding, "I'm not too strong yet; I can't go to chapel on my own. I need two arms rather than one. It's a little humiliating, but what can I do? I must submit, since the good Lord wants it that way."[80]

"The warm days will make me well again this time," she confided to her sister Toinette, in a more hopeful letter.[81]

Actually, her health did continue to improve. On July 1, she again informed her brother, Jean-Marie, of a "usual state of suffering";[82] yet, in August she was able to make the retreat preached by Père H. Nurit, S.J., and to leave the choir loft when he began to talk about her.[83]

In August of 1876, Soeur Joseph Biermann found her "sweeping up the infirmary." "I ran over to replace her," she relates. "She indicated that I was out of order, and grabbing the broom out of my hands with a certain amount of energy, for there was a bit of a scuffle between us, she said pleasantly, 'You can't have it. Conquer or die!'"[84]

In the wake of France's defeat in 1870, a military spark had been struck in Bernadette's soul. In this same summer of 1876, she told Soeur Joseph Cassagnes, who interrupted her reading, "Oh, this book! It makes me want to go off to war!"[85]

"I suffer very little," she wrote to her godchild, Bernadette Nicolau, on August 26, 1876.[86]

"I don't suffer much," she confided to Soeur Mathilde Pomian of September 7, 1876.[87]

What she discovered, now that the red curtain of violent sufferings had been drawn open, was a "weakness like no other."[88] She had to cut short her letter of September 7, for, she said, "My hand is shaking like an old woman's."[89]

Likewise, on September 13, to Rachel Dufo: "I leave you [te] now, I can't hold my pen any longer. I'm not too sure of what I'm saying to you [vous]. Adieu...."[90]

She wavered between the formal *vous* she had used in Lourdes with this young girl from one of the first families in town, and the familiar *tu*, which Rachel had strongly insisted on. For Rachel, this would be the last letter. Bernadette was exhausted, at the end of her strength. She was living on nothing. Her stomach "refused nourishment."[91]

At the end of September 1876, she was in bed when she received Soeur Joseph Cassagnes, a newly arrived postulant, escorted by Mère Vauzou.[92] Her health seemed to be holding up, however. On November 3, she even wrote to her cousin Lucile, "I'm a little better."[93]

Likewise to Jean-Marie in that same month: "My health is getting a little better."[94]

But it was always on the occasion of a relative "better" that she wrote. Hence, this paradox: she always spoke of some improvement, while on the contrary the situation was slowly growing worse.

Bernadette wanted to keep her family from worrying. She particularly highlighted the comfortable atmosphere where she was kept "very warm in the infirmary"[95] and the care she was receiving.

"I feel a little better once again; don't worry about it," she wrote to her godchild, Bernadette Nicolau, on August 26, 1876. "I'm being taken care of like a little baby."[96]

This was because she had slipped to a point where she could no longer do anything for herself. She continued, "I am really embarrassed by all the kindnesses our venerable Mother General lavishes on me, not to mention the tender care I get from the infirmarian. All the dear sisters are very good to me. They very often tell me, each one would like to take a bit of my sickness so that I could run like I used to. I start laughing and say, 'My biggest suffering, for the moment, is not being able...to follow the community schedule...."[97]

In this same letter, she added, "I ask you not to tell my sister that I am sick."[98]

This was because Toinette had just lost her little Bernadette on August 12 and her grief was at its peak.

Through all these kind words, we catch a glimpse of the courage of the patient. "Where there's a will, there's a way," she wrote to Jean-Marie in the above mentioned letter of November, 1876.[99]

In October 1876, Abbé Febvre, former Curé of Fourchambault and now chaplain at the motherhouse, made his first visit to Bernadette. He noted "the terrible gasping" of "asthma." He was "quite impressed by her patience."[100]

On December 16, 1876, Bishop de Ladoue, Bishop of Nevers, went up to the infirmary because he was going to Rome and hoped to bring a letter from the visionary of Lourdes in order to please Pius IX and win his good graces. He held out to Bernadette the hope of "a blessing from the Holy Father" and concluded, "The surest way of obtaining one is to write to him."

It was in bed that Bernadette received the bishop, and it was in bed that she wrote the letter. Soeur Gabrielle de Vigouroux held the wooden desk steady on her patient's knees. She wrote a rough draft.[101] The superiors looked it over. Had she not carelessly copied down the bishop's comment on "the best way to obtain a blessing"? It was trivial, and the bishop would not be happy if the friendly familiarity of his remark were misused. That had to be deleted. Further on, Bernadette said, alluding to the valiant soldiers who had come to defend the Vatican: "For a long time, though unworthy, I have been a *zouave* (soldier) of Your Holiness: My weapons are prayer and sacrifice."

That was a striking turn of phrase. The sisters had used it in a welcoming speech to the Nuncio, Bishop Chigi, when he came to Saint-Gildard's on November 15, 1868: "We are soldiers of duty, zouaves of prayer...." Indeed, recalling the troops of Monsieur de Charette could only gladden the heart of the Holy Father; but as it was, it was too blunt. Some kind of preamble had to lead up to it, for instance, "I can only continue what I have done up to now, that is, suffer and pray. Some years ago now, I appointed myself, though unworthy, Your Holiness' little zouave."

Rough draft of the letter to the Pope. Bernadette wrote this using a patient's desk. She was hard put to spell the word "zouave."

The word "appointed" elevated the tone of the statement which could thus touch the exalted soul of the Holy Father, while the adjective "little" would give a more modest aspect to the claim of imitating the glorious defenders of the Holy See.

Bernadette ended by saying, "It seems to me...that the Blessed Virgin must often look down from heaven upon you, Most Holy Father, since you proclaimed her Immaculate, and because, four years later, this good Mother came on earth to say, 'I am the Immaculate.' I did not know what that meant. I had never heard the word before. Ever since, in thinking it over, I say to myself, 'The Blessed Virgin is good; one could say she came to confirm the statement of our Holy Father.'"

The letter could not end so abruptly. A farewell, more in keeping with custom, had to be used: "This is what makes me think that she must be protecting you in a special way. I hope that this good Mother will have mercy on her children, and that she will deign to put her foot once more on the head of the cursed serpent, and, in this way, put an end to the cruel trials of Holy Mother Church and to the sorrows of her august and beloved Pontiff...."

Once the corrections were made, a sister recopied this second draft on official stationery bearing the letterhead of the congregation.[102] In her turn, Bernadette copied this handwritten letter on her portable desk. But she got confused in the famous closing paragraph about the head of the "cursed serpent," and left out a phrase. She added it above the line.[103] There were also some misspellings. For the Pope this was unthinkable! She had to start all over again. She went back to work. It was this final draft that Bishop de Ladoue would submit to Pius IX.

On January 14, 1877, he would bring back the Pope's blessing, whose wording he had had composed in Italian before his departure.

On December 28, 1876, Bernadette wrote to Abbé Pomian, "For a month now, I've been able to keep down a little more food."[104]

She was hopeful.... She said to Doctor Robert Saint-Cyr: "It's very long."[105]

The doctor, who considered her a "bizarre patient," answered her,[106] "You have a terrible enemy."

"At that," relates Bernadette, "he took to his heels.... I'm starting to think he's losing his wits!"[107]

J. M. J.

Très-Saint Père,

Je n'aurais jamais osé prendre la plume pour écrire à Votre Sainteté, moi pauvre petite Sœur, si notre Digne Évêque, Monseigneur de Tarbes, ne m'eût encouragée, malgré le vif désir que j'éprouvais de venir me jeter à genoux à vos pieds, Très Saint Père, pour vous prier de me donner votre bénédiction apostolique, qui sera, j'en suis sûre, une nouvelle force pour mon âme si faible. J'ai craint, tout d'abord, d'être trop indiscrète; puis il m'est venu à la pensée que Notre Seigneur aime à être importuné aussi bien par le petit que par le grand, par le pauvre que par le riche, qu'il se donne à chacun de nous sans distinction. Cette pensée m'a donné du courage; aussi je ne crains plus, je viens à vous, Très Saint Père, comme une pauvre petite enfant au plus tendre des Pères, pleine d'abandon et de confiance. Que pourrais-je faire, très-Saint Père, pour vous témoigner mon

The first good copy of the letter to the Pope (the one which has been kept in the archives)

The year 1876 finished badly. "It's over a year now that I've been in my white chapel," she wrote to Peyramale on December 28.[108]

She left her bed only to be carried or helped along to Mass in her better moments, as she made clear in that letter to her old Curé.

The day before (December 27), she gave a sign of improvement to her sister Toinette. "My health is better, but I still can't leave the infirmary, except on Sundays, to attend Mass."[109]

1877 ℓ

June 8, 1877, the feast of the Sacred Heart, saw a drama in the infirmary.

"A violent storm occurred at eleven o'clock, lightning struck the window near Soeur Marie-Bernard's bed, scorched the shutter, and fell on the small roof between the sacristy and Saint Luke's.... The gas pipe melted all along the roof and flames soared several yards into the air."[110]

Here, as always, high emotions skewed the testimony. Was Bernadette in any condition "to leap to the foot of her bed," screaming *"Oh! Le grappin!"* [i.e. Satan], as Soeur Casimir Callery said, or even to "kneel down in the middle of the room...her hands folded and lifted up toward heaven"? In any case, the witnesses were impressed by her calmness and prayer, which they tried to imitate.

According to Soeur Julie Ramplou, she supposedly said, "Why get frightened like that?... It's the devil who's furious over the feast day celebrated here with so much solemnity."[111]

In those days, they went to extremes in seeing the supernatural in life's everyday occurrences.

The summer of 1877 marked a new stage of improvement that would last until September 15, 1877.[112] Bernadette would move about again. "I walk every day in the garden to regain my strength," she wrote to her brother Bernard-Pierre on July 17, 1877.[113]

"My health has grown much stronger. I can follow a good deal of the community exercises; I go for walks and I have a hearty appetite," she also wrote to Abbé Pomian on September 15.[114]

During that same period, reports Soeur Victorine Laborde, she came "on Sundays" to the novitiate recreation, which took place in the community room. She would arrive, "always accompanied by one of the older sisters, who was often the Secretary General, Soeur Eléonore Cassagnes.

"We would have liked to spend the whole recreation with her, but she had to move quickly to visit with each group. She left us after a few minutes, and, although she said or did nothing (special), she left us with...an impression of peace.

"That's how I saw her every Sunday or thereabouts, from July to October."[115]

She could walk easily enough for them to give her errands to do. "Having come to Nevers on October 25, 1877, to make my perpetual vows, I met the Venerable Sister carrying the registers where the names of the professed were recorded. When I told her how sad I was for one of my sick companions, she said to me, 'Don't worry, it'll be a good while before that sister dies. You'll still have time to look after her.'"[116]

During that happy period, we often find Bernadette coming and going. Summer was definitely good to her.

On August 19, she came down to the novitiate; they wished her a happy feast day: the feast of Saint Bernard.

"Mère Louise Ferrand, an assistant, who was with her, said, 'Yes, Sisters, you will pray for her conversion.'

"Since everyone was making a lot of noise, Bernadette raised her voice and said, 'Sisters, listen to what dear Sister Assistant has to say.'

"Hearing her familiar voice, everyone stopped talking and came closer. Mère Louise then said, 'I'm saying that Soeur Marie-Bernard has received many graces and we must pray for her.'

"Then Soeur Marie-Bernard, in a very emotional and serious voice repeated, 'Yes, it's true, I have received many graces.'"[117]

In September 1877, she was working in the "Sainte-Croix (Holy Cross) room" near the infirmary, assembling pictures she had been assigned to make. She told Soeur Marie Delbrel, "I'll glue the hearts. You make the flames and write the inscription. Then they can truthfully say, 'Soeur Marie-Bernard made them.'"[118]

She had regained an astonishing ability to move, confirmed by all the witnesses of that period. There was no more question of bed, nor even of a cane. With the help of her own courage, she walked up to the third-floor attic. She had a reason. Jeanne Jardet, a kitchen worker, who so much enjoyed seeing Bernadette when she came to the kitchen, had fallen sick. She had left the stoves, badly perspired, to catch a breath of cool night air on the porch and had consequently fallen ill. The following is her account:

"Bernadette had not been assigned to look after me; that duty fell on the sisters in the kitchen. Nevertheless, she used to come see me...out of the goodness of her heart...in the workers' dormitory, at the top of the house. I knew her right away by her footstep and also by the habit she had of humming. As soon as I heard her little hymn melody, I'd say, 'Here she is!' And I was happy. When she came in, she'd begin by bowing to a statue of the Virgin above the cupboard facing the door; then she'd turn toward my bed, which was the first on the left against the wall. She arrived a little out of breath. I noticed that her stomach was 'pounding'.... She said, 'Here I am. How are you doing today?'

"Usually, I barely had the strength to answer her, but enjoyed having her there. She fluffed up my pillow, straightened out the bolster, sponged away my perspiration, and held my hand.... It happened that I had moments of weakness when she was with me. Then she immediately got some vinegar from the cupboard, and with a napkin, she rubbed some on my lips and had me inhale. I remember biting on the napkin to suck on it, I was so thirsty. While taking care of my needs, she would say something pious, for example, one that I remember: 'We must suffer a little for the good Lord, my child. He suffered so much for us.'

"She also told me, 'When we're in heaven, we'll be happy, but here below....'

"She finished her sentence with a gesture that meant, 'Don't count on this life.' One day I told her how sorry I was to be sick, far away from my mother. Then...pointing at the Virgin over the cupboard, she said, 'There's your mother, my child. She is mother of us all.'

"Then she said something else that gave me less pleasure, 'Ask her to call you.'

"But you can well imagine that at the age of twenty, I wasn't anxious to die. I didn't say a word. Then, without scolding me, she took my hand and said, 'Courage, my child, I'll be back to see you as soon as I can.'

"One day I thought I was going to die, and I was crying. She told me, 'Don't cry. The good Lord is the Master. You'll see your mother again....' When I saw Bernadette again, I asked her to bring me some Lourdes water. She answered, 'I'd like to, but I don't have permission.'

"A few days later, she brought me some in a tiny bottle. I said, 'That's not enough. That won't do me any good.'

"Bernadette smiled. 'The amount isn't important. Don't take it all at once.'

"On another day, she gave me a picture as a gift: on one side was the Blessed Virgin and on the other, a prayer. She recommended that I recite this prayer every night, and for sixty years, I've never missed once."[119]

During the retreat of September 1 to 8, 1877, Bernadette was kept waiting a long time for her turn to go to confession and even had to "save a place" for Soeur Irène Ganier, in front of Abbé Febvre's busy confessional in Saint Hélène's second floor infirmary chapel. "After waiting so long, I had to leave without going to confession," relates Soeur Irène. "Soeur Marie-Bernard...came back the next day, found that I was again the last in line and asked me how come. I told her that, while I was away, the book marking my place had been pushed back. Since lunchtime had arrived, Soeur Marie-Bernard said to me, 'I'll save your place; go and have lunch.'

"When I returned, I saved her place while she herself went to eat. But the other sisters kept going ahead of us, and the day was over: we still hadn't been able to go to confession. The next day the same thing happened. Soeur Marie-Bernard, feeling tired, said to me, 'I'm going to the infirmary, and I'll go to confession there. It bothers me to disturb the chaplain, with all the work he has to do.'

"I offered to ask a dear sister to let her go ahead, which she would have gladly done. But Soeur Marie-Bernard's humility balked at this. A few moments later, noticing a sister "cutting in," she got up quickly, left and came back again. A few minutes later, Mother Assistant arrived. Then Soeur Marie-Bernard, filled with the spirit of justice, stood up, spoke spiritedly, and described what she had just witnessed. Good Mother Louise listened to her, then very gently, said a few appropriate words and left.

"Soeur Marie-Bernard understood that her act of charity had become...impatience. Ashamed, she left and that very night she made amends for her fault."

The truth is, reporting someone like that was not Bernadette's style. She did it, relates Soeur Irène out of indignation at the "injustice done to me."[120]

Bernadette confirmed her return to health in the previously cited letter of September 15, 1877, to Abbé Pomian.[121] She had recovered so much of her strength, that by the end of October (between the twenty-fifth and the thirty-first) she was well enough to exert herself physically, as certified by Soeur Marguerite Magnié:[122] "In the month of October (before professions on the twenty-fifth) ...after the grape harvest...the community, after the prayer concluding recreation, went to Saint Joseph's Chapel as was the custom, to recite a short daily prayer. All of a sudden, (Bernadette)...noticed a beautiful bunch of grapes, inadvertently left hanging from the vine on the big wall facing the chapel, just above the latticed water tank that irrigates the garden. 'What a shame to let such beautiful grapes go to waste,' said Soeur Marie-Bernard. 'If we tried to get them, we could enjoy them.'

"No sooner said than done. Soeur Saint Michel Graffeuil, Soeur Bernard Dalias, another sister whose name I forget, and yours truly hastened to crisscross our hands to form a kind of stepladder to help permit her to reach our goal. After taking off her shoes, our companion jumped on and climbed up...and soon came back down triumphantly holding in her hands the beautiful golden cluster of grapes. After admiring it...[Soeur Marie-Bernard] headed off toward our venerable Mother, who was walking a few steps ahead of us, no doubt to offer it to her or to ask permission to divide it out [which she actually did, according to Soeur Marguerite's first testimony.]"[123]

There is no doubt that they chose to hoist Bernadette because she was so light, but it would be the last wall she would climb.

All the same, her improvement lasted until Wednesday, November 21, 1877. On that day, the feast of the Presentation, Bernadette could still come down for the renewal of vows. It was she who read the formula in the name of the "renewers"; but her voice, usually clear and strong, was weakened by an asthma attack.[124]

The Winter of 1877–1878

In December, winter did its work. Soeur Véronique Crillon, superior at Montceau-les-Mines, found her sick in the infirmary. Soeur Thaïs Carteron, assigned to the hospital at Nevers, accompanied the visitor. Referring to the time when Bernadette was in charge of the infirmary, she said, "Can you believe that Soeur Véronique is a superior, but not me! Yet we were professed together. You, at least are the superior of the infirmary."

Soeur Marie-Bernard replied seriously, "Understand, Sister, that I seek only to become superior of myself, and I can't seem to manage that."[125]

One night toward the end of 1877, Soeur Rosalie Pérasse came with another novice to bring firewood. Bernadette "had a painful knee that day and was staying in her room. When we opened the door, the sun poured in with us and filled the room with gladness."

It was the evening sun, slanting its way through the large corridor windows.

"Oh," she said, "those little diabolical tempters who come to show me the sun, when I'm stuck in my armchair!"[126]

From December 1877–January 1878, Soeur Marie-Bernard regained enough mobility to go to the novices' infirmary. She helped them set up the Christmas crèche and she was the one who arranged the Infant Jesus, saying, "You must have been very cold, my poor little Jesus, in the stable in Bethlehem." One of the novices recalls, "And she turned toward us, saying, 'They were heartless, those residents of Bethlehem, not to give hospitality to the Infant Jesus.'"[127]

She came over to admire a doll, made by the novices "for the caretaker's little girl" for New Year's Day.

"She took it in her arms and, making it hop, said, 'O my poor little doll! You look like those unfortunate girls who frequent the park. How unhappy they are....'"[128]

She was thinking of the prostitutes who at that time were the only ones who could wear makeup.

During one of those recreations, Soeur Stanislas—another sick novice—looked for a way "to get her to touch" her religious articles.... "Look, my dear Soeur Marie-Bernard, how rusty my rosary beads are!"

"My good friend, they get rusty because you don't say them enough...."[129]

Over the month of January 1878, Soeur Claire was getting better; Bernadette less so. And no doubt, that was the reason why they were put in the same room, so that the healthier one could keep an eye on the other.

"One night, when I was in bed nearby," recalls Soeur Claire, "I heard her heave a deep sigh, and, since I was afraid, I called out to her.... She answered softly, 'Stay calm, I won't die yet.'"[130]

It was the condition of her knee that was growing worse. Soeur Ambroise Fenasse, who came to Nevers for the Chapter of January 28, 1878, where Mère Adélaïde was elected superior general, replacing the ailing Mère Joséphine, found "Soeur Marie-Bernard in bed immobilized by a white tumor on her knee, which was covered by a silicate dressing."[131]

Silicate was an experimental treatment. Recently Doctor Flament was amazed that it was known at that time.

At the beginning of February, there was noticeable improvement, but on the tenth, Bernadette "relapsed and coughed up blood."[132] She needed a night nurse. According to Soeur Julie Durand, assigned to this duty, she supposedly said, "Don't disturb yourself so often. They think I'm going to die. I have more than six months to go."

"The next day," affirms Soeur Julie, "I repeated these words to Mère Marie-Thérèse, then mistress of novices, who laughed and said to her, 'You're a silly little thing.... You knew you weren't going to die and you disturbed the chaplain and everyone else as well!'

"'But, Mother, you didn't ask me if I was going to die!'

"'Very well, my daughter, the next time, we'll ask....'"[133]

However, this testimony seems suspect. According to Soeur Julie, Bernadette received the Anointing of the Sick that day, which seems impossible. Was she not getting confused with Bernadette's profession *at the point of death,* mentioned in Bishop Forcade's account?

Everything went wrong at the beginning of 1878: Bernadette had problems with her knee, her stomach and her chest. She was suffocating. She liked to keep the windows open, but that was against the "hygenics of the day." Under that heading, *The Religious Calendar for the Sisters of Charity* was quite clear: "Whatever the heat, one must never go to bed with the windows open, because it is too easy to catch cold and to contract rheumatic pains."[134]

Bernadette's instincts ran contrary to this rule. The following incident, reported by Soeur Julie, testifies to this. "Having spent the night with her, at the beginning of May 1878, the patient had me open the window early in the morning. At 5:30, I saw our venerable

Mère Marie-Thérèse Vauzou arrive and tell her, 'Thoughtless creature, this is your doing. Why did you have the window open? To
catch a bit more cold?'

"At that, I closed it, then heard, 'Shh! Shh! Mother didn't say to
close it; she only scolded me for having it open.'"[135]

Bernadette was in bed on Monday, June 17, 1878, when Soeur
Claire came to say good-bye. "Cheer up!" she told Soeur Claire.
"You're going to the orphans; really love those little girls; tell them
to pray for me, and I'll be praying for them."[136] She felt the need of
prayers in return.[137]

One of Bernadette's sufferings was thirst. During the previous
year, she had already begun to drink during the night. Once while
the young novice, assigned to night watch, was asleep, Bernadette
got up and took a drink from the water pitcher.

"I cried out," relates Soeur Casimir Callery, "but Bernadette
stopped me": 'Shh!... Don't wake the poor sister up. She's sleeping
so soundly.'"[138]

Angéle Letord, who prepared the room on days when they
brought her Communion, came on the morning of June 24, 1878:
"Bernadette was surprised to see me and said, 'What's happening
today?'

"'My dear Sister, it's the feast of Saint John the Baptist.'

"'Ah! I'd forgotten about that. I drank something during the
night....'

"Indeed she had some herbal tea at hand to quench her thirst
during the long nights of fever and insomnia."[139]

In those days the rules for the Eucharistic fast were strict. Any
liquid taken after midnight ruled out going to Communion. Bernadette did not "burst out in loud lamentations," continued Soeur
Angéle. "She merely said, 'Go tell the sacristan not to bother....' She
was simple."[140]

In July 1878, Soeur Alexis Féral came to the infirmary to say
good-bye before leaving for a community in the South. Bernadette
was on her feet, but she had to depend "on her crutches," to go get
a holy picture memento.

"We'll meet again in heaven," she said as she gave Soeur Alexis
the picture.[141]

The Final Summer

Bernadette's last summer, the summer of 1878, was characterized, like all the others, by a remission. When Soeur Victoire Cassou came back from Lourdes on September 13, 1878, Bernadette was able to come down.

"They gave Soeur Marie-Bernard and me permission to spend a whole afternoon together, from half past two until about five o'clock. We were allowed to walk in the garden. Afraid of giving bad example to the novices, who would see us together too long, and also to keep from being disturbed, she said to me: 'Come on!' And she made me get into the community coach then closed the door. There we talked about the grotto, our families, Père Sempé and many other things.

"I told her how lucky she was to have seen the Blessed Virgin and also to be guaranteed of going to heaven. She answered, 'Certainly I'm lucky, but so are you; all you have to do is walk the straight and narrow. The Blessed Virgin made use of me as she did the oxen of Bétharram. You come from there, you know the story.'"[142]

Here, the witness must have been confused. The oxen in question were from Sarrance (near Oloron); they allegedly fell to their knees before the tree where a statue of the Virgin had been hidden.

"During the retreat of 1878 (September 13–21)," relates Soeur Irène Ganier, "Bernadette suffered very much from decay of the bone in one knee. In spite of her pain, she came to chapel just the same and knelt during the exercises. During one of the preacher's talks she attended, she told me, 'I'm exhausted; I won't be coming back again; I'll stay in the infirmary.'"

During this retreat which was preparing Bernadette for perpetual vows, Soeur Eudoxie Bagnol, who was taking her vows at the same time, also saw her saying "her rosary on her knees at our Lady's altar in the novitiate."

Sister asked her for prayers. "I will pray for you," she said, "but you pray for me, too. I'm proud."[143]

Bernadette was still able to go down to the chapel on September 22. There she made her perpetual vows and came out radiant. She headed straight for Soeur Joseph Garnier, a bubbly Parisian, who had directed the singing. She "incensed" her with her apron, exclaiming, "Oh! How beautifully you sang! I thought I was in heaven."[144]

That same day, she repeated, "I thought I was in heaven. If I were dead I'd have nothing to worry about because vows are a second baptism."[145]

Soeur Gonzague Champy, whom Bernadette had first met on July 4, 1866, while stopping at Bordeaux, then in 1871 and again during her novitiate in 1872, was taking part in the retreat. She came to ask for a holy picture for Soeur Philippine Molinéry, Bernadette's former infirmarian. "Yes, I'll give Soeur Philippine a picture," Bernadette responded, "and doesn't Soeur Gonzague want one, too?"

"I never would've dared to ask you for one," answered Soeur Gonzague.

"Oh! That's not very nice of you; you should act more naturally with me," replied Bernadette.[146]

With Soeur Germaine Gibergues, Bernadette shared one of her deepest sorrows: "You're very lucky, you people; you can do good, while I just wait around like some useless good-for-nothing."[147]

Soeur Stanislas Tourriol found her weary of all the requests for prayers, which grew more numerous that day of her profession and finished by testing her sincerity. "Yes, yes, I'll pray," she said, "but not in this world; I have so little time to live, I'm so sick."[148]

"That same day or the day after," relates Soeur Joseph Caldairou, "I found her at the end of her rope, very emotional, like someone who's upset. Taking her arm and giving it a squeeze I said, 'Hey! Soeur Marie-Bernard, what's wrong?'

"[She answered] 'Leave me alone; pray for me.'"[149]

During those days it became impossible for Bernadette to take part in community exercises, especially the lectures. One sister said to her, pointing at the cane she was leaning on to support herself, "Why be…sad? You hold in your hands one of the most eloquent of preachers."

This was a reference to a saying of Saint Ignatius, frequently quoted at the time: "A religious should be like a staff in the hands of her superiors." Bernadette caught the allusion. "Yes," she answered, "but that's not always easy. It takes a lot out of me."[150]

She was in a state of exhaustion. Her courage hung by a thread. It was, then, a healthy response for her to defend herself….

A recollection of Soeur Léontine Villaret reflects the same thought. "While I was making my novitiate at Saint Mary's (July–September, 1878), I came to the motherhouse with a few professed sisters. We went to greet our Mothers in the community.... Soeur Marie-Bernard arrived...very tired and very sick, walking with much difficulty because of a tumor on her knee. One of us told her she shouldn't have come down. Mère Marie-Thérèse then made a stinging remark, directed at Bernadette. Soeur Marie-Bernard, who was in a great deal of pain, said, 'Oh, Mistress!...' As if to say, 'She's always picking on me!' At least, that's what I understood.

"Then Mère Marie-Thérèse retorted, 'Ah! We struck that little self-pride of yours.'

"I thought that long-suffering Bernadette would have overlooked that little compliment. Nevertheless, I was surprised at Bernadette's criticism.... We were so devoted to our Mother Mistress that I could not tolerate anyone's answering her in such a fashion."[151]

The last two sentences quoted above were added in the margin of the beatification proceedings when the testimony was reviewed, because this reaction from Bernadette posed a problem for the cause. The promoter of the cause questioned Soeur Léontine on this point once again on May 15, 1918. She gave the following explanation: "Soeur Marie-Bernard had been professed at the time for almost ten years and, consequently, was no longer under Mère Marie-Thérèse Vauzou's authority. She could, therefore, respond politely, as she did, without undermining her authority in the least."[152]

It was also in September 1878 that Soeur Eugénie Calmès, having come to Nevers for the same retreat before perpetual vows, met Bernadette dragging herself along in the infirmary corridor. Her knee was giving her trouble and she needed to use a cane.[153]

There was some improvement at the end of September or the beginning of October, 1878. She could come down to the garden. It was there that the chaplain, Abbé Febvre, arranged to introduce her to his cousin, Jean-Marie, who recalls that his uncle asked him, "Would you like to meet Bernadette?"

"At my affirmative answer, he stood up, so did I, and on the way, he said, 'Our dear Bernadette is doing poorly, and since it's a nice evening, it's almost certain that Mother Superior will have her come down to the garden.'

"Once there, we found ourselves about one hundred feet away from two religious, walking in the upper end of the garden.

"'There they are,' said the chaplain. At that moment, the superior caught sight of us and came over. The short, humble religious stayed a few steps behind. I did the same behind Abbé Febvre, then a short conversation took place between the superior and the chaplain. Suddenly, I heard the superior give Soeur Marie-Bernard this order, 'Go down to the wall at the foot of the garden and pick some grapes to give this young man, who has just made a rather long journey.'

"Coming to the top of the steps, she [Soeur Marie-Bernard] looked at me and held out some fruit. 'Young man,' she said to me, 'you're in the seminary, and you want to become a priest, don't you?'

"'Yes, Sister, if God calls me.'

"'Yes, you'll be a priest all right! Oh, how beautiful—a priest at the altar! But you know,' she said, looking at the community bell tower, 'when the priest is at the altar, he is always Jesus Christ on the cross. You'll have to work and suffer. Don't lose heart!'

"Those were pretty much her exact words. She bowed and disappeared."

On October 7, 1878, she wrote, as she usually did, a reassuring letter to her brother Bernard-Pierre: "Little by little, my strength is coming back. I still limp a bit. It's been three months since I put away the crutches (in favor of a simple cane). It's nothing serious. Just a touch of sciatica in my knee, that gave me some trouble, true, but it's over now."[154]

Arriving at the novitiate October 24, Soeur Thérèse Lecoste found Bernadette "ailing" but still working.

"Her total attention was focused on coloring small pictures or in drawing the crown of thorns around the Sacred Heart of Jesus. Soeur Marie-Bernard told me a little impishly, though quite seriously, 'If you wish to become a religious, Mademoiselle, you'll have to learn to love suffering. Our Lord gives his crown of thorns to his friends on earth. Expect no better.'"[155]

Her Final Home

On October 30, 1878, the infirmaries at Saint-Gildard's changed locations. The one for the professed sisters was relocated to Sainte

Croix Hall in the other wing of the building. This was to be Bernadette's last home.

Yet another remission allowed her to come downstairs again, on the 12 or 13 of November, to see the new postulants. One of them, Soeur Marguerite Chardon, was an only child; her father and mother had brought her from Beaucaire themselves on November 7. She relates, "It had been four or five days since I got there. I was feeling very homesick. This short sister came by, her veil pulled round in front, fully covering her shoulders. She went straight to the 'little caps' [the postulants] and asked one of us, 'Who is the latest arrival?'

"'I am, dear Sister,' I replied.

"At the same time, I kept looking at this sister and I was struck by her kindly smile and something indescribably pleasing about her features. She said to me, 'Are you homesick?'

"'Oh, yes, very much!'

"Then she put her hand on my shoulder and said, 'Come now, set your mind at ease; you will persevere in the congregation.'"[156]

There were times when Bernadette could no longer manage to put on a happy face. She would try to break away in time. During 1878, at a period when she was still able to get around, Soeur Michel Duhême saw her "pirouette," as a friendly kind of joke, bringing an end to the interview after answering several questions. This "pirouette" was one of her last. In fact, on December 11, 1878, "she was confined to her bed for good," according to Henri Lasserre:[157] a confinement which permitted her to go only from her bed to her armchair and back again.

The final phase of her life had begun.

The "White Chapel"

Bernadette herself gives us the most telling metaphor for this last stage of her life: "I am in my white chapel."[158]

On the curtains surrounding her sick bed she had pinned holy pictures that helped her to pray. It was an adaptation of a regional custom. She had already built little altars in the meadows of Bartrès. Jean-Marie Doucet, the sick child she visited at the Piqué Farm in March, 1858, had done the same thing by his fireside. In the first days of August 1876, Soeur Agathe de Filiquier and her companion took note of "the picture of Saint Bernard near her."

Above: Bernadette's "white chapel" in the Sainte-Croix Infirmary, her last home.

Below: crosses mark the two windows of Sainte-Croix overlooking the front courtyard

"You pray to your patron."

"Indeed I do," she said, "but I don't imitate him very much. Saint Bernard loved suffering, while I avoid it as much as I can."[159]

To Soeur Valentine Audidier, a visitor that same year, she showed a little golden monstrance fastened to the curtain, adding that seeing it gave her the desire, the strength even, to offer herself in sacrifice whenever she became more sensitive to her isolation and suffering.[160]

To Soeur Ambroise Fenasse, in January 1879, "she pointed out a picture pinned to her bed curtain, depicting the elevation of the host at the Holy Sacrifice.

"'Yes, although I'm so close to chapel, I've been unable to attend Holy Mass for quite some time; but to make up, I attend night and day, the one being said without interruption.... Masses are being celebrated perpetually at one place or another on the globe. I unite myself to all those Masses, especially during my occasional sleepless nights.'

"She said this quite earnestly, then becoming playful again, she added, 'What upsets me is that little altar boy who never rings the bells.' And pointing to the altar boy in the picture: 'I sometimes get the urge to give him a good shake.'"[161]

As sacristan, Bernadette used to help the altar boys get dressed; she liked it when they were full of life.

Eggs and Hearts

Immobilized beneath the white curtains, Bernadette didn't remain inactive; she accomplished a good deal of work, attested Abbé Febvre.

In August 1876, Soeur Agathe de Filiquier found her sitting on her bed, shredding linen.

At Easter 1877, she "penknifed" decorations on eggs, as described by Soeur Casimir Callery, who was helping her: "I did the drawing, Soeur Marie-Bernard did the scraping and that's how we turned out the complete product. This work was getting on my nerves. 'What difference does it make,' she said to me, 'reaching heaven by scraping eggs or by doing something else?'"[162]

On June 21, 1877, Soeur Eugénie Calmès also found her "sitting on her bed, keeping busy with small manual chores," which she did not specify. Bernadette cheerfully interrupted her work to welcome the visitor: "Ah! good Mère Joséphine! You're bringing me a postulant!"[163]

She was one more postulant Bernadette encouraged.

The activity mentioned most frequently was the making of hearts, which she embroidered or painted.[164]

Soeur Victoire Cassou, who visited on September 8, 1877, asked her for one with her superior's permission. "Don't you have a heart?" Bernadette said affably. "Here, take one...."[165] Pointing to the many samples scattered around her, she added, "They can't say Soeur Marie-Bernard has no heart!"

In September 1877,[166] she said almost the same thing to Soeur Valérie Perrinet, with one difference—this time the hearts were not "embroidered" but "painted." "If anyone tells you I have no heart, just say that I make them all day long."[167]

At Easter 1878, Soeur Joseph Caldairou was astonished at something else she made: "dyed eggs...on which she engraved superb designs." She exclaimed: "How lovely your eggs are!"

"Don't say that.... It's a job like any other."[168]

The Burden of Suffering (1875–1878)

The keynote of this period was—along with thoughtfulness toward others—the acceptance of suffering. For Bernadette this meant, first and foremost, silence. But occasionally, when the pain grew too severe, or when she was asked for advice, she uttered a few words, briefly and unpretentiously.

Many times in her sufferings, she was heard to say, "My God, your will be done! I accept suffering, since it is your will."[169]

She advised others to conform their will to God's. To one of the sisters she often said, "This is the path the good Lord lays out before you: to suffer."[170]

To Soeur Marcelline Durand, who offered her something to drink after a "rather violent coughing spell," she replied, "I'll wait a little while longer...for the souls in purgatory."[171]

Unable to attend Mass, just like Soeur Claire Lecoq in the next bed, she said, "That poor Soeur Claire keeps tossing and turning, squirming like a worm that's been cut in half, because she wants to go to Mass. As for me, I remain calm. They tell me to stay here, I obey."[172]

She helped this sister to die by asking her, with infectious composure, to deliver "her messages for heaven."[173]

More than one visitor tactlessly reminded her of what weighed her down the most: "So you're still in the infirmary?"

"Yes," she answered, with a gracious smile. "Still in the infirmary, still 'good for nothing,' still being taken care of and unable to take care of anyone else."[174]

She added these words, which give meaning to her smile: "The good Lord did well not to allow me to choose my way of life. I definitely would never have chosen this inactivity I've been reduced to. I would have loved so much to have an occupation."

When Soeur Victoire asked her, "Do you pray for those who don't pray?"

She answered, "That's all I have left to do. I'm good for nothing. My prayer is my only weapon. All I can do is pray and suffer."[175]

This was the theme of her letter to the Pope: "My weapons are prayer and sacrifice, which I will grip firmly till my dying breath. Only then will the weapon of sacrifice fall, but prayer will come along with me to heaven where it will be much more powerful."[176]

When Soeur Victoire expressed envy at her remaining at the motherhouse, Bernadette repeated, remembering the humiliation at the announcement of her first assignment: "What would they have done with me anywhere else? I'm good for nothing."[177] This preoccupied and saddened her, but not bitterly.

A breath of fresh air and mercy came to Saint-Gildard's in the person of Abbé Febvre, the new chaplain at the motherhouse. He succeeded Père Douce, whose austere spirituality Bernadette expressed in this acrostic:

D *Douleur*   (Sorrow)
O *Oubli*   (Oblivion)
U *Union*   (Union)
C *Confiance*   (Confidence)
E *Exigeant*   (Exacting)

For the letter "E" Bernadette had at first written *Eprouvant,* (Trying). She crossed it out, but this very action spoke volumes.

The words of the new chaplain inspired confidence. And that was why Bernadette was willing to hobble over to the choir loft to listen to his talks. At one of his first, in October 1876, Soeur Casimir Callery recounts, "Abbé Febvre preached a sermon on sin. Since I

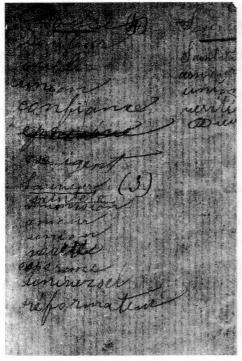
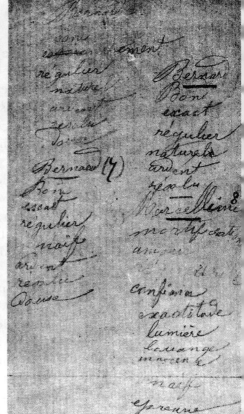

Acrostics Composed by Bernadette on the Theme of "How to Inscribe in My Heart the Name of...."

Left: Acrostic for Père **DOUCE** and of Jesus our Savior ("**SAUVEUR**"):

Sainteté (Soumission) —— Holiness (Obedience)
Amour ———— Love
Union ———— Union
Vérité ———— Truth
Espérance ——— Hope
Universel ——— Universal
Réformateur —— Reformer

(It is interesting that this last word had a positive meaning for Bernadette.)

Right: Three acrostics for the name **BERNARD:**

First draft (column one, top half)
Bon ———— Good
EspéranceEpanchement —— Hope/Outpouring
Régulier ——— Orderly
Naturel ———— Natural
Ardent ——— Fervent
Résolu ———— Determined
Doux ———— Gentle

Bernadette fell back on more direct and less original terminology:
(column one, bottom half):

Bon ———— Good
Exact ———— Punctual
Régulier ——— Orderly
Naïf ———— Straightforward
Ardent ——— Fervent
Résolu ———— Determined
Doux ———— Gentle

Her third draft (top half, column two) restore "Naturel" and left out the final D.

Second half of column two, the acrostic for Soeur **MARCELLINE** (Lannessans)

Mortification —— Asceticism
Amour ———— Love
Répara[tion?] —— Atonement
Confiance ——— Confidence
Exactitude ——— Punctuality
Lumière ———— Light
Louange ———— Praise
Innocence ——— Innocence
Naïf ———— Straightforward
Epreuve ———— Ordeal

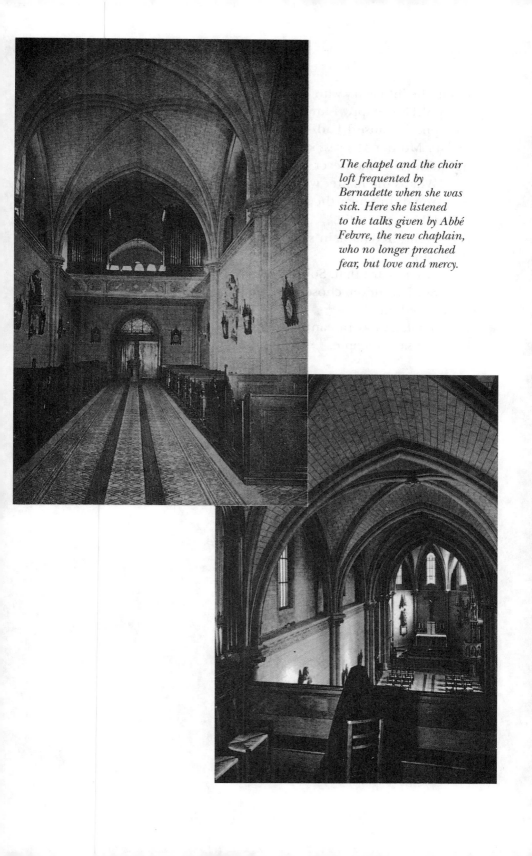

The chapel and the choir loft frequented by Bernadette when she was sick. Here she listened to the talks given by Abbé Febvre, the new chaplain, who no longer preached fear, but love and mercy.

was in the infirmary with Soeur Marie-Bernard, she said to me, 'Oh, Seraph! How happy I am!...' Soeur Marie-Bernard used to call me 'Seraph,' because I had been the seraph in a dialogue we recited for our Mother Mistress's feast day. The name *Casimir* kept slipping her mind; she had never known a Casimir before....

"'What's the matter with you?' I said.

"'You didn't hear the sermon?'

"'Of course, I did.'

"'Well, the chaplain said that when we don't choose to sin, we don't sin.'

"'Yes, I heard that. So what?'

"'So, I've never chosen to commit a sin; therefore, I've never committed one.'

"Her face was radiant with joy.... I envied her happiness, for I couldn't say the same."[178]

Chapter 20

— ⚜ —

The Last Deposition

On December 8, 1878, Père Emmanuel de Montagnac, who was preaching a retreat to the sisters at the hospital of Nevers, was given permission to see Bernadette in the infirmary. He gave her the cord of the Third Order of Saint Francis and questioned her about the apparitions.

"The Blessed Virgin always spoke to me in patois," Bernadette confirmed repeating the words, *'Que soy l'Immaculada Conceptiou.'*[1]

She always said *l'Immaculada,* with the *l'* (or even *l'Immaculée*) whereas the article *era* would have been more common in the patois of Lourdes.

This was only a private conversation. Another ordeal awaited Bernadette: a final deposition, intended for history.

An Historical Project

It seemed that everything was over and done with after *"The Protest"* and *"The Counter-Protest,"* of which the superiors of Saint-Gildard's and Bernadette herself had such painful memories.

But an official project was underway. The bishop of Tarbes and of Lourdes, Bishop Jourdan, sized up the historical inadequacy of

the books publicizing Lourdes. The difficulty was still the same as
it had been in 1868–1869. Lasserre could not tolerate any book
that did not present itself as a humble echo of his own account. He
fought them. And people were very afraid because he was known to
be a man who carried out his threats, ever since he had printed, at
his own expense and distributed in Rome and among the bishops,
the memoir entitled: *A very humble petition and memoir addressed by
Monsieur Henri Lasserre to the Sacred Congregation of the Holy Roman
Office, on certain abuses, very prejudicial to religion, committed in the diocese of Tarbes.*[2]

Lasserre had been dismissed by the Holy Office. But his threat-
ening letters discouraged several initiatives.

Finally, in 1876, a major project took shape. Père Sempé received permission from the Jesuits to have Père Cros, a painstaking
and qualified historian, interrupt his work-in-progress on the history of the Society of Jesus and undertake the history of Lourdes, an
idea inspired by his second meeting with Bernadette on October
23–24, 1865.

In November 1877, permission was granted. On the seventeenth
of that month, Cros received from his superiors and from Père
Sempé, with the authorization of Bishop Jourdan, the responsibility
of assembling the documentation and of writing the history of
Lourdes.[3]

The historian promised to make himself available the following
May, and that was when he began in Lourdes the extraordinary investigation without which our knowledge of the 1858 occurrence
would have been reduced to a rough outline.

The problem, the obsession really, remained the same: how to
avoid Lasserre's attacks. Lasserre was powerful—powerful in his un-
failing conviction, powerful in his highly placed connections, powerful in the reputation built on the tremendous success of his book
on Lourdes, powerful because of the "Brief of Praise" the book had
received from Pius IX. Would not the rewriting of the history so honored by "the Vicar of Christ," be branded as an act of high treason?

It was, therefore, essential for the new project to be sanctioned
by the Pope's blessing. Progress was being made, not without difficulty, when Pius IX died on February 7, 1878.

Undeterred, Cros began his work anyway. He questioned more
than two hundred witnesses, had them write down their recollec-

tions, discovered in two "attics, or storage rooms" many diocesan papers, once thought to be lost; and, thanks to an incredible police investigation, unearthed most of the official papers that had been shifted around by civil servants in 1858. In a word, Père Cros examined everything Lasserre had ignored, everything that would furnish the basis for a scientific history.

Père Cros's Battles and Disappointments

The central witness, however, Bernadette herself, remained inaccessible. On August 24, 1878, Cros tried to push his luck. He went to Nevers to present for Bernadette's consideration the difficulties she alone could clear up. He had the recommendations of the bishop of Tarbes and Père Sempé. He received some support from the Bishop of Nevers and the good will of the bishop's manservant, but collided head on with the sisters' refusal. There was no question of stirring up a recurrence of *"The Protest,"* nor of putting a declining Bernadette through an ordeal like that again.

Once again, Cros displayed his powers of persuasion and mobilized reason and emotions—including fear. Ernest Renan, it was said, was preparing a dreadful story against Lourdes; he must be beaten to the punch.... But Cros stumbled up against a wall of unshakable determination. He tried to wrench the decision from higher up. He went back to the Bishop of Nevers and humbly implored, addressing him in the third person: "The sisters will consent if the bishop gives his permission."

The bishop replied, "If Mother General agrees, I am not opposed."

"Well then, Bishop," Père Cros responded, "be good enough, I pray, to just write those words down. They are all I'll need."

The bishop answered, "Yes, but I will have to add that I think it inadvisable to give permission."

"Oh, Bishop, that would be giving with one hand and taking away with the other."

After more discussion, Père Cros made another attempt: "If the Bishop of Tarbes asks you to grant us this favor, you will not refuse."

"Ah! If the Bishop of Tarbes asks me...well!"

Cros withdrew after one last appeal: "Today is the feast of the Heart of Mary. May it please our Lady to incline the bishop's heart to grant us our request."[4]

With that, he went directly to the telegraph office. While Père Sempé was busy in Lourdes soliciting the support of the Bishop of Tarbes, Père Cros went back to see Soeur Nathalie, the general assistant, who seemed the most amenable to him, in order to negotiate conditions for a meeting with Bernadette. He thought he had succeeded, and so he went to the superior general's office, only to hear over and over again: "Questions?... I won't listen. It is useless to insist, you'll get nowhere.... Whatever steps you take will be useless." This was said stiffly, coldly, almost rudely.

Père Cros controlled his anger and, with a smile, repeated the *ferverino* he had just used with the bishop: "Very Reverend Mother, today is the feast of the Heart of Mary; throughout the day, say an occasional 'Gentle Heart of Mary,' so that our Lady will incline your heart toward what is most in keeping with her wishes."

She answered, "I do not fall short in praying to the Blessed Virgin."[5]

He stressed the point, "Entreat her to incline your heart."

She replied, "My heart is not inclined; it is upright!"[6]

Cros went downtown and managed to get the postal workers (who were very reluctant) to admit that a telegram from Tarbes had indeed been delivered to the bishop's house. Off he went and found the bishop's valet—friendly, trusting and pessimistic: "The bishop has just told me that he will see no one. And he already saw you coming."

"Well, then, my good man, simply ask him this, 'Bishop, Père Cros requests that you let him know whether he should leave tonight or wait....'"

"Shortly after," Cros recalls, "I heard a voice, upset and shrill with anger, then silence; and my friend the valet returned...a downcast look on his face.

"'Well?' I said to him.

"'The bishop told me to tell you that he has just written a letter to Mother General, and she will tell you what you have to do....'"

In the stairway of the bishop's house, Vicar General Dubarbier led Père Cros to believe that a letter addressed to the superior general had been left on the bishop's desk. Cros asked the valet to "get it back to him."

"'The bishop has just looked; he found nothing,' said the valet when he returned.

"Arriving at the gates of Saint-Gildard's," continued Cros, "I asked the portress, 'Has anyone brought Mother General a letter from the bishop?'

"'Yes, Father.'

"I walked up to the sisters' entrance and asked Sister Portress to send for Soeur Nathalie on my behalf. She took her time in coming, and on entering, told me: 'I've got nothing but bad news. Mother is all upset. She says they're trying to force her hand. She's angry that Soeur Marie-Bernard's name was mentioned in a telegram.'"

Père Cros waged one final battle with the benevolent assistant; he knew it was futile, but his honor was at stake. He took the night train to Limoges.

Leo XIII's "Brief"

Certainly, a papal "Brief" had to be obtained at all costs.

Père Cros had been working on the project for a year (since November 1877). In November 1878, "the Bishop of Rheims and the Bishop of Tarbes" agreed to place the matter before the Pope.

On December 8, Bishop Langénieux announced that the case had been won. A few days later, Père Cros received the text of his "Brief," translated into Latin and signed by Leo XIII on December 10. The document contained this clause, essential for the work to continue: "Also, Venerable Brother, not content to approve your plan.... We declare in advance our gratitude to anyone who, at your invitation, comes forward to help you bring this project to a happy conclusion, and to this end, submits into your hands written documents or gives sworn testimony as a witness."[7]

Negotiations ensued. At Nevers, Père Cros was no longer welcome; but Père Sempé, who had proven himself to be tasteful, open-minded, and moderate in his requests at the time of *"The Counter-Protest,"* would be allowed to put the historian's questions to Bernadette.

The Interrogation of December 12, 1878[8]

On December 12, Père Sempé was in the infirmary together with Vicar General Dubarbier, the superior general, the two assistants and the secretary, Mère Eléonore Cassagnes, who took turns with

*Thanks to the Brief of Leo XIII, Père Sempé was able
to question Bernadette with Soeur Eléonore Cassagnes*

her superior writing down Bernadette's answers. The superior and Père Sempé each had in front of them a sheet of paper, bearing the letterhead of the Archdiocese of Tarbes. Père Cros's questions each numbered, were on the left. The right half was left blank. Père Sempé began reading number one, dealing with things prior to the apparitions:

"Did Bernadette visit Bétharram before 1858?"

On her sickbed, Soeur Marie-Bernard hesitated.

Sempé wrote in pencil: "I don't think so."

The superior general said, "She does not remember."

This last expression, or others like it, was the one that would recur most often throughout the interrogation.

The most significant answers were the following: Bernadette "hardly went to the teacher's at Bartrès where she learned nothing." She seldom went to catechism. She "expressed a desire to return to Lourdes" to make her "First Communion." She had "never gone to Massabielle before February 1858." *Aqueró* seemed "very young."

The different points of the protest, scattered among the thirty-three questions, met only with Bernadette's not remembering, except for question seven:

"How many prayers and which ones did (Bernadette) know in the month of February 1858?"

"I only knew the *Pater, Ave, Credo,* and this one in French: 'O Mary, conceived without sin,'" wrote Sempé.

But the superior general did not jot down this last phrase. She only wrote:

"She knew the *Pater,* the *Ave Maria* and the *Credo* in French."

"Does Bernadette remember having sometimes scolded or corrected her brothers and sister before February 1858, for their lack of devotion, frivolity, etc" (question nine).

"When I saw them doing something inappropriate, I corrected them," noted Sempé.

"Yes, I sometimes corrected them," noted the superior general.

"Was she sometimes beaten by her sister and brothers?" (question ten).

"There were some arguments with her sister, 'neither of us willing to give in,'" recorded Sempé.

"Sometimes, without malice," wrote the superior general.

"At home, did she sometimes say night prayers or the rosary before the apparitions?" (question eleven).

"It was after the apparitions, in front of a little altar of the Blessed Virgin," noted Sempé.

"Yes, sometimes, after the [apparitions]," noted the superior general, leaving the last sentence hanging before writing that last word.

From question fourteen on the secretary general took over, and from that point on, the notes on both sheets are identical, which confirms Père Sempé's precise accuracy.

Question twenty raised, in ambiguous language, the question of the apparition's welcoming gesture, well established by the early evidence,[9] but which Bernadette had quickly forgotten, now remembering only the usual pose, hands folded.

"What was the position, or what were the positions or the successive gestures of the apparition on February 11?" she was asked.

"She always kept her hands folded, except on March 25; when she said, *'I am the Immaculate Conception';* she greeted me by nodding her head.

Recalling Jeanne Abadie's swearword, the scene at the mill, the candle left at the grotto, etc., triggered no recollection on Bernadette's part. What came back to her most clearly were the Virgin's words, which were recorded then and there by Vicar General Dubarbier.[10]

On this subject, they again asked, "Was Bernadette ever called 'Bernadette' by our Lady? If so, how did she say it in patois? Did our Lady call her 'My child,' 'My daughter'? What were the words in patois?"

"Never by her name nor by any other. Always 'vous,'" noted Sempé.

"'Vous' and never by her name," wrote Soeur Eléonore briefly.

The first series of thirty-three questions was over. They began the second, which opened up with one of the burning issues of *"The Protest."*

"Toinette [also called Marie] Soubirous attests that Bernadette said on February 11, after crossing the stream, 'I find the water very warm, as if it were dishwater.' Monsieur Estrade affirms that Bernadette said the same to him. What does Bernadette say?"

"She remembers it to be mild. She may have compared it to dishwater," noted Sempé (question one).

Soeur Eléonore wrote the same thing, with this variant: "She may have said, 'like water for doing the dishes.'"

As to the rest, eight out of nineteen questions brought back no recollection; others received short, definite answers: *Aqueró* "spoke patois." A few days after the first apparition, Bernadette remembers "having gone to see Monsieur Pomian in the confessional, but does not remember the day." (It was actually February 13.) When she spoke of the Virgin, "she usually called her *Aqueró*. She may have said *Damizella*."[11]

The investigators noted in identical terms, almost word for word, her answers concerning Monday, February 22, a day with no apparition: "She was criticized for play acting. At the hospice gates, it was impossible for her to go any further. She went to the grotto by the castle road." (Here the secretary, Soeur Eléonore, says *path* instead of *road*.)

The last question that stirred up any recollection was the seventeenth:

"What were the main words, either mocking, harsh or severe of the superior of the hospice and of the sisters about her in the early days of the apparitions?"

The echo of the words spoken by "Monsieur Curé came to her": She repeated, in French and patois: "What is that lady?"

"Quauquaré!" (Something!)

Everything went well with the questioning.

"She answered with the greatest innocence, joy and simplicity," noted Père Sempé in the minutes of the interrogation.

The Interview of December 13

The next day, before leaving, Sempé saw Bernadette again "in bed, feeling better than yesterday, very happy," he noted. The interview was informal:

"She told me that her uncle, her godmother's husband, came back from Bétharram with a number of small rings for her companions. They were all too big for Bernadette's little fingers. She was very sad over this. Her uncle consoled her by promising to bring back one that would fit. He kept his promise and brought back a small ring. Alas! It was so small it wouldn't go on. Bernadette was not discouraged; using her teeth, she forced the ring on. But then her finger started to hurt and soon to swell; the swelling grew worse along with the pain. They had to saw the ring off with a small file."

Laughing heartily, Soeur Marie-Bernard said, "I never wanted a ring again."[12]

The day before, Sempé had written enthusiastically to Père Cros: "Give thanks to the Blessed Virgin! My mission is accomplished. Bernadette has forgotten most of the details, but she does not deny them. She only says—and it is true—that she has forgotten. I have the patois words, etc."

Other Patois Words

Père Cros, in the middle of his work, could not be satisfied. To begin with, the patois text of two of the Virgin's statements were missing. On December 21, 1878, he wrote a letter asking for them and received them immediately:

The Blessed Virgin, after having told Bernadette: *"Anat bébé a la houn et b'y laoua,"* added immediately after Bernadette obeyed, *"Anat baïsat la terra, per penitenza tas pecadous et mingot ta quelle herba."*[13]

The Interrogation of January 12, 1879[14]

On December 31, Père Cros forwarded to Nevers two new sets of long and detailed questions that he considered absolutely necessary. The superior general decided to submit them to Bernadette on January 12, 1879. The first question concerned the description of the apparition.

Cros transcribed the prosecutor's examination and the memoir of the sculptor Fabisch on *Aqueró's* shortness of stature and youthfulness.

Soeur Adélaïde Dons wrote the answers as follows:

"*Aqueró* was short rather than tall, but our sister does not remember making comparisons between the vision's height and her own, nor with the statue in church. The Blessed Virgin looked very young. The child could not tell clearly if what she saw under the veil was hair."

The second question went back over the first two apparitions. Here, Cros submitted to Bernadette the interview that A. Clarens conducted with her on March 4, 1858. She had then described the welcoming gesture (apparently disputed by *"The Protest,"* in 1868) and, in great detail, "the white dress, gathered at the neck by a drawstring...a cord with several knots, hanging like a necklace," etc. On the first point, Bernadette repeated the conventional wording of the preceding interview. She had forgotten the brief welcoming gesture; all she remembered was the folded hands and their having been held open on March 25.

On the clothing, the superior general noted her answer thus: "No recollection at all of the cord with several knots; a negative idea rather than affirmative."[15]

The next section of Clarens' text dealt with the second apparition and the scene at the mill. Here, as elsewhere, he had expressed Bernadette's remarks rather freely in his own style. Bernadette's response to Clarens' account was written by the superior general as follows: "Remembers the hurled stone, but not the words spoken by Jeanne Abadie. The latter, standing above the grotto, could have said them without having been heard by Bernadette, who was in front of the grotto. The crack of the stone breaking and bouncing into the Gave, frightened the child. Bernadette rebuked her companion for this rudeness, but she never lost consciousness. She could not have said: 'I recovered "my spirits" only long afterwards,' because she did not know the expression. She heard it for the first time at our motherhouse and she thought we were making a mistake, since she was convinced that a single person could not have several spirits."

As for Madame Milhet and Antoinette Peyret's insisting on taking her to the grotto for the third time, on February 18, the answer she gave, very vaguely, was that she: "felt attracted and needed no urging. Madames Milhet and Peyret may have told her to come to the grotto with them."

The third question submitted a long passage from the Clarens memoir, concerning the same apparition. The sisters transcribed Bernadette's answer as follows: "Soeur Marie-Bernard does not remember placing the pen and paper on a rock," noted Mère Adélaïde Dons, "but she remembers offering both to our Lady, saying: *'Boulet avoué la bouenté dé mettré vosté noun pér éscrit.'*

"Our Lady answered: *'N'es pas necessairo.'* She added: *'Boulet avoué la gracio de bié aci penden quinzé dios.'*"

Here Bernadette took the initiative to add, agreeing with Fourcade's booklet: "the same day she told the child to go speak to the priests, to go drink, to wash herself, and to pray for sinners. She made this last request several times."

She assigned to February 18, the first of the fifteen days, all the words heard from that day until March 4. This concentration was already fixed in her mind in November 1858.[16]

The fourth question placed before Bernadette regarded her own hesitant answer to the Episcopal Commission in 1858, concerning the procession. On this point, we may recall, Bernadette's memories were traumatically disturbed from the very outset by the horrendous reception at the rectory that day.[17] Père Sempé had already asked her this question on the previous December 12, and all he could record was this: "No recollection: vague request to come in procession."[18]

On January 12, the answer was equally evasive: "Soeur Marie-Bernard thinks that the Blessed Virgin spoke to her once about her procession, but cannot be certain."[19]

The fifth question was about the order of her visits on March 2: "Did Bernadette go first 'to Monsieur Pomian...or...to Monsieur le Curé?' For: 'I am the Immaculate Conception,' would not the reverse be true? Everything points to a mix-up."

Mother General wrote down this answer: "Neither can she be sure whether Monsieur le Curé or Monsieur Pomian was the one to whom she first brought the command to build the chapel, since she told both of them. Monsieur le Curé was the one to whom she first went when our Lady told her: 'I am the Immaculate Conception.' She went from the grotto to the rectory with her godmother. All along the way, she repeated the words of the vision so as not to forget them."

The sixth question focused on a very controversial point. On Wednesday, March 3, Bernadette had not seen the apparition in the morning; but five witnesses, whose testimony Cros submitted to Bernadette, certified that she came back during the day. Here the answer was succinct: "Soeur Marie-Bernard has no recollection of the circumstances surrounding the March 3 apparition. All she knows is that she saw our Lady every day for two weeks, except a *Monday* and a *Friday*. She has no idea of the dates."

The seventh question, a very brief one, concerned the last apparition, that of July 16, when Bernadette saw "at night...in the

Pimorin meadow...across the Gave." The answer was clear and concise: "Bernadette could not get near the grotto, which was barricaded, and was in the meadow, across the Gave, when our Lady appeared in the usual place, but without saying anything to her. Since then, she has never seen her again."

A second series of questions bore on a few thorny details:

1. "Is it true, as so many witnesses affirm, that Bernadette did not soil her clothes at all, climbing on her knees during the apparitions over the muddy ground to the grotto rock?"

"Bernadette heard that her clothes did not get dirty when she climbed on her knees across a muddy piece of ground. She does not remember noticing this herself."

2. "Does she remember Doctor Dozous' experiment, touching a candle flame to her hand? Did this experiment take place at the grotto or else, as the demoiselles Tardhivail affirm, in the house of these ladies?"

"Doctor Dozous never touched a candle to the child's hand. He came to her parents' home to observe that her hand, held a long time over the candle at the grotto during this apparition, was not injured, even though it should have been burned to a crisp."[20]

The following questions on the "alternation between joy and sorrow observed on her face," and the "gaze of our Lady...on a few individuals in particular," brought back no recollection to Bernadette's memory. "But that may very well be," she conceded.[21]

Mother General asked the fifth question:

5. "Did she experience a general weariness, particularly eye fatigue after the apparitions?"

"She experienced no weariness after the apparitions. Her eyes felt the same as they do when one goes from bright sunlight to a dark place."

6. "Is it true that she gave away the rosary she used during the apparitions to a priest from Bordeaux...Junqua, who boasted of this in a published article?"

"She did not give away the rosary she used during the apparitions. She refused to exchange it for a rosary with a gold chain offered her by an archbishop at Monsieur le Curé's. One day, after having said her rosary, she put it in her pocket. That night she could not find it, neither in her pocket nor in the house, despite all her searching. This gave her great sorrow."

Here the superior quoted Bernadette's own words, "If someone claims to have it," she said, "it's because he stole it from me; I never agreed to give it to anyone."

The superior added that Bernadette "had no other during the apparitions." In a postscript, she answered a question, submitted later no doubt, but the text of which has not come down to us.

The Blessed Virgin taught Bernadette the words of a prayer, but for her alone.[22]

The Interrogation of January 30[23]

These answers had barely arrived when Père Cros, on fire with his writing, sent out on January 22, 1879 a new series of twenty questions...plus a few additions. The papal Brief of Leo XIII and the fear that Père Cros might return to Nevers, armed with this instrument and his legendary impulsiveness, won the day. On January 30, the superiors began a new interrogation.

Cros now had a better idea of Bernadette's memory. He stirred up her recollections; he tried to prompt her memory by mentioning what this or that witness had said so that she would have to react. In this way, he was able to draw out a few more precise answers, in particular that Bernadette "knew not one prayer in patois before the apparitions," so she prayed in French without fully understanding what she was saying.

Only five questions brought back no recollection.

Despite these shock tactics, certain silences indicate to what extent the passage of time and especially illness had dimmed Bernadette's memory. Quite often, up to now, and again on October 6, 1874, while talking to Charlotte de Vigoroux, she had recalled on her own that the apparition had blue eyes.[24] The twelfth question on January 30 had been put in these words: "Were our Lady's eyes blue?"

Bernadette simply replied, "Soeur Marie-Bernard thinks she remembers that our Lady's eyes were blue."[25]

It was an ordeal for her to come to grips with this haziness and occasional total lapse of memory.

Finally, Cros opposed with might and main—sworn testimony to support him—a remark Bernadette had repeated during the preceding inquiries: "I repeat that Bernadette is mistaken in thinking that the apparition was absent on a Monday and a Friday; it was on a Monday (February 22) and a Wednesday (March 3)."

Here Cros presented the impressive but shaky argument with which he had reconstructed the apparition of Friday, February 26, contrary to the constant testimony of the visionary. Bernadette's proverbial stubbornness did not fail; she dug her heels in even more. The reply, written down under her dictation, was categorical: "Soeur Marie-Bernard still believes that it was a Monday and a *Friday* that the apparition was missing. She doesn't know the dates. She remembers kissing the ground as our Lady ordered, in the sight of many witnesses, but not the day when it took place.

"She has no recollection of what is contained in Jacomet's account regarding March 3."[26]

In this instance Bernadette, not Cros, was right. He, nevertheless, stuck to his own account.[27] His talent for synthesis and his critical sense failed to match his extraordinary gifts as a researcher.

The wording of the twentieth and final question was no less provocative: "Another significant error, but I don't know whether it comes from Bernadette. It seems, however, that she shares in it, for she thinks she saw the apparition on Easter Monday. That apparition took place not on Monday, April 5, but on Wednesday, April 7. There is no question (the proofs follow: testimony from the day itself and this conclusion). Very Reverend Mother, do not immediately accept Bernadette's declarations as certain, even should they be supported by books. There are a host of proven facts that she has lost sight of and which she'll have to be reminded of with our Lord's help."

Soeur Adélaïde wrote the answer thus: "No recollection either of the apparition of April 7, Easter Wednesday. Soeur Marie-Bernard says that it is necessary to refer back to statements she made to the time of the apparitions."[28]

In short, Bernadette did not establish the dates, as she had said more than once.

At the end of the questionnaire, Cros attached an example related to other errors: "Assuredly, the vision appeared to her the first time with arms extended, as on the Miraculous Medal. Our Lady made this gesture in greeting her. Assuredly Bernadette said several times: 'She is *my height*...she is *my age*.' And likewise with many other seriously significant elements. Whether she remembers them or not, they will be presented for what they are, that is, as facts that are certain, supported by proofs. But pray to our Lady so that Bernadette will recover her memories, and obtain from her as many factual details as possible."

Mère Adélaïde noted the answer thus: "Bernadette maintains that our Lady had her hands folded, except when she said, *'I am the Immaculate Conception,'* and that she looked very young.

"As for the height of the apparition, Bernadette gave the dimensions for the statue standing in the grotto as our Lady's height. So the Blessed Virgin was about as tall as the statue in the niche at the grotto seems to be."

This argument is not based on recollection. It is deceptive. We have seen, in fact, that the sculptor made the statue taller than stipulated, so much so that he had to chip away the ledge, already cleared of the layer of soil and the rosebush on which had rested the feet of *Aqueró.* So if the statue, which measures five feet, ten inches, "stands in the grotto at our Lady's height," it means that it is much taller—by about twenty inches—than was the apparition.[29]

The last part of the interrogation shows traces of Bernadette's fatigue. Yet she still had to answer a postscript of Père Cros's, challenging her chronology. He reproduced Bernadette's answer to the third question on January 12, just as the sister had transcribed it, in the third person: "The same day, (the apparition) told the child:

'—Tell the priests to have a chapel built
—to drink
—to wash
—to pray for sinners.'"

Père Cros objected: "I have difficulty believing that Bernadette said 'the same day,' February 18, the day of the third apparition.... I'm afraid that one of your sisters took that from the 1861 account, written by Bernadette, and in which no attention was paid to chronology. It is certain that these three quotations were not said on the same day—and not one of them was said on the eighteenth.

"Very Reverend Mother, I beg you to send me only the answers *of Bernadette herself.*"

Bernadette's positions hardened. Her answer was expressed thus: "Soeur Marie-Bernard maintains that at the third apparition, our Lady told her: to come for fifteen days, to go tell the priests to have a chapel built, to go drink and wash at the spring, to pray for sinners. Our Lady repeated these words to her during several apparitions. Soeur Marie-Bernard affirms that her May 28, 1861 account is substantially accurate."

The defense of Bernadette's 1861 handwritten account, thrown into question by Cros, is, however, qualified by what followed: "...without keeping track of chronology, bearing in mind that she did not know the days of the month."

Indeed, it is very clear that Bernadette quickly lost track of chronology and just as clear that she did not receive the request to go drink before February 25,[30] nor the chapel request before March 2.[31] The identical answers given by Bernadette to the first investigators and the quantity of cross-references are unimpeachable.

Clearly Bernadette, strongly convinced that Fourcade's brochure was authenticity itself, and perhaps encouraged by the sisters who were eager to support her consistency, felt antagonized by Père Cros's aggressive requests. By the tenth question she was already beginning to lose patience. Cros asked, "Monsieur Pène and others heard Bernadette speak about our Lady's veil as if this veil were a mere trifle, a piece, a bit of veil. What should we say? I'd like a complete description of the veil: arrangement, length, width, folds, material, etc."

"Here," notes the superior general, "Soeur Marie-Bernard made an expressive gesture and said, 'Can I remember all that? If he wants to know, let him make her come back...'"

The official record softens Bernadette's strong patois expression, having her say, "They can go look for themselves!"[32]

After this outburst of impatience, Bernadette nevertheless answered the essential:

"The veil allowed our Lady's height to be seen, since it fell over her shoulders and came down each side, almost to the hem of the gown. The material of the veil and of the gown cannot be compared to anything Soeur Marie-Bernard has ever seen."

Ending her letter to Père Cros, Mère Adélaïde Dons bore witness to another reaction of Bernadette who had lost all patience with these petty details. She wrote, "The short account first published (that of Fourcade) contained everything in its simplicity. That's what was best about it. In our eagerness to embellish, we only distort."[33]

"These are Soeur Marie-Bernard's own words," declared Mère Adélaïde, who was protecting herself in advance against any offensive measure from the historian. "If you still have difficulty, would you speak to the bishop of Nevers? We no longer have the heart, without his express order, to further torment our sister, so sick at this moment."

The Interrogation of March 3, 1879[34]

But before this letter reached him, on February 1, 1879, Père Cros had sent a new series of eight questions. On February 19, he also sent a written apology, but without eliminating any of the questions. He even added a ninth question, attempting a kindlier tone: "Please, Very Reverend Mother. Imitate Abraham and bring to completion what you so kindly began. The questions I had the honor of submitting to you will be indispensable. I started to laugh as I read that Soeur Marie-Bernard is afraid that we wish to embellish the history of Our Lady of Lourdes. It's just the opposite; it must be trimmed down: a great benefit for our Lady and for souls, since no one has the right to embellish the works of God."

Thanks to Leo XIII's "Brief" and the support of the bishops, he again got what he wanted. Four of the nine questions brought back no recollection, especially the one dealing with the last point of *"The Protest"*: the candle on March 25 (question eight). The others received a reply.

Concerning the collar of the apparition: "The gown was fastened by a drawstring. One cord hung down. No recollection of any knots."

Concerning the "secrets," Bernadette did not go into the assumptions that had been made about them, but recalled briefly, "Three secrets and a prayer, with the command not to tell anyone" (question seven).

She confirmed that she had no recollection of the words Henri Lasserre had attributed to our Lady and which the missionaries had repeated with great delight in their *Petite histoire;* "Madame Milhet and Antoinette Peyret...can return...and others too. *I want to see people here.*"

The superior concluded, "Since Soeur Marie-Bernard was very tired, I admit, Reverend Father, that it pains me very much to further torment her. I beg you again to take into consideration the condition of our dear patient, who has been seriously sick for some time. She cannot understand why anyone would go over the matter again after everything the Episcopal Commission wrote, under her dictation, at the time of the great event."

This was the upshot of Bernadette's most vigorous opposition. She explicitly intended not to deviate whatsoever from the official deposition, recorded in the minutes of the first commission of inquiry.

From that time on, Cros would make no more attempts, for the final questionnaire had been so unproductive, and Bernadette's end was near.

Chapter 21

— ⚜ —

The Last Illness

The motives given by the sisters to stop Père Cros were not diplomatic ones. A few months later, they described Bernadette's condition during the interrogations of the final winter: "A tumor produced rigidity in her knee...horrible sufferings...knee swollen, leg atrophied. They did not know how to move her; sometimes it took an hour to find a good position. Her face had changed; she took on a cadaverous appearance; she who had been so strong in suffering was now overcome by pain. Even in her sleep, the slightest movement of her leg tore a scream from her (and these) sharp screams kept her fellow patients from sleeping. She went through whole nights without sleep. In her sufferings, she lost weight...(she had) slipped away to nothing."[1]

Jean-Marie's Visit

When Jean-Marie, Bernadette's brother, appeared at the motherhouse to see his sister on December 18, 1878, the situation posed a problem.

In August 1892, at Lourdes, Emile Zola described the circumstances of this meeting in this way: "A gentleman had promised him

Above: Jean-Marie Soubirous
Below: With his brother Bernard-Pierre

money for the trip. Days passed. At last, the money arrived. The gentleman was in Nevers to act as guide for the brother."[2]

What followed was learned from bits of gossip, which was growing worse at that time against Père Sempé, who, wrote Zola, was allegedly "seen coming out of the convent...."

In fact, Père Sempé had come for the interrogation on December 12 and had returned to Lourdes on the thirteenth, five days before Jean-Marie Soubirous arrived. The comparison of the two men was therefore pointless.

"At first, the brother was refused admission [to the convent]. He had the worst trouble getting in to see her.... He threatened to create a scandal."[3]

Although wrongly interpreted, these last details were not without foundation. The visit presented a problem. Even though, strictly speaking, churchmen could be brought to the infirmary for the same reason as a confessor, lay people in general—and certainly not men—could not enter the convent cloister. To grant an exception was to risk the wrath of all those who had met with a refusal in similar circumstances and to create "a precedent," which would multiply problems in the future.

Without doubt, it took some determination, perhaps even a "fine show of Pyrénéenne temper" on the one hand, and negotiations on the other, to arrive at the solution they adopted. Taking advantage of a remission, the sisters brought Bernadette downstairs [to the parlor] in her armchair.

Zola continues, "The brother found his sister tired, resigned. She thought he had been given an easy, well-paying job at the grotto, lighting candles. But he worked there as a manual laborer and earned only forty-five sous a day. She promised to write to Père Sempé."[4]

No trace of such a letter was ever found, even though Bernadette still wrote several to her family after this date.

Zola learned the rest from Jean-Marie himself. He questioned him in his "shop on the Plateau de la Merlasse." Jean-Marie had not seen his sister since her departure from Lourdes in July 1866. "He found her quite changed, sick, talking little but affectionately of her family; showing an interest in her relatives, with quiet tenderness. She did not complain; she gave him some good advice."[5]

One piece of advice concerned Bernard-Pierre Soubirous, Bernadette's other brother, as he disclosed at the apostolic Process of

Beatification in Tarbes on February 15, 1917: "If Bernard-Pierre has
to go into business, advise him not to sell anything on Sundays."[6]

"Let him not return"

In January, Doctor Robert Saint-Cyr grew desperate over his patient's
condition: "huge knee, withered leg."[7] Her remissions and relapses
confused him. He was tense, terse. He continued to consider her "a
bizarre patient." We have already heard him say by way of diagnosis
in December of 1876: "You have a terrible enemy...."[8] and turn on
his heels with no further comment. That was traumatic for the patient. Seeing him, hearing him, aggressive and powerless, though
he meant well, Bernadette lost what little courage she had left. She
said, "No more of this—let him not return."[9]

In January 1879, she confessed to being worn out by a "sister
from outside the community," who gave her thirty-six recommendations, asking her for all kinds of prayers....

"She let nothing show, even though at that time she was suffering terribly," relates Soeur Victoire Cassou. "On the contrary, she
was very gracious. However, when the sister had left, she could not
help saying, 'I like seeing her heels better than the tip of her nose.
When you're sick, you need to be alone.'

"I said to her, 'You'll say the same about me when I'm gone.'

"She answered, 'Oh! No, my dear friend, it's not the same
thing!'"[10]

Her next to the last letter, dated January 5, 1879, tried once
again to reassure her family: "I'm doing better; I've been coughing
less since the weather has grown a little milder."[11]

She breathed not a word about her knee or her stomach and
ended on this hopeful note: "Our venerable Mother asked me to
make a novena to Our Lady of Lourdes for me to be healed; it will
end Saturday. I urge you to join me in this intention; I'm making
the same request to the whole family. If I'm cured I would ask all of
you to go to the grotto in thanksgiving for such a great favor."[12]

Her very last letter, five days later, gave no more news of any
kind. There was none to give. She could no longer be left alone at
night. The sisters took turns at her bedside. Soeur Michel Duhême
testifies: "In February 1879, while still a novice, I kept watch one
night at Sainte-Croix. Soeur Marie-Bernard, quite ill, was in bed,
with her right leg outside the bed, supported on a chair. The night

was very distressing, with constant, uninterrupted moaning...." It was, she stated more precisely in later testimony, "a kind of muffled moan, half stifled between her teeth, interspersed with brief moments of silence. I suspected she was making an effort to hold back for my sake.... She realized that I was staying awake.... At one moment, to obey the charge I had been given, I told her, 'My dear sister, you no doubt need something. Can I be of service?'

"'No,' she answered, 'sleep, sleep.... I'll call you if I need anything....'

"I had been forcing myself to remain completely motionless so as to give...the illusion that I was asleep; but this didn't fool her. When I took leave of her to go to prayer, she said, 'You didn't sleep, did you?'

"The sister infirmarian came to inform me that I would not be returning to tend the patient.... Bernadette herself had said to her, 'I don't want that sister on night duty anymore.... I want sisters who can sleep.'"[13]

Sometimes she said, "I ask your forgiveness for complaining so much."[14] Or again, "Don't take my contortions too seriously."[15]

She also knew how to say "thank you" for what was being done for her; however, she was unable to taste a thing. "It's perfect," she said to the sister who brought her bouillon.

And when the infirmarian expressed the spiritual desire of also dying soon, Soeur Marie-Bernard exclaimed, "Don't die before me.... I wouldn't get nice bouillon anymore."[16]

"I'm looked after better than a princess," she also said.[17]

Visitors of March 1879

On March 18, there was a final visit from her family: her sister Marie, called Toinette, accompanied by her husband, Joseph Sabathé, came.[18]

No details have been given on the place or the circumstances. (Were the sisters able to bring Bernadette downstairs again? Was her brother-in-law able to see her too?) We only know that she was "very sick."

The superior general came to see her regularly. "When I drew close to receive her *culp*, or because she wanted to ask permission to receive Communion, she had such an attitude of respect, of devotion, that I did not recognize her."[19]

Abbé Febvre, one of the most frequent visitors those last months, drew up the following list of her ailments at that time: "Chronic asthma, chest pains accompanied by the spitting up of blood, that lasted for two years; an aneurysm (enlargement of the aorta), stomach pains, a tumor on the knee, which, during a sizable length of time, forced the servant of God to remain motionless.... Finally, over the last two years, decay of the bones to such an extent that her poor body was subjected to all kinds of pains. Meanwhile, abscesses formed in Soeur Marie-Bernard's ears and caused partial deafness which was very painful for her and continued until shortly before her death.

"Ever since her perpetual vows (on September 22, 1878)," he observed, "the pains grew more intense and ended only at death. Her desire, which she kept secret as best she could, was to be a... victim for the heart of Jesus."[20]

A little later, on March 19, the feast of Saint Joseph, Bernadette confided to the chaplain, "I asked him for the grace of a happy death."[21]

The hope of recovery she had expressed in her letter of January 5 was gone.[22] If mention was made of a novena, she replied, "Ask for my recovery? Certainly not!"[23]

There was a deep understanding between Bernadette and the chaplain. He discerned in her life a "direction" guided from above and from within, which he had to follow, not map out. Most often his words of encouragement were very appropriate. One day he spoke to her about the happiness of soon joining Christ and meeting the Virgin of the apparitions again. "Oh, yes!... That thought does me good," she answered.[24]

But occasionally, even encouraging words were burdensome. One day, Abbé Febvre said to her, "Courage, Sister! Remember Mary's promises. Joy, reward and happiness are waiting at the end."

"Yes," she answered, "but how long it's taking for the end to come!"[25]

Bernadette revealed that she could no longer meditate. The chaplain urged her to fall back on simpler, more basic forms of prayer: "Remain interiorly prostrate at the foot of the Cross...lose yourself." Sometimes she could be heard to murmur, "My God, I offer this up to you."[26] "My God, give me patience."[27]

The sisters still brought her novices who were having difficulty settling in. That was the case with Soeur Camille Labaume, who had arrived on March 20, 1879. "I was roaming through the novitiate cloisters," she relates. "'Where are you going, Mademoiselle?' [a sister asked].

"'To Saint-Gertrude, dear Sister.'

"'Have you seen Bernadette?'

"'No, dear Sister.'

"'Well then! Come along with me....'

"Opening the door of the Sainte-Croix Infirmary, she said, 'Look, Soeur Marie-Bernard, I'm bringing you a little postulant.'

"Soeur Marie-Bernard was in bed. She fixed her gaze on me... then said, 'Mademoiselle, I'm too sick; I can't embrace you, but I will pray for you.'

"I didn't know what to say. 'Thank you, dear Sister.'

"Whereupon...Soeur Elisabeth told me, 'Now go, and don't say a word.'

"It seems it was forbidden to go to Sainte-Croix. I went back downstairs very happy."[28]

The Fourth Anointing of the Sick

On Friday, March 28, Bernadette was advised once more, for at least the fourth time since 1858, to receive the sacrament of the Anointing of the Sick. Having learned from experience, she protested, "I got better each time I received it...."[29]

Her hesitancy was ignored. The chaplain arrived at 2:30 in the afternoon: "I gave her Holy Communion as Viaticum, then the sacrament of Extreme Unction. After the brief words I addressed to her before she received our Lord Jesus Christ, she spoke up before a large number of assembled sisters, in a strong, clear voice. She said something like this: 'My dear Mother, I ask your forgiveness for all the trouble I have caused you by my failures in religious life and I also ask forgiveness of my companions for the bad example I have given them...especially by my pride.'"[30]

She had "stressed" the "last phrase," which she had added on her own to the general formula used for a *culp* made before the community.

"The conviction in her voice struck everyone; hers was a voice of thunder...like a preacher seeking to make himself heard...."[31]

"She's not that sick," said the secretary general.[32]

After "Extreme Unction," as this sacrament was then called, since it was considered "ultimate," the sisters lovingly gathered around the dying patient. In keeping with custom, Bernadette received "their errands for heaven."[33] "Yes, I won't forget anyone," she told them.[34]

The following day, March 29, Abbé Greuzard, Curé of the cathedral parish, paid her a visit in the infirmary, together with Abbé Febvre.

"They showed her a photograph of a statue of Our Lady of Lourdes, sculpted by Armand Caillat, the famous artist from Lyons.... They asked her what she thought of it. She softened and said, 'It's the least flawed.'"

But, once again, she added, "I don't know why the Blessed Virgin is shown this way. I've always said that she did not have her head tilted so far back. That's not how she was when she looked up toward heaven...."[35]

Around the end of March 1879, Soeur Philomène Roques received "permission to spend one night at her bedside."

"For some days we had been taking turns," she relates. "Around the middle of the night, the patient had a terrible nightmare. At her anguished groans, I ran over to her bed: 'What's wrong, dear sister? Are you in pain?'"

Was it the stone thrown at the grotto by Jeanne Abadie that haunted this bad dream?

"She answered, 'Oh! I was back there, and a little boy was throwing stones in the river.'

"'No, dear Sister, you're in your own bed.'

"I wiped away the perspiration that covered her and offered her something to drink.

"'Thank you,' she said, 'I'm fine; go sit by the fire....'"

In the "morning," continues Soeur Philomène, "they had to position a drawsheet. I called the sister infirmarian, following the instructions given me. She made me stand on a chair at the head of the bed to lift the patient up. We could feel her atrocious sufferings as we tried to find her a new position on a rubber cushion....

"'Her poor body is nothing but one wound,' the infirmarians told me. 'There is no more skin on her lower body....' This happened about two weeks before she died."[36]

About the same date, the "newly professed" were given permission to pay her a visit. Bernadette recognized Soeur Marcella Poujade, who had assisted her during her last walks. "She stretched her arms outside the bed," drew her "gently to herself," and embraced her.

Easter was approaching. Again that year, Bernadette summoned enough strength for one last task.

"One day," relates Soeur Alphonse Guerre, another infirmarian, "I found her sitting up, looking even gaunter and paler between the white curtains. She was holding a beautiful pink Easter egg in one hand and a small penknife in the other, and was scraping the egg to make the white shell appear.... With a smile, she said, 'Men no longer have hearts, so I put some on the eggs.'"[37] This was a thought she repeated time and again to amuse the sisters who came to visit.

Soeur Angèle Letord, whose testimony is hard to date—it could have been a few months earlier—tells us that Soeur Marie-Bernard always kept a few eggs in the drawer of her nightstand. She would get them from there when she was well enough to work.

"One day, in too much of a hurry, I took hold of the table on the wrong side. The drawer slid out onto the floor, spilling all its contents...a half dozen eggs that Bernadette had decorated. They were all cracked to pieces...unusable. Bernadette...uttered a little exclamation, something like 'Ah!' but not impatiently. Then she said, without the least emotion, 'You will advise sister sacristan and dear Sister Mistress [of Novices].'

"'Why dear Sister Mistress?'

"'Because it's customary. When a novice commits a blunder, she makes her culp.'"[38]

During the last weeks, toward the end of Lent, Soeur Alphonse Guerre also tells us this: "One morning, I took off her cap to comb her hair. I cried out: *'Tè!'* (Soeur Alphonse was from Nîmes) 'They've cut your hair off!'

"She replied, 'Do you know why?'

"'No.'

"'Well, to ransom an African woman.'"[39]

In those days, the sisters' hair was periodically cut off and donated to missionary groups who derived a little income from selling it in order to ransom slaves. This was one of Bernadette's last visible acts of service....

CHAPTER 22

— ⚜ —

THE LAST DAYS

During Holy Week (April 6–13, 1879) Bernadette's bedsores became intolerable. She told Soeur Pagés, pharmacist in another of their Nevers communities, "If you could find something in your pharmacy to soothe my lower back; I'm all chafed...."[1]

She still struggled. "Look among your drugs...for something... that will revive me. I'm so weak I can't breath.... Send me some really strong vinegar to inhale."[2]

But Bernadette had arrived at the final stage of her life. "Just a few days...before her death, she...had them remove all the holy pictures which had been pinned to the curtains of her bed." Why? Pointing to her crucifix, she replied, "This is enough for me."[3]

On Monday, April 7, she started thinking about the interrogations and bickerings of the historians. She had the secretary general, Mère Eléonore Cassagnes, draw near and said to her, "I told what happened. Let them go back to what I said the first time. I may have forgotten, and the others too may have forgotten. The simplest version will be the best. When I read the Passion, I am more moved than when it is explained to me."

On the subject of "arguments involving Lasserre," she added, "I strongly advised my family to keep out of this. Personally, I want no arguments."[4]

On Easter Sunday, April 13, 1879, "she coughed continually." "After lunch," relates Soeur Saint-Cyr Jollet, "a few of us went up to see her. In all simplicity, she told us, 'This morning after Holy Communion, I asked our Lord for a five-minute respite so I could talk comfortably with him, but he was unwilling to give it to me. My passion will last until I die.'"[5]

That same day, she received a final visit from the outside. Père Moïse, a Capuchin, who was preaching a Lenten series at Saint-Etienne de Nevers, received permission to see her, in order to give her "general absolution and the plenary indulgence for Franciscan tertiaries." He made her repeat in patois—certainly it was the last time—the words of March 25, 1858: *"Que souy l'Immaculada Counceptioun,"* which he wrote down (always with the *"l,"* which surprises experts in southern French dialects, but is widely used in Tarbes).

Easter Monday brought a visit from Soeur Bernard Dalias, who was then teaching at the boarding school of Our Lady of the Angels. A group accompanied her. "The curtains had been pushed back.... The patient kept her face toward the wall and would not budge (She did not like these group visits)....

"I leaned over the foot of her bed for a moment to see her one last time. Then...with one of those childish ways she had always kept, she opened one eye and looked at me, making a little gesture for me to come closer.... Her wasted hand lightly touched mine."

"'Adieu...Bernard,' she said to me, 'this time it's all over.'

"In a burst of devotion, I was about to bring that little hand to my lips, but she quickly put it back under the blankets....[6]

"Twelve years earlier, when (referring to her) I had spoken that humiliating expression, which must have wrenched her heart, 'Bernadette? Nothing but that!' she had offered me that same hand with a smile. Today, she pulled it back. Our twelve years of loving friendship were thus enclosed between two handclasps....

"She had not noticed the presence of my companions; this is what afforded me the privilege of a personal farewell."[7]

That same Easter Monday, Soeur Cecile Pagès, the pharmacist, asked her, "Well, Soeur Marie-Bernard, have you come back to life a little?"

"Oh, no! I feel no relief. The chaplain told me that the good Lord wants me to earn merits for as long as I am on earth. I have to resign myself...." She then added, "Tell me, couldn't you find something in your pharmacy to restore my courage?"[8]

Her pains weighed heavily on her that day. Exhaustion could be read on her "congested face." There came back to her a childhood memory: the crushing and grinding millstones of the Boly Mill. She told Soeur Léontine Villaret, "I'm being ground down like a grain of wheat...." She added, "I wouldn't have thought it took so much suffering to die."[9]

During Easter Monday night, she began her spiritual agony. She was heard repeating several times, "Begone, Satan!" assures her confessor. "On Tuesday morning, she told me the devil had tried to frighten her, but she had invoked the Holy Name of Jesus and everything had disappeared.[10]

"Tuesday...she received Holy Communion again, but as the morning went on, she experienced a severe shortness of breath.

"She sent for me and wanted to receive the sacrament of Penance. Afterwards, I gave her the plenary indulgence reserved for the moment of death. As I was telling her to renew with love the sacrifice of her life, she replied with surprising energy, 'What sacrifice? It's no sacrifice to give up a miserable life where we encounter so many hardships to belong to God.'"[11]

She made every effort to repeat the invocations suggested to her but this exercise put too much strain on her. She said, "How right the author of the *Imitation [of Christ]* is to teach that we mustn't wait until the last minute to serve God! We can do so little."[12]

"At seven o'clock that night," Soeur Nathalie arrived at Bernadette's bedside. She narrates the following, referring to herself as "the religious" and speaking of herself in the third person: "She was in the chapel, in front of the Blessed Virgin's altar and was praying to our divine Mother for her privileged child, whose condition was growing worse and worse. Finishing her prayer, the religious was strongly inspired to go visit the patient, who saw her and said, 'Dear Sister, I'm afraid. I've received so many graces and profited so little.'

"'All the merits of the heart of Jesus are ours,' said the sister. 'Offer yourself to God in payment for your debts and in thanksgiving for all his kindness.'

"Then, after promising the patient always to *help her* give thanks to the Blessed Virgin for the favors with which she had deigned to honor her, the religious whispered a few more words."[13]

They were words of mercy, according to Père Sempé's interpretation,[14] but "the religious" does not specify. She leaves us only with the reply: "'Oh, I thank you!' said the patient, who seemed to be freed from a heavy burden."[15] Bernadette was completing her last day on earth.

Knee Tumor and Bone Decay

The tumor on the knee, which was Bernadette's most intense physical suffering, had been pointed out in January 1878, by Mère Ambroise Fenasse.[16]

But the "silicate dressing" seems to have brought about a temporary cure, as Bernadette certified in her letter of October 7, 1878.[17] In fact, she was healthy up to the end of autumn, according to many witnesses.

The tumor (stemming from tuberculosis) was again confirmed by many witnesses, beginning in January 1879.[18] Most of the witnesses also spoke of "bone decay."[19]

Shortly after Bernadette's death, the superior general, Mère Adélaïde gave more details to Père Cros: "[she had] a tumor that stiffened the knee, [she was in] excruciating pain—we did not know how to move her; huge knee, withered leg. Sometimes, [it took] one hour to find her a [bearable] position."[20] There was also the testimony of Soeur Alphonse Guerre, who remained at Bernadette's bedside during the last night.[21]

CHAPTER 23

— ⚜ —

THE LAST MOMENTS

During the night of April 15–16, 1879, Soeur Alphonse Guerre, a novice, kept watch over Soeur Marie-Bernard. "I went up to the infirmary after night prayers, around nine o'clock," she relates. "The dear patient...answered me softly, weakly. I found her so worn out that I thought it wise not to go to bed like those who had preceded me. I sat beside her bed, alert and ready to help her out.

"From time to time, the pain would tear a weak moan from her, which made me shiver in my chair. She asked me a number of times to help her turn over so she could find a bit of comfort, because her poor body was raw and one could say she was lying right on her sores. So we tried to synchronize ourselves to execute this difficult maneuver. I took the foot of her diseased leg (you know her knee was terribly swollen by bone decay) and I took great care to follow closely the movements of her body so that she could turn over all at once, without having to bend her leg. During that endless night I noticed that she expressed no word of impatience or annoyance.... The rest has escaped my memory."[1]

The next day Bernadette still found the strength to receive Mère Marie-Louise Bourgeot, superior of the boarding school in Beau-

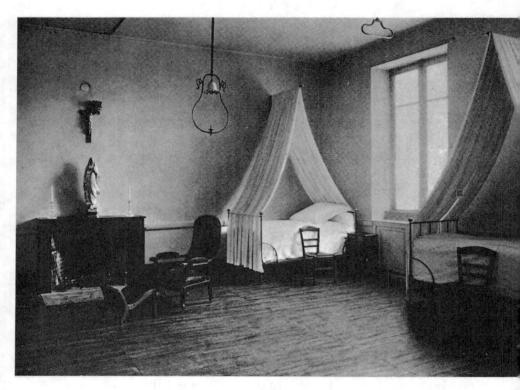

The "white chapel" with the last armchair of Bernadette

mont (Oise), and gave her "a holy card" for Soeur Madeleine Bounaix, a sister at this school.[2]

At 11:30 A.M. that morning she wanted to get up. The sisters sat her in an armchair. Then she noticed the time by the sound of the bell. She apologized to those companions who were by her side for making them late for the midday meal.[3]

"The armchair" was placed "opposite the crucifix on which her eyes gazed with rapt attention," added Mère Eléonore Cassagnes.[4]

"Between noon and one o'clock," during the meal, Mère Marie-Joséphine Forestier was the one who assisted her.

"I was near her. I found her attempting, with an unsteady hand, to take a little food, but with no success. Her extremely weak condition struck me so deeply that I thought it my duty to warn the infirmarian and to alert the community."[5] Abbé Febvre was "hastily summoned."

"I found the patient...sitting in an armchair," he relates, "breathing with difficulty and suffering the most agonizing pains. She went to confession again...invoked the name of Jesus.... Then we recited the prayers of the dying.

"It was moving to hear her repeat, in a weak but clear voice, all the prayers we suggested to her."[6]

Mère Eléonore was struck by the intensity of her "gaze...on the crucifix on the wall.[7]

"In a calmer moment I approached her and counseled her to put into practice those words of Scripture with which the divine Spouse asks the faithful soul to place him as a seal upon her heart (Cant 8:6) so that he may take possession of her...forever.

"We saw her clutch her crucifix and place it on her heart, squeezing it mightily. She longed to have it remain there forever, and we even fastened it on with a cord, for fear it would be dislodged by involuntary movements brought on by the pain."[8]

Between 1:30 and 2:00 P.M., Mère Eléonore Cassagnes said to her, "You are...on the cross."

"She stretched both arms toward the crucifix, 'My Jesus! Oh, how I love him!'"[9]

At 2:15 she received a visit from one of her companions, who asked, "Sister, are you suffering a lot?"

"This is all good for heaven," Bernadette replied.

"I am going to ask our Immaculate Mother to give you comfort."

"No!" the patient answered, "not comfort but strength and patience."[10]

"That was when Bernadette remembered the special blessing that the Sovereign Pontiff, Pius IX, had bestowed on her for the moment of death.

"She asked for the document which granted the favor, seeking to hold it in her hands in order to put it into effect. They told her that that was not necessary; it was enough for her to make the intention, while invoking the name of Jesus.[11]

"At that moment, she tried to sit up a bit, leaning her right hand on the arm of her chair; she raised her eyes toward heaven and brought her left hand to her forehead. Her eyes had a piercing expression and for a few seconds remained focused on a fixed point. The expression on her face conveyed a kind of melancholy pensiveness. Then, in a tone of voice, difficult to describe, expressing surprise rather than pain, and increasing in volume, she cried out this triple exclamation: 'Oh! Oh! Oh!' and her whole body trembled."[12]

Some unjustifiably sought to interpret that cry, that attitude, as a sign of a final vision.

"Then she gently dropped her trembling hand on her heart, lowered her eyes, and in a very clear voice uttered these words, 'My God, I love you with all my heart, all my soul, all my strength.'"[13]

At 2:55, the bell rang for the litanies which the community recited each day in the chapel. Bernadette expressed a "desire to take a little rest." The confessor left. One of the sisters said to the others present, "Let us leave and go recite the litanies; we can be of more help to her only by observing our Rule and praying for her."[14]

A few seconds later, she was offered a reason to be hopeful: "The Blessed Virgin will come down to meet you...."

"Oh, yes! I hope so!" she answered.[15]

"At about three o'clock in the afternoon, the patient seemed to be undergoing the agonies of some inexpressible, interior suffering. Alarmed, the infirmary sisters quickly got some holy water, sprinkled it several times on the dying Sister and suggested some invocations. The patient seized her crucifix (brought back from Rome by Bishop de Ladoue in 1877) looked lovingly at it for a moment, then slowly kissed the wounds of Christ one by one."[16]

At that moment, Soeur Nathalie arrived. She relates the following, always referring to herself in the third person: "She entered the infirmary and approached the dying one, who seemed completely absorbed in contemplating her crucifix. All of a sudden, she raised her head, held her arms toward the sister and, looking at her with an indescribable expression, said, 'My dear Sister, forgive me.... Pray for me.... Pray for me.'

"(Soeur Nathalie) and the two infirmarians fell on their knees to pray. The patient joined in their invocations, which she repeated in a whisper.[17]

"Then she recollected herself a few moments, her head leaning toward the sister infirmarian on her left, and with an expression of pain and utter surrender she raised her eyes toward heaven, stretched her arms out in the form of a cross and cried out loudly: 'My God!...'

"A shiver...went through the three sisters, still on their knees.[18]

"(Bernadette) again joined her companions in prayer.... 'Holy Mary, Mother of God....'

"The dying Sister found new strength...twice she repeated, 'Holy Mary, Mother of God, pray for me, a poor sinner.'[19]

"Death was at hand. She seemed to be engaged in a terrible battle.... The patient tossed about for a moment and twice silently renewed her plea to the sister (Nathalie) by holding her arms out to her, her eyes fixed on the sister."

Soeur Nathalie had taught the deaf. She had learned to understand without the use of words. That is how, she explained elsewhere, she understood what Bernadette's expression meant—and "questioned Bernadette with a look of her own": *Why are you holding your arms to me like that? What are you looking for from me?*

Not one word was spoken, but the dying one understood. She said "in a strong voice": "For you to help me...."[20]

"Then Sister remembered her promise of the night before...."

She had promised to help Bernadette thank the Virgin to the very end.

"A few moments later, the patient gestured, indicating something to drink. She made a large sign of the cross, took the vial of medicine they handed her, twice swallowed a few drops and, bowing her head, gently surrendered her soul."[21]

Soeur Gabrielle de Vigouroux came in at that moment: "I arrived in time to receive her last breath, which she exhaled very gently, leaning on my arm. She held her crucifix in her hand, resting it on her heart; they had even fastened it, I believe. She was leaning over to the right, but with her eyes closed. I remember having had trouble closing her right eye, which opened several times."[22]

"Lasserre saw her in death," wrote Zola in his *Journal* of 1892. He said "she was very beautiful."

Bernadette was beatified on Sunday, June 14, 1925. Eight years later, on December 8, 1933—the Feast of the Immaculate Conception—she was declared a saint by Pope Pius XI. Her body remains incorrupt to this day.

Bernadette lies in state in a white-draped coffin

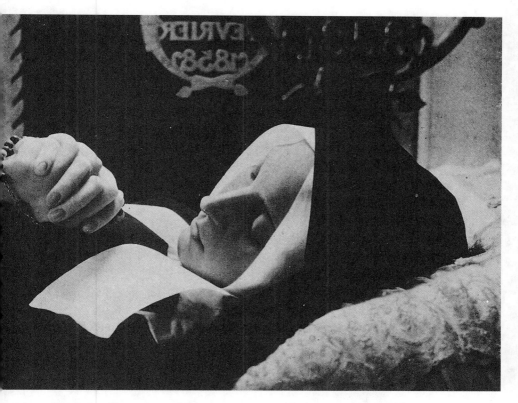

The body of Bernadette in its presesnt reliquary at Saint-Gildard's Convent. The face has been covered with a thin layer of wax, which has conventionalized her features.

PART FOUR

— ⚜ —

BERNADETTE'S SIGNIFICANCE AND RELEVANCE TODAY

CHAPTER 24

— ⚜ —

WHO IS BERNADETTE?

We have finally reached the end of that life, or rather the end of this book, which has presented, day by day, the words of Bernadette.

She had to be allowed to speak for herself as much as possible, keeping explanations to a minimum. She did not like commentaries. We have heard her say, "I'm more touched when I read the Passion than when it is explained to me."[1]

Above all, Bernadette was simple. This was the word most often used to describe her. This simplicity must not be betrayed, neither must the instruction she addressed to historians: "In our eagerness to embellish, we only distort." That advice seems to invite us to stop right here.

Nevertheless, the reader rightfully asks for more. He seeks to penetrate the significance of those words that grow more meaningful for him as time goes on. He also wonders about the shadowy areas, which have made Bernadette "the most secretive of all the saints," as the classical expression puts it.

In fact, her mistress of novices, Mère Marie-Thérèse Vauzou, though skilled in directing souls, found this characteristic of Bernadette's a stumbling block.

The life of Bernadette was enveloped between two zones of mystery: initial silence and final ordeal. Between the two, she received secrets for herself alone.

In light of this, it might seem wise to give up. Is it not impossible, is it not indiscreet to try to expose this "secret mission," a secret kept so well by Bernadette herself?

Should we conclude that Bernadette's holiness is something unapproachable and esoteric, having no connection with ourselves?

Just the opposite is true.

Let us clearly distinguish between the possible and the impossible, the useful and the useless. Indeed, it would be futile to try to discover the hidden details that Bernadette refused to reveal. They would only satisfy idle curiosity.

But there is a solid truth here: the holiness of Bernadette does make sense. It has meaning both for Bernadette and for those seeking guidance.

Bernadette's last confessor correctly discerned this. Many Christians and many of the sick still profitably relate to her today. For them she is a beacon in the night.

Yes, the holiness of Bernadette still shines. There may be shades and shadows, but there is also light—similar to the luminous pillar of cloud that guided the Israelites in the desert: dark by day and bright by night.

We will begin then with what is clear. From there we will attempt to examine the zones of obscurity: the unexplored regions and silences of her childhood, the secrets received during the apparitions, and her final trials.

The clearer areas correspond roughly to the two major periods of Bernadette's life: the testimony given at Lourdes from 1858–1866 (Chapter 25), and the private realization of the message at Nevers from 1866–1879 (Chapter 26).

An examination of these two periods is the object of the next two chapters.

CHAPTER 25

— ⚜ —

BERNADETTE'S
OBJECTIVE TESTIMONY

1. Value

The quality of Bernadette's testimony, as it manifested itself day after day at Lourdes from 1858 to 1866, then from time to time at Nevers, drew unanimous praise. Consequently, we had to slowly prune away the admiring comments of visitors and investigators about the intensity, clarity, intelligibility, simplicity, authority and charm of the testimony. In his pastoral letter, acknowledging the authenticity of the apparitions (January 18, 1862), Bishop Laurence conveyed this general impression in the most concise and authoritative way:

"Who on drawing near her cannot but admire the simplicity, the nobility, and the modesty of this child? While everyone was talking about the marvels that had been revealed, she alone remained silent. She spoke only when questioned; then she related all, with no affectation, with a touching innocence; and to the many questions asked of her, without hesitation she gave clear, precise answers, to the point and marked by a strong conviction. Subjected to severe tests, she was never shaken by threats. To the most generous offers, she replied with a noble indifference. Ever true to herself, in the various interrogations she was put through, she constantly adhered to what she had already said, without ever adding or retracting anything. Bernadette's sincerity is therefore unquestionable.... It is unquestioned. Her opponents, when she had any, have themselves given her this compliment."[1]

There is nothing to delete from this high praise, so unconditional does it appear.

And Bernadette did nothing to merit the loss of any of this esteem from 1862, the year Bishop Laurence wrote these words, until 1879, when she breathed her last. This book, based on the evidence, is proof of that.

The structure and nature of this testimony has been studied in *l'Histoire authentique des apparitions*.[2] The parameters were already defined. They do nothing to lessen the value of this testimony. They show the limits of its poverty, a poverty perfectly focused on the essential.

2. Limits

Bernadette's memory was not conspicuously vivid, precise, or retentive. It was ordinary, average. It deteriorated with time. "Bernadette has forgotten a lot," observed the historians who questioned her throughout her lifetime. Each year the weakening of her memory became more and more evident.

But her memory was of a rare purity. It did not distort. It did not exaggerate. This is amazing, since, as time goes by, outstanding recollections normally acquire more details and stature. They grow more perfect, fully developed, and marvelously embellished.

With Bernadette, memory did not grow more colorful with time. It became impoverished. It slipped away. Not through images did the message mature within her. It did not blossom into words but deeds. It was something to be sensed, not seen—visceral, not visible. Her memory did not degenerate; there was no external evolution, but an inner transformation that moved toward greater simplicity. Yet Bernadette's memory was not a passive one. It had structure, as does a tradition. It sorted out and synthesized the important elements: the sign of the apparition itself, the words spoken, the essential gestures; in a word, the significance. It automatically left out details and certain time sequences. It concentrated and condensed. It scanned the story and kept the reality.

Bernadette's imagination was subdued. She kept to simple stylized symbols: pebble, stick, poplar, bird, apple or grape and above all the crucifix—without romanticism or adornments. (The list of these symbols may be found in the index of the third volume of the *Logia*.[3])

A framework formed by daily repetition underpinned her account of the apparition and her testimony. Sometimes the living flame of memory flared up. At other times, it seemed almost extinguished by weariness and the separation of time. At those times, the pattern was reduced to its simplest form. Apart from that, Bernadette was modest. She only said, "I don't remember," "I don't know," or "Why bother?"

Whatever the condition of her memory, her answers were accurate and well framed, with no inconsistency on the essentials. Bernadette rebuffed inappropriate questions, bringing the questioner back to something solid, something that mattered. She disarmed the adversary with her candor. She never crossed swords with anyone. It was as if she had a secret defense that, from a distance, struck down the sword of criticism and quarreling.

Even on this strong point, however, let us guard against idealizing, generalizing or mythologizing. Bernadette's talent for repartee was uneven. It had its limits. She didn't always understand the questions that were put to her. The weakness of her French gave her trouble in this area. Sometimes she was tired. At other times she thought it useless to say anything against an opponent already entrenched in his own unshakable, ready-made ideas. On those occasions she fell back into silence or vague irrelevant remarks which the questioner could take for approval—at least on minor points, or on what was not his business: notably, the secrets.[4] In 1864, Paul de Lajudie and Dominique Mariote observed this wariness that comes from old peasant wisdom. Bernadette let the tactless person speak while she gave him a friendly smile that he could interpret, if he so desired, as approval, but she kept to herself what could not be expressed.

Bernadette's testimony was not consistently expressed in an outburst of bewildering answers like Joan of Arc's. It implied a humble awareness of human limitations, her own and her questioners'. These very limitations helped to establish what Abbé Peyramale and Abbé Pomian had early on put into words: the best proof of the apparition is Bernadette herself.

CHAPTER 26

— ⚜ —

THE PRIVATE REALIZATION
OF THE MESSAGE

Bernadette's entrance into the convent at Nevers marked a milestone in her life, a transformation.

It was not only the occasion of being placed on new ground in a new context. For that matter, her six years with the sisters at the hospice of Lourdes and her gradual postulancy had been a transition.

Leaving Lourdes was, above all, an uprooting, one that was painful to the point of tears. And yet, Bernadette did not lack courage. But her roots were there: her family, her culture, her language, and lastly, the grotto. It was a break, a relocation that affected her whole life.

It was also a new direction. In Lourdes her life had been devoted to giving testimony. Various Church officials were unwilling to relieve her of this unique responsibility. For years she had borne it by herself, out in the open, with its risks and hazards. At the hospice she had lived in a more artificial, more regulated atmosphere, where contact with visitors was coupled with conventional humiliations; she remained at the daily beck and call of all kinds of people.

When she left the Pyrénées, Lourdes was established; *her mission was ended.* Abbé Peyramale, Mère Vauzou and Abbé Perreau, the assistant chaplain at Saint-Gildard's, repeated this in similar words. Bernadette was aware of this herself.

"Would you enjoy seeing the grotto again?" Soeur Ursule Lassalle asked her. She answered, "My mission in Lourdes is ended. What would I do there?"[1]

Abbé Perreau went so far as to say that she "*repeated over and over that her mission as a visionary was accomplished.*"[2]

She had come to Nevers "to hide."[3] These were not just words. Bernadette had no desire to show off; she delighted in passing unnoticed. From this came her tendency to run away from the curious and to wrap herself up in her veil. One day, as we have seen, she had herself locked in so as not to be disturbed; but she immediately realized how excessive this protection was and put an end to the subterfuge.[4]

We have seen her hide in the convent coach[5] or in the office of Sainte-Croix[6] to talk or work in peace, etc. Henceforth, she would testify only by exception and with reluctance.

Her confessor, Abbé Febvre, noticed this reconversion, this change of orbit, as well as the significance of this new stage and its driving force.

"When the humble visionary came knocking at the convent door of the Sisters of Nevers," he wrote, "*she already possessed insights, instructions, and, in a way, a course of action that would orient and at the same time help her directors and superiors guide her in the ways of perfection.*"

The apparitions provided Bernadette's life with direction. For her, this direction was not an external rule that had to be followed and applied. She lived the apparitions as an inner driving force, animated by daily grace and stirred up by the impact of events. Her confessor continues: "From the meditative memory of the words, recommendations, or secrets communicated to her by *the Immaculate Conception,* and from her understanding of the mysterious actions at the grotto, she would draw rules of conduct destined to help her attain the ideal of sanctity she insisted on.

"Moreover, like the prophets of the Old Law, whose life and actions served as a visible confirmation of the great truths they proclaimed, she would in no way have as her sole mission the transmission of heaven's directives. Rather she would perform actions that spoke and her constant state of suffering would teach souls both the way and the necessity of penance in order to be happy, not in this world, but in the next."[7]

In short, Bernadette's mission was the personal realization of the message...not in words but in actions, in praxis as we would say today—in "actions that speak," as Abbé Febvre so clearly put it.

Here is a telling test: as I looked for a framework with which to organize the overall conclusions of the *Logia,* the format fell into place on its own. What most completely and harmoniously gathered together and linked the dust of Bernadette's sparse words were the key words of the message of Lourdes. We have clearly determined elsewhere[8] that this message was not restricted to the words spoken by *Aqueró,* but included the important actions in an adventure which took place in the midst of a people.

We have singled out and summed up this message, at the end of the *Histoire authentique des apparitions.*[9] It can be condensed in a few words that Bernadette kept in mind and which she wrote down several times. We put them together chronologically as follows:

Our Lady's Words

I. February 18

    1. *"It is not necessary."*
    This was said in answer to Bernadette's question, "Would you be good enough to put your name in writing?"
    2. *"Would you do me the favor of coming here for fifteen days?"*
    3. *"I do not promise to make you happy in this world, but in the next."*

II. February 23—Words of Penance (Repeated on subsequent days)

    4. *"Penance! Penance! Penance!"*
    5. *"Pray to God for sinners."*
    6. *"Go kiss the ground as a penance for the conversion of sinners."*

III. February 25

    7. *"Go drink at the spring and wash there."*
    8. *"Eat the grass that is there."*

IV. March 2

    9. "Go tell the priests to have people come here in procession
       and to have a chapel built here."
    10. "Go tell the priests to have a chapel built here."

V. Dates Uncertain

    11. "I forbid you to tell this to anyone."
    (This statement concerned the three secrets and the secret
    prayer. It was repeated several times.[10])

VI. March 25

    12. "I am the Immaculate Conception."

The patois version of these statements is given in Lourdes: Histoire authentique.[11]

It may be surprising that we have set these words apart like this
instead of inserting them where they occur in the narrative. It was
done not only to avoid repetition, but especially to point out two
things:

1. Bernadette did not have these words before her eyes, but in
her heart. They were present to her inwardly more than externally,
like a spirit or motivational force, a grace received, not a law. She did
not "apply" the message; she lived it instinctively as a spiritual gift.

Herein lies the aim of this book. There was no question of publishing a new edition of the commentary on the message as an
object in itself;[12] the purpose was to come to understand how Bernadette lived it. This goes further and is of far greater consequence
—especially for our own age, one which is so allergic to words and
so inclined to accept only living testimony.

2. The message of Lourdes goes beyond the words spoken by
our Lady. It is all of one piece: the apparition itself, the Virgin's
gaze, her bodily movements and posture (which Bernadette mim-
icked in such a startling way) and also the impact of the message in
Bernadette's personal life and in the surrounding environment. A
prophetic message always goes beyond words. It is a leaven in the
dough of the human community through which it makes its way.

That is why, as we have stated in the *Histoire authentique,* the key words of the message are not only the words spoken explicitly: "Prayer," "Penance and conversion," "Immaculate Conception."

The key is first of all "poverty."

In the person of Bernadette, the prophetic message of Lourdes came to remind us how blessed are the poor: their existence, their worth, their honor.[13] This message again gives meaning to the fundamental words of the Gospel, which had been largely forgotten at Bernadette's time: "The poor have the good news proclaimed to them" (Mt 11:5; Lk 4:18; Is 61:1).

That prophetic message was important for the nineteenth century, an age when poverty was particularly disregarded, derided, reduced to a ruinous state of misery for the benefit of triumphant wealth.

It was a time when industrial development produced exploitation, child labor, urban slums and all the rest. It was a time when the "development" of the first "developed" country, England, began to cause on a large scale the underdevelopment of countries in Asia. The replacement of food production with the production of textiles tore the economy of India apart and gave rise to famine. The civilization of China, the most ancient and magnificent in the world, was reduced to servitude and fell apart. Under the influence of the opium wars, under the regime of dependence and one-sided treaties, this nation plunged into misery.

In France, the triumph of middle-class capitalism, the separation of profit from labor was at its height. Worth, social prestige and, to a certain extent, political ability was openly based on income. The personal fortune of civil servants was a factor in their advancement. Wealth was seen as a certificate of morality, hard work, honesty, merit. The bourgeois and capitalistic society, founded on money, was at its peak.

It is important then to begin with the lived testimony of Bernadette on matters of poverty.

1. Poverty

Chosen by God, Bernadette splendidly demonstrates the happiness of the poor. This child, unknown or disregarded, would be proclaimed blessed by all....

She lived poverty—this personal aspect of the apparitions—consciously and explicitly.

"I want to stay poor," she spontaneously told the journalist who was laying out before her the prospect of wealth.[14]

Money Is Fire

We have seen her turn down money repeatedly, spontaneously, steadfastly. This sprung from a deep inner strength. With the apostle Saint James, Bernadette understood that money is fire (Jas 5:1–3).

"It burns me," we've heard her say, rejecting the gold pieces they tried to slip into her pocket.

Rarely has this biblical teaching been expressed so vividly, to such a charismatic and prophetic degree. Bernadette was unwilling to accept to transfer money, except under obedience.[15]

This was not contempt, because she knew its worth and the deprivation of its lack. It was her declaration of independence. Her witness remained steadfast, despite the thousand and one attempts to corrupt her, from the most Machiavellian to the most naive, from the most subtle to those inspired by thoughtfulness and friendship.

For her, poverty was not merely a shortage of and a refusal of money; it was an evangelical attitude as much concerned with being as it is with having—a state of humility.

Chosen because of Her Poverty

Bernadette was aware of having been looked upon out of pure grace because of her poverty. Abbé Raffin testified to this at the beatification process: "She delighted in saying that if she had been chosen by preference to be the confidante and messenger of the Blessed Virgin, it was because of her littleness, her lowliness, so that all honor would revert to the Blessed Virgin and to the glory of God."[16]

"If the Blessed Virgin chose me, it was because I was the most ignorant," she replied to Mère Sophie Cresseil, who was filled with admiration over her good fortune.[17]

"I had no right to that favor," she told Soeur Madeleine Bounaix, in 1870.[18]

In this, Bernadette was the reflection of the Virgin of the Magnificat. She too was aware of having been chosen for her poverty: "The Lord has looked upon the poverty of his handmaid" (Lk 1:48).

This feeling of having been chosen in her poverty, even because of her poverty, she expressed in symbols and parables, it seems, in several contexts and under different forms.

"The Blessed Virgin *picked me up* like a pebble."[19]

A pebble, to her, symbolized something commonplace and worthless, but also something rock-hard, a quality that was hers on many grounds.

"Oh! A pebble, that's it, hardheaded."[20]

As early as 1867, she told Soeur Stéphanie Vareillaud, "I'm a stone; what can you get from a stone?"[21]

At the end of a conversation on the apparitions, she suggested a more vivid parable to Soeur Philippine Molinéry, who recalls Bernadette asking, "What do you do with a broom when you're done sweeping?"

"Surprised, I answered, 'What kind of a question is that?'

"'Yes, I'm asking you where you put it when you're done with it?'

"'...In a corner, behind the door.'

"Then gleefully she said, 'Well, I was like a broomstick for the Blessed Virgin; when she no longer needed me, she put me in my place behind the door.'

"And with a clap of her hands, she added, 'Here I am and here I'll stay.'

"Both her voice and gesture were very happy," the witness went on to say.[22]

Material Poverty

Poverty is not simply need. According to the Gospel, it is an essential value—the revelation of what is best in a human being made to the image of God. It is a way of living one's life without worrying about the future, of simply being, relying not on the riches of the world, but on life and on him who is the source of life. Here the number of examples in Bernadette's life abound, from the most trivial to the most sublime.

Like all who are genuinely poor, Bernadette didn't like to see anyone waste water,[23] or bread[24] or damage things[25] or "lack poverty" in little things.[26] It was in this sense, too, that she told Soeur Marcelline Lannessans, "Patching is our business."[27]

She came from a poverty that was free from romanticism or pretense of any kind. Like the prophets and the sages of the Bible, she knew from experience the physical and moral disgrace of poverty. We find neither masochism nor smugness in her. She did not like to wear "hand-me-downs," as she called them, [28] in other words, dresses in the final stages of wear and tear. Neither did she like excessive and unreasonable patching. She avoided it with her common sense, even to the point of apparent disobedience. Had she not looked one day among the rejects for a better cornet than the one they had given her to repair...to test her? [29]

But Bernadette wasn't attached to things provided her for her use and gladly gave them away, as we have already seen. When a sister "seemed displeased at having something she valued taken away, she was able to tease her (to bring her to detachment). She could not understand how anyone could be so attached to such trifles." [30]

If she could joyfully thank those who cared for her "like a princess," it was with the evangelical preoccupation that: "The poor are not treated like this." [31]

When she said, "I want to stay poor," it was not an empty statement. In 1860, when she became a "boarding student" with the sisters, her strong desire was not to leave the charity students.

However, she harbored no bitterness toward the rich. She adhered to what is constructive in the Gospel, keeping her distance from maledictions: She believed that we can be poor by mastering our desires. "When we desire nothing, we have what we need," she told Soeur Vincent Garros in 1871. [32]

Among the Poor

From that reasoning came Bernadette's affection for the poor, which was intentional and at the same time spontaneous. "They're the friends of God," she used to say. [33]

She was sorry she had nothing to give them; she would have deprived herself to comfort them. [34] "...She gladly worked for them," relates Soeur Joseph Garnier. "Since I was assigned to visit them, she often questioned me about them. She loved the poor as our Lord's suffering members." [35]

But it was not just a matter of words and pious wishes. As we have seen, when Jeanne Jardet, the scullery maid at Saint-Gildard's was sick in 1877, Bernadette went to visit her in her attic room, in spite of her weakness and shortness of breath. Jeanne's testimony clearly indicates that the visit took place in an atmosphere of friendship.[36]

It was this friendship, this contact with the poor that made Bernadette aware of her vocation. In the words of Abbé Pomian, her confessor, it was in nursing "very disgusting," old women that she felt drawn to the religious family of the Sisters of Nevers.

She confirmed the importance of this awareness in her advice to Soeur Vincent Garros: "The more disgusting the poor man, the more you must love him."[37] And again, "The vocation of the Sisters of Nevers is precious, because it makes one love the poor."

With Bernadette, this was not a veneer; it was not escapism. She was not one of those formalistic religious, who, by way of compensation, desire for those they love the wealth they themselves have renounced. The hopes she expressed for her family were no different from what she sought for herself. She said, "I only hope they don't get rich."[38] "I do not ask that they be rich" (words spoken to Soeur Aurélie Gouteyron in 1873).[39]

In this way, she was committed to following Christ himself. "A well trained wife must follow her husband and enter more deeply into his heart," she said on this very point.[40]

Humility

Bernadette took no pride whatsoever in the spiritual favors that had catapulted her into hagiography. She was aware that she had received them undeservedly. Of course, she had been told this again and again ad nauseam. But without deep humility, such treatment, far from strengthening humility, would have provoked reactions, compensations, secret or eye-catching retaliations, or even the contrived excesses of false humility. She was able to strike the right note—a rare sign of authenticity, already obvious during her time in Lourdes. This remained true during the period she spent in Nevers.

Bernadette fled admiration with skillful discretion. "Look for her, she's always hiding," was the reply given to her former companion, Soeur Catherine Fourcade, who had come to see her in Nevers.[41]

Instinctively, Bernadette discouraged the atmosphere of veneration, which had a way of cropping up around her: "I am not a saint; I'm being canonized quite erroneously," she told Soeur Marie Delbrel.[42]

One day she had escaped from the infirmary and gone "to the little balcony that extended along the tribune." Soeur Casimir Callery found her there and asked her, "What are you doing here?"

"I'm putting myself in a niche while I live, for fear that I won't be there after I die," Bernadette replied.[43]

Jeanne Marsan recalls a time she was fervently watching Bernadette. "... she put her hands over my eyes and said, 'My dear, don't look at me like that.'"[44]

Another day, "on the way to Our Lady of the Waters, Bernadette happened to catch the indiscreet gestures of a postulant" who must have kissed or touched her veil in passing.

"She stopped for a second, looking very displeased, [and said,] 'Mademoiselle, you know that's not allowed!'"[45]

"People think I'm something that I'm not," she told Soeur Vincent Garros in 1872.[46] "I say nothing, as if I didn't understand."

But above all, Bernadette discouraged veneration by all that she was—with a unique touch of humor—and a humor that can step back and smile at oneself and one's limitations is the touchstone of true humility. Such humility was quite evident in Bernadette.

People multiplied excuses to have her touch objects: medals, holy pictures, etc. They would say to her, "Choose one," having arranged things so that everything fell into her hands. She was not taken in.... "Come on now! You're going to make me do something foolish," she would say.[47]

In Lourdes, she had been forbidden to touch objects. Before that, even at the time of the apparitions, she used to say, "And after I touch it, how much more will it be worth?"[48]

At Nevers, "a mistress in the novitiate had someone bring her a reliquary in the infirmary. She wanted Bernadette to be the one who cleaned it. 'Even the inside?' Bernadette asked the one who brought it.

"'Yes, especially the inside.'

"(She) smiled and did what she was asked."[49]

To those sisters who turned to her, clearly considering her to be an oracle, she said, "To give you an answer is not my mission."[50]

One day, Félicité Benoît, "a formidable woman with thick glasses, the infirmarian and pharmacist" at the minor seminary at Pignelin, paid a visit to her friends, the sisters in Varennes. She knew that Soeur Marie-Bernard was in the house. That "evening" she was walking with a short, unfamiliar sister and asked her, "Could I see Bernadette?"

"Oh, Mademoiselle!" the sister replied most sincerely, "Bernadette is just like everyone else."

And when she asked another sister the same question, Félicité heard, "What? You don't recognize her? Why just a little while ago you were strolling with her."[51]

Was Bernadette's phrase, "just like everyone else," inspired by something Mère Marie-Thérèse Vauzou had said, or vice versa? The fact remains that, after the death of the visionary of Lourdes, the former mistress of novices used the same phrase: "One day, when she was visiting their house in Durango in Biscay, the little Spanish girls begged her to talk to them about Bernadette.

"'Oh!' Mother answered 'Bernadette was just like everyone else.'

"And she steered the conversation to another topic."

"We stood flabbergasted," said one of those who witnessed this episode.[52]

We have also seen how skillfully Bernadette could move beyond taking self-satisfaction in her works,[53] and devote herself to the task itself, not to what glittered.[54]

Without bitterness, she accepted criticism and acknowledged her faults...including pride. According to Soeur Marthe du Rais, "the superior general, the mistresses and even the infirmarian" told her, "You're nothing but a show-off."[55]

Why this reprimand? It was apparently due to a certain quality in Bernadette's behavior, a certain self-confidence. She had an innate sense of how to adjust her behavior to any situation and didn't like to change arbitrarily on a simple admonition, even from a superior.[56] When they censured this "fault," she simply replied with great humility and sincerity, "It's very true."[57]

She would also say, "The mistress is right; I am very proud."[58] Sometimes she would add, "Pray for my conversion."[59]

But Bernadette knew that "pride," understood in this sense, dwelt in the heart of every living human being. From this realization came a parable in action: "During recreation, one day, while we were talking about self-esteem, Soeur Marie-Bernard made a circle with the thumb and forefinger of her hand and said, 'Let her who hasn't any put her finger here.'"[60]

Probably without even giving it a thought, she repeated Jesus' challenge in the presence of the woman taken in adultery, but for a subtler, more hidden fault. With her, humility involved action, hard work and will power. She told others and herself as well: "This act of humility must be done."[61]

The hardest thing for Bernadette to accept was the label "good-for-nothing," which was repeatedly used with her. The wound hurt and grew more and more painful as illness crushed her and those three words came true. Consequently, this theme often found its way to her lips, "I would have liked to do what everyone else does; I'm the only one who is good for nothing."[62]

"I'm only good for raking out ashes," she told Soeur Joseph Ducout in 1871.[63]

"I'm good for nothing; the only thing I can do is pray."[64]

"I'm here like some useless creature," she remarked to Soeur Gibergues in 1878.[65]

Bernadette accepted this without bitterness as a condition directed by Providence; it never paralyzed within her the gratitude that is the indisputable test of authentic poverty. "She thought herself particularly bound by gratitude to our Congregation, saying that she had been accepted out of charity, and that she was a burden on the motherhouse," Soeur Marthe du Rais candidly observed.

However, Bernadette didn't accept humiliation passively, like a corpse. She received it as a living person who feels and feels deeply, yet without giving in to resentment. According to Soeur Marthe's testimony, "when she received...undeserved...reprimands, she would say, 'The good Lord sees my intentions. Fiat!' And she preserved the same serenity of soul.

"I would tell her, 'You're very lucky. You let nothing show on the outside. You're unemotional! I can't be like that.'

"She remained as friendly as before toward people who had caused her pain."[66]

We have encountered in the course of her life so many words of resignation, tingled with humor: "I don't know how to conjugate a verb."[67] "Ten centimes, that's all I'm worth."[68] "I accept just the same."[69] "All that is sugar."[70] And again, "My Sisters, how little I'm worth."[71] "Yes, Bernadette is only that!"[72]

Did this humility exert an influence in the form of miracles or prophecies during her lifetime? This is a delicate question that we've discussed in the *Logia*.[73] The difficulty is to discern the dividing line between Bernadette's natural good judgment and an intuitive knowledge that would effectively be miraculous—between the words of encouragement or hope she lavished on her companions in their troubles and everything their fervor might see in retrospect and call premonition. In an age when the gift of miracles and prophecies was ranked first among the signs of sanctity, people tended to detect them in Bernadette. It is very hard to judge the significance of these accounts made after the fact, some of which are obvious exaggerations or pure speculations. It is a reliable fact that Bernadette was blessed with the widening influence given to those who live transparently in God's friendship.

The secret of her humility was, in the final analysis, the keen awareness of having been given everything, without the spirit of ownership. It was the conviction of having been an instrument and of being nothing by herself before the love that overwhelmed her.

Obedience

Humility was the source of Bernadette's obedience. "She never failed in this virtue," declared Soeur Marie Delbrel.[74]

This was not an easy thing for her, because at that time, obedience was understood as something absolute, strict and meticulous; and Bernadette was endowed with an exceptionally robust self-assurance and self-will, like the good Bigorre peasant girl she was.

It was in this sense that in 1872 she assured Soeur Eudoxie Chatelain, "You will find happiness in obedience."[75]

She was careful "not to do anything without permission,"[76] and she did not presume permission when she could ask for it, stated Soeur Joseph Garnier.[77]

Her obedience was unflinching, in keeping with the spirituality of the times, both in Lourdes as well as in Nevers. We have seen Bernadette, the infirmarian, demand of others the strict obedience she practiced herself. Nevertheless, her sensitivity to life and other people softened in her the severity she had been taught. On the one hand, it was an impulse: Bernadette was "alert at the first sound of the bell...at the first call," said Soeur Marie Delbrel; "mindful...to obey at the first indication," recalls Soeur Bernard Dalias (1867 statement). "The slightest command made her fly," affirmed Soeur Stanislas Tourriol (statement of 1867).

On the other hand, that obedience was flexible. Bernadette understood enough not to hide behind a command in order to exempt herself from an act of charity or service.

One day, a sister brought her a holy picture for her to inscribe. She replied, "I don't have permission."[78]

But in order not to hurt the visitor's feelings she "made a cross with her fingernail" on the picture. Above all, the depth of her obedience was dependent on its relationship to God. In fact, he is the one whom she obeyed in all things.

From this comes a distinctive feature, all the more striking because we understand Bernadette's fear of her superior general. "Mère Joséphine Imbert sent word to Soeur Marie-Bernard telling her not to go to Mass the next day, which was a Sunday. Nevertheless, Soeur Marie-Bernard attended Mass from the gallery. The superior, who was in the large gallery, saw her. As soon as Soeur Marie-Bernard came back to the infirmary, the superior stood at the threshold of the door and roundly scolded her.

"'What!' she said. 'I sent you word not to go to Mass and you went just the same!'

"I was present, and I was so astonished, that those were the only words of the superior I remember. Soeur Marie-Bernard made no reply; but after the superior had left, she said: 'What do you expect! I fulfilled the precept.'"[79]

Little by little, we have discovered this flexibility in an obedience that didn't passively take refuge behind the will of others, but remained open to human values and purposes.[80]

Bernadette's inner freedom surfaced and occasionally emerged, when she "answered Mère Vauzou," or again in the following incident, which was investigated at the beatification process. Mère Bordenave received the following account from two sisters, whose names she did not give: "One day, a Sunday, after Mass, they found Soeur Marie-Bernard lying on her bed in the infirmary in full habit. They were quite moved because this is the way we are on our deathbed. They informed the superior general who had them tell Bernadette to get up, which she did immediately.

"'But,'" added one of the sisters, "'the superior probably should have specified not to do this again.'

"So they were surprised the following Sunday, to see Bernadette again lying on her bed. They remarked that their surprise came from knowing her scrupulosity when it came to obedience."

"I want to point out," added the witness, Mère Marie-Thérèse Bordenave, "that their reaction was based on a 'probability.'"[81]

In keeping with this spiritual freedom, which places human beings before the Sabbath, Bernadette could say, "Happiness on earth is obedience."[82]

The Hidden Life

Another facet of Bernadette's humility was her relish for the hidden life. Bishop Lelong understood this in his funeral oration: "She came wholeheartedly to bury herself and her "secret mission" in solitude. She too discovered and proclaimed that it was an extremely good thing.... *Sacramentum regis abscondere bonum est.* " ("It is good to conceal the sacred secret of the king.")

Bishop Forcade had already said that she "wanted nothing more for herself than to disappear from sight," and we shall see that he had a bone to pick with this tendency of hers. Accordingly, he went so far as to say, "Her main attraction obviously was for the hidden life."[83]

This attraction asserted itself right from the outset of her religious life: she came to Nevers to "hide" herself.[84] Certain behaviors expressed this deep-rooted intention. To disappear from sight, she instinctively wrapped herself in her hooded cloak at the grotto or in her veil at Nevers. She had cut down on her correspondence with her family, because her letters were being circulated everywhere. She begged that they be destroyed.[85] We have heard her evade questions which people asked her as if asking an oracle. "To give you an answer is not my mission," she said to Soeur Marthe du Rais, who nonetheless kept insisting.[86]

On this point of hiddenness she gave many bits of good advice drawn from common sense and her own experience:

To Soeur Bounaix in 1871: "Don't place yourself first."[87]

To Julie Garros in 1871: "Think of yourself as the last."[88] Again to Julie that same year: "Don't wait for compliments."[89]

Each statement was an echo of the Gospel (cf. Lk 14:10; 18:14; 22:26).

2. Prayer and Penance

The most explicit elements in the message of Lourdes are prayer and penance.

These two points were so tightly bound together in Bernadette's life and words that it is impossible to present them separately.

They spring from the message itself. The Virgin asked Bernadette to pray and to do penance for sinners, or "for the conversion of sinners."

For her, prayer, penance and conversion were all one, because prayer is doing, not dreaming; it involves the will; it is the act whereby we turn toward God (this is the meaning of conversion), and the rest follows. So prayer for the conversion of others is intimately tied to personal conversion.

Here, as with poverty (linked to humility, humor and obedience), the themes we shall present separately should not be isolated from one another. They are part of a living whole.

Silence

The prayer of Bernadette was first and foremost rooted in her silence. This is one of the characteristic traits of the woman whom the breviary calls *"custos silentii"* ("guardian of silence"). Her confessor attests to this,[1] and we have seen it emerge, as it were, beginning with her inconspicuous and impoverished childhood, which left no retrievable words or traces. Silence was one of Bernadette's fundamental traits. Bishop Forcade, who was both bishop and her confessor, expressed it clearly, "Although people delight in attributing to her today countless beautiful sayings, that I, for my part have never heard, I have always observed that she suffered, like everything else she did, simply and without words."[2]

"She never spoke unless questioned," remarked Soeur Joseph Caldairou.[3]

This silence was not escapism from the world, nor a lack of ability, for Bernadette was a ready talker who possessed infectious enthusiasm, and a lively repartee with her friends as well as in recreation. But she was fond of recollection, in which she found God. The rule of silence, very strict at the time, helped and liberated her. It was a "directive in the [Congregation's] Rule that she particularly treasured," noted Abbé Febvre.[4] For this reason, she hardly ever allowed herself to be caught unawares by unexpected questions during times of silence.[5] Time and time again we have seen her observing this rule or reminding others of it. "I asked her a few unnecessary questions in the cloister. She looked annoyed, reproached me for this, and when she saw me coming after that, she fled,[6] as though I carried the plague," added Soeur Caldairou.[7]

Yet hers was not a rigid or routine attitude. "She engaged in small talk out of charity, but it was a hardship for her to depart from the rule and from silence," noted Soeur Joseph Garnier.[8]

Recollection

In prayer, as in her practice of silence, there was nothing to single Bernadette out. It was very simply and unaffectedly that she threw her whole self into the "large sign of the cross," which she would make "before each religious exercise."[9] Her recollection seemed transparent. She understood how to prolong it. Did she have an aptitude for doing this? We know nothing. All we know is that she had trouble meditating. This is surprising, but the reason is simple. Her gifts were free and intuitive, in line with her life. The methods of prayer in vogue at the time cramped her spontaneity.

Formulas

Bernadette liked to multiply those short prayers that the spiritual authors call "ejaculatory prayers." This odd expression refers to the flight of a javelin (*jaculum*) hurled toward the sky. It was an impulse that made Bernadette repeat formulas such as these:

"My God, I offer it up to you, my God, I love you!"

"My God I believe in you, I hope in you, I love you."

She explained to Soeur Marthe du Rais, "I can't say long prayers. I make up with ejaculatory prayers."[10]

Bernadette recommended this form of prayer to her patients and to the dying.

She appreciated prayer in common, which "gives greater glory to Jesus Christ," noted Abbé Febvre.[11] She felt exiled when she could not participate. She then had to be reassured.[12] Lastly, and especially, she felt that prayer in common "enriched her poverty."[13]

The Cross and the Eucharist

For her time, Bernadette practiced a minimum of "private devotions." She told Soeur Philippine Molinéry, "What do you want? Making the Stations of the Cross, participating at Mass, receiving Holy Communion—those are the big devotions."[14]

The cross and the Eucharist...it would be difficult to go more directly to the essential. The Mass held a central place in her piety. From her sickbed, she united herself to the sacrifice being celebrated around the world, following the sun's daily cycle.[15] In conformity with the spirit of her time, she strongly emphasized the real and personal presence of the Lord.[16] She prepared for her Communions very energetically, just as we prepare for an important meeting, and preferred to abstain rather than approach this sacrament poorly. "I'm very much at peace," she told Soeur Germaine J. Gibergues, "because I never receive Holy Communion when I have a doubt on my conscience."[17]

In that case, she made a "spiritual communion," a frequent practice with her, day or night. To Soeur Henri Bonnefoy, her companion in the infirmary, she said one day, "If you wake up tonight, call me."

"And since Soeur Henri expressed the desire to know the reason for this request, Soeur Marie-Bernard replied, 'It's because I want to make a spiritual communion.'"[18]

Linked to this respect for the Eucharist was her respect for priests, given concrete expression in the familiar aphorisms she liked to repeat: "The priest at the altar is always Jesus on earth."[19] "If you encounter a priest and an angel, the priest should be acknowledged first."[20]

Bernadette was subjected to endless requests for prayers, wearying in their frequency, their persistence and the whole background of pious wiles people kept coming up with to obtain them.

"Superiors and teaching sisters used to come begging for prayers for their students. They quickly spotted the group where Bernadette was and preferably made their requests there. The bolder ones sometimes insisted on adding, 'Soeur Marie-Bernard, did you understand that all right?'

"'Yes, yes, I understood.'"[21]

She would tell her suppliants, "I will pray for you."[22]

But she understood this in the interchange of the communion

of saints: "Yes, but you pray for me....[23] I also need prayers."[24] Or again, "I don't give something for nothing."[25]

For Sinners

The message of Lourdes directed Bernadette's prayer toward sinners. In reciting the rosary, Bernadette strongly stressed the words *pauvres pécheurs* (poor sinners). Someone mentioned this to her one day. She answered, "Oh, yes! We must pray for sinners, it was a directive of the Blessed Virgin."[26] "You can never do enough for the conversion of sinners," she also said in recreation.[27]

This concern of hers was obvious. Mère Adélaïde Dons noticed the sadness of "her expression..." when she spoke of sinners.[28]

"'So you have a whole collection of sinners?' asked Soeur Marthe du Rais.

"She answered, 'Unfortunately, there are always some.'"[29]

The deep concern that motivated her was not limited to generalities. Her prayer was personalized by all sorts of specific intentions entrusted to her. Over and above these cases, like a fisherman casting his line or spreading his nets in the secretly inhabited waters, she kept dreaming of the big fish....

"When they brought her some distasteful medicine (which happened often), she would make the sign of the cross and say, 'It's for the big sinner.'

"Once," relates Soeur Marthe du Rais, "I asked her, 'So where is this big sinner of yours?'

"'Oh! The Blessed Virgin knows who he is.'"[30]

"She had made a pact with our Lord to offer up her sufferings each day for the conversion of one sinner," affirmed Abbé Perreau.[31]

Sins of the flesh seemed to disturb her. Did this stem from the time when she waited on customers at her Aunt Bernarde's tavern? It would be difficult to pinpoint. In any event, we can discern neither obsession nor signs of trauma when she worried about the "behavior of soldiers," or when she scolded her loudly-painted "doll," recalling the brightly made up streetwalkers of Nevers.[32] Here the allegory was light and playful.

For the intention of sinners recommended by our Lady, Bernadette offered in a very special way her Communions,[33] her Stations of the Cross,[34] her bitter medicine[35] and the even more bitter visiting sessions,[36] etc. "For sinners," she would say.

She advised Soeur Michel Gaillard, "Every time you go to the chapel, recite an act of contrition for them."[37]

She had the rosary said for that intention[38] and would urge, "Let us offer up our sufferings for sinners."[39] Or again, "We are not mortifying ourselves enough for them. We must mortify ourselves even more."[40]

In applying blister-raising medication on Soeur Marthe du Rais, Bernadette encouraged her, "There, my little one, put up with it for sinners."[41]

Even the cause of the souls in purgatory, for whom she prayed,[42] paled in comparison: "They are certain of their happiness...but sinners are in danger."[43]

Conversion and Penance

A significant fact is that Bernadette did not often use the word "penance" (found only five times in the Nevers writings).[44] Even more seldom did she use the word "conversion." It is not officially authenticated among her words. (Very uncertain or hazy are some uses of this term,[45] and even once in a later testimony,[46] it was added in.) In the lengthy collection of her *Ecrits* (Writings), we find only once the verb "convert," which she applied to herself in this wish: "That I may finally be converted for the good"[47]—and not one single use of the word "conversion" during the Nevers period. (The Lourdes writings use it only when Bernadette repeated our Lady's words, for the "conversion of sinners.") However, the term appears forcefully in a letter dated April 6, 1869, discovered by Dom Bernard Billet after the publication of the *Ecrits:* "Ask the good Lord and the most Blessed Virgin for my conversion."[48]

Bernadette's infrequent use of the word does not indicate that she forgot our Lady's invitation to do "penance for the conversion of sinners." It rises from what we said at the beginning: for Bernadette, penance and conversion were realities more than conventional expressions. She lived, she internalized the message; she formulated it and externalized it only by rare exception.

3. Aqueró

The fact is still more striking in what relates to the Virgin. We could be astonished that Bernadette's words do not refer to the dogma of the *Immaculate Conception,* except when the interviewers make her repeat—without further explanation—the words she heard on March 25.

Here again, Bernadette did not enter into speculation or speak of doctrinal developments. For a long time, she did not even know what name to give the apparition: *Aqueró,* "That," is what she used to say. And yet, it was enough for her. *"Immaculate Conception"* was not one of her themes for doctrinal reflection; it was the name, the overall title of the Mother of Jesus.

A Presence

Here again, the essential is to be found in the quality of a certain silence. The life of Bernadette is linked to the presence of the Immaculate, expressed very simply in word and deed. She lived the message of Lourdes in relationship with the Messenger, who later turned up in Bernadette's words and writings on almost every page.

A Mother

Bernadette usually called the Blessed Virgin "My good Mother," observed Soeur Casimir Callery.[49]

"When she had said, 'My Mother in heaven,' she had said everything," confirmed Soeur Marthe du Rais.[50]

The death of her own mother on the *Feast of the Immaculate Conception* in 1866 had a meaning for her. Bernadette later spoke of it to Soeur Casimir, consoling her on the loss of her father: "I too lost my mother on December 8. The Blessed Virgin wanted it that way to show me that she would replace my mother, whom I had lost."[51]

This explains the words addressed to Jeanne Jardet, who was pining away far from her mother: "Your Mother—here she is; she is the Mother of us all."[52]

There was nothing extraordinary in all this. It was a simple affection, a secret assurance within the darkness of faith. The "memory" of the apparition faded away. What had been clear in 1858 could no longer be recalled, but there remained a connection, a conviction expressed by the gift of self. "If you only knew how good the Blessed Virgin is," Bernadette said one day to Soeur Emilienne Duboé, during her novitiate.[53] And again, "Ah! If people only knew!"[54]

Fabisch's statue (1864).
Bernadette's main criticisms: The expression of the face, the hair hidden by the veil, the position of the head, the neck, "long and distorted," what she sometimes called the goiter—much more noticeable in other photos taken from below. The hands are soft and too far apart. For no reason at all, the knee shows under the dress, which should have been flared. Sash, veil and tunic do not fall simply enough. In general Bernadette remarked that there was a lack of simplicity, straightness, symmetry and youthfulness. The height was too tall.

"You could feel her love for the Blessed Virgin," reported Soeur Joseph Caldairou in her notes of 1867. She sometimes expressed this in simple, everyday language: "My children, love the Blessed Virgin," she told the orphan girls at Varennes.[55] "Love the Blessed Virgin very much," she advised Julie Garros.[56]

She spoke freely of the Virgin, reported Soeur Casimir;[57] she especially expressed her "great trust" in her.[58]

For Bernadette, the experience of the apparitions had eclipsed the attractions of this world. From this came her intensity when she was asked if this or that beautiful woman, admired at the time, could give some idea of the Virgin of Massabielle. "When you've seen her, you can't love this world anymore," she told Soeur Madeleine Bounaix in 1870.

And Soeur Eléonore Cassagnes heard her answer with some emotion the question:

"Was she beautiful?"

"So beautiful that when you've seen her once, you can't wait to die to see her again."[59] This was part of her attraction to heaven.[60] Bernadette was confident that after the long night, the Virgin "would come to get her."[61]

But emotionalism was unusual for her; she gave in to it in reply to a question from a child, the little Darfeuille girl, who asked her plainly whether the Blessed Virgin was beautiful.

Ordinarily, Bernadette spoke of the Virgin briefly, objectively, reservedly and always by request. The accounts taken down by the best witnesses, from Jacomet to Soeur Vigouroux, clearly reflect how plainly she spoke.[62]

The Internal Image and the Statues

Even in her mind's eye, Bernadette "could no longer see" what she had seen at the grotto. The color of the apparition's eyes was clear to her in Lourdes. By 1879, she had forgotten it.[63]

The impression she had about the beauty, the indescribable simplicity of *Aqueró* was expressed essentially in a negative way when she was asked her opinion about this or that statue—something she was asked many times. Her fear of hurting an artist's feelings or of offending piety usually kept her reactions limited to tactful and carefully measured words, which those around her still twisted.

"It's the least poorly done," or "the least like a dancer," she supposedly said to the sculptor Cabuchet in 1876, in reference to his statue.[64]

"It's one of the least ugly," she told Soeur Casimir Callery, referring to Our Lady of the Sacred Heart at Issoudun.[65]

When she did acknowledge some resemblance, people often exaggerated its significance. When this was done in her presence, she reacted.

"You find it beautiful? I don't," she told Soeur Stanislas Tourriol, referring to the novitiate statue of the Virgin.[66]

And after stating her favorable reaction to a reproduction of the Virgin of Saint Luke—the only one in the whole album that evoked such a response—she immediately added, "That's not it. No, that's not it."[67]

In Lourdes, her preference was for the simple statues of the parish church. She referred to one of these as a point of comparison in speaking with Prosecutor Dutour during the two weeks of the apparitions.

Among the statues at Nevers, Our Lady of the Waters was the one Bernadette ranked first: "It's my favorite Virgin," she maintained, according to Soeur Stanislas Tourriol.[68]

"It's the only one I like," Soeur Marie Delbrel assures us she heard her say.[69] But Bernadette added, "They aren't beautiful here."[70]

"Here," probably compared with her home parish. Yet Bernadette enjoyed praying before the statue of Our Lady of the Waters at the far end of the convent garden beneath the little hill. Was it because it stood out in the open, in a natural setting and "in a kind of grotto," as she herself said?[71] Perhaps. But there is more. Concurring declarations state that Bernadette detected some resemblance there: "It reminds me more than the others of the Blessed Virgin."[72]

"When I saw it for the first time, this Virgin made an impression on me," she also confided.[73]

"This is the one that most resembles the real one," Soeur Marguerite-Marie Magnié even had her saying.[74]

But none of this tells us where the resemblance lies. Is it in the gesture of welcome, similar to the one the Virgin made on February 11, or on the Miraculous Medal? Is it in the simpler appearance and the softer expression of this statue? This latter reason was attested to by Soeur Casimir Callery, who reported Bernadette as having said,

These four images received Bernadette's flattering or lenient criticisms:

1. Top left: Cabuchet's crowned statue: "The least like a dancer," Bernadette supposedly said, according to a tradition within the sculptor's family.

2. Top right: Armand Cait's Virgin (the base of a monstrance executed in 1879). "The least poorly done," Bernadette is reported to have graciously commented on March 29 of that year. Perhaps the reasons are its straightness, the simplicity of the position of the head, and a certain youthfulness.

3. Bottom left: The Virgin of Saint Luke. Bernadette saw it in an album brought by Fabisch. At that time it was not a photograph but a drawing similar to this one.

4. Bottom right: Our Lady of Issoudun (1869). The resemblance to Our Lady of Lourdes is seen in the gesture of welcome which Bernadette also saw in the Virgin of the Miraculous Medal, but "without the rays," as she specified.

Statues in the parish church of Lourdes in 1858. There were four. Which one did Bernadette have in mind when she told Prosecutor Dutour on February 25, 1858, that the apparition (Aqueró) resembled the statue of the Virgin in the parish church? Probably the welcoming Virgin, whose open arms resembled the apparition at the very beginning. That statue (bottom right) is preserved today at the cachot.

Our Lady of the Waters, at the far end of the garden at Saint-Gildard's

"The Blessed Virgin is always depicted with a stern look, or at least cold and solemn. The Blessed Virgin is gracious and smiling. That's why I prefer Our Lady of the Waters."[75]

Yet these favorable reactions must not be exaggerated nor taken out of a limited context. Even Our Lady of the Waters did not escape Bernadette's criticism. According to Soeur Julie Durand, it was in front of this very statue that Bernadette exclaimed, "Oh! How the one who did this will get caught in heaven!"[76]

The reason for her dissatisfaction with attempts to portray the Virgin of Lourdes was elementary: it was because the apparition was indescribable. Among other things Bernadette said, "The difference is like heaven and earth."[77] "Here below, nothing comes close."[78] "No matter how hard they try, they will never be able to duplicate her."[79]

As for details, her main criticism centered on the tendency of sculptors to bend the head back and roll the eyes up toward heaven.[80] Bernadette clung to the impression of a look focused downwards on her.[81] That gaze was raised only for an instant, before the words, *"I am the Immaculate Conception."* "She raised *only* her eyes," and not her head, Bernadette insisted.[82]

"They gave her a goiter," she told Soeur Casimir Callery.[83]

On these grounds, she offended a sculptor Count, who had come recommended by a bishop, to show her his work.[84] And yet she had toned down her reaction. When she was observed unawares, she was heard to exclaim, "Good Mother, how they disfigure you!"[85]

"Oh! How ugly!"[86]

"I don't understand how they can make her look so ugly."[87]

"No statue was right," summed up Soeur Charles Ramillon.[88]

Nonetheless, it would be a mistake to think that Bernadette drew strength from some marvelous mental picture. She remembered that the apparition was wonderful, but she could no longer see the picture. What she had perceived in a sensory way had become something internal, visceral. She could no doubt recall it "sometimes, but not always," as she told one of her infirmary companions.[89]

More than once, someone hinted at what Bernadette could have done had she been an artist.[90] One day, she replied, "I can't. I don't know how. For myself, I don't need [a picture]." She was said to have added, "I have it in my heart."[91] Or again, "It's engraved in my heart."[92] "Forget it? It's in here!"[93]

The witnesses seem to have understood this to mean a vivid pic-

Photo submitted to Bernadette November 12, 1872. She gave the following critique: "The rosary did not go around her arm twice...it simply hung. Each rose was at the tip of the feet, which were hidden...the rose is placed much too high."
Bernadette "gasped on seeing these inaccuracies," but the rest was "fine," added the good-natured Soeur Nathalie, in her reply to Abbé Roger, who had sent the photo (Grotto Archives, file drawer ten).

ture. But it seems to be something more deep-rooted than visual memory. Bernadette was not interested in describing the apparition externally but in assimilating it personally within the ascetic context of faith.

An Ordinary Piety

Bernadette's piety toward the Virgin contained nothing extraordinary. She spoke of her in simple words, words everyone uses: "Love the Blessed Virgin, pray to the Blessed Virgin."[94] "Make others love the Blessed Virgin."[95] "Your Mother, here she is!"[96] "We'll make this sacrifice for the Blessed Virgin."[97] "I have great confidence in her."[98]

Sometimes, when asked for prayers, she said, "I'll speak to the Blessed Virgin."[99]

She advised the impatient to persevere.... "The Virgin wants us to pray to her for a long time."[100]

Her prayer was neither particularly emotional nor even observable. Occasionally, however, Bernadette's voice was tinged with feeling when she gave a talk on the Virgin or when she sang the hymn, *"Ah, c'est ma Mère!"* (Ah! She is my Mother!).[101]

The Rosary

Bernadette's conversation with God expressed itself particularly, and over a long period of time, by the first form of prayer she had learned (and with difficulty)—the rosary. They affirmed this at Bartrès, where Emile Zola jotted down this remark on August 28, 1892: "They had trouble teaching her the rosary; after that she never abandoned it."

She recommended the rosary to others.[102] "You will never say it in vain," she counseled.[103] And again, "Go to sleep reciting it...like little children who fall asleep saying 'Mama.'"[104]

It was definitely a daughterly attitude that governed Bernadette's piety toward the Virgin.

4. *"Not happy in this world..."*

The message of the apparition included a stern promise for Bernadette's immediate present: "I do not promise to make you happy in this world...."[1]

Bernadette rarely commented on these words, heard on February 18, 1858, the first day *Aqueró* spoke. She lived them in a spirit of penance.

This statement already described for her a past that had been filled with bitter experiences, sickness, hunger, scorn, cultural and religious illiteracy. Her desires, including her spiritual longings, were generally frustrated. At over fourteen years of age, she was still waiting to make her First Communion.

After the apparitions, this ordeal was eased, but it made way for others: harassment by the police and the administration, curiosity, maddening flattery and the intrusiveness of visitors, the discomfort of being taken for what she was not. At Nevers the trial progressively took on new forms.

The Uprooting

First, it was being torn away from Lourdes, where she had solid family roots. "[Leaving was] a big sacrifice," she confided to Soeur Joseph Garnier.[2] "The biggest sacrifice of my life," she "often" told Soeur Marthe du Rais.[3]

We have already analyzed the elements of this human and spiritual uprooting, which, as she said, made her "water" with her tears, the first days spent at Nevers. "The longing to see the grotto again" —haunted her,[4] but without bitterness and eventually without regret, because it was temporary. When she was questioned, she admitted her secret dream: "To see without being seen,"[5] "like a little bird,"[6] or even "in a balloon."[7] She didn't dwell on these daydreams. This exile was identified in her mind with her earthly exile. "Lourdes isn't heaven," she would say.[8] And again, "In heaven, it will be more beautiful."[9]

Family Worries

A second chapter of Bernadette's trials was concern over her family. We have seen what the function and the matriarchal authority of the eldest daughter meant in Lourdes. Distance did not abrogate this responsibility. She fulfilled it in prayer, but also in action, through her letters of advice, of reproach (some so personal that they had to be edited for publication), and even of intercession, when her influence in Lourdes could arrange for a position for one of her relatives in the service of the bishop or Père Sempé. We have seen Bernadette's cares multiply on this score. Toinette's periods of mourning over her inability to keep a single child, the abortive vocation of her brother Jean-Marie and the problem of his shop, the festering family quarrels—all of these were cause for worry. Had she not heard that her brother Bernard-Pierre had thumbed his nose[10] at his brother-in-law and his sister, Joseph and Marie Sabathé? Her family's setting themselves up in the religious goods business ran counter to the personal requirement she had made them respect when she was in Lourdes.[11] She didn't want "her name to be used as an advertisement,"[12] or her family to "do business on Sunday,"[13] or even desire "them to get rich,"[14] as we have seen.

The Curious

One trial, more personal and more agonizing, kept cropping up time and time again: visits. Bernadette had had her fill of these in Lourdes. She had left her hometown assured that it was over. But the visits always began again, and at the wrong time. We have seen countless examples and the dates they occurred. Here are a few others; the first, given by an eyewitness, Soeur Victoire Seurre: "In the two instances when Soeur Marie-Bernard came to Coulanges (about two miles from Nevers), her recreation was cut short.... She stayed with us only half an hour, or one hour at most. She was called out, because some important people—I think they were bishops—were waiting for her at the motherhouse. She was honestly having fun.... They summoned her suddenly. I understood her sacrifice when I heard her say to me, 'God doesn't want me to enjoy myself anymore....' I admired her resignation.... Once I told her, 'Let it not be said that you left without tasting our pastry and drinking our delicious milk.' She exploded with childlike merriment and she began eating with pleasure what I offered her."[15]

"She did not hide her great distaste [for visits]," recalls Soeur Gonzague Champy.[16] "Oh! How tiresome this is!" she said.[17]

She would sigh, "When will they stop treating me like a strange animal?"[18]

Objections were her defense, her only weapon. And if she used them, it was because she felt that this was her right. Consequently, she expressed her gratitude when she was excused from such visits.[19] When she was not dispensed, she would say, "But they promised me."[20]

One day, Soeur Augustin Faur testifies, she told Mother General, "My dear Mother, I will go only if you command me under holy obedience."[21] That time, the superior did not insist and Bernadette did not go.

Another day, a sister invited her to come down to the parlor, where she had been granted an audience for one of her cousins. Bernadette inquired further and was told, "Our venerable Mother gives you permission...but she leaves you free."

"She leaves me free!" exclaimed Soeur Marie-Bernard, "Well then, no!"[22]

She seemed to be particularly fearful of visits from bishops, not only because they were bishops, but because they were the only ones authorized to see her. Because of this they were most numerous and the awareness of their own importance sometimes made them imprudent. "Those poor bishops would do better to stay home in their dioceses," she said.[23]

In their presence her ability to defend herself remained intact. We have seen her outmaneuver many a ploy "to put her on display,"[24] or "to have her touch objects,"[25] for instance, the violet skullcap that fell from one bishop's hand as the result of an obviously deliberate accident.

Two other incidents cannot be dated:

"One day, she caught sight of the bishop of Nevers, accompanied by an unknown clergyman, coming to the convent. They were heading for the infirmary. Immediately Soeur Marie-Bernard disappeared and hid, where, I don't know.... She ended up being discovered.

"'Quick! Quick! Soeur Marie-Bernard, Reverend Mother is calling for you. The bishop has come to see you.'

"She replied, 'The bishop hasn't come to see me; he's come to show me off.'"[26]

At the time she was sacristan, "a group of lay people" came up to her while "she was preparing the Blessed Virgin's altar."

"'Good sister, where is Bernadette's place? Today is a profession day and we were told that she would be at the ceremony.... Might we be able to see her?'

"'Oh! No, no! That's impossible. She won't be in her usual place today.' And even as she spoke, she disappeared."[27]

One day, a lady came into the sacristy at Saint-Gildard's in Nevers and, turning to a sister who happened to be there, asked, "Sister, may I see Soeur Marie-Bernard?"

"'I'll go get her.'

"A moment later, another sister came along and asked, 'What do you wish?'

"'I wish to see Soeur Marie-Bernard.'

"'Why she's the one who just went out!...' And she did not come back."[28]

But when trapped—especially by obedience[29] she forced herself with a smile.

"Having arrived, she made a graceful curtsy and complied...[30] but briefly and simply."[31]

Her hostility resurfaced, however when she was asked tactless questions.[32] For this she was reprimanded. She "promised to do better," but relapsed.

Struggling against Nature

Here we touch upon another trial—what spiritual writers used to call, "the struggle against nature." It was not that Bernadette had evil tendencies, but, according to her confessor, Abbé Febvre, "She was really a girl from the mountains, accustomed in her early years to a life of freedom, movement and action."[33] It was hard for her to adjust to the enclosed and strictly regulated religious life of that time. Her spontaneous reactions tended to shake up the administration. Her responses had a way of escaping her. She herself was surprised by them. She suffered all the more for having been trained in an absolute respect for the rule and for law.

Lastly, the times she lived in saw little value in naturalness and spontaneity. Bernadette was made to feel ashamed of these qualities. "I hear myself being very often called headstrong. I am ashamed of this, and, nevertheless, I cannot correct myself," she wrote in an April 8, 1869 letter to Mère Alexandrine, the superior of the Lourdes hospice.[34]

The image that keeps coming back in her speech is one of an exuberance that was difficult to control. "My boiling nature again!"

she said.[35] And another time, "It boils inside; you can't see what's going on inside."[36] She added, "We'd have no merit if we didn't control ourselves."[37]

Hers was a battle full of alternatives: "The first movement does not belong to us. The second does."[38]

Soeur Marthe du Rais[39] occasionally found her crushed. "I'm discouraged," she would say.[40]

But better moments left her more optimistic. "By dint of putting the stick to an animal, you end up taming it," she told the same witness.[41] And again, "Now I feel nothing."[42]

Bernadette's failures were an occasion for her to count more on grace. "How I need the help of God!" she said.[43]

In this spirit she accepted the purification of suffering. At the height of her asthma attacks, she would say, in the words of Saint Paul, "The old man must die. Alas! He is still very much alive."[44]

Feeling Useless

What weighed upon her more than all else was inactivity. "She loved the active life," Soeur Marthe informs us.[45] In fact, we saw her intentionally choose this type of life. Her confessor, Abbé Febvre, confirmed this, almost in the same words: "By temperament...she always felt a particular attraction to the active life. That's where God was waiting for her. He made her pass through a life completely opposed to...her own inclinations and tastes.... He imposed on her the crucifixion of a life of inactivity, solitude and retreat."

Here, too, Bernadette saw no virtue in keeping her sorrow silent.[46] "To...a sick companion...she said one day, 'You get away with three blistering medications; but me, nothing gets me away from this....'

"She added, 'My God! Be praised by all. We each have...our own way to get to you.'"[47]

To Soeur Philippine Molinéry, who enjoyed robust health, she said "many times," "How lucky you are.... Ah! If I could only have strong arms like yours, how hard I would work.... But here I still am in my bed doing nothing.... Well, it's the good Lord's will!... I must submit."[48]

Bernadette was attracted by every work of the Congregation: the children, the orphan girls, the elderly and the sick. Like Thérèse of the Child Jesus, she would have liked to have chosen them all. She told Soeur Marthe and some others, "You're lucky to be able to work."[49] Sometimes she added, "I'm only good for raking out the ashes at Saint-Gildard's."[50]

As the sight of food sharpens the appetite of the hungry, seeing each task to be done stirred up her thirst for being useful.

"One day, when she was visiting the children's home of La Chaumière (in Nevers), she told Soeur Saint-Cyr that she would have liked to teach the youngest children."

But her greatest desire was "to care for the sick in the hospitals."

"It's really unfortunate that I can't do this," she confided to Soeur Marthe.[51]

Yes, feeling herself useless was the bitterest of Bernadette's trials,[52] the one that wrung from her the most regrets. Her courage, which was great in accepting sufferings, was here outmatched because she felt that she was a burden.

"Here I am, sick again. Still good for nothing, being given care and able to give none," she said, according to Lasserre.[53]

The Sternness of Her Superiors

We have slowly become acquainted with another of Bernadette's trials—the sternness of her superiors: Mère Joséphine Imbert, the mother general (deceased March 1, 1878), and particularly Mère Marie-Thérèse Vauzou, the mistress of novices.

The trial was genuine. It was acknowledged by many witnesses and by Bernadette herself, both in writings[1] and in speech.[2]

But the facts reported have often been exaggerated. The myth of the "persecuted saint" was unfairly developed with astonishing success by Père Petitot in his *Histoire exacte de le vie intérieure et religieuse de sainte Bernadette*[3] (A Detailed History of the Interior and Religious Life of Saint Bernadette). This corresponded to a personal experience. His own master of novices abnormally practiced the "classic" art of testing the novices, even going so far one day as to spit in his face. Père Petitot had made it through the test, but had not accepted it. He denounced it in typical fashion by identifying himself with the emblematic Bernadette. This explains both the intensity and the ambiguity of his argumentation.

The gripping theme of the "persecuted saint," which conformed to popular taste, was worked by the gifted Franz Werfel into his fine novel, *The Song of Bernadette,* and into the bad motion picture that prolonged its impact by further influencing movies which were even worse.

This impact was made all the stronger by Mère Vauzou, who embodied an age and a lifestyle which our own has abandoned with a one-sided and inflexible reaction that wars against similar situations. But we must be fair.

The question of Bernadette's treatment at the hands of her superiors has taken on an exaggerated importance for the following reasons:

1. At Saint-Gildard's, the superiors' sternness made a striking impression on the novices and religious in keeping with their respect for the visionary of Lourdes.

2. The inquiries and canonization process dwelt minutely on this point which had an effect on the chapters dealing with obedience and the acceptance of trials. It therefore took on a great material significance.

3. Since the various documents regarding Bernadette were not made available to the public, people had the feeling that something was being hidden to protect the memory of Mère Vauzou, who later became superior general.

An unbiased focus is a must. It has to be thorough, leaving aside not the slightest significant observation. Père Petitot and Monseigneur Trochu had access to only some of the documents in the archives—one fourth of the complete documentation which we were able to bring together for this present study.

Before drawing up an inventory of the *facts*—and we were amazed at finding it so meager after such an investigation—the situation must be clarified.

The arrival of "the visionary from Lourdes" at Saint-Gildard's presented a real problem. The fervor whose object Bernadette was, posed a danger to herself as well as to the house. Her superiors had to provide her with as normal a religious life as possible and not allow her any privileges that might create a singular situation.

This legitimate concern was forever being thwarted by events: books and articles arrived continually, singing the praise of "the blessed visionary," "our Lady's favored one." Let us not forget that Henri Lasserre's *Notre-Dame de Lourdes* (1869) was the religious best seller of the nineteenth century. Bernadette's presence attracted bishops, prominent persons, the curious, the unbalanced; it even drew one marriage proposal.[4] Generally speaking, visitors couldn't go to the motherhouse without talking about her. In short, there was a tidal wave of attention.

It was hard to maintain a balanced position in regard to Bernadette without becoming inflexible. As a result, the superiors asked the novices "not to mention" her "in their correspondence";[5] and they reminded them that it was forbidden to talk to her about the apparitions.[6]

These reasons seem to fully explain the attitude of the superior general, Mère Joséphine Imbert: her coldness, her concern over "humiliating" Bernadette, her neglecting to show her the kindness she was capable of personally demonstrating to each one, for fear of giving in to favoritism. Here, for example is one incident that occurred in 1870, "On her return from Rome...where...people had spoken a great deal to her [Mère Joséphine] about Bernadette...all the novices were waiting for her in the cloister and...in their midst...Soeur Marie-Bernard. The superior general embraced each one with a kind word.... When she came to Bernadette, she embraced her without saying a thing."

It was Mère Joséphine who planned and carried out the humiliation of denying Bernadette a new assignment at the time of her profession of vows. What can we find on the debit side? Mère Joséphine kept a strict account of Bernadette's infractions: notably the famous open window scene. She labeled her a "useless person" and perhaps a "little fool," although evidence of this latter remark has not been given in a definitive way.[7] What is certain is that we have heard Bernadette exclaim, "Mère Joséphine! Oh, how afraid I am of her!"[8]

The lengthy documentation of confidences made under the seal of secrecy and given under oath, with complete candor, contains *nothing more*.

The examples relating to Mère Marie-Thérèse are more numerous, but do not go any further. She spoke to Bernadette in "cold, curt language"[9] with "never a word of encouragement."[10]

"Should she [Bernadette] arrive late...(and even if not through her own fault) she had to kneel down to receive a severe reprimand and...had to kiss the floor...."

*Mère Joséphine Imbert, superior general from
December 29, 1863 until her death on March 1, 1878*

But at that time this was a common practice for all novices, as indeed it was for all convents.

"I'd be searching in vain for the novitiate floor stone that I haven't kissed," we have heard Soeur Julienne Capmartin comment concerning her personal experience.

Mère Marie-Thérèse called Bernadette "a fool" and "arrogant."[11] She tended to make her feel ashamed of her strong-willed temperament.

She humiliated her fairly frequently,[12] "more than the others,"[13] said Soeur Joseph Caldairou. "She never let an occasion slip by when she could subject her to some humiliation," declared Soeur Lucie Cloris.[14]

Finally, Mère Marie-Thérèse would send Bernadette out of the room whenever they read a book on the apparitions,[15] which was normal; and dismissed her from a lecture in the novitiate when she was a professed sister,[16] which was also in order.

As to what concerns the negative treatment Bernadette endured, there are *no other specific examples.*

"Bernadette was uneasy," affirmed Soeur Marthe du Rais. "In the infirmary where the two of us were, the mistress of novices often came to see us...and at each visit, she made remarks to test us, and she was good at it. So the Venerable would say to me when she heard her coming, 'What's going to happen to us?'"[17]

Here, we see that Bernadette was not the only one to be treated strictly.

In short, none of the reported incidents went beyond what ordinarily happened to the other novices. Bernadette suffered "reprimands," not "indignities," noted Père C. Payrard.[18] Only she was given a stronger dose and the testing was prolonged, due to the fact that Mère Marie-Thérèse "still enjoyed, following the illness" of the superior general, complete authority over the professed sisters and prevailing influence in the house.[19]

Most of the witnesses comment on this negative treatment in general terms: "I would not have wanted to be in her place," says Soeur Stéphanie Vareillaud, a fellow novice of Bernadette's.[20]

"I said to myself in my lack of fervor, 'What luck not to be Bernadette!'" wrote the same sister in a letter, dated October 16, 1908.[21]

Mère Marie-Thérèse Vauzou
(1825–1907)
Mistress of Novices from July 1861 to January 1881

"It is not good to be Bernadette here," likewise noted Père C. Payrard.[22]

Two witnesses saw a lack of fairness here, even a lack of justice.

"I was painfully impressed by the way our Mère Marie-Thérèse treated Soeur Marie-Bernard. I thought there was something unjust," says Soeur Valentine Gleyrose, who lived at the motherhouse from 1866–1877.[23]

"She was rebuked, most often undeservedly," observed Soeur Marthe du Rais.[24]

However, this was not the general impression. Four witnesses said just the opposite.

"I heard...that the mistress of novices was hard on her.... As for me I noticed nothing," said another fellow novice, Soeur Stanislas Paschal.[25]

"I heard that Soeur Marie-Bernard had to suffer at the hands of the mistress of Novices," recalls another companion, Soeur Eugénie Calmès, "but in the novitiate, I noticed nothing at all. I found it strange, however, that they made so little of the Venerable."[26]

"I don't know anything in particular about the relationship between the Servant of God and the mistress of novices," Soeur Emilie Marcillac answered under oath, "except that it seemed excellent."[27] And yet she was Bernadette's fellow novice from July to November 1866.

Soeur Julienne Capmartin later made a similar statement. Nevertheless, she had personally experienced Mère Marie-Thérèse's severity. The mistress of novices had "really worked me over," to use her own terminology. For a full week she had kept her kneeling in the refectory during the entire lunch, for having missed a meal without permission. She had intentionally skipped over her name while reading out the list of novices called to profession in order to test her. Soeur Julienne showed nothing less than the greatest devotion toward Mère Marie-Thérèse and declared, "I never noticed anything whatsoever that might look like an injustice or an unkindness.... When she spoke to Soeur Marie-Bernard, she maintained her usual attitude and manner; and I am convinced that she always treated her like the others, without deference to be sure, but without any injustice either."[28]

Along with the dark side, we can detect some light. Mère Marie-

Thérèse appreciated Bernadette because she so often sent her troubled novices, as we have seen. So, in her letters, Bernadette sincerely called her, "our good and worthy mistress."[29]

And we have heard Bernadette say, "I owe her much gratitude for the good she has done my soul."[30]

The situation was complicated, as we have seen. It involved a combination of attraction and repression: the "cough signal" that the mistress of novices exchanged with Bernadette when walking by the infirmary is an indication. This unspoken exchange meant on both their parts: "I'm here. I'm waiting for you, aren't you going to call me?" Neither one of them dared take the next step, which would have inevitably brought on resistance in each of them.[31]

Positive incidents are numerous, but we must admit that as far as we can date them, they all took place at the beginning of Bernadette's religious life. Mère Marie-Thérèse set out with a favorable presumption as expressed by her announcement of the visionary's arrival: "You understand...what a grace and what a favor it is for us to welcome Mary's privileged child, and how grateful we must prove to be. For me, it will be one of the greatest joys of my life to see the eyes that have seen the Blessed Virgin."[32]

In the early days, the novices thought they noticed that Mère Marie-Thérèse was "delighted to have Bernadette close by her." She did not deny this but recalled that Bernadette had "resumed the common path."[33]

One day, in the early months, she told Bernadette to go up early to the dormitory, then told the novices Bernadette's story. She repeated to them that they were: "greatly favored by being able to gaze upon the eyes that had seen the Blessed Virgin," relates Soeur Cécile Pagès. "She told us to pay attention when Bernadette raised her eyes to heaven, that her eyes had a heavenly brilliance...."

In giving Bernadette her name in religion on July 29, 1866, Mère Marie-Thérèse stated publicly, "It is only right that I give her the name of the Blessed Virgin, whose privileged child she is."[34]

During Bernadette's first illness, "she visited her every day in the infirmary," related Soeur Emilie Marcillac,[35] "and appeared rather well-disposed."

During this initial period, Mère Marie-Thérèse let slip, "I'm always afraid someone will steal her from us."[36]

And when they thought they would lose her, at the time of her near-death profession (October, 1866), Mère Marie-Thérèse said, "We are not worthy to have her...but we must storm heaven."

After that the atmosphere clouded over. But the mistress of novices had warned Bernadette that "the testing time was about to begin."[37]

For one who has been advised that their pain has meaning, suffering is lessened. My childhood dentist used to tell his patients, "Mister So-and-So, I know that I'm hurting you." And this was greatly appreciated; it calmed the fear and anxiety that the dentist might be making some mistake.

After giving Bernadette this notice, Mère Marie-Thérèse initiated her regime of sternness, without much of a break in the clouds from then on.

How can we explain this attitude? Before all else, it appears to be a failure to understand, a closed-mindedness toward the case of Bernadette.

According to the authoritative witnesses, Mère Marie-Joséphine Forestier[38] and Mère Marie-Thérèse Vauzou, the mistress of novices "did not like Soeur Marie-Bernard."[39] Mère Bordenave even went so far as to say [about the latter], "On those occasions when she spoke to me about the Venerable, I was unable to detect a feeling of friendliness toward her."[40]

The novice mistress was unable to acknowledge Bernadette's holiness, even after her death. Mère Bordenave was amazed at this, for Mère Marie-Thérèse should have appreciated Bernadette's spiritual notes; they had depth and often went in the direction she liked. She used to get letters, testifying to miracles obtained through Soeur Marie-Bernard's intercession.[41]

Despite all that, Mère Marie-Thérèse said and said again, contrary to general opinion and—to tell the truth—in a partly superficial manner: "Bernadette is an ordinary religious."

This was one of her most common expressions. She used it again with Père N. Burosse, chaplain of the orphanage in Lourdes who asked, "Well, Mother, what do you have to say about our little Bernadette?"

"She was a good, ordinary religious."

"Was she devout?"

"Oh, very devout."

"Was she humble?"

"Yes, very humble. She never took pride in the graces she had received."

"Was she obedient?"

"Oh, very obedient!"

"Then, Mother, what more do you want to be able to say that she was a holy religious?"[42]

Mère Marie-Thérèse made comparisons to the benefit of other religious.

"At that time, there was an assistant mistress, Soeur Saint-Michel Graffeuil, a privileged soul who lived constantly with our Lord in the Garden of Olives and to whom the good Lord had given the gift of tears. Our Mother...concluded that Soeur Saint-Michel's devotion was extraordinary, while Soeur Marie-Bernard's was ordinary."[43]

During Bernadette's lifetime, Mère Vauzou had reacted when Soeur Bernard Dalias had said, "I think the first sister to be canonized will be a shepherdess."

"No, no" she snapped, thinking of Père de Laveyne [the founder of the Sisters of Nevers], "it isn't right for the daughter to go before the father!"[44]

When the "Introduction of the Cause of Canonization" was under consideration, Mère Marie-Thérèse's reservations persisted. Soeur Stanislas Paschal heard her exclaim with a "negative" gesture: "Oh! To be able to cast my vote at Bernadette's canonization...."[45]

"On returning from one of my trips to Rome, in 1906," relates Mère Marie-Joséphine Forestier, "as...I was telling her that they had spoken to me about the possibility of introducing Bernadette's cause, she replied, 'Wait until I'm dead!'"[46]

Mère Henri Fabre[47] and Mère Bordenave[48] were all the more surprised since Mère Marie-Thérèse Vauzou offered no serious objection to Bernadette's sanctity other than the incident in which the visionary traced a circle on the ground saying, "Let her who has no self-esteem put her finger here."[49]

The mistress of novices seemed to have understood that Bernadette would have put her own finger there and would have bragged about being free from all pride. But this was definitely not Bernadette's feeling.

What were the motives behind Mère Vauzou's harsh judgments? The witnesses at the beatification process have carefully assembled them:

1. The one that astounded them the most was Mère Vauzou's comparative skepticism about Lourdes. She "scarcely believed" in it, says Soeur Valentine Gleyrose, who heard her influencing the superior general on the matter.[50]

Mère Bordenave, who reported this incident continued, "To myself she said very wistfully one day, 'All the same, the rosebush didn't bloom.' However, she did add, 'The Blessed Virgin showed good taste in choosing that site to appear in.' So I think what Soeur Valentine Gleyrose said was an overstatement."

Likewise, only with reservation do we cite the deposition of J. Le Cerf, echoing the memoirs of Mère Henri Fabre: "Sometimes looking down at the activities of the crowds at the grotto, which she [Mère Vauzou] could see from the window of her room (during the last years of her life) she felt on edge and slammed her shutters."[51]

Following a rousing sermon he had preached at the motherhouse, Canon Boillot had a conversation that he related at the beatification process:

"You're convinced of the events at Lourdes?" Mère Vauzou asked him.

"Certainly, Mother. I'm very convinced of the reality of the wondrous events that have taken place in Lourdes and those that are still taking place."

"And yet, there are bishops who don't believe. I could offer you as an example Bishop Dupanloup, Bishop of Orléans."

"It seems to me, however, that when we study the fact..."

At that point the superior general cut things short with this observation, "If the Blessed Virgin wanted to appear somewhere on earth, why would she choose a vulgar peasant girl with no education, instead of a virtuous and well educated religious?"[52]

"A few days later," Canon Boillot continues, "I had the opportunity to see three sisters on the Council and I shared with them my astonishment at the superior general's observation.[53]

"They answered me, 'Why, you don't know that our venerable Mother has no relish at all for this Lourdes business? She used the very same language with us.'"

This very modern hesitation regarding exceptional supernatural events was due particularly to Mère Vauzou's traditionalism and her suspicion of "new fangled devotions."[54] It was perhaps even more strongly rooted in rigorous Christocentrism. She was in large measure responsible for spreading devotion to the Sacred Heart within the Congregation.[55] She was on the alert for any Marian polarity that might have pushed Christ into the background.

That attitude shocked those who knew her. They even went so far as to say that she "Did not believe in the apparitions."

"That was obviously overstated," noted J. Le Cerf. [56]

On this point, the right note was struck by Soeur Eléonore Cassagnes: "Since they had been speaking about visionaries who had duped the public (after the apparitions) perhaps there remained in Mère Marie-Thérèse Vauzou's mind some doubts on the truth of the apparitions."[57]

"She was not interested in the Lourdes matter," Abbé Jouin also accurately said.[58]

This inflexibility toward the fact of the apparitions eased off as she lay close to death.

She died uttering these words, "Our Lady of Lourdes, safeguard the hour of my death."[59]

2. A second, more conventional motive for Mère Vauzou's judgments was the difference in class, background and education, brought up by Mère Bordenave[60] and numerous other witnesses. "'Oh! She was a little peasant girl,' she used to say.[61] Or else, "I cannot understand the Blessed Virgin's revealing herself to Bernadette. There are so many other souls so refined and so well bred.... Oh, well!"[62]

All of which made Père Payrard think of this comparison: "I compare Bernadette with Joan of Arc...and I believe that Mère Marie-Thérèse would have found Joan of Arc very poorly reared."[63]

3. A third motive, the most pivotal, clearly explains the misunderstandings and tensions: "Mother Marie-Thérèse really wanted the young sisters to lay bare their souls to her.... She found Bernadette too closemouthed."[64]

"She evaluated the piety of the novices in terms of their openness toward her," confirmed Mère Bordenave.[65] Judging from Bernadette's reticence, the mistress of novices "questioned her sensitivity of heart..." "She told me this herself," confides Mère Bordenave.[66]

The silent treatment was mutual. In fact, according to Abbé Febvre, Bernadette was free only with "unsophisticated people like herself," and "would fall silent with less simple people."[67]

Mère Vauzou, "who had a great talent for opening souls when she showed kindness, could also close them when she appeared stern."[68]

Her position grew even more unyielding because Bernadette freely opened up to other superiors, notably to Mère Eléonore Cassagnes, who had her confidence. From this point came "a little resentment in the mind of Mère Marie-Thérèse."[69]

"It also happened that...the Venerable confided her troubles to Soeur Nathalie Portat, the second assistant.... From that, feathers were somewhat ruffled."[70]

Soeur Joseph Garnier attributed this "lack of openness" to Bernadette's shyness: something Mère Bordenave took up again with more nuancing.

The cause appears to be deeper. If Bernadette could not open up, it was because she was not introspective. She avoided analytical probing; she was allergic to learned discussions on the spiritual life. She had nothing to say. It was not her gift to verbalize.

Nevertheless, the witnesses were surprised at Mère Vauzou's failure to understand, given her intelligence, her usually keen judgment and Bernadette's conformity with the essential virtues that Mother loved to find in souls. "Mère Thérèse's lack of sympathy toward Soeur Marie-Bernard is all the more difficult to explain since the Servant of God possessed everything that the mistress of novices valued in souls," said Mère Bordenave.[71] And also, "I can guarantee that if Mère Marie-Thérèse could have penetrated that soul, she would have been so delighted that her affection for her novice might have been too great and Soeur Marie-Bernard's sanctity would have been the loser. She, in fact, had everything the mistress of novices loved best: simplicity, innocence, union with God, love of suffering and surrender to God's good pleasure....

"If all this escaped the all-seeing eye of Mère Marie-Thérèse, it could only be because God allowed it so that she would be able to justify to her delicate conscience the severity she practiced toward Soeur Marie-Bernard."[72]

4. Leaving out these mystical explanations involving "God's permission," the witnesses are in agreement in explaining the misunderstanding between Bernadette and her novice mistress by emphasizing that Mère Vauzou was "impressionable" and "set in her ideas." "With her, impression often overruled reason," wrote Mère Forestier.[73]

"Her impressions of certain people were lasting, and it was difficult to get her to reconsider; we didn't even try," wrote Mère Bordenave.[74]

In this connection, "she was not aware" of her toughness, observed the same witness.[75] In such a shrewd and intuitive person, there was no question of an impenetrable lack of understanding, but rather one riddled with uneasiness. During her first stays in Lourdes, Mère Vauzou said to Mère Villaret, "Every time I had something to say to Bernadette, I tended to say it harshly.... In the novitiate I had novices before whom I would have knelt rather than kneel before Bernadette."[76]

To Père Charles Payrard, a Marist priest, she also said "she realized that sometimes she had been hard on Bernadette. Nevertheless, she believed she was not wrong and thought she was carrying out her duty."[77]

During her retreat in Lourdes, Mère Marie-Thérèse Vauzou revealed her doubts to Père Jean Léonard, abbot of the Cistercian monastery of Fontfroide. She came out of his confessional saying: "I am very happy to have seen this holy man. I was worried about my dealings with Soeur Marie-Bernard; I was afraid I had been too strict with her. I told him why I had acted as I did. Père Jean reassured me and now I am at peace on that subject."[78]

As a result, two months before her death, she said, "God allowed Mère Joséphine Imbert...and me to be severe with Soeur Marie-Bernard in order to keep her humble."[79]

The words of advice that reassured Mère Marie-Thérèse after the fact matched those she received during Bernadette's lifetime. Mère Joséphine the superior general, who half-fashioned her own conduct in agreement with Mère Marie-Thérèse, must have informed the novice mistress about this conversation she had with Abbé Peyramale. "Do you grant any favors, any privileges to Soeur Marie-Bernard? Do you treat her better than her companions?" asked the Curé of Lourdes.

The superior general answered, "Not at all."

"Is that the way it really is?"

"Why yes, I assure you."

Then Monseigneur Peyramale replied, "How happy you make me; otherwise, you would have gone down ten degrees in my estimation, because you could have lost her for me through pride."

If Mère Marie-Thérèse Vauzou was influenced by impressions, she never gave into them except for conscious, well thought out motives, the first being the one that motivated Peyramale and all those who, at that time, were responsible for Bernadette: concern about keeping her humble. On this point the testimonies are countless as well as commonplace.

"Our Mère Marie-Thérèse, before her very delicate and upright conscience, justified the excessive severity with which she treated Bernadette, in the sense that she thought it a duty in light of the glorious mission laid upon her, to strengthen her against temptations to pride or vainglory—something she was wary of in all her girls," wrote, for example, Mère Bordenave.[80]

"The way Mélanie behaved cast doubt on the apparition of the Blessed Virgin at La Salette: this was a reason for caution regarding her novice," she further specified.[81]

5. Another cause for the tension between Bernadette and Mère Vauzou is related to the concealment of emotions typical of that time. Bernadette had her own temperament; she reacted honestly, without pretense. She would occasionally express disagreement and objection—something rarely done by the very young, very submissive girls who came to the novitiate. Consequently, Mère Vauzou wrote in her "confidential comments on the novices" this evaluation of Bernadette: "Inflexible character, very excitable."[82]

She made it a point of honor to test Bernadette on this weakness, and all the more since Bernadette, unable to lose her naturalness, continued to react or to make some "facial expression."[83] Hence the remark we have heard: "Ah! We've wounded that little self-esteem of yours."[84]

Let us not overlook the other half of the picture. Mère Marie-Thérèse recognized Bernadette's good qualities. We have heard her acknowledge to Père Burosse that she was "pious, humble, obedient"[85] and the confidential comment we have just cited ended with these words: "Pious, modest, devout; she was orderly."[86]

In December 1906, shortly before her death, Mère Marie-Thérèse testified, "What struck me about Soeur Marie-Bernard was her coolness toward the world; her disinterestedness, which always made her refuse what was offered to her or her family; her accuracy in giving accounts of the apparitions, which I have heard several times. This appeared to me as the supernatural side of this child, as well as the look in her eyes which had something heavenly about it."[87]

Already in 1869, she had been telling the novices to "look closely when Bernadette raised her eyes to heaven, that her eyes had a very heavenly brilliance."[88]

Lastly, Mère Vauzou had enough sentiment to make, as Abbé Febvre had, an observation as perceptive as this one: "Soeur Marie-Bernard never looked more pleasant than when she was suffering greatly."[89]

Let us add that this positive side surfaced at the end of Mother Vauzou's life.

"In 1897," related Soeur Julienne Capmartin, "I became so sick they thought I was past recovery. Mère Marie-Thérèse came to see me at the clinic on the Rue Blomet in Paris. During her visit, she said, 'Speak to Soeur Marie-Bernard; you'll see that she will get you out of this. We have already prayed to her for you.'"[90]

In Mère Marie-Thérèse's final comments, which read like her last will and testament, we find an echo of her first impressions: "Do not forget how much Mary loves our Institute, since she gave us her privileged child.... Be happy over this predilection of Mary Immaculate."[91]

It remains to be seen how her trying relationship with Mère Vauzou was experienced from Bernadette's point of view.

In the context of Bernadette's desire "to do well," of her keen sensitivity and of the attraction which the personality of the mistress of novices exerted on her, the trial was hard to bear. Bernadette's companions help us feel the strength of Mère Vauzou's influence, made more apparent by the fact that the novitiate was totally dependent on her. There was in her presence something spellbinding which Soeur Justine Pelat's enthusiasm expresses so simply: "Our Mother seemed set on attracting all our hearts and burying them within her own."[92]

The religious never stopped praising her qualities. "She had a very lively faith, genuine piety, great love for the interior life, zeal for souls, a heart of gold. Beneath her cold exterior, she needed to give and also receive a great deal of affection. She exerted a kind of attraction on us and we loved her very much. Her prestige at the motherhouse and in the Institute was considerable and her influence almost decisive, given the sickly condition of Mother General," noted Mère Joséphine Forestier.[93]

"Mère Marie-Thérèse had a high degree of piety; she brought to an active life a very intense interior life," said Mère Bordenave in a similar vein.[94] "She was a noble soul, highly intelligent, large hearted."[95]

Thus Mère Vauzou was elected to head the Congregation in 1881. Her term of office as superior general lasted eighteen years and was one of the most impressive.

"It's as if there were within her a magnet that attracted. She was one of those persons about whom no one could be indifferent. You had to either fear her very much or love her very much. It happened often enough that we did both at the same time. Her manner was such that she brought about torment or enjoyment," wrote Mère Bordenave.[96]

So Bernadette suffered in proportion to her attachment—and the community's attachment—to the mistress of novices.

"When the novice mistress came to see her in the infirmary, I noticed that Soeur Marie-Bernard was very happy to see her and her face beamed," noted Soeur Marcelline Durand.[97]

And we remember with what an "excessively natural" enthusiasm she had leaped to embrace the mistress at one particular homecoming.[98]

Bernadette also suffered in proportion to her other trials which "would have cried out for the soothing help of a mother's sympathy."[99]

It was in this sense that some of the hearsay evidence at the beatification process went so far as to say, "It was a continual martyrdom of the heart."[100] "She suffered greatly from these trials."[101] "She felt acutely the humiliations she was subjected to; she would blush," relates Soeur Joseph Garnier.[102]

Bernadette calmly referred to this suffering in her personal journal in connection with her struggle not to be bested by it.[103]

What particularly impressed the witnesses was that, in her suffering, Bernadette did not "seek out human support,"[104] nor "comfort from her friends."[105] She did not even resort to "making the first move," to which Mère Forestier alluded as follows: "I loved our Mother very much, but then I sometimes certainly had to put up with her temper, especially in the early years. When I later became more intimately acquainted with her nature, I would humbly make the first moves, jumping up to embrace her, and so for a moment the coldness came to a halt; but that wasn't always successful. Did Bernadette understand that this was the way it had to be?"[106]

Most certainly not. But if she had succeeded along that line, would she not have leveled off at a high point of human satisfaction? Would she have become Saint Bernadette?

Furthermore, if she had shown some affection for this prestigious woman to the extent of "burying her heart," to quote Soeur Justine Pelat, [107] would she not have destroyed the personality which is at the human foundation of all her spiritual value?

One other point struck the witnesses: Bernadette "never complained."

"Soeur Marie-Bernard suffered a good deal. I saw her cry, but complain, never," said Soeur Elisabeth Manhès, who had lived with Soeur Marie-Bernard from 1872 to 1879.[108] (This was reported by Mère Bordenave. Soeur Valentine Gleyrose, who knew Bernadette from 1866 to 1871, said the same thing.)[109]

"Soeur Marie-Bernard accepted this very well.... I never heard her say a word against her superiors, nor against anyone else," confirmed Soeur Joseph Caldairou.[110]

"I never heard her complain about what she had to suffer at the hands of the mistress of novices," recalled Soeur Marcelline Durand.[111]

And Mère Eléonore Cassagnes, who one day "found her crying near Saint Joseph's Chapel," testified, "She never complained, although she surely suffered."[112]

Bernadette had so much self-control that Soeur Marthe du Rais said to her one day: "You're very lucky, you are, to let nothing show on the outside; you're unemotional."[113]

Bernadette's attitude toward her mistress of novices was neither bitter nor retreating;[114] even less was it hardened. We have seen her agreeably disagree with the sternness of the mistress of novices,[115] as well as with that of the superior general.[116]

Here, as elsewhere, she appeared "pleasant toward people who had caused her pain."[117] She harbored no grudge against the mistress of novices, who did not spare her. "She always managed to remain remarkably even-tempered...gracious and kind," noted Soeur

Casimir Callery, adding, "She did not allow herself to get discouraged over the difficulties coming from the superior general."[118]

Concerning these difficulties with authority, Bernadette religiously accepted criticism.

"When Mère Marie-Thérèse Vauzou rebuked her, which surprised her companions, she said, 'She's quite right, I'm so proud.'[119] Or again, 'She is quite right.'[120] 'Ah! I understand.'"[121] "I owe her a debt of gratitude for the good she's doing for my soul."[122]

If she was afraid of being scolded by the mistress of novices, she used to say after Mère Vauzou left, "That went really well!" or "All that for heaven!"[123]

In a word, Bernadette assumed the trial on two serious foundations: on the one hand, she readily admitted her limits and her faults, as we have seen. On the other hand, she made an effort "to see God in her superiors."[124] "She never said a single word against them," attested Soeur Joseph Caldairou.[125] That was one trial well under control.

The conclusions of a thorough examination cannot possibly have the flash and flare of the pamphlets and novels that have left their mark on general opinion.

The difficulties between Bernadette and Mère Vauzou stemmed primarily from an objective problem, which was also the case with the superior general: to find a place within the accepted order for an exceptional individual.

They also originated from a very complex network of psychological problems: the lack of understanding between social environments and cultures; between two strong temperaments; between two spiritualities firmly set on different paths and; lastly, from the discomfort of the mistress of novices in confronting the secret of a privileged soul. Facing this extraordinary situation that was beyond her reach, Mère Marie-Thérèse felt a sort of resentment, similar to Doctor Robert Saint-Cyr's having taken the offensive when he realized that his science could not help the visionary of Lourdes he would have so much liked to cure.

Difficulties of this nature were not at all exceptional in those days when religious communities were maintained in very strict hierarchies and encouraged an excessive identicalness. Those individuals who did not rise to the maternal position of superior were generally made to suffer.

Physical Suffering

The most impressive of Bernadette's trials, and the most torment-ing, was definitely sickness. From the age of six, "her stomach, her spleen,"[126] and probably asthma all gave her trouble. After the chol-era epidemic of the summer of 1855, her life was an almost continu-ous series of illnesses whose history we have traced, month by month.

In this trial that left her helpless, Bernadette saw meaning, a ful-fillment of the promise made to her at the grotto....

A superior who came to see her said, "What do you do here, you lazy little thing?"

"Mother, I do my job."

"What is your job?"

"Being sick," she answered pleasantly.[127]

"Suffering is my job," she also told Soeur Marthe du Rais.[128]

What struck most witnesses was her patience, as well as her cour-age. "She had to undergo an operation for a boil under her arm," related Soeur Marthe. "She was so weak that the doctor was reluc-tant. They used no anesthetic to deaden the pain, but she never let out a whimper, neither during the operation nor afterwards.... The doctor was amazed at this...."[129]

"You can pull; I'm pain-proof, like cats," we heard her say on another occasion.[130]

"Not one complaint," other witnesses stressed.[131] It took an aw-ful combination of suffering and weakness to make her groan. "Pay no attention to my contortions; I'm happy to suffer," she would say.[132]

The way she sent out news about herself in her letters showed us how little preoccupied she was about herself. She mentioned her health only when asked, with no lengthy descriptions and always stressing the positive side. Her attitude was the same in her conver-sations. "Dear Sister, how are you feeling today?" Soeur Apolline asked her. Bernadette smiled at her and said, "The same today as yesterday and yesterday as today."[133]

She was usually cheerful, available to visitors, focused on them and not on herself—on this all those who knew her were in agree-ment.

"She was able to submit and repeat her 'Let it be done,'" said her confessor, Abbé Febvre.[134]

She indicated the motive for acceptance as follows: "There is no way at all of not accepting it, since this comes from the good Lord."[135] More simply put, "The good Lord sends it to me."[136]

To Soeur Marthe du Rais, she said, "It would be a shame to suffer so much and lose all the merit."[137]

And if any of the sisters felt sorry for her, she would even say, according to Soeur Dominique Brunet, "It is so good, so sweet and above all, so beneficial to suffer."[138]

The witness was probably exaggerating, because Bernadette was not moving toward "dolorism." She accepted suffering, but didn't go looking for it. On hearing Mademoiselle Claire's heroic remark: "I suffer a lot, but it is not enough; may the good Lord bring on more," Bernadette declared both wisely and humbly, "I wouldn't do that much."[139]

It was through experience that she took comfort from traditional recommendations and encouragements concerning sufferings: "They must be accepted; nothing happens without God's permission."[140] "You'll be rewarded for this one day."[141]

There was a more meaningful test: we have seen her maintain her sense of humor and joke about her troubles.[142] When pain was most unbearable, she took refuge in the cross of Christ. It was her landmark, "the bedrock" of her "thoughts," said Soeur Marthe du Rais.

"Every Friday at three o'clock, she never failed to recall the sufferings of our Lord."[143]

Drowning in pain, she would kiss her crucifix, related Soeur Gabrielle Vigouroux;[144] and during her final hours, when she was no longer able to hold it, she had it pinned to her, as we have seen. It was not merely for protection; it was an identification: "I am like him."[145]

"In her bed," she confided to Soeur Bernard Dalias, "she sometimes held her arms out in the form of a cross to unite herself to our Lord's passion."[146]

It was on the level of identification that she could find joy in suffering: "What folly to withdraw within oneself when our Lord asks for our hand to drive a nail through it." "From now on, the more I am crucified, the more I shall rejoice," she wrote.[147] And again, "I'm happier with my crucifix on my bed of pain than a queen on her throne."[148]

This chapter has dealt with the clear areas of her trial. We have reserved for the next chapter a discussion of her hidden trial, which we can only glimpse in its obscurity and which Bernadette herself felt was the most serious.

5. "...But in the next"

Bernadette made an effort to see in her sufferings a pledge and a promise: "The Blessed Virgin did not lie to me."[1]

She was referring to the words of February 18, "I do not promise to make you happy in this world, but in the next."

The fulfillment of the first part guaranteed the fulfillment of the last, which formed the positive, hidden aspect of the promise. Bernadette commented, "The first part of these words is coming true; that, I'm holding on to, I'm sure of getting it...."[2]

Like Saint Paul, she was anxious "to finish the race" (2 Tm 4:7). "The end is long in coming," she said.[3]

To Soeur Marthe du Rais, who nursed her very often during her attacks those last four years, she said several times on regaining consciousness, "It won't be this time, not yet. That's really too bad."[4]

Recalling her "deathbed profession" Bernadette commented, "It's too bad that I didn't pass on. I missed my chance. Here, we just soil ourselves...."[5]

In this same regard she confided to Soeur Marthe, "They say there are saints who didn't go straight to heaven because they didn't desire it enough. That won't be true in my case."[6] And again, from the depths of her sufferings: "Heaven! Heaven! Happy are those who are there!"[7]

This was a theme of her encouragements to those who were suffering: "One day we'll go to heaven" (to Louise Brusson in 1868).[8]

"Just a few more hours of suffering" (to Soeur Julie Ramplou in 1873).[9]

"In heaven...we are happy" (to Jeanne Jardet in 1877).[10]

"Heaven": this word has little appeal for people today. They feel overwhelmed by the afterlife, unable to picture another world that would not simply duplicate this one. Caught in the grim current of "demythologizing," they limit themselves to a dynamic perception of a hidden love, destined to last and to be revealed after being fulfilled in this life. In Bernadette's day, heaven was preached straightforwardly. That word defined in a real, though often naive, physically perceptible and even customized way, the eschatological hopes essential to Christ's message. Nevertheless, Bernadette did not "mythicize" on this theme. She didn't "picture" the hereafter. She took it as a word of God, according to the Gospel, which cannot lie. She did not rest on the promise received on February 18, of being "happy in the next world."

Soeur Marthe du Rais expressed her surprise to Bernadette, "I don't understand this fear. You're sure of your fate."

"Not too sure,"[11] Bernadette replied.

She considered the Virgin's promise as conditional. "One proud thought would be enough..." she told Soeur Marcelline Lannessans.[12]

She repeated countless times, probably in different forms, an observation that struck a number of witnesses: "They think I'm a saint.... When I'm dead, they'll come and touch holy pictures and rosaries to me, and all the while I'll be getting broiled on a grill in purgatory. At least...promise me you'll pray a lot for the repose of my soul."[13] Or again, "They'll say, 'Oh! That little saint'[14]...and it will be very hot in purgatory."[15]

To Père Payrard who reminded her of the promise of happiness made by the Virgin of Massabielle, Bernadette answered, "Yes, but only if I do what is required."[16]

For her, heaven was not a shining fantasy, a glowing meditation; it was the mysterious fulfillment of a promise, the conclusion of an obligation, the incentive to action.

"All that is good for heaven."[17]

"All that is nothing. You really have to suffer to deserve heaven."[18]

"Let's work for heaven; all the rest is nothing."[19]

That is what she told a discouraged sister: "Have confidence; this is only for a while...you'll be rewarded in heaven."[20] And also, "Let's do everything to earn heaven; let's offer up our work, our sufferings."[21]

"It's an installment for purgatory and it will count toward heaven."[22]

She didn't understand the hereafter in a magical sense, but as Saint Paul explained it. "It is necessary for the old man to die," she told Soeur Philippine Molinéry.[23]

In the same way, Bernadette didn't turn toward the oversimplified contrast according to which a maximum of dissatisfaction was required to buy a maximum of satisfaction; servitude, to achieve freedom. She expressed the contrast between earthly riches and the joys of heaven according to the logic of salvation: given but at the same time merited, future, yet already present.

But she had a sense of the continuity between the present time and the age to come. And so she considered the novitiate to be "heaven on earth," an expression she often repeated orally as well as in writing.

Here, too, her experience was linked with Saint Paul's. She could glimpse in this "earthly death," a pledge, a down payment, so that heaven would be nothing other than an unveiling. She knew that even "wounds would become glorious."[24] That is why, although tested beyond all imagining, Bernadette is a joyful saint. She knew how to cling to everything she lived as a gift of God. She saw in suffering itself "a caress of the Divine Spouse," as she one day told Julie Garros. She considered it "madness to withdraw within oneself."[25]

Bernadette knew how to live—not in a private conservation with a lonely God—but in a steadfast love of others in Jesus Christ. It was not in the sense of isolation that she spoke of Jesus alone.

She did not understand heaven in an individualistic sense, but as permanence and the fulfillment of every friendship. "I won't forget anyone," she said.[26]

Likewise in her letter to the Pope in 1876:[27] "The weapon of sacrifice will fall but that of prayer will follow me to heaven, where it will be much more powerful."

Sister Thérèse of the Child Jesus would later say with greater style, "I want to spend my heaven doing good on earth."

Thus did Bernadette in her shattered body radiate joy and even cheerfulness—not sadness. Thus did several of her correspondents recall from her letters this fact before all else: she was happy.[28]

It was on the level of love, freely given, that Bernadette, condemned to "uselessness," was capable of consciously discovering her job. This brings us to what was deepest in her life, something that explains all the rest: charity.

6. Charity

Bernadette didn't consider the words she heard during the apparitions as a message of salvation sufficient unto itself. She saw them as guidelines orienting her toward the love revealed in a tradition she could adopt.

This was the tradition she had received in her family and in her parish, then later, within the framework of her religious family. The spirituality of the Sisters of Charity, founded by Dom de Laveyne in 1683, and the message of Lourdes—poverty, prayer and penance—coincided exactly. The great themes of Lourdes were also the major themes of the Congregation, which Père Ravier sums up in these words: "Prayer, penance, poverty, service of souls, charity toward the sick and the poor."[29]

It was within this framework, weighed down by the nineteenth century's resistance to change, that Bernadette would discover her path and her life.

Bernadette's Fundamental Attitude

The major contribution of the Congregation was probably to help her center everything explicitly on charity. The founder Dom de Laveyne had grasped its critical role according to Saint Paul. Bernadette could read in the handbook, given to each religious: "Your greatest rule is the one Jesus Christ has laid down for you, that is, charity. It is enough for you to be charitable to fulfill your rule perfectly, because he who has charity fulfills the whole of God's law, according to Saint Paul" (Rom 13:8–15; Gal 5:14).

To Bernadette charity was surely the heart of the matter, the essential. Here too, it was not so much a word, but rather an exacting attitude. Her whole life expressed this, even in the smallest matters.

"I never heard her say an unbecoming word, nor fail in charity," said Soeur Marie Delbrel.[30]

"Never did I hear a word against anyone slip from her mouth," confirmed Soeur Bernard Dalias.

"Never...a word against anyone whatsoever," maintained Soeur Philippine Molinéry.[31]

"Never a single spiteful word," recalled Soeur Madeleine Bounaix.[32]

Even her repartees, often sharp and witty, were "never hurtful," Soeur Joseph Garnier noted.[33] We could multiply these statements indefinitely.[34]

Bernadette knew how to keep her place, acknowledge her faults and "ask forgiveness for a spontaneous reaction that hurt others."[35]

"I witnessed some of her temperamental quips," relates Soeur Philippine Molinéry,[36] "but I never left the room without seeing our

Dom de Laveyne
(1653–1719)
Founder of the Sisters of Charity of Nevers

dear patient make amends for her momentary slips with a sincere apology. One time, among others, I had upset her a bit by being careless with her linen. She snipped at me, 'Now it will have to be mended....' Realizing that this hurt me, she said to me with tears in her eyes, 'I ask you to forgive me for speaking to you like that. Pray for my conversion.'"[37]

When she was reminded that, on the other hand, someone might have hurt her, she would say, "I've forgotten all about it." The usual state of her soul was not to remember the annoyances she suffered.[38]

We have heard the full story of those kind or comforting words with which Bernadette was gifted. We have seen her accept disappointments good-naturedly. The "burnt stew," which "she ate laughingly," as if it had been perfect,[39] has a symbolic value.

She knew how to keep her companions from being reprimanded. "A sister who clumsily broke a saucer did not dare admit it to the sister bursar. 'Give that to me,' said Soeur Marie-Bernard. She brought it to the sister bursar and received the scolding that would have been given to her companion."[40]

We have seen her, throughout her sicknesses, facilitate the work of her caregivers, show concern for their attendance at divine worship and insist that "her night-watchers sleep."[41]

To her fellow patient who got up to help her during her asthma attacks, she said, "Please, don't get up; you're really annoying me. If I can't sleep during the night, I can make up for it later. It's not the same for you. Calmly get your rest."[42]

"A sister who had taken care of her for three months in the infirmary...told her, 'How well you accept everything I bring you.'

"'I have to,' Bernadette responded, 'it's the good Lord who sends it to me.'"[43]

Her Humanness

There was nothing overly submissive or calculated about these attitudes. They originated not from virtuous trickery but from the heart. They were the expressions of a lively and sometimes sharp temperament.

Bernadette had "character," as they say. She was no "cushy feather bed," where good and evil could disappear and blend together in a kind of fuzzy neutral zone. She could react and elicit reactions from others.

She had an energy, a capacity for reaction and "distraction," in Pascal's sense of the word, which was accounted as one of her "liabilities." People were surprised to see her "become erratic," especially in the extremes of her endless sufferings.

"Certain signs of impatience, certain tendencies toward anger, even certain sharp comments sometimes made a sorry impression on the sisters who were taking care of her," wrote Bishop Forcade.[44]

He added, "These little peculiarities came solely from the uncontrollable agitation brought on by some of her attacks.... She was not at all responsible. In the very depths of her soul, she remained just as submissive and resigned, even thankful and joyful."[45]

Abbé Febvre adds a modification which at first sight differs. Although Bishop Forcade seems to situate these abnormalities in times of sickness, her confessor observed "her temperamental whims, especially when she was feeling well. Gripped by illness, she became more cheerful. The erraticism disappeared."

If we understand correctly, we must differentiate two things:

1. On the one hand, the almost clownish "whims" or "jokes" with which she would react when sickness laid her low. It was the doctor, as we have seen, who served as the target of Bernadette's colorful remarks, even in her letters: "Let him not return."[46] And in a letter of December 8, 1876, "I'm beginning to think that he's losing his wits."[47]

Certain medications may have brought on the hyperactivity mentioned by Bishop Forcade.

2. On the other hand, there were defensive reactions in moments of relative health: healthy responses, with no bitterness or ulterior motives.

"Madame X...of Nevers came to the community one day to tell Soeur Victoire, then portress, that her little boy was quite sick. She brought a crocheted baby blanket, convinced that if Bernadette worked on this blanket and it were then placed over her child, he would be cured. After getting permission from our venerable Mère, Soeur Victoire went upstairs to the infirmary where Soeur Marie-Bernard was, and said in a questioning tone of voice, speaking to all the sisters who were there with the visionary, 'Madame X...brought this blanket, which she has botched up, I think, and asks if someone might not be able to fix it for her.'

"'Well, isn't this nice,' teased Soeur Marie-Bernard. 'These fine ladies ruin their work and we're the ones who have to mend it. Oh well, give it to me anyway; I'll try to straighten it out.'"[48]

And indeed, she did. The blanket was placed over the little boy, who got well, affirmed the witness, Soeur Louise de Guiran.[49]

Soeur Philippine Molinéry also noted a sharp comment aimed at Soeur Gabrielle de Vigouroux, who had replaced her as head infirmarian on November 5, 1873:[50] "There was a little uneasiness between Bernadette and the infirmarian.... One day, the latter was tired and went to bed. An elderly religious, Soeur Elisabeth Auvray... came into the infirmary and said to the ones who were there, 'You have made your infirmarian sick.'

"'If she's sick,' retorted Soeur Marie-Bernard, 'so are we; and if she got tired being with us, it's her duty.'"[51]

Bernadette's temperament contained a normal dose of assertiveness, in the sense of a defensive instinct. It was a force, a quality, which facilitated the carrying out of her responsibilities. It was the human side of her charity, for in order to love, one must first exist. It takes an impetus and even some violence, to convert ourselves to communion with others. Otherwise, there are only theoretical connections among people. Bernadette was alert to this conversion and quick to make amends for the rough flare-ups of her nature. We have seen this throughout her life.

Sense of Humor

Another aspect of Bernadette's human face was the distance she maintained in all circumstances—regarding herself, the people around her, and even her sufferings. This is something we shall call, if you will, her cheerfulness or her sense of humor. Her confessor underlined this quality. It is an indefinable grace, beyond the reach of those who are unable to keep a similar distance, to conceal their tenderness behind this reserve. For Bernadette, just as for all those who have received and nurtured this gift, it was not a question of any specific or definite activity. At one point we had considered assembling some examples in a "humor section." We had to give up this idea, however, because it involved a condition of being, a dimension of the person. One who possesses a sense of humor always has it; one who does not will never have it.[52]

In the active and generous life of Bernadette we discover the deep roots of her attitude toward others.

Friendship

Friendship was not some abstract virtue for Bernadette, but a lively sensitivity to others.

She had her natural preferences. That which she had for her father during her childhood bothered her briefly. She appreciated music and musicians: Soeur Joseph Garnier, who directed the singing,[53] and Soeur Claire Lecoq, the organist,[54] who was a friend to her. And Soeur Claire was not Bernadette's only friend.

"She had a true friendship for me, which she always kept. I had replaced her close friend, Soeur Claire Lecoq, at the organ; and when she died, I took her place in the infirmary," confided Soeur Casimir Callery.[55]

Bernadette saw no virtue in hiding her affections. "I loved your sister very much," she told Soeur Gonzague Champy.[56]

And we have seen the warm welcome she could give her countrywomen: among others, Léontine Mouret, her fellow postulant,[57] and Julie Garros.[58]

We have observed her attraction to children, closely connected with her attraction to the poor, in keeping with the Gospel (Mt 18:2–5; 19:13–14; cf. 11:25). She acknowledged this weakness for "whatever was small," beginning with the lambs she had shepherded at Bartrès.[59] We have seen her spontaneously take a respite on the busy day of March 4, 1858, to play with the little Clarens girls, and have noted that she found herself on an equal footing with very young children just about everywhere she went: Cauterets, Bagnères, Momères, and Nevers, when the children visited her.[60]

"She loved children and was beloved by them," said her cousin Jeanne Védère.[61] This was true throughout her life.

"I love the little orphan girls very much," she told Soeur Claire Bordes, who was leaving for her assignment at Mâcon.[62]

"I really love the 'little bonnets,'" she said about the postulants,[63] who, at that time, arrived long before the age of twenty and were often very childish.

She was able to recognize or create bonds between herself and her various companions with the insignificant trifles that form the fabric of daily life. She loved Soeur Bernard Dalias, because she too was "a Bernard," and Soeur Marcillac, because she was the same height (four feet, six inches). "She would stand next to me," said the latter, "move her hand over our heads and say pleasantly, 'How could you expect me not to like you? You're my match.'"[64]

We have seen her make acrostics with the names of her friends, Soeur Bernard Dalias and Soeur Marcelline Lannessans. She explained the meaning of these word and letter games with this introductory phrase:[65] "A way of inscribing in my heart the name of...."[66]

Soeur Marthe du Rais, a beneficiary of these acrostics, drew a portrait of Bernadette's friendship: "She was an excellent friend, keeping a faithful remembrance of those she loved. She was not free with her friendship, but when she had given it, she never took it back. As for me, I was the object of her friendship; she remained my friend till she died...she sometimes took me to task severely, but I knew it was for my own good; and if she noticed that she had hurt my feelings, she would come quickly to apologize...."[67]

This friendship found appropriately distinctive expressions. "One day," says Soeur Emilie Marcillac, "I went to Nevers and went to get something to drink at the infirmary as I always did. She was interested in my work, in my health. That day, she said, 'Ah! There you are! I had a feeling you'd be coming today.' As I was leaving her, I asked for her prayers. She replied, 'How could I not pray for you? I owe you that for several reasons. You've taken care of me; we were clothed with the habit together, professed together, were born the same month, almost the same day—I cannot forget you.'"[68]

To Julie Garros, at the moment of their final separation she happily remarked, "There's no need to give a memento when we love each other."[69]

If Bernadette avoided the visits of curiosity seekers,[70] she welcomed those of friends, the simple of heart, or visits from home.

One day, a soldier turned up at Saint-Gildard's. He came from Lourdes and had been Bernadette's childhood friend. Soeur Dominique, who was sent to tell her, knew Bernadette's distaste for visitors. Sister prepared her defense, "Dear Sister, this time it's someone from your hometown. It's young Piarre."

"Oh," said Bernadette. "If it's young Piarre, I'll be right there."

"So she went down and spent a long time chatting with the soldier from Lourdes. As he was leaving...Piarre...asked her if she would be willing to see a few of his comrades who wanted to meet her. Bernadette agreed...and prepared a whole variety of religious objects...spoke a brief word of encouragement to them and then distributed her treasures among them."[71]

Bernadette's friendships found a home in her prayer. She roved freely in the communion of saints with a predilection for Saint Aloysius Gonzaga, Saint Stanislaus Kostka, Saint Bernard, her patron, and especially Saint Joseph—the saint she spoke of most frequently.[72] She put him first after the Virgin and used to say, "He's my father."[73]

7. God Alone

In all of this, Bernadette was living only one love: the love of God, "the focus of all her thoughts and all her words."[74] Everything was directed toward this center.

Often, and on the spur of the moment, she would say, "How good God is!"[75] "Let us love the good Lord!"[76] Hers was a love founded on gratitude.

During a retreat, Soeur Hortense Gauthier found her crying. "What's wrong, Soeur Marie-Bernard?" she asked.

"I have received so many graces and I'm afraid I haven't measured up."

God was the One from whom she expected everything.

"How I need God's help," she told her confessor, Abbé Febvre.[77]

Before everything else, God's will was her reference point, right from her childhood.

"God wants it; we must always want what he wants," she said, according to Soeur Gonzague Champy.[78] Or, "My God, whatever you want and however you want it!"[79]

She often told God in her sufferings, "I offer them up to you. Your will be done."[80] "It's the good Lord who wants this, the good Lord who permits this."[81] "...The good Lord's will, this I prefer to everything else."[82] "Nothing happens without God's will."[83] "We must accept what the good Lord sends."[84] "I submit myself to God's will; I want nothing but His will."[85]

We could multiply such quotations.

Soeur Gabrielle de Vigouroux, her infirmarian, observed count-less signs of a "constant union with God."[86]

"When she received unmerited scoldings...Bernadette would say, 'The good Lord sees my intentions. *Fiat!*' And she maintained the same inner tranquillity...."[87]

"You're very lucky, you are, not to let anything show externally...I can't do that," Soeur Marthe du Rais told her.[88]

From her union with God, came her concern for the spread of the Gospel[89] and her horror of sin, for others as well as for herself: "If only I could shake the dust from my soul like we shake the dust from the altar rugs," she said (probably when she was sacristan).[90]

This desire sprang not from fear but from love. "I love the good Lord; I don't want to offend him," she said.[91] This was also the reason for her outburst of joy when Abbé Febvre explained that lacking intention, there was no mortal sin.[92]

Bernadette's statements on the love of God are the most vital and perhaps the most numerous. She said, "Love the good Lord, it's all there."[93]

"My God, take my heart. Set it on fire!" Julie Garros heard her say.[94]

Such longings explain the spontaneous desire she expressed during her novitiate: "Mother, bring me back the love of God!"[95]

One of her most frequent prayers was, "My God, I love you."[96]

To express the all-encompassing nature of this transcendent love, Bernadette would occasionally use exclusive and radical phrasing: "Let us seek *only* the glory of God."[97] "Let us work *only* for God."[98] "Don't work for creatures, you're wasting your time; work for God."[99] And following another version from the same witness: "We mustn't linger over creatures; we must go straight to God."[100]

In a more colorful way, she also said, "Run along, creatures; we've got God."[101]

In one particular instance, she went so far as to assert to Soeur Julienne Capmartin, "What we love too much, God does not love."[102]

Bernadette's whole attitude contradicts anything negative or re-strictive that could be found in these exclusions. She didn't look down on human beings. She didn't dichotomize soul and body. She loved the whole person and every person in God himself; and this, in large measure, explains her preferences: "The poor are God's friends," she told Soeur Marthe du Rais.[103]

For her, God was not an abstract idea. He was Jesus Christ. She was united with him particularly in his humanity, in his sufferings, which she had the feeling she was continuing. We have seen this, little by little, through her reflections: "Put yourself in the Garden of Olives."[104] "See yourself like our Lord on the cross."[105]

Her writings also corroborate this outlook. She lived the life of a spouse as indicated in the ritual for the reception of the habit,[106] as a complete gift of herself that no obstacle, no suffering could discourage. This theme, which restraint and modesty concealed in her conversations, was expressed forcefully and soberly in her writings.[107] She knew Jesus Christ, not on the elementary level of human attraction, but as God. And it is on this level that we must understand this theme, so evident in her writings: "Jesus alone."[108]

She found the final word of her spirituality inscribed over the main entrance of Saint-Gildard's. There had been engraved this motto, also featured on the coat of arms of the Congregation: *God alone.*[109] These words, which she repeated without prompting, sum up in a powerful phrase what had been for her a constant orientation.

Such is Bernadette's sanctity on the level of clear expressions and explicit words, the object of our study. These words may appear hackneyed and lusterless. And they are. Yet a living light can be glimpsed through the trite language, like the torches carried by Gideon's soldiers.... Can we go beyond appearances and allow ourselves to be touched by this hidden light?

Chapter 27

— ⚜ —

Bernadette's Secret

What do people mean when they call Bernadette "the most secretive of all the saints"?

This mythical expression seems to have been suggested by the "secrets" received by Bernadette during the apparitions, which so intrigued those around her, as we have gradually seen. We must begin here, if only to demythologize.

1. The Secrets of Massabielle

We have elsewhere made an exhaustive study of all the facts relating to the three secrets and the prayer entrusted to Bernadette on the bank of the Gave with this stipulation: "I forbid you to tell this to anyone."

She strictly observed this order and kept these confidences solely to herself. She always answered prying people by saying something like, "You're too curious; you won't find out anything."[1] "Do you know what a secret is?"[2] "I was ordered to be silent."[3]

However undiscoverable, these secrets are not mysterious. The exhaustive study of the data[4] leads to the following two conclusions:

1. They do not concern "France or the world or the Church or the Pope or others"; they concern only Bernadette herself.

"This secret is for me," she told Abbé Sacareau.[5]

"I alone," she emphasized to Père de Lajudie.[6]

In Nevers, she kept on repeating, "They're mine."[7] "It's my business."[8]

2. The secrets probably involved short and simple words, like all the words in the Lourdes message: words tailored to the visionary, who had not received much schooling and had great difficulty remembering sentences containing ten to twelve syllables.

As for the daily prayer she had been taught, Bernadette reportedly said to one of her companions, "All I know is my little prayer. It is geared to my afflictions. It wouldn't teach you anything at all."[9]

In a word, all of this was given to her as a help in leading a difficult life.

Certain theories have been put forward: aren't the secrets directed toward Bernadette's testimony, money to be turned down, certain aspects of her vocation, her sufferings or her death?[10] This is pure speculation.

What really matters is that the secrets played a part in Bernadette's life. They were manifested in her behavior, even though we can't clearly pinpoint where. They are part of a whole, in which their role is not discernible. Nevertheless this whole is decipherable. That is what is important.

2. The Secret Trial of the Final Years

Over and above the "secrets" entrusted during the apparitions, another particular mystery has aroused the curiosity of biographers—the personal trial Bernadette referred to when she told Julie Garros in 1873: "It's really painful not to be able to breath, but it's much worse to be tortured by interior distress. It's horrible."[11]

Now the attacks of suffocation she had were very serious, so serious that people wondered at times whether she would survive.

Soeur Marthe du Rais gives similar testimony: "One day, I found her all in tears—that often happened to her. I said to her, 'Soeur Marie-Bernard, why are you crying? Are you sick?'

"She answered, 'Oh, no! It's not that.... If you only knew everything that's going on inside me.... Pray for me!'"[12]

Soeur Marthe thought attacks from the devil were involved. This cliché casts no light for us on the nature of the trial, even if the following commentary from the same witness is tacked on: "Several times, I saw her sprinkling her bed with holy water and on several occasions heard her saying, 'Begone grappin!... Leave me alone. I want nothing to do with you.'"[13]

That Bernadette blamed her trials on the spirit of darkness and that Soeur Stanislas Tourriol heard her say: "Go away!"[14] does not tell us what the trial was. In his *Histoire intime des apparitions* (Intimate History of the Apparitions), published in 1898, Estrade described it thus: "During the final years of her life, she was assailed with spiritual terrors, a thousand times more terrifying than physical sufferings. She confessed imaginary faults and considered herself a great sinner. The innocent child spoke of the apparitions only to say that she 'had been unworthy' and that 'through her lack of gratitude' she deserved to be condemned.... God put an end to this anguish only at the moment when he was preparing to crown his beloved daughter."[15]

Indeed, we must make allowances for Estrade's literary exhibitionism. But he was embroidering on a hard fact he may have gotten from Père Sempé.

Bernadette's last confesssor, Abbé Febvre, corroborated, "She often blamed herself...for not 'giving back' to God in return for the graces received. Consequently, she asked her companions to pray for her.

"'I'm afraid,' she would say. 'I've received so many graces and made so little use of them.'"[16]

To Soeur Hortense Gauthier, who found her crying—just as Soeur Marthe had—she also indicated the reason for her distress: "I've received so many graces! And I'm worried that I haven't really lived up to them."[17]

There we see a definite trial for Bernadette, and Père Ravier stands on extremely solid ground when he concludes that Bernadette's trial was her fear of not corresponding with grace.[18]

However, this was one of the sufferings most clearly described by Bernadette. It was verified very soon, as early as 1867.[19] So this is not the secret trial which seems to become apparent from 1874 onward.

If it seems plausible that she could find herself in this quandary, then what might the new and secret element be?

We find ourselves drawn toward two working hypotheses. In 1877, Bernadette expressed to Bishop Bourret the fear of "being mistaken" about the apparitions. This phrase opens up horizons that lay unsuspected in her writings. It tends to reveal a trial that took place at the very core of the ardor that gave Bernadette's life its direction.

Beyond this precise fact, we are led to wonder whether or not there had been more seriously, over and above the well-known trial that struck Bernadette in the sensitive area of her hope, a trial touching her very faith.

3. Transparency

The preceding analysis has enabled us to put Bernadette's "secrets" in their proper perspective. They do not constitute an aberration or area of mystery. The secrets are instead elements difficult to define within a complex whole, precisely because they are transparent. They are a bit like a particular note, a particular beat that reveals a musician's personality without making it easily identifiable at first sight, and without allowing one to separate the note or beat from the overall piece.

The Secret of the Gospel

The real question concerns not the particular secrets, which we have just recalled, but an all-embracing secret, better called "mystery," which Christ expressed this way in the Gospel: "I bless you, Father, Lord of heaven and earth, for hiding these things from the learned and clever and revealing them to mere children" (Mt 11:25).

Bernadette's real secret is perhaps, quite simply, simplicity. Nothing is more hidden than transparency. So let us try to decipher this inclusive mystery, of which the "secrets" are but individual elements.

1. Bernadette's secret is first of all the impenetrable silence of early childhood. Our research was unable to reveal much about this anonymous little girl. The first chapter of this book is evidence of that. It covers more than a third of Bernadette's life, but remains virtually a blank like the "unexplored territories" on ancient maps of the world. And yet, the little we do know, beginning with the very silence of Bernadette, bears an amazing resemblance to what developed later and whose culmination was the suffering and total abandonment of her final days. It is tempting to think that everything was already there in the poor little urchin of Lourdes, in the shep-

herdess of Bartrès, humbly devoted to God in the underdevelopment and suffering which were her destiny.

This is only a theory, of course, but it offers so much light that it is hard to discount. One thing must be considered as certain: on the threshold of the apparitions, everything about Bernadette was already present in principle—the essential had been given, her story of grace had already reached its first stage of maturity. Besides, isn't it one of the laws of God's action that the fundamental elements of the gift come before its outward revelation? And so, at the very outset of the Annunciation, the moment she emerged from the shadows, the Virgin Mary was hailed as the *Kecharitoméne,* the "highly favored one of God." Everything that followed brought out the grace that over a long and hidden period the Lord had been planting in her.

Certain aspects of Bernadette's childhood revealed this preapparition light. One of these was the little saying she used to repeat to herself in her many difficulties: "When the good Lord permits it, we don't complain. When we desire nothing, we have what we need."

In the same sense we remember the rosary she automatically clutched in her apron pocket seconds before the first apparition. This was already the instrument of her modest prayer, now an automatic reaction. It was already the sign of a presence at the moment when there appeared before her in the shadowed niche, the woman clothed with the sun.

In a word, everything was already, more or less clearly, in place at that moment when Bernadette entered history: poverty, prayer, penance, a certain habitual presence of the Virgin Mary in the communion of saints. From that time on, there is a feeling that the rest was nothing more than the unfolding of that earlier, fundamental gift. The remainder of Bernadette's life—what we have called the zone of clarity, including the grace of the apparitions—would be a development of her obscure beginnings.

Doesn't acknowledging that everything was given to Bernadette very early on amount to an obvious observation? She gratuitously received baptism, which, in a sense, contains everything. Indeed, that factor counts for something. But here we are thinking of holiness; in other words, the lived evolution of this fundamental gift. Why does it appear so pure in Bernadette? This too is a mystery of a free gift, but it is also the mystery of a response freely given, of an instinct that could faithfully adhere to the essential.

Bernadette did not live all this in isolation. She owed much to the surroundings that formed her. From her environment, a Christian environment, she received faith and baptism, which are inseparable, for the sacraments are the signs of a communal faith. They have no meaning, they are inconceivable apart from faith. But to say that Bernadette received her faith in the context of a Christian community that was for her the concrete realization of the People of God, is to state an ordinary fact.

More precisely, Bernadette knew how to bring to life, in an exceptionally pure way, good examples given to her in her own impoverished family. The generosity of her parents, the quality of their hospitality, their spontaneity of heart, their mutual understanding, even in ruin and its accompanying slander, in spite of everything that was done to divide them, one against the other, these are the qualities best supported by the evidence. The way they were able to accept all this before God and their fidelity to prayer—these too are clearly in evidence. Despite a great lack of verbal and intellectual skills, which connects her to Mary of Galilee, Bernadette was able to discern, benefit from, and live in an exceptionally pure manner the grace of the poor in keeping with the heart of God. And so the child was ready to receive the severe message of February 18, 1858, which summed up her past so well and at the same time indicated the plan for her vocation on earth and beyond: "I do not promise to make you happy in this world but in the next."

2. The message of the apparitions expressed and confirmed what Bernadette was already living. It commanded her not only to repeat the words of the simple message over which she sometimes stumbled—especially those words directed toward establishing the pilgrimage—but also to bear witness to the grace she was already living, by letting it shine through her entire being: poverty, prayer, penance, daughterly self-surrender to the Blessed Virgin, and with the Virgin, to God. It is in this sense that Bernadette was very quickly considered to be the best proof of the message of Lourdes.

3. Her life in Nevers went in the same direction. Dom de Laveyne wanted his religious "to be, first of all, perfect Christians, models for the people."[20] Your life always "lies open to the eyes of all," he told them, "and you are destined to teach them by your ex-

Dom de Laveyne's cell in the sacristy of the Church of Saint-Saulge.
It was here that he rediscovered the secret of the Gospel.

ample how the Gospel truths must be practiced, how to be authentic Christians."[21]

Bernadette instinctively returned to that source. At the height of the nineteenth century, that is to say, when legalism was at its strongest, she returned spontaneously to the original spirit of the Gospel without criticizing the oppressive atmosphere of the times in which she lived.

Here too, the true secret of Bernadette was her transparency, the simplicity that made her accept so many things—some out of inclination, others out of obedience—without ever ceasing to be herself.

She had the ability to derive benefit from human realities and divine demands; from humiliations and admiration; from her own temperament and obedience; from the Rule and the Gospel. Her secret was her ability to respond to human demands and the promptings of the Holy Spirit.

She undertook all this humbly, day by day, forgetful of herself, very simply giving of herself, looking upward toward God and reaching out toward others. Her secret, in the final analysis, was a secret of patience, of suffering, of submerging herself in the love of the hidden God. Thus did Bernadette invent—or better, did the Holy Spirit invent or reveal in her, with her spontaneous and conscious cooperation—a form of Christian holiness without fanfare, or works, or learning—one that returned to the root of the Gospel and to the love God gives and receives. From the very outset, Bernadette's lot was the simple faithfulness typical of the middle classes of holiness. There is a message here that must not be lost to our era of constant change. The jolts caused by change today highlight the debate about and the expansion of "human values." Bernadette invites us not to forget the rest, which she was able to live in her poverty.

4. What she lived in this way reached its final culmination in the suffering and silence that grew more severe toward the end of her life. During this time of complete abandonment, Bernadette attained full maturity in God. Her gesture of removing all the holy pictures with which she had decorated her sickbed, keeping only the crucifix, was in its own way a symbol.

In short, the contribution of Père Ravier, the editor of the *Ecrits de Bernadette* (Bernadette's Writings) was in showing that by the grace of the apparitions, her sanctity had already taken shape before her entrance into the convent at Nevers. The study of her sayings, which allows us to go further back in this story of grace, leads to one more step in the same direction: Bernadette's sanctity seems to precede the exceptional grace of the apparitions. She had been prepared in the poverty of her childhood. The apparitions revealed this to the world.

Are we speaking here about a sanctity fully formed, with neither growth nor evolution? Certainly not. But it did involve a consistent development, in which the obvious charism made the hidden gift flourish and become fully visible.

Bernadette and Thérèse

The difficulty is to go beyond the writings and sayings, conditioned by Bernadette's environment and arrive at her own contribution to spirituality, for this element of originality lies concealed beneath the surface. If we can penetrate the shell of conventionality, we find that Bernadette is close to our own time, skeptical about words, but believing in life.

To expose this underpinning, it would be tempting to compare Bernadette to another saint who belongs to the same current, the same "phylum," so to speak, of holiness: Saint Thérèse of the Child Jesus, who was six-and-a-half years old when Bernadette died, and who herself died less than twenty years later on September 30, 1897.

This comparison may come as a surprise, for on the surface, there are many differences that immediately come to mind.

Bernadette belonged to the "lower class," as it used to be called then; Thérèse to the middle class. There was on the one hand, poverty; on the other, comfort. Academically, Bernadette was a late bloomer: she began to read at the age of fourteen; Thérèse, learned to read at three. Bernadette was silent; Thérèse, prolific in speech. Her driving force was something impetuous and white-hot. Bernadette's was the product of peasant patience—earthy and passive.

If we wanted to describe the two saints in terms of their resemblance to the four elements, Bernadette reminds us of water and earth: there is something of rock in her faith and in her hardheadedness. Thérèse is related to air and fire.

If these contrasts are striking, it is because they appear among many similarities occurring in the most diverse places. Thérèse and

Bernadette were born in January, twenty-nine years apart (1844 and 1873). Both were sent out to nurse. Both suffered from respiratory ailments. Their lives were short (twenty-four and thirty-five years). Both were sociable and had the gift of mimicry: Bernadette made others laugh by imitating colorful characters, especially the Curé of Lourdes and Doctor Robert Saint-Cyr. In each, there appears at certain times the spirit of a warrior. Both were concerned about letting their infirmarians sleep and had little talent for singing, even though they enjoyed it. But these details are not important.

More significantly, each desired to reach the very limits of sanctity. The love that filled them fed boundless ambitions, the desire to accomplish every work, every service. And in the end, both accepted —or better, learned how to accept, without reserve or resentment— the assignment of suffering for love's sake. Both prayed passionately for sinners. And while these sinners lived free from anxiety, these two women experienced, in their stead, the fear of having lost God's friendship—like Christ, seated at the sinners' table; Christ, agonizing in Gethsemane (Mt 26:36–42); Christ abandoned on Golgotha (Mt 27:46), "having been made sin for us" (2 Cor 5:21).

The similarity that concerns us here rests on an essential point. Without knowing one another, yet one being the extension of the other, both saints rediscovered a Gospel-based path to holiness, one that by-passed great deeds and glory: "the assignment of being sick," as Bernadette pithily expressed it. She lived this path, like a seed sown in the ground; her sanctity remaining hidden from her own eyes as well as from those of her novice mistress. Thérèse was also conscious of this new way. She became its spokeswoman, thanks to her verbal abilities.

It is not our intention to detail here the spirituality of Thérèse of the Child Jesus, brought to light so well in these past few years, but to draw attention to a "pattern" in order to understand better what Bernadette unwittingly discovered: a "little way" which is great in the eyes of love and which consists in love. This was truly the cry from Bernadette's heart when she was asked point-blank for the object of her desires: "Bring me the love of God!"[22]

In her private notes, she wrote in the same vein: "I will not live one moment that is not spent in loving."[23] Bernadette followed this orientation so implicitly that she rarely uttered the abstract noun *love*. The verb *to love* was adequate for her straightforward, simple language. The platitudes of sanctity's middle classes exacted a high toll from her. But hers was indeed the same Gospel-based inspiration as that of Thérèse of the Child Jesus, the same abandonment, the same relish for the straight Gospel expressed when she said, for example, on Easter Sunday, 1879, three days before she died: "When I read the Passion, I am more touched than when it is explained to me."[24]

It is interesting that Bernadette should say this shortly before she died; it is almost an instruction to historians on how the history of Lourdes should be written.

Likewise, both Thérèse and Bernadette reacted against the conventional biographies of the saints. Just as Thérèse disliked sermons that betrayed the humble simplicity of the Virgin Mary, so too Bernadette insisted on being told "the faults of the saints" and how they overcame them.

Thérèse and Bernadette were sisters in suffering. They each experienced similar self-abandonment on three levels:

1. The first separation severed their very deep natural and family ties.

Like Bernadette, but with less restraint, more expansiveness and many embellishments, Thérèse adored her father. According to their games and their use of nicknames, which continued in her letters at the beginning of her religious life, she was his little "blond scamp" and especially his "little queen." And he was her "King." Thérèse capitalized this word thirty-seven times in her writings. The two of them had created their own universe in their intimate conversations. Then, all of a sudden, Thérèse's "beloved king," "the king of France and Navarre," was stricken with "general paralysis": a shameful madness, even morally speaking, during the initial phase of manic excitement and mental lapses over which the historians' customary attention to the smallest detail has left a veil. On February 12, 1889, he had to be committed to a mental institution.[25] Thérèse suddenly responded with self-assurance: "Our great treasure," she wrote, speaking of this trial, the worst she could have imagined.[26] And again, "Far from complaining to Jesus about the cross he sends us, I cannot understand the infinite love that made him treat us like this."[27] And yet, she felt all the anguish and humiliation.

In a more commonplace and less dramatic way, Bernadette was torn away in one sweep from her regional and family roots, from the land and the locale that had been her milieu of nature and of grace. She was able to get beyond her tears, even to the point of no longer wishing to return to Lourdes.

2. A second trial stripped both Bernadette and Thérèse of extraordinary graces in order to reinsert them into the life of ordinary, common faith. About that trial, Bernadette gave no details. It was by accident that she revealed it when she told Bishop Bourret, who was questioning her about the apparitions, "I don't like to talk about them.... What if I were mistaken?"[28]

The luminous experiences of Massabielle had slipped back into the night until they became a source of doubt and suffering.

Thérèse of the Child Jesus, too, had seen the Virgin on May 13, 1883, and this vision had brought an end to her grave childhood sickness.[29] But after talking about this favor, she grew fearful of having been mistaken; even more, of "having lied."[30] Even though it was more private, Bernadette's trial was probably no less severe on this score.

3. It seems necessary to push this parallel even further.

In the last phase of her life, Thérèse was tried no longer on the basis of one apparition and one special favor, but in her *very faith*. Up to then, heaven had been nothing but fascinating and transparent. Now, it seemed unreal. The feeling of being deceived about the essential gripped her soul. She interrupted this passage in her autobiography to say, "I do not wish to write any more about this, I'd be afraid of committing blasphemy."[31] And in this final letting go, her sanctity reached the fullness of Gethsemane and Golgotha, a love fit for God.

Did Bernadette experience this third separation on a theological level? Definitely, in her hope, as we have seen.

Was her faith also overtaken by this spiritual darkness? The secretive Bernadette said nothing about it. And, in any event, it was not possible for her to share her thoughts because she did not possess Thérèse's ability to express herself on this difficult matter, bordering on blasphemy. But something on this order would best account for the silence she maintained about her trials, as well as the heartbreaking request she made to Soeur Nathalie during the last hours of her life: *"Help me."*[32]

Bewildered in this agony, Bernadette sought human help, just as Jesus had with his disciples in Gethsemane (Mt 26:37–38). Might that not be the secret of indescribable suffering that was hers at three o'clock in the afternoon, a few moments before she died?[33]

What is definite and what really matters is that Bernadette was tested right to the root of her theological confidence, whatever the circumstances might have been. The important thing is that she found herself thereby brought to the cross. It was the moment when she could do nothing more except identify herself with Christ in his passion, to have herself tied to the crucifix the way she did shortly before she died.

From this point of view, Bernadette's final secret, the "secret" trial—a topic of lengthy discussions—also seems like a secret of transparency, of simplicity. We cannot positively identify it in every detail, but we can perceive how it shines in the heart of a total picture, like the luminous cloud, symbol of the mystery of God present day and night among us. In this respect, too, we are faced not so much with a secret as with a mystery.

Beyond Action and Contemplation

One and the same passion served as the foundation of Bernadette's life. That solid, continuous line, detected by Abbé Febvre, gives the historian no warrant to describe "developmental stages," or even progress.

Then how may we categorize her style of holiness in terms of the classic criteria of the active versus the contemplative life?

The charism given to Bernadette during the apparitions was contemplative. That was her first attraction to religious life, leading her to consider joining Carmel and then the "Bernadines." But given her circumstances, her poverty and the condition of her health, such an avenue was closed to her.

That was when Bernadette found the solution to her problem. She discerned in the faces of the poor the living image of Christ in his passion. In keeping with her own quiet manner, she discovered a certain active silence which reaches beyond appearances to God: "What you did to the least of my own, you did to me" (Mt 25:40, 45). She believed she had found her path in "action," understood in that sense. And this was the way she followed at the hospice of Lourdes and later as infirmarian at Nevers until 1873.

It was then that we saw her gradually stumble upon a final

path—one that would appear more like a precipice—neither traditional contemplation, for which she seemed to have no talent, nor
active service, but the utter self-destruction caused by suffering. She
experienced the inactivity of an overburdened body, of an exhausted spirit. Not yet thirty years old, Bernadette, after a long novitiate of suffering, saw being realized in her own life Jesus' words to
Peter: "When you were young, you fastened your own belt and went
wherever you wished. But when you grow old, you will stretch out
your hands and someone else will fasten a belt around you and take
you where you do not wish to go" (Jn 21:18).

Jesus "said that," the evangelist points out, "to indicate the kind
of death by which Peter would glorify God." And that was when Jesus
invited Peter, "Follow me."

Bernadette seems to have discovered a similar call, not in so
many words, but within her very sufferings. Isolated from the world,
eager for the next life, she was aware of this vocation. Hence, on
learning of the death of Abbé Peyramale, with whom she wished to
be reunited, she said, "First, I must do another kind of dying."[34] On
Easter Sunday, 1879, she likewise said, "My passion will last until my
death."[35]

Bernadette lived the final stage of her life in neither action nor,
in the traditional sense, contemplation. Must it be said that she was
a failure in both?

Should we not rather say that beyond action and contemplation,
she practiced what is essential to each? She lived the love that is
their essence: love of God and of others, of God in others and of
others in God. At the end of this life's story of Bernadette, her fundamental commitment to the *Via Dolorosa,* her sharing in the cross
of Christ, seemed to call for this last answer.

Thus did she fulfill the wish of the founder of the Sisters of Charity, Dom de Laveyne, when he wrote, before everything else, in the
very *Prologue* of his *Oeuvres spirituelles* (Spiritual Works): "Consider,
my dear sisters, in the Rules that are being given to you, two forms
of life that you have to observe: one is that of Martha and the other
that of Mary. Martha is the symbol of the active life, busy in the service of the neighbor out of the obligation of charity; and Mary is the
symbol of the contemplative life, focused solely on God out of love

of the truth.... You must love these two kinds of life, bring them together within you like sisters."[36]

The essential element of contemplation, contemplative love, eager to rediscover the One seen obscurely in the night, dwelt within Bernadette's own poverty...from the time in Lourdes when she said, "All right, I don't know how to meditate," right up until her death-bed, when she told Abbé Febvre, "I can't meditate anymore."[37]

The essential element of the active life was also unfailingly present in her. It was a constant attention to others, a way of welcoming whose encouraging nature and attitudes we have already seen. Bernadette knew how to shut the door to idle curiosity, while opening it to genuine needs: those of the poor, the young, and those learning how to adjust to or live out their religious vocation. For this reason, Mère Vauzou, who was so reticent toward Bernadette in many respects, regularly sent troubled novices to her. In this area, the novice mistress was never disappointed.

Is it an exaggeration to say all this? Isn't it recreating a myth, beyond action and contemplation? And shouldn't we expose the ambiguous nature of Bernadette's influence? Didn't this influence stem from blind admiration for the one "who had seen the Blessed Virgin," who in her own lifetime had become the subject of books, sermons, stained glass windows and hagiography? Didn't she function as a fetish, a symbol, offering some amusement in the otherwise austere and closed convent environment? Wasn't it by way of superficial diversion that it was possible for her to dissipate minor dramas and psychological blocks? These factors undoubtedly came into play. But the truth is that Bernadette in no way staged them. She discouraged such polarization by her refusals as well as by her welcomes, by her way of acting and, above all, of being.

Her influence was unconscious, like that of a flower unaware of its own color: "Look at the lilies of the field, they neither toil nor spin; yet, even Solomon in all his glory was not clothed like one of these" (Mt 6:28–29). The "myth of Bernadette" could only have done damage. But she was a healer. And this was the reason why Mère Vauzou sent her novices to her. Bernadette's influence, generally non-directive, was not at all in competition with her own. Bernadette brought out the best in each person.

Bernadette's Passion

As paradoxical as this conclusion might be at the end of a collection of Bernadette's sayings, her sanctity was characterized less by her words than by a certain active silence, giving rise to "deeds that speak," which her confessor compared to the actions of the prophets. Here too, it involved essentially silent deeds resembling not action as much as a passion similar to Christ's. For Bernadette's poor, humiliating, sickly childhood was indeed a passion, a passion carried out with the loving conviction that "when the good Lord wishes, all is well and we do not complain."

Passion is not passivity. To be "passionate" is not to be inactive or neutral. However, passion is something received. In this sense, it is the opposite of a deed.

"She worked less than she was worked on," said Bernadette's confessor on November 29, 1879.[38] He added, "The passive virtues abounded in her: a life of penance, sanctified by divine action... shaped by crosses."

But Bernadette's passion became action in the realm of love. And so she takes her place among those who carry on the work of Christ, whose death, inflicted by others, was accepted as an act of redemptive love (Jn 10:18; also 7:30, 44; 8:20; 12:27; 13:1–3; 17:19; 18:4–6; 19:28).

Yes, it was indeed a Passion that Christ humanly suffered. And it was human beings who humanly forced him to flee and hide himself; it was human beings who arrested him, condemned him, nailed him to a cross and put him to death; they tore his life from him as they would have that of any of their enemies.

And yet, Jesus said, "No one takes my life from me" (Jn 10:18).

This is true on two levels. The first is unique to Christ, and this is what traditional theology emphasizes. At the high point of his Passion, he could continue to say, "My Father is still working and I also am working" (Jn 5:17), that is to say, on the level of divine action, no one could stop his work.

But it is also true to say that no one took Christ's life from him on the level of consent that transforms the accepted into the chosen, into an act of redeeming love. And here is something that can be imitated and shared. The love of Jesus, who consented to the Passion and accomplished the salvation of humanity, was also a human love.

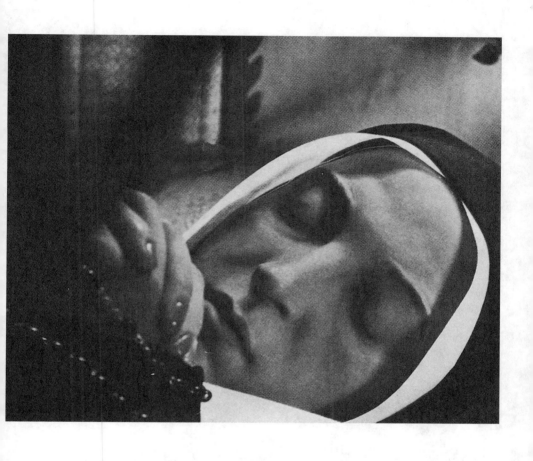

The Gave looking toward the grotto in 1861 (above) and 1873 (below)

In this human and divine crucible, the act of dying is identified as glory, according to Saint John. In this context, translucent as it is, we are given some idea of the secret—or call—the mystery of Bernadette.

She was vaguely aware of this, as her identification with Christ on the cross makes clear.[39] She was conscious of the passion and death she had to "*accomplish.*"[40] This word signifies an *action,* a free choice.

In the early months of 1879, when she had lost her ability to pray, the advice that actually guided her toward the inevitable outcome was her confessor's invitation to "lose herself completely" in the "cross of the Savior."[41] Little by little, everything for her came down to this blind contact with the cross: "This is enough for me."[42]

Here we reach the foundation of Bernadette's sanctity: a love tried and true, pointing to the ultimate freedom—the freedom to accept the unacceptable.

On his deathbed, Cardinal Veuillot said, "Tell priests not to speak about suffering; they don't know what it is...."

Suffering is beyond all telling, beyond all understanding. It is senseless. It goes against logic. In her own way, Bernadette truly realized this absurdity. She was fascinated by the reading of Isaiah, which she summed up in this way, "Our Lord was treated like a broken pot."[43]

If suffering has any meaning here on earth, it is in relationship to Christ, that is, to the redeeming love that destroys sin by humanly taking upon itself the evil that flows from sin. Suffering here is the decisive test, the irrefutable proof of authentic love. It is in times of suffering that we discover who our true friends are: those who, with nothing to gain, stand by us in adversity. Here on earth, love worthy of the name undergoes an ordeal far more demanding than breaking the sound barrier is for a ballistic missile. Such a love finds a way through the "suffering barrier." Christ, our Passover, is that way.

Must we admit that our century is called to live this love in forms more deeply involved in the history and life of people today: forms nearer to the passion of Camillo Torres or Martin Luther King than to Bernadette's? Perhaps, in one sense, but only on condition that the list of examples be expanded and that we clearly realize that all are united, more than they appear to be, on the level of poverty, of self-giving, of suffering and of death lived as a gift of life. Everything must begin with bread broken and shared, but the climax of redeeming love is found in the image of the cross.

Bernadette's sanctity developed from meager resources: the spirituality of a regimented era, the trough of the post-Trent wave. It went beyond the legalism and voluntarism of her day without casting them aside. Bernadette spiritually soared above these by the quality of the love she was able to bring forth within their narrow confines.

In that austere era, which she learned to accept just as it was, she lived her dark night: a night like the one experienced by people today, by the modern-day "non-believer." Here we touch her relevance for today, a relevance for all ages.

From this point of view, as from every other, the secret of Bernadette's sanctity is also a secret of the Gospel: the secret of the grain sown in the earth, which dies in order to bear fruit (Jn 12:24).

Two days before she died, Bernadette offered another metaphor for the same mystery—rougher, nearer to bread broken. Out of the depths of her agony came rising to the surface the grinding of the millstones that had lullabied her to sleep as a baby and accompanied her first sufferings as a child at the Boly mill: "I am ground like a grain of wheat."[44]

GLOSSARY

Abbé: a parish priest; he would be addressed as *Monsieur l'Abbé* (similar to "Reverend Father").

Aqueró: "that" in Bernadette's native dialect; the term by which she referred to the young lady of the apparition prior to learning that the "lady" was in fact the Blessed Virgin.

Cachot: a dungeon or prison cell.

Curé: the pastor of a parish; he would be addressed as *Monsieur le Curé* (similar to "Reverend Pastor").

Demoiselle: a young woman.

Grappin: Berndette's name for Satan; it means "grappling hook" or "grabber."

Maï: in Bernadette's dialect, the familiar term for "Mother."

Mère: mother; also the title given to superiors in Bernadette's religious congregation.

Monseigneur: literally, "my Lord"; a title of honor reserved to members of the French episcopacy ("Bishop") and to Church prelates ("Monsignor").

Patois: a provincial dialect.

Père: father.

Soeur: sister.

Sou: a copper coin of very little value.

Sources

— ⚜ —

(The abbreviations in the left column are those used in the Notes.)

A I–A V	Part of the CROS archives.
A VI	Part of the CROS archives, reserved for the testimony of pilgrims to Lourdes.
A VII	Père CROS' Journal of Inquiry (1878–1881).
A VIII	Part of the CROS archives.
ANDL	*Annales de Notre-Dame de Lourdes* (1866–1944).
ARCH	Archives.
AZUN	T. M. J. AZUN DE BERNETAS, *La grotte des Pyrénées,* Tarbes, Larrieu, 1861.
BARBET	J. BARBET, *Bernadette Soubirous,* Pau, 1909. We cite the 1923 Tarbes edition.

637

BRTL	*Bulletin religieux du diocèse de Tarbes.*
BORDENAVE	Mère Marie-Thérèse BORDENAVE, *Sainte Bernadette Soubirous, la confidente de l'Immaculée,* Nevers, 1933.
CROS	L. J. M. CROS, S.J., *Histoire de Notre-Dame de Lourdes,* Paris, Beauchesne, 1927, 3 volumes (posthumous edition).
D	R. LAURENTIN, *Lourdes. Documents authentiques,* 6 volumes, Paris, Lethielleux. Volumes 3–6 in collaboration with Dom Bernard BILLET, sole editor of Volume 7.
ESB	A. RAVIER, S.J., *Ecrits de sainte Bernadette,* Paris, Lethielleux, 1961.
GUYNOT 1936	E. GUYNOT, *Sainte Bernadette, souvenirs inédits,* Paris, Spes, 1936.
GUYNOT 1956	E. GUYNOT, *Sainte Bernadette, souvenirs inédits,* Paris G. Victor, 1956. This collection repeats some of the preceding material.
H	R. LAURENTIN, *Lourdes. Histoire authentique,* 6 volumes, Paris, Lethielleux, 1961–1964.
JGL	*Journal of the Lourdes Grotto,* established in 1898, replacing the newspaper, *Lavedan.*
Journ. Com.	Journal of the community of the Sisters of Charity at Nevers.
Logia	See the following.
N	R. LAURENTIN & Marie-Thérèse BOURGEADE, *Logia de Bernadette. Etude critique de ses paroles de 1866 à 1879* (3 volumes).

1. *La vie active* (July 7, 1866–January 17, 1873)
2. *L'emploi de malade* (January 17, 1873–April 16, 1879)
3. *Le secret de Bernadette. Partie synthétique,* Paris, Apostolat de Editions, P. Lethielleux et Oeuvre de la Grotte. "N" indicates the reference number of the word cited.

OG   M. OLPHE-GAILLIARD, *Lourdes, 1858. Témoins de l'événement,* Paris, Lethielleux, 1957.

PANev   *Procès apostolique de Nevers,* archives of the Convent of St. Gildard.

PATarb   *Procès apostolique de Tarbes,* archives of the Diocese of Tarbes.

PONev   *Procès ordinaire de Nevers,* archives of the Convent of St. Gildard.

RAM   *Hommage à la bienheureuse Bernadette Soubirous,* special issue of the *Revue d' ascétique et de mystique,* 10, (1929) pp. 1–174.

RC   Register of her contemporaries: preliminary inquiry of the Superior General of Nevers for the canonization process (November 1907).

Rev. Bern.   *Revue Bernadette,* published in Nevers (1922–1940).

RSL   *Recherches sur Lourdes,* edited by Dom B. BILLET, Oeuvre de la Grotte, Lourdes.

SEMPÉ   R. SEMPÉ and J. M. DUBOÉ, *Notre-Dame de Lourdes,* Paris, Letouzey, 1931 (a republication of the 1868–1869 original found in ANDL).

VÉDÈRE   *Bernadette et Jeanne Védère,* Auros, 1933. We have checked this edition against the manuscript, whose style has been polished.

ZOLA   E. ZOLA, *Mes voyages. Lourdes, Rome,* Journals published by René Ternois, Paris. Fasquelle, 1958.

For further bibliographical details, see *Logia 3,* pp. 319–322, and H 1, pp. 177–179.

NOTES

— ⚜ —

Chapter 1
BERNADETTE'S CHILDHOOD

1. H 2, p. 16, note 24.
2. D 2, p. 19.
3. H 2, p. 31.
4. A VII, p. 173, n. 73.
5. A VII, p. 123, n. 813; H 2, p. 35.
6. H 2, p. 59, note 170.
7. D 5, p. 325.
8. H 2, p. 56.
9. PONev 1239v.
10. H 2, p. 62.
11. A VII, p. 184.
12. H 2, p. 55, note 157.
13. Estrade, p. 27, etc.
14. H 2, p. 58.
15. Ibid., note 170.
16. PONev 1230v; H 2, p. 59, note 170.
17. H 2, pp. 61–62, note 175.
18. Guy de Pierrefeux, *Le Triomphe de Lourdes*, Paris, Flammarion, 1893, pp. 258–259.
19. Zola, p. 96.
20. Ibid.
21. Ibid.
22. Lasserre, p. 18.

23. Zola, pp. 100–101.
24. H 2, p. 61.
25. H 2, p. 50.
26. November 9, 1879; H 2, p. 50.
27. H 2, p. 60.
28. A VII, p. 173.
29. H 2, p. 50.
30. H 2, p. 61.
31. H 2, p. 33.
32. Zola, p. 96.
33. PONev 894.
34. A VII, p. 151.
35. A VII, pp. 32–34; H 2, p. 65, note 184.
36. A VII, p. 187.
37. A VII, p. 151; H 2, pp. 64–66.

Chapter 2
THE FIRST THREE APPARITIONS

1. H 2, p. 152, note 8.
2. H 2, p. 109 and 153, note 16.
3. H 2, p. 109.
4. H 2, p. 156, note 28.
5. H 2, p. 158, note 34.
6. H 2, p. 160, note 46.
7. H 2, p. 161, note 47.
8. H 2, p. 162, note 48.

9. H 3, p. 163, notes 49–50.

10. H 2, p. 108, note 109.

11. H 2, p. 180, note 100 and pp. 138–140.

12. H 2, p. 180, note 112.

13. H 2, p. 181, note 115.

14. H 2, p. 184, note 122.

15. H 2, p. 186, note 130.

16. H 2, p. 186.

17. H 2, pp. 186 and 111.

18. H 2, p. 187.

19. Ibid.

20. H 2, p. 189, note 140.

21. H 2, pp. 111–112, note 190.

22. H 2, pp. 196–200.

23. H 2, pp. 202 and 205.

24. Ibid.

25. H 2, p. 202, n. 2.

26. H 2, p. 256.

27. H 2, p. 261, note 68.

28. H 2, pp. 262–263.

29. H 2, pp. 225 and 272.

30. H 2, pp. 224 and 275.

31. H 2, p. 276.

32. H 2, p. 290, note 9.

33. H 2, p. 291.

34. H 2, p. 292.

35. Ibid.

36. H 2, p. 301.

37. H 2, p. 357.

38. H 2, p. 361.

39. H 2, p. 364.

40. Ibid.

41. H 2, p. 366.

42. H 2, p. 367.

43. Ibid.

44. H 2, p. 369.

45. H 2, p. 362.

46. H 2, pp. 347–348 and 362.

47. H 2, pp. 349 and 363.

Chapter 3
TWO WEEKS OF APPARITIONS

1. H 4, p. 13.

2. H 4, p. 39.

3. Ibid.

4. *Mémoire Pène,* January 8, 1879, p. 11.

5. Ibid., p. 7.

6. H 4, p. 63.

7. H 2, p. 76.

8. H 4, p. 77.

9. H 4, p. 123.

10. H 4, p. 162.

11. H 4, p. 176

12. H 4, p. 225.

13. Ibid.

14. H 4, p. 309.

15. H 4, p. 311.

16. H 4, p. 312.

17. H 4, p. 313.

18. Ibid.

19. H 4, p. 314.

20. H 4, p. 224, note 100.

21. H 4, p. 187, note 6.

22. H 4, p. 406.

23. H 4, p. 424.

24. H 4, p. 425.

25. Ibid.

26. H 4, p. 428.

27. Ibid.

28. Ibid.

29. H 4, p. 438.

30. H 4, p. 439.

31. H 4, p. 441.

32. H 4, p. 442.

33. D 1, p. 177.

34. H 4, p. 443.

35. H 4, p. 444.

36. H 4, p. 445.

37. H 1, p. 134.

38. H 2, pp. 76–80.

39. H 4, p. 447.

40. H 4, p. 488, note 267.

41. Ibid.

42. H 5, p. 24.

43. H 5, pp. 49–50.

44. H 5, p. 51.

45. H 5, p. 90, note 57.

46. H 5, pp. 90–91.

47. H 5, p. 166.

48. H 5, pp. 174–175.

49. H 5, p. 175.

50. Ibid.

51. H 5, p. 177.

52. H 5, p. 179.

53. H 5, p. 180.

54. H 5, p. 181.

55. H 5, p. 190.

56. H 5, p. 191.

57. H 5, p. 192.

58. Ibid.

59. H 5, p. 193.
60. Ibid.
61. H 5, pp. 193–194.
62. H 5, p. 194.
63. Ibid.
64. H 5, p. 231.
65. H 5, p. 233.
66. H 5, p. 235.
67. H 5, p. 237.
68. Ibid.
69. H 5, p. 307.
70. H 5, p. 309.
71. H 5, p. 310.
72. Ibid.
73. H 5, p. 313.
74. H 5, p. 327.
75. H 5, p. 329.
76. H 5, pp. 332–333.
77. H 5, p. 335.
78. H 5, p. 336.
79. Ibid.
80. H 5, p. 337.
81. Ibid.
82. H 5, p. 343.
83. H 5, p. 345.
84. Ibid.
85. H 5, p. 354.
86. H 5, p. 355.

Chapter 4
THE LAST THREE APPARITIONS

1. D 5, p. 11.
2. H 6, p. 20.
3. Ibid.
4. Jean-Marie's First Journal, p. 60;
Second Journal, p. 39.
5. H 6, p. 22.
6. Ibid.
7. H 6, p. 23.
8. H 6, p. 24.
9. First Journal, p. 68.
10. H 6, p. 24.
11. Ibid.
12. First Journal, p. 69.
13. H 6, p. 24.
14. H 6, pp. 27–29.
15. D 1, p. 256.
16. D 1, pp. 257–260; H 6, pp. 33–35.
17. D 1, p. 260; H 6, pp. 34–35.
18. H 6, p. 35, note 87.

19. H 6, p. 112.
20. H 6, p. 110.
21. H 6, p. 117.
22. H 6, pp. 95–99 and 121.
23. H 6, pp. 124–125.
24. H 6, p. 126.
25. H 6, p. 127.
26. H 6, p. 128.
27. H 6, p. 129.
28. Ibid.
29. H 6, p. 130.
30. D 1, pp. 284–286.
31. D 1, p. 298, n. 104.
32. A III, "folio 109," n. 2, p. 2.
33. D 1, pp. 297–298.
34. D 1, p. 300.
35. D 1, p. 301.
36. PONev 728v.
37. Deposition of 1879–, A III, "folio
109," n. 2, p. 20.
38. PONev 728v.
39. Letter of March 29, 1858; D 5, p. 76.
40. A III; cf. OG, p. 241.
41. D 5, p. 76.
42. D 5, p. 77.
43. H 6, p. 138, note 16.
44. H 6, p. 140.
45. H 6, p. 214.
46. H 6, p. 215.
47. H 6, pp. 216–217.
48. H 6, p. 218.
49. Ibid.
50. Letter of April 10; D 2, p. 154.
51. D 2, p. 154; cf. D 5, p. 292, lines 18–22.
52. H 6, p. 133.
53. D 2, p. 154.
54. D 2, pp. 128–133
55. D 2, p. 221.
56. Ibid.
57. H 1, pp. 41–82; especially pp. 68–77.
58. D 2, p. 243, n. 193.
59. D 2, p. 269, n. 226.
60. D 2, p. 296, n. 253.
61. D 2, p. 317; cf. pp. 33–34.
62. Memoir of October 11, 1879; A III;
cf. A VIII, p. 622, n. 1241.
63. Letter of Abbé Péré to his cousin,
Sister Gonzague Péré, a Sister of Charity
of Nevers at Montpellier, 1908—Arichives
of Nevers.

64. D 3, p. 378.

65. Peyramale letter, D 2, n. 314, p. 359; cf. Lasserre, *Bernadette,* pp. 120–121; other editions, p. 184; PONev 2, 344; 4, 874; PANev 2, 366v; 6, 1485 and 7, 1800.

66. From Mother Fabre, PONev 2260; Barbet, *Bernadette,* 1929, p. 813; other editions, p. 126, Barbet, PONev 4925; cf. Mother Forestier, PANev 196, and Perreau, PANev 109.

67. A VII, p. 184.

68. Ibid.

69. A VI, pp. 255–256; A VIII, p. 712.

70. D 3, pp. 11, 15, 17–18.

71. Védère, pp. 53–54; RAM, 9–22, 129; OG, pp. 187–188; D 3, pp. 70–71; H 6, p. 345. (We paid little attention to the minor variations between the two copies of Védère.)

72. D 3, p. 120.

73. A VII, p. 129.

74. A VII, p. 129; H 3, p. 177.

75. H 6, p. 250, note 24.

76. H 6, p. 250.

77. A VII, p. 101; H 6, p. 251, note 27.

78. H 6, pp. 227–252.

79. D 5, p. 49.

80. H 5, p. 354, note 280.

81. D 5, p. 49.

82. Védère, p. 53.

83. D 3, p. 236.

84. D 5, p. 49, line 2 (where we should read "September" and not "May" 1858).

Chapter 5
GIVING PUBLIC TESTIMONY

1. D 5, p. 292, line 10.

2. H 1, p. 154.

3. D 3, pp. 235–236, n. 475.

4. D 3, p. 239, n. 475.

5. D 3, p. 240, n. 476.

6. Ibid.

7. Estrade, p. 315; other editions, p. 291.

8. *Premier Mémoire d'Estrade,* PONev 489v.

9. D 3, pp. 31–32.

10. *Mémoire d'Estrade,* 1878.

11. D 3, p. 33.

12. PATarb 105.

13. D 7, p. 33, note 116; Barbet, PONev 4, 924v.

14. D 3, pp. 210–214, n. 449.

15. D 3, p. 224.

16. Letter of Sister Saint-Antonin, Cros Archives, A VI; cf. Cros 2, pp. 301–302.

17. A VII, p. 136, n. 903; cf. D 3, p. 42.

18. D 3, p. 43.

19. D 4, p. 91.

20. D 4, p. 89.

21. D 3, p. 47.

22. A VII, p. 204, n. 191.

23. S. Carrère, *Histoire de Notre-Dame de Lourdes,* Paris, Beauchemin, 1912, p. 88.

24. A VII, p. 204.

25. D 3, pp. 74–75; A VII, p. 204, n. 192.

26. A VI.

27. A VII, p. 204, n. 192.

28. Preserved in the Cros Archives, A VI.

29. Cros Archives, A VI.

30. Ibid.

31. D 4, p. 225, note 1.

32. D 4, p. 245.

33. D 5, p. 292, lines 10–13.

34. D 4, p. 73, note 160; Letter of Fonteneau, July 5, 1878, p. 2, in A VI.

35. Letters of Moreau: November 8, and December 6, 1878; and June 20, 1879 in A VI.

36. PONev 1, 164.

37. Guy de Pierrefeux, *Le Triomphe de Lourdes,* Paris, Flammarion, 1893 edition pp. 119–121. Account reproduced in the *Annuaire de Saint-Pé,* 2, 1909, pp. 22–24; cf. PONev 3, 662 and PANev 2, 347; 6, 1477.

38. D 3, p. 253.

39. Cf. 1 Kings 19:8.

40. D 4, p. 73, note 161.

41. D 5, p. 221.

42. D 2, p. 165.

43. D 4, p. 74, note 163.

44. D 4, p. 74, note 165.

45. PONev 4, 965.

46. A VIII, 696.

47. D 3, p. 74; PONev 4, 965; OG, p. 296.

48. D 2, pp. 62–71.

49. A. Tardhivail, A VII, p. 205.

50. *Rosier de Marie 4,* 1858, n. 183, October 1.

51. Letter of Abbé Liesta, Jean-Marie's pastor, January 6, 1879, Grotto Archives, record rack 12, p. 5.

52. *Courrier Français,* September 26; D 4, pp. 76–77; facsimile; and n. 748, pp. 245–249.

53. Ibid., p. 247.

54. D 4, p. 248, n. 748.

55. Henri de Courrèges, *Souvenirs,* published in *La Source,* 4, 1922, pp. 3– 4.

56. *Premier Mémoire d'Estrade,* first part, re-edited during the summer of 1858; D 3, p. 326.

57. D 3, p. 326.

58. D 5, p. 23.

59. D 5, p. 25, note 47; cf. H 6, p. 180.

60. H 5, pp. 26 and 217, n. 820, note 3.

61. H 1, p. 64.

62. H 1, pp. 72–73.

63. D 5, p. 142, n. 820.

64. H 6, p. 28, note 67.

65. D 5, p. 142, n. 820.

66. Sister Marie Géraud, cited by Barbet, p. 124; 1926 edition, p. 170.

67. A VII, p. 180.

68. Interview of November 12, Azun, p. 172; D 5, p. 329, n. 912.

69. D 5, pp. 185–187; ESB, pp. 552–556.

70. D 5, p. 161.

71. D 7, p. 126, note 700.

72. OG, p.170; D 5, pp. 161–162.

73. D 5, pp. 62 and 328, note 13.

74. D 5, p. 51, note 124.

75. H 1, pp. 80–81.

76. D 5, p. 288.

77. D 5, pp. 51–52 and 281–288.

78. D 5, p. 290.

79. D 5, p. 294, n. 900.

80. Ibid.

81. Ibid.

82. D 5, p. 340.

83. D 5, pp. 318–319, n. 907.

84. D 5, p. 319.

85. Ibid.

86. D 5, pp. 315–320, n. 907.

87. D 5, p. 320.

88. D 5, pp. 340–341, n. 914.

89. Ibid.

90. D 5, p. 341.

91. Azun, p. 169; D 5, p. 328.

92. Which can be read in D 5, pp. 325–327.

93. Ibid., p. 329.

94. E. Boyer, *Une visite à la grotte,* second edition, p. 51.

95. Védère, p. 42; RAM, p. 123.

96. D 5, p. 344, n. 915.

97. D 5, pp. 344–345.

98. H 4, p. 416.

99. D 5, p. 345.

100. D 5, p. 346, n. 915.

101. Ibid., p. 347.

102. D 5, pp. 347–348.

103. D 5, p. 348.

104. D 5, p. 303, n. 903.

105. PANev folio 1212.

106. Depostion of Elfrida Lacrampe, A VII, p. 197; OG, p. 104.

107. D 6, p. 74, note 180.

108. D 6, p. 74, note 181.

109. *Rev. Bern.,* December 1969, n. 44.

110. PONev 744v.

111. D 6, p. 88, note 240.

112. D 6, p. 110.

113. PANev 1142.

114. D. Calmels, RC, pp. 4–5.

115. A VII, p. 63, n. 145; D 6, p. 76, note 190.

116. D 6, p. 77, note 191.

117. D 6, p. 77, note 196.

118. Barbet, pp. 129–130; D 6, p. 77, notes 194–195.

119. D 1, pp. 95–128.

120. D 6, p. 77, notes 198–199; and p. 220, n. 930.

121. D 6, pp. 78–79.

Chapter 6
BERNADETTE THE BOARDER

1. D 4, p. 248.

2. D 6, p. 80, note 202.

3. D 6, p. 80, note 203.

4. D 6, p. 146, note 940.

5. D 6, p. 80, note 204.

6. D 6, pp. 181–184, n. 984; H 1, inset related to pp. 78–79.

7. D 6, p. 80, note 206.

8. PATarb 228.

9. *La Croix,* May 11, 1939.

10. *La Croix,* May 11, 1939; cf. H 3, p. 46 on her shortness of breath.

11. Barbet, p. 130.

12. A VII, p. 191, n. 136; D 6, p. 81, note 208.

13. A VII, p. 191, n. 136; D 6, p. 81, note 209.

14. D 6, p. 81, note 210; PONev 1061.

15. *Positio super virtutibus,* published papers of the beatification process, Rome, 1922. *Animadversiones Promotoris,* folio 27, *et responsio,* ibid., folio 59.

16. D 6, p. 82, note 212.

17. D 6, p. 82, note 213.

18. D 6, p. 82, note 214.

19. A VII, p. 197, n. 167.

20. D 6, p. 83, note 216.

21. D 6, p. 83, note 217.

22. A VII, p. 191, n. 136; RSL, n. 15, p. 106.

23. D 6, p. 83, note 220 bis.

24. RSL, n. 15, p. 107.

25. D 6, p. 84, note 222.

26. D 6, p. 84, note 223.

27. D 6, p. 84, note 224.

28. D 6, p. 84, note 225.

29. D 5, p. 86, note 226; PATarb 157, 201, etc.

30. PATarb 283; D 7, p. 29.

31. PATarb 187.

32. Ibid.

33. A VII, p. 191, n. 137.

34. D 5, pp. 60-62.

35. Ibid.

36. A VII, p. 191.

37. A VII, p. 198.

38. A VII, p. 191.

39. A VII, p. 198.

40. PONev 3, 764v; D 7, p. 112, note 623.

41. D 7, p. 112, according to C. Yver, *L'humble Bernadette,* Paris, 1935, p. 186.

42. A VII, p. 198, n. 169 bis.

43. PATarb p. 229, n. 49.

44. M. Géraud, cited by Zola, *Journal,* August 31, 1892, p. 113.

45. A VII, p. 197, n. 167; RSL, n. 15, p. 108.

46. PATarb p. 229, n. 49.

47. A VII, p. 197.

48. A VII, p. 191; RSL, p. 108.

49. D 7, p. 423, n. 1722.

50. Philomène Camès, in *La Croix,* May 11, 1939.

51. A VII, p. 191.

52. A VII, p. 198.

53. A VII, p. 191.

54. A VII, p. 198; RSL, p. 108.

55. A VII, p. 191, n. 140.

56. A VII, p. 198.

57. Marie Fourcade, Memoir, October 16, 1879; OG, p. 239.

58. Ibid.

59. A VII, p. 198.

60. Ibid.

61. PATarb 103.

62. PANev 5, 1121; D 7, p. 95, note 539.

63. D 7, p. 95, note 541.

64. Letter of January 19, 1863, Grotto Archives, record rack 21.

65. D 6, p. 87, note 238.

66. D 6, p. 87, note 239.

67. D 6, pp. 87-88, note 240.

68. D 6, p. 88, nn. 932, 945.

69. Barbet, pp. 132-134; 1926 edition, pp. 181-184.

70. Ibid.; D 6, p. 88; PONev 447v.

71. D 6, p. 89, note 243.

72. D 6, p. 89, note 244.

73. D 6, p. 89 and 202-205, n. 1012.

74. Ibid., note 249.

75. D 6, p. 36, n. 1022.

76. D 6, note 250.

77. D 6, p. 213, n. 1022.

78. D 6, p. 91, note 259.

79. D 6, note 260.

80. D 6, p. 92.

81. Ibid., note 262.

82. D 6, pp. 237-245.

83. D 6, p. 91, note 255.

84. D 6, p. 91 and 257, n. 1046.

85. D 6, p. 91.

86. Ibid., note 257.

87. D 6, p. 92, note 263.

88. D 6, p. 93, note 265.

89. D 6, p. 93, note 266.

90. H 4, p. 432.

91. D 6, p. 93, note 267.

92. D 6, p. 93, note 268.

93. D 6, p. 93, note 269.

94. D 6, p. 94, note 270.

95. D 6, p. 94, note 271.

96. D 6, p. 94, note 272.

97. D 6, p. 95, note 273.

98. D 6, p. 96, note 275.

99. D 6, p. 96, note 276.

100. D 6, p. 95.

101. D 6, p. 360, n. 1300.

102. D 6, p. 364, n. 1306.

103. D 6, pp. 360–361, n. 1300; cf. p. 97, note 277.

104. Guynot, *Rev. Bern.,* December 1936, n. 25, p. 50.

105. D 7, pp. 91 and 159.

106. D 7, p. 170.

107. D 7, p. 171.

108. Ibid.

109. D 6, p. 401.

110. D 7, p. 244, n. 1457.

111. D 7, p. 93, note 533.

112. D 7, pp. 255–256, n. 1476.

113. D 7, p. 259, n. 1482 and pp. 266–268, n. 1485.

114. D 7, p. 263, n. 1484.

115. D 7, pp. 262–264, n. 1484.

116. *Mémoire Langlade,* A III; D 7, p. 274.

117. D 7, p. 25.

118. D 7, p. 167, n. 1377.

119. D 7, pp. 177–178, n. 1390.

120. PONev 698.

121. *Souvenirs de Soeur Philomène Roques,* September 19, 1930, Nevers Archives; D 7, p. 90, note 520.

122. BRTL, 14, 1935, December 8, n. 49, pp. 543–546.

123. D 7, pp. 275–276, n. 1496.

Chapter 7
THE SHEPHERDESS AND THE SCULPTOR

1. D 7, p. 281.

2. D 7, p. 287, n. 1509.

3. D 7, p. 270, n. 1488.

4. Memoir of October 7, 1878, p. 3.

5. D 7, p. 280, n. 1500.

6. H 3, p. 214, n. 83.

7. D 7, p. 278, n. 1499.

8. Letter of September 18, 1863; D 7, p. 280, n. 1500.

9. Memoir of 1878.

10. D 7, p. 279, n. 1499.

11. Memoir of October 7, 1878.

12. D 7, p. 279.

13. D 7, pp. 279–280.

14. Memoir of October 7, 1878, p. 4.

15. Memoir of October 7, 1878.

16. A VII, p. 136; and *Voix du peuple,* September 9, 1894.

17. D 7, p. 282, n. 1503.

18. Estrade, p. 369, note 2.

19. D 7, p. 282.

20. Sempé, p. 224; H 3, p. 138, note 12.

21. D 7, p. 309.

22. D 7, p. 281, n. 1501.

23. D 4, facing p. 61.

24. D 7, n. 309, n. 1543.

25. D 7, p. 48; cf. p. 323, n. 1565.

26. Letter of November 30, 1863; D 7, pp. 309–310.

27. D 7, p. 337.

28. Ibid., n. 1595; cf. p. 108.

29. Memoir of 1894 in the *Bulletin religieux de Tarbes et de Lourdes,* 1931, pp. 491–494; JGL 1931, November 15, n. 46; D 7, p. 52, note 272.

30. *Mémoire Ollivier,* cf. Sempé, p. 224.

31. Memoir of October 7, 1878, p. 8.

32. H 3, p. 210.

33. D 7, p. 468, n. 1777.

34. D 7, p. 331.

35. Ibid.

36. D 7, p. 51.

37. Ibid.

38. Letter of September 10, 1879.

39. Letter of September 10, 1879, pp. 16–18; Védère, pp. 73–75; OG, p. 198; D 7, p. 58, note 313. Using the two versions, we complete one with the other.

40. PATarb 237.

Chapter 8
BERNADETTE'S VOCATION

1. PONev 1202v; D 7, p. 109.

2. D 2, p. 149.

3. A VII, p. 174, n. 80.

4. PANev 1328; *Logia,* N 777.

5. D 4, pp. 232–234; D 7, p. 83, note 485.

6. Ibid.

7. A VII, p. 174, n. 80.

8. Védère, September 10, 1879, p. 10; Védère, pp. 67–68; OG, pp. 191–192.

9. D 7, p. 97, note 555.

10. D 7, p. 98, note 555.

11. October 14, 1862, Nevers Archives.

12. Letter of September 10, 1879, question 2; Védère, p. 63; OG, p. 190.

13. OG, p. 199.

14. Védère, p. 63; cf. p. 22; OG, p. 190; cf. p. 177.

15. Letter of September 10, 1879; question 2; Védère, pp. 64–65; OG, p. 191.

16. Letter of September 10, 1879; Védère, p. 82; OG, p. 197. The Blagnac manuscript repeats this text from beginning to end with slight variations.

17. Letter of September 10, 1879, p. 7; D 7, p. 84, note 493.

18. Letter of September 10, 1879, pp. 6–8; Védère, pp. 63–66; D 7, p. 85, n. 495.

19. Védère, p. 68.

20. Cf. D 7, p. 86, n. 498.

21. Letter of October 2, 1879, pp. 2–3; Védère, pp. 86–87.

22. D 7, pp. 86–88.

23. D 7, p. 99, note 757.

24. PANev 1328.

25. Letter of October 2, 1879; Védère, p. 85.

26. Letter of September 10, 1879; Védère, p. 66; OG, p. 191.

27. A VII, p. 189.

28. A VII, p. 174.

29. A. Labayle, PONev 761v.

30. PANev 5, 1227; JGL 104, 1955, n. 17; D 7, p. 99.

31. Archives of the Sisters of St. Vincent de Paul.

32. RSL, n. 8; D 7, p. 89, note 516.

33. A VII, p. 189.

34. Barbet, 1929 ed., p. 189.

35. Letter of September 10, 1879; Védère, p. 71; OG, pp. 192–193.

36. PANev 909; cf. 1328 and PONev 1069v.

37. D 7, p. 160, n. 1369.

38. Barbet, p. 146; D 7, p. 100, note 561.

39. Rough notes of Sisters Aurélie and Damien, RSL, n. 13, p. 9; D 7, p. 101.

40. Forcade, pp. 7–9.

41. Forcade, pp. 11–12.

42. Forcade, pp. 9–14.

43. Letter of September 10, 1879, p. 13; Védère, p. 70.

44. Letter of Jeanne Védère, September 10, 1879, p. 13. The text has been retouched and softened in Védère, pp. 70–71; an accurate version is found in OG, p. 193.

45. OG, p. 178; Védère, p. 24.

46. PANev 1547; cf. PONev 737 and 1110v.

47. PONev 5, 1128; D 7, p. 109, note 606.

48. PANev 5, 1301v.

49. A VII, p. 187, n. 367.

50. Ursule Court, PONev 1244v.

51. PANev 1119v; D 7, pp. 122–123.

52. PONev 5, 729v.

53. H 5, p. 319, n. 907.

54. Ibid.

55. D 3, p. 240, n. 476.

56. V. Cassou, PONev 1259v.

Chapter 9
THE YEAR 1864

1. PANev 5, 1128v; D 7, p. 108, note 601.

2. Védère, p. 71.

3. Védère, pp. 22–23; D 7, p. 108, note 601.

4. D 7, p. 111, note 615.

5. D 7, p. 351, n. 1611.

6. D 7, pp. 351–352, n. 1611.

7. D 7, p. 352.

8. Ibid.

9. D 7, p. 350, n. 1610; cf. p. 110, note 609.

10. Guynot, in Rev. Bern., n. 1, 1934, pp. 42–49.

11. JGL, 102, 1953, n. 4, February 15, p. 4, col. 4.

12. D 7, p. 374, n. 1648; cf. p. 111.

13. D 7, p. 373.

14. D 7, pp. 387–391, n. 1464; cf. p. 111.

15. D 7, p. 388.

16. D 7, pp. 388–389, n. 1664.

17. D 7, p. 389.

18. D 7, p. 390.

19. Ibid.

20. D 7, p. 395, n. 1673.

21. D 7, pp. 139–140; H 1, pp. 95–104.

22. D 7, pp. 19–20.

23. Letter of September 10, 1879, p. 22; Védère, p. 79; OG, p. 195.

24. Letter of September 10, 1879, p. 23; Védère, pp. 78–79; OG, pp. 195–196.

25. Letter of September 10, 1879, Védère, p. 79; OG, p. 196.

26. Notes gathered by Mother Hildegarde, July 2–5, 1879, p. 8; Védère, p. 22; OG, p. 177.

27. Letter of September 10, 1879, p. 23; Védère, p. 79; OG, p. 196.

28. Védère, p. 89.

29. Letter of September 10, 1879, p. 2; Védère, pp. 67–68; cf. p. 89; OG, pp. 191–192.

30. Letter of September 10, 1879, p. 23; Védère, p. 81; OG, p. 196.

31. D 7, p. 293, n. 1518.

32. A VII, p. 179, n. 89; cf. PANev 7, 1731; D 7, p. 108, note 598.

33. Letter of September 10, 1879, p. 23; Védère, p. 80; OG, p. 196.

34. Letter of September 10, 1879, pp. 23–24; Védère, p. 80; OG, p. 196.

35. Ibid.

36. Letter of September 10, 1879, p. 25; Védère, p. 81.

37. Letter of September 10, 1879, p. 25; Védère, p. 82; OG, p. 97.

38. Letter of October 2, 1879, p. 9; Védère, p. 91; OG, p. 201.

39. Letter of October 2, 1879, pp. 12–13; Védère, pp. 93–95.

40. Letter of August 8, 1879, question 6, pp. 6–7; Védère, pp. 38–39; OG, p. 181.

41. Letter of September 10, 1879, question 2, p. 10; Védère, p. 68; cf. p. 86–87; OG, p. 192.

42. Letter of October 2, 1879, question 4, p. 5; Védère, p. 88; OG, p. 200. (The date November 23, 1864, verified in the civil registers of Bartrès, n. 579, confirms Jeanne Védère's precision.)

43. Letter of October 2, 1879, question 6, p. 11; Védère, p. 93; OG, p. 202.

44. Letter of August 8, 1879, question 6, p. 8; Védère, p. 40; OG, p. 181.

45. Védère, p. 22; OG, p. 177.

46. PANev 202v.

47. Ibid.

48. Ibid.

49. B. Billet, in *Mélanges,* J. Coppin, Lille, 1967, pp. 75–76.

50. PONev 747; D 7, p. 109; B. Billet, *Mélanges,* J. Coppin, p. 78, note 40, for the correction of the date.

51. D 7, p. 421, n. 1717.

Chapter 10
THE YEAR 1865

1. D 3, pp. 74–75 and D 4, pp. 244–245.

2. *Rev. Bern.* p. 232; D 7, p. 432.

3. D 7, pp. 431–432; *Mémoire Clavé,* A VII and the *Souvenirs* of Father Clauzel, published in the *Rev. Bern.* 5, 1937, n. 6, pp. 230–234.

4. D 7, p. 442, n. 1759.

5. D 7, p. 444.

6. Ibid.

7. D 5, p. 77, note 191.

8. D 7, p. 492, n. 1813.

9. D 7, pp. 451–455, n. 1766.

10. D 7, pp. 451–452, n. 1766; cf. p. 116, note 641.

11. D 7, p. 452.

12. D 7, pp. 454–455.

13. D 7, p. 455.

14. Ibid.

15. D 7, p. 467, n. 1777.

16. D 7, pp. 467–469, n. 1777.

17. H 3, p. 236; cf. D 7, pp. 469–470.

18. D 7, p. 469.

19. Ibid.

20. D 7, p. 470, n. 1777.

21. D 7, p. 470.

22. D 7, p. 466.

23. Ibid.

24. D 1, p. 230, n. 44 bis.

25. D 1, p. 233, n. 50; cf. volume 4, p. 269, n. 766b.

26. D 1, p. 298, n. 104.

27. D 4, p. 247, n. 748.

28. D 5, p. 343, n. 915.

29. D 6, p. 212, n. 1022.

30. D 7, p. 160, n. 1369a.

31. D 7, p. 264, n. 1484.

32. BRTL 1933, p. 544.

33. D 7, p. 387, n. 1664.

34. D 7, p. 467, n. 1777.

35. Letter of January 7, 1924, Grand Séminaire de Tarbes.

36. D 1, p. 268 or D 1, p. 230, 232, 238, 298; D 2, p. 240; D 3, p. 129; D 4, p. 247, 265; D 5, p. 247.

37. D 7, p. 468.

38. *Histoire Naturelle,* volume 4, p. 238.

39. J. J. Rousseau, *L'Emile,* book 4, Garnier Publications classic, p. 251.

40. Cf. D 1, p. 230.

Chapter 11
THE FINAL MONTHS IN LOURDES

1. D 7, pp. 118–119.

2. RC, p. 78, repeated by later witnesses; PONev 121; PANev 210 and 317–318.

3. Letter of Souviron, November 27, 1878.

4. D 7, p. 121, note 666.

5. D 7, p. 496.

6. PONev 1100v; ESB, p. 181, n. 48.

7. D 7, p. 498, 1822.

8. PONev 810.

9. B. Billet, *Mélanges*, J. Coppin, Lille, 1967, p. 79.

10. PONev p. 15, art. 22.

11. PANev 5, 1227.

12. D 7, p. 421, n. 1717 and p. 114.

13. B. Billet, *Mélanges*, J. Coppin, Lille, 1967, pp. 76, 78–79.

14. PANev 202v.

15. B. Billet, *Mélanges*, J. Coppin, p. 76.

16. PONev 86v.

17. Ibid., p. 102, already cited.

18. D 7, p. 499, n. 1823; cf. p. 78, note 467.

19. D 7, p. 499.

20. PANev 1855v; cf. PONev 1243v; 1187v; D 7, p. 75, note 447.

21. Védère, pp. 75–76.

22. PANev 380; D 7, p. 76, note 449.

23. PONev 1243v.

24. D 7, p. 76, notes 450 and 452.

25. Anastasie Carrière, PANev 909 and PONev 624.

26. PONev 1243v.

27. D 7, p. 77.

28. ANDL 42, 1910, p. 311.

29. ANDL 1910, p. 307.

30. D 7, p. 528, n. 1582, cf. p. 121, note 671.

31. D 7, pp. 121 and 528; ESB, pp. 189–190.

32. D 7, p. 502, n. 1826; ESB, pp. 99–106.

33. ESB, p. 107.

Chapter 12
GOOD-BYES AND DEPARTURE

1. D 7, p. 122, note 673.

2. D 7, p. 122, note 676.

3. D 7, p. 493, n. 1814.

4. *Logia* 3, p. 236.

5. D 7, p. 531, n. 1857.

6. D 7, p. 430, n. 1856.

7. U. Court, PONev 1244; cf. PANev 1720v.

8. Hildegarde notes, p. 6; Védère, p. 21.

9. PONev 982.

10. PANev 1774v.

11. A VII, p. 308, n. 589.

12. PONev 979.

13. D 7, pp. 404–405, n. 1690; PONev 979.

14. D 7, p. 125, note 691.

15. ANDL 42, 1910, p. 311; D 7, p. 125, note 693.

16. A VII, p. 183, n. 96.

17. PANev 1289; cf. 1157.

18. Barbet, PONev 928.

19. PANev 218.

20. PANev 1707.

21. PONev article 23 of the Process, p. 15.

22. PONev 113; 21; 1438v.

23. PANev 3, 692v; cf. PONev 202 and 203; D 7, p. 126, note 697.

24. PONev 810v.

25. Marguerite Carassus, PATarb p. 315.

26. A VII, p. 287, n. 556.

27. PANev 1241v.

28. Letter of Sister Savinien Beyssière, July 17, 1866.

29. PONev 4, 831v; D 7, p. 126, note 698.

30. PONev 810v.

31. ANDL 42, 1910, p. 308.

32. PONev 846; PATarb p. 230.

33. D 7, p. 127, note 206.

34. A recollection recorded by Dom Bernard, January 20, 1861.

35. D 7, p.127, note 206.

36. ANDL 42, 1910, pp. 308–309.

Chapter 13
ARRIVAL AT NEVERS AND POSTULANCY

1. ESB, p. 241.

2. N 1.

3. ESB, p. 181.

4. RC, p. 82.

5. RC, p. 29; PONev 1100v.

6. N 3v and x.

7. D 7, pp. 122–123.

8. N 3.

9. Journ. Com.

10. PONev 701.

11. N 6; Sister Emilienne Duboé; PONev 699v.

12. RC, p. 55.

13. N 453.

14. ESB, p. 241.

15. Ibid.

16. N 16; RC, p. 81.

17. Ibid.
18. N 17.
19. N 14; RC, p. 81; Mother Marie Thérèse Bordenave, p. 124.
20. N 7; PONev 698v–699.
21. RC, p. 55.
22. N 20.
23. N 15.
24. RC, p. 55.
25. N 9; RC, p. 55.
26. N 9; PONev 699.
27. N 11; PONev 699v.
28. N 12; PONev 700.
29. N 10; PONev 699.
30. N 18; RC, p. 99.
31. P. Lemaitre, *Rev. Bern.*, June 1939, n. 41, p. 153.
32. N 19.
33. ESB, pp. 232–233.
34. PONev 110.
35. N 21 i.

Chapter 14
THE NOVITIATE

1. RSL, January 1967, n. 17, pp. 20–22.
2. *La Salette, Lourdes, Pontmain,* Paris, 1872, reproduced in *Rev. Bern.*, October 1939, n. 43, p. 24.
3. *The Spiritual Treasury of the Sisters of Charity,* Nevers. P. Bégat, 1860, p. 296; cf. RSL, Janaury 1967, n. 17, pp. 20–21. On the espousal theme, see RSL, October 1967, n. 20, pp. 178–179 and 183.
4. L. Cloris, RC, p. 30.
5. N 23; PANev 1809.
6. N 23; PANev 1809.
7. N 23.
8. N 26.
9. N 24.
10. N 25.
11. Sempé, p. 103.
12. N 28.
13. N 29; cf. RSL, October 1967, n. 20, pp. 171–175 on the hidden life.
14. N 31.
15. N 30.
16. N 32.
17. N 33.
18. RC, pp. 60–62.
19. N 41.

20. N 34.
21. PANev 747; N 49.
22. PONev 741v.
23. N 35.
24. N 37.
25. N 50; PANev 748.
26. N 39.
27. PONev 534v; N 48.
28. N 42; PANev 746v.
29. N 42; RC, p. 62.
30. N 43.
31. N 44.
32. Ibid.; *La confidante,* p. 131.
33. N 45.
34. N 46.
35. N 47.
36. PONev 738v.
37. N 51.
38. Ibid.
39. N 54.
40. Ibid.
41. N 64.
42. N 54.
43. Ibid.
44. N 53.
45. Ibid.
46. A VII, p. 191, n. 138; RSL, n. 15, p. 106, notes 1 and 2.
47. N 55.
48. N 56.
49. N 57.
50. N 58.
51. N 59; PONev 1135v.
52. N 60; RC, p. 111.
53. N 106.
54. N 96.
55. N 95.
56. N 56; PONev 1129.
57. N 62.
58. ESB, p. 296.
59. N 65.
60. H 5, pp. 222–223; N 214, etc.
61. N 66.
62. ESB, p. 252.
63. N 69.
64. PANev 1123.
65. RC, pp. 34–35.
66. RC, pp. 129–130.
67. R. Pignol, RC, p. 120.

68. PONev 659v; 62v.
69. RC, p. 121.
70. RC, pp. 71–72.
71. PONev 1170v.
72. PANev 1886.
73. Ibid.
74. PONev 659v.
75. N 91.
76. PANev 1159v; N 91.
77. N 13.
78. RC, p. 83.
79. N 90; PONev 1175.
80. S. Tourriol, PONev 1116v.
81. N 88.
82. N 73.
83. N 80.
84. Ibid.
85. N 68; PONev 1296–1297.
86. N 92.
87. N 109.
88. N 74.
89. N 70.
90. N 77.
91. N 89.
92. PONev 1176.
93. PANev 1098.
94. N 93.
95. N 94.
96. N 107.
97. *Notice,* 1879, p. 19; N 78.
98. N 79.
99. N 84.
100. N 97.
101. N 98.
102. N 99, etc.
103. N 71.
104. RC, pp. 129–130.
105. N 486: synthesis of both testimonies of C. Bordes; RC, p. 51; PANev 950v.
106. N 487.
107. N 85.
108. N 86; PANev 1526v.
109. N 189.
110. Ibid.
111. N 287.
112. N 370.
113. N 104.
114. N 123.
115. N 81.
116. N 72.

Chapter 15
Profession of Vows

1. N 110.
2. N 110; cf. RSL, October 1967, n. 20, pp. 169–185.
3. N 110.
4. Forcade, p. 32.
5. A. Carrière, PONev 624v–625.
6. PONev 1297v.
7. PONev 533v.
8. Forcade, p. 32.
9. Ibid.
10. RC, p. 167.
11. PONev 1297v.
12. N 111.
13. J. Caldairou, PONev 1297v; PANev 1890.
14. RC, p. 76.
15. N 114–115.
16. N 113; RC, p. 94.

Chapter 16
Bernadette Employed

1. N 117.
2. Ibid., iii.
3. N 117, i.
4. N 117.
5. N 128.
6. H 6, p. 252.
7. October 2, 1869; N 151.
8. N 70 and 152.
9. *Logia* 1, p. 168.
10. *Testament d'un antisémite,* pp. 299, 305, 308–309.
11. ANDL, pp. 68–69.
12. ANDL, 1, 1868, p. 69.
13. Ibid.
14. H 2, p. 111.
15. ANDL, Ibid.
16. ANDL, August 1868, p. 70.
17. ANDL, p. 71.
18. Ibid.
19. Ibid.
20. H 2, p. 135 and note 48, pp. 161–162.
21. Ibid., p. 71.
22. H 2, pp. 136–162, note 49; pp. 180–181, note 112.
23. ANDL, p. 72.
24. ANDL, p. 73.
25. H 2, p. 178, note 102.

26. ANDL, p. 74.

27. H 2, pp. 138–140.

28. A VII, p. 218, n. 226; H 2, p. 140.

29. ANDL, p. 75.

30. Ibid.

31. Ibid.

32. Testimonies and discussions on this may be found in H 2, pp. 140–144; cf. p. 193, notes 154–158.

33. ANDL, September 1868, p. 86.

34. H 2, p. 258, notes 46–47.

35. H 2, p. 87.

36. H 2, pp. 248–252 and 259.

37. H 2, pp. 248–252.

38. ANDL, pp. 87–88.

39. H 2, p. 261, notes 67–70, where are cited the Clarens' interview, which goes back to March 4, 1858, and Toinette's testimonies.

40. ANDL, pp. 87–88.

41. H 2, pp. 240–248; cf. 264–272.

42. D 7, p. 265.

43. ANDL, p. 89.

44. ANDL, pp. 92–93.

45. H 2, pp. 364–366, especially note 85.

46. ANDL, October 1868, p. 103.

47. ANDL, August 1868, p. 72.

48. Ibid., p. 72 of the copy kept in the Lasserre Archives.

49. H 3, pp. 175–176, note 173; cf. p. 182, note 210 for the light persisting after the apparition.

50. *Petite histoire*, in ANDL, November 1868, p. 114.

51. H 6, pp. 122–123, note 78, where the eight testimonies on this point are discussed.

52. H 5, pp. 305–307.

53. Forcade, p. 57.

54. Forcade, p. 58.

55. *Logia* 1, p. 290.

56. Letter of November 5, 1871, to the Bishop of Tarbes.

57. Letter of November 17, 1869, pp. 1–2.

58. Letter of November 17, 1869, p. 2, Archives of the grotto.

59. D 1, p. 52, account 2, in which we corrected the spelling.

60. *Logia* 1, p. 291.

61. *Logia* 1, p. 292.

62. Ibid.

63. H 3, p. 175, note 176.

64. H 2, pp. 132–144, 161–162, 177, 184, 219, 240–253; H 3, pp. 171–176, 207; H 5, p. 305, note 58; H 6, pp. 122–123, note 78.

65. *Logia* 1, p. 412; N 295.

66. Paris, 1891, pp. 300–314.

67. *Mémoire Sempé*, 1873.

Chapter 17
BERNADETTE THE INFIRMARIAN

1. N 119.

2. N 136.

3. N 137.

4. N 139.

5. N 141.

6. N 140.

7. N 144.

8. N 154.

9. N 155.

10. N 130.

11. N 122.

12. N 161, 164, 165, etc.

13. ESB, p. 311.

14. ESB, p. 312.

15. N 161; PANev 1354.

16. N 164.

17. N 165.

18. N 166; PANev 1367.

19. N 192.

20. N 190.

21. N 311.

22. N 176.

23. N 177.

24. N 305.

25. Ibid.

26. N 305c; PANev 881v.

27. N 305c.

28. N 313.

29. N 282.

30. N 304.

31. N 269.

32. N 270.

33. N 274.

34. ESB, p. 309.

35. RSL, n. 21, January 1968, p. 25.

36. N 153.

37. Journ. Com.

38. N 160; RC, p. 122.

39. ESB, pp. 287 and 295.

40. ESB, p. 280

41. ESB, p. 316.
42. Journ. Com.
43. Ibid., cf. N 318.
44. ESB, p. 321; cf. p. 319.
45. N 321.
46. N 320.
47. Journ. Com.; ESB, p. 263.
48. N 325.
49. N 134.
50. Ibid.
51. N 124.
52. N 132.
53. N 272.
54. N 179.
55. N 265.
56. Ibid.
57. Journ. Com., November 16, 1869.
58. D 6, pp. 259–282, n. 1049; cf. pp. 232–234, n. 1040.
59. N 223.
60. N 133.
61. N 156.
62. N 281.
63. N 171.
64. Journ. Com.
65. N 172.
66. N 174.
67. PONev 1163.
68. N 183.
69. N 184.
70. ESB, p. 395.
71. Cros, III, p. 223; ESB, p. 279.
72. ESB, p. 280.
73. N 182; RC, p. 44.
74. ESB, p. 282.
75. ESB, p. 283.
76. ESB, p. 32.
77. N 162.
78. PANev 1202.
79. N 193.
80. N 194.
81. N 195.
82. Ibid.; PANev 1209v, testimony of 1918.
83. N 195; RC, p. 116.
84. N 195; PONev 1063.
85. N 197.
86. N 198; PONev 1062v.
87. H 5, pp. 137–140.
88. N 199.
89. N 200.
90. N 201.
91. N 202.
92. N 251.
93. N 202; PANev 1282v.
94. N 204.
95. N 206.
96. N 203.
97. N 208.
98. N 209.
99. N 210.
100. N 212.
101. N 211.
102. N 213.
103. Ibid.
104. N 214.
105. N 222.
106. N 215.
107. N 216.
108. N 217.
109. N 220.
110. N 221; PANev 1211.
111. N 222.
112. N 224; PANev 1210.
113. N 226; PANev 1210v.
114. N 227.
115. N 228.
116. N 253.
117. N 230.
118. N 233.
119. N 235.
120. N 243.
121. N 252.
122. N 244.
123. N 245.
124. N 249.
125. Ibid.
126. N 324.
127. Mk 8:35; Mt 10:39; 16:25; Lk 9:24; 17:33; Jn 12:25.
128. N 236.
129. N 237.
130. N 239.
131. N 238.
132. N 240.
133. N 232.
134. N 241.
135. N 242.
136. N 248.
137. N 247.

138. N 256.
139. N 234.
140. N 254.
141. N 257.
142. N 258.
143. N 255.
144. N 259.
145. N 260.
146. N 261.
147. N 264.
148. ESB, p. 262.
149. N 267.
150. N 268.
151. N 292.
152. N 293.
153. N 295.
154. *Notice,* pp. 47–51.
155. N 295 III.
156. N 295.
157. N 314.
158. N 318.
159. N 329.
160. N 332.
161. ESB, p. 280.
162. N 332.
163. Zola, 1892, p. 82.
164. Lasserre, *Bernadette,* 1879, p. 323.
165. N 334.
166. N 335.
167. N 336.
168. N 338.
169. N 345b, 422b, 426.
170. N 340.
171. ESB, p. 281.
172. N 341.
173. ESB, p. 305.
174. N 342.
175. N 343.
176. N 344.
177. N 345.
178. N 231.

Chapter 18
BERNADETTE'S FINAL ACTIVITIES

1. N 683.
2. PONev 1280v.
3. July Retreat 1875, ESB, p. 409 (On her relations with G. de Vigouroux, see present text, p. 608 and the table of the *Logia*).

4. PONev 1061.
5. N 348.
6. N 352.
7. N 349.
8. N 350.
9. N 355.
10. N 347.
11. N 157.
12. N 289.
13. N 361; Guynot 1936, pp. 232–233.
14. N 358.
15. N 351.
16. N 357.
17. N 356.
18. N 360.
19. N 359.
20. N 360.
21. N 363.
22. N 365.
23. N 368.
24. 1906 edition, p. 316.
25. N 369.
26. H 1, p. 61, line 500.

Chapter 19
THE LAST ASSIGNMENT

1. N 374.
2. N 378.
3. Journ. Com.
4. N 381; RC, p. 74, J. Ramplou.
5. N 387.
6. Ibid.
7. N 395.
8. N 403; RC, p. 97.
9. N 416.
10. N 427.
11. N 433.
12. N 434.
13. N 435.
14. N 502.
15. N 452.
16. N 453.
17. N 455.
18. N 458.
19. N 490.
20. N 494, a synthesis of two testimonies a and b.
21. N 497.
22. N 504.
23. N 472.

24. N 507.
25. N 471.
26. N 530.
27. N 530.
28. N 538.
29. N 450.
30. N 411.
31. N 377.
32. N 415.
33. Letter of December 28, 1876; ESB, p. 473.
34. Cf. N 409, etc.
35. N 397.
36. ESB, p. 425.
37. N 396.
38. N 441.
39. N 406.
40. N 405.
41. N 402.
42. N 399.
43. N 400.
44. N 407.
45. N 401.
46. N 375; Guynot 1936, p. 202.
47. N 390.
48. N 391.
49. ESB, p. 275.
50. N 454.
51. Chapter 26.
52. N 510.
53. Ibid.
54. Ibid.
55. N 522.
56. N 511.
57. N 512.
58. N 398.
59. Ibid.
60. N 467 i.
61. N 467 ii.
62. N 468.
63. Ibid.
64. ESB, pp. 481, 489, 500.
65. N 469.
66. Letter of E. Rigal, June 5, 1879; N 470.
67. N 460; PONev 1270v.
68. N 460.
69. N 461.
70. Ibid.
71. According to Guynot, 1936, p. 201.

72. Journ. Com.
73. N 383.
74. Journ. Com.
75. ESB, p. 475; cf. p. 418.
76. Journ. Com.
77. ESB, p. 419.
78. ESB, p. 475.
79. Letter of June 27, 1876; ESB, p. 428.
80. ESB, p. 424.
81. June 25, 1876; ESB, pp. 421–422.
82. ESB, p. 430.
83. Guynot 1936, p. 169.
84. N 413.
85. N 417.
86. ESB, p. 434.
87. ESB, p. 436.
88. ESB, p. 426, cf. p. 434.
89. ESB, p. 437.
90. ESB, p. 439.
91. Letter of September 7; ESB, p. 436.
92. Guynot 1936, p. 278.
93. ESB, p. 447.
94. ESB, p. 444.
95. Ibid.
96. ESB, p. 434.
97. Ibid.
98. Ibid.
99. ESB, p. 444.
100. N 419 bis.
101. ESB, pp. 453–454.
102. ESB, p. 458.
103. ESB, p. 451.
104. ESB, p. 473.
105. Ibid.
106. N 546.
107. Letter of December 28, 1876; ESB, p. 473.
108. ESB, p. 475.
109. ESB, p. 472.
110. N 451.
111. Ibid.
112. ESB, p. 491.
113. ESB, p. 486.
114. ESB, p. 491.
115. N 474.
116. N 473.
117. N 456.
118. N 466.
119. N 459; Guynot 1936.
120. N 465.

121. ESB, p. 491.

122. N 477.

123. RC, pp. 84–85; N 477, synthesis of three testimonies.

124. N 478.

125. N 481.

126. N 479.

127. N 484.

128. N 488.

129. N 491, a synthesis of the first two testimonies of C. Bordes.

130. Testimony of C. Bordes, N 492.

131. N 499.

132. Journ. Com.

133. N 501.

134. The religious calendar in use by the Sisters of Charity, Nevers, 1858 edition, p. 46.

135. N 505; RC, p. 14.

136. N 506.

137. N 383, 518, 525, 540.

138. N 447.

139. N 508.

140. Ibid.

141. N 509.

142. N 513.

143. N 518.

144. N 519.

145. N 520.

146. N 521.

147. N 523.

148. N 524.

149. N 525.

150. N 526; M. Delbrel, PONev 1037.

151. N 527.

152. Ibid.

153. Guynot 1936, p. 173; M. Delbrel; PONev 1037.

154. ESB, pp. 503–504.

155. N 529.

156. N 530.

157. Lasserre, *Bernadette*, 1879, p. 349

158. Letter to Peyramale, December 28, 1876; ESB, p. 475.

159. N 410.

160. N 411b.

161. N 500.

162. N 429.

163. N 452.

164. N 457; PONev 1205.

165. N 462.

166. N 463.

167. Ibid.

168. N 503.

169. N 392.

170. N 393.

171. N 394.

172. N 418, at the end of September 1876.

173. N 419.

174. N 499.

175. N 515.

176. ESB, p. 453.

177. N 516.

178. N 420.

Chapter 20
THE LAST DEPOSITION

1. N 532.

2. Octavo of 64 pp., 14.5 x 22.5.

3. A VII and L.J.M. Cros, *Notre-Dame de Lourdes, récits et mystères*, Toulouse, Privat, 1901, pp. viii–ix.

4. A VII, p. 265.

5. Ibid.

6. A VII, p. 267.

7. A VII, n. 1124; Cros, *Récits et mystères*, Toulouse, 1901, p. 12.

8. N 533.

9. D 2, pp. 167–168, notes 69–71.

10. N 534.

11. Ibid., question 12.

12. N 535.

13. Letter of Sister Adélaïde Dons, December 22, 1878; N 536.

14. N 547.

15. Ibid., question 2.

16. H 1, p. 63; H 4, pp. 365–368; H 5, pp. 143–156.

17. H 5, p. 142, note 94.

18. N 534, question 14.

19. N 547, question 4.

20. The evolution of this delicate point can be found in H 6, pp. 196–200.

21. N 547, second series, question 4.

22. Cf. H 3, pp. 256–257 and 270–271.

23. N 548.

24. H 3, p. 161, note 97.

25. N 548, question 12.

26. N 548, question 19.

27. Cros, I, pp. 289–298.

28. N 548, question 20.

29. H 3, p. 156; cf. present text, pp. 222–224.

30. D 4, pp. 365–368.

31. D 5, pp. 142–151.

32. N 549.

33. N 550.

34. N 552.

Chapter 21
THE LAST ILLNESS

1. Stenography of Father Cros, A I; ESB, p. 516.

2. N 537; Zola, p. 64.

3. Ibid.

4. Ibid.

5. Zola, pp. 97–98; cf. p. 65.

6. N 537.

7. ESB, p. 516.

8. December 1876.

9. N 546.

10. N 545.

11. ESB, p. 508.

12. Ibid.

13. N 551.

14. N 555.

15. N 556.

16. N 562.

17. N 563.

18. N 565.

19. N 564.

20. N 554.

21. N 566.

22. ESB, p. 508.

23. N 561.

24. N 579.

25. N 578.

26. N 557.

27. N 558.

28. N 567.

29. N 568.

30. N 569 I.

31. Cf. H 3, p. 56, note 101.

32. N 569 iv.

33. N 419.

34. N 570; PONev 213v.

35. N 571.

36. N 572.

37. N 575.

38. N 544.

39. N 574.

Chapter 22
THE LAST DAYS

1. N 577.

2. Ibid.

3. N 580.

4. N 576, Ib.

5. N 581.

6. N 583, a synthesis of four testimonies by B. Dalias.

7. N 583 d.

8. N 584.

9. N 585.

10. N 586.

11. N 587.

12. N 588.

13. N 589.

14. Sempé, p. 285.

15. N 589, Sister Nathalie's notes, April 15, 1879.

16. *Logia* 2, p. 177; cf. p. 162.

17. ESB, p. 504.

18. *Logia* 2, pp. 243, 277, 279, 283, 305, 330.

19. *Logia* 2, pp. 243, 277, 283, 305, 330.

20. ESB, p. 507.

21. *Logia* 2, p. 330.

Chapter 23
THE LAST MOMENTS

1. N 590.

2. N 592.

3. N 593.

4. Ibid.

5. N 594.

6. N 595.

7. N 593 ii.

8. N 596.

9. N 597.

10. N 599, deposition of Abbé Febvre, April 26, 1879.

11. N 600.

12. N 601.

13. N 602.

14. N 603.

15. N 604; Lasserre, *Bernadette*, p. 118.

16. N 605.

17. N 606.

18. N 607.

19. N 608.
20. N 609.
21. N 611.
22. Ibid.

Chapter 24
Who Is Bernadette?
1. N 576.

Chapter 25
Bernadette's Objective Testimony
1. H 6, p. 240.
2. H 1, pp. 77–82.
3. *Logia* 3, p. 314, col. 2.
4. H 1, p. 82.

Chapter 26
The Private Realization of the Message
1. N 660.
2. N 29 bis.
3. N 29.
4. N 411.
5. N 513.
6. N 466.
7. N 665.
8. H 6, pp. 257–258.
9. Ibid.
10. H 3, pp. 249–271.
11. H 3, p. 230, cf. pp. 231–347.
12. H 6, pp. 253–287.
13. H 6, pp. 266–271.
14. D 4, p. 248.
15. N 26.
16. N 666; PANev 1800v.
17. N 268, in 1871.
18. N 170, in 1870.
19. N 667–668.
20. N 667; cf. 668 a variant.
21. N 81.
22. N 669; PONev 1278v.
23. N 166, in 1870.
24. N 228, in 1871.
25. L. Brusson notes, 1867.
26. N 348, June 4, 1874.
27. N 66, in 1866.
28. N 287.
29. N 189.
30. N 672.
31. N 670.

32. N 246.
33. N 673.
34. Ibid.
35. N 674; PANev 1547.
36. N 459.
37. N 356, in 1874.
38. N 406, in 1876.
39. N 341.
40. N 676.
41. OG, p. 339; N 690.
42. N 685.
43. N 449.
44. N 296.
45. N 686.
46. N 353.
47. N 687.
48. H 5, p. 336.
49. N 687.
50. N 691.
51. N 678.
52. Ibid.
53. N 324.
54. N 124.
55. N 683.
56. N 283 and 505.
57. N 683.
58. N 10, in 1866.
59. N 683.
60. N 682.
61. N 693.
62. N 78, in 1867.
63. N 276.
64. N 518 bis.
65. N 523; cf. N 267, 276, 516.
66. N 684.
67. N 18, in 1866.
68. N 104, in 1867.
69. N 130, in 1869.
70. N 254, in 1871.
71. N 366, Perreau, in 1874.
72. N 172, in 1867.
73. N 698–699.
74. N 700; cf. 7, 8, 19 bis, 67, etc.
75. N 305.
76. N 703; cf. N 33, 704, 705.
77. N 704; cf. 459.
78. N 702.
79. N 705.
80. N 108, 370, 505.
81. PANev 378v–379.

82. N 305, in 1872.
83. N 690, *Notice,* p. 37.
84. N 29.
85. N 692.
86. N 691.
87. N 192.
88. N 250.
89. N 249.

Chapter 26 contd.
PRAYER AND PENANCE

1. PONev 1325; N 709.
2. Forcade, p. 36.
3. 1867, preparatory notes.
4. PONev 1325v; N 709.
5. N 136, 137, 229, 281, 709.
6. PONev 1061v.
7. PANev 1227v.
8. Cited by Mother Bordenave, PONev 337v; cf. N 312 and 314.
9. N 712.
10. PANev 370; N 710.
11. N 711.
12. N 712.
13. N 713.
14. N 714; PONev 1282.
15. N 500 and 718.
16. N 232, 240, 411 bis, etc.
17. N 717; RC, p. 91.
18. N 719.
19. N 528, in 1878.
20. N 233, in 1871.
21. N 722.
22. N 138 and parallel numbers in N 722.
23. N 115.
24. N 747 and parallels in *Logia* 3, p. 136.
25. N 125, in 1868.
26. N 723.
27. N 45, in 1866.
28. N 727.
29. Ibid.
30. N 730; PONev 1146v.
31. N 730; *Conservateurs,* April 20, 1879.
32. N 488.
33. N 736.
34. N 735.
35. N 744.
36. N 745.
37. N 732.
38. N 734.

39. N 738.
40. N 739.
41. N 740.
42. N 260, 394, etc.
43. N 725; Lasserre, *Bernadette,* 1879, p. 205.
44. ESB, p. 365, 376, 408, 409, 507.
45. N 45, 172, 456.
46. N 683.
47. ESB, p. 428.
48. RSL, n. 21, January 1968, p. 28.
49. N 445, 604, 752.
50. N 751.
51. N 434.
52. N 459.
53. N 6.
54. N 1.
55. N 320.
56. N 359 I a.
57. N 432.
58. N 443.
59. N 657.
60. N 329, 334.
61. N 604.
62. N 639.
63. N 548, question 12; *Logia* 2, p. 257.
64. N 637 and 388.
65. N 442.
66. N 106.
67. H 3, p. 214, n. 83.
68. N 106.
69. N 641.
70. Ibid.
71. ESB, p. 241.
72. N 639.
73. N 638.
74. N 640.
75. N 432.
76. N 642; RC, p. 41.
77. N 632.
78. N 634.
79. N 643; cf. 658.
80. H 3, p. 187, note 227.
81. N 635.
82. N 636.
83. N 432.
84. N 631; RC, p. 90.
85. N 476.
86. N 628.
87. N 630.

88. N 629.
89. N 653.
90. Ibid.
91. N 654.
92. N 655.
93. N 656.
94. N 753.
95. N 543.
96. N 459.
97. N 247.
98. N 443.
99. N 750.
100. N 154.
101. N 331.
102. N 25, 491; cf. 380.
103. N 754.
104. N 755; cf. 25, 491.

Chapter 26 contd.
"NOT HAPPY IN THIS WORLD…"

1. H 2, pp. 348–349.
2. N 756; PANev 1544v.
3. N 757; PANev 1330v.
4. N 579; cf. 6, 30, 145, 328, 335, etc.
5. N 399.
6. N 332, 367, 399, 421.
7. N 402.
8. N 759; cf. 195.
9. N 329; cf. 334.
10. ESB, p. 481 and 486.
11. N 198.
12. N 441.
13. N 537.
14. N 406.
15. N 767.
16. G. Champy, PANev 848.
17. N 760.
18. N 768v.
19. B. Dalias, note in 1867.
20. N 761.
21. N 764; PONev 1202v.
22. Lasserre, *Bernadette,* 1879, p. 297; N 763.
23. N 766.
24. N 411, 466, 513, 760 III.
25. N 175, etc.
26. N 765.
27. N 771.
28. N 770.
29. N 762.
30. A I, n. 12.

31. Autographed letter of N. Portat.
32. N 760 III.
33. Febvre-Picq notice, p. 75, Archives of Nevers.
34. RSL, n. 21, January 1968, p. 25.
35. N 772, Mother Bordenave; PANev 339.
36. N 773; Marthe du Rais, PANev 339.
37. Ibid.
38. N 253.
39. PONev 1156v.
40. N 774.
41. N 776; PANev 1343.
42. N 368.
43. Febvre-Picq, PANev 1416.
44. N 775; RC, pp. 171–172.
45. PANev 1328.
46. N 795.
47. N 778; cf. 394 bis.
48. Ph. Molinéry, N 779.
49. N 779.
50. N 276.
51. N 782.
52. N 783.
53. N 781.

Chapter 26 contd.
THE STERNNESS OF HER SUPERIORS

1. ESB, p. 409 and 410.
2. N 784, 785, 786, 787, etc.
3. Paris, Desclée de Brower, 1936.
4. *Logia* 3, pp. 236–240.
5. PONev 1210v.
6. Sister Paschal, PANev 1157; N 661.
7. Forcade, p. 26.
8. N 502; cf. present text, pp. 593, 597–598; *Logia* 3, pp. 55 and 154.
9. B. Dalias, PONev 660.
10. B. Dalias, PANev 1475v.
11. N 683.
12. PONev 1296.
13. PANev 1887v–1888.
14. PONev 1101.
15. *Logia* 1, pp. 239, 241, 252–253, 373.
16. Ibid., p. 272.
17. N 785.
18. PANev 1253.
19. PANev 335.
20. PANev 327–328.
21. Ibid.

22. PANev 1253.

23. PANev 335v.

24. N 684; PANev 1341v.

25. PONev 1175.

26. PANev 1771.

27. PONev 533.

28. Guynot 1936, pp. 86–92.

29. ESB, p. 422.

30. Mother Bordenave, PANev 361v.

31. N 281.

32. N 1.

33. B. Dalias, written memoir, folio 13; cf. L. Cloris, PANev 1089v.

34. L. Cloris, PONev 1120.

35. PONev 533; PANev 738v.

36. A. Carrière, PANev 919.

37. N 69.

38. PONev 104v.

39. Ibid.

40. PANev 327.

41. PANev 336.

42. Mother Bordenave, PANev 336; cf. Picq, PONev 1319.

43. PANev 327–328.

44. PANev 1475v.

45. PANev 1087; PANev 1087v.

46. PONev 104; cf. Mother Bordenave, PONev 323–324; PANev 414.

47. PONev 1269.

48. PANev 414.

49. N 682; PONev 269, etc.

50. PANev 326.

51. PANev 986v.

52. PANev 1228 and Mother Bordenave's version, PANev 327–328.

53. PANev 1228–1229.

54. Mother Bordenave, PANev 326 and 412v–413.

55. Mother Bordenave, *Notice on our venerable Mother Marie-Thérèse Vauzou,* in the religious calendar in use by the Sisters of Charity, Nevers, 1910, p. 58, 71–74 and the testimony of oral tradition.

56. PANev 986v.

57. A deposition obtained by Mother M. A. Crapard, PANev 1438v.

58. PANev 1708.

59. Mother Bordenave, PANev 337v.

60. PANev 326.

61. Cf. testimony of Boillot, present text, p. 590.

62. PANev 327–328.

63. PONev 1089–1089v.

64. PANev 225.

65. PANev 327–328.

66. PANev 326.

67. Cros III, pp. 265–266; ESB, p. 515.

68. Mother Bordenave, PANev 327v–328.

69. Mother Bordenave, PANev 335.

70. J. Garnier, PANev 1545v.

71. PONev 324.

72. Mother Bordenave, PANev 412v–414.

73. PANev 1224.

74. PONev 322–323.

75. PANev 336.

76. L. Villaret, PANev 1123.

77. PANev 1251v.

78. Mother Forestier, PONev 1014v; cf. PANev 225, 335, etc.

79. Mother Forestier, PONev 104v; cf. PANev 335, etc.

80. PANev 327.

81. PANev 326; cf. PANev 412v.

82. PANev 324.

83. B. Dalias, PONev 662v.

84. N 527.

85. PANev 336.

86. Mother Bordenave, PONev 324; PANev 334–335.

87. PONev 269v.

88. C. Pagès, PONev 1049.

89. Evaluation in 1906, N 795; PANev 1410.

90. Guynot 1936, p. 91.

91. L. Cloris, PANev 1087v.

92. RC, pp. 129–130.

93. PANev 224.

94. PANev 326v–328.

95. Ibid., 412v–413.

96. PANev 326–327.

97. PANev 1064.

98. N 90.

99. J. LeCerf, PANev 978.

100. PANev 978.

101. Abbé Jouin, PANev 1708.

102. PONev 1210v.

103. ESB, p. 409.

104. C. Payrard, PANev 1251.

105. S. Tourriol, PANev 1194.

106. PANev 224–225.

107. RC, pp. 129–130.

108. Mother Bordenave, PANev 334–336v.

109. Ibid.

110. PONev 1296v.

111. PANev 1064.

112. PANev 1438v.

113. PANev 1341v.

114. C. Callery, PONev 1181v–1182v.

115. N 69, 156.

116. N 505.

117. N 684.

118. PANev 1181.

119. C. Payrard, N 786.

120. N 10.

121. N 48.

122. N 787.

123. N 785.

124. N 130.

125. N 68 II.

126. H 5, p. 327.

127. B. Lauzeral, N 788; RC, p. 37.

128. N 789.

129. N 791.

130. N 153.

131. N 38.

132. N 556; Mother Bordenave, PANev 370.

133. N 794.

134. N 799.

135. N 792.

136. N 35.

137. N 796.

138. N 793.

139. N 202.

140. G. Champy, N 797.

141. Ph. Molinéry, N 798.

142. N 256, etc.

143. N 804.

144. N 800 and 801.

145. N 805.

146. N 802.

147. ESB, p. 376.

148. N 803.

Chapter 26 contd.
"...BUT IN THE NEXT"

1. N 790.

2. Ibid.

3. N 578.

4. N 812.

5. N 817.

6. N 810.

7. N 811; PANev 1330v.

8. N 82.

9. N 337.

10. N 459.

11. N 814.

12. N 61.

13. N 822.

14. N 475.

15. N 219.

16. N 813.

17. N 816; E. Marcillac; cf. 46, 556, 818.

18. N 818.

19. N 815 to Marthe du Rais; cf. 244.

20. N 819, G. Champy.

21. N 821, I. Ganier.

22. N 819, I. Ganier.

23. N 755.

24. ESB, p. 377.

25. ESB, p. 376.

26. N 570.

27. ESB, p. 542.

28. RSL, n. 17, January 1967, p. 22.

29. ESB, p. 228.

30. N 824 I.

31. N 824 IV.

32. N 824 VII.

33. N 824 III.

34. N 824.

35. Marthe du Rais, PANev 1343v.

36. RC, p. 170.

37. N 832; cf. PONev 1280.

38. N 830.

39. N 827.

40. N 826.

41. N 34, 49, 447, 492, 551, 829.

42. N 828.

43. Mother Bordenave, PANev 367v; N 35.

44. Forcade, p. 35.

45. Forcade, pp. 35–36.

46. N 546.

47. ESB, p. 473.

48. N 831.

49. RC, p. 108.

50. ESB, p. 411

51. N 833.

52. Ibid.; *Logia* 3, pp. 214–215; cf. 1, pp. 30–31.

53. N 519, present text, pp. 481–482.

54. PANev 1182v.

55. Ibid.

56. N 458.

57. N 75.

58. N 193–264; 349–360.

59. N 612.

60. *Logia* 3, p. 304—"children."

61. Védère, p. 79; OG, p. 196.

62. N 506.

63. N 297.

64. N 836.

65. Edited by Ravier, ESB, pp. 394–395.

66. Ibid., facsimile, facing p. 394.

67. N 835.

68. N 834.

69. N 360.

70. ESB, p. 515, n. 5.

71. N 838.

72. N 62, 238, 239, 303, 384, 839–841.

73. N 840.

74. N 849.

75. N 851, to G. Champy.

76. N 852, to I. Ganier.

77. *Notice of 1907;* PONev 1330v; cf. PANev 1416v.

78. PANev 844v.

79. N 842 IV; cf. N 554.

80. N 843; Marthe du Rais, PANev 1340v.

81. N 844; Ph. Molinéry, PONev 1280.

82. N 846; Mother Bordenave, PANev 339v.

83. N 845, G. Champy, PANev 844v.

84. N 165; A. Lompech.

85. N 274, C. Chassan, in 1871.

86. N 855; PONev 1071.

87. N 684.

88. PANev 1341v.

89. PANev 314–315.

90. N 854.

91. N 853.

92. N 420.

93. N 304, in 1872.

94. N 264, in 1871.

95. N 71, in 1867.

96. N 557, 602, 710.

97. N 98, in 1867.

98. N 290, in 1871; N 437, in 1877.

99. N 850, to Marthe du Rais.

100. N 850; PANev 733.

101. N 373, in 1871.

102. N 311, in 1872.

103. N 673.

104. N 236.

105. N 242.

106. RSL, 1967, n. 20. pp. 177, 179, 183.

107. ESB, p. 537.

108. ESB, p. 377.

109. N 857.

Chapter 27
BERNADETTE'S SECRET

1. N 60.

2. N 646.

3. N 648.

4. H 3, pp. 249–272.

5. H 3, p. 265, n. 52.

6. H 3, p. 253, note 32.

7. N 644.

8. N 645; etc. See H 3, p. 253, note 33.

9. H 3, pp. 256–257 and 271.

10. H 3, pp. 254–256.

11. N 345.

12. N 806.

13. N 808; cf. N 586.

14. PANev 1201.

15. N 807.

16. N 589.

17. N 809.

18. ESB, p. 217.

19. N 37; present text, pp. 341–342.

20. *Oeuvres spirituelle,* P. Bouix edition, Nevers, 1871, p. 159.

21. Ibid., p. 163.

22. May 13, 1867, N 71.

23. ESB, p. 345.

24. N 576.

25. *Correspondence,* Paris, Cerf, 1972, volume 1, letter 82.

26. Manuscript A.

27. *Correspondence générale,* Paris, Cerf, 1972, volume 1, letter 82; cf. letters 85, 86, 87, 91, 101, 108.

28. N 461.

29. *Manuscripts autobiographiques,* Carmel de Lisieux, 1957, p. 71.

30. *Manuscripts autobiographiques,* Carmel de Lisieux, 1957, p. 73.

31. *Manuscripts autobiographiques,* Carmel de Lisieux, 1957, pp. 252–253; cf. p. 250 and *Novissima verba,* p. 16, 164, 175.

32. N 609; cf. 589.

33. N 605.
34. N 470.
35. N 581.
36. *Oeuvres spirituelles du père de Laveyne,*
ed. Bouix, Nevers, 1871, pp. 1–2.
37. N 560.
38. ESB, p. 515.
39. *Logia* 3, pp. 183–186.
40. N 470.
41. N 560.
42. N 580.
43. N 480, in 1877.
44. N 585.

Lourdes in 1858

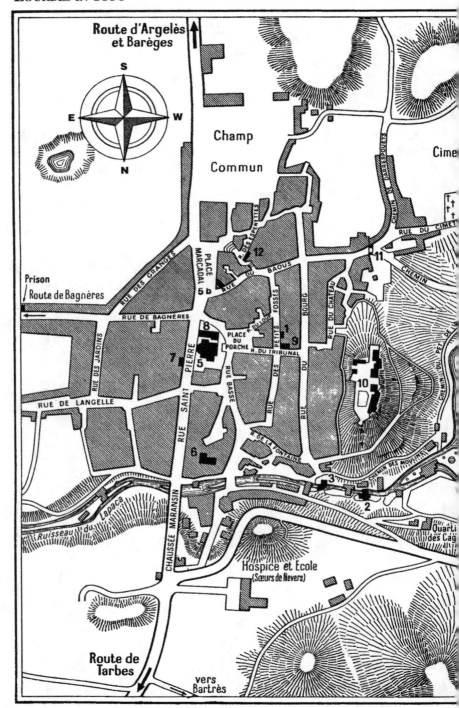

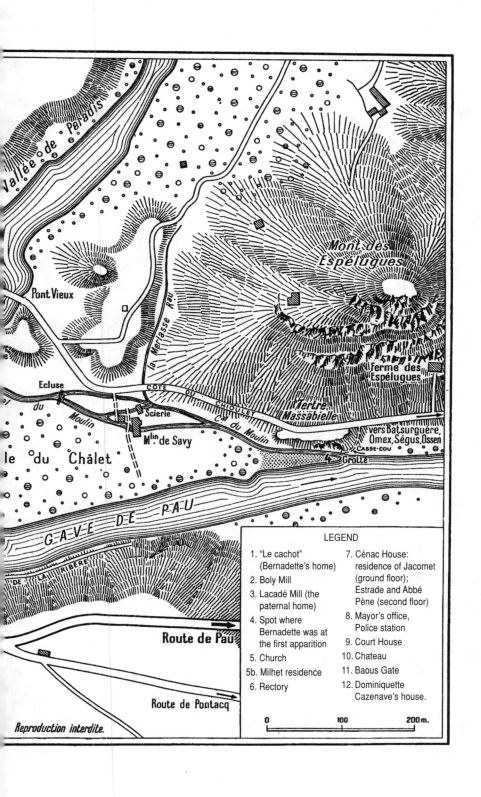

Vallée de Paradis

Pont Vieux

Mont des Espélugues

Ferme des Espélugues

la Merlasse Nau

Ecluse
du
Moulin

Scierie

Mⁱⁿ de Savy

le du Châlet

CÔTE DU CHOULET

Cⁱᵉ du Moulin

Tertre Massäbielle

vers Batsurguère,
Omex, Ségus, Ossen

CASSE-COU

Grotte

GAVE DE PAU

DE LA RIBÈRE

Route de Pau

Route de Pontacq

Reproduction interdite.

LEGEND

1. "Le cachot" (Bernadette's home)
2. Boly Mill
3. Lacadé Mill (the paternal home)
4. Spot where Bernadette was at the first apparition
5. Church
5b. Milhet residence
6. Rectory
7. Cénac House: residence of Jacomet (ground floor); Estrade and Abbé Pène (second floor)
8. Mayor's office, Police station
9. Court House
10. Chateau
11. Baous Gate
12. Dominiquette Cazenave's house.

0   100   200 m.

BOOKS & MEDIA

The Daughters of St. Paul operate book and media centers at the following addresses. Visit, call or write the one nearest you today, or find us on the World Wide Web, www.pauline.org

CALIFORNIA
3908 Sepulveda Blvd., Culver City, CA 90230   310-397-8676
5945 Balboa Ave., San Diego, CA 92111   858-565-9181
46 Geary Street, San Francisco, CA 94108   415-781-5180

FLORIDA
145 S.W. 107th Ave., Miami, FL 33174   305-559-6715

HAWAII
1143 Bishop Street, Honolulu, HI 96813   808-521-2731
Neighbor Islands call: 800-259-8463

ILLINOIS
172 North Michigan Ave., Chicago, IL 60601   312-346-4228

LOUISIANA
4403 Veterans Memorial Blvd., Metairie, LA 70006   504-887-7631

MASSACHUSETTS
Rte. 1, 885 Providence Hwy., Dedham, MA 02026   781-326-5385

MISSOURI
9804 Watson Rd., St. Louis, MO 63126   314-965-3512

NEW JERSEY
561 U.S. Route 1, Wick Plaza, Edison, NJ 08817   732-572-1200

NEW YORK
150 East 52nd Street, New York, NY 10022   212-754-1110
78 Fort Place, Staten Island, NY 10301   718-447-5071

OHIO
2105 Ontario Street (at Prospect Ave.), Cleveland, OH 44115
  216-621-9427

PENNSYLVANIA
9171-A Roosevelt Blvd., Philadelphia, PA 19114   215-676-9494

SOUTH CAROLINA
243 King Street, Charleston, SC 29401   843-577-0175

TENNESSEE
4811 Poplar Ave., Memphis, TN 38117   901-761-2987

TEXAS
114 Main Plaza, San Antonio, TX 78205   210-224-8101

VIRGINIA
1025 King Street, Alexandria, VA 22314   703-549-3806

CANADA
3022 Dufferin Street, Toronto, Ontario, Canada M6B 3T5
  416-781-9131
1155 Yonge Street, Toronto, Ontario, Canada M4T 1W2;
  416-934-3440

¡También somos su fuente para libros, videos y música en español!